# HONDA | PILOT/ACURA
## 2001-07 REPAIR

Covers all U.S. and Canadian models of
Honda Pilot (2003 through 2007) and
Acura MDX (2001 through 2007)

by John A Wegmann

**CHILTON** *Automotive Books*

PUBLISHED BY **HAYNES NORTH AMERICA. Inc.**

Manufactured in USA
©2007 Haynes North America, Inc.
ISBN-13: 978-1-56392-692-1
ISBN-10: 1-56392-692-X
Library of Congress Control Number 2007940012

**Haynes Publishing Group**
Sparkford Nr Yeovil
Somerset BA22 7JJ England

**Haynes North America, Inc**
861 Lawrence Drive
Newbury Park
California 91320 USA

ABCDE
FGHIJ
KLMNO
PQRS

# Contents

**Author and mechanic with a 2005 Honda Pilot**

## ACKNOWLEDGEMENTS

Technical writers who contributed to this project include Joe Hamilton, Mike Stubblefield and Rob Maddox. Wiring diagrams provided exclusively for the publisher by Solution Builders.

## About this manual

### ITS PURPOSE

The purpose of this manual is to help you get the best value from your vehicle. It can do so in several ways. It can help you decide what work must be done, even if you choose to have it done by a dealer service department or a repair shop; it provides information and procedures for routine maintenance and servicing; and it offers diagnostic and repair procedures to follow when trouble occurs.

We hope you use the manual to tackle the work yourself. For many simpler jobs, doing it yourself may be quicker than arranging an appointment to get the vehicle into a shop and making the trips to leave it and pick it up. More importantly, a lot of money can be saved by avoiding the expense the shop must pass on to you to cover its labor and overhead costs. An added benefit is the sense of satisfaction and accomplishment that you feel after doing the job yourself.

### USING THE MANUAL

The manual is divided into Chapters. Each Chapter is divided into numbered Sections, which are headed in bold type between horizontal lines. Each Section consists of consecutively numbered paragraphs.

At the beginning of each numbered Section you will be referred to any illustrations which apply to the procedures in that Section. The reference numbers used in illustration captions pinpoint the pertinent Section and the Step within that Section. That is, illustration 3.2 means the illustration refers to Section 3 and Step (or paragraph) 2 within that Section.

Procedures, once described in the text, are not normally repeated. When it's necessary to refer to another Chapter, the reference will be given as Chapter and Section number. Cross references given without use of the word "Chapter" apply to Sections and/or paragraphs in the same Chapter. For example, "see Section 8" means in the same Chapter.

References to the left or right side of the vehicle assume you are sitting in the driver's seat, facing forward.

Even though we have prepared this manual with extreme care, neither the publisher nor the author can accept responsibility for any errors in, or omissions from, the information given.

➡**NOTE**

A *Note* provides information necessary to properly complete a procedure or information which will make the procedure easier to understand.

### ❋❋ CAUTION

A *Caution* provides a special procedure or special steps which must be taken while completing the procedure where the Caution is found. Not heeding a Caution can result in damage to the assembly being worked on.

### ❋❋ WARNING

A *Warning* provides a special procedure or special steps which must be taken while completing the procedure where the Warning is found. Not heeding a Warning can result in personal injury.

## Introduction

This manual covers the Honda Pilot and Acura MDX sport utility vehicles. All Acura MDX models are all-wheel drive. All Honda Pilot models through 2005 are also all-wheel drive, but beginning in 2006, a front-wheel drive model was available. The engine in all Acura models through 2006 and Honda models through 2007 is a 3.5L SOHC V6. 2007 Acura MDX models are equipped with a 3.7L SOHC V6 engine. All engines are equipped with Programmed Fuel Injection (PGM-FI), a "sequential multiport" system. The engine is mated to a five-speed automatic transaxle.

Independent suspension, featuring coil spring/strut damper units, is used on the front, while the rear suspension utilizes trailing arms, shock absorbers, coil springs, and one upper and two lower control arms per side.

The power-assisted rack-and-pinion steering unit is mounted behind the engine.

Disc brakes are used at all four wheels. An Anti-lock Braking System is standard on all models.

## Vehicle Identification Numbers

Modifications are a continuing and unpublicized process in vehicle manufacturing. Since spare parts manuals and lists are compiled on a numerical basis, the individual vehicle numbers are essential to correctly identify the component required.

### VEHICLE IDENTIFICATION NUMBER (VIN)

This very important identification number is stamped on a plate attached to the dashboard inside the windshield on the driver's side of the vehicle (see illustration). It can also be found on the certification label located on the driver's side door post. The VIN also appears on the Vehicle Certificate of Title and Registration. It contains information such as where and when the vehicle was manufactured, the model year and the body style.

### VIN ENGINE AND MODEL YEAR CODES

Two particularly important pieces of information found in the VIN are the body/engine code and the model year code. Counting from the left, the body/engine code letter designations are the 4th through 6th digits and the model year code letter designation is the 10th digit.

On the models covered by this manual the body/engine codes are:

**Honda**

| | | |
|---|---|---|
| 2003, 2004 | | |
| YF1 | ............................ | Pilot/J35A4 (3.5L V6 w/VTEC) |
| 2005 | | |
| YF1 | ............................ | Pilot/J35A6 (3.5L V6 w/VTEC) |
| 2006, 2007 | | |
| YF1 | ............................ | Pilot 4WD/J35A9 (3.5L V6 w/VTEC) |
| YF2 | ............................ | Pilot 2WD/J35Z1 (3.5L V6 w/iVTEC) |

**Acura**

| | | |
|---|---|---|
| 2001, 2002 | | |
| YD1 | ............................ | MDX/J35A3 (3.5L V6 w/VTEC) |
| 2003 through 2006 | | |
| YD1 | ............................ | MDX/J35A5 (3.5L V6 w/VTEC) |
| 2007 | | |
| YD2 | ............................ | MDX/J37A1 (3.7L V6 w/VTEC) |

On the models covered by this manual the model year codes are:

| | | |
|---|---|---|
| 1 | ............................ | 2001 |
| 2 | ............................ | 2002 |
| 3 | ............................ | 2003 |
| 4 | ............................ | 2004 |
| 5 | ............................ | 2005 |
| 6 | ............................ | 2006 |
| 7 | ............................ | 2007 |

### CERTIFICATION LABEL

The certification label is attached to the driver's door post (see illustration). The plate contains the name of the manufacturer, the month and year of production, the Gross Vehicle Weight Rating (GVWR), the Gross Axle Weight Rating (GAWR) and the certification statement.

### ENGINE IDENTIFICATION NUMBERS

The engine serial number can be found on the front side of the engine (see illustration).

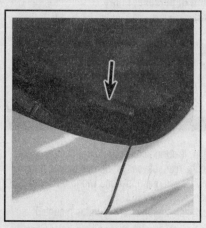

The Vehicle Identification Number (VIN) is located on a plate on top of the dash (visible through the windshield)

The vehicle certification label is located on the driver's door post

The engine serial number is located on the front side of the block

## Recall information

Vehicle recalls are carried out by the manufacturer in the rare event of a possible safety-related defect. The vehicle's registered owner is contacted at the address on file at the Department of Motor Vehicles and given the details of the recall. Remedial work is carried out free of charge at a dealer service department.

If you are the new owner of a used vehicle which was subject to a recall and you want to be sure that the work has been carried out, it's best to contact a dealer service department and ask about your indi-

vidual vehicle - you'll need to furnish them your Vehicle Identification Number (VIN).

The table below is based on information provided by the National Highway Traffic Safety Administration (NHTSA), the body which oversees vehicle recalls in the United States. The recall database is updated constantly. For the latest information on vehicle recalls, check the NHTSA website at www.nhtsa.gov, or call the NHTSA hotline at 1-888-327-4236.

| Recall date | Recall campaign number | Model(s) affected | Concern |
|---|---|---|---|
| Aug 30, 2002 | 02V226000 | 2002 MDX<br><br>2003 Pilot | On certain minivans, sedans, coupes, and sport utility vehicles equipped with V6 engines, a timing belt tensioner pulley on the water pump is misaligned and could cause the timing belt to contact a bolt on the cylinder head. Eventually the belt could be damaged and fail. If the timing belt breaks, the engine will stall, increasing the risk of a crash. |
| Apr 21, 2004 | 04V176000 | 2001, 2002 MDX<br><br>2003, 2004 Pilot | On some mini vans, sport utility and passenger vehicles, certain operating conditions can result in heat build-up between the countershaft and secondary shaft second gears in the automatic transmission, eventually leading to gear tooth chipping or gear breakage. Gear failure could result in transmission lockup, which could result in a crash. |
| Aug 11, 2004 | 04V389000 | 2004 Pilot | Certain sport utility vehicle's certification labels may contain incorrect vehicle weight and tire size information. |
| Nov 10, 2004 | 04V541000 | 2005 MDX<br><br>2005 Pilot | On certain sport utility vehicles, some fuel tanks were improperly manufactured. In a crash, the fuel tank could be damaged and leak fuel. Fuel leakage, in the presence of an ignition source, could result in a fire. |
| Jan 25, 2005 | 05V039000 | 2005 Pilot | On certain minivans and sport utility vehicles, the steering column may be incorrectly assembled, which could result in a loss of steering control. |
| Oct 11, 2005 | 05V385000 | 2001, 2002 MDX | On certain sport utility vehicles originally sold in or currently registered in the states of Connecticut, Delaware, Illinois, Indiana, Iowa, Kentucky, Maine, Maryland, Massachusetts, Michigan, Minnesota, Missouri, New Hampshire, New Jersey, New York, Ohio, Pennsylvania, Rhode Island, Vermont, Virginia, West Virginia, Wisconsin and the District of Columbia, in areas where large quantities of road salt are used, the front suspension coil springs have insufficient corrosion protection, and may be susceptible to corrosion. Excessive corrosion can cause spring failure and a broken spring could puncture a front tire, which increases the risk of a crash. |

## Buying parts

Replacement parts are available from many sources, which generally fall into one of two categories - authorized dealer parts departments and independent retail auto parts stores. Our advice concerning these parts is as follows:

**Retail auto parts stores:** Good auto parts stores will stock frequently needed components which wear out relatively fast, such as clutch components, exhaust systems, brake parts, tune-up parts, etc. These stores often supply new or reconditioned parts on an exchange basis, which can save a considerable amount of money. Discount auto parts stores are often very good places to buy materials and parts needed for general vehicle maintenance such as oil, grease, filters, spark plugs, belts, touch-up paint, bulbs, etc. They also usually sell tools and general accessories, have convenient hours, charge lower prices and can often be found not far from home.

**Authorized dealer parts department:** This is the best source for parts which are unique to the vehicle and not generally available elsewhere (such as major engine parts, transmission parts, trim pieces, etc.).

**Warranty information:** If the vehicle is still covered under warranty, be sure that any replacement parts purchased - regardless of the source - do not invalidate the warranty!

To be sure of obtaining the correct parts, have engine and chassis numbers available and, if possible, take the old parts along for positive identification.

## Maintenance techniques, tools and working facilities

## MAINTENANCE TECHNIQUES

There are a number of techniques involved in maintenance and repair that will be referred to throughout this manual. Application of these techniques will enable the home mechanic to be more efficient, better organized and capable of performing the various tasks properly, which will ensure that the repair job is thorough and complete.

### Fasteners

Fasteners are nuts, bolts, studs and screws used to hold two or more parts together. There are a few things to keep in mind when working with fasteners. Almost all of them use a locking device of some type, either a lockwasher, locknut, locking tab or thread adhesive. All threaded fasteners should be clean and straight, with undamaged threads and undamaged corners on the hex head where the wrench fits. Develop the habit of replacing all damaged nuts and bolts with new ones. Special locknuts with nylon or fiber inserts can only be used once. If they are removed, they lose their locking ability and must be replaced with new ones.

Rusted nuts and bolts should be treated with a penetrating fluid to ease removal and prevent breakage. Some mechanics use turpentine in a spout-type oil can, which works quite well. After applying the rust penetrant, let it work for a few minutes before trying to loosen the nut or bolt. Badly rusted fasteners may have to be chiseled or sawed off or removed with a special nut breaker, available at tool stores.

If a bolt or stud breaks off in an assembly, it can be drilled and removed with a special tool commonly available for this purpose. Most automotive machine shops can perform this task, as well as other repair procedures, such as the repair of threaded holes that have been stripped out.

Flat washers and lockwashers, when removed from an assembly, should always be replaced exactly as removed. Replace any damaged washers with new ones. Never use a lockwasher on any soft metal surface (such as aluminum), thin sheet metal or plastic.

### Fastener sizes

For a number of reasons, automobile manufacturers are making wider and wider use of metric fasteners. Therefore, it is important to be able to tell the difference between standard (sometimes called U.S.

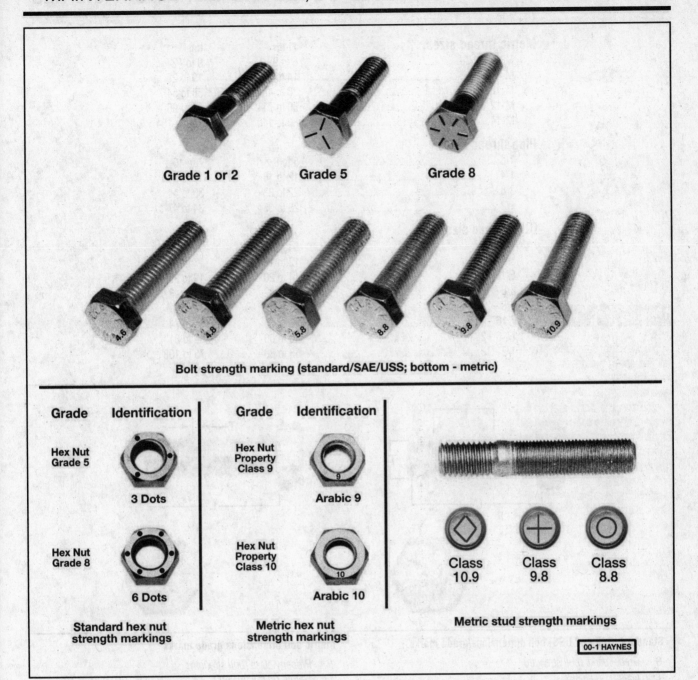

Grade 1 or 2    Grade 5    Grade 8

4.6    4.8    5.8    8.8    9.8    10.9

Bolt strength marking (standard/SAE/USS; bottom - metric)

| Grade | Identification |
|---|---|
| Hex Nut Grade 5 | 3 Dots |
| Hex Nut Grade 8 | 6 Dots |

**Standard hex nut strength markings**

| Grade | Identification |
|---|---|
| Hex Nut Property Class 9 | Arabic 9 |
| Hex Nut Property Class 10 | Arabic 10 |

**Metric hex nut strength markings**

Class 10.9    Class 9.8    Class 8.8

**Metric stud strength markings**

00-1 HAYNES

or SAE) and metric hardware, since they cannot be interchanged.

All bolts, whether standard or metric, are sized according to diameter, thread pitch and length. For example, a standard 1/2 - 13 x 1 bolt is 1/2 inch in diameter, has 13 threads per inch and is 1 inch long. An M12 - 1.75 x 25 metric bolt is 12 mm in diameter, has a thread pitch of 1.75 mm (the distance between threads) and is 25 mm long. The two bolts are nearly identical, and easily confused, but they are not interchangeable.

In addition to the differences in diameter, thread pitch and length, metric and standard bolts can also be distinguished by examining the bolt heads. To begin with, the distance across the flats on a standard bolt head is measured in inches, while the same dimension on a metric bolt is sized in millimeters (the same is true for nuts). As a result, a standard wrench should not be used on a metric bolt and a metric wrench should not be used on a standard bolt. Also, most standard bolts have slashes

radiating out from the center of the head to denote the grade or strength of the bolt, which is an indication of the amount of torque that can be applied to it. The greater the number of slashes, the greater the strength of the bolt. Grades 0 through 5 are commonly used on automobiles. Metric bolts have a property class (grade) number, rather than a slash, molded into their heads to indicate bolt strength. In this case, the higher the number, the stronger the bolt. Property class numbers 8.8, 9.8 and 10.9 are commonly used on automobiles.

Strength markings can also be used to distinguish standard hex nuts from metric hex nuts. Many standard nuts have dots stamped into one side, while metric nuts are marked with a number. The greater the number of dots, or the higher the number, the greater the strength of the nut.

Metric studs are also marked on their ends according to property class (grade). Larger studs are numbered (the same as metric bolts), while smaller studs carry a geometric code to denote grade.

### Metric thread sizes

| | Ft-lbs | Nm |
|---|---|---|
| M-6 | 6 to 9 | 9 to 12 |
| M-8 | 14 to 21 | 19 to 28 |
| M-10 | 28 to 40 | 38 to 54 |
| M-12 | 50 to 71 | 68 to 96 |
| M-14 | 80 to 140 | 109 to 154 |

### Pipe thread sizes

| | | |
|---|---|---|
| 1/8 | 5 to 8 | 7 to 10 |
| 1/4 | 12 to 18 | 17 to 24 |
| 3/8 | 22 to 33 | 30 to 44 |
| 1/2 | 25 to 35 | 34 to 47 |

### U.S. thread sizes

| | | |
|---|---|---|
| 1/4 - 20 | 6 to 9 | 9 to 12 |
| 5/16 - 18 | 12 to 18 | 17 to 24 |
| 5/16 - 24 | 14 to 20 | 19 to 27 |
| 3/8 - 16 | 22 to 32 | 30 to 43 |
| 3/8 - 24 | 27 to 38 | 37 to 51 |
| 7/16 - 14 | 40 to 55 | 55 to 74 |
| 7/16 - 20 | 40 to 60 | 55 to 81 |
| 1/2 - 13 | 55 to 80 | 75 to 108 |

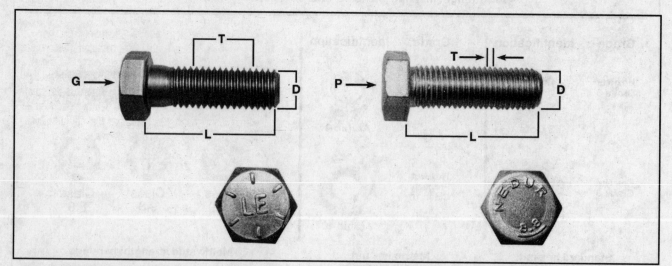

**Standard (SAE and USS) bolt dimensions/grade marks**

G   Grade marks (bolt strength)
L   Length (in inches)
T   Thread pitch (number of threads per inch)
D   Nominal diameter (in inches)

**Metric bolt dimensions/grade marks**

P   Property class (bolt strength)
L   Length (in millimeters)
T   Thread pitch (distance between threads in millimeters)
D   Diameter

It should be noted that many fasteners, especially Grades 0 through 2, have no distinguishing marks on them. When such is the case, the only way to determine whether it is standard or metric is to measure the thread pitch or compare it to a known fastener of the same size.

Standard fasteners are often referred to as SAE, as opposed to metric. However, it should be noted that SAE technically refers to a non-metric fine thread fastener only. Coarse thread non-metric fasteners are referred to as USS sizes.

Since fasteners of the same size (both standard and metric) may have different strength ratings, be sure to reinstall any bolts, studs or nuts removed from your vehicle in their original locations. Also, when replacing a fastener with a new one, make sure that the new one has a strength rating equal to or greater than the original.

### Tightening sequences and procedures

Most threaded fasteners should be tightened to a specific torque value (torque is the twisting force applied to a threaded component such as a nut or bolt). Overtightening the fastener can weaken it and cause it to break, while undertightening can cause it to eventually come loose. Bolts, screws and studs, depending on the material they are made of and their thread diameters, have specific torque values, many of which are noted in the Specifications at the end of each Chapter. Be sure to follow the torque recommendations closely. For fasteners not assigned a specific torque, a general torque value chart is presented here as a guide. These torque values are for dry (unlubricated) fasteners threaded into steel or cast iron (not aluminum). As was previously mentioned, the size and grade of a fastener determine the amount of torque that can

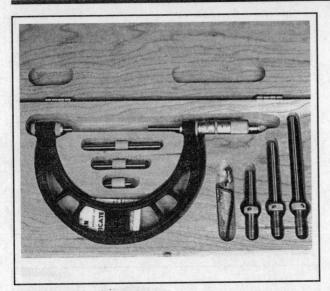

**Micrometer set**

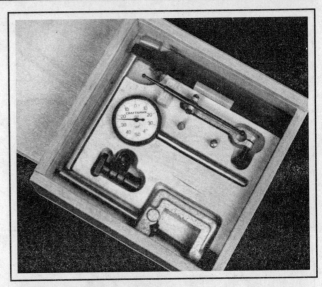

**Dial indicator set**

safely be applied to it. The figures listed here are approximate for Grade 2 and Grade 3 fasteners. Higher grades can tolerate higher torque values.

Fasteners laid out in a pattern, such as cylinder head bolts, oil pan bolts, differential cover bolts, etc., must be loosened or tightened in sequence to avoid warping the component. This sequence will normally be shown in the appropriate Chapter. If a specific pattern is not given, the following procedures can be used to prevent warping.

Initially, the bolts or nuts should be assembled finger-tight only. Next, they should be tightened one full turn each, in a criss-cross or diagonal pattern. After each one has been tightened one full turn, return to the first one and tighten them all one-half turn, following the same pattern. Finally, tighten each of them one-quarter turn at a time until each fastener has been tightened to the proper torque. To loosen and remove the fasteners, the procedure would be reversed.

## Component disassembly

Component disassembly should be done with care and purpose to help ensure that the parts go back together properly. Always keep track of the sequence in which parts are removed. Make note of special characteristics or marks on parts that can be installed more than one way, such as a grooved thrust washer on a shaft. It is a good idea to lay the disassembled parts out on a clean surface in the order that they were removed. It may also be helpful to make sketches or take instant photos of components before removal.

When removing fasteners from a component, keep track of their locations. Sometimes threading a bolt back in a part, or putting the washers and nut back on a stud, can prevent mix-ups later. If nuts and bolts cannot be returned to their original locations, they should be kept in a compartmented box or a series of small boxes. A cupcake or muffin tin is ideal for this purpose, since each cavity can hold the bolts and nuts from a particular area (i.e. oil pan bolts, valve cover bolts, engine mount bolts, etc.). A pan of this type is especially helpful when working on assemblies with very small parts, such as the carburetor, alternator, valve train or interior dash and trim pieces. The cavities can be marked with paint or tape to identify the contents.

Whenever wiring looms, harnesses or connectors are separated, it is a good idea to identify the two halves with numbered pieces of masking tape so they can be easily reconnected.

## Gasket sealing surfaces

Throughout any vehicle, gaskets are used to seal the mating surfaces between two parts and keep lubricants, fluids, vacuum or pressure contained in an assembly.

Many times these gaskets are coated with a liquid or paste-type gasket sealing compound before assembly. Age, heat and pressure can sometimes cause the two parts to stick together so tightly that they are very difficult to separate. Often, the assembly can be loosened by striking it with a soft-face hammer near the mating surfaces. A regular hammer can be used if a block of wood is placed between the hammer and the part. Do not hammer on cast parts or parts that could be easily damaged. With any particularly stubborn part, always recheck to make sure that every fastener has been removed.

Avoid using a screwdriver or bar to pry apart an assembly, as they can easily mar the gasket sealing surfaces of the parts, which must remain smooth. If prying is absolutely necessary, use an old broom handle, but keep in mind that extra clean up will be necessary if the wood splinters.

After the parts are separated, the old gasket must be carefully scraped off and the gasket surfaces cleaned. Stubborn gasket material can be soaked with rust penetrant or treated with a special chemical to soften it so it can be easily scraped off.

---

**✳✳ CAUTION:**

**Never use gasket removal solutions or caustic chemicals on plastic or other composite components.**

---

A scraper can be fashioned from a piece of copper tubing by flattening and sharpening one end. Copper is recommended because it is usually softer than the surfaces to be scraped, which reduces the chance of gouging the part. Some gaskets can be removed with a wire brush, but regardless of the method used, the mating surfaces must be left clean and smooth. If for some reason the gasket surface is gouged, then a gasket sealer thick enough to fill scratches will have to be used during reassembly of the components. For most applications, a non-drying (or semi-drying) gasket sealer should be used.

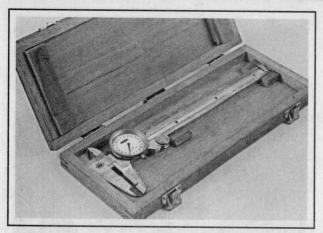

**Dial caliper**

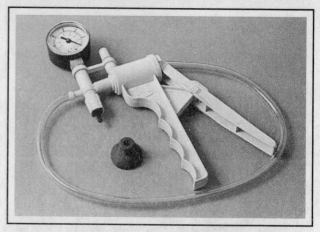

**Hand-operated vacuum pump**

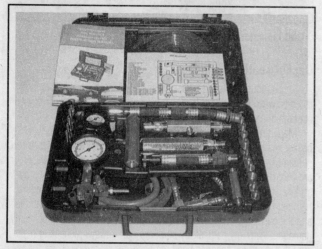

**Fuel pressure gauge set**

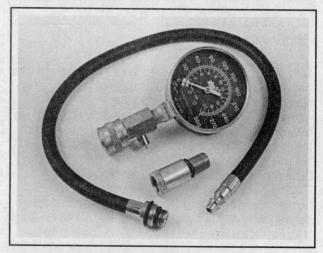

**Compression gauge with spark plug hole adapter**

## Hose removal tips

> ❋❋ **WARNING:**
>
> **If the vehicle is equipped with air conditioning, do not disconnect any of the A/C hoses without first having the system depressurized by a dealer service department or a service station.**

Hose removal precautions closely parallel gasket removal precautions. Avoid scratching or gouging the surface that the hose mates against or the connection may leak. This is especially true for radiator hoses. Because of various chemical reactions, the rubber in hoses can bond itself to the metal spigot that the hose fits over. To remove a hose, first loosen the hose clamps that secure it to the spigot. Then, with slip-joint pliers, grab the hose at the clamp and rotate it around the spigot. Work it back and forth until it is completely free, then pull it off. Silicone or other lubricants will ease removal if they can be applied between the hose and the outside of the spigot. Apply the same lubricant to the inside of the hose and the outside of the spigot to simplify installation.

As a last resort (and if the hose is to be replaced with a new one anyway), the rubber can be slit with a knife and the hose peeled from the spigot. If this must be done, be careful that the metal connection is not damaged.

If a hose clamp is broken or damaged, do not reuse it. Wire-type clamps usually weaken with age, so it is a good idea to replace them with screw-type clamps whenever a hose is removed.

## TOOLS

A selection of good tools is a basic requirement for anyone who plans to maintain and repair his or her own vehicle. For the owner who has few tools, the initial investment might seem high, but when compared to the spiraling costs of professional auto maintenance and repair, it is a wise one.

To help the owner decide which tools are needed to perform the tasks detailed in this manual, the following tool lists are offered: *Maintenance and minor repair, Repair/overhaul and Special.*

The newcomer to practical mechanics should start off with the *maintenance and minor repair* tool kit, which is adequate for the simpler jobs performed on a vehicle. Then, as confidence and experience grow, the owner can tackle more difficult tasks, buying additional tools as they are needed. Eventually the basic kit will be expanded into the *repair and overhaul* tool set. Over a period of time, the experienced do-it-yourselfer will assemble a tool set complete enough for most repair and overhaul procedures and will add tools from the special category when it is felt that the expense is justified by the frequency of use.

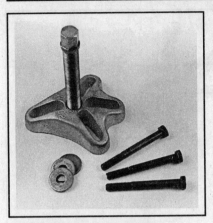

**Damper/steering wheel puller**

**General purpose puller**

**Hydraulic lifter removal tool**

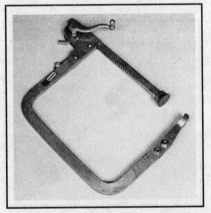

**Valve spring compressor**

**Valve spring compressor**

**Ridge reamer**

## Maintenance and minor repair tool kit

The tools in this list should be considered the minimum required for performance of routine maintenance, servicing and minor repair work. We recommend the purchase of combination wrenches (box-end and open-end combined in one wrench). While more expensive than open end wrenches, they offer the advantages of both types of wrench.

>   *Combination wrench set (1/4-inch to 1 inch or 6 mm to 19 mm)*
>   *Adjustable wrench, 8 inch*
>   *Spark plug wrench with rubber insert*
>   *Spark plug gap adjusting tool*
>   *Feeler gauge set*
>   *Brake bleeder wrench*
>   *Standard screwdriver (5/16-inch x 6 inch)*
>   *Phillips screwdriver (No. 2 x 6 inch)*
>   *Combination pliers - 6 inch*
>   *Hacksaw and assortment of blades*
>   *Tire pressure gauge*
>   *Grease gun*
>   *Oil can*
>   *Fine emery cloth*
>   *Wire brush*
>   *Battery post and cable cleaning tool*
>   *Oil filter wrench*
>   *Funnel (medium size)*
>   *Safety goggles*
>   *Jackstands (2)*
>   *Drain pan*

➡ **Note: If basic tune-ups are going to be part of routine maintenance, it will be necessary to purchase a good quality stroboscopic timing light and combination tachometer/dwell meter. Although they are included in the list of special tools, it is mentioned here because they are absolutely necessary for tuning most vehicles properly.**

## Repair and overhaul tool set

These tools are essential for anyone who plans to perform major repairs and are in addition to those in the maintenance and minor repair tool kit. Included is a comprehensive set of sockets which, though expensive, are invaluable because of their versatility, especially when various extensions and drives are available. We recommend the 1/2-inch drive over the 3/8-inch drive. Although the larger drive is bulky and more expensive, it has the capacity of accepting a very wide range of large sockets. Ideally, however, the mechanic should have a 3/8-inch drive set and a 1/2-inch drive set.

>   *Socket set(s)*
>   *Reversible ratchet*
>   *Extension - 10 inch*
>   *Universal joint*
>   *Torque wrench (same size drive as sockets)*
>   *Ball peen hammer - 8 ounce*
>   *Soft-face hammer (plastic/rubber)*
>   *Standard screwdriver (1/4-inch x 6 inch)*
>   *Standard screwdriver (stubby - 5/16-inch)*
>   *Phillips screwdriver (No. 3 x 8 inch)*
>   *Phillips screwdriver (stubby - No. 2)*
>   *Pliers - vise grip*

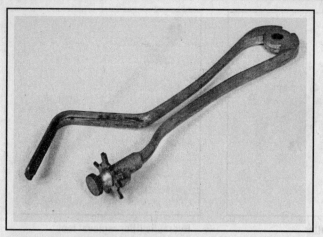

**Piston ring groove cleaning tool**

**Ring removal/installation tool**

**Ring compressor**

**Cylinder hone**

**Brake hold-down spring tool**

Pliers - lineman's
Pliers - needle nose
Pliers - snap-ring (internal and external)
Cold chisel - 1/2-inch
Scribe
Scraper (made from flattened copper tubing)
Centerpunch
Pin punches (1/16, 1/8, 3/16-inch)
Steel rule/straightedge - 12 inch
Allen wrench set (1/8 to 3/8-inch or 4 mm to 10 mm)
A selection of files
Wire brush (large)
Jackstands (second set)
Jack (scissor or hydraulic type)

➡**Note: Another tool which is often useful is an electric drill with a chuck capacity of 3/8-inch and a set of good quality drill bits.**

## Special tools

The tools in this list include those which are not used regularly, are expensive to buy, or which need to be used in accordance with their manufacturer's instructions. Unless these tools will be used frequently, it is not very economical to purchase many of them. A consideration would be to split the cost and use between yourself and a friend or friends. In addition, most of these tools can be obtained from a tool rental shop on a temporary basis.

This list primarily contains only those tools and instruments widely available to the public, and not those special tools produced by the vehicle manufacturer for distribution to dealer service depart-

ments. Occasionally, references to the manufacturer's special tools are included in the text of this manual. Generally, an alternative method of doing the job without the special tool is offered. However, sometimes there is no alternative to their use. Where this is the case, and the tool cannot be purchased or borrowed, the work should be turned over to the dealer service department or an automotive repair shop.

Valve spring compressor
Piston ring groove cleaning tool
Piston ring compressor
Piston ring installation tool
Cylinder compression gauge
Cylinder ridge reamer
Cylinder surfacing hone
Cylinder bore gauge
Micrometers and/or dial calipers
Hydraulic lifter removal tool
Balljoint separator
Universal-type puller
Impact screwdriver
Dial indicator set
Stroboscopic timing light (inductive pick-up)
Hand operated vacuum/pressure pump
Tachometer/dwell meter
Universal electrical multimeter
Cable hoist
Brake spring removal and installation tools
Floor jack

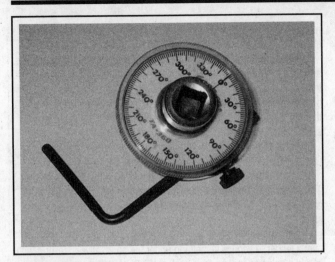

**Torque angle gauge**

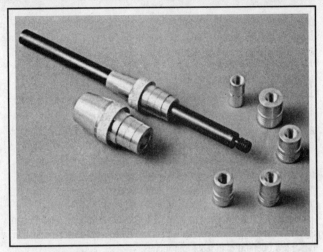

**Clutch plate alignment tool**

## Buying tools

For the do-it-yourselfer who is just starting to get involved in vehicle maintenance and repair, there are a number of options available when purchasing tools. If maintenance and minor repair is the extent of the work to be done, the purchase of individual tools is satisfactory. If, on the other hand, extensive work is planned, it would be a good idea to purchase a modest tool set from one of the large retail chain stores. A set can usually be bought at a substantial savings over the individual tool prices, and they often come with a tool box. As additional tools are needed, add-on sets, individual tools and a larger tool box can be purchased to expand the tool selection. Building a tool set gradually allows the cost of the tools to be spread over a longer period of time and gives the mechanic the freedom to choose only those tools that will actually be used.

Tool stores will often be the only source of some of the special tools that are needed, but regardless of where tools are bought, try to avoid cheap ones, especially when buying screwdrivers and sockets, because they won't last very long. The expense involved in replacing cheap tools will eventually be greater than the initial cost of quality tools.

## Care and maintenance of tools

Good tools are expensive, so it makes sense to treat them with respect. Keep them clean and in usable condition and store them properly when not in use. Always wipe off any dirt, grease or metal chips before putting them away. Never leave tools lying around in the work area. Upon completion of a job, always check closely under the hood for tools that may have been left there so they won't get lost during a test drive.

Some tools, such as screwdrivers, pliers, wrenches and sockets, can be hung on a panel mounted on the garage or workshop wall, while others should be kept in a tool box or tray. Measuring instruments, gauges, meters, etc. must be carefully stored where they cannot be damaged by weather or impact from other tools.

When tools are used with care and stored properly, they will last a very long time. Even with the best of care, though, tools will wear out if used frequently. When a tool is damaged or worn out, replace it. Subsequent jobs will be safer and more enjoyable if you do.

## HOW TO REPAIR DAMAGED THREADS

Sometimes, the internal threads of a nut or bolt hole can become stripped, usually from overtightening. Stripping threads is an all-too-

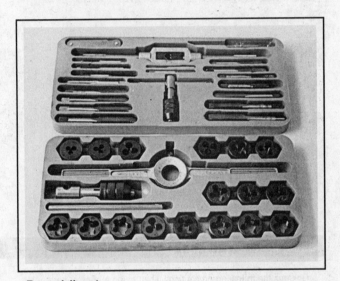

**Tap and die set**

common occurrence, especially when working with aluminum parts, because aluminum is so soft that it easily strips out.

Usually, external or internal threads are only partially stripped. After they've been cleaned up with a tap or die, they'll still work. Sometimes, however, threads are badly damaged. When this happens, you've got three choices:

1) *Drill and tap the hole to the next suitable oversize and install a larger diameter bolt, screw or stud.*

2) *Drill and tap the hole to accept a threaded plug, then drill and tap the plug to the original screw size. You can also buy a plug already threaded to the original size. Then you simply drill a hole to the specified size, then run the threaded plug into the hole with a bolt and jam nut. Once the plug is fully seated, remove the jam nut and bolt.*

3) *The third method uses a patented thread repair kit like Heli-Coil or Slimsert. These easy-to-use kits are designed to repair damaged threads in straight-through holes and blind holes. Both are available as kits which can handle a variety of sizes and thread patterns. Drill the hole, then tap it with the special included tap. Install the Heli-Coil and the hole is back to its original diameter and thread pitch.*

Regardless of which method you use, be sure to proceed calmly and carefully. A little impatience or carelessness during one of these relatively simple procedures can ruin your whole day's work and cost you a bundle if you wreck an expensive part.

## WORKING FACILITIES

Not to be overlooked when discussing tools is the workshop. If anything more than routine maintenance is to be carried out, some sort of suitable work area is essential.

It is understood, and appreciated, that many home mechanics do not have a good workshop or garage available, and end up removing an engine or doing major repairs outside. It is recommended, however, that the overhaul or repair be completed under the cover of a roof.

A clean, flat workbench or table of comfortable working height is an absolute necessity. The workbench should be equipped with a vise that has a jaw opening of at least four inches.

As mentioned previously, some clean, dry storage space is also

required for tools, as well as the lubricants, fluids, cleaning solvents, etc. which soon become necessary.

Sometimes waste oil and fluids, drained from the engine or cooling system during normal maintenance or repairs, present a disposal problem. To avoid pouring them on the ground or into a sewage system, pour the used fluids into large containers, seal them with caps and take them to an authorized disposal site or recycling center. Plastic jugs, such as old antifreeze containers, are ideal for this purpose.

Always keep a supply of old newspapers and clean rags available. Old towels are excellent for mopping up spills. Many mechanics use rolls of paper towels for most work because they are readily available and disposable. To help keep the area under the vehicle clean, a large cardboard box can be cut open and flattened to protect the garage or shop floor.

Whenever working over a painted surface, such as when leaning over a fender to service something under the hood, always cover it with an old blanket or bedspread to protect the finish. Vinyl covered pads, made especially for this purpose, are available at auto parts stores.

## Booster battery (jump) starting

Observe the following precautions when using a booster battery to start a vehicle:

a) *Before connecting the booster battery, make sure the ignition switch is in the Off position.*
b) *Turn off the lights, heater and other electrical loads.*
c) *Your eyes should be shielded. Safety goggles are a good idea.*
d) *Make sure the booster battery is the same voltage as the dead one in the vehicle.*
e) *The two vehicles MUST NOT TOUCH each other.*
f) *Make sure the transmission is in Park.*
g) *If the booster battery is not a maintenance-free type, remove the vent caps and lay a cloth over the vent holes.*

Connect the red jumper cable to the positive (+) terminals of each battery.

Connect one end of the black cable to the negative (-) terminal of the booster battery. The other end of this cable should be connected to a good ground on the engine block (see illustration). Make sure the cable will not come into contact with the fan, drivebelts or other moving parts of the engine.

Start the engine using the booster battery, then, with the engine running at idle speed, disconnect the jumper cables in the reverse order of connection.

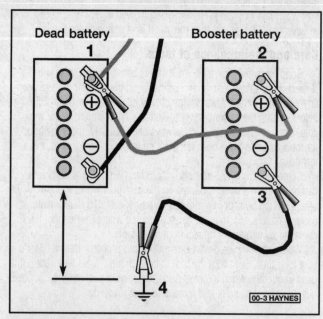

**Make the booster battery cable connections in the numerical order shown (note that the negative cable of the booster battery is NOT attached to the negative terminal of the dead battery)**

## Jacking and towing

### JACKING

The jack supplied with the vehicle should only be used for raising the vehicle for changing a tire or placing jackstands under the frame.

### ✳✳ WARNING:

**Never crawl under the vehicle or start the engine when the jack is being used as the only means of support.**

All models are supplied with a scissors-type jack. When jacking the vehicle, it should be engaged with the rocker panel flange, between the two cutouts (see illustration).

The vehicle should be on level ground with the wheels blocked and the transmission in Park. Pry off the hub cap (if equipped) using the tapered end of the lug wrench. Loosen the lug nuts one-half turn and leave them in place until the wheel is raised off the ground.

Place the jack under the side of the vehicle in the indicated position. Use the supplied wrench to turn the jackscrew clockwise until the wheel is raised off the ground. Remove the lug nuts, pull off the wheel and install the spare.

With the beveled side in, install the lug nuts and tighten them until snug. Lower the vehicle by turning the jackscrew counterclockwise. Remove the jack and tighten the nuts in a diagonal pattern to the torque listed in the Chapter 1 Specifications. If a torque wrench is not available, have the torque checked by a service station as soon as possible. Install the hubcap by placing it in position and using the heel of your hand or a rubber mallet to seat it.

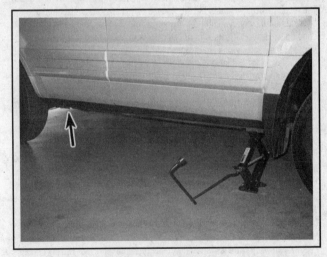

**The jack fits over the rocker panel flange (there are two jacking points on each side of the vehicle)**

### TOWING

The manufacturer states that the only safe way to tow these vehicles is with a flatbed-type car carrier. Other methods could cause damage to the drivetrain.

## Automotive chemicals and lubricants

A number of automotive chemicals and lubricants are available for use during vehicle maintenance and repair. They include a wide variety of products ranging from cleaning solvents and degreasers to lubricants and protective sprays for rubber, plastic and vinyl.

## CLEANERS

*Carburetor cleaner and choke cleaner* is a strong solvent for gum, varnish and carbon. Most carburetor cleaners leave a dry-type lubricant film which will not harden or gum up. Because of this film it is not recommended for use on electrical components.

*Brake system cleaner* is used to remove brake dust, grease and brake fluid from the brake system, where clean surfaces are absolutely necessary. It leaves no residue and often eliminates brake squeal caused by contaminants.

*Electrical cleaner* removes oxidation, corrosion and carbon deposits from electrical contacts, restoring full current flow. It can also be used to clean spark plugs, carburetor jets, voltage regulators and other parts where an oil-free surface is desired.

*Demoisturants* remove water and moisture from electrical components such as alternators, voltage regulators, electrical connectors and fuse blocks. They are non-conductive and non-corrosive.

*Degreasers* are heavy-duty solvents used to remove grease from the outside of the engine and from chassis components. They can be sprayed or brushed on and, depending on the type, are rinsed off either with water or solvent.

## LUBRICANTS

*Motor oil* is the lubricant formulated for use in engines. It normally contains a wide variety of additives to prevent corrosion and reduce foaming and wear. Motor oil comes in various weights (viscosity ratings) from 0 to 50. The recommended weight of the oil depends on the season, temperature and the demands on the engine. Light oil is used in cold climates and under light load conditions. Heavy oil is used in hot climates and where high loads are encountered. Multi-viscosity oils are designed to have characteristics of both light and heavy oils and are available in a number of weights from 5W-20 to 20W-50.

*Gear oil* is designed to be used in differentials, manual transmissions and other areas where high-temperature lubrication is required.

*Chassis and wheel bearing grease* is a heavy grease used where increased loads and friction are encountered, such as for wheel bearings, balljoints, tie-rod ends and universal joints.

*High-temperature wheel bearing grease* is designed to withstand the extreme temperatures encountered by wheel bearings in disc brake equipped vehicles. It usually contains molybdenum disulfide (moly), which is a dry-type lubricant.

*White grease* is a heavy grease for metal-to-metal applications where water is a problem. White grease stays soft under both low and high temperatures (usually from -100 to +190-degrees F), and will not wash off or dilute in the presence of water.

*Assembly lube* is a special extreme pressure lubricant, usually containing moly, used to lubricate high-load parts (such as main and rod bearings and cam lobes) for initial start-up of a new engine. The assembly lube lubricates the parts without being squeezed out or washed away until the engine oiling system begins to function.

*Silicone lubricants* are used to protect rubber, plastic, vinyl and nylon parts.

*Graphite lubricants* are used where oils cannot be used due to contamination problems, such as in locks. The dry graphite will lubricate metal parts while remaining uncontaminated by dirt, water, oil or acids. It is electrically conductive and will not foul electrical contacts in locks such as the ignition switch.

*Moly penetrants* loosen and lubricate frozen, rusted and corroded fasteners and prevent future rusting or freezing.

*Heat-sink grease* is a special electrically non-conductive grease that is used for mounting electronic ignition modules where it is essential that heat is transferred away from the module.

## SEALANTS

*RTV sealant* is one of the most widely used gasket compounds. Made from silicone, RTV is air curing, it seals, bonds, waterproofs, fills surface irregularities, remains flexible, doesn't shrink, is relatively easy to remove, and is used as a supplementary sealer with almost all low and medium temperature gaskets.

*Anaerobic sealant* is much like RTV in that it can be used either to seal gaskets or to form gaskets by itself. It remains flexible, is solvent resistant and fills surface imperfections. The difference between an anaerobic sealant and an RTV-type sealant is in the curing. RTV cures when exposed to air, while an anaerobic sealant cures only in the absence of air. This means that an anaerobic sealant cures only after the assembly of parts, sealing them together.

*Thread and pipe sealant* is used for sealing hydraulic and pneumatic fittings and vacuum lines. It is usually made from a Teflon compound, and comes in a spray, a paint-on liquid and as a wrap-around tape.

## CHEMICALS

*Anti-seize compound* prevents seizing, galling, cold welding, rust and corrosion in fasteners. High-temperature anti-seize, usually made with copper and graphite lubricants, is used for exhaust system and exhaust manifold bolts.

*Anaerobic locking compounds* are used to keep fasteners from vibrating or working loose and cure only after installation, in the absence of air. Medium strength locking compound is used for small nuts, bolts and screws that may be removed later. High-strength locking compound is for large nuts, bolts and studs which aren't removed on a regular basis.

*Oil additives* range from viscosity index improvers to chemical treatments that claim to reduce internal engine friction. It should be noted that most oil manufacturers caution against using additives with their oils.

*Gas additives* perform several functions, depending on their chemical makeup. They usually contain solvents that help dissolve gum and varnish that build up on carburetor, fuel injection and intake parts. They also serve to break down carbon deposits that form on the inside surfaces of the combustion chambers. Some additives contain upper cylinder lubricants for valves and piston rings, and others contain chemicals to remove condensation from the gas tank.

## MISCELLANEOUS

*Brake fluid* is specially formulated hydraulic fluid that can withstand the heat and pressure encountered in brake systems. Care must be taken so this fluid does not come in contact with painted surfaces or plastics. An opened container should always be resealed to prevent contamination by water or dirt.

*Weatherstrip adhesive* is used to bond weatherstripping around doors, windows and trunk lids. It is sometimes used to attach trim pieces.

*Undercoating* is a petroleum-based, tar-like substance that is designed to protect metal surfaces on the underside of the vehicle from corrosion. It also acts as a sound-deadening agent by insulating the bottom of the vehicle.

*Waxes and polishes* are used to help protect painted and plated surfaces from the weather. Different types of paint may require the use of different types of wax and polish. Some polishes utilize a chemical or abrasive cleaner to help remove the top layer of oxidized (dull) paint on older vehicles. In recent years many non-wax polishes that contain a wide variety of chemicals such as polymers and silicones have been introduced. These non-wax polishes are usually easier to apply and last longer than conventional waxes and polishes.

## CONVERSION FACTORS

### LENGTH (distance)

| | | | | | |
|---|---|---|---|---|---|
| Inches (in) | X | 25.4 | = Millimeters (mm) | X | 0.0394 | = Inches (in) |
| Feet (ft) | X | 0.305 | = Meters (m) | X | 3.281 | = Feet (ft) |
| Miles | X | 1.609 | = Kilometers (km) | X | 0.621 | = Miles |

### VOLUME (capacity)

| | | | | | |
|---|---|---|---|---|---|
| Cubic inches (cu in; in$^3$) | X | 16.387 | = Cubic centimeters (cc; cm$^3$) | X | 0.061 | = Cubic inches (cu in; in$^3$) |
| Imperial pints (Imp pt) | X | 0.568 | = Liters (l) | X | 1.76 | = Imperial pints (Imp pt) |
| Imperial quarts (Imp qt) | X | 1.137 | = Liters (l) | X | 0.88 | = Imperial quarts (Imp qt) |
| Imperial quarts (Imp qt) | X | 1.201 | = US quarts (US qt) | X | 0.833 | = Imperial quarts (Imp qt) |
| US quarts (US qt) | X | 0.946 | = Liters (l) | X | 1.057 | = US quarts (US qt) |
| Imperial gallons (Imp gal) | X | 4.546 | = Liters (l) | X | 0.22 | = Imperial gallons (Imp gal) |
| Imperial gallons (Imp gal) | X | 1.201 | = US gallons (US gal) | X | 0.833 | = Imperial gallons (Imp gal) |
| US gallons (US gal) | X | 3.785 | = Liters (l) | X | 0.264 | = US gallons (US gal) |

### MASS (weight)

| | | | | | |
|---|---|---|---|---|---|
| Ounces (oz) | X | 28.35 | = Grams (g) | X | 0.035 | = Ounces (oz) |
| Pounds (lb) | X | 0.454 | = Kilograms (kg) | X | 2.205 | = Pounds (lb) |

### FORCE

| | | | | | |
|---|---|---|---|---|---|
| Ounces-force (ozf; oz) | X | 0.278 | = Newtons (N) | X | 3.6 | = Ounces-force (ozf; oz) |
| Pounds-force (lbf; lb) | X | 4.448 | = Newtons (N) | X | 0.225 | = Pounds-force (lbf; lb) |
| Newtons (N) | X | 0.1 | = Kilograms-force (kgf; kg) | X | 9.81 | = Newtons (N) |

### PRESSURE

| | | | | | |
|---|---|---|---|---|---|
| Pounds-force per square inch (psi; lbf/in$^2$; lb/in$^2$) | X | 0.070 | = Kilograms-force per square centimeter (kgf/cm$^2$; kg/cm$^2$) | X | 14.223 | = Pounds-force per square inch (psi; lbf/in$^2$; lb/in$^2$) |
| Pounds-force per square inch (psi; lbf/in$^2$; lb/in$^2$) | X | 0.068 | = Atmospheres (atm) | X | 14.696 | = Pounds-force per square inch (psi; lbf/in$^2$; lb/in$^2$) |
| Pounds-force per square inch (psi; lbf/in$^2$; lb/in$^2$) | X | 0.069 | = Bars | X | 14.5 | = Pounds-force per square inch (psi; lbf/in$^2$; lb/in$^2$) |
| Pounds-force per square inch (psi; lbf/in$^2$; lb/in$^2$) | X | 6.895 | = Kilopascals (kPa) | X | 0.145 | = Pounds-force per square inch (psi; lbf/in$^2$; lb/in$^2$) |
| Kilopascals (kPa) | X | 0.01 | = Kilograms-force per square centimeter (kgf/cm$^2$; kg/cm$^2$) | X | 98.1 | = Kilopascals (kPa) |

### TORQUE (moment of force)

| | | | | | |
|---|---|---|---|---|---|
| Pounds-force inches (lbf in; lb in) | X | 1.152 | = Kilograms-force centimeter (kgf cm; kg cm) | X | 0.868 | = Pounds-force inches (lbf in; lb in) |
| Pounds-force inches (lbf in; lb in) | X | 0.113 | = Newton meters (Nm) | X | 8.85 | = Pounds-force inches (lbf in; lb in) |
| Pounds-force inches (lbf in; lb in) | X | 0.083 | = Pounds-force feet (lbf ft; lb ft) | X | 12 | = Pounds-force inches (lbf in; lb in) |
| Pounds-force feet (lbf ft; lb ft) | X | 0.138 | = Kilograms-force meters (kgf m; kg m) | X | 7.233 | = Pounds-force feet (lbf ft; lb ft) |
| Pounds-force feet (lbf ft; lb ft) | X | 1.356 | = Newton meters (Nm) | X | 0.738 | = Pounds-force feet (lbf ft; lb ft) |
| Newton meters (Nm) | X | 0.102 | = Kilograms-force meters (kgf m; kg m) | X | 9.804 | = Newton meters (Nm) |

### VACUUM

| | | | | | |
|---|---|---|---|---|---|
| Inches mercury (in. Hg) | X | 3.377 | = Kilopascals (kPa) | X | 0.2961 | = Inches mercury |
| Inches mercury (in. Hg) | X | 25.4 | = Millimeters mercury (mm Hg) | X | 0.0394 | = Inches mercury |

### POWER

| | | | | | |
|---|---|---|---|---|---|
| Horsepower (hp) | X | 745.7 | = Watts (W) | X | 0.0013 | = Horsepower (hp) |

### VELOCITY (speed)

| | | | | | |
|---|---|---|---|---|---|
| Miles per hour (miles/hr; mph) | X | 1.609 | = Kilometers per hour (km/hr; kph) | X | 0.621 | = Miles per hour (miles/hr; mph) |

### FUEL CONSUMPTION *

| | | | | | |
|---|---|---|---|---|---|
| Miles per gallon, Imperial (mpg) | X | 0.354 | = Kilometers per liter (km/l) | X | 2.825 | = Miles per gallon, Imperial (mpg) |
| Miles per gallon, US (mpg) | X | 0.425 | = Kilometers per liter (km/l) | X | 2.352 | = Miles per gallon, US (mpg) |

### TEMPERATURE

Degrees Fahrenheit = (°C x 1.8) + 32          Degrees Celsius (Degrees Centigrade; °C) = (°F - 32) x 0.56

*It is common practice to convert from miles per gallon (mpg) to liters/100 kilometers (l/100km), where mpg (Imperial) x l/100 km = 282 and mpg (US) x l/100 km = 235

# FRACTION/DECIMAL/MILLIMETER EQUIVALENTS

## DECIMALS TO MILLIMETERS

| Decimal | mm | Decimal | mm |
|---|---|---|---|
| 0.001 | 0.0254 | 0.500 | 12.7000 |
| 0.002 | 0.0508 | 0.510 | 12.9540 |
| 0.003 | 0.0762 | 0.520 | 13.2080 |
| 0.004 | 0.1016 | 0.530 | 13.4620 |
| 0.005 | 0.1270 | 0.540 | 13.7160 |
| 0.006 | 0.1524 | 0.550 | 13.9700 |
| 0.007 | 0.1778 | 0.560 | 14.2240 |
| 0.008 | 0.2032 | 0.570 | 14.4780 |
| 0.009 | 0.2286 | 0.580 | 14.7320 |
|  |  | 0.590 | 14.9860 |
| 0.010 | 0.2540 |  |  |
| 0.020 | 0.5080 |  |  |
| 0.030 | 0.7620 |  |  |
| 0.040 | 1.0160 | 0.600 | 15.2400 |
| 0.050 | 1.2700 | 0.610 | 15.4940 |
| 0.060 | 1.5240 | 0.620 | 15.7480 |
| 0.070 | 1.7780 | 0.630 | 16.0020 |
| 0.080 | 2.0320 | 0.640 | 16.2560 |
| 0.090 | 2.2860 | 0.650 | 16.5100 |
|  |  | 0.660 | 16.7640 |
| 0.100 | 2.5400 | 0.670 | 17.0180 |
| 0.110 | 2.7940 | 0.680 | 17.2720 |
| 0.120 | 3.0480 | 0.690 | 17.5260 |
| 0.130 | 3.3020 |  |  |
| 0.140 | 3.5560 |  |  |
| 0.150 | 3.8100 |  |  |
| 0.160 | 4.0640 | 0.700 | 17.7800 |
| 0.170 | 4.3180 | 0.710 | 18.0340 |
| 0.180 | 4.5720 | 0.720 | 18.2880 |
| 0.190 | 4.8260 | 0.730 | 18.5420 |
|  |  | 0.740 | 18.7960 |
| 0.200 | 5.0800 | 0.750 | 19.0500 |
| 0.210 | 5.3340 | 0.760 | 19.3040 |
| 0.220 | 5.5880 | 0.770 | 19.5580 |
| 0.230 | 5.8420 | 0.780 | 19.8120 |
| 0.240 | 6.0960 | 0.790 | 20.0660 |
| 0.250 | 6.3500 |  |  |
| 0.260 | 6.6040 |  |  |
| 0.270 | 6.8580 | 0.800 | 20.3200 |
| 0.280 | 7.1120 | 0.810 | 20.5740 |
| 0.290 | 7.3660 | 0.820 | 21.8280 |
|  |  | 0.830 | 21.0820 |
| 0.300 | 7.6200 | 0.840 | 21.3360 |
| 0.310 | 7.8740 | 0.850 | 21.5900 |
| 0.320 | 8.1280 | 0.860 | 21.8440 |
| 0.330 | 8.3820 | 0.870 | 22.0980 |
| 0.340 | 8.6360 | 0.880 | 22.3520 |
| 0.350 | 8.8900 | 0.890 | 22.6060 |
| 0.360 | 9.1440 |  |  |
| 0.370 | 9.3980 |  |  |
| 0.380 | 9.6520 |  |  |
| 0.390 | 9.9060 |  |  |
|  |  | 0.900 | 22.8600 |
| 0.400 | 10.1600 | 0.910 | 23.1140 |
| 0.410 | 10.4140 | 0.920 | 23.3680 |
| 0.420 | 10.6680 | 0.930 | 23.6220 |
| 0.430 | 10.9220 | 0.940 | 23.8760 |
| 0.440 | 11.1760 | 0.950 | 24.1300 |
| 0.450 | 11.4300 | 0.960 | 24.3840 |
| 0.460 | 11.6840 | 0.970 | 24.6380 |
| 0.470 | 11.9380 | 0.980 | 24.8920 |
| 0.480 | 12.1920 | 0.990 | 25.1460 |
| 0.490 | 12.4460 | 1.000 | 25.4000 |

## FRACTIONS TO DECIMALS TO MILLIMETERS

| Fraction | Decimal | mm | Fraction | Decimal | mm |
|---|---|---|---|---|---|
| 1/64 | 0.0156 | 0.3969 | 33/64 | 0.5156 | 13.0969 |
| 1/32 | 0.0312 | 0.7938 | 17/32 | 0.5312 | 13.4938 |
| 3/64 | 0.0469 | 1.1906 | 35/64 | 0.5469 | 13.8906 |
| 1/16 | 0.0625 | 1.5875 | 9/16 | 0.5625 | 14.2875 |
| 5/64 | 0.0781 | 1.9844 | 37/64 | 0.5781 | 14.6844 |
| 3/32 | 0.0938 | 2.3812 | 19/32 | 0.5938 | 15.0812 |
| 7/64 | 0.1094 | 2.7781 | 39/64 | 0.6094 | 15.4781 |
| 1/8 | 0.1250 | 3.1750 | 5/8 | 0.6250 | 15.8750 |
| 9/64 | 0.1406 | 3.5719 | 41/64 | 0.6406 | 16.2719 |
| 5/32 | 0.1562 | 3.9688 | 21/32 | 0.6562 | 16.6688 |
| 11/64 | 0.1719 | 4.3656 | 43/64 | 0.6719 | 17.0656 |
| 3/16 | 0.1875 | 4.7625 | 11/16 | 0.6875 | 17.4625 |
| 13/64 | 0.2031 | 5.1594 | 45/64 | 0.7031 | 17.8594 |
| 7/32 | 0.2188 | 5.5562 | 23/32 | 0.7188 | 18.2562 |
| 15/64 | 0.2344 | 5.9531 | 47/64 | 0.7344 | 18.6531 |
| 1/4 | 0.2500 | 6.3500 | 3/4 | 0.7500 | 19.0500 |
| 17/64 | 0.2656 | 6.7469 | 49/64 | 0.7656 | 19.4469 |
| 9/32 | 0.2812 | 7.1438 | 25/32 | 0.7812 | 19.8438 |
| 19/64 | 0.2969 | 7.5406 | 51/64 | 0.7969 | 20.2406 |
| 5/16 | 0.3125 | 7.9375 | 13/16 | 0.8125 | 20.6375 |
| 21/64 | 0.3281 | 8.3344 | 53/64 | 0.8281 | 21.0344 |
| 11/32 | 0.3438 | 8.7312 | 27/32 | 0.8438 | 21.4312 |
| 23/64 | 0.3594 | 9.1281 | 55/64 | 0.8594 | 21.8281 |
| 3/8 | 0.3750 | 9.5250 | 7/8 | 0.8750 | 22.2250 |
| 25/64 | 0.3906 | 9.9219 | 57/64 | 0.8906 | 22.6219 |
| 13/32 | 0.4062 | 10.3188 | 29/32 | 0.9062 | 23.0188 |
| 27/64 | 0.4219 | 10.7156 | 59/64 | 0.9219 | 23.4156 |
| 7/16 | 0.4375 | 11.1125 | 15/16 | 0.9375 | 23.8125 |
| 29/64 | 0.4531 | 11.5094 | 61/64 | 0.9531 | 24.2094 |
| 15/32 | 0.4688 | 11.9062 | 31/32 | 0.9688 | 24.6062 |
| 31/64 | 0.4844 | 12.3031 | 63/64 | 0.9844 | 25.0031 |
| 1/2 | 0.5000 | 12.7000 | 1 | 1.0000 | 25.4000 |

## Safety first!

Regardless of how enthusiastic you may be about getting on with the job at hand, take the time to ensure that your safety is not jeopardized. A moment's lack of attention can result in an accident, as can failure to observe certain simple safety precautions. The possibility of an accident will always exist, and the following points should not be considered a comprehensive list of all dangers. Rather, they are intended to make you aware of the risks and to encourage a safety conscious approach to all work you carry out on your vehicle.

## ESSENTIAL DOS AND DON'TS

**DON'T** rely on a jack when working under the vehicle. Always use approved jackstands to support the weight of the vehicle and place them under the recommended lift or support points.

**DON'T** attempt to loosen extremely tight fasteners (i.e. wheel lug nuts) while the vehicle is on a jack - it may fall.

**DON'T** start the engine without first making sure that the transmission is in Neutral (or Park where applicable) and the parking brake is set.

**DON'T** remove the radiator cap from a hot cooling system - let it cool or cover it with a cloth and release the pressure gradually.

**DON'T** attempt to drain the engine oil until you are sure it has cooled to the point that it will not burn you.

**DON'T** touch any part of the engine or exhaust system until it has cooled sufficiently to avoid burns.

**DON'T** siphon toxic liquids such as gasoline, antifreeze and brake fluid by mouth, or allow them to remain on your skin.

**DON'T** inhale brake lining dust - it is potentially hazardous (see *Asbestos* below).

**DON'T** allow spilled oil or grease to remain on the floor - wipe it up before someone slips on it.

**DON'T** use loose fitting wrenches or other tools which may slip and cause injury.

**DON'T** push on wrenches when loosening or tightening nuts or bolts. Always try to pull the wrench toward you. If the situation calls for pushing the wrench away, push with an open hand to avoid scraped knuckles if the wrench should slip.

**DON'T** attempt to lift a heavy component alone - get someone to help you.

**DON'T** rush or take unsafe shortcuts to finish a job.

**DON'T** allow children or animals in or around the vehicle while you are working on it.

**DO** wear eye protection when using power tools such as a drill, sander, bench grinder, etc. and when working under a vehicle.

**DO** keep loose clothing and long hair well out of the way of moving parts.

**DO** make sure that any hoist used has a safe working load rating adequate for the job.

**DO** get someone to check on you periodically when working alone on a vehicle.

**DO** carry out work in a logical sequence and make sure that everything is correctly assembled and tightened.

**DO** keep chemicals and fluids tightly capped and out of the reach of children and pets.

**DO** remember that your vehicle's safety affects that of yourself and others. If in doubt on any point, get professional advice.

## ASBESTOS

Certain friction, insulating, sealing, and other products - such as brake linings, brake bands, clutch linings, torque converters, gaskets, etc. - may contain asbestos. Extreme care must be taken to avoid inhalation of dust from such products, since it is hazardous to health. If in doubt, assume that they do contain asbestos.

## FIRE

Remember at all times that gasoline is highly flammable. Never smoke or have any kind of open flame around when working on a vehicle. But the risk does not end there. A spark caused by an electrical short circuit, by two metal surfaces contacting each other, or even by static electricity built up in your body under certain conditions, can ignite gasoline vapors, which in a confined space are highly explosive. Do not, under any circumstances, use gasoline for cleaning parts. Use an approved safety solvent.

Always disconnect the battery ground (-) cable at the battery before working on any part of the fuel system or electrical system. Never risk spilling fuel on a hot engine or exhaust component. It is strongly recommended that a fire extinguisher suitable for use on fuel and electrical fires be kept handy in the garage or workshop at all times. Never try to extinguish a fuel or electrical fire with water.

## FUMES

Certain fumes are highly toxic and can quickly cause unconsciousness and even death if inhaled to any extent. Gasoline vapor falls into this category, as do the vapors from some cleaning solvents. Any draining or pouring of such volatile fluids should be done in a well ventilated area.

When using cleaning fluids and solvents, read the instructions on the container carefully. Never use materials from unmarked containers.

Never run the engine in an enclosed space, such as a garage. Exhaust fumes contain carbon monoxide, which is extremely poisonous. If you need to run the engine, always do so in the open air, or at least have the rear of the vehicle outside the work area.

If you are fortunate enough to have the use of an inspection pit, never drain or pour gasoline and never run the engine while the vehicle is over the pit. The fumes, being heavier than air, will concentrate in the pit with possibly lethal results.

## THE BATTERY

Never create a spark or allow a bare light bulb near a battery. They normally give off a certain amount of hydrogen gas, which is highly explosive.

Always disconnect the battery ground (-) cable at the battery before working on the fuel or electrical systems.

If possible, loosen the filler caps or cover when charging the battery from an external source (this does not apply to sealed or maintenance-free batteries). Do not charge at an excessive rate or the battery may burst.

Take care when adding water to a non maintenance-free battery and when carrying a battery. The electrolyte, even when diluted, is very corrosive and should not be allowed to contact clothing or skin.

Always wear eye protection when cleaning the battery to prevent the caustic deposits from entering your eyes.

## HOUSEHOLD CURRENT

When using an electric power tool, inspection light, etc., which operates on household current, always make sure that the tool is correctly connected to its plug and that, where necessary, it is properly grounded. Do not use such items in damp conditions and, again, do not create a spark or apply excessive heat in the vicinity of fuel or fuel vapor.

## SECONDARY IGNITION SYSTEM VOLTAGE

A severe electric shock can result from touching certain parts of the ignition system (such as the spark plug wires) when the engine is running or being cranked, particularly if components are damp or the insulation is defective. In the case of an electronic ignition system, the secondary system voltage is much higher and could prove fatal.

## Troubleshooting

## CONTENTS

This section provides an easy reference guide to the more common problems which may occur during the operation of your vehicle. Various symptoms and their possible causes are grouped under headings denoting components or systems, such as Engine, Cooling system, etc. They also refer to the Chapter and/or Section that deals with the problem.

Remember that successful troubleshooting isn't a mysterious art practiced only by professional mechanics. It's simply the result of knowledge combined with an intelligent, systematic approach to a problem. Always use a process of elimination, starting with the simplest solution and working through to the most complex - and never overlook the obvious. Anyone can run the gas tank dry or leave the lights on overnight, so don't assume that you're exempt from such oversights.

Finally, always establish a clear idea why a problem has occurred and take steps to ensure that it doesn't happen again. If the electrical system fails because of a poor connection, check all other connections in the system to make sure they don't fail as well. If a particular fuse continues to blow, find out why - don't just go on replacing fuses. Remember, failure of a small component can often be indicative of potential failure or incorrect functioning of a more important component or system.

## ENGINE AND PERFORMANCE

### 1   Engine will not rotate when attempting to start

1   Battery terminal connections loose or corroded (Chapter 1).
2   Battery discharged or faulty (Chapter 1).
3   Automatic transaxle not completely engaged in Park (Chapter 7).
4   Broken, loose or disconnected wiring in the starting circuit (Chapters 5 and 12).
5   Starter motor pinion jammed in flywheel ring gear (Chapter 5).
6   Starter solenoid faulty (Chapter 5).
7   Starter motor faulty (Chapter 5).
8   Ignition switch faulty (Chapter 12).
9   Neutral start switch faulty (Chapter 7).
10  Starter pinion or driveplate teeth worn or broken (Chapter 5).

### 2   Engine rotates but will not start

1   Fuel tank empty.
2   Battery discharged (engine rotates slowly) (Chapter 5).
3   Battery terminal connections loose or corroded (Chapter 1).
4   Leaking fuel injector(s), fuel pump, pressure regulator, etc. (Chapter 4).
5   Fuel not reaching fuel injection system (Chapter 4).
6   Ignition components damp or damaged (Chapter 5).
7   Worn, faulty or incorrectly gapped spark plugs (Chapter 1).
8   Broken, loose or disconnected wiring in the starting circuit (Chapter 5).
9   Broken, loose or disconnected wires at the ignition coil(s) or faulty coil(s) (Chapter 5).

### 3   Engine hard to start when cold

1   Battery discharged or low (Chapter 1).
2   Fuel system malfunctioning (Chapter 4).
3   Emissions or engine control system malfunctioning (Chapter 6).

### 4   Engine hard to start when hot

1   Air filter clogged (Chapter 1).
2   Fuel not reaching the fuel injection system (Chapter 4).
3   Corroded battery connections, especially ground (Chapter 1).
4   Emissions or engine control system malfunctioning (Chapter 6).

### 5   Starter motor noisy or excessively rough in engagement

1   Pinion or driveplate gear teeth worn or broken (Chapter 5).
2   Starter motor mounting bolts loose or missing (Chapter 5).

### 6   Engine starts but stops immediately

1   Loose or faulty electrical connections at coil pack or alternator (Chapter 5).
2   Insufficient fuel reaching the fuel injectors (Chapter 4).
3   Vacuum leak at the gasket between the intake manifold/plenum and throttle body (Chapters 1 and 4).
4   Restricted exhaust system (most likely the catalytic converter) (Chapters 4 and 6).

### 7   Oil puddle under engine

1   Oil pan gasket and/or oil pan drain bolt seal leaking (Chapters 1 and 2).
2   Oil pressure sending unit leaking (Chapter 2).
3   Rocker arm cover gaskets leaking (Chapter 2).
4   Engine oil seals leaking (Chapter 2).

### 8   Engine lopes while idling or idles erratically

1   Vacuum leakage (Chapter 4).
2   Leaking EGR valve or plugged PCV valve (Chapter 6).
3   Air filter clogged (Chapter 1).
4   Fuel pump not delivering sufficient fuel to the fuel injection system (Chapter 4).
5   Leaking head gasket (Chapter 2).
6   Camshaft lobes worn (Chapter 2).

### 9   Engine misses at idle speed

1   Spark plugs worn or not gapped properly (Chapter 1).
2   Faulty ignition coil(s) (Chapter 5).
3   Vacuum leaks (Chapters 1 and 4).
4   Uneven or low compression (Chapter 2B).

### 10   Engine misses throughout driving speed range

1   Fuel filter clogged and/or impurities in the fuel system (Chapters 1 and 4).
2   Low fuel output at the injector (Chapter 4).
3   Faulty or incorrectly gapped spark plugs (Chapter 1).
4   Faulty emission system components (Chapter 6).
5   Low or uneven cylinder compression pressures (Chapter 2B).
6   Weak or faulty ignition coil(s) (Chapter 5).
7   Vacuum leak in fuel injection system, intake manifold or vacuum hoses (Chapter 4).

## 11 Engine stumbles on acceleration

1 Spark plugs fouled (Chapter 1).
2 Fuel injection system needs adjustment or repair (Chapter 4).
3 Fuel filter clogged (Chapter 1).
4 Intake manifold air leak (Chapter 4).

## 12 Engine surges while holding accelerator steady

1 Intake air leak (Chapter 4).
2 Fuel pump faulty (Chapter 4).
3 Loose fuel injector harness connections (Chapter 4).
4 Defective PCM (Chapter 6).

## 13 Engine stalls

1 Idle speed incorrect (Chapter 1).
2 Fuel filter clogged and/or water and impurities in the fuel system (Chapters 1 and 4).
3 Ignition components damp or damaged (Chapter 5).
4 Faulty emissions system components (Chapter 6).
5 Faulty or incorrectly gapped spark plugs (Chapter 1).
6 Vacuum leak in the intake manifold or vacuum hoses (Chapter 4).

## 14 Engine lacks power

1 Faulty or incorrectly gapped spark plugs (Chapter 1).
2 Restricted exhaust system (most likely the catalytic converter (Chapters 4 and 6).
3 Fuel injection system malfunctioning (Chapter 4).
4 Faulty coil(s) (Chapter 5).
5 Brakes binding (Chapter 1).
6 Automatic transaxle fluid level incorrect (Chapter 1).
7 Fuel filter clogged and/or impurities in the fuel system (Chapter 1).
8 Emission control system not functioning properly (Chapter 6).
9 Low or uneven cylinder compression pressures (Chapter 2B).

## 15 Engine backfires

1 Emissions system not functioning properly (Chapter 6).
2 Fuel injection system malfunctioning (Chapter 4).
3 Vacuum leak at fuel injectors, intake manifold or vacuum hoses (Chapter 4).
4 Valves sticking (Chapter 2).

## 16 Pinging or knocking engine sounds during acceleration or uphill

1 Incorrect grade of fuel.
2 Fuel injection system malfunctioning Chapter 4).
3 Improper or damaged spark plugs or wires (Chapter 1).
4 Worn or damaged ignition components (Chapter 5).
5 Faulty emissions system (Chapter 6).
6 Vacuum leak (Chapter 4).

## 17 Engine runs with oil pressure light on

1 Low oil level (Chapter 1).
2 Short in wiring circuit (Chapter 12).
3 Faulty oil pressure sender (Chapter 2B).
4 Oil viscosity too low or oil diluted.
5 Worn engine bearings and/or oil pump (Chapter 2).

## 18 Engine diesels (continues to run) after switching off

1 Excessive engine operating temperature (Chapter 3).
2 Excessive carbon deposits on valves and pistons.

# ENGINE ELECTRICAL SYSTEM

## 19 Battery will not hold a charge

1 Alternator drivebelt defective or not adjusted properly (Chapter 1).
2 Battery terminals loose or corroded (Chapter 1).
3 Alternator not charging properly (Chapter 5).
4 Loose, broken or faulty wiring in the charging circuit (Chapter 5).
5 Short in vehicle wiring (Chapters 5 and 12).
6 Internally defective battery (Chapters 1 and 5).

## 20 Voltage warning light fails to go out

1 Faulty alternator or charging circuit (Chapter 5).
2 Alternator drivebelt defective or out of adjustment (Chapter 1).
3 Alternator voltage regulator inoperative (Chapter 5).

## 21 Voltage warning light fails to come on when key is turned on

1 Warning light bulb defective (Chapter 12).
2 Fault in the printed circuit, dash wiring or bulb holder (Chapter 12).

# FUEL SYSTEM

## 22 Excessive fuel consumption

1 Dirty or clogged air filter element (Chapter 1).
2 Emissions system not functioning properly (Chapter 6).
3 Fuel injection system malfunctioning (Chapter 4).
4 Low tire pressure or incorrect tire size (Chapter 1).

## 23 Fuel leakage and/or fuel odor

1 Leak in a fuel feed or vent line (Chapter 4).
2 Tank overfilled.
3 Evaporative emissions control canister defective (Chapters 1 and 6).
4 Fuel injector seals faulty (Chapter 4).

## COOLING SYSTEM

### 24  Overheating

1  Insufficient coolant in system (Chapter 1).
2  Water pump drivebelt defective or out of adjustment (Chapter 1).
3  Radiator core blocked or grille restricted (Chapter 3).
4  Thermostat faulty (Chapter 3).
5  Electric cooling fan blades broken or cracked (Chapter 3).
6  Radiator cap not maintaining proper pressure (Chapter 3).

### 25  Overcooling

Incorrect (opening temperature too low) or faulty thermostat (Chapter 3).

### 26  External coolant leakage

1  Deteriorated/damaged hoses or loose clamps (Chapters 1 and 3).
2  Water pump seal defective (Chapters 1 and 3).
3  Leakage from radiator core (Chapter 3).
4  Engine drain or water jacket core plugs leaking (Chapter 2).

### 27  Internal coolant leakage

1  Leaking cylinder head gasket (Chapter 2).
2  Cracked cylinder bore or cylinder head (Chapter 2).

### 28  Coolant loss

1  Too much coolant in system (Chapter 1).
2  Coolant boiling away because of overheating (Chapter 3).
3  Internal or external leakage (Chapter 3).
4  Faulty radiator cap (Chapter 3).

### 29  Poor coolant circulation

1  Inoperative water pump (Chapter 3).
2  Restriction in cooling system (Chapters 1 and 3).
3  Water pump drivebelt defective or out of adjustment (Chapter 1).
4  Thermostat sticking (Chapter 3).

## AUTOMATIC TRANSAXLE

➡**Note: Due to the complexity of the automatic transaxle, it's difficult for the home mechanic to properly diagnose and service this component. For problems other than the following, the vehicle should be taken to a dealer service department or a transmission shop.**

### 30  Fluid leakage

1  Automatic transmission fluid is a deep red color. Fluid leaks should not be confused with engine oil, which can easily be blown by airflow to the transaxle.
2  To pinpoint a leak, first remove all built-up dirt and grime from the transaxle housing with degreasing agents and/or steam cleaning.

Drive the vehicle at low speeds so air flow will not blow the leak far from its source. Raise the vehicle and determine where the leak is coming from. Common areas of leakage are:
a)  Fluid pan
b)  Fill plug (Chapter 1)
c)  Fluid cooler lines (Chapter 7)
d)  Vehicle Speed Sensor (Chapter 6)

### 31  Transaxle fluid brown or has a burned smell

Transaxle overheated. Change fluid (Chapter 1).

### 32  General shift mechanism problems

1  Chapter 7 deals with checking and adjusting the shift cable on automatic transaxles. Common problems which may be attributed to a poorly adjusted cable are:
a)  Engine starting in gears other than Park or Neutral.
b)  Indicator on shifter pointing to a gear other than the one actually being used.
c)  Vehicle moves when in Park.
2  Refer to Chapter 7 for the shift cable adjustment procedure.

### 33  Engine will start in gears other than Park or Neutral

Transmission range switch malfunctioning (Chapter 6).

### 34  Transaxle slips, shifts roughly, is noisy or has no drive in forward or reverse gears

There are many probable causes for the above problems, but the home mechanic should be concerned with only one possibility - fluid level. Before taking the vehicle to a repair shop, check the level and condition of the fluid as described in Chapter 1.

Correct the fluid level as necessary or change the fluid and filter if needed. If the problem persists, have a professional diagnose the probable cause.

## DRIVEAXLES

### 35  Clicking noise in turns

Worn or damaged outer CV joint. Check for cut or damaged boots (Chapter 1). Repair as necessary (Chapter 8).

### 36  Knock or clunk when accelerating after coasting

Worn or damaged CV joint. Check for cut or damaged boots (Chapter 1). Repair as necessary (Chapter 8).

### 37  Shudder or vibration during acceleration

1  Worn or damaged CV joints. Repair or replace as necessary (Chapter 8).
2  Sticking inner joint assembly. Correct or replace as necessary (Chapter 8).

## DRIVESHAFT

➡Note: Refer to Chapter 8, unless otherwise specified, for service information.

### 38  Leaks at front of driveshaft

Defective transfer case seal.

### 39  Knock or clunk when transmission is under initial load (just after transmission is put into gear)

1   Loose or disconnected rear suspension components. Check all mounting bolts and bushings (Chapter 10).
2   Loose driveshaft bolts. Inspect all bolts and nuts and tighten them securely.
3   Worn or damaged universal joint bearings.
4   Worn sleeve yoke and mainshaft spline.

### 40  Metallic grating sound consistent with vehicle speed

1   Pronounced wear in the universal joint bearings. Replace driveshaft.
2   Worn center support bearing. Replace driveshaft.

### 41  Vibration

➡Note: Before blaming the driveshaft, make sure the tires are perfectly balanced and perform the following test.

1   Install a tachometer inside the vehicle to monitor engine speed as the vehicle is driven. Drive the vehicle and note the engine speed at which the vibration (roughness) is most pronounced. Now shift the transmission to a different gear and bring the engine speed to the same point.
2   If the vibration occurs at the same engine speed (rpm) regardless of which gear the transmission is in, the driveshaft is NOT at fault since the driveshaft speed varies.
3   If the vibration decreases or is eliminated when the transmission is in a different gear at the same engine speed, refer to the following probable causes:

a) *Bent or dented driveshaft. Inspect and replace as necessary.*
b) *Undercoating or built-up dirt, etc. on the driveshaft. Clean the shaft thoroughly.*
c) *Worn universal joint bearings. Replace the driveshaft.*
d) *Driveshaft and/or companion flange out of balance. Check for missing weights on the shaft. Remove driveshaft and reinstall 180-degrees from original position, then recheck. Have the driveshaft balanced if problem persists.*
e) *Loose driveshaft mounting bolts/nuts.*
f) *Worn center support bearing. Replace the driveshaft.*
g) *Worn transfer case rear bushing.*

### 42  Scraping noise

Make sure there is nothing, such as an exhaust heat shield or safety loop, rubbing on the driveshaft.

## REAR DIFFERENTIAL

➡Note: For differential servicing information, refer to Chapter 8, unless otherwise specified.

### 43  Noise - same when in drive as when vehicle is coasting

1   Road noise. No corrective action available.
2   Tire noise. Inspect tires and check tire pressures (Chapter 1).
3   Hub bearings worn or damaged (Chapter 10).
4   Insufficient differential oil (Chapter 1).
5   Defective differential.

### 44  Knocking sound when starting or shifting gears

Worn differential.

### 45  Noise when turning

Worn differential.

### 46  Vibration

See probable causes under *Driveshaft*. Proceed under the guidelines listed for the driveshaft. If the problem persists, check the rear hub bearings by raising the rear of the vehicle and spinning the wheels by hand. Listen for evidence of rough (noisy) bearings. Remove and inspect.

### 47  Oil leaks

1   Pinion oil seal damaged.
2   Driveaxle oil seals damaged.
3   Loose filler or drain plug on differential (Chapter 1).
4   Clogged or damaged breather on differential.

## BRAKES

➡Note: Before assuming that a brake problem exists, make sure . . .

a) *The tires are in good condition and properly inflated (Chapter 1).*
b) *The front end alignment is correct (Chapter 10).*
c) *The vehicle isn't loaded with weight in an unequal manner.*

### 48  Vehicle pulls to one side during braking

1   Incorrect tire pressures (Chapter 1).
2   Front end out of alignment (have the front end aligned).
3   Unmatched tires on same axle.
4   Restricted brake lines or hoses (Chapter 9).
5   Sticking caliper piston (Chapter 9).
6   Loose suspension parts (Chapter 10).
7   Contaminated brake pad material (Chapter 9).

**49  Noise (grinding or high-pitched squeal) when the brakes are applied**

Disc brake pads worn out. Replace pads with new ones immediately (Chapter 9).

**50  Brake roughness or chatter (pedal pulsates)**

1  Excessive brake disc lateral runout (Chapter 9).
2  Parallelism of disc not within specifications (Chapter 9).
3  Uneven pad wear caused by caliper not sliding due to improper clearance or dirt (Chapter 9).
4  Defective brake disc (Chapter 9).

**51  Excessive pedal effort required to stop vehicle**

1  Malfunctioning power brake booster (Chapter 9).
2  Partial system failure (Chapter 9).
3  Excessively worn pads (Chapter 9).
4  One or more caliper pistons seized or sticking (Chapter 9).
5  Brake pads contaminated with oil or grease (Chapter 9).
6  New pads installed and not yet seated. It will take a while for the new material to seat.

**52  Excessive brake pedal travel**

1  Partial brake system failure (Chapter 9).
2  Insufficient fluid in master cylinder (Chapters 1 and 9).
3  Air trapped in system (Chapter 9).
4  Faulty master cylinder (Chapter 9).

**53  Dragging brakes**

1  Master cylinder pistons not returning correctly (Chapter 9).
2  Restricted brake lines or hoses (Chapters 1 and 9).
3  Incorrect parking brake adjustment (Chapter 9).
4  Defective brake calipers (Chapter 9).

**54  Grabbing or uneven braking action**

1  Malfunction of proportioning valve (Chapter 9).
2  Malfunction of power brake booster unit (Chapter 9).
3  Binding brake pedal mechanism (Chapter 9).
4  Contaminated brake linings (Chapter 9).

**55  Brake pedal feels spongy when depressed**

1  Air in hydraulic lines (Chapter 9).
2  Master cylinder mounting bolts loose (Chapter 9).
3  Master cylinder defective (Chapter 9).

**56  Brake pedal travels to the floor with little resistance**

Little or no fluid in the master cylinder reservoir caused by leaking caliper, or loose, damaged or disconnected brake lines (Chapter 9).

**57  Parking brake does not hold**

Parking brake cables improperly adjusted (Chapter 9).

## SUSPENSION AND STEERING SYSTEMS

➡**Note: Before attempting to diagnose the suspension and steering systems, perform the following preliminary checks:**
*a) Check the tire pressures and look for uneven wear.*
*b) Check the steering universal joints or coupling from the column to the steering gear for loose fasteners and wear.*
*c) Check the front and rear suspension and the steering gear assembly for loose and damaged parts.*
*d) Look for out-of-round or out-of-balance tires, bent rims and loose and/or rough wheel bearings.*

**58  Vehicle pulls to one side**

1  Mismatched or uneven tires (Chapter 10).
2  Broken or sagging springs (Chapter 10).
3  Wheel alignment incorrect (Chapter 10).
4  Front brakes dragging (Chapter 9).

**59  Abnormal or excessive tire wear**

1  Front wheel alignment incorrect (Chapter 10).
2  Sagging or broken springs (Chapter 10).
3  Tire out-of-balance (Chapter 10).
4  Worn strut or shock absorber (Chapter 10).
5  Overloaded vehicle.
6  Tires not rotated regularly.

**60  Wheel makes a "thumping" noise**

1  Blister or bump on tire (Chapter 1).
2  Improper strut or shock absorber action (Chapter 10).

**61  Shimmy, shake or vibration**

1  Tire or wheel out-of-balance or out-of-round (Chapter 10).
2  Loose or worn wheel bearings (Chapter 10).
3  Worn tie-rod ends (Chapter 10).
4  Worn balljoints (Chapter 10).
5  Excessive wheel runout (Chapter 10).
6  Blister or bump on tire (Chapter 1).

**62  Hard steering**

1  Lack of lubrication at balljoints, tie-rod ends and steering gear assembly (Chapter 10).
2  Front wheel alignment incorrect (Chapter 10).
3  Low tire pressure (Chapter 1).

## 63 Steering wheel does not return to center position correctly

1 Lack of lubrication at balljoints and tie-rod ends (Chapters 1 and 10).
2 Binding in steering column (Chapter 10).
3 Defective rack-and-pinion assembly (Chapter 10).
4 Front wheel alignment problem (Chapter 10).

## 64 Abnormal noise at the front end

1 Lack of lubrication at balljoints and tie-rod ends (Chapter 1).
2 Loose upper strut mount (Chapter 10).
3 Worn tie-rod ends (Chapter 10).
4 Loose stabilizer bar (Chapter 10).
5 Loose wheel lug nuts (Chapter 1).
6 Loose suspension bolts (Chapter 10).

## 65 Wander or poor steering stability

1 Mismatched or uneven tires (Chapter 10).
2 Lack of lubrication at balljoints or tie-rod ends (Chapters 1 and 10).
3 Worn struts or shock absorbers (Chapter 10).
4 Loose stabilizer bar (Chapter 10).
5 Broken or sagging springs (Chapter 10).
6 Front wheel alignment incorrect.
7 Worn steering gear clamp bushing (Chapter 10).

## 66 Erratic steering when braking

1 Wheel bearings worn (Chapter 10).
2 Broken or sagging springs (Chapter 10).
3 Leaking caliper (Chapter 9).
4 Warped brake discs (Chapter 9).
5 Worn steering gear clamp bushing (Chapter 10).
6 Wheel alignment incorrect.

## 67 Excessive pitching and/or rolling around corners or during braking

1 Loose stabilizer bar (Chapter 10).
2 Worn struts/shock absorbers or mounts (Chapter 10).
3 Broken or sagging springs (Chapter 10).
4 Overloaded vehicle.

## 68 Suspension bottoms

1 Overloaded vehicle.
2 Worn struts or shock absorbers (Chapter 10).
3 Incorrect, broken or sagging springs (Chapter 10).

## 69 Cupped tires

1 Front wheel alignment incorrect (Chapter 10).
2 Worn struts or shock absorbers (Chapter 10).
3 Hub bearings worn (Chapter 10).
4 Excessive tire or wheel runout (Chapter 10).
5 Worn balljoints (Chapter 10).

## 70 Excessive tire wear on outside edge

1 Inflation pressures incorrect (Chapter 1).
2 Excessive speed in turns.
3 Wheel alignment incorrect (excessive toe-in or positive camber). Have professionally aligned.
4 Suspension arm bent or twisted (Chapter 10).

## 71 Excessive tire wear on inside edge

1 Inflation pressures incorrect (Chapter 1).
2 Wheel alignment incorrect (toe-out or excessive negative camber). Have professionally aligned.
3 Loose or damaged steering components (Chapter 10).

## 72 Tire tread worn in one place

1 Tires out-of-balance.
2 Damaged or buckled wheel. Inspect and replace if necessary.
3 Defective tire (Chapter 1).

## 73 Excessive play or looseness in steering system

1 Hub bearings worn (Chapter 10).
2 Tie-rod end loose or worn (Chapter 10).
3 Steering gear loose (Chapter 10).

## 74 Rattling or clicking noise in steering gear

1 Steering gear mounting bolts loose (Chapter 10).
2 Steering gear defective (Chapter 10).

1

TUNE-UP
AND ROUTINE
MIANTENANCE

**Section**

## 1 Maintenance schedule

The maintenance intervals in this manual are provided with the assumption that you, not the dealer, will be doing the work. These are the minimum maintenance intervals recommended by the factory for vehicles that are driven daily. If you wish to keep your vehicle in peak condition at all times, you may wish to perform some of these procedures even more often. Because frequent maintenance enhances the efficiency, performance and resale value of your car, we encourage you to do so. If you drive in dusty areas, tow a trailer, idle or drive at low speeds for extended periods or drive for short distances (less than four miles) in below freezing temperatures, shorter intervals are also recommended.

When your vehicle is new, follow the maintenance schedule to the letter, record the maintenance performed in your owners manual and keep all receipts to protect the new vehicle warranty. In many cases, the initial maintenance check is done at no cost to the owner.

### EVERY 250 MILES (400 KM) OR WEEKLY, WHICHEVER COMES FIRST

Check the engine oil level (Section 4)
Check the engine coolant level (Section 4)
Check the windshield washer fluid level (Section 4)
Check the brake fluid level (Section 4)
Check the power steering fluid level (Section 4)
Check the automatic transaxle fluid level (Section 4)
Check the rear differential fluid (Section 4)
Check the tires and tire pressures (Section 5)
Check the operation of all lights
Check the horn operation

### EVERY 3000 MILES (4800 KM) OR 3 MONTHS, WHICHEVER COMES FIRST

All items listed above plus:
Change the engine oil and oil filter (Section 6)

### EVERY 7500 MILES (12,000 KM) OR 6 MONTHS, WHICHEVER COMES FIRST

All items listed above plus:
Inspect (and replace, if necessary) the windshield wiper blades (Section 7)
Check and service the battery (Section 8)
Check the cooling system (Section 9)
Rotate the tires (Section 10)
Check the seat belts (Section 11)
Inspect the brake system (Section 12)

### EVERY 15,000 MILES (24,000 KM) OR 12 MONTHS, WHICHEVER COMES FIRST

All items listed above plus:
Inspect the suspension and steering components (Section 13)*
Inspect and replace, if necessary, all underhood hoses (Section 14)
Replace the air filter (Section 15)*
Replace the interior ventilation filter (Section 16)
Inspect the fuel system (Section 17)
Check the exhaust system (Section 18)
Check the driveaxle boots (Section 19)

### EVERY 30,000 (48,000 KM) MILES OR 24 MONTHS, WHICHEVER COMES FIRST

All items listed above plus:
Check the engine drivebelts (Section 20)
Replace the brake fluid (Section 21)
Change the automatic transaxle fluid (Section 22)**
Change the rear differential lubricant (Section 23)

### EVERY 45,000 MILES (72,400 KM) OR 36 MONTHS, WHICHEVER COMES FIRST

Service the cooling system (drain, flush and refill) (Section 24)

### EVERY 105,000 MILES (169,000 KM) OR 84 MONTHS, WHICHEVER COMES FIRST

Replace the spark plugs (see Section 25)
Check and adjust, if necessary, the engine idle speed (Section 26)
Check and adjust, if necessary, the valve clearance (see Chapter 2A)
Replace the timing belt, and inspect the water pump (see Chapter 2A and Chapter 3)

*This item is affected by "severe" operating conditions as described below. If your vehicle is operated under "severe" conditions, perform all maintenance indicated with a * at 7500 mile/6 month intervals. Severe conditions are indicated if you mainly operate your vehicle under one or more of the following conditions:

Operating in dusty areas
Towing a trailer
Idling for extended periods and/or low speed operation
Operating when outside temperatures remain below freezing and when most trips are less than five miles

**If operated under one or more of the following conditions, change the automatic transaxle fluid every 15,000 miles:

In heavy city traffic where the outside temperature regularly reaches 90-degrees F (32-degrees C) or higher
In hilly or mountainous terrain

**Typical engine compartment layout**

| | | | | | |
|---|---|---|---|---|---|
| 1 | Fuse/relay block | 5 | Engine oil dipstick | 9 | Battery |
| 2 | Windshield washer fluid reservoir | 6 | Radiator cap | 10 | Air filter housing |
| 3 | Engine coolant reservoir | 7 | Engine oil filler cap | 11 | Brake fluid reservoir |
| 4 | Power steering fluid reservoir | 8 | Automatic transaxle fluid dipstick | | |

**Typical front underside components**

| | | | | | |
|---|---|---|---|---|---|
| 1 | Front disc brake caliper | 4 | Catalytic converter | 6 | Engine oil drain plug |
| 2 | Radiator drain fitting | 5 | Exhaust pipe | 7 | Engine oil filter |
| 3 | Automatic transaxle drain plug | | | | |

**Typical rear underside components**

| | | | | | |
|---|---|---|---|---|---|
| *1* | Muffler | *3* | Differential drain plug | *5* | Fuel tank |
| *2* | Rear disc brake caliper | *4* | Driveaxle boot | *6* | Exhaust system hanger |

## 2 Introduction

This Chapter is designed to help the home mechanic maintain the Pilot and MDX with the goals of maximum performance, economy, safety and reliability in mind.

Included is a master maintenance schedule, followed by procedures dealing specifically with each item on the schedule. Visual checks, adjustments, component replacement and other helpful items are included. Refer to the accompanying illustrations of the engine compartment and the underside of the vehicle for the locations of various components.

Servicing the vehicle, in accordance with the mileage/time maintenance schedule and the step-by-step procedures will result in a planned maintenance program that should produce a long and reliable service life. Keep in mind that it is a comprehensive plan, so maintaining some items but not others at the specified intervals will not produce the same results.

As you service the vehicle, you will discover that many of the procedures can - and should - be grouped together because of the nature of the particular procedure you're performing or because of the close proximity of two otherwise unrelated components to one another.

For example, if the vehicle is raised for chassis lubrication, you should inspect the exhaust, suspension, steering and fuel systems while you're under the vehicle. When you're rotating the tires, it makes good sense to check the brakes since the wheels are already removed. Finally, let's suppose you have to borrow or rent a torque wrench. Even if you only need it to tighten the spark plugs, you might as well check the torque of as many critical fasteners as time allows.

The first step in this maintenance program is to prepare yourself before the actual work begins. Read through all the procedures you're planning to do, then gather up all the parts and tools needed. If it looks like you might run into problems during a particular job, seek advice from a mechanic or an experienced do-it-yourselfer.

### OWNER'S MANUAL AND VECI LABEL INFORMATION

Your vehicle owner's manual was written for your year and model and contains very specific information on component locations, specifications, fuse ratings, part numbers, etc. The Owner's Manual is an important resource for the do-it-yourselfer to have; if one was not supplied with your vehicle, it can generally be ordered from a dealer parts department.

Among other important information, the Vehicle Emissions Control Information (VECI) label contains specifications and procedures for applicable tune-up adjustments and, in some instances, spark plugs (see Chapter 6 for more information on the VECI label). The information on this label is the exact maintenance data recommended by the manufacturer. This data often varies by intended operating altitude, local emissions regulations, month of manufacture, etc.

This Chapter contains procedural details, safety information and more ambitious maintenance intervals than you might find in manufacturer's literature. However, you may also find procedures or specifications in your Owner's Manual or VECI label that differ with what's printed here. In these cases, the Owner's Manual or VECI label can be considered correct, since it is specific to your particular vehicle.

## 3 Tune-up general information

The term tune-up is used in this manual to represent a combination of individual operations rather than one specific procedure.

If, from the time the vehicle is new, the routine maintenance schedule is followed closely and frequent checks are made of fluid levels and high wear items, as suggested throughout this manual, the engine will be kept in relatively good running condition and the need for additional work will be minimized.

More likely than not, however, there will be times when the engine is running poorly due to lack of regular maintenance. This is even more likely if a used vehicle, which has not received regular and frequent maintenance checks, is purchased. In such cases, an engine tune-up will be needed outside of the regular routine maintenance intervals.

The first step in any tune-up or diagnostic procedure to help correct a poor running engine is a cylinder compression check. A compression check (see Chapter 2B) will help determine the condition of internal engine components and should be used as a guide for tune-up and repair procedures. If, for instance, a compression check indicates serious internal engine wear, a conventional tune-up will not improve the performance of the engine and would be a waste of time and money. Because of its importance, the compression check should be done by someone with the right equipment and the knowledge to use it properly.

The following procedures are those most often needed to bring a generally poor running engine back into a proper state of tune.

### MINOR TUNE-UP

Check all engine related fluids (Section 4)
Clean, inspect and test the battery (Section 8)
Check the cooling system (Section 9)
Check all underhood hoses (Section 14)
Check the air filter (Section 15)
Check and adjust the drivebelts (Section 20)

### MAJOR TUNE-UP

**All items listed under minor tune-up, plus . . .**

Replace the air filter (Section 15)
Check the fuel system (Section 17)
Replace the spark plugs (Section 25)
Check the idle speed (Section 26)

### 4 Fluid level checks (every 250 miles [400km] or weekly)

1 Fluids are an essential part of the lubrication, cooling, brake, clutch and other systems. Because these fluids gradually become depleted and/or contaminated during normal operation of the vehicle, they must be periodically replenished. See *Recommended lubricants and fluids and Capacities* at the end of this Chapter before adding fluid to any of the following components.

➡ **Note: The vehicle must be on level ground before fluid levels can be checked.**

## ENGINE OIL

▶ **Refer to illustrations 4.2, 4.4 and 4.6**

2 The engine oil level is checked with a dipstick located at the front side of the engine (see illustration). The dipstick extends through a metal tube from which it protrudes down into the engine oil pan.

3 The oil level should be checked before the vehicle has been driven, or about 5 minutes after the engine has been shut off. If the oil is checked immediately after driving the vehicle, some of the oil will remain in the upper engine components, producing an inaccurate reading on the dipstick.

4 Pull the dipstick from the tube and wipe all the oil from the end with a clean rag or paper towel. Insert the clean dipstick all the way back into its metal tube and pull it out again. Observe the oil at the end of the dipstick. At its highest point, the level should be between the upper and lower marks (see illustration).

5 It takes one quart of oil to raise the level from the lower mark to the upper mark on the dipstick. Do not allow the level to drop below the lower hole or oil starvation may cause engine damage. Conversely, overfilling the engine (adding oil above the upper mark) may cause oil fouled spark plugs, oil leaks or oil seal failures.

6 Remove the threaded cap from the valve cover to add oil (see illustration). Use an oil can spout or funnel to prevent spills. After adding the oil, install the filler cap hand tight. Start the engine and look

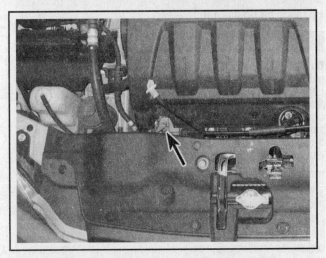

**4.2 The engine oil dipstick is located at the front side of the engine**

carefully for any small leaks around the oil filter or drain plug. Stop the engine and check the oil level again after it has had sufficient time to drain from the upper block and cylinder head galleries.

7 Checking the oil level is an important preventive maintenance step. A continually dropping oil level indicates oil leakage through damaged seals, from loose connections, or past worn rings or valve guides. If the oil looks milky in color or has water droplets in it, a cylinder head gasket may be blown or the oil cooler could be leaking. The engine should be checked immediately. The condition of the oil should also be checked. Each time you check the oil level, slide your thumb and index finger up the dipstick before wiping off the oil. If you see small dirt or metal particles clinging to the dipstick, the oil should be changed (see Section 6).

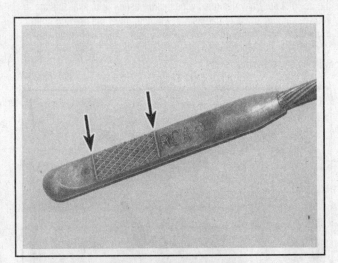

**4.4 The oil level should be in the safe range**

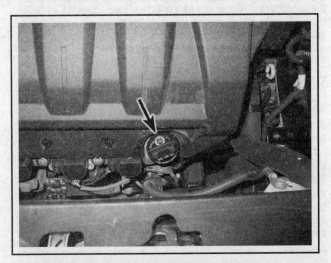

**4.6 The oil filler cap is located on the front valve cover - always make sure the area around the opening is clean before unscrewing the cap to prevent dirt from contaminating the engine**

## ENGINE COOLANT

♦ **Refor to illustration 4.9**

> ❊❊ **WARNING:**
>
> **Do not allow antifreeze to come in contact with your skin or painted surfaces of the vehicle. Flush contaminated areas immediately with plenty of water. Don't store new coolant or leave old coolant lying around where it's accessible to children or pets - they're attracted by its sweet smell. Ingestion of even a small amount of coolant can be fatal! Wipe up garage floor and drip pan spills immediately. Keep antifreeze containers covered and repair cooling system leaks as soon as they're noticed.**

8    All vehicles covered by this manual are equipped with a pressurized coolant recovery system. A coolant reservoir, located on the right side of the engine compartment, is connected by a hose to the base of the radiator filler neck. If the coolant heats up during engine operation, coolant can escape through the pressurized filler cap, then through the connecting hose into the reservoir. As the engine cools, the coolant is automatically drawn back into the cooling system to maintain the correct level.

9    The coolant level in the reservoir should be checked regularly. It must be between the MAX and MIN lines on the tank. The level will vary with the temperature of the engine. When the engine is cold, the coolant level should be at or slightly above the MIN mark on the tank. Once the engine has warmed up, the level should be at or near the MAX mark. If it isn't, allow the fluid in the tank to cool, then remove the cap from the reservoir (see illustration) and add coolant to bring the level up to the MAX line.

> ❊❊ **WARNING:**
>
> **Do not remove the radiator cap to check the coolant level when the engine is warm! Use only the recommended coolant and water in the mixture ratio listed in this Chapter's Specifications. Do not use supplemental inhibitors or additives. If only a small amount of coolant is required to bring the system up to the proper level, water can be used. However, repeated additions of water will dilute the recommended antifreeze and water solution. In order to maintain the proper ratio of antifreeze and water, it is advisable to top up the coolant level with the correct mixture.**

10    If the coolant level drops within a short time after replenishment, there may be a leak in the system. Inspect the radiator, hoses, engine coolant filler cap, drain plugs and water pump. If no leak is evident, have the radiator cap pressure tested.

> ❊❊ **WARNING:**
>
> **Never remove the radiator cap or the coolant reservoir cap when the engine is running or has just been shut down, because the cooling system is hot. Escaping steam and scalding liquid could cause serious injury.**

11    If it is necessary to open the radiator cap, wait until the system has cooled completely, then wrap a thick cloth around the cap and turn it to the first stop. If any steam escapes, wait until the system has cooled further, then remove the cap.

12    When checking the coolant level, always note its condition. It should be relatively clear. If it is brown or rust colored, the system

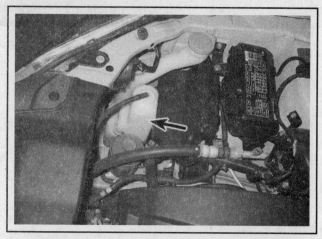

**4.9 The coolant reservoir is located at the right-front corner of the engine compartment**

should be drained, flushed and refilled. Even if the coolant appears to be normal, the corrosion inhibitors wear out with use, so it must be replaced at the specified intervals.

13    Do not allow antifreeze to come in contact with your skin or painted surfaces of the vehicle. Flush contacted areas immediately with plenty of water.

## WINDSHIELD WASHER FLUID

♦ **Refer to illustration 4.14**

14    Fluid for the windshield washer system is stored in a plastic reservoir which is located at the right front corner of the engine compartment (see illustration). Check the fluid level by detaching the cap and pulling up the dipstick. In milder climates, plain water can be used to top up the reservoir, but the reservoir should be kept no more than 2/3 full to allow for expansion should the water freeze. In colder climates, the use of a specially designed windshield washer fluid, available at your dealer and any auto parts store, will help lower the freezing point of the fluid. Mix the solution with water in accordance with the manufacturer's directions on the container. Do not use regular antifreeze. It will damage the vehicle's paint.

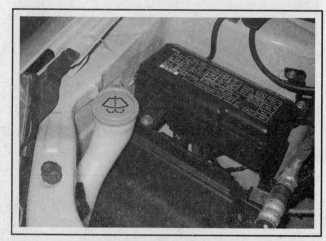

**4.14 The windshield/rear window washer fluid reservoir is located in the right front corner of the engine compartment**

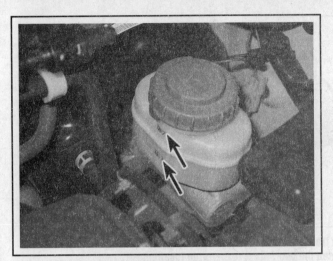

**4.16 The brake fluid level should be kept between the MIN and MAX marks on the translucent plastic reservoir**

## BRAKE FLUID

▶ **Refer to illustration 4.16**

15  The brake master cylinder is located on the driver's side of the engine compartment firewall.

16  The level should be maintained at the MAX mark on the reservoir (see illustration).

17  If additional fluid is necessary to bring the level up, use a rag to clean all dirt off the top of the reservoir. If any foreign matter enters the master cylinder when the cap is removed, blockage in the brake system lines can occur. Also, make sure all painted surfaces around the master cylinder are covered, since brake fluid will ruin paint. Carefully pour new, clean brake fluid into the master cylinder. Be careful not to spill the fluid on painted surfaces. Be sure the specified fluid is used; mixing different types of brake fluid can cause damage to the system. See *Recommended lubricants and fluids* at the end of this Chapter or your owner's manual.

18  At this time the fluid and the master cylinder can be inspected for contamination. If deposits, dirt particles or water droplets are seen in the fluid, the system should be drained and refilled with fresh fluid (see

**4.23 The power steering fluid reservoir is located at the right front of the engine compartment**

Section 21).

19  Reinstall the master cylinder cap.

20  The brake fluid in the master cylinder will drop slightly as the brake pads at each wheel wear down during normal operation. If the master cylinder requires repeated replenishing to keep the level up, it's an indication of leaks in the brake system, which should be corrected immediately. Check all brake lines and connections, along with the brake calipers and booster (if there's fluid in the booster, the master cylinder is leaking) (see Chapter 9 for more information on the brake system).

21  If you discover that the reservoir is empty or nearly empty, the brake system should be filled, bled (see Chapter 9) and checked for leaks.

## POWER STEERING FLUID

▶ **Refer to illustration 4.23**

22  Check the power steering fluid level periodically to avoid steering system problems, such as damage to the pump.

**⁂ CAUTION:**

**DO NOT hold the steering wheel against either stop (extreme left or right turn) for more than five seconds. If you do, the power steering pump could be damaged.**

23  The power steering reservoir, located at the right side of the engine compartment (see illustration), has MIN and MAX fluid level marks on the side. The fluid level can be seen without removing the reservoir cap.

24  Park the vehicle on level ground and apply the parking brake.

25  Run the engine until it has reached normal operating temperature. With the engine at idle, turn the steering wheel back and forth about 10 times to get any air out of the steering system. Shut the engine off with the wheels in the straight-ahead position.

26  Note the fluid level on the side of the reservoir. It should be between the two marks.

27  Add small amounts of fluid until the level is correct.

**⁂ CAUTION:**

**Do not overfill the reservoir. If too much fluid is added, remove the excess with a clean syringe or suction pump.**

28  Check the power steering hoses and connections for leaks and wear.

## AUTOMATIC TRANSAXLE FLUID

▶ **Refer to illustrations 4.32a, 4.32b and 4.34**

29  The level of the automatic transaxle fluid should be carefully maintained. Low fluid level can lead to slipping or loss of drive, while overfilling can cause foaming, loss of fluid and transaxle damage.

30  The transaxle fluid level should only be checked when the transaxle is hot (at its normal operating temperature). If the vehicle has just been driven over 10 miles (15 miles in a frigid climate), and the fluid temperature is 160 to 175-degrees F, the transaxle is hot.

4.32a The transaxle dipstick is located on the left side of the engine compartment, near the battery

4.32b The automatic transaxle fluid level should be between the two holes in the dipstick - if it isn't, add enough fluid to bring the level to or near the upper hole

4.34 Automaitc transaxle fill plug location

**⁂ CAUTION:**

**If the vehicle has just been driven for a long time at high speed or in city traffic in hot weather, or if it has been pulling a trailer, an accurate fluid level reading cannot be obtained. Allow the fluid to cool down for about 30 minutes.**

31 If the vehicle has not just been driven, park the vehicle on level ground, set the parking brake and start the engine. While the engine is idling, depress the brake pedal and move the selector lever through all the gear ranges, beginning and ending in Park.

32 With the engine still idling, remove the dipstick from its tube (see illustration). Check the level of the fluid on the dipstick (see illustration) and note its condition.

33 Wipe the fluid from the dipstick with a clean rag and reinsert it back into the tube until the cap seats.

34 Pull the dipstick out again and note the fluid level. The fluid level should be in the operating temperature range (between the upper and lower mark). If the level is at the low side of either range, add the

specified automatic transmission fluid through the fill plug opening (see illustration).

35 With the engine off and the fill plug removed, add just enough of the recommended fluid to fill the transaxle to the proper level. It takes about one pint to raise the level from the low mark to the high mark when the fluid is hot, so add the fluid a little at a time and keep checking the level until it is correct.

**⁂ CAUTION:**

**It's important to not overfill the transaxle.**

36 The condition of the fluid should also be checked along with the level. If the fluid at the end of the dipstick is black or a dark reddish brown color, or if it emits a burned smell, the fluid should be changed (see Section 22). If you are in doubt about the condition of the fluid, purchase some new fluid and compare the two for color and smell.

## REAR DIFFERENTIAL LUBRICANT LEVEL (AWD MODELS)

▶ Refer to illustration 4.38

37 Raise the vehicle and support it securely on jackstands.

**⁂ WARNING:**

**If the vehicle is equipped with electronically modulated air suspension, make sure that the height control switch is turned off.**

38 Using the appropriate wrench, unscrew the plug from the rear differential (see illustration).

39 Use a finger to reach inside the housing to feel the lubricant level. The level should be at or near the bottom of the plug hole. If it isn't, add the recommended lubricant through the plug hole with a syringe or squeeze bottle.

40 Install the plug and tighten it securely. Check for leaks after the first few miles of driving.

4.38 Rear differential check/fill plug (A) and drain plug (B)

## 5  Tire and tire pressure checks (every 250 miles [400 km] or weekly)

▶ **Refer to illustrations 5.2, 5.3, 5.4a, 5.4b and 5.8**

1  Periodic inspection of the tires may spare you from the inconvenience of being stranded with a flat tire. It can also provide you with vital information regarding possible problems in the steering and suspension systems before major damage occurs.

2  Normal tread wear can be monitored with a simple, inexpensive device known as a tread depth indicator (see illustration). When the tread depth reaches the specified minimum, replace the tire(s).

3  Note any abnormal tread wear (see illustration). Tread pattern irregularities such as cupping, flat spots and more wear on one side than the other are indications of front end alignment and/or balance problems. If any of these conditions are noted, take the vehicle to a tire shop or service station to correct the problem.

4  Look closely for cuts, punctures and embedded nails or tacks. Sometimes a tire will hold its air pressure for a short time or leak down very slowly even after a nail has embedded itself into the tread. If a slow leak persists, check the valve core to make sure it is tight (see illustration). Examine the tread for an object that may have embedded itself into the tire or for a "plug" that may have begun to leak (radial tire punctures are repaired with a plug that is installed in a puncture). If a puncture is suspected, it can be easily verified by spraying a solution of soapy water onto the puncture area (see illustration). The soapy solution will bubble if there is a leak. Unless the puncture is inordinately large, a tire shop or gas station can usually repair the punctured tire.

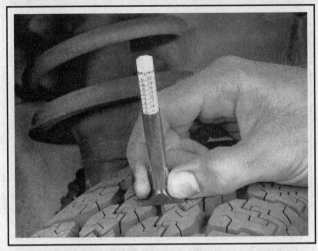

**5.2  A tire tread depth indicator should be used to monitor tire wear - they are available at auto parts stores and service stations and cost very little**

5  Carefully inspect the inner side of each tire for evidence of brake fluid leakage. If you see any, inspect the brakes immediately.

6  Correct tire air pressure adds miles to the lifespan of the tires,

**INCORRECT TOE-IN OR EXTREME CAMBER**

**UNDERINFLATION**

**CUPPING**

**Cupping may be caused by:**
- **Underinflation and/or mechanical irregularities such as out-of-balance condition of wheel and/or tire, and bent or damaged wheel.**
- **Loose or worn steering tie-rod or steering idler arm.**
- **Loose, damaged or worn front suspension parts.**

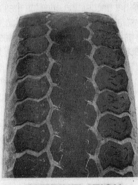

**OVERINFLATION**

**FEATHERING DUE TO MISALIGNMENT**

**5.3  This chart will help you determine the condition of your tires, the probable cause(s) of abnormal wear and the corrective action necessary**

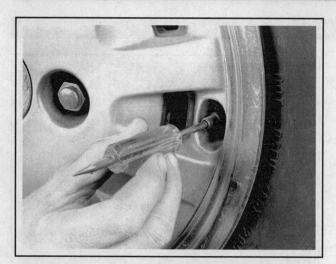

**5.4a  If a tire loses air on a steady basis, check the valve core first to make sure it's snug (special inexpensive wrenches are commonly available at auto parts stores)**

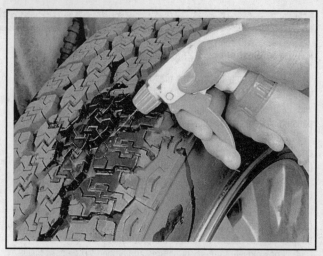

**5.4b  If the valve core is tight, raise the corner of the vehicle with the low tire and spray a soapy water solution onto the tread as the tire is turned slowly - slow leaks will cause small bubbles to appear**

improves mileage and enhances overall ride quality. Tire pressure cannot be accurately estimated by looking at a tire, particularly if it is a radial. A tire pressure gauge is therefore essential. Keep an accurate gauge in the glovebox. The pressure gauges fitted to the nozzles of air hoses at gas stations are often inaccurate.

7    Always check tire pressure when the tires are cold. "Cold," in this case, means the vehicle has not been driven over a mile in the three hours preceding a tire pressure check. A pressure rise of four to eight pounds is not uncommon once the tires are warm.

8    Unscrew the valve cap protruding from the wheel or hubcap and push the gauge firmly onto the valve (see illustration). Note the reading on the gauge and compare this figure to the recommended tire pressure shown on the tire placard on the left door jamb. Be sure to reinstall the valve cap to keep dirt and moisture out of the valve stem mechanism. Check all four tires and, if necessary, add enough air to bring them up to the recommended pressure levels.

9    Don't forget to keep the spare tire inflated to the specified pressure (consult your owner's manual). Note that the air pressure specified for the compact spare is significantly higher than the pressure of the regular tires.

**5.8  To extend the life of your tires, check the air pressure at least once a week with an accurate gauge (don't forget the spare!)**

## 6    Engine oil and oil filter change  (every 3000 miles [4800 km] or 3 months)

♦ **Refer to illustrations 6.2, 6.7, 6.12 and 6.14**

1    Frequent oil changes are the best preventive maintenance the home mechanic can give the engine, because aging oil becomes diluted and contaminated, which leads to premature engine wear.

2    Make sure you have all the necessary tools before you begin this procedure (see illustration). You should also have plenty of rags or newspapers handy for mopping up any spills.

3    Access to the underside of the vehicle is greatly improved if the vehicle can be lifted on a hoist, driven onto ramps or supported by jackstands.

**✳✳ WARNING:**

**Do not work under a vehicle which is supported only by a bumper, hydraulic or scissors-type jack.**

4    If this is your first oil change, get under the vehicle and familiarize yourself with the locations of the oil drain plug and the oil filter. The engine and exhaust components will be warm during the actual work, so try to anticipate any potential problems before the engine and accessories are hot.

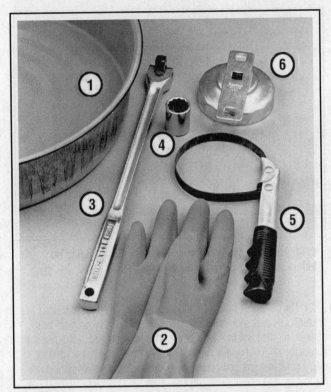

**6.2 These tools are required when changing the engine oil and filter**

1. **Drain pan** - *It should be fairly shallow in depth, but wide in order to prevent spills*
2. **Rubber gloves** - *When removing the drain plug and filter, it is inevitable that you will get oil on your hands (the gloves will prevent burns)*
3. **Breaker bar** - *Sometimes the oil drain plug is pretty tight and a long breaker bar is needed to loosen it*
4. **Socket** - *To be used with the breaker bar or a ratchet (must be the correct size to fit the drain plug)*
5. **Filter wrench** - *This is a metal band-type wrench, which requires clearance around the filter to be effective*
6. **Filter wrench** - *This type fits on the bottom of the filter and can be turned with a ratchet or beaker bar (different size wrenches are available for different types of filters)*

5   Park the vehicle on a level spot. Start the engine and allow it to reach its normal operating temperature. Warm oil and sludge will flow out more easily. Turn off the engine when it's warmed up. Remove the filler cap from the valve cover.

6   Raise the vehicle and support it securely on jackstands.

**✳✳ WARNING:**

**Never get beneath the vehicle when it is supported only by a jack. The jack provided with your vehicle is designed solely for raising the vehicle to remove and replace the wheels. Always use jackstands to support the vehicle when it becomes necessary to place your body underneath the vehicle.**

7   Being careful not to touch the hot exhaust components, place the drain pan under the drain plug in the bottom of the pan and remove the plug (see illustration). You may want to wear gloves while unscrewing

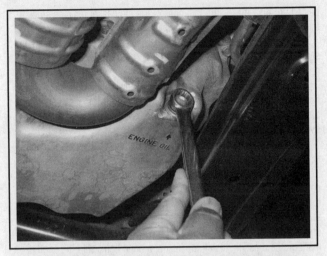

**6.7 Use a proper size box-end wrench or socket to remove the oil drain plug and avoid rounding it off**

**6.12 Use an oil filter wrench to remove the filter**

the plug the final few turns if the engine is hot.

8   Allow the old oil to drain into the pan. It may be necessary to move the pan farther under the engine as the oil flow slows to a trickle. Inspect the old oil for the presence of metal shavings and chips.

9   After all the oil has drained, wipe off the drain plug with a clean rag. Even minute metal particles clinging to the plug would immediately contaminate the new oil.

10   Clean the area around the drain plug opening, reinstall the plug and tighten it securely, but do not strip the threads.

11   Move the drain pan into position under the oil filter.

12   Loosen the oil filter (see illustration) by turning it counterclockwise with an oil filter wrench. Once the filter is loose, use your hands to unscrew it from the block. Keep the open end pointing up to prevent the oil inside the filter from spilling out.

**✳✳ WARNING:**

**The exhaust system may still be hot, so be careful.**

13   With a clean rag, wipe off the mounting surface on the block. If a residue of old oil is allowed to remain, it will smoke when the block is

heated up. Also make sure that none of the old gasket remains stuck to the mounting surface. It can be removed with a scraper if necessary.

14 Compare the old filter with the new one to make sure they are the same type. Smear some clean engine oil on the rubber gasket of the new filter (see illustration).

15 Attach the new filter to the engine, following the tightening directions printed on the filter canister or packing box. Most filter manufacturers recommend against using a filter wrench due to the possibility of overtightening and damaging the seal.

16 Remove all tools, rags, etc. from under the vehicle, being careful not to spill the oil in the drain pan, then lower the vehicle.

17 Add new oil to the engine through the oil filler cap in the valve cover. Use a funnel, if necessary, to prevent oil from spilling onto the top of the engine. Pour four quarts of fresh oil into the engine. Wait a few minutes to allow the oil to drain into the pan, then check the level on the oil dipstick (see Section 4). If the oil level is at or near the upper mark on the dipstick, install the filler cap hand tight, start the engine and allow the new oil to circulate.

18 Allow the engine to run for about a minute. While the engine is running, look under the vehicle and check for leaks at the oil pan drain plug and around the oil filter. If either is leaking, stop the engine and tighten the plug or filter.

19 Wait a few minutes to allow the oil to trickle down into the pan, then recheck the level on the dipstick and, if necessary, add enough oil to bring the level to the upper mark on the dipstick.

20 During the first few trips after an oil change, make it a point to check frequently for leaks and proper oil level.

**6.14 Lubricate the oil filter gasket with clean engine oil before installing the filter on the engine**

21 The old oil drained from the engine cannot be reused in its present state and should be disposed of. Check with your local auto parts store, disposal facility or environmental agency to see if they will accept the oil for recycling. After the oil has cooled it can be drained into a container (capped plastic jugs, topped bottles, milk cartons, etc.) for transport to one of these disposal sites. Don't dispose of the oil by pouring it on the ground or down a drain!

## 7  Windshield wiper blade inspection and replacement (every 7500 miles [12,000 km] or 6 months)

▶ **Refer to illustrations 7.5a and 7.5b**

1 The windshield wiper and blade assembly should be inspected periodically for damage, loose components and cracked or worn blade elements.

2 Road film can build up on the wiper blades and affect their efficiency, so they should be washed regularly with a mild detergent solution.

3 The action of the wiping mechanism can loosen bolts, nuts and fasteners, so they should be checked and tightened, as necessary, at the same time the wiper blades are checked.

4 If the wiper blade elements are cracked, worn or warped, or no longer clean adequately, they should be replaced with new ones.

5 Lift the arm assembly away from the glass for clearance, press on the release lever, then slide the wiper blade assembly out of the hook at the end of the arm (see illustrations).

6 Attach the new wiper to the arm. Connection can be confirmed by an audible click.

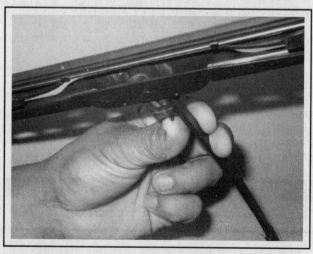

**7.5a  To release the blade holder, push the release lever . . .**

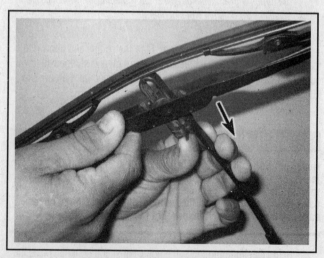

**7.5b  . . . and pull the wiper blade in the direction of the arrow to separate it from the arm**

## 8 Battery check, maintenance and charging (every 7500 miles [12,000 km] or 6 months)

▶ Refer to illustrations 8.1, 8.6a, 8.6b, 8.7a and 8.7b

### ※ WARNING:

Certain precautions must be followed when checking and servicing the battery. Hydrogen gas, which is highly flammable, is always present in the battery cells, so keep lighted tobacco and all other open flames and sparks away from the battery. The electrolyte inside the battery is actually diluted sulfuric acid, which will cause injury if splashed on your skin or in your eyes. It will also ruin clothes and painted surfaces. When removing the battery cables, always detach the negative cable first and hook it up last!

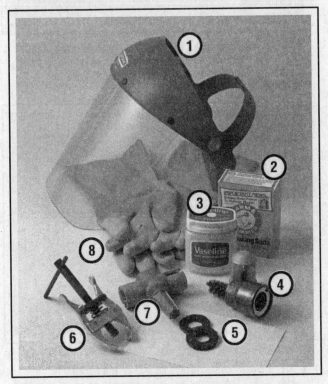

**8.1 Tools and materials required for battery maintenance**

1  **Face shield/safety goggles** - *When removing corrosion with a brush, the acidic particles can easily fly up into your eyes*
2  **Baking soda** - *A solution of baking soda and water can be used to neutralize corrosion*
3  **Petroleum jelly** - *A layer of this on the battery posts will help prevent corrosion*
4  **Battery post/cable cleaner** - *This wire brush cleaning tool will remove all traces of corrosion from the battery posts and cable clamps*
5  **Treated felt washers** - *Placing one of these on each post, directly under the cable clamps, will help prevent corrosion*
6  **Puller** - *Sometimes the cable clamps are very difficult to pull off the posts, even after the nut/bolt has been completely loosened. This tool pulls the clamp straight up and off the post without damage*
7  **Battery post/cable cleaner** - *Here is another cleaning tool which is a slightly different version of number 4 above, but it does the same thing*
8  **Rubber gloves** - *Another safety item to consider when servicing the battery; remember that's acid inside the battery!*

1  A routine preventive maintenance program for the battery in your vehicle is the only way to ensure quick and reliable starts. But before performing any battery maintenance, make sure that you have the proper equipment necessary to work safely around the battery (see illustration).

2  There are also several precautions that should be taken whenever battery maintenance is performed. Before servicing the battery, always turn the engine and all accessories off and disconnect the cable from the negative terminal of the battery (see Chapter 5, Section 1).

3  The battery produces hydrogen gas, which is both flammable and explosive. Never create a spark, smoke or light a match around the battery. Always charge the battery in a ventilated area.

4  Electrolyte contains poisonous and corrosive sulfuric acid. Do not allow it to get in your eyes, on your skin on your clothes. Never ingest it. Wear protective safety glasses when working near the battery. Keep children away from the battery.

5  Note the external condition of the battery. If the positive terminal and cable clamp on your vehicle's battery is equipped with a rubber protector, make sure that it's not torn or damaged. It should completely cover the terminal. Look for any corroded or loose connections, cracks in the case or cover or loose hold-down clamps. Also check the entire length of each cable for cracks and frayed conductors.

6  If corrosion, which looks like white, fluffy deposits (see illustration) is evident, particularly around the terminals, the battery should be removed for cleaning. Loosen the cable clamp bolts with a wrench, being careful to remove the ground cable first, and slide them off the terminals (see illustration). Then disconnect the hold-down clamp bolt and nut, remove the clamp and lift the battery from the engine compartment.

7  Clean the cable clamps thoroughly with a battery brush or a terminal cleaner and a solution of warm water and baking soda (see illustration). Wash the terminals and the top of the battery case with the same solution but make sure that the solution doesn't get into the battery. When cleaning the cables, terminals and battery top, wear safety goggles and rubber gloves to prevent any solution from coming in contact with your eyes or hands. Wear old clothes too - even diluted, sulfuric acid splashed onto clothes will burn holes in them. If the terminals have been extensively corroded, clean them up with a terminal cleaner (see illustration). Thoroughly wash all cleaned areas with plain water.

8  Make sure that the battery tray is in good condition and the hold-

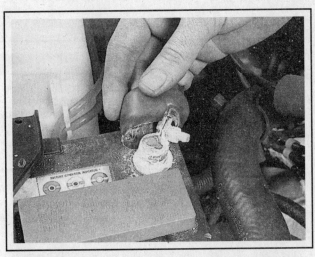

**8.6a Battery terminal corrosion usually appears as light, fluffy powder**

**8.6b Removing a cable from the battery post with a wrench - sometimes a pair of special battery pliers are required for this procedure if corrosion has caused deterioration of the nut hex (always remove the ground (-) cable first and hook it up last!)**

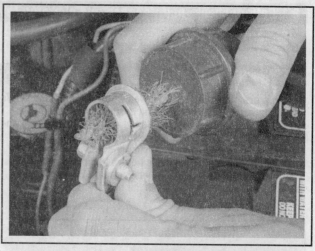

**8.7a When cleaning the cable clamps, all corrosion must be removed (the inside of the clamp is tapered to match the taper on the post, so don't remove too much material)**

**8.7b Regardless of the type of tool used to clean the battery posts, a clean, shiny surface should be the result**

down clamp fasteners are tight. If the battery is removed from the tray, make sure no parts remain in the bottom of the tray when the battery is reinstalled. When reinstalling the hold-down clamp bolts, do not over-tighten them.

9   Information on removing and installing the battery can be found in Chapter 5. If you disconnected the cable(s) from the negative and/or positive battery terminals, see Chapter 5, Section 1. Information on jump starting can be found at the front of this manual. For more detailed battery checking procedures, refer to the *Haynes Automotive Electrical Manual*.

## CLEANING

10   Corrosion on the hold-down components, battery case and surrounding areas can be removed with a solution of water and baking soda. Thoroughly rinse all cleaned areas with plain water.

11   Any metal parts of the vehicle damaged by corrosion should be covered with a zinc-based primer, then painted.

## CHARGING

### ✳✳ WARNING:

**When batteries are being charged, hydrogen gas, which is very explosive and flammable, is produced. Do not smoke or allow open flames near a charging or a recently charged battery. Wear eye protection when near the battery during charging. Also, make sure the charger is unplugged before connecting or disconnecting the battery from the charger.**

12   Slow-rate charging is the best way to restore a battery that's discharged to the point where it will not start the engine. It's also a good way to maintain the battery charge in a vehicle that's only driven a few miles between starts. Maintaining the battery charge is particularly important in the winter when the battery must work harder to start the engine and electrical accessories that drain the battery are in greater use.

13   It's best to use a one or two-amp battery charger (sometimes called a "trickle" charger). They are the safest and put the least strain on the battery. They are also the least expensive. For a faster charge, you can use a higher amperage charger, but don't use one rated more than 1/10th the amp/hour rating of the battery. Rapid boost charges that claim to restore the power of the battery in one to two hours are hardest on the battery and can damage batteries not in good condition. This type of charging should only be used in emergency situations.

14   The average time necessary to charge a battery should be listed in the instructions that come with the charger. As a general rule, a trickle charger will charge a battery in 12 to 16 hours.

## 9 Cooling system check (every 7500 miles [12,000 km] or 6 months)

▶ Refer to illustration 9.4

1   Many major engine failures can be attributed to a faulty cooling system. The cooling system also cools the transaxle fluid and thus plays an important role in prolonging transaxle life.

2   The cooling system should be checked with the engine cold. Do this before the vehicle is driven for the day or after the engine has been shut off for at least three hours.

3   Remove the radiator cap by turning it to the left until it reaches a stop. If you hear a hissing sound (indicating there is still pressure in the system), wait until it stops. Now press down on the cap with the palm of your hand and continue turning to the left until the cap can be removed. Thoroughly clean the cap, inside and out, with clean water. Also clean the filler neck on the radiator. All traces of corrosion should be removed. The coolant inside the radiator should be relatively transparent. If it's rust colored, the system should be drained and refilled (see Section 24). If the coolant level isn't up to the top, add additional antifreeze/coolant mixture (see Section 4).

4   Carefully check the large upper and lower radiator hoses along with the smaller diameter heater hoses which run from the engine to the firewall. Inspect each hose along its entire length, replacing any hose which is cracked, swollen or shows signs of deterioration. Cracks may become more apparent if the hose is squeezed (see illustration). Regardless of condition, it's a good idea to replace hoses with new ones every two years.

5   Make sure that all hose connections are tight. A leak in the cooling system will usually show up as white or rust colored deposits on the areas adjoining the leak. If wire-type clamps are used at the ends of the hoses, it may be a good idea to replace them with more secure screw-type clamps.

6   Use compressed air or a soft brush to remove bugs, leaves, etc. from the front of the radiator or air conditioning condenser. Be careful not to damage the delicate cooling fins or cut yourself on them.

7   Every other inspection, or at the first indication of cooling system problems, have the cap and system pressure tested. If you don't have a pressure tester, most gas stations and repair shops will do this for a minimal charge.

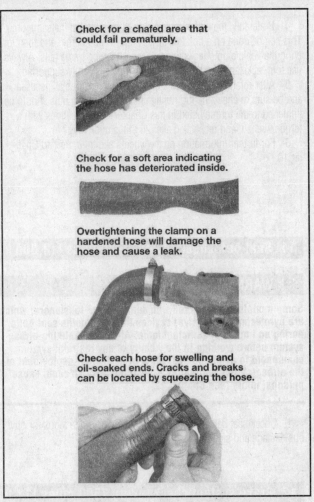

Check for a chafed area that could fail prematurely.

Check for a soft area indicating the hose has deteriorated inside.

Overtightening the clamp on a hardened hose will damage the hose and cause a leak.

Check each hose for swelling and oil-soaked ends. Cracks and breaks can be located by squeezing the hose.

**9.4  Hoses, like drivebelts, have a habit of failing at the worst possible time - to prevent the inconvenience of a blown radiator or heater hose, inspect them carefully as shown here**

## 10 Tire rotation (every 7500 miles [12,000 km] or 6 months)

▶ Refer to illustrations 10.2a and 10.2b

1   The tires should be rotated at the specified intervals and whenever uneven wear is noticed. Since the vehicle will be raised and the tires removed anyway, check the brakes (see Section 12) at this time.

2   Radial tires must be rotated in a specific pattern (see illustrations). Most models are equipped with non-directional tires, but some models may have directional tires, which have a different rotation pattern. When rotating tires, examine the sidewalls. Directional tires have arrows on the sidewall that indicate the direction they must turn.

3   Refer to the information in *Jacking and towing* at the front of this manual for the proper procedures to follow when raising the vehicle and changing a tire. If the brakes are to be checked, do not apply the parking brake as stated. Make sure the tires are blocked to prevent the vehicle from rolling.

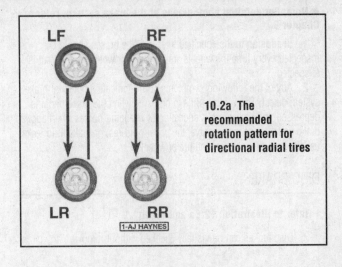

**10.2a The recommended rotation pattern for directional radial tires**

LF    RF

LR    RR

1-AJ HAYNES

4   Preferably, the entire vehicle should be raised at the same time. This can be done on a hoist or by jacking up each corner and then lowering the vehicle onto jackstands placed under the frame rails. Always use four jackstands and make sure the vehicle is firmly supported.

5   After rotation, check and adjust the tire pressures as necessary and be sure to check the lug nut tightness. Ideally, lug nuts should be tightened to the torque listed in this Chapter's Specifications with a torque wrench, and rechecked after 25 miles of driving.

6   For further information on the wheels and tires, refer to Chapter 10.

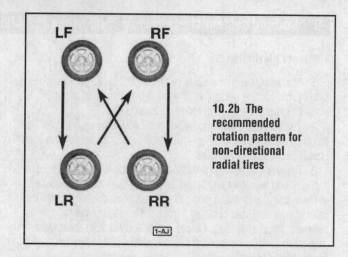

**10.2b The recommended rotation pattern for non-directional radial tires**

## 11  Seat belt check (every 7500 miles [12,000 km] or 6 months)

### ✳✳ WARNING:

**Some models are equipped with seat belt pre-tensioners, which are pyrotechnic (explosive) devices that tighten the seat belts during an impact of sufficient force. Always disable the airbag system before working in the vicinity of any restraint system component to avoid the possibility of accidental deployment of the airbag(s) and seat belt pre-tensioners, which could cause personal injury (see Chapter 12).**

1   Check seat belts, buckles, latch plates and guide loops for obvious damage and signs of wear.

2   See if the seat belt reminder light comes on when the key is turned to the Run or Start position. A chime should also sound. On passive restraint systems, the shoulder belt should move into position in the A-pillar.

3   The seat belts are designed to lock up during a sudden stop or impact, yet allow free movement during normal driving. Make sure the retractors return the belt against your chest while driving and rewind the belt fully when the buckle is unlatched.

4   If any of the above checks reveal problems with the seat belt system, replace parts as necessary.

## 12  Brake system check (every 7500 miles [12,000 km] or 6 months)

### ✳✳ WARNING:

**The dust created by the brake system is harmful to your health. Never blow it out with compressed air and don't inhale any of it. An approved filtering mask should be worn when working on the brakes. Do not, under any circumstances, use petroleum-based solvents to clean brake parts. Use brake system cleaner only!**

➡Note: For detailed photographs of the brake system, refer to Chapter 9.

1   In addition to the specified intervals, the brakes should be inspected every time the wheels are removed or whenever a defect is suspected.

2   Any of the following symptoms could indicate a potential brake system defect: The vehicle pulls to one side when the brake pedal is depressed; the brakes make squealing or dragging noises when applied; brake pedal travel is excessive; the pedal pulsates; or brake fluid leaks, usually onto the inside of the tire or wheel.

### DISC BRAKES

▶ Refer to illustration 12.6a and 12.6b

3   Disc brakes can be visually checked without removing any parts

except the wheels. Remove the hub caps (if applicable) and loosen the wheel lug nuts a quarter turn each.

4   Raise the vehicle and place it securely on jackstands.

### ✳✳ WARNING:

**Never work under a vehicle that is supported only by a jack!**

5   Remove the wheels. Now visible is the disc brake caliper which contains the pads. There is an outer brake pad and an inner pad. Both must be checked for wear.

6   Measure the thickness of the outer pad at each end of the caliper and the inner pad through the inspection hole in the caliper body (see illustrations). Compare the measurement with the limit given in this Chapter's Specifications; if any brake pad thickness is less than specified, then all brake pads must be replaced (see Chapter 9).

7   If you're in doubt as to the exact pad thickness or quality, remove them for measurement and further inspection (see Chapter 9).

8   Check the disc for score marks, wear and burned spots. If any of these conditions exist, the disc should be removed for servicing or replacement (see Chapter 9).

9   Before installing the wheels, check all the brake lines and hoses for damage, wear, deformation, cracks, corrosion, leakage, bends and

**12.6a  You will find an inspection hole like this in each caliper through which you can view the thickness of remaining friction material for the inner pad (front caliper shown, rear caliper similar)**

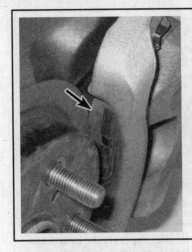

**12.6b  The outer pad is more easily checked at the edge of the caliper**

twists, particularly in the vicinity of the rubber hoses and calipers.

10  Install the wheels, lower the vehicle and tighten the wheel lug nuts to the torque given in this Chapter's Specifications.

## BRAKE BOOSTER CHECK

11  Sit in the driver's seat and perform the following sequence of tests.

12  With the brake fully depressed, start the engine - the pedal should move down a little when the engine starts.

13  With the engine running, depress the brake pedal several times - the travel distance should not change.

14  Depress the brake, stop the engine and hold the pedal in for about 30 seconds - the pedal should neither sink nor rise.

15  Restart the engine, run it for about a minute and turn it off. Then firmly depress the brake several times - the pedal travel should decrease with each application.

16  If your brakes do not operate as described, the brake booster has failed. Refer to Chapter 9 for the replacement procedure.

## 13  Steering and suspension check (every 15,000 miles [24,000 km] or 12 months)

➡Note: For detailed illustrations of the steering and suspension components, refer to Chapter 10.

### WITH THE WHEELS ON THE GROUND

1  With the vehicle stopped and the front wheels pointed straight ahead, rock the steering wheel gently back and forth. If freeplay is excessive, a front wheel bearing, steering shaft universal joint or lower arm balljoint is worn or the steering gear is out of adjustment or broken. Refer to Chapter 10 for the appropriate repair procedure.

2  Other symptoms, such as excessive vehicle body movement over rough roads, swaying (leaning) around corners and binding as the steering wheel is turned, may indicate faulty steering and/or suspension components.

3  Check the shock absorbers by pushing down and releasing the vehicle several times at each corner. If the vehicle does not come back to a level position within one or two bounces, the shocks/struts are worn and must be replaced. When bouncing the vehicle up and down, listen for squeaks and noises from the suspension components.

4  Check the struts and shock absorbers for evidence of fluid leakage. A light film of fluid is no cause for concern. Make sure that any fluid noted is from the struts or shocks and not from some other source. If leakage is noted, replace the struts or shocks as a set.

5  Check the struts and shocks to be sure they are securely mounted and undamaged. Check the upper mounts for damage and wear. If damage or wear is noted, replace the struts or shocks as a set (both front or both rear).

6  If the struts or shocks must be replaced, refer to Chapter 10 for the procedure.

### UNDER THE VEHICLE

▶ **Refer to illustrations 13.10 and 13.11**

7  Raise the vehicle with a floor jack and support it securely on jackstands. See *Jacking and towing* at the front of this book for the proper jacking points.

8  Check the tires for irregular wear patterns and proper inflation. See Section 5 in this Chapter for information regarding tire wear and Chapter 10 for information on wheel/hub bearing replacement.

9  Inspect the universal joint between the steering shaft and the steering gear housing. Check the steering gear housing for lubricant leakage. Make sure that the dust seals and boots are not damaged and that the boot clamps are not loose. Check the steering linkage for looseness or damage. Check the tie-rod ends for excessive play. Look for loose bolts, broken or disconnected parts and deteriorated rubber bushings on all suspension and steering components. While an assistant turns the steering wheel from side to side, check the steering components for free movement, chafing and binding. If the steering components do not seem to be reacting with the movement of the steering wheel, try to determine where the slack is located.

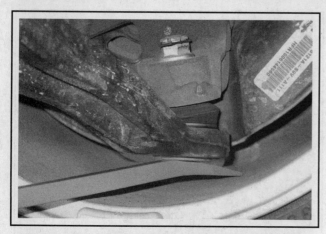

**13.10 To check a balljoint for wear, try to pry the control arm up and down to make sure there is no play in the balljoint (if there is, replace it)**

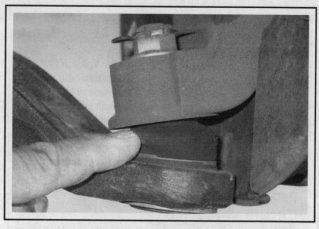

**13.11 Push on the balljoint boot to check for tears and grease**

10  Check the balljoints for wear by trying to move each control arm up and down with a prybar (see illustration) to ensure that its balljoint has no play. If any balljoint does have play, replace it. See Chapter 10 for the balljoint replacement procedure.

11  Inspect the balljoint boots for damage and leaking grease (see illustration). Replace the balljoints with new ones if they are damaged (see Chapter 10).

12  At the rear of the vehicle, inspect the suspension arm bushings for deterioration. Additional information on suspension components can be found in Chapter 10.

## 14  Underhood hose check and replacement (every 15,000 miles [24,000 km] or 12 months)

**✳✳ WARNING:**

**Replacement of air conditioning hoses must be left to a dealer service department or air conditioning shop that has the equipment to depressurize the system safely. Never remove air conditioning components or hoses until the system has been depressurized.**

### GENERAL

1  High temperatures under the hood can cause deterioration of the rubber and plastic hoses used for engine, accessory and emission systems operation. Periodic inspection should be made for cracks, loose clamps, material hardening and leaks.

2  Information specific to the cooling system hoses can be found in Section 9.

3  Most (but not all) hoses are secured to the fittings with clamps. Where clamps are used, check to be sure they haven't lost their tension, allowing the hose to leak. If clamps aren't used, make sure the hose has not expanded and/or hardened where it slips over the fitting, allowing it to leak.

### PCV SYSTEM HOSE

4  To reduce hydrocarbon emissions, crankcase blow-by gas is vented through the PCV valve in the rocker arm cover to the intake manifold via a rubber hose (on most models). The blow-by gases mix with incoming air in the intake manifold before being burned in the combustion chambers.

5  Check the PCV hose for cracks, leaks and other damage. Disconnect it from the valve cover and the intake manifold and check the inside for obstructions. If it's clogged, clean it out with solvent.

### VACUUM HOSES

6  It's quite common for vacuum hoses, especially those in the emissions system, to be color coded or identified by colored stripes molded into them. Various systems require hoses with different wall thickness, collapse resistance and temperature resistance. When replacing hoses, be sure the new ones are made of the same material.

7  Often the only effective way to check a hose is to remove it completely from the vehicle. If more than one hose is removed, be sure to label the hoses and fittings to ensure correct installation.

8  When checking vacuum hoses, be sure to include any plastic T-fittings in the check. Inspect the fittings for cracks and the hose where it fits over each fitting for distortion, which could cause leakage.

9  A small piece of vacuum hose (1/4-inch inside diameter) can be used as a stethoscope to detect vacuum leaks. Hold one end of the hose to your ear and probe around vacuum hoses and fittings, listening for the "hissing" sound characteristic of a vacuum leak.

**✳✳ WARNING:**

**When probing with the vacuum hose stethoscope, be careful not to come into contact with moving engine components such as drivebelts, the cooling fan, etc.**

## FUEL HOSE

10  The fuel lines are usually under pressure, so if any fuel lines are to be disconnected, be prepared to catch spilled fuel.

11  Check all flexible fuel lines for deterioration and chafing. Check especially for cracks in areas where the hose bends and just before fittings, such as where a hose attaches to the fuel pump, fuel filter and fuel rail.

12  When replacing a hose, use only hose that is specifically designed for your fuel injection system.

13  Spring-type clamps are sometimes used on fuel return or vapor lines. These clamps often lose their tension over a period of time, and can be "sprung" during removal. Replace all spring-type clamps with screw clamps whenever a hose is replaced. Some fuel lines use spring-lock type couplings, which require a special tool to disconnect. See Chapter 4 for more information on this type of coupling.

## METAL LINES

14  Sections of metal line are often used for fuel line between the fuel pump and the fuel injection unit. Check carefully to make sure the line isn't bent, crimped or cracked.

15  If a section of metal fuel line must be replaced, use seamless steel tubing only, since copper and aluminum tubing do not have the strength necessary to withstand vibration caused by the engine.

16  Check the metal brake lines where they enter the master cylinder and brake proportioning unit (if used) for cracks in the lines and loose fittings. Any sign of brake fluid leakage calls for an immediate thorough inspection of the brake system.

## 15  Air filter replacement (every 15,000 miles [24,000 km] or 12 months)

▶ **Refer to illustrations 15.1a and 15.1b**

1  The air filter is located inside a housing at the left (driver's) side of the engine compartment. To remove the air filter, loosen the screw securing the two small coolant pipes to the cover and detach the pipes, remove the screws securing the two halves of the air filter housing together, then separate the cover halves and remove the air filter element (see illustrations).

2  Inspect the outer surface of the filter element. If it is dirty, replace it. If it is only moderately dusty, it can be reused by blowing it clean from the back to the front surface with compressed air. Because it is a pleated paper type filter, it cannot be washed or oiled. If it cannot be cleaned satisfactorily with compressed air, discard and replace it. While the cover is off, be careful not to drop anything down into the housing.

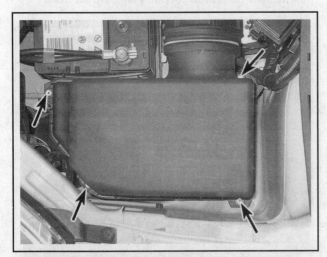

**15.1a  Remove the screws securing the two halves of the air cleaner housing**

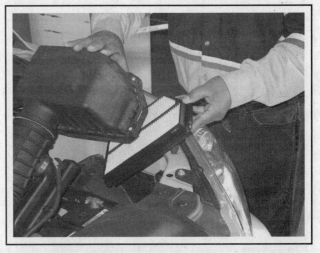

**15.1b  Pull the cover out of the way and lift the element out**

Never drive the vehicle with the air cleaner removed. Excessive engine wear could result and backfiring could even cause a fire under the hood.

3  Wipe out the inside of the air cleaner housing.
4  Place the new filter into the air cleaner housing, making sure it seats properly.
5  Installation of the housing is the reverse of removal.

## 16  Interior ventilation filter replacement (every 15,000 miles [24,000 km] or 12 months)

▶ Refer to illustrations 16.3, 16.4, 16.5 and 16.6

The models covered by this manual are equipped with a Supplemental Restraint System (SRS), more commonly known as airbags. Always disable the airbag system before working in the vicinity of any airbag system component to avoid the possibility of accidental deployment of the airbag, which could cause personal injury (see Chapter 12).

1  These models are equipped with an air filtering element in the air conditioning system, located in a housing next to the evaporator, under the right side of the instrument panel.
2  Refer to Chapter 11 for removal of the glove box.
3  If you're changing the filter for the first time, you'll need to cut out the plastic cross brace (see illustration).
4  Remove the glove box frame (see illustration).
5  Release the tab at the top and remove the filter door (see illustration).
6  Remove the filter from the evaporator housing (see illustration).
7  Installation is the reverse of the removal procedure.

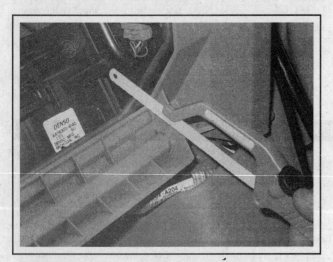

16.3  Cut and remove the plastic cross brace

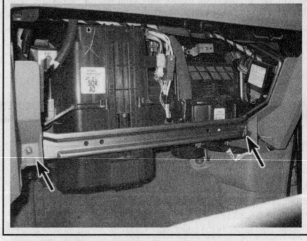

16.4  Remove the fasteners securing the glove box frame

16.5  Release the tab securing the filter door

16.6  Slide the filter from the housing

## 17  Fuel system check (every 15,000 miles [24,000 km] or 12 months)

1   If you smell gasoline while driving or after the vehicle has been sitting in the sun, inspect the fuel system immediately.

2   Remove the fuel filler cap and inspect if for damage and corrosion. The gasket should have an unbroken sealing imprint. If the gasket is damaged or corroded, install a new cap.

3   Inspect the fuel feed line for cracks. Make sure that the connections between the fuel lines and the fuel injection system.

4   Since some components of the fuel system - the fuel tank and the fuel lines, for example - are underneath the vehicle, they can be inspected more easily with the vehicle raised on a hoist. If that's not possible, raise the vehicle and support it on jackstands.

5   With the vehicle raised and safely supported, inspect the gas tank and filler neck for punctures, cracks and other damage. The connection between the filler neck and the tank is particularly critical. Sometimes a rubber filler neck will leak because of loose clamps or deteriorated rubber. Inspect all fuel tank mounting brackets and straps to be sure that the tank is securely attached to the vehicle.

6   Carefully check all hoses and lines leading away from the fuel tank. Check for loose connections, deteriorated hoses, crimped lines and other damage. Repair or replace damaged sections as necessary (see Chapter 4).

## 18  Exhaust system check (every 15,000 miles [24,000 km] or 12 months)

▶ Refer to illustration 18.2

1   With the engine cold (at least three hours after the vehicle has been driven), check the complete exhaust system from the engine to the end of the tailpipe. Ideally, the inspection should be done with the vehicle on a hoist to permit unrestricted access. If a hoist isn't available, raise the vehicle and support it securely on jackstands.

2   Check the exhaust pipes and connections for evidence of leaks, severe corrosion and damage. Make sure that all brackets and hangers are in good condition and tight (see illustration).

3   At the same time, inspect the underside of the body for holes, corrosion, open seams, etc. which may allow exhaust gases to enter the passenger compartment. Seal all body openings with silicone or body putty.

4   Rattles and other noises can often be traced to the exhaust system, especially the mounts and hangers. Try to move the pipes, muffler and catalytic converter. If the components can come in contact with the body or suspension parts, secure the exhaust system with new mounts.

5   Check the running condition of the engine by inspecting inside the end of the tailpipe. The exhaust deposits here are an indication of engine state-of-tune. If the pipe is black and sooty or coated with white deposits, the engine may need a tune-up, including a thorough fuel system inspection and adjustment.

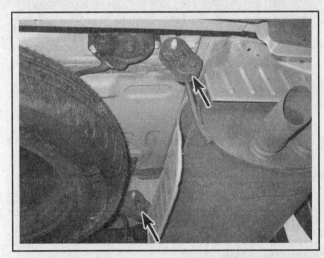

**18.2  Check the exhaust system for rust, damage, or worn rubber hangers**

## 19 Driveaxle boot check (every 15,000 miles [24,000 km] or 12 months)

♦ **Refer to illustration 19.2**

1   The driveaxle boots are very important because they prevent dirt, water and foreign material from entering and damaging the constant velocity (CV) joints. Oil and grease can cause the boot material to deteriorate prematurely, so it's a good idea to wash the boots with soap and water. Because it constantly pivots back and forth following the steering action of the front hub, the outer CV boot wears out sooner and should be inspected regularly.

2   Inspect the boots for tears and cracks as well as loose clamps (see illustration). If there is any evidence of cracks or leaking lubricant, they must be replaced as described in Chapter 8.

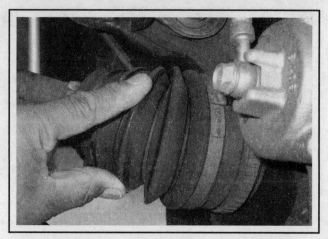

**19.2  Flex the driveaxle boots by hand to check for tears, cracks and leaking grease**

## 20 Drivebelt check and replacement (every 30,000 miles [48,000 km] or 24 months)

### ✳✳ WARNING:

**The electric cooling fan(s) on these models can activate any time the ignition switch is in the ON position. Make sure the ignition is OFF when working in the vicinity of the fan(s).**

1   The drivebelt(s) play an important role in the operation of the vehicle and its components. Due to their function and material makeup, drivebelts are prone to failure after a period of time and should be inspected and adjusted periodically to prevent major damage.

2   2001 and 2002 Acura and 2003 and 2004 Honda models are equipped with two belts. One belt transmits power from the crankshaft to the alternator and air conditioning compressor. The power steering pump is driven by its own belt. 2003 and later Acura and 2005 and later Honda models are equipped with a single serpentine drivebelt that drives the alternator, air conditioning compressor and power steering pump.

## CHECK

♦ **Refer to illustrations 20.3a, 20.3b, 20.4 and 20.5**

3   With the engine off, open the hood and use your fingers (and a flashlight, if necessary), to move along the belt, checking for cracks and separation of the belt plies. Also check for fraying and glazing, which gives the belt a shiny appearance, and check the ribs on the underside of the belt. They should all be the same depth, with none of the surface uneven (see illustrations).

4   On models with a separate power steering pump drivebelt, the power steering belt tension is checked by pushing on it at a distance halfway between the pulleys. Apply about 20 pounds of force with your thumb and see how much the belt moves down (deflects). Measure the deflection with a ruler (see illustration). The belt should deflect about

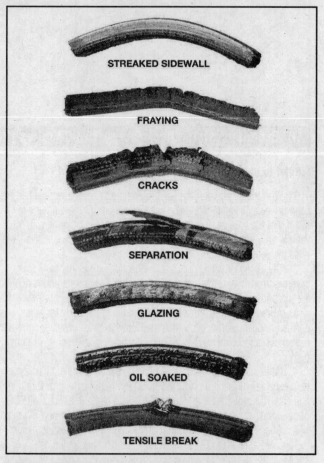

**20.3a  Look for these signs of wear or damage on V-belt drivebelts**

STREAKED SIDEWALL

FRAYING

CRACKS

SEPARATION

GLAZING

OIL SOAKED

TENSILE BREAK

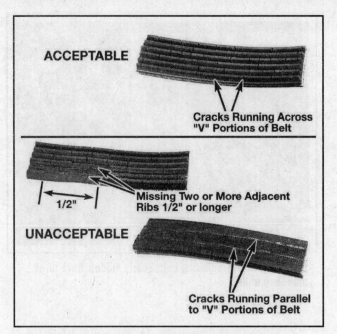

**20.3b Here are some of the more common problems associated with ribbed drivebelts (check the belts very carefully to prevent an untimely breakdown)**

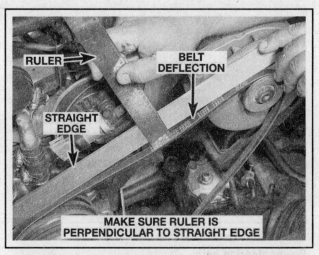

**20.4 Measure V-belt deflection with a straightedge and ruler - make sure the ruler is perpendicular to the straightedge**

**20.5 Details of the drivebelt tensioner**

1   *Maximum length (belt worn out)*
2   *Belt length indicator*

**20.6 Power steering pump belt adjustment details**

1   *Power steering pump mounting bolt and nut*
2   *Adjustment nut*

1/4-inch if the distance between pulleys is between 7 and 11 inches and around 1/2-inch if the distance is between 12 and 16 inches.

5   The tension on ribbed belts is adjusted by an automatic tensioner. Look at the wear indicator on the tensioner (see illustration). The marks should be within the specified range; if not, the belt will have to be replaced.

## ADJUSTMENT (POWER STEERING BELT)

▶ **Refer to illustration 20.6**

➡**Note: This procedure applies to 2001 and 2002 Acura/2003 and 2004 Honda models only.**

6   Loosen the power steering pump mounting bolt and nut, then turn the adjuster bolt to set the belt tension (see illustration). When you have obtained the desired tension, tighten the pump fasteners securely.

## REPLACEMENT

7   Disconnect the cable from the negative terminal of the battery (see Chapter 5, Section 1).

### Ribbed drivebelt

▶ **Refer to illustration 20.8**

8   The automatic tensioner must be released to allow drivebelt replacement. Place a wrench or a socket on the upper tensioner pulley bolt and rotate it clockwise until the belt can be removed (see illustration). Remove the belt and slowly release the tensioner.

9   Install the new belt, then rotate the tensioner clockwise to allow the belt to slip over it. Release the tensioner slowly until it contacts the drivebelt.

10  When installing the belt, make sure the belt is centered on the pulleys.

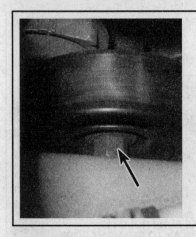

20.8 With a wrench placed on the upper pulley bolt, rotate the tensioner counterclockwise to release the tension

### Power steering belt

➡**Note: This procedure applies to 2001 and 2002 Acura/2003 and 2004 Honda models only.**

11 Remove the alternator/air conditioning compressor drivebelt (see Steps 8 through 10).

12 Follow Step 6 for drivebelt adjustment, but loosen the belt and slip the belt off the pulleys and remove it.

13 When installing the belt, make sure the belt is centered on the pulleys.

14 Adjust the belt as described in Step 6.

## AUTOMATIC TENSIONER REPLACEMENT

▶ **Refer to illustrations 20.17**

15 Disconnect the cable from the negative terminal of the battery

20.17 Tensioner mounting bolts (early models have three mounting bolts)

(see Chapter 5, Section 1).

16 Remove the drivebelt (see Step 8).

17 Unscrew the tensioner mounting bolts and remove the tensioner (see illustration).

➡**Note: On 2001 and 2002 Acura/2003 and 2004 Honda models, the tensioner is secured by three bolts; on other models it's secured by two.**

18 Install the new tensioner assembly by reversing the removal procedure. Tighten the mounting bolt to the torque listed in this Chapter's Specifications.

19 Install the drivebelt as described previously in this Section.

---

### 21 Brake fluid change (every 30,000 miles [48,000 km] or 24 months)

**✳ WARNING:**

**Brake fluid can harm your eyes and damage painted surfaces, so use extreme caution when handling or pouring it. Do not use brake fluid that has been standing open or is more than one year old. Brake fluid absorbs moisture from the air. Excess moisture can cause a dangerous loss of braking effectiveness.**

1 At the specified intervals, the brake fluid should be drained and replaced. Since the brake fluid may drip or splash when pouring it, place plenty of rags around the master cylinder to protect any surrounding painted surfaces.

2 Before beginning work, purchase the specified brake fluid (see *Recommended lubricants and fluids* at the end of this Chapter).

3 Remove the cap from the master cylinder reservoir.

4 Using a hand suction pump or similar device, withdraw the fluid

from the master cylinder reservoir.

5 Add new fluid to the master cylinder until it rises to the base of the filler neck.

6 Bleed the brake system as described in Chapter 9 at all four brakes until new and uncontaminated fluid is expelled from the bleeder screw. Be sure to maintain the fluid level in the master cylinder as you perform the bleeding process. If you allow the master cylinder to run dry, air will enter the system.

7 Refill the master cylinder with fluid and check the operation of the brakes. The pedal should feel solid when depressed, with no sponginess.

**✳ WARNING:**

**Do not operate the vehicle if you are in doubt about the effectiveness of the brake system.**

## 22  Automatic transaxle fluid change (every 30,000 miles [48,000 km] or 24 months)

**◆ Refer to illustration 22.6**

1  The automatic transaxle fluid should be changed at the recommended intervals.

2  Before beginning work, purchase the specified transmission fluid (see *Recommended lubricants and fluids* at the end of this Chapter).

3  Other tools necessary for this job include jackstands to support the vehicle in a raised position, wrenches, a drain pan capable of holding at least four quarts, newspapers and clean rags.

4  The fluid should be drained immediately after the vehicle has been driven. Hot fluid is more effective than cold fluid at removing built up sediment.

### ✵ WARNING:

**Fluid temperature can exceed 350-degrees F in a hot transaxle. Wear protective gloves.**

5  After the vehicle has been driven to warm up the fluid, raise the front of the vehicle and support it securely on jackstands.

### ✵ WARNING:

**Never work under a vehicle that is supported only by a jack!**

6  Place the drain pan under the drain plug and remove the fill plug (see illustration 4.34) and the drain plug (see illustration). Be sure the drain pan is in position, as fluid will come out with some force. Once the fluid is drained, reinstall the drain plug, tightening it to the torque listed in this Chapter's Specifications. Measure the amount of fluid

**22.6  Transaxle drain plug location**

drained and write down this figure for reference when refilling.

7  Lower the vehicle.

8  With the engine off and the fill plug removed, add new fluid to the transaxle (see *Recommended lubricants and fluids* for the recommended fluid type). Begin the refill procedure by initially adding 1/3 of the amount drained. Then, with the engine running, add 1/2-pint at a time (cycling the shifter through each gear position between additions) until the level is correct on the dipstick.

9  If desired, repeat Steps 5 through 8 once to flush any contaminated fluid from the torque converter.

## 23  Rear differential lubricant change (AWD models) (30,000 miles [48,000 km] or 24 months)

1  Raise the rear of the vehicle and support it securely on jackstands. Place a drain pan under the rear differential.

2  Remove the check/fill plug, then remove the drain plug and drain the lubricant (see illustration 4.38).

3  Reinstall the drain plug and tighten it securely.

4  Add new lubricant until it is even with the lower edge of the filler hole (see Section 4). See *Recommended lubricants and fluids* for the specified lubricant type.

5  Reinstall the check/fill plug and tighten it securely.

## 24  Cooling system servicing (draining, flushing and refilling) (every 60,000 miles [96,000 km] or 36 months)

### ✵ WARNING:

**Do not allow antifreeze to come in contact with your skin or painted surfaces of the vehicle. Rinse off spills immediately with plenty of water. Antifreeze is highly toxic if ingested. Never leave antifreeze lying around in an open container or in puddles on the floor; children and pets are attracted by its sweet smell and may drink it. Check with local authorities about disposing of used antifreeze. Many communities have collection centers which will see that antifreeze is disposed of safely. Never dump used antifreeze on the ground or pour it into drains.**

1  Periodically, the cooling system should be drained, flushed and refilled to replenish the antifreeze mixture and prevent formation of rust and corrosion, which can impair the performance of the cooling system and cause engine damage. When the cooling system is serviced, all hoses and the radiator cap should be checked and replaced if necessary.

## DRAINING

▶ **Refer to illustrations 24.3 and 24.4**

**✳✳ WARNING:**

The engine must be completely cool before beginning this procedure.

   2  Apply the parking brake and block the wheels. Turn the ignition switch On. If the vehicle is equipped with automatic climate control, set the system to 90-degrees F (32-degrees C). On other models, turn the heater control to maximum heat. Now turn the ignition switch Off.

   3  Move a large container under the radiator drain to catch the coolant. The radiator drain plug is located on the right side lower corner of the radiator (see illustration). Unscrew the drain plug until coolant starts flowing from the drain hole (a pair of pliers may be required to turn it).

   4  Remove the radiator cap and allow the radiator to drain, then, move the container under the engine. Loosen the engine block drain plug and allow the coolant in the block to drain (see illustration). While the coolant is draining, check the condition of the radiator hoses, heater hoses and clamps (refer to Section 9, if necessary).

   5  Remove the coolant reservoir (see Chapter 3) and drain the coolant, then reinstall the reservoir.

   6  Replace any damaged clamps or hoses. Tighten the drain plug securely.

## FLUSHING

▶ **Refer to illustration 24.9**

   7  Once the system is completely drained, remove the thermostat from the engine (see Chapter 3), then reinstall the thermostat housing without the thermostat. This will allow the system to be thoroughly flushed.

   8  Turn the heating system controls to Hot, so that the heater core will be flushed at the same time as the rest of the cooling system.

   9  Disconnect the upper radiator hose from the radiator, then place a garden hose in the upper radiator inlet and flush the system until the water runs clear at the upper radiator hose (see illustration).

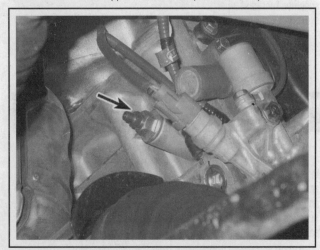

**24.4  The engine has a coolant drain plug located on the rear side of the engine**

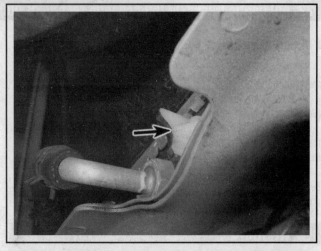

**24.3  The drain fitting is located at the bottom of the radiator**

10  In severe cases of contamination or clogging of the radiator, remove the radiator (see Chapter 3) and have a radiator repair facility clean and repair it if necessary.

11  Many deposits can be removed by the chemical action of a cleaner available at auto parts stores. Follow the procedure outlined in the manufacturer's instructions.

➡**Note: When the coolant is regularly drained and the system refilled with the correct antifreeze/water mixture, there should be no need to use chemical cleaners or descalers.**

12  Remove the overflow hose from the coolant recovery reservoir. Drain the reservoir and flush it with clean water, then reconnect the hose.

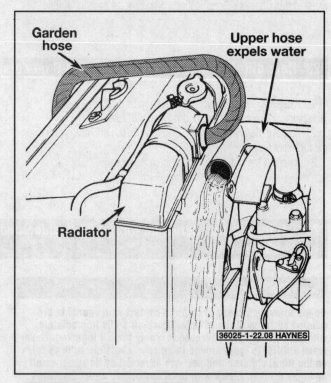

**24.9  With the thermostat removed, disconnect the upper radiator hose and flush the radiator and engine block with a garden hose**

## REFILLING

13 Reconnect the upper radiator hose and reinstall the thermostat.

14 Fill the cooling system with the proper type and mixture of anti-freeze (see this Chapter's Specifications), up to the base of the radiator cap filler neck.

15 Start the engine and run it at approximately 1500 rpm until the radiator fan comes on two times. Feel the upper radiator hose - it should be warm, indicating the thermostat has opened.

16 Turn off the engine and let it cool down. Slowly remove the radiator cap and check the coolant level, adding as necessary.

### ✳✳ WARNING:

**If you hear a hissing sound as you unscrew the cap, STOP. Let the engine cool down longer.**

17 Place the heater control to minimum heat. Start the engine and run it at approximately 1500 rpm for five minutes.

18 Turn off the engine and let it cool down. Slowly remove the radiator cap and check the coolant level, adding as necessary.

### ✳✳ WARNING:

**If you hear a hissing sound as you unscrew the cap, STOP. Let the engine cool down longer.**

19 Place the heater control to maximum heat. Start the engine and run it at approximately 1500 rpm for five minutes.

20 Turn off the engine and let it cool down. Slowly remove the radiator cap and check the coolant level, adding as necessary.

### ✳✳ WARNING:

**If you hear a hissing sound as you unscrew the cap, STOP. Let the engine cool down longer.**

21 Place the heater control to minimum heat. Start the engine and run it at approximately 1500 rpm for three minutes.

22 Turn off the engine and let it cool down. Slowly remove the radiator cap and check the coolant level, adding as necessary.

### ✳✳ WARNING:

**If you hear a hissing sound as you unscrew the cap, STOP. Let the engine cool down longer.**

23 Place the heater control to maximum heat. Start the engine and run it at approximately 1500 rpm for three minutes.

24 Turn off the engine and let it cool down. Slowly remove the radiator cap and check the coolant level, adding as necessary.

### ✳✳ WARNING:

**If you hear a hissing sound as you unscrew the cap, STOP. Let the engine cool down longer.**

25 Repeat Steps 21 through 24 until the cooling system no longer requires any more coolant, then install the radiator cap, but don't tighten it.

26 Place the heater control to minimum heat. Start the engine and run it at approximately 2500 rpm for one minute.

27 Place the front and rear heater controls to maximum heat and check the temperature of the air coming out of the rear floor vents; it should be quite warm, if not actually hot. If it isn't, repeat Steps 21 through 24 a few more times, then repeat this Step.

28 With the engine running, listen for the sound of flowing water at the rear heater unit, which would indicate that air is still in the system. If you do hear flowing water, repeat Steps 21 through 24 a few more times until you don't.

29 Let the engine cool down completely, then check the coolant level in the radiator again, adding as necessary. Fill the coolant reservoir up to the MIN mark, if necessary.

30 Start the engine, allow it to reach normal operating temperature and check for leaks.

## 25  Spark plug check and replacement (every 105,000 miles [169,000 km] or 84 months, whichever comes first)

▶ **Refer to illustrations 25.2, 25.5, 25.8, 25.10, 25.11, 25.12a and 25.12b**

1 The spark plugs are located in the center of each cylinder head.

2 In most cases the tools necessary for spark plug replacement include a spark plug socket which fits onto a ratchet (this special socket is padded inside to protect the porcelain insulators on the new plugs and hold them in place), various extensions and a feeler gauge to check the spark plug gap (see illustration). Since these engines are equipped with aluminum cylinder heads, a torque wrench should be used when tightening the spark plugs.

3 The best approach when replacing the spark plugs is to purchase the new spark plugs beforehand, check the gaps and then replace each plug one at a time. When buying the new spark plugs, be sure to obtain the correct plug for your specific engine. This information can be found in the Specification Section at the front of this Chapter, or in your owner's manual

4 Allow the engine to cool completely before attempting to remove any of the plugs. During this cooling off time, each of the new spark plugs can be inspected for defects and the gaps can be checked.

5 The gap is checked by inserting the proper thickness gauge between the electrodes at the tip of the plug (see illustration). The gap between the electrodes should be as listed in this Chapter's Specifications or in your owner's manual.

### ✳✳ CAUTION:

**The manufacturer recommends against adjusting the gap on platinum- or iridium-tipped spark plugs; if the gap is out of specification, replace the plug. Also, at this time check for cracks in the spark plug body (if any are found, the plug must not be used).**

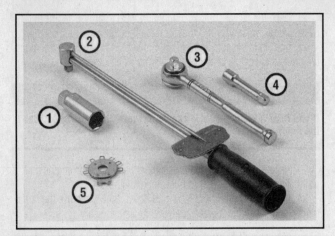

**25.2 Tools required for changing spark plugs**

1. **Spark plug socket** - *This will have special padding inside to protect the spark plug porcelain insulator*
2. **Torque wrench** - *Although not mandatory, use of this tool is the best way to ensure that the plugs are tightened properly*
3. **Ratchet** - *Standard hand tool to fit the plug socket*
4. **Extension** - *Depending on model and accessories, you may need special extensions and universal joints to reach one or more of the plugs*
5. **Spark plug gap gauge** - *This gauge for checking the gap comes in a variety of styles. Make sure the gap for your engine is included*

6 Cover the fender to prevent damage to the paint. Fender covers are available from auto parts stores but an old blanket will work just fine.

7 Remove the engine cover and the ignition coil cover (see Chapter 2A, illustration 6.3).

8 Remove the ignition coils (see illustration).

9 If compressed air is available, use it to blow any dirt or foreign material away from the spark plug area.

**✳✳ WARNING:**

**Wear eye protection! The idea here is to eliminate the possibility of material falling into the cylinder through the spark plug hole as the spark plug is removed.**

10 Place the spark plug socket over the plug and remove it from the engine by turning it in a counterclockwise direction (see illustration).

11 Compare the spark plug to those shown on this chart to get an indication of the overall running condition of the engine (see illustration).

12 Apply a small amount of anti-seize compound to the spark plug threads (see illustration). Install one of the new plugs into the hole until you can no longer turn it with your fingers, then tighten it with a torque wrench (if available) or the ratchet. It is a good idea to slip a short length of rubber hose over the end of the plug to use as a tool to thread it into place (see illustration). The hose will grip the plug well enough to turn it, but will start to slip if the plug begins to cross-thread in the hole - this will prevent damaged threads and the accompanying repair costs.

13 Attach the coil to the new spark plug using a twisting motion until it is firmly seated on the end of the spark plug. Tighten the mounting bolts securely.

14 Repeat the procedure for the remaining spark plugs.

**25.5 Spark plug manufacturers recommend using a wire-type gauge to check the spark plug gap - if the wire doesn't slide between the electrodes with a slight drag, adjustment is required**

**25.8 To remove the coils, disconnect the electrical connector (A) then remove the retaining screw (B)**

**25.10 Use a ratchet and extension to remove the spark plug**

A normally worn spark plug should have light tan or gray deposits on the firing tip.

A carbon fouled plug, identified by soft, sooty, black deposits, may indicate an improperly tuned vehicle. Check the air cleaner, ignition components and engine control system.

An oil fouled spark plug indicates an engine with worn piston rings and/or bad valve seals allowing excessive oil to enter the chamber.

This spark plug has been **left in the engine too long,** as evidenced by the extreme gap. Plugs with such an extreme gap can cause misfiring and stumbling accompanied by a noticeable lack of power.

A **physically damaged** spark plug may be evidence of severe detonation in that cylinder. Watch that cylinder carefully between services, as a continued detonation will not only damage the plug, but could also damage the engine.

A **bridged or almost bridged** spark plug, identified by a build-up between the electrodes caused by excessive carbon or oil build-up on the plug.

**25.11  Inspect the spark plug to determine engine running conditions**

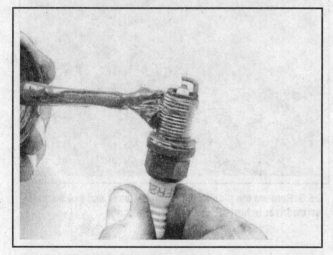

**25.12a  Apply a thin coat of anti-seize compound to the spark plug threads - DO NOT get any on the electrodes!**

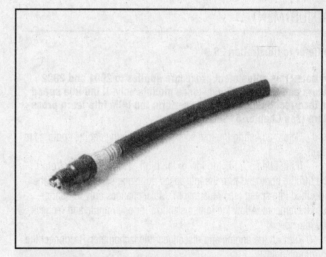

**25.12b  A length of snug-fitting rubber hose will save time and prevent damaged threads when installing the spark plugs**

**26  Idle speed check and adjustment (105,000 miles [169,000 km] or 84 months)**

## CHECK

▶ **Refer to illustration 26.4**

1   Engine idle speed is the speed at which the engine operates when no accelerator pedal pressure is applied, as when stopped at a traffic light. The speed is critical to the performance of the engine itself, as well as many subsystems.

2   Set the parking brake firmly and block the wheels to prevent the vehicle from rolling. Place the transaxle in Park.

3   Connect a hand-held tachometer in accordance with the tool manufacturer's instructions.

4   Disconnect the two-pin electrical connector from the EVAP purge control solenoid (see illustration).

5   Start the engine and run it at 3000 rpm until it warms up to normal operating temperature (the cooling fan comes on).

6   Slowly release the accelerator until the idle drops to normal speed. Make sure all accessories are turned off and the transaxle is in Neutral.

7   Note the idle speed on the tachometer and compare it to that listed on the VECI label or in this Chapter's Specifications.

➡**Note: If the idle speed listed on the VECI label is different than that listed in this Chapter's Specifications, use the specification shown on the VECI label.**

## ADJUSTMENT

▶ **Refer to illustration 26.9**

➡**Note: This adjustment procedure applies to 2001 and 2002 Acura and 2003 and 2004 Honda models only. If the idle speed is incorrect on other models, perform the PCM idle learn procedure (see Chapter 5, Section 1).**

8   Before adjusting the idle speed, make sure the engine cooling fan is off.

9   If the idle speed is too low or too high, remove the plug from the throttle body and turn the idle speed adjusting screw to obtain the specified idle speed (see illustration). Make changes only in quarter-turn increments. Allow the idle to stabilize for one minute and recheck the idle speed.

10  Turn off the engine and disconnect the tachometer. Reconnect the EVAP solenoid.

**26.4  Depress the tab and disconnect the electrical connector from the canister purge solenoid (it's located at the left end [driver's side] of the intake manifold)**

**26.9  Remove the plug from the throttle body and use a small screwdriver to turn the idle adjustment screw**

## Specifications

### Recommended lubricants and fluids

➡Note: The fluids and lubricants listed here are those recommended by the manufacturer at the time this manual was written. Vehicle manufacturers occasionally upgrade their fluid and lubricant specifications, so check with your local auto parts store for the most current recommendations.

Engine oil
    Type                            API "Certified for gasoline engines"
    Viscosity
        Pilot                     SAE 5W-20
        MDX
                2001 models        SAE 5W-30
                2002 and later models    SAE 5W-20

Automatic transmission fluid       Honda ATF-Z1 or equivalent
Brake fluid type                  DOT 3 brake fluid
Power steering system fluid        Honda power steering fluid or equivalent
Rear differential
    Pilot                       Honda VTM-4 Differential fluid
    MDX
        2006 and earlier models    Honda VTM-4 Differential fluid
        2007 models            Honda ATF-Z1 or equivalent
Fuel type
    Pilot
        2005 and earlier models    Unleaded gasoline, 86 octane or higher
        2006 and 2007 models     Unleaded gasoline, 87 octane or higher
    MDX                     Unleaded gasoline, 91 octane or higher
Engine coolant                 Honda All Season Antifreeze/Coolant Type 2 or equivalent 50/50 mixture of non-silicate antifreeze and water (the genuine Honda antifreeze is a pre-mixed solution - don't add water to it)

### Capacities*

Engine oil (including oil filter)
    Pilot
        2004 and earlier models    5.1 quarts (4.8 liters)
        2005 and later models     4.5 quarts (4.3 liters)
    MDX
        2001 and 2002 models     5.0 quarts (4.7 liters)
        2003 and later models     4.5 quarts (4.3 liters)
Automatic transaxle fluid (drain and refill)**
    Pilot
        2004 and earlier models    3.2 quarts (3.0 liters)
        2005 models           3.9 quarts (3.7 liters)
        2006 and later models
             without AWD (2WD)    4.0 quarts (3.8 liters)
            with AWD (4WD)       3.5 quarts (3.3 liters)
    MDX
        2002 and earlier models    3.2 quarts (3.0 liters)
        2003 through 2006 models   2.9 quarts (2.7 liters)
        2007 models            3.0 quarts (2.8 liters)

## Capacities* (continued)

Cooling system
  Routine coolant change      up to 2 gallons (7.3 liters)
  After engine overhaul      up to 3 gallons (11 liters)

*All capacities approximate. Add as necessary to bring to appropriate level.*
**If you want to flush the converter during a fluid change, purchase twice the amount of fluid listed here.*

## Ignition system

Spark plug type and gap
Type
  Pilot
    2004 and earlier models      NGK: PZFR5F-11 or
         DENSO: PKJ16CR-L11

    2005 and later models      NGK: IZFR5K-11 or
         DENSO SKJ16DR-M11

  MDX
    2002 and earlier models      NGK: PZFR5F-11 or
         DENSO: PKJ16CR-L11

    2003 through 2006 models      NGK: IZFR5K-11 or
         DENSO SKJ16DR-M11

    2007 models      NGK: IZFR6K-11 or
         DENSO SKJ20DR-M11

Gap      0.039 to 0.043 inch (1.0 to 1.1 mm)
Engine firing order      1-4-2-5-3-6

```
┌─────────────────────────────────┐
│  ①   ②   ③        FRONT OF      │
│                    VEHICLE       │
│  ④   ⑤   ⑥          ↓           │
│      1-4-2-5-3-6                 │
│      42035-B-SPECS HAYNES        │
└─────────────────────────────────┘
```

**Cylinder locations**

## Engine idle speed (in Park or Neutral)

Pilot
  2005 and earlier models      730+/-50 rpm
  2006 and later models
    VTEC engine      730+/-50 rpm
    i-VTEC engine      650+/-50 rpm
MDX
  2006 and earlier models      730+/-50 rpm
  2007 models      710+/-50 rpm

## Brakes

Disc brake pad lining thickness (minimum),
  front or rear      1/16-inch (1.6 mm)
Drum brake shoe lining thickness (minimum)      5/64-inch (2.0 mm)

| Torque specifications | Ft-lbs (unless otherwise indicated) | Nm |
|---|---|---|
| Engine oil drain plug | 29 | 39 |
| Automatic transaxle | | |
|     Drain plug | 36 | 49 |
|     Filler plug | 33 | 44 |
| Spark plugs | 156 in-lbs | 18 |
| Wheel lug nuts | 80 | 108 |

**2A**

ENGINES

## Section

## Reference to other Chapters

## 1    General information

This Part of Chapter 2 is devoted to in-vehicle repair procedures for the 3.5L and 3.7L V6 engines. Since these procedures are based on the assumption that the engine is installed in the vehicle, many of the steps outlined in this Part of Chapter 2 will not apply if the engine has been removed.

A "VTEC" system is used on all 4WD models. The VTEC system is Honda's design for Variable Valve Timing and Lift Electronic Control. Refer to Chapter 6 for additional information.

2WD models are equipped with a Variable Cylinder Management (VCM) system which disengages the intake and exhaust valves on the rear bank cylinder head under certain conditions such as cruising and fuel cutoff (deceleration). Refer to Chapter 6 for additional information.

The Specifications included in this Part of Chapter 2 apply only to the procedures contained in this Part. Information concerning engine/transaxle removal and engine overhaul can be found in Part B of this Chapter.

## 2    Repair operations possible with the engine in the vehicle

Many major repair operations can be accomplished without removing the engine from the vehicle.

Clean the engine compartment and the exterior of the engine with some type of degreaser before any work is done. It will make the job easier and help keep dirt out of the internal areas of the engine.

When working on the engine, cover the fenders to prevent damage to the paint. Special pads are available, but an old bedspread or blanket will also work.

If vacuum, exhaust, oil or coolant leaks develop, indicating a need for gasket or seal replacement, the repairs can generally be made with the engine in the vehicle. The intake and exhaust manifold gaskets, oil pan gasket, crankshaft front oil seal and cylinder head gaskets are all accessible with the engine in place.

Exterior engine components, such as the intake and exhaust mani-

folds, the oil pan, the oil pump, the water pump (see Chapter 3), the starter motor, the alternator, the ignition coils (see Chapter 5) and the fuel system components (see Chapter 4) can be removed for repair with the engine in place.

Since the cylinder heads can be removed without pulling the engine, valve component servicing can also be accomplished with the engine in the vehicle. Replacement of the camshafts, timing belt and sprockets is also possible with the engine in the vehicle.

In extreme cases caused by a lack of necessary equipment, repair or replacement of piston rings, pistons, connecting rods and rod bearings is possible with the engine in the vehicle. However, this practice is not recommended because of the cleaning and preparation work that must be done to the components involved.

## 3    Top Dead Center (TDC) for number one piston - locating

▶ **Refer to illustrations 3.5 and 3.6**

1    Top Dead Center (TDC) is the highest point in the cylinder that each piston reaches as it travels up-and-down during crankshaft rotation. Each piston reaches TDC on the compression stroke and again on the exhaust stroke, but TDC generally refers to piston position on the compression stroke.

2    Positioning the piston(s) at TDC is an essential part of certain repair procedures discussed in this manual.

3    Before beginning this procedure, be sure to place the transaxle in Neutral and apply the parking brake or block the rear wheels. Remove the spark plugs, as this will make the crankshaft much easier to turn (see Chapter 1).

4    In order to bring any piston to TDC, the crankshaft must be turned using one of the methods outlined below. When looking at the front of the engine, normal crankshaft rotation is clockwise.

### ☀ WARNING:

**If method b) or c) is used, disable the fuel system (see Chapter 4, Section 2).**

a)  *The preferred method is to turn the crankshaft with a socket and ratchet attached to the bolt threaded into the front of the crankshaft.*

b)  *A remote starter switch, which may save some time, can also be used. Follow the instructions included with the switch. Once the piston is close to TDC, use a socket and ratchet as described in the previous paragraph.*

c)  *If an assistant is available to turn the ignition switch to the Start position in short bursts, you can get the piston close to TDC without a remote starter switch. Make sure your assistant is out of the vehicle, away from the ignition switch, then use a socket and ratchet as described in Paragraph a) to complete the procedure.*

5    Turn the crankshaft until the TDC notch on the crankshaft pulley is aligned with the pointer on the timing belt lower cover (see illustration).

6    Locate the camshaft sprocket timing mark on the front cylinder bank. Look through the hole in the timing belt cover to check that the camshaft sprocket timing mark is aligned with the mark on the rear cover (see illustration). If no mark is present, rotate the crankshaft clockwise one revolution and realign the marks.

7    When the crankshaft pulley timing marks are aligned, and the camshaft sprocket timing marks are aligned, the number one piston is at TDC on the compression stroke.

8    After the number one piston has been positioned at TDC on the compression stroke, TDC for any of the remaining pistons can be located by turning the crankshaft and following the firing order, aligning the cylinder number on the camshaft sprocket with the pointer on the timing belt cover (they're arranged in the firing order).

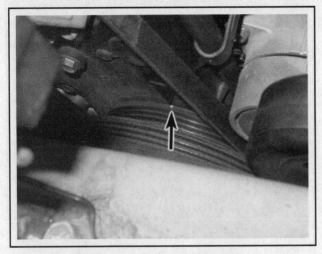

**3.5  Align the TDC mark on the crankshaft pulley with the pointer**

**3.6  Position the inspection hole cover aside and check the alignment of the camshaft sprocket timing mark with the mark on the timing belt cover (there is an inspection hole on each cylinder bank) - the numeral 1 is visible when the number 1 piston is at TDC**

## 4  Valve covers - removal and installation

### REMOVAL

▶ **Refer to illustrations 4.9a and 4.9b**

1  Disconnect the cable from the negative terminal of the battery (see Chapter 5, Section 1).

2  Remove the ignition coils (see Chapter 5).

3  Remove the engine oil dipstick.

4  Remove the upper intake manifold (see Section 6).

5  On Honda 2WD models, disconnect the injector connectors, the rocker arm oil control solenoid connector and rocker arm engine oil pressure (EOP) switch connector.

6  Detach the PCV hose from the valve cover.

7  At the rear valve cover, remove the bolt retaining the power steering hose bracket and move the hose aside, if necessary.

8  Remove the harness bracket bolts and disconnect the heated oxygen sensor connectors, the EGR valve connector and the ECT sensor connectors (see Chapter 6).

9  Remove the retaining bolts (see illustrations), then lift the valve cover off. If the cover is stuck to the head, bump the end with a block of wood and a hammer to jar it loose.

### ✳✳ CAUTION:

**Don't pry at the cover-to-head joint or damage to the sealing surfaces may occur, leading to oil leaks after the cover is reinstalled.**

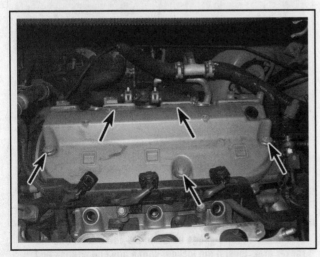

**4.9a  Valve cover retaining bolts (rear valve cover)**

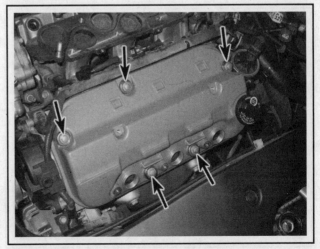

**4.9b  Valve cover retaining bolts (front valve cover)**

10 Remove the original gasket and seal washers and clean the mating surfaces of the cylinder head and valve cover. If you removed the front valve cover, remove and inspect the PCV valve (see Chapter 1).

## INSTALLATION

▶ **Refer to illustration 4.12**

11 Position a new gasket in the groove and install new sealing washers on the bolts.

12 Install the cover and tighten the bolts, a little at a time, to the torque listed in this Chapter's Specifications. Follow the correct torque sequence (see illustration).

13 Reinstall the remaining components.

14 Reconnect the battery. Refer to Chapter 5, Section 1.

15 Run the engine and check for oil leaks.

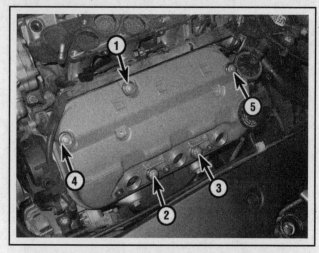

**4.12 Valve cover tightening sequence - front shown, rear valve cover tightening sequence is identical**

## 5   Valve clearance - check and adjustment

## CHECK

1   The valve clearance generally does not need adjustment unless valvetrain components have been replaced or a valve job has been performed, or if the valves are noisy.

2   The simplest check for proper valve adjustment is to listen carefully to the engine running with the hood open. If the valvetrain is noisy, adjustment is necessary.

3   The valve clearance must be checked and adjusted with the engine cold.

## ADJUSTMENT

▶ **Refer to illustrations 5.6, 5.7 and 5.9**

4   Remove the valve covers (see Section 4).

5   Rotate the crankshaft clockwise and position the number one piston at TDC (see Section 3). When positioned correctly at TDC, the pointer on the front timing belt cover will align with the sprocket mark (see illustration 3.6).

6   In this position, adjust the valves for cylinder number one (see illustration). There are four valves for each cylinder.

7   Starting with the intake valve, insert a feeler gauge of the correct thickness (see this Chapter's Specifications) between the valve stem and the rocker arm (see illustration). Withdraw it; you should feel a slight drag. If there's no drag or a heavy drag, loosen the adjuster nut and back off the adjuster screw. Carefully tighten the adjuster screw until you can feel a slight drag on the feeler gauge as you withdraw it.

8   Hold the adjuster screw with a screwdriver to keep it from turning and tighten the locknut. Recheck the clearance to make sure it hasn't changed. Repeat the procedure in this Step and the previous Step on

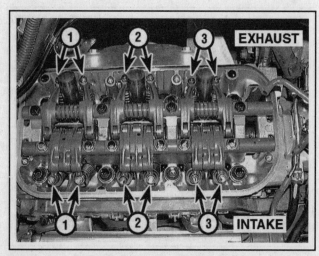

**5.6  Valve layout for the rear cylinder head**

**5.7  Insert a feeler gauge between the valve stem and the rocker arm, loosen the locknut with a box end wrench and adjust the clearance with a screwdriver**

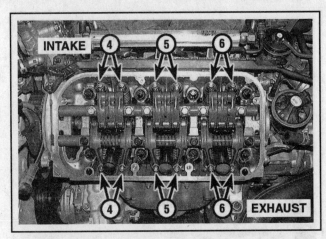

**5.9 Valve layout for the front cylinder head**

the other intake valve, then on the two exhaust valves.

9   Rotate the crankshaft pulley clockwise until the number 4 on the camshaft sprocket is aligned with the pointer on the timing belt cover (see illustration 3.6). Check and adjust the number 4 cylinder valves (see illustration).

10  Rotate the crankshaft pulley 120-degrees clockwise until the number 2 cylinder is at TDC. Check and adjust the number 2 cylinder valves.

11  Rotate the crankshaft pulley clockwise, follow the firing order listed in this Chapter's Specifications and adjust the remaining valves.

12  Refer to Section 4 and install the valve covers.

## 6   Intake manifold - removal and installation

### ⁕⁕ WARNING:

**Wait until the engine is completely cool before beginning this procedure.**

## UPPER INTAKE MANIFOLD

▶ **Refer to illustrations 6.3, 6.10, 6.11, 6.12, 6.13a, 6.13b and 6.13c**

1   Relieve the fuel pressure (see Chapter 4).

2   Disconnect the cable from the negative terminal of the battery (see Chapter 5, Section 1).

3   Remove the engine cover (see illustration).

4   Remove the breather hose and the air intake duct (see Chapter 4), then disconnect the accelerator cable, vacuum hoses and other connections from the throttle body (see Chapter 4).

➡Note: Early Acura models (2001 and 2002) and Honda models (2003 and 2004) are equipped with accelerator cables, while all other models are equipped with the Electronic Throttle Control (ETC) system.

5   Remove the EVAP hose and the transaxle vent hose mounting bracket, if equipped.

6   Clamp-off the coolant hoses to the throttle body, then detach them. Be prepared for a little coolant spillage.

7   Disconnect the brake booster hose and the PCV hoses from the intake manifold.

8   Remove the engine harness connectors (IAT, TPS, IAC, MAP, EVAP canister [early models]) from their respective components. Label each connector with tape to insure correct reassembly.

➡Note: On models equipped with the Intake Manifold Tuning (IMT) valve system, label and disconnect the harness connectors (see Chapter 6).

9   Remove the intake manifold cover.

➡Note: Follow the reverse order of the tightening sequence (see illustrations 6.13b and 6.13c).

10  Following the reverse of the tightening sequence (see illustration 6.12), remove the bolts and nuts and remove the manifold (see illustration).

**6.3 Rotate the locking tabs to release the engine cover from the intake manifold**

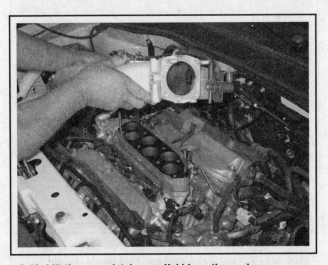

**6.10 Lift the upper intake manifold from the engine . . .**

**6.11 . . . then remove the spacer plate, if equipped**

**6.12 Upper intake manifold bolt tightening sequence**

11 If equipped, remove the spacer plate and gaskets (see illustration).

12 To install the upper manifold, clean the mounting surfaces of the upper and lower manifold and remove all traces of the old gasket material or sealant. Install the new gasket over the studs on the lower manifold, then install the spacer (if equipped) and upper intake manifold. Tighten the nuts and bolts in sequence (see illustration) to the torque listed in this Chapter's Specifications.

13 Install the intake manifold cover and tighten the bolts in sequence (see illustrations) to the torque listed in this Chapter's Specifications.

14 The remainder of installation is the reverse of the removal procedure. Reconnect the battery (refer to Chapter 5, Section 1). Check the coolant level and add some, if necessary (see Chapter 1).

## LOWER INTAKE MANIFOLD

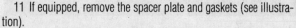

▶ **Refer to illustration 6.17**

15 Remove the upper intake manifold (and the spacer plate, on models so equipped).

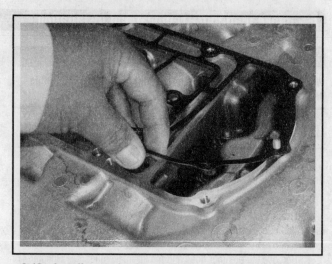

**6.13a Install a new intake manifold cover gasket on the upper intake manifold**

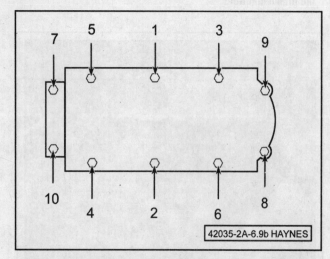

42035-2A-6.9b HAYNES

**6.13b Intake manifold cover bolt tightening sequence on 2001 and 2002 Acura and 2003 and 2004 Honda models**

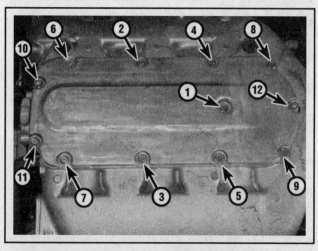

**6.13c Intake manifold cover bolt tightening sequence on 2003 and later Acura and 2005 and later Honda models**

**6.17 Location of the lower intake manifold mounting nuts - the four corner nuts are hidden from view**

16 Remove the fuel rails from the lower intake manifold (see Chapter 4).

17 Remove the mounting nuts and bolts, then detach the two lower intake manifold sections from the cylinder heads (see illustration). If they are stuck, don't pry between the gasket mating surfaces or damage may result.

18 Carefully use a scraper to remove all traces of old gasket material and sealant from the manifold and cylinder heads, then clean the mating surfaces with lacquer thinner or acetone.

19 Install new gaskets, then position the lower manifolds on the cylinder heads. Make sure the gaskets and manifolds are aligned over the dowels in the cylinder heads and install the nuts/bolts.

20 Tighten the fasteners, a little at a time, to the torque listed in this Chapter's Specifications. Work from the center out towards the ends to avoid warping the manifolds.

21 Install the upper intake manifold.

22 The remainder of the installation is the reverse of the removal procedure. Check the coolant level and add some, if necessary (see Chapter 1). Run the engine and check for fuel, vacuum and coolant leaks.

## 7   Exhaust manifolds - removal and installation

### ✴✴ WARNING:

**The engine must be completely cool before beginning this procedure.**

➡Note: Only 2001 and 2002 Acura models and 2003 and 2004 Honda models are equipped with exhaust manifolds. Later models are not equipped with separate exhaust manifolds but instead use catalytic converter assemblies bolted directly to the cylinder heads. Refer to Chapter 6 for additional information.

### REMOVAL

▸ **Refer to illustrations 7.3, 7.4, 7.5 and 7.6**

1   Disconnect the cable from the negative terminal of the battery (see Chapter 5, Section 1).

2   Spray penetrating oil on the exhaust manifold fasteners and allow it to soak in.

3   Block the rear wheels to prevent the vehicle from rolling. Set the parking brake and place the transaxle in Park. Raise the front of the vehicle and support it securely on jackstands. Remove the splash guard from below the engine compartment (see illustration).

4   Disconnect the exhaust pipes from the manifolds (see illustration).

**7.4 Remove the exhaust pipe-to-manifold nuts**

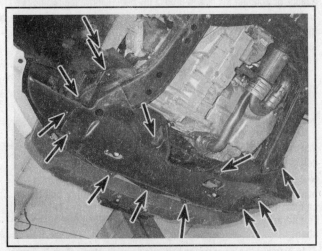

**7.3 Location of the engine splash shield fasteners - some hidden from view**

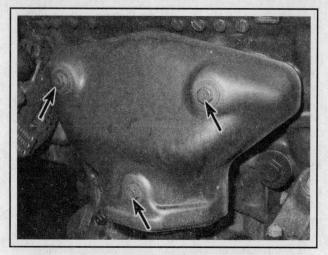

**7.5 Remove the heat shield bolts and the heat shield**

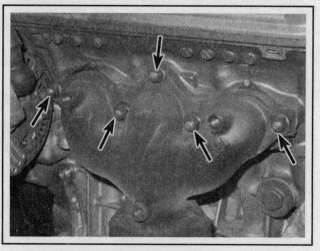

**7.6 Location of the exhaust manifold nuts**

5   Remove the bolts and the heat shields from each manifold (see illustration).

6   Remove the self-locking nuts retaining the manifold to the cylinder head and remove the manifold (see illustration). Discard the self-locking nuts and obtain new ones for reassembly.

7   Carefully inspect the manifold for cracks and warpage. If the manifold is cracked or warped, replace it with a new one.

## INSTALLATION

8   Use a scraper to remove any traces of old gasket material and carbon deposits from the manifold and cylinder head mating surfaces.

9   Position a new gasket over the cylinder head studs.

10  Install the manifold and thread the mounting nuts into place. Working from the center out, tighten the nuts to the torque listed in this Chapter's Specifications in three equal steps.

11  Reinstall the remaining parts in the reverse order of removal. Apply engine oil to the studs and install new self-locking nuts.

12  Reconnect the battery. Refer to Chapter 5, Section 1.

13  Run the engine and check for exhaust leaks.

## 8   Timing belt and sprockets - removal, inspection and installation

### REMOVAL

▶ **Refer to illustrations 8.11a, 8.11b, 8.12, 8.13a, 8.13b, 8.14, 8.15, 8.16, 8.17, 8.18, 8.19 and 8.20**

1   Disconnect the cable from the negative terminal of the battery (see Chapter 5, Section 1).

2   Place the transaxle in Park, apply the parking brake and block the rear wheels.

3   Remove the drivebelts (see Chapter 1).

4   Remove the spark plugs to make it easier to turn the crankshaft (see Chapter 1), then position the number one piston at TDC (see Section 3).

5   Loosen the lug nuts on the right front wheel. Raise the front of the vehicle and support it securely on jackstands. Remove the right front wheel.

6   Remove the right front inner fender splash shield (see Chapter 11).

7   Remove the engine cover (see illustration 6.3).

8   Remove the alternator (see Chapters 5).

9   Remove the power steering pump without disconnecting the power steering fluid lines and position the assembly off to the side (see Chapter 10).

10  Support the engine by placing a floor jack under the oil pan with a block of wood on the jack to protect the pan. Remove the two bolts and the wiring harness retainer holding the passenger-side engine mount to the block, remove the through-bolt, and remove the mount (see Section 17). Remove the engine mount bracket.

11  Remove the upper timing belt covers (see illustrations).

12  If you intend to re-use the belt, mark the belt to indicate the direction of rotation (see illustration).

13  Make sure the timing marks are properly aligned (see illustrations).

14  Remove the torque converter cover, wedge a large screwdriver into the driveplate ring gear teeth, then unscrew the crankshaft pulley bolt (see illustration).

➡**Note: When the crankshaft pulley bolt is loosened, the position of the timing marks on the crankshaft pulley and the camshafts may be disturbed. Check and align them again. Temporarily reinstall the crankshaft pulley bolt to turn the crankshaft.**

15  Remove the lower timing belt cover (see illustration), then remove the Crankshaft Position (CKP) sensor (see Chapter 6).

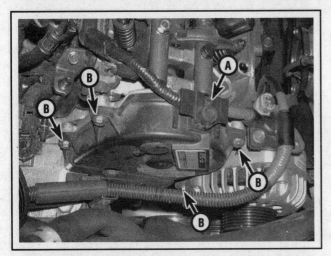

8.11a Detach the wiring harness from the retainer (A) and remove the bolts (B) from the upper timing belt cover (front cylinder bank)

8.11b Remove the upper timing belt cover (arrows indicate two of the four bolts) from the rear cylinder bank

8.12 Mark the direction of rotation on the timing belt

8.13a Camshaft timing marks (front cylinder bank) - align the mark on the sprocket with the mark on the rear cover

8.13b Camshaft sprocket timing marks - rear cylinder bank

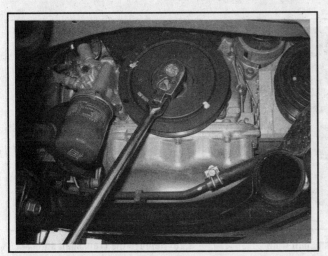

8.14 Use a long ratchet or breaker bar to loosen the crankshaft pulley bolt, as it can be very tight

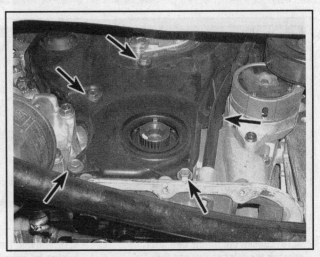

8.15 Remove the bolts and the lower timing belt cover

**8.16 Crankshaft sprocket timing marks - early model shown**

**8.17 Thread the long battery hold-down bolt (A) into the boss as shown to hold the timing belt adjuster (B) in position**

16 Slip the timing belt guide plate off the crankshaft sprocket, noting how it's installed. Also note the alignment of the crankshaft sprocket timing marks (see illustration).

17 Remove one of the long hold-down bolts from the battery tray and bevel the threaded end somewhat with a file or grinder. Thread the bolt into the boss so that it pushes against the timing belt adjuster - the bolt is used to hold the adjuster in position (see illustration). Do not apply any more than hand pressure in tightening.

18 Remove the engine mount bracket upper and lower halves and remove the idler pulley bolt (see illustration), then remove the timing belt.

19 The camshaft sprockets can be removed at this point, if they are damaged or to replace the oil seals (see illustration). Remove the keys from the shafts so they don't fall out and get lost.

## ✳✳ CAUTION:

**Don't allow the camshaft(s) to turn.**

20 If it's worn or damaged, or if you're replacing the crankshaft front oil seal, the crankshaft sprocket can now be removed (see illustration).

If it won't come off by hand, carefully pry it off. Also remove the timing belt guide, noting how it's installed.

## INSPECTION

21 Inspect the sprocket teeth for wear and damage. Check the timing belt for any cracks or oil residue. Also check the camshaft for excessive endplay (see Section 11). Check the timing belt tensioner for smooth operation. Replace any worn parts with new ones.

22 Now that the timing belt is removed, inspect the water pump (see Chapter 3).

➡**Note: Because of the work involved in getting at the water pump, it is advisable you replace the water pump anytime the timing belt is removed.**

## INSTALLATION

23 Remove all dirt and oil from the timing belt area. Clean the teeth of the sprockets with lacquer thinner.

**8.18 Loosen the timing belt idler, remove the idler pulley and the timing belt**

**8.19 Prevent the camshaft from turning by inserting a two-pin spanner through the holes in the sprocket while you loosen the bolt**

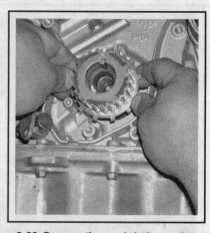

**8.20 Remove the crankshaft sprocket**

24 If any of the timing belt sprockets were removed, install them now with their keys and tighten the bolts to the torque listed in this Chapter's Specifications.

25 If removed, install the timing belt guide over the crankshaft sprocket with the chamfered edge facing away from the belt.

26 Recheck the position of the timing marks (see illustrations 8.13a, 8.13b and 8.16). Install the timing belt in a clockwise direction, starting at the crankshaft sprocket and tensioner pulley, then rear camshaft sprocket, water pump, front camshaft sprocket, and idler pulley. If you're re-using the original belt, the arrow you made in Step 12 should point in the normal direction of rotation.

➡**Note: If the tensioner piston has extended and you're unable to install the timing belt, remove the tensioner and compress the piston as described below.**

27 Install the outer timing belt guide over the crankshaft sprocket with the concave side facing away from the belt.

28 Tighten the idler pulley bolt to the torque listed in this Chapter's Specifications. Remove the battery hold-down bolt that was holding the tensioner pulley in position (see illustration 8.17).

29 Turn the crankshaft slowly six revolutions clockwise using a socket and breaker bar on the crankshaft pulley bolt to seat the belt, then return to TDC. Recheck the alignment of cam and crank sprocket timing marks.

### ❊❊ CAUTION:

**If you feel any resistance, back up and recheck the belt timing. Do not force the crankshaft to turn or engine damage will occur!**

30 Install the lower timing belt cover.

31 Install the crankshaft pulley, aligning the pulley keyway with the crankshaft key. Install the bolt and tighten it to the torque listed in this Chapter's Specifications. Use the method described in Step 14 to keep the crankshaft from turning.

32 Recheck the timing marks (see illustrations 8.13a, 8.13b and 8.16).

### ❊❊ CAUTION:

**If the timing marks are not aligned exactly as shown, repeat the timing belt installation procedure. DO NOT start the engine until you're absolutely certain that the timing belt is installed correctly. Serious and costly engine damage could occur if the belt is installed incorrectly.**

**8.37 Compress the tensioner by prying against the pulley (A) until the holes on the rod and the tensioner body are in alignment, then insert a pin (B) with a diameter of 0.08 inch (2.0 mm), locking the tensioner in a retracted position**

33 Reinstall the remaining parts in the reverse order of removal.

34 Reconnect the battery. Refer to Chapter 5, Section 1.

## TENSIONER RETRACTING/REPLACEMENT

▶ **Refer to illustration 8.37**

35 The belt tensioner does not normally need to be removed for a timing belt replacement procedure, but there are other engine procedures (water pump replacement, etc.) that require the tensioner be removed. Once removed, the tensioner piston will extend in length. The following Steps apply only if the tensioner has been removed from the engine.

36 Remove the long bolt used in Step 17, and unbolt the tensioner from the block.

37 Using a long screwdriver or prybar, lever the tensioner pulley toward the tensioner and insert a drill bit or other pin into the tensioner to hold it in the retracted position (see illustration).

38 Unbolt the tensioner from the engine.

39 Install the tensioner, being careful not to dislodge the locating pin, and tighten the mounting bolts to the torque listed in this Chapter's Specifications. After completing the remainder of the timing belt installation procedure, remove the tensioner locating pin.

## 9   Crankshaft front oil seal - replacement

▶ **Refer to illustrations 9.2 and 9.4**

1   Remove the crankshaft position sensor (see Chapter 6), then remove the timing belt and crankshaft sprocket (see Section 8).
2   Carefully pry the seal out of the engine with a screwdriver or seal removal tool (see illustration). If you use a screwdriver, don't scratch the housing bore or damage the crankshaft (if the crankshaft is scratched, the new seal will end up leaking).
3   Clean the oil seal bore and coat the outer edge of the new seal with a small amount of engine oil to ease installation. Apply multi-purpose grease to the seal lip.
4   Using a seal driver or a socket with an outside diameter slightly smaller than the outside diameter of the seal, carefully drive the new seal into place with a hammer (see illustration). Make sure it's installed squarely and driven in to the same depth as the original.
5   Reinstall the crankshaft sprocket and timing belt (see Section 8).
6   Run the engine and check for oil leaks at the front seal.

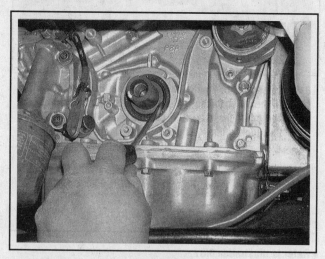

**9.2  Carefully pry out the oil seal**

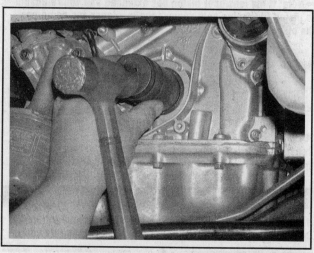

**9.4  Lubricate the seal lip and tap the new crankshaft seal into place with a seal driver or a large socket and a hammer**

## 10   Rocker arm assembly - removal, inspection and installation

### REMOVAL

▶ **Refer to illustration 10.4**

1   Remove the valve cover (see Section 4).
2   Remove the timing belt (see Section 8).
3   Loosen the rocker shaft mounting bolts (or bridge mounting bolts if you're working on a 2WD Honda model) 1/4-turn at a time, in the reverse of the tightening sequence, until the spring pressure is relieved (see illustration 10.11a, 10.11b and 10.11c).
4   Lift the rocker arms and shaft assembly from the cylinder head (see illustration). Do not remove the shaft mounting bolts; they will keep the rocker arm assembly components together.

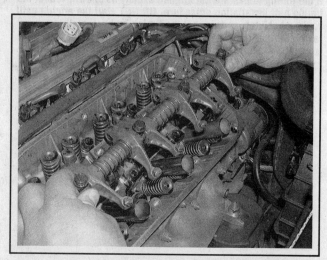

**10.4  Leave the rocker assembly mounting bolts in place as you remove the assembly (this will keep the components in order on the shafts)**

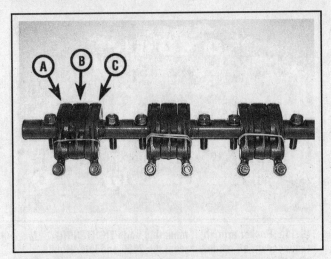

**10.5 VTEC intake rocker arm components (note the rubber bands installed to hold the components together)**

A   Primary intake rocker arm
B   Mid intake rocker arm
C   Secondary intake rocker arm

## INSPECTION

▸ **Refer to illustrations 10.5, 10.6, 10.7 and 10.8**

5   If you wish to disassemble and inspect the rocker arm assembly, a good idea as long as you have them off, remove the mounting bolts and slip the rocker arms and springs off the shafts (see illustration). Keep the parts in order so you can reassemble them in the same positions.

➥ **Note: Keep the rocker arms for each cylinder together by wrapping them with a heavy rubber band.**

6   Thoroughly clean the parts and inspect them for wear and damage. Check the rocker arm faces that contact the camshaft and the rocker arm tips (see illustration). Check the surfaces of the shafts that the rocker arms ride on, as well as the bearing surfaces inside the rocker arms, for scoring and excessive wear. Replace any parts that are damaged or excessively worn. Also, make sure the oil holes in the

**10.7 Push down on the plunger of each lost motion assembly - they should move smoothly**

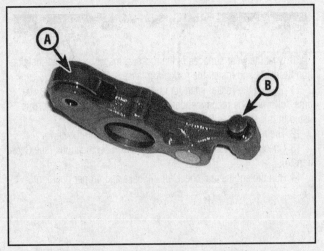

**10.6 Inspect the rockers arms for wear and damage at the roller (A) and the valve stem end of the adjusters (B)**

shafts are not plugged. Check the roller tips for wear and smoothness of operation.

7   Remove the lost motion assemblies from the cylinder head (see illustration), and clean them. Check for smoothness of plunger operation by pushing down gently with your finger.

8   Check the smoothness of operation of the VTEC pistons in each intake rocker arm (see illustration).

## INSTALLATION

▸ **Refer to illustrations 10.11a, 10.11b and 10.11c**

9   Lubricate all components with engine oil and reassemble the shafts. When installing the rocker arms, shafts and springs, note the markings and the difference between the left and right side parts. If you're installing the rocker arm assembly on the rear cylinder head of a 2006 or later 2WD model, apply gasket sealant to the surface of the left end (driver's side) of the cylinder head where the rocker arm bridge seats.

**10.8 Check for smooth movement of the piston in each VTEC rocker arm**

10 Coat the wear surfaces of the rocker arms with camshaft installation lubricant and install the rocker arm assembly.

11 Tighten the rocker shaft (or bridge) mounting bolts a little at a time, following the recommended tightening sequence, to the torque listed in this Chapter's Specifications (see illustrations).

12 The remainder of installation is the reverse of removal.

13 Check the valve clearance and adjust to Specifications (see Section 5).

14 Run the engine and check for oil leaks and proper operation.

**10.11a Rocker arm/shaft mounting bolts TIGHTENING sequence on all models except the 2006 and later Honda Pilot 2WD models**

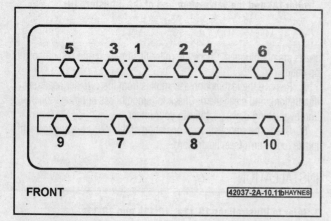

**10.11b Rocker arm/shaft mounting bolt TIGHTENING sequence on the front cylinder head on 2006 and later Honda Pilot 2WD models**

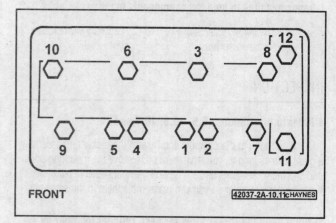

**10.11c Rocker arm bridge mounting bolt TIGHTENING sequence on the rear cylinder head on 2006 and later Honda Pilot 2WD models**

## 11 Camshafts - removal, inspection and installation

### ❄❄❄ WARNING:

**Wait until the engine is completely cool before beginning this procedure.**

### REMOVAL

▶ Refer to illustrations 11.7, 11.8 and 11.9

1 If you're going to remove the camshaft from the front cylinder head, drain the engine coolant (see Chapter 1)

2 Remove the valve covers (see Section 4) and the timing belt (see Section 8).

3 Remove the rocker arms/shafts as an assembly (see Section 10).

➡**Note: Refer to the Inspection procedures below and check camshaft endplay before removing the camshafts.**

4 Remove the camshaft sprockets (see Section 8).

5 If you're removing the camshaft from the front cylinder head, remove the battery and the battery tray (see Chapter 5).

6 If you're removing the camshaft from the front cylinder head, detach the upper radiator hose from the coolant passage (see Chapter 3). If you're removing the camshaft from the rear cylinder head, detach the brake lines from the master cylinder (see Chapter 9).

7 If you're removing the camshaft from the front cylinder head, remove the EGR valve to access the camshaft retainer plate (see illustration). If you're removing the camshaft from the rear cylinder head, remove the two nuts and detach the EVAP purge joint bracket from the rear camshaft retainer plate.

8 Remove the camshaft retainer plate (see illustration).

9 Carefully slide the camshaft out of the cylinder head, being careful not to nick the lobes or journals as you withdraw it (see illustration).

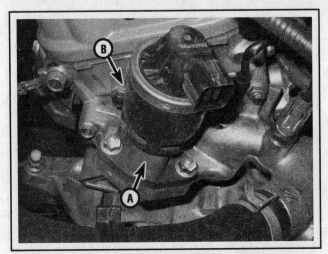

**11.7 To access the retainer plate for the front camshaft, remove the EGR valve (A), then the two bolts on the plate (B) located behind the EGR valve**

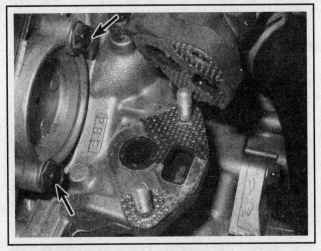

**11.8 Remove the bolts and the camshaft retainer plate**

**11.9 Pull the camshaft straight out of the cylinder head, taking care not to nick the journals or bearings**

## INSPECTION

▶ **Refer to illustrations 11.12a and 11.12b**

10 Keeping careful track of the location of the components (see illustration 10.5), remove the rocker arms and springs from the rocker shafts (or bridge) and bolt the bare rocker shafts (or bridge) to the cylinder head, tightening them to the torque listed in this Chapter's Specifications.

11 Mount a dial indicator so that it contacts the nose of the camshaft. Pry the camshaft forwards and back with a screwdriver, with the tip taped to prevent damage to the camshaft. Record the movement of the dial indicator and compare it to this Chapter's Specifications. If the endplay is excessive, install a new retainer plate and check the endplay again. If the endplay is still excessive, the camshaft must be replaced.

12 Remove the retainer plate and slide the camshaft out of the head. Measure the journal diameters and lobe heights on each camshaft, comparing your measurements to this Chapter's Specifications. Check also for visual signs of wear, scoring, pitting or overheating.

➡**Note: The arrangement of lobes is different between the front and rear camshafts (see illustrations).**

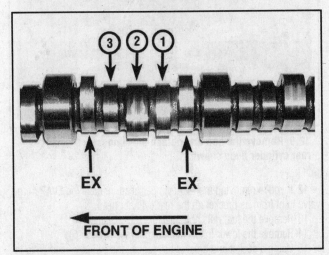

**11.12a Arrangement of camshaft lobes on the left cylinder bank (front) camshaft (VTEC models shown)**

1 Primary intake lobe
2 Mid intake lobe
3 Secondary intake lobe

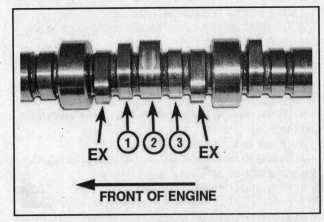

**11.12b Arrangement of camshaft lobes on the right cylinder bank (rear) camshaft (VTEC models shown)**

1 Primary intake lobe
2 Mid intake lobe
3 Secondary intake lobe

## INSTALLATION

▶ **Refer to illustration 11.13**

13  The camshaft oil seal should be replaced whenever a camshaft is removed or replaced. Remove the timing belt rear covers from each cylinder head to access the camshaft seals (see illustration).

14  Pry the old seal out with a screwdriver or seal removal tool.

15  Lubricate the lips with engine oil, then install a new camshaft oil seal by driving it in squarely with a seal installation tool to the same depth as the original seal. A socket of the appropriate size will also work.

16  Clean the camshaft thoroughly with solvent, then lubricate the journals and lobes with camshaft installation lubricant and carefully install the camshaft into the cylinder head.

17  Lubricate and install a new O-ring on the camshaft retainer plate. Install the retainer plate and tighten the bolts to the torque listed in this Chapter's Specifications.

18  Reinstall the remaining components in the reverse order of removal. Refer to Section 5 for the valve adjustment procedure. If the coolant was drained, refill the cooling system (see Chapter 1). If the brake lines were detached from the master cylinder, bleed the brake system (see Chapter 9).

19  Run the engine and check for oil leaks at the camshaft seals. Run the engine at low speed for five minutes to allow the air to bleed from

**11.13  Remove the two bolts and the timing belt rear cover from each cylinder head**

the lost motion assemblies, then check for leaks and proper operation.

➡**Note: There will be some tappet noise during the first few minutes of operation. If the noise continues, it may indicate a problem with one of the lost motion assemblies.**

## 12  Cylinder heads - removal and installation

❊❊ **WARNING:**

**Allow the engine to cool completely before beginning this procedure.**

## REMOVAL

▶ **Refer to illustrations 12.9, 12.10a, 12.10b and 12.16**

1  Relieve the fuel system pressure (see Chapter 4).

2  Disconnect the cable from the negative terminal of the battery (see Chapter 5, Section 1).

3  Drain the cooling system, including both block drains (see Chapter 1).

4  Remove the power steering pump and set it aside without disconnecting the power steering fluid lines (see Chapter 10).

5  If you're removing the front cylinder head, remove the alternator (see Chapter 5).

6  Remove the upper intake manifold (see Section 6).

7  Remove the exhaust manifolds (see Section 7) or the catalytic converter assemblies (see Chapter 6).

8  Remove the timing belt and the camshaft sprockets (see Section 8).

9  Remove the connector brackets from the transaxle side of the front and rear cylinder heads (see illustration).

10  Remove the coolant passage from the cylinder heads (see illustrations).

11  Remove the valve cover (see Section 4) and the rocker arms/shafts assembly (see Section 10).

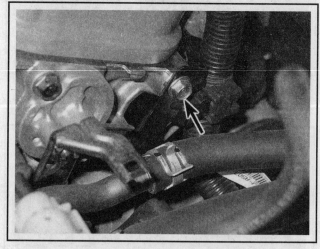

**12.9  Remove the bolt and detach the connector brackets - rear cylinder head shown**

12  If you're removing the rear cylinder head, remove the EVAP purge valve joint from its bracket on the rear cylinder head.

13  Remove the fuel rails and injectors (see Chapter 4).

14  Remove the lower intake manifold(s) (see Section 6).

15  Using a socket and breaker bar, loosen the cylinder head bolts in 1/4-turn increments until they can be removed by hand. Loosen them in a sequence opposite that of the tightening sequence (see illustration 12.23)

16  Lift the cylinder head off the engine block. If the head is stuck, pry against an external casting protrusion (see illustration).

**12.10a Remove the harness ground connectors from the coolant passage**

**12.10b Remove the coolant passage mounting bolts from both cylinder heads - lightly tap the passage with a soft-faced hammer to break the gasket seal and remove the coolant passage**

※※ **CAUTION:**

**Don't pry between the head and block. The gasket surfaces may be damaged and leaks could result.**

## INSTALLATION

▸ **Refer to illustration 12.23**

17 The mating surfaces of the cylinder heads and block must be perfectly clean when the heads are installed. Use a gasket scraper to remove all traces of carbon and old gasket material. Be careful not to gouge the delicate aluminum. Clean the mating surfaces with lacquer thinner or acetone. If there's oil on the mating surfaces when the head is installed, the gasket may not seal correctly and leaks could develop. When working on the block, stuff the cylinders with clean shop rags to keep out debris. Use a vacuum cleaner to remove material that falls into the cylinders.

18 Check the block and head mating surfaces for nicks, deep scratches and other damage. If damage is slight, it can be removed with

a file; if it's excessive, machining may be the only alternative.

19 Use a tap of the correct size to chase the threads in the head bolt holes, then clean the holes with compressed air - make sure that nothing remains in the holes.

※※ **WARNING:**

**Wear eye protection when using compressed air!**

20 Mount each bolt in a vise and run a die down the threads to remove corrosion and restore the threads. Dirt, corrosion, sealant and damaged threads will affect torque readings.

21 Clean the oil-control orifices thoroughly and reinstall them with new O-rings. Position the new gaskets over the oil-control orifices and locating dowels in the block.

22 Carefully set the head on the block without disturbing the gasket.

23 Before installing the head bolts, apply a small amount of clean engine oil to the threads and under the bolt heads. Install the bolts and special washers and tighten them finger tight. Following the recommended sequence (see illustration), tighten the bolts to the torque listed

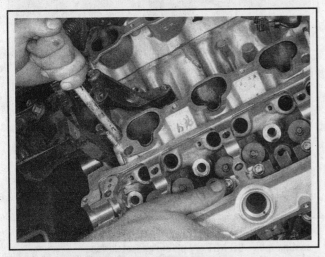

**12.16 Pry up carefully on a casting protrusion**

**12.23 Cylinder head bolt TIGHTENING sequence**

in this Chapter's Specifications in three steps.

➡**Note: On 2001 through 2006 Acura and 2003 through 2005 Honda models, perform each step twice, i.e., torque all bolts to the Specification for the first step, then again torque all to the same Specification before proceeding to the second step.**

24  The remaining installation steps are the reverse of removal.

25  Reconnect the battery (see Chapter 5, Section 1).

26  Refill the cooling system, change the oil and filter (see Chapter 1), then run the engine and check for leaks. Run the engine at low speed for five minutes to allow the air to bleed from the lost motion assemblies, then check for leaks and proper operation.

➡**Note: There will be some tappet noise during the first few minutes of operation. If the noise continues, it may indicate a problem with one of the lost motion assemblies.**

## 13  Oil pan - removal and installation

### REMOVAL

▶ **Refer to illustrations 13.6, 13.8a and 13.8b**

1  Disconnect the cable from the negative terminal of the battery (see Chapter 5, Section 1).

2  Block the rear wheels and set the parking brake.

3  Raise the front of the vehicle and support it securely on jackstands.

4  Remove the engine splash shield (see illustration 7.3).

5  Drain the engine oil and remove the oil filter (see Chapter 1).

6  Remove the crossmember (see illustration).

7  Unbolt the exhaust pipes from the exhaust manifold/catalytic converter assemblies and from the rear portion of the exhaust system (see Chapter 4). Remove the front portion of the exhaust system.

8  Remove the torque converter cover, then remove the bolts/nuts (see illustration) and lower the oil pan. The bolts at the timing belt end of the engine can be removed with a 1/4-inch drive flex-socket, extension and ratchet. If the pan is stuck, carefully pry at the tabs on the casting corners (see illustration). Don't damage the mating surfaces of the pan and block or oil leaks could develop.

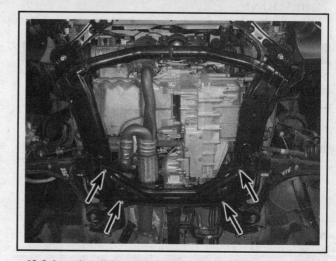

**13.6  Location of the crossmember mounting bolts**

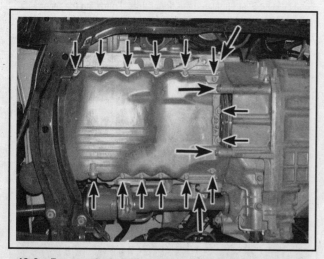

**13.8a  Remove the bolts from around the perimeter of the oil pan and the oil pan-to-transaxle bolts (four bolts hidden from view behind subframe)**

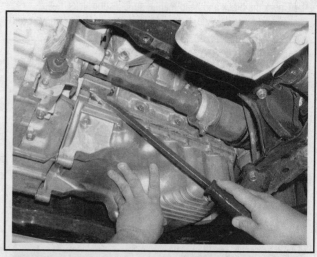

**13.8b  Use a prybar or screwdriver to pry the pan loose at the casting tabs - DO NOT pry on the gasket surface**

## INSTALLATION

◆ **Refer to illustration 13.13**

9   Use a scraper to remove all traces of old sealant from the block and oil pan. Be careful not to gouge the delicate aluminum surfaces. Clean the mating surfaces with lacquer thinner or acetone.

10   Make sure the threaded bolt holes in the block are clean.

11   Inspect the oil pump pick-up screen assembly for damage and a blocked strainer (see Section 14).

12   Apply a bead of sealant to the mating surface of the oil pan.

➡**Note: Install the oil pan within 4 minutes of sealant application.**

13   Carefully position the oil pan on the engine block and install the bolts. Follow the correct torque sequence (see illustration) and tighten them a little at a time to the torque listed in this Chapter's Specifications. After the oil pan-to-block bolts have been tightened, tighten the pan-to-transaxle bolts to the torque listed in this Chapter's Specifications.

14   The remainder of installation is the reverse of removal. Be sure to add oil and install a new oil filter.

➡**Note: Wait 30 minutes (to allow the sealant to cure) before adding oil.**

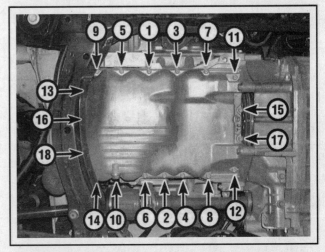

**13.13 Oil pan bolt tightening sequence. (Once the pan bolts are tightened, tighten the pan-to-transaxle bolts to the torque listed in this Chapter's Specifications)**

15   Reconnect the battery (see Chapter 5, Section 1).

16   Run the engine and check for oil pressure and leaks.

## 14   Oil pump - removal, inspection and installation

### REMOVAL

◆ **Refer to illustrations 14.3 and 14.5**

1   Remove the crankshaft position sensor (see Chapter 6).

2   Remove the timing belt, crankshaft sprocket and idler pulley (see Section 8).

3   Remove the oil pan (see Section 13) and oil pick-up screen (see illustration). If equipped, remove the oil level sensor.

4   Remove the oil filter adapter housing/VTEC solenoid assembly (4WD models) from the front of the oil pump (see Chapter 6).

5   Remove the bolts and detach the oil pump housing from the engine (see illustration). You may have to pry carefully between the main bearing cap and the pump housing with a screwdriver.

**14.3  Oil pick-up screen bolt locations**

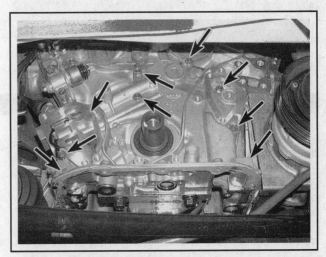

**14.5  Oil pump housing bolt locations**

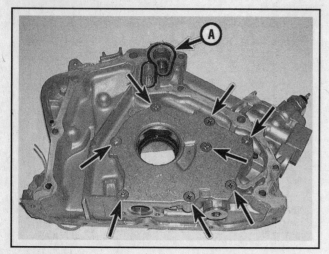

**14.6 Remove the screws from the pump cover and replace the O-ring seal (A)**

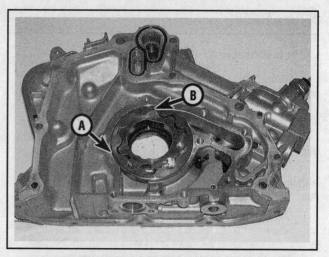

**14.7 Inspect the condition of the rotors and the inside of the cover - with feeler gauges, measure the clearances at (A) (outer rotor-to-housing) and (B) (inner rotor-to-outer rotor). Also lay a straightedge across the face of the pump housing and measure the housing-to-rotor axial clearance**

## INSPECTION

▶ **Refer to illustrations 14.6 and 14.7**

6   Use a Phillips screwdriver to remove the screws holding the pump cover to the rear of the housing (see illustration).

7   Lift the cover off and inspect the pump rotors (see illustration). If any wear or damage is evident, replace the pump. Check the rotor clearance with a feeler gauge and compare it to this Chapter's Specifications.

8   Use a scraper to remove any traces of old sealant from the pump body and engine block, being careful not to damage the delicate aluminum.

## INSTALLATION

9   Replace the old crankshaft oil seal (see Section 9). Apply engine oil or multi-purpose grease to the seal lip.

10   Pack the pump cavities with petroleum jelly and install the cover. Apply thread-locking compound to the threads and tighten the screws to the torque listed in this Chapter's Specifications following a criss-cross pattern.

11   Use acetone or lacquer thinner and a clean rag to remove all traces of oil from the gasket surfaces.

12   Apply a bead of anaerobic sealant to the oil pump flange and the threads of the mounting bolts. Avoid using an excessive amount of sealant, especially around oil passages and bolt holes. Parts must be assembled within five minutes of sealant application, otherwise the material must be removed and reapplied. Wherever O-rings are employed, use new ones.

13   Engage the flat surfaces on the oil pump drive rotor with the matching flats on the crankshaft and slide the pump into place.

14   Install the pump mounting bolts in their original locations and tighten them to the torque listed in this Chapter's Specifications in a criss-cross pattern.

15   Using a new O-ring, install the oil pick-up screen and tighten the fasteners to the torque listed in this Chapter's Specifications.

16   Reinstall the remaining parts in the reverse order of removal.

17   Wait 30 minutes to allow the sealant to cure, then add oil, start the engine and check for oil leaks and pressure.

18   Recheck the engine oil level after operating the engine.

## 15   Driveplate - removal and installation

1   Remove the engine and transaxle (see Chapter 2B), then separate the transaxle from the engine (see Chapter 7).

2   Remove the bolts that secure the driveplate to the crankshaft.

3   Clean the driveplate and inspect the surface for cracks. Check for worn, cracked or broken ring-gear teeth. Lay the driveplate on a flat surface and use a straightedge to check for warpage.

4   Clean and inspect the mating surfaces of the driveplate and the crankshaft. If the crankshaft oil seal is leaking, replace it before rein-stalling the driveplate (see Section 16).

5   Position the driveplate against the crankshaft. Note that offset bolt holes ensure correct installation.

6   Follow a criss-cross pattern and tighten the bolts in several stages to the torque listed in this Chapter's Specifications.

7   The remainder of installation is the reverse of the removal procedure.

## 16 Rear main oil seal - replacement

◆ **Refer to illustration 16.2**

1   Remove the driveplate (see Section 15).

2   The seal can be replaced without removing the oil pan or removing the seal retainer. However, the lip of the seal is quite stiff and it's possible to cock the seal in the retainer bore or damage it during installation. Pry out the old seal with a screwdriver (see illustration).

3   Apply multi-purpose grease to the crankshaft seal journal and the lip of the new seal, then carefully drive the new seal into place with a seal driver. The lip is stiff, so carefully work it onto the seal journal of the crankshaft. Don't rush it or you may damage the seal.

➡**Note: Drive the seal in squarely and only until it is flush with the back of the seal plate, no further. Make sure the spring side is facing in.**

4   The remaining steps are the reverse of removal.

**16.2  Carefully pry the rear main seal out - don't damage the surface of the crankshaft or the new seal will leak**

## 17 Powertrain mounts - check and replacement

### CHECK

**❋❋ CAUTION:**

The front and rear mounts on 2WD models are computer-controlled (see Section 18). The following check procedure does not include the 2WD models. Refer to Section 18 for the checking procedure for the Engine Mount Control system.

1   There are four engine mounts on these models.

2   During the check, the engine must be raised slightly to remove the weight from the mounts.

3   Raise the vehicle and support it securely on jackstands, then position a floor jack under the engine oil pan. Place a large block of wood between the jack head and the oil pan, then carefully raise the engine just enough to take the weight off the mounts.

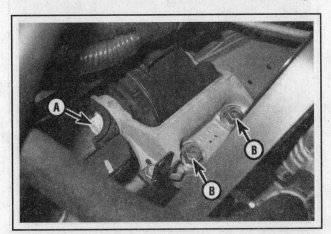

**17.9  Location of the through-bolt (A) and the bracket bolts (B) on the passenger's side engine mount - 2005 Honda Pilot shown**

**❋❋ WARNING:**

DO NOT place any part of your body under the engine when it's supported only by a jack!

4   Check the mounts to see if the rubber is cracked, hardened or separated from the casing.

5   Check for relative movement between the mount plates and the engine or subframe. Use a large screwdriver or prybar to attempt to move the mounts. If movement is noted, lower the engine and tighten the mount fasteners.

6   Apply the parking brake, block the rear wheels, raise the front of the vehicle and support it securely on jackstands (if not already done).

### REPLACEMENT

◆ **Refer to illustrations 17.9, 17.13, 17.16 and 17.29**

**Right (passenger-side) mount**

7   Remove the PCM (see Chapter 6) and position it off to the side without disconnecting the wiring harness.

8   Use a floor jack under the engine to take the weight from the mount. Place a large block of wood between the jack head and the oil pan, then carefully raise the engine just enough to take the weight off the mount.

**❋❋ WARNING:**

DO NOT place any part of your body under the engine when it's supported only by a jack!

9   Remove the through-bolt from the mount (see illustration), then remove the bolts holding the engine bracket in place. Remove the mount-to-chassis bolts and remove the mount.

10   Installation is the reverse of removal.

➡Note: Tighten the bolts securely only after the engine/transaxle weight is back onto the mounts and the jack is removed.

### Left (driver's-side) mounts

11 The driver's-side mounts are between the bottom of the transaxle and the subframe.

12 Use a floor jack under the transaxle to take the weight from the mount. Place a large block of wood between the jack head and the oil pan, then carefully raise the transaxle just enough to take the weight off the mount.

13 Remove the two nuts from below the subframe, the two bolts at the transaxle, and remove the mount (see illustration).

14 Installation is the reverse of removal.

➡Note: Tighten the bolts securely only after the engine/transaxle weight is back onto the mounts and the jack is removed.

### Front mount

15 The front mount is located between the engine and radiator.

### 4WD models

16 Remove the large nut where the mount stud goes through the engine bracket (see illustration).

17 Use a floor jack under the engine to take the weight from the mount. Place a large block of wood between the jack head and the oil pan, then carefully raise the engine just enough to take the weight off the mount.

> **✳✳ WARNING:**
>
> **DO NOT place any part of your body under the engine when it's supported only by a jack!**

18 Remove the bolts holding the mount to the mount base, and the bolts holding the mount base to the subframe. Raise the engine slightly, slide the mount base forward, then remove the mount.

19 Installation is the reverse of removal.

➡Note: Tighten the bolts securely only after the engine/transaxle weight is back onto the mounts and the jack is removed.

### 2WD models

20 Remove the battery and the battery tray (see Chapter 5).

21 Use a floor jack under the engine to take the weight from the mount. Place a large block of wood between the jack head and the oil pan, then carefully raise the engine just enough to take the weight off the mount.

> **✳✳ WARNING:**
>
> **DO NOT place any part of your body under the engine when it's supported only by a jack!**

22 Disconnect the electrical connector from the engine mount.

23 Remove the nuts securing the mount stop to the mount.

24 Remove the bolts holding the mount to the chassis, the upper bolt holding the mount to the bracket and the bolts holding the mount to the subframe.

25 Raise the engine slightly and remove the mount. Installation is the reverse of removal.

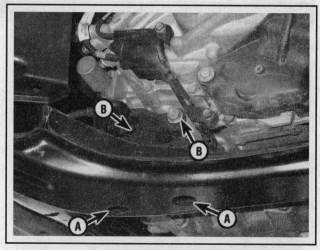

**17.13 Remove the lower bolts through the access holes (A) in the subframe and the upper bolts (B)**

### Rear mount

26 Remove the air intake duct and the air filter housing (see Chapter 4).

### 4WD models

27 Raise the front of the vehicle and support it securely on jackstands.

28 Remove the bolts holding the mount to the subframe. Lower the vehicle.

29 Use a floor jack under the engine to take the weight from the mount. Place a large block of wood between the jack head and the oil pan, then carefully raise the engine just enough to take the weight off the mount. Remove the through-bolt from the rear engine mount (see illustration).

30 Raise the engine enough for the mount to clear the upper bracket and remove the mount.

31 Installation is the reverse of removal.

➡Note: Tighten the bolts securely only after the engine/transaxle weight is back onto the mounts and the jack is removed.

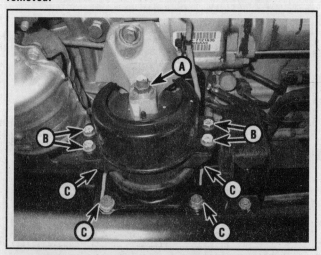

**17.16 Remove the upper nut (A) from the mount stud on the front engine mount, the bolts securing the mount to the mount base (B) and the four mount base bolts (C)**

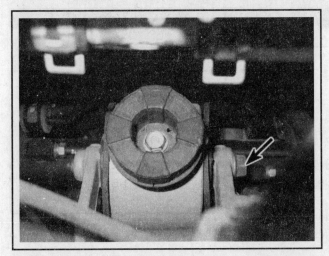

**17.29 Remove the through-bolt from the rear engine mount**

### 2WD models

32  Raise the front of the vehicle and support it securely on jackstands.

33  Remove the mount-to-subframe bolts, then lower the vehicle.

34  Use a floor jack under the engine to take the weight from the

mount. Place a large block of wood between the jack head and the oil pan, then carefully raise the engine just enough to take the weight off the mount.

### ✱✱ WARNING:

**DO NOT place any part of your body under the engine when it's supported only by a jack!**

35  Disconnect the electrical connector from the engine mount.

36  Remove the nuts securing the mount stop to the mount.

37  Remove the bolts holding the mount to the chassis, the upper bolt holding the mount to the bracket and the bolts holding the mount to the subframe.

38  Raise the engine slightly and remove the mount. Installation is the reverse of removal.

### Final tightening, all mounts

39  To ensure maximum bushing life and prevent excessive noise and vibration, the vehicle should be level and the engine weight should be on the mounts during the final tightening stage.

➥**Note: Use non-hardening thread locking compound on the nuts/bolts. Ensure that the bushings are not twisted or offset. If you have replaced more than one mount, or when you are installing the engine, tighten the mounts in the following order: front, rear, passenger-side and driver's-side.**

## 18  Engine Mount Control System - description and check

### DESCRIPTION

1  2006 and later Honda 2WD models have special front and rear engine mounts that are computer-controlled to reduce vibrations during idle and when the engine is in cylinder pause mode (when the Variable Cylinder Mangement system deactivates the rear bank cylinders). The interior of the liquid-filled mount has two chambers. When the engine is idling, the Powertrain Control Module (PCM) signals a control solenoid valve in the mount which induces a "counter-vibration," to reduce  nor-

mal vibrations. At engine speeds over 1,000 rpm, the solenoid is shut off and the engine mount changes to its normal mode.

### CHECK

2  Aside from checking the mounts for loose electrical connectors and fluid leakage, testing of this system must be performed by a dealer service department or other qualified automotive repair facility.

## Specifications

### General

Cylinder numbers (timing belt end-to-transaxle end)
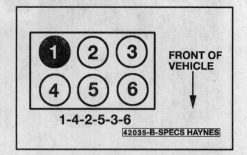

**Cylinder locations**

| | |
|---|---|
| Rear (firewall) side | 1-2-3 |
| Front (radiator) side | 4-5-6 |
| Firing order | 1-4-2-5-3-6 |

Bore
| | |
|---|---|
| 2007 Acura models | 3.54 inches (90.0 mm) |
| All other models | 3.50 inches (89.0 mm) |

Stroke
| | |
|---|---|
| 2007 Acura models | 3.78 inches (96.0 mm) |
| All other models | 3.66 inches (93.0 mm) |

Displacement
| | |
|---|---|
| 2007 Acura models | 224 cubic inches (3.7 liters) |
| All other models | 212 cubic inches (3.5 liters) |

### Valve adjustment

| | |
|---|---|
| Intake | 0.008 to 0.009 inch (0.20 to 0.22 mm) |
| Exhaust | 0.011 to 0.013 inch (0.28 to 0.32 mm) |

### Camshaft and rocker arms

Camshaft to holder oil clearance
| | |
|---|---|
| Standard | 0.0020 to 0.0035 inch (0.050 to 0.089 mm) |
| Service limit | 0.006 inch (0.15 mm) |

Camshaft lobe height

Acura models

2001 and 2002

Intake
| | |
|---|---|
| Primary | 1.3676 inches (34.737 mm) |
| Mid | 1.4348 inches (36.445 mm) |
| Secondary | 1.3748 inches (34.919 mm) |
| Exhaust | 1.4302 inches (36.326 mm) |

2003 through 2006

Intake
| | |
|---|---|
| Primary | 1.3796 inches (35.041 mm) |
| Mid | 1.4348 inches (36.445 mm) |
| Secondary | 1.3891 inches (35.284 mm) |
| Exhaust | 1.4302 inches (36.326 mm) |

2007

Intake
| | |
|---|---|
| Primary | 1.3824 inches (35.112 mm) |
| Mid | 1.4328 inches (36.394 mm) |
| Secondary | 1.3824 inches (35.112 mm) |
| Exhaust | 1.4326 inches (36.389 mm) |

Honda models
    2003 and 2004 4WD models
        Intake
            Primary                1.3676 inches (34.737 mm)
            Mid                   1.4348 inches (36.445 mm)
            Secondary          1.3748 inches (34.919 mm)
        Exhaust              1.4302 inches (36.326 mm)
    2005 and later 4WD models
        Intake
            Primary                1.3796 inches (35.041 mm)
            Mid                   1.4348 inches (36.445 mm)
            Secondary          1.3891 inches (35.284 mm)
        Exhaust              1.4302 inches (36.326 mm)
    2006 and later 2WD models
        Front camshaft
            Intake                 1.4232 inches (36.149 mm)
            Exhaust         1.4120 inches (35.864 mm)
        Rear camshaft
            Intake                 1.3817 inches (35.096 mm)
            Exhaust         1.4374 inches (36.509 mm)
Camshaft endplay
    Standard                   0.002 to 0.008 inch (0.05 to 0.20 mm)
    Service limit             0.008 inch (0.20 mm)
Camshaft runout limit (total indicator reading)    0.002 inch (0.04 mm)
Rocker arm-to-shaft oil clearance
    Acura models
        Intake
            Standard              0.0010 to 0.0026 inch (0.026 to 0.067 mm)
            Service limit        0.0026 inch (0.067 mm)
        Exhaust
            Standard              0.0010 to 0.0030 inch (0.026 to 0.077 mm)
            Service limit        0.0030 inch (0.077 mm)
    Honda models
        2003 and later 4WD models
            Intake
                Standard              0.0010 to 0.0026 inch (0.026 to 0.067 mm)
                Service limit        0.0026 inch (0.067 mm)
            Exhaust
                Standard              0.0010 to 0.0030 inch (0.026 to 0.077 mm)
                Service limit        0.0030 inch (0.077 mm)
        2006 and later 2WD models
            Intake
                Standard              0.0007 to 0.0026 inch (0.019 to 0.067 mm)
                Service limit        0.0026 inch (0.067 mm)
            Exhaust
                Standard              0.0006 to 0.0018 inch (0.015 to 0.046 mm)
                Service limit        0.0018 inch (0.046 mm)

### Oil pump

Outer rotor-to-body clearance

Acura models

| | |
|---|---|
| 2001 and 2002 | 0.006 to 0.007 inch (0.14 to 0.19 mm) |
| 2003 and later | 0.004 to 0.007 inch (0.10 to 0.19 mm) |

Honda models

| | |
|---|---|
| 2003 and 2004 | 0.006 to 0.007 inch (0.14 to 0.19 mm) |
| 2005 and later | 0.004 to 0.007 inch (0.10 to 0.19 mm) |
| Outer rotor-to-inner rotor clearance | 0.002 to 0.006 inch (0.05 to 0.15 mm) |
| Housing-to-rotor clearance | 0.001 to 0.003 inch (0.02 to 0.07 mm) |

| Torque specifications | Ft-lbs (unless otherwise indicated) | Nm |
|---|---|---|
| Camshaft thrust plate bolts | 16 | 22 |
| Camshaft sprocket bolts | | |
|     2007 Acura models | 68 | 91 |
|     All other models | 67 | 90 |
| Coolant passage | | |
|     Small bolts | 104 in-lbs | 12 |
|     Large bolts | 16 | 22 |
| Crankshaft pulley bolt | | |
|     2001 and 2002 Acura and 2003 and | | |
|     2004 Honda models | 181 | 245 |
|     All other models | | |
|         Step 1 | 47 | 64 |
|         Step 2 | Tighten an additional 60 degrees | |
| Crossmember bolts | 40 | 54 |
| Cylinder head bolts (in sequence - see illustration 12.25) | | |
|     Acura models | | |
|         2001 through 2006 | | |
|             Step 1* | 29 | 39 |
|             Step 2* | 51 | 69 |
|             Step 3* | 72 | 98 |
|         2007 | | |
|             Step 1 | 22 | 29 |
|             Step 2 | Tighten an additional 90 degrees | |
|             Step 3 | Tighten an additional 90 degrees | |
|             Step 4 (with new head bolts only) | Tighten an additional 90 degrees | |
|     Honda models | | |
|         2003 through 2005 | | |
|             Step 1* | 29 | 39 |
|             Step 2* | 51 | 69 |
|             Step 3* | 72 | 98 |
|         2006 and later | | |
|             Step 1 | 22 | 29 |
|             Step 2 | Tighten an additional 90 degrees | |
|             Step 3 | Tighten an additional 90 degrees | |
|             Step 4 (with new head bolts only) | Tighten an additional 90 degrees | |
| Drivebelt tensioner bolt | 19 | 25 |

*Perform each Step twice*

| Torque specifications | Ft-lbs (unless otherwise indicated) | Nm |
|---|---|---|
| Driveplate bolts | 54 | 74 |
| Exhaust manifold nuts | | |
|     2001 and 2002 Acura models | 16 | 22 |
|     2003 and 2004 Honda models | 23 | 31 |
| Exhaust heat shield bolts | 16 | 22 |
| Intake manifold upper cover bolts | 104 in-lbs | 12 |
| Intake manifold bolts | | |
|     Upper intake manifold | 16 | 22 |
|     Lower intake manifold(s) | 16 | 22 |
| Oil pan bolts | 104 in-lbs | 12 |
| Oil pan-to-transaxle bolts | | |
|     2001 and 2002 Acura and 2003 through | | |
|         2005 Honda models | 28 | 38 |
|     All other models | 54 | 74 |
| Oil pick-up screen mounting bolts | 104 in-lbs | 12 |
| Oil pump housing mounting bolts | 104 in-lbs | 12 |
| Oil pump cover screws | 48 in-lbs | 6 |
| Rocker arm shaft bolts | | |
|     4WD models (see illustration 10.11a) | 17 | 24 |
|     2WD models | | |
|         Front cylinder head (see | | |
|             illustration 10.11b) | 17 | 24 |
|         Rear cylinder head (see | | |
|             illustration 10.11c) | 16 | 22 |
| Timing belt adjuster bolt | 19 | 25 |
| Timing belt tensioner bolts | 104 in-lbs | 12 |
| Timing belt idler pulley bolt | 33 | 44 |
| Timing belt cover bolts | 104 in-lbs | 12 |
| Rear main oil seal retainer bolts | 104 in-lbs | 12 |
| Valve cover bolts | 104 in-lbs | 12 |

**Notes**

**Section**

**Reference to other Chapters**
CHECK ENGINE light on - See Chapter 6

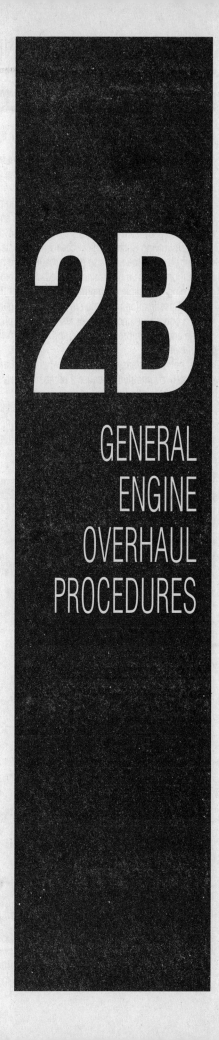

# 2B

## GENERAL ENGINE OVERHAUL PROCEDURES

## 1 General information - engine overhaul

▶ **Refer to illustrations 1.1, 1.2, 1.3, 1.4, 1.5 and 1.6**

Included in this portion of Chapter 2 are general information and diagnostic testing procedures for determining the overall mechanical condition of your engine.

The information ranges from advice concerning preparation for an overhaul and the purchase of replacement parts and/or components to detailed, step-by-step procedures covering removal and installation.

The following Sections have been written to help you determine whether your engine needs to be overhauled and how to remove and install it once you've determined it needs to be rebuilt. For information concerning in-vehicle engine repair, see Chapter 2A.

The Specifications included in this Part are general in nature and include only those necessary for testing the oil pressure and checking the engine compression. Refer to Chapter 2A for additional engine Specifications.

It's not always easy to determine when, or if, an engine should be completely overhauled, because a number of factors must be considered.

High mileage is not necessarily an indication that an overhaul is needed, while low mileage doesn't preclude the need for an overhaul. Frequency of servicing is probably the most important consideration. An engine that's had regular and frequent oil and filter changes, as well as other required maintenance, will most likely give many thousands of miles of reliable service. Conversely, a neglected engine may require an overhaul very early in its service life.

Excessive oil consumption is an indication that piston rings, valve seals and/or valve guides are in need of attention. Make sure that oil leaks aren't responsible before deciding that the rings and/or guides are bad. Perform a cylinder compression check to determine the extent of the work required (see Section 3). Also check the vacuum readings under various conditions (see Section 4).

Check the oil pressure with a gauge installed in place of the oil pressure sending unit and compare it to this Chapter's Specifications (see Section 2). If it's extremely low, the bearings and/or oil pump are probably worn out.

Loss of power, rough running, knocking or metallic engine noises, excessive valve train noise and high fuel consumption rates may also point to the need for an overhaul, especially if they're all present at the same time. If a complete tune-up doesn't remedy the situation, major mechanical work is the only solution.

An engine overhaul involves restoring the internal parts to the specifications of a new engine. During an overhaul, the piston rings are replaced and the cylinder walls are reconditioned (rebored and/ or honed) (see illustrations 1.1 and 1.2). If a rebore is done by an

**1.1 An engine block being bored. An engine rebuilder will use special machinery to recondition the cylinder bores**

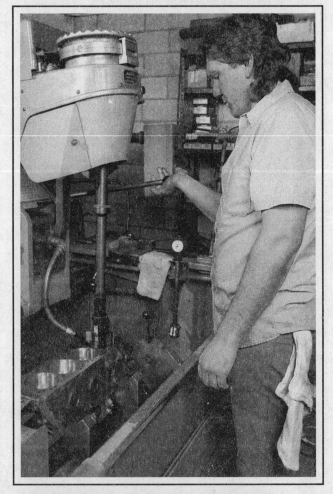

**1.2 If the cylinders are bored, the machine shop will normally hone the engine on a machine like this**

**1.3  A crankshaft having a main bearing journal ground**

**1.4  A machinist checks for a bent connecting rod, using specialized equipment**

automotive machine shop, new oversize pistons will also be installed. The main bearings, connecting rod bearings and camshaft bearings are generally replaced with new ones and, if necessary, the crankshaft may be reground to restore the journals (see illustration 1.3). Generally, the valves are serviced as well, since they're usually in less-than-perfect condition at this point. While the engine is being overhauled, other components, such as the distributor, starter and alternator, can be rebuilt as well. The end result should be similar to a new engine that will give many trouble free miles.

➡**Note: Critical cooling system components such as the hoses, drivebelts, thermostat and water pump should be replaced with new parts when an engine is overhauled. The radiator should be checked carefully to ensure that it isn't clogged or leaking (see Chapter 3). If you purchase a rebuilt engine or short block, some rebuilders will not warranty their engines unless the radiator has been professionally flushed. Also, we don't recommend overhauling the oil pump - always install a new one when an engine is rebuilt.**

Overhauling the internal components on today's engines is a difficult and time-consuming task which requires a significant amount of specialty tools and is best left to a professional engine rebuilder (see illustrations 1.4, 1.5 and 1.6). A competent engine rebuilder will handle the inspection of your old parts and offer advice concerning the reconditioning or replacement of the original engine, never purchase parts or have machine work done on other components until the block has been thoroughly inspected by a professional machine shop. As a general rule, time is the primary cost of an overhaul, especially since the vehicle may be tied up for a minimum of two weeks or more. Be aware that some engine builders only have the capability to rebuild the engine you bring them while other rebuilders have a large inventory of rebuilt exchange engines in stock. Also be aware that many machine shops could take as much as two weeks time to completely rebuild your engine depending on shop workload. Sometimes it makes more sense to simply exchange your engine for another engine that's already rebuilt to save time.

**1.5  A bore gauge being used to check the main bearing bore**

**1.6  Uneven piston wear like this indicates a bent connecting rod**

## 2 Oil pressure check

**▶ Refer to illustration 2.2**

1   Low engine oil pressure can be a sign of an engine in need of rebuilding. A "low oil pressure" indicator (often called an "idiot light") is not a test of the oiling system. Such indicators only come on when the oil pressure is dangerously low. Even a factory oil pressure gauge in the instrument panel is only a relative indication, although much better for driver information than a warning light. A better test is with a mechanical (not electrical) oil pressure gauge.

2   Locate the oil pressure indicator sending unit on the engine block. The oil pressure sending unit is located on the oil pump housing behind the oil filter adapter.

3   Unscrew and remove the oil pressure sending unit and then screw in the hose for your oil pressure gauge (see illustration). If necessary, install an adapter fitting. Use Teflon tape or thread sealant on the threads of the adapter and/or the fitting on the end of your gauge's hose.

4   Connect an accurate tachometer to the engine, according to the tachometer manufacturer's instructions.

5   Check the oil pressure with the engine running (normal operating temperature) at the specified engine speed, and compare it to this Chapter's Specifications. If it's extremely low, the bearings and/or oil pump are probably worn out.

**2.2 The oil pressure sending unit is located on top of the oil pump housing**

## 3 Cylinder compression check

**▶ Refer to illustration 3.6**

1   A compression check will tell you what mechanical condition the upper end of your engine (pistons, rings, valves, head gaskets) is in. Specifically, it can tell you if the compression is down due to leakage caused by worn piston rings, defective valves and seats or a blown head gasket.

**➡Note: The engine must be at normal operating temperature and the battery must be fully charged for this check.**

2   Begin by cleaning the area around the ignition coils before you remove the spark plugs (compressed air should be used, if available).

The idea is to prevent dirt from getting into the cylinders as the compression check is being done.

3   Remove all of the spark plugs from the engine (see Chapter 1).

4   Block the throttle open. On models that have an accelerator cable connected to the throttle body, you can simply depress the accelerator pedal when the engine is cranked over. On models with the Electronic Throttle Control (ETC) system, remove the air intake duct from the throttle body (see Chapter 4) and use a wood dowel or something similar to block the throttle plate open.

### ✳✳ CAUTION:

**Be certain that whatever is used to block the throttle open doesn't scratch the throttle body bore or get sucked into the intake manifold.**

5   Disable the fuel system (see Chapter 4, Section 2).

6   Install a compression gauge in the spark plug hole (see illustration).

7   Crank the engine over at least seven compression strokes and watch the gauge. The compression should build up quickly in a healthy engine. Low compression on the first stroke, followed by gradually increasing pressure on successive strokes, indicates worn piston rings. A low compression reading on the first stroke, which doesn't build up during successive strokes, indicates leaking valves or a blown head gasket (a cracked head could also be the cause). Deposits on the undersides of the valve heads can also cause low compression. Record the highest gauge reading obtained.

8   Repeat the procedure for the remaining cylinders and compare the results to this Chapter's Specifications.

**3.6 Use a compression gauge with a threaded fitting for the spark plug hole, not the type that requires hand pressure to maintain the seal**

9   Add some engine oil (about three squirts from a plunger-type oil can) to each cylinder, through the spark plug hole, and repeat the test.

10  If the compression increases after the oil is added, the piston rings are definitely worn. If the compression doesn't increase significantly, the leakage is occurring at the valves or head gasket. Leakage past the valves may be caused by burned valve seats and/or faces or warped, cracked or bent valves.

11  If two adjacent cylinders have equally low compression, there's a strong possibility that the head gasket between them is blown. The appearance of coolant in the combustion chambers or the crankcase would verify this condition.

12  If one cylinder is slightly lower than the others, and the engine has a slightly rough idle, a worn lobe on the camshaft could be the cause.

13  If the compression is unusually high, the combustion chambers are probably coated with carbon deposits. If that's the case, the cylinder heads should be removed and decarbonized.

14  If compression is way down or varies greatly between cylinders, it would be a good idea to have a leak-down test performed by an automotive repair shop. This test will pinpoint exactly where the leakage is occurring and how severe it is.

## 4   Vacuum gauge diagnostic checks

▶ **Refer to illustrations 4.4 and 4.6**

A vacuum gauge provides inexpensive but valuable information about what is going on in the engine. You can check for worn rings or cylinder walls, leaking head or intake manifold gaskets, incorrect carburetor adjustments, restricted exhaust, stuck or burned valves, weak valve springs, improper ignition or valve timing and ignition problems.

Unfortunately, vacuum gauge readings are easy to misinterpret, so they should be used in conjunction with other tests to confirm the diagnosis.

Both the absolute readings and the rate of needle movement are important for accurate interpretation. Most gauges measure vacuum in inches of mercury (in-Hg). The following references to vacuum assume the diagnosis is being performed at sea level. As elevation increases (or atmospheric pressure decreases), the reading will decrease. For every 1,000 foot increase in elevation above approximately 2,000 feet, the gauge readings will decrease about one inch of mercury.

**4.4  A simple vacuum gauge can be handy in diagnosing engine condition and performance**

Connect the vacuum gauge directly to intake manifold vacuum, not to ported (throttle body) vacuum (see illustration). Be sure no hoses are left disconnected during the test or false readings will result.

Before you begin the test, allow the engine to warm up completely. Block the wheels and set the parking brake. With the transaxle in Park, start the engine and allow it to run at normal idle speed.

### ✳ WARNING:

**Keep your hands and the vacuum gauge clear of the fans.**

Read the vacuum gauge; an average, healthy engine should normally produce about 17 to 22 in-Hg with a fairly steady needle (see illustration). Refer to the following vacuum gauge readings and what they indicate about the engine's condition:

1   A low, steady reading usually indicates a leaking gasket between the intake manifold and cylinder head(s) or throttle body, a leaky vacuum hose, late ignition timing or incorrect camshaft timing. Check and eliminate all possible causes before you remove the timing belt cover to check the timing marks.

2   If the reading is three to eight inches below normal and it fluctuates at that low reading, suspect an intake manifold gasket leak at an intake port or a faulty fuel injector.

3   If the needle has regular drops of about two-to-four inches at a steady rate, the valves are probably leaking. Perform a compression check or leak-down test to confirm this.

4   An irregular drop or down-flick of the needle can be caused by a sticking valve or an ignition misfire. Perform a compression check or leak-down test and read the spark plugs.

5   A rapid vibration of about four in-Hg vibration at idle combined with exhaust smoke indicates worn valve guides. Perform a leak-down test to confirm this. If the rapid vibration occurs with an increase in engine speed, check for a leaking intake manifold gasket or head gasket, weak valve springs, burned valves or ignition misfire.

6   A slight fluctuation, say one inch up and down, may mean ignition problems. Check all the usual tune-up items and, if necessary, run the engine on an ignition analyzer.

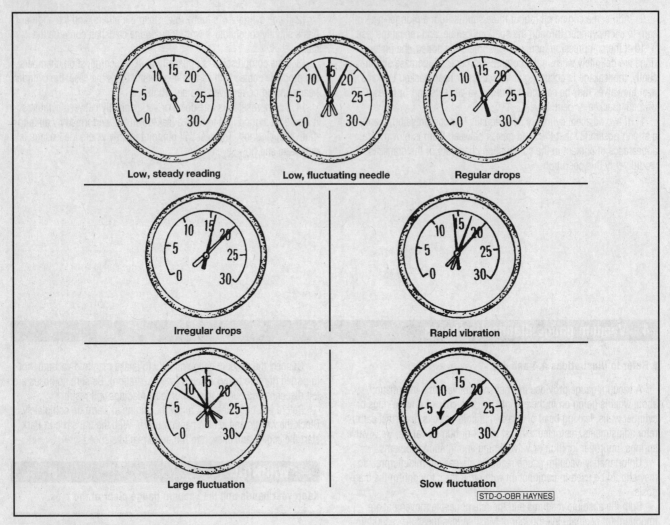

Low, steady reading

Low, fluctuating needle

Regular drops

Irregular drops

Rapid vibration

Large fluctuation

Slow fluctuation

STD-O-OBR HAYNES

**4.6 Typical vacuum gauge readings**

7   If there is a large fluctuation, perform a compression or leak-down test to look for a weak or dead cylinder or a blown head gasket.

8   If the needle moves slowly through a wide range, check for a clogged PCV system, incorrect idle fuel mixture, throttle body or intake manifold gasket leaks.

9   Check for a slow return after revving the engine by quickly snapping the throttle open until the engine reaches about 2,500 rpm and let it shut. Normally the reading should drop to near zero, rise above normal idle reading (about 5 in-Hg over) and then return to the previous idle reading. If the vacuum returns slowly and doesn't peak when the throttle is snapped shut, the rings may be worn. If there is a long delay, look for a restricted exhaust system (often the muffler or catalytic converter). An easy way to check this is to temporarily disconnect the exhaust ahead of the suspected part and redo the test.

## 5   Engine rebuilding alternatives

The do-it-yourselfer is faced with a number of options when purchasing a rebuilt engine. The major considerations are cost, warranty, parts availability and the time required for the rebuilder to complete the project. The decision to replace the engine block, piston/connecting rod assemblies and crankshaft depends on the final inspection results of your engine. Only then can you make a cost effective decision whether to have your engine overhauled or simply purchase an exchange engine for your vehicle.

Some of the rebuilding alternatives include:

**Individual parts** - If the inspection procedures reveal that the engine block and most engine components are in reusable condition, purchasing individual parts and having a rebuilder rebuild your engine may be the most economical alternative. The block, crankshaft and piston/connecting rod assemblies should all be inspected carefully by a machine shop first.

**Short block** - A short block consists of an engine block with a crankshaft and piston/connecting rod assemblies already installed. All new bearings are incorporated and all clearances will be correct. The existing camshafts, valve train components, cylinder head and external parts can be bolted to the short block with little or no machine shop work necessary.

**Long block** - A long block consists of a short block plus an oil pump, oil pan, cylinder head, valve cover, camshaft and valve train components, timing sprockets and timing cover. All components are installed with new bearings, seals and gaskets incorporated throughout. The installation of manifolds and external parts is all that's necessary.

**Low mileage used engines** - Some companies now offer low mileage used engines which is a very cost effective way to get your vehicle up and running again. These engines often come from vehicles which have been totaled in accidents or come from other countries which have a higher vehicle turn over rate. A low mileage used engine also usually has a similar warranty like the newly remanufactured engines.

Give careful thought to which alternative is best for you and discuss the situation with local automotive machine shops, auto parts dealers and experienced rebuilders before ordering or purchasing replacement parts.

## 6  Engine removal - methods and precautions

▶ **Refer to illustrations 6.1, 6.2, and 6.3**

If you've decided that an engine must be removed for overhaul or major repair work, several preliminary steps should be taken. Read all removal and installation procedures carefully prior to committing to this job. These engines are removed by lowering the engine to the floor, along with the transaxle, and then raising the vehicle sufficiently to slide the assembly out; this will require a vehicle hoist as well as an engine hoist.

Locating a suitable place to work is extremely important. Adequate work space, along with storage space for the vehicle, will be needed. If a shop or garage isn't available, at the very least a flat, level, clean work surface made of concrete or asphalt is required.

Cleaning the engine compartment and engine before beginning the removal procedure will help keep tools clean and organized (see illustrations 6.1 and 6.2).

An engine hoist will also be necessary. Make sure the hoist is rated in excess of the combined weight of the engine and transaxle. Safety is of primary importance, considering the potential hazards involved in removing the engine from the vehicle.

If you're a novice at engine removal, get at least one helper. One person cannot easily do all the things you need to do to remove a big heavy engine and transaxle assembly from the engine compartment. Also helpful is to seek advice and assistance from someone who's experienced in engine removal.

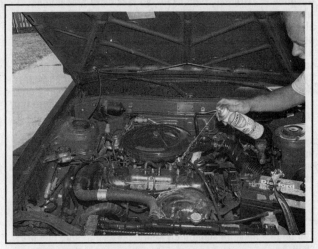

**6.1  After tightly wrapping water-vulnerable components, use a spray cleaner on everything, with particular concentration on the greasiest areas, usually around the valve cover and lower edges of the block. If one section dries out, apply more cleaner**

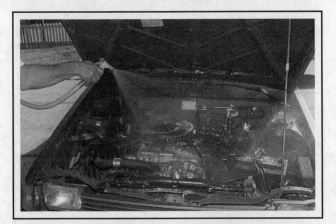

**6.2  Depending on how dirty the engine is, let the cleaner soak in according to the directions and then hose off the grime and cleaner. Get the rinse water down into every area you can get at; then dry important components with a hair dryer or paper towels**

**6.3  Get an engine stand sturdy enough to firmly support the engine while you're working on it. Stay away from three-wheeled models; they have a tendency to tip over more easily, so get a four-wheeled unit**

Plan the operation ahead of time. Arrange for or obtain all of the tools and equipment you'll need prior to beginning the job (see illustration 6.3). Some of the equipment necessary to perform engine removal and installation safely and with relative ease are (in addition to a vehicle hoist and an engine hoist) a heavy duty floor jack (preferably fitted with a transmission jack head adapter), complete sets of wrenches and sockets as described in the front of this manual, wooden blocks, plenty of rags and cleaning solvent for mopping up spilled oil, coolant and gasoline.

Plan for the vehicle to be out of use for quite a while. A machine shop can do the work that is beyond the scope of the home mechanic. Machine shops often have a busy schedule, so before removing the engine, consult the shop for an estimate of how long it will take to rebuild or repair the components that may need work.

## 7  Engine - removal and installation

### ✳✳ WARNING 1:

**Gasoline is extremely flammable, so take extra precautions when you work on any part of the fuel system. Don't smoke or allow open flames or bare light bulbs near the work area, and don't work in a garage where a gas-type appliance (such as a water heater or clothes dryer) is present. Since gasoline is carcinogenic, wear fuel-resistant gloves when there's a possibility of being exposed to fuel, and, if you spill any fuel on your skin, rinse it off immediately with soap and water. Mop up any spills immediately and do not store fuel-soaked rags where they could ignite. The fuel system is under constant pressure, so, if any fuel lines are to be disconnected, the fuel pressure in the system must be relieved first (see Chapter 4 for more information). When you perform any kind of work on the fuel system, wear safety glasses and have a Class B type fire extinguisher on hand.**

### ✳✳ WARNING 2:

**The engine must be completely cool before beginning this procedure.**

➡ **Note 1: Engine removal on these models is a difficult job, especially for the do-it-yourself mechanic working at home. Because of the vehicle's design, the manufacturer states that the engine and transaxle have to be removed as a unit from the bottom of the vehicle, not the top. With a floor jack and jackstands, the vehicle can't be raised high enough and supported safely enough for the engine/transaxle assembly to slide out from underneath. The manufacturer recommends that removal of the engine transaxle assembly only be performed on a frame-contact type vehicle hoist.**

➡ **Note 2: Read through the entire Section before beginning this procedure. The engine and transaxle are removed as a unit from below and then separated outside the vehicle.**

➡ **Note 3: Keep in mind that during this procedure you'll have to adjust the height of the vehicle to perform certain operations.**

## REMOVAL

▶ **Refer to illustrations 7.8, 7.10, 7.20, 7.28a, 7.28b, 7.28c, 7.29, 7.36a and 7.36b**

1  Park the vehicle on a frame-contact type vehicle hoist, then engage the arms of the hoist with the jacking points of the vehicle. Raise the hoist arms until they contact the vehicle, but not so much that the wheels come off the ground.

2  Place the hood in the wide-open position (with the prop rod in the lowest hole).

3  Relieve the fuel system pressure (see Chapter 4), then disconnect the cable from the negative terminal of the battery (see Chapter 5, Section 1).

4  Remove the engine cover (see Chapter 2, Section 6).

5  Remove the air filter housing and the air intake duct (see Chapter 4).

6  Disconnect the accelerator cable and cruise control cable (if equipped) from the throttle body.

7  Remove the battery and the battery tray (see Chapter 5).

8  Remove the coolant reservoir for access to the Powertrain Control Module (PCM), then disconnect the electrical connectors from the PCM (see illustration).

9  Disconnect the engine harness connectors near the battery tray and remove the ground cable, the harness bracket and the alternator

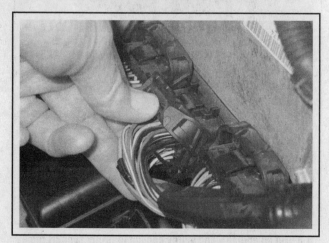

**7.8  To disconnect the electrical connectors from the PCM, depress the button on top of the connector, swing the connector lock forward, then pull the connector out**

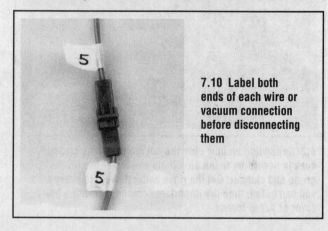

**7.10  Label both ends of each wire or vacuum connection before disconnecting them**

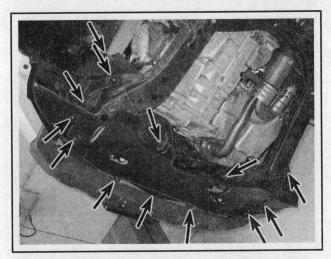

**7.20 Location of the engine splash shield fasteners - some hidden from view**

**7.28a Disconnect the power steering return hose from the rear of the pipe on the right side of the subframe . . .**

cable. Position the components off to the side. Follow all wiring harnesses from the engine and transaxle and disconnect the electrical connectors leading to the vehicle wiring harnesses.

10  Clearly label and disconnect all vacuum lines, emissions hoses, and ground straps between the engine and the engine compartment. Masking tape and/or a touch up paint applicator work well for marking items (see illustration). Take instant photos or sketch the locations of components and brackets.

11  Disconnect the fuel line(s) from the fuel rail (see Chapter 4).

12  Loosen the driveaxle/hub nuts (see Chapter 8) and the front wheel lug nuts, then raise the vehicle on the hoist.

13  Remove the drivebelts (see Chapter 1).

14  Detach the power steering pressure hose from the power steering pump, then remove the power steering pump (see Chapter 10). Also remove the bracket securing the hose to the rear cylinder head.

15  Drain the cooling system (see Chapter 1).

16  Detach the heater hoses at the firewall (see Chapter 3).

17  Remove the cooling fan(s) and radiator (see Chapter 3). Also detach the radiator hoses from the engine.

18  Remove the air conditioning compressor without disconnecting the hoses (see Chapter 3). Support the compressor with a piece of rope, tying it to the radiator lower crossmember.

19  Working inside the driver's compartment, remove the driver's side lower trim panel and remove the pinch bolt from the intermediate shaft and steering gear input shaft connector (see Chapter 10). Be sure to paint a mark across the connector to insure correct alignment on reassembly.

20  Raise the vehicle and remove the engine splash shield (see illustration).

21  Drain the engine oil and the automatic transaxle fluid (see Chapter 1).

22  Remove the crossmember (see illustration 7.46).

23  Detach the stabilizer bar links from the stabilizer bar (see Chapter 10).

24  Detach the tie-rod ends from the steering knuckle arms (see Chapter 10).

25  On 4WD models, remove the driveshaft and the transfer case (see Chapter 8).

26  Remove the driveaxles (see Chapter 8).

27  Disconnect the shift cable from the transaxle (see Chapter 7).

28  Disconnect the power steering return hose from the pipe near the right steering gear boot (see illustration). Follow the pipe along the subframe and detach the hose from its forward end, then free the hose clips from the subframe (see illustrations).

29  Unplug the electrical connector from the power steering pressure switch (see illustration).

**7.28b . . . follow the pipe forward and detach the hose from it . . .**

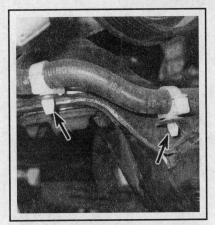

**7.28c . . . then free the hose clips from the subframe**

**7.29 Unplug the electrical connector from the power steering pressure switch**

**7.36a Right-side engine lifting bracket (near power steering pump)**

**7.36b Left-side lifting bracket (on transaxle)**

30 Detach the exhaust pipe from the exhaust manifold/catalytic converter assemblies and from the rear portion of the exhaust system, then remove the front portion of the exhaust system (see Chapter 4).

31 On 2WD models, disconnect the electrical connectors from the front and rear engine mounts (see Chapter 2A).

32 Remove the torque converter cover. Mark the position of the torque converter to the driveplate, then remove the torque converter bolts.

33 Unbolt the left (driver's side) transaxle mounts from the subframe (see Chapter 2A).

34 Unbolt the rear engine mount from the subframe (see Chapter 2A).

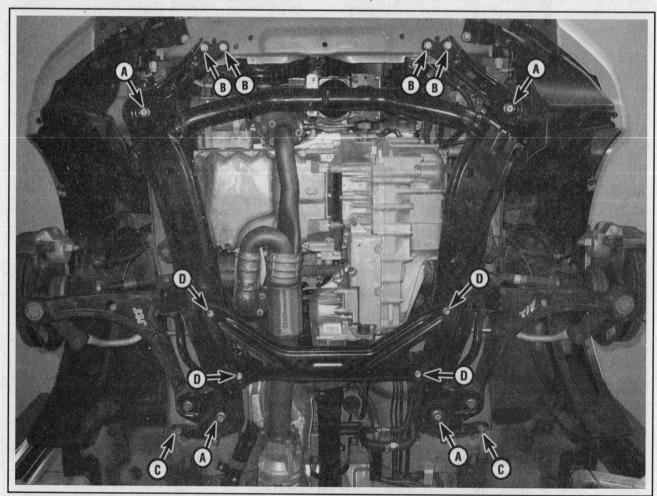

**7.46 Location of the main subframe mounting bolts (A), the bracket bolts (B and C) and the crossmember bolts (D)**

35  Lower the vehicle.

36  Attach one end of an engine lifting sling or chain to the lift bracket near the power steering pump (see illustration). Attach the other end of the sling or chain to a lift bracket bolted to the transaxle (see illustration). Be sure the positioning of the chain or sling will support the engine and transaxle in a balanced attitude.

➡Note: The sling or chain must be long enough to allow the engine hoist to lower the engine/transaxle assembly to the ground, without letting the hoist arm contact the vehicle.

37  Roll the hoist into position and attach the sling or chain to it. Take up the slack until there is slight tension on the hoist.

➡Note: Depending on the design of the engine hoist, it may be helpful to position the hoist from the side of the vehicle, so that when the engine/transaxle assembly is lowered, it will fit between the legs of the hoist.

38  Carefully mark the position of the subframe in relation to the vehicle chassis. Remove the nut from the stud at the top of the front engine mount (see Chapter 2A).

39  Support the subframe with two floor jacks (one on each side) and remove the subframe mounting bolts (see illustration 7.46). Lower the subframe to the floor and remove it from under the vehicle.

40  Unbolt the passenger's side engine mount from the bracket on the engine (see Chapter 2A).

41  Recheck to be sure nothing is still connecting the engine or transaxle to the vehicle. Disconnect and label anything still remaining.

42  Slowly lower the engine/transaxle assembly to the floor.

43  Once the powertrain assembly is on the floor, disconnect the engine lifting hoist and raise the vehicle using the vehicle hoist until it clears the powertrain assembly.

44  Reconnect the chain or sling and raise the engine and transaxle.

Support the engine with blocks of wood or another floor jack, while leaving the sling or chain attached to the right-side mounting boss. Support the transaxle with another floor jack, preferably one with a transmission jack head adapter. At this point the transaxle can be unbolted and removed from the engine. Be very careful to ensure that the components are supported securely so they won't topple off their supports during disconnection.

45  Reconnect the lifting chain to the engine, then raise the engine and attach it to an engine stand.

## INSTALLATION

♦ **Refer to illustration 7.46**

46  Installation is the reverse of removal, noting the following points:

a)  *Check the engine/transaxle mounts. If they're worn or damaged, replace them.*

b)  *Attach the transaxle to the engine following the procedure described in Chapter 7.*

c)  *Add coolant, engine oil, power steering and transmission fluids (see Chapter 1).*

d)  *Align the subframe reference marks before tightening the bolts.*

e)  *Tighten the subframe mounting bolts and bracket bolts to the torque listed in this Chapter's Specifications. Note the locations of the various size bolts (see illustration). Replace all the large subframe bolts (A) with new bolts.*

f)  *Reconnect the negative battery cable (see Chapter 5, Section 1).*

g)  *Run the engine and check for proper operation and leaks. Shut off the engine and recheck fluid levels.*

## 8  Engine overhaul - disassembly sequence

1  It's much easier to remove the external components if the engine is mounted on a portable engine stand. A stand can often be rented quite cheaply from an equipment rental yard. Before the engine is mounted on a stand, the driveplate should be removed from the engine.

2  If a stand isn't available, it's possible to remove the external engine components with it blocked up on the floor. Be extra careful not to tip or drop the engine when working without a stand.

3  If you're going to obtain a rebuilt engine, all external components must come off first, to be transferred to the replacement engine. These components include:

*Driveplate*
*Ignition system components*
*Emissions-related components*
*Engine mounts and mount brackets*
*Engine rear cover (spacer plate between driveplate and engine block)*
*Intake/exhaust manifolds*

*Fuel injection components*
*Oil filter*
*Spark plugs*
*Thermostat and housing assembly*
*Water pump*

➡Note: When removing the external components from the engine, pay close attention to details that may be helpful or important during installation. Note the installed position of gaskets, seals, spacers, pins, brackets, washers, bolts and other small items.

4  If you're going to obtain a short block (assembled engine block, crankshaft, pistons and connecting rods), then remove the timing belt, cylinder heads, oil pan, oil pump pick-up tube, oil pump and water pump from your engine so that you can turn in your old short block to the rebuilder as a core. See *Engine rebuilding* alternatives for additional information regarding the different possibilities to be considered.

**9   Pistons and connecting rods - removal and installation**

## REMOVAL

▶ **Refer to illustrations 9.1, 9.3 and 9.4**

➡**Note: Prior to removing the piston/connecting rod assemblies, remove the cylinder heads and oil pan (see Chapter 2A).**

1   Use your fingernail to feel if a ridge has formed at the upper limit of ring travel (about 1/4-inch down from the top of each cylinder). If carbon deposits or cylinder wear have produced ridges, they must be completely removed with a special tool (see illustration). Follow the manufacturer's instructions provided with the tool. Failure to remove the ridges before attempting to remove the piston/connecting rod assemblies may result in piston breakage.

2   After the cylinder ridges have been removed, turn the engine so the crankshaft is facing up.

3   Before the connecting rods are removed, check the connecting rod endplay with feeler gauges. Slide them between the first connecting rod and the crankshaft throw until the play is removed (see illustration).

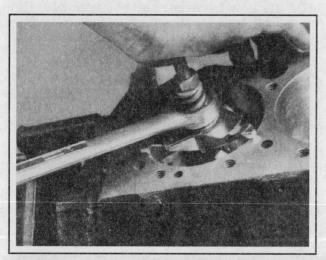

**9.1  Before you try to remove the pistons, use a ridge reamer to remove the raised material (ridge) from the top of the cylinders**

**9.3  Checking the connecting rod endplay (side clearance)**

Repeat this procedure for each connecting rod. The endplay is equal to the thickness of the feeler gauge(s). Check with an automotive machine shop for the endplay service limit (a typical endplay should measure between 0.005 to 0.015 inch [0.127 to 0.396 mm]). If the play exceeds the service limit, new connecting rods will be required. If new rods (or a new crankshaft) are installed, the endplay may fall under the minimum allowable. If it does, the rods will have to be machined to restore it. If necessary, consult an automotive machine shop for advice.

4   Check the connecting rods and caps for identification marks. If they aren't plainly marked, use paint or marker (see illustration) to clearly identify each rod and cap (1, 2, 3, etc., depending on the cylinder they're associated with).

**✳ CAUTION:**

**Do not use a punch and hammer to mark the connecting rods or they may be damaged.**

5   Loosen each of the connecting rod cap bolts 1/2-turn at a time until they can be removed by hand.

➡**Note: New connecting rod cap bolts must be used when reassembling the engine, but save the old bolts for use when checking the connecting rod bearing oil clearance.**

6   Remove the number one connecting rod cap and bearing insert. Don't drop the bearing insert out of the cap.

7   Remove the bearing insert and push the connecting rod/piston assembly out through the top of the engine. Use a wooden or plastic hammer handle to push on the upper bearing surface in the connecting rod. If resistance is felt, double-check to make sure that all of the ridge was removed from the cylinder.

8   Repeat the procedure for the remaining cylinders.

9   After removal, reassemble the connecting rod caps and bearing inserts in their respective connecting rods and install the cap bolts finger tight. Leaving the old bearing inserts in place until reassembly will help prevent the connecting rod bearing surfaces from being accidentally nicked or gouged.

10  The pistons and connecting rods are now ready for inspection and overhaul at an automotive machine shop.

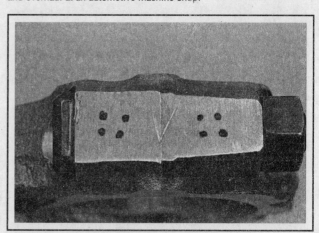

**9.4  If the connecting rods or caps are not marked, use permanent ink or paint to mark the caps to the rods by cylinder number (for example, this would be number 4 cylinder connecting rod)**

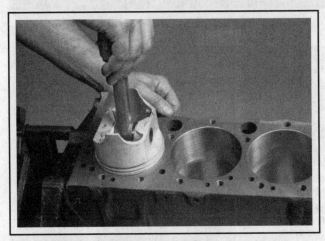

**9.13  Install the piston ring into the cylinder then push it down into position using a piston so the ring will be square in the cylinder**

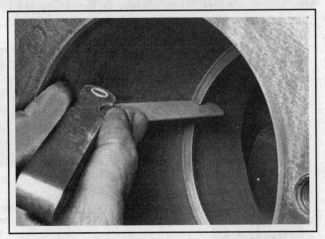

**9.14  With the ring square in the cylinder, measure the ring end gap with a feeler gauge**

## PISTON RING INSTALLATION

▶ **Refer to illustrations 9.13, 9.14, 9.15, 9.19a, 9.19b and 9.22**

11  Before installing the new piston rings, the ring end gaps must be checked. It's assumed that the piston ring side clearance has been checked and verified correct.

12  Lay out the piston/connecting rod assemblies and the new ring sets so the ring sets will be matched with the same piston and cylinder during the end gap measurement and engine assembly.

13  Insert the top (number one) compression ring into the first cylinder and square it up with the cylinder walls by pushing it in with the top of the piston (see illustration). The ring should be near the bottom of the cylinder, at the lower limit of ring travel.

14  To measure the end gap, slip feeler gauges between the ends of the ring until a gauge equal to the gap width is found (see illustration). The feeler gauge should slide between the ring ends with a slight amount of drag. A typical ring gap should fall between 0.010 and 0.020 inch (0.25 to 0.50 mm) for compression rings and up to 0.030 inch (0.76 mm) for the oil ring steel rails. If the gap is larger or smaller than specified, double-check to make sure you have the correct rings before proceeding.

15  If the gap is too small, it must be enlarged or the ring ends may come in contact with each other during engine operation, which can cause serious damage to the engine. If necessary, increase the end gaps by filing the ring ends very carefully with a fine file. Mount the file in a vise equipped with soft jaws, slip the ring over the file with the ends contacting the file face and slowly move the ring to remove material from the ends. When performing this operation, file only by pushing the ring from the outside end of the file towards the vise (see illustration).

16  Excess end gap isn't critical unless it's greater than 0.040 inch (1.01 mm). Again, double-check to make sure you have the correct ring type.

17  Repeat the procedure for each ring that will be installed in the first cylinder and for each ring in the remaining cylinders. Remember to keep rings, pistons and cylinders matched up.

18  Once the ring end gaps have been checked/corrected, the rings can be installed on the pistons.

19  The oil control ring (lowest one on the piston) is usually installed first. It's composed of three separate components. Slip the spacer/expander into the groove (see illustration). If an anti-rotation tang is used, make sure it's inserted into the drilled hole in the ring groove. Next, install the upper side rail in the same manner (see illustration). Don't use a piston ring installation tool on the oil ring side rails, as

**9.15  If the ring end gap is too small, clamp a file in a vise as shown and file the piston ring ends - be sure to remove all raised material**

**9.19a  Installing the spacer/expander in the oil ring groove**

**9.19b  DO NOT use a piston ring installation tool when installing the oil control side rails**

# ENGINE BEARING ANALYSIS

## Debris

Babbitt bearing embedded with debris from machinings

Microscopic detail of debris

Microscopic detail of gouges

Overplated copper alloy bearing gouged by cast iron debris

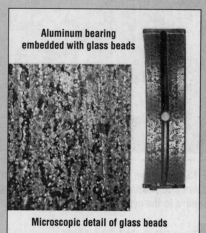

Aluminum bearing embedded with glass beads

Microscopic detail of glass beads

Damaged lining caused by dirt left on the bearing back

## Misassembly

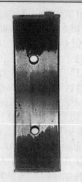

Result of a lower half assembled as an upper - blocking the oil flow

Excessive oil clearance is indicated by a short contact arc

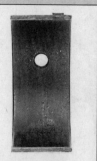

Polished and oil-stained backs are a result of a poor fit in the housing bore

Result of a wrong, reversed, or shifted cap

## Overloading

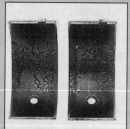

Damage from excessive idling which resulted in an oil film unable to support the load imposed

Damaged upper connecting rod bearings caused by engine lugging; the lower main bearings (not shown) were similarly affected

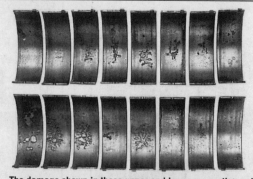

The damage shown in these upper and lower connecting rod bearings was caused by engine operation at a higher-than-rated speed under load

# Misalignment

A warped crankshaft caused this pattern of severe wear in the center, diminishing toward the ends

A poorly finished crankshaft caused the equally spaced scoring shown

A tapered housing bore caused the damage along one edge of this pair

A bent connecting rod led to the damage in the "V" pattern

# Lubrication

Result of dry start: The bearings on the left, farthest from the oil pump, show more damage

Result of a low oil supply or oil starvation

Severe wear as a result of inadequate oil clearance

# Corrosion

Microscopic detail of corrosion

Corrosion is an acid attack on the bearing lining generally caused by inadequate maintenance, extremely hot or cold operation, or inferior oils or fuels

Microscopic detail of cavitation

Example of cavitation - a surface erosion caused by pressure changes in the oil film

Damage from excessive thrust or insufficient axial clearance

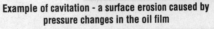

Bearing affected by oil dilution caused by excessive blow-by or a rich mixture

**9.22 Use a piston ring installation tool to install the number 2 and the number 1 (top) rings - be sure the directional mark on the piston ring(s) is facing toward the top of the piston**

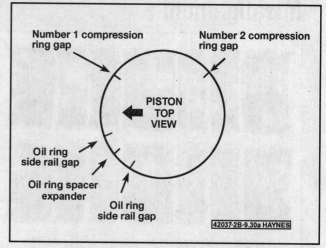

**9.30a Location of the piston ring end gaps on 2001 and 2002 Acura models**

they may be damaged. Instead, place one end of the side rail into the groove between the spacer/expander and the ring land, hold it firmly in place and slide a finger around the piston while pushing the rail into the groove. Finally, install the lower side rail.

20 After the three oil ring components have been installed, check to make sure that both the upper and lower side rails can be rotated smoothly inside the ring grooves.

21 The number two (middle) compression ring is installed next. It's usually stamped with a mark which must face up, toward the top of the piston. Do not mix up the top and middle rings, as they have different cross-sections.

➡ Note: Always follow the instructions printed on the ring package or box - different manufacturers may require different approaches.

22 Use a piston ring installation tool and make sure the identification mark is facing the top of the piston, then slip the ring into the middle groove on the piston (see illustration). Don't expand the ring any more than necessary to slide it over the piston.

23 Install the number one (top) compression ring in the same manner. Make sure the mark is facing up. Be careful not to confuse the number one and number two compression rings.

24 Repeat the procedure for the remaining pistons and rings.

## INSTALLATION

25 Before installing the piston/connecting rod assemblies, the cylinder walls must be perfectly clean, the top edge of each cylinder bore must be chamfered, and the crankshaft must be in place.

26 Remove the cap from the end of the number one connecting rod (refer to the marks made during removal). Remove the original bearing inserts and wipe the bearing surfaces of the connecting rod and cap with a clean, lint-free cloth. They must be kept spotlessly clean.

### Connecting rod bearing oil clearance check

▸ **Refer to illustrations 9.30a, 9.30b, 9.35, 9.37 and 9.41**

27 Clean the back side of the new upper bearing insert, then lay it in place in the connecting rod.

28 Make sure the tab on the bearing fits into the recess in the rod.

Don't hammer the bearing insert into place and be very careful not to nick or gouge the bearing face. Don't lubricate the bearing at this time.

29 Clean the back side of the other bearing insert and install it in the rod cap. Again, make sure the tab on the bearing fits into the recess in the cap, and don't apply any lubricant. It's critically important that the mating surfaces of the bearing and connecting rod are perfectly clean and oil free when they're assembled.

30 Position the piston ring gaps at the specified intervals around the piston as shown (see illustrations).

31 Lubricate the piston and rings with clean engine oil and attach a piston ring compressor to the piston. Leave the skirt protruding about 1/4-inch to guide the piston into the cylinder. The rings must be compressed until they're flush with the piston.

32 Rotate the crankshaft until the number one connecting rod journal is at BDC (bottom dead center) and apply a liberal coat of engine oil to the cylinder walls.

33 With the arrow on the top of the piston crown facing the front (timing belt end) of the engine, gently insert the piston/connecting rod assembly into the number one cylinder bore and rest the bottom edge of the ring compressor on the engine block. Install the pistons with the cavity mark(s) facing toward the timing belt.

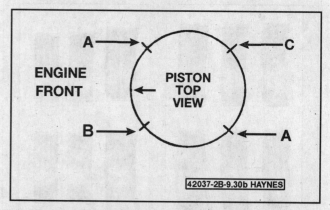

**9.30b Location of the piston ring end gaps on all other models**

A   Oil ring side rail gaps
B   Top compression ring gap and oil ring spacer gap
C   Second compression ring gap

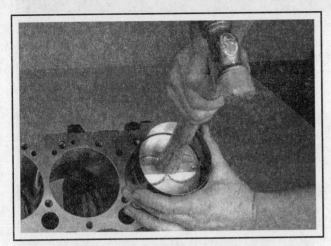

**9.35  Use a plastic or wooden hammer handle to push the piston into the cylinder**

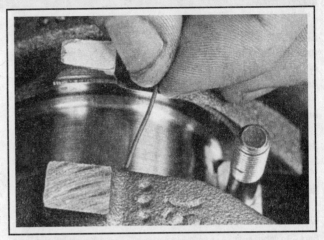

**9.37  Place Plastigage on each connecting rod bearing journal parallel to the crankshaft centerline**

34  Tap the top edge of the ring compressor to make sure it's contacting the block around its entire circumference.

35  Gently tap on the top of the piston with the end of a wooden or plastic hammer handle (see illustration) while guiding the end of the connecting rod into place on the crankshaft journal. The piston rings may try to pop out of the ring compressor just before entering the cylinder bore, so keep some downward pressure on the ring compressor. Work slowly, and if any resistance is felt as the piston enters the cylinder, stop immediately. Find out what's hanging up and fix it before proceeding. Do not, for any reason, force the piston into the cylinder - you might break a ring and/or the piston.

36  Once the piston/connecting rod assembly is installed, the connecting rod bearing oil clearance must be checked before the rod cap is permanently installed.

37  Cut a piece of the appropriate size Plastigage slightly shorter than the width of the connecting rod bearing and lay it in place on the number one connecting rod journal, parallel with the journal axis (see illustration).

38  Clean the connecting rod cap bearing face and install the rod cap. Make sure the mating mark on the cap is on the same side as the mark

on the connecting rod (see illustration 9.4).

39  Install the old rod bolts, at this time, and tighten them to the torque listed in this Chapter's Specifications.

➡**Note: Use a thin-wall socket to avoid erroneous torque readings that can result if the socket is wedged between the rod cap and the bolt or nut. If the socket tends to wedge itself between the fastener and the cap, lift up on it slightly until it no longer contacts the cap. DO NOT rotate the crankshaft at any time during this operation.**

40  Remove the fasteners and detach the rod cap, being very careful not to disturb the Plastigage. Discard the cap bolts at this time as they cannot be reused.

➡**Note: You MUST use new connecting rod bolts.**

41  Compare the width of the crushed Plastigage to the scale printed on the Plastigage envelope to obtain the oil clearance (see illustration). The connecting rod oil clearance is usually about 0.001 to 0.002 inch. Consult an automotive machine shop for the clearance specified for the rod bearings on your engine.

42  If the clearance is not as specified, the bearing inserts may be the wrong size (which means different ones will be required). Before deciding that different inserts are needed, make sure that no dirt or oil was between the bearing inserts and the connecting rod or cap when the clearance was measured. Also, recheck the journal diameter. If the Plastigage was wider at one end than the other, the journal may be tapered. If the clearance still exceeds the limit specified, the bearing will have to be replaced with an undersize bearing.

> ❈❈ **CAUTION:**
>
> **When installing a new crankshaft always use a standard size bearing.**

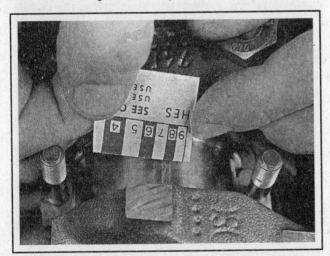

**9.41  Use the scale on the Plastigage package to determine the bearing oil clearance - be sure to measure the widest part of the Plastigage and use the correct scale; it comes with both standard and metric scales**

### Final installation

43  Carefully scrape all traces of the Plastigage material off the rod journal and/or bearing face. Be very careful not to scratch the bearing - use your fingernail or the edge of a plastic card.

44  Make sure the bearing faces are perfectly clean, then apply a uniform layer of clean moly-base grease or engine assembly lube to both of them. You'll have to push the piston into the cylinder to expose the face of the bearing insert in the connecting rod.

# GLOSSARY

## B

**Backlash** - The amount of play between two parts. Usually refers to how much one gear can be moved back and forth without moving the gear with which it's meshed.

**Bearing Caps** - The caps held in place by nuts or bolts which, in turn, hold the bearing surface. This space is for lubricating oil to enter.

**Bearing clearance** - The amount of space left between shaft and bearing surface. This space is for lubricating oil to enter.

**Bearing crush** - The additional height which is purposely manufactured into each bearing half to ensure complete contact of the bearing back with the housing bore when the engine is assembled.

**Bearing knock** - The noise created by movement of a part in a loose or worn bearing.

**Blueprinting** - Dismantling an engine and reassembling it to EXACT specifications.

**Bore** - An engine cylinder, or any cylindrical hole; also used to describe the process of enlarging or accurately refinishing a hole with a cutting tool, as to bore an engine cylinder. The bore size is the diameter of the hole.

**Boring** - Renewing the cylinders by cutting them out to a specified size. A boring bar is used to make the cut.

**Bottom-end** - A term which refers collectively to the engine block, crankshaft, main bearings and the big ends of the connecting rods.

**Break-in** - The period of operation between installation of new or rebuilt parts and time in which parts are worn to the correct fit. Driving at reduced and varying speed for a specified mileage to permit parts to wear to the correct fit.

**Bushing** - A one-piece sleeve placed in a bore to serve as a bearing surface for shaft, piston pin, etc. Usually replaceable.

## C

**Camshaft** - The shaft in the engine, on which a series of lobes are located for operating the valve mechanisms. The camshaft is driven by gears or sprockets and a timing chain. Usually referred to simply as the cam.

**Carbon** - Hard, or soft, black deposits found in combustion chamber, on plugs, under rings, on and under valve heads.

**Cast iron** - An alloy of iron and more than two percent carbon, used for engine blocks and heads because it's relatively inexpensive and easy to mold into complex shapes.

**Chamfer** - To bevel across (or a bevel on) the sharp edge of an object.

**Chase** - To repair damaged threads with a tap or die.

**Combustion chamber** - The space between the piston and the cylinder head, with the piston at top dead center, in which air-fuel mixture is burned.

**Compression ratio** - The relationship between cylinder volume (clearance volume) when the piston is at top dead center and cylinder volume when the piston is at bottom dead center.

**Connecting rod** - The rod that connects the crank on the crankshaft with the piston. Sometimes called a con rod.

**Connecting rod cap** - The part of the connecting rod assembly that attaches the rod to the crankpin.

**Core plug** - Soft metal plug used to plug the casting holes for the coolant passages in the block.

**Crankcase** - The lower part of the engine in which the crankshaft rotates; includes the lower section of the cylinder block and the oil pan.

**Crank kit** - A reground or reconditioned crankshaft and new main and connecting rod bearings.

**Crankpin** - The part of a crankshaft to which a connecting rod is attached.

**Crankshaft** - The main rotating member, or shaft, running the length of the crankcase, with offset throws to which the connecting rods are attached; changes the reciprocating motion of the pistons into rotating motion.

**Cylinder sleeve** - A replaceable sleeve, or liner, pressed into the cylinder block to form the cylinder bore.

## D

**Deburring** - Removing the burrs (rough edges or areas) from a bearing.

**Deglazer** - A tool, rotated by an electric motor, used to remove glaze from cylinder walls so a new set of rings will seat.

## E

**Endplay** - The amount of lengthwise movement between two parts. As applied to a crankshaft, the distance that the crankshaft can move forward and back in the cylinder block.

## F

**Face** - A machinist's term that refers to removing metal from the end of a shaft or the face of a larger part, such as a flywheel.

**Fatigue** - A breakdown of material through a large number of loading and unloading cycles. The first signs are cracks followed shortly by breaks.

**Feeler gauge** - A thin strip of hardened steel, ground to an exact thickness, used to check clearances between parts.

**Free height** - The unloaded length or height of a spring.

**Freeplay** - The looseness in a linkage, or an assembly of parts, between the initial application of force and actual movement. Usually perceived as slop or slight delay.

**Freeze plug** - See Core plug.

## G

**Gallery** - A large passage in the block that forms a reservoir for engine oil pressure.

**Glaze** - The very smooth, glassy finish that develops on cylinder walls while an engine is in service.

## H

**Heli-Coil** - A rethreading device used when threads are worn or damaged. The device is installed in a retapped hole to reduce the thread size to the original size.

## I

**Installed height** - The spring's measured length or height, as installed on the cylinder head. Installed height is measured from the spring seat to the underside of the spring retainer.

## J

**Journal** - The surface of a rotating shaft which turns in a bearing.

## K

**Keeper** - The split lock that holds the valve spring retainer in position on the valve stem.

**Key** - A small piece of metal inserted into matching grooves machined into two parts fitted together - such as a gear pressed onto a shaft - which prevents slippage between the two parts.

**Knock** - The heavy metallic engine sound, produced in the combustion chamber as a result of abnormal combustion - usually detonation. Knock is usually caused by a loose or worn bearing. Also referred to as detonation, pinging and spark knock. Connecting rod or main bearing knocks are created by too much oil clearance or insufficient lubrication.

## L

**Lands** - The portions of metal between the piston ring grooves.

**Lapping the valves** - Grinding a valve face and its seat together with lapping compound.

**Lash** - The amount of free motion in a gear train, between gears, or in a mechanical assembly, that occurs before movement can begin. Usually refers to the lash in a valve train.

**Lifter** - The part that rides against the cam to transfer motion to the rest of the valve train.

## M

**Machining** - The process of using a machine to remove metal from a metal part.

**Main bearings** - The plain, or babbitt, bearings that support the crankshaft.

**Main bearing caps** - The cast iron caps, bolted to the bottom of the block, that support the main bearings.

## O

**O.D.** - Outside diameter.

**Oil gallery** - A pipe or drilled passageway in the engine used to carry engine oil from one area to another.

**Oil ring** - The lower ring, or rings, of a piston; designed to prevent excessive amounts of oil from working up the cylinder walls and into the combustion chamber. Also called an oil-control ring.

**Oil seal** - A seal which keeps oil from leaking out of a compartment. Usually refers to a dynamic seal around a rotating shaft or other moving part.

**O-ring** - A type of sealing ring made of a special rubberlike material; in use, the O-ring is compressed into a groove to provide the sealing action.

**Overhaul** - To completely disassemble a unit, clean and inspect all parts, reassemble it with the original or new parts and make all adjustments necessary for proper operation.

## P

**Pilot bearing** - A small bearing installed in the center of the flywheel (or the rear end of the crankshaft) to support the front end of the input shaft of the transmission.

**Pip mark** - A little dot or indentation which indicates the top side of a compression ring.

**Piston** - The cylindrical part, attached to the connecting rod, that moves up and down in the cylinder as the crankshaft rotates. When the fuel charge is fired, the piston transfers the force of the explosion to the connecting rod, then to the crankshaft.

**Piston pin (or wrist pin)** - The cylindrical and usually hollow steel pin that passes through the piston. The piston pin fastens the piston to the upper end of the connecting rod.

**Piston ring** - The split ring fitted to the groove in a piston. The ring contacts the sides of the ring groove and also rubs against the cylinder wall, thus sealing space between piston and wall. There are two types of rings: Compression rings seal the compression pressure in the combustion chamber; oil rings scrape excessive oil off the cylinder wall.

**Piston ring groove** - The slots or grooves cut in piston heads to hold piston rings in position.

**Piston skirt** - The portion of the piston below the rings and the piston pin hole.

**Plastigage** - A thin strip of plastic thread, available in different sizes, used for measuring clearances. For example, a strip of plastigage is laid across a bearing journal and mashed as parts are assembled. Then parts are disassembled and the width of the strip is measured to determine clearance between journal and bearing. Commonly used to measure crankshaft main-bearing and connecting rod bearing clearances.

**Press-fit** - A tight fit between two parts that requires pressure to force the parts together. Also referred to as drive, or force, fit.

**Prussian blue** - A blue pigment; in solution, useful in determining the area of contact between two surfaces. Prussian blue is commonly used to determine the width and location of the contact area between the valve face and the valve seat.

## R

**Race (bearing)** - The inner or outer ring that provides a contact surface for balls or rollers in bearing.

**Ream** - To size, enlarge or smooth a hole by using a round cutting tool with fluted edges.

**Ring job** - The process of reconditioning the cylinders and installing new rings.

**Runout** - Wobble. The amount a shaft rotates out-of-true.

## S

**Saddle** - The upper main bearing seat.

**Scored** - Scratched or grooved, as a cylinder wall may be scored by abrasive particles moved up and down by the piston rings.

**Scuffing** - A type of wear in which there's a transfer of material between parts moving against each other; shows up as pits or grooves in the mating surfaces.

**Seat** - The surface upon which another part rests or seats. For example, the valve seat is the matched surface upon which the valve face rests. Also used to refer to wearing into a good fit; for example, piston rings seat after a few miles of driving.

**Short block** - An engine block complete with crankshaft and piston and, usually, camshaft assemblies.

**Static balance** - The balance of an object while it's stationary.

**Step** - The wear on the lower portion of a ring land caused by excessive side and back-clearance. The height of the step indicates the ring's extra side clearance and the length of the step projecting from the back wall of the groove represents the ring's back clearance.

**Stroke** - The distance the piston moves when traveling from top dead center to bottom dead center, or from bottom dead center to top dead center.

**Stud** - A metal rod with threads on both ends.

## T

**Tang** - A lip on the end of a plain bearing used to align the bearing during assembly.

**Tap** - To cut threads in a hole. Also refers to the fluted tool used to cut threads.

**Taper** - A gradual reduction in the width of a shaft or hole; in an engine cylinder, taper usually takes the form of uneven wear, more pronounced at the top than at the bottom.

**Throws** - The offset portions of the crankshaft to which the connecting rods are affixed.

**Thrust bearing** - The main bearing that has thrust faces to prevent excessive endplay, or forward and backward movement of the crankshaft.

**Thrust washer** - A bronze or hardened steel washer placed between two moving parts. The washer prevents longitudinal movement and provides a bearing surface for thrust surfaces of parts.

**Tolerance** - The amount of variation permitted from an exact size of measurement. Actual amount from smallest acceptable dimension to largest acceptable dimension.

## U

**Umbrella** - An oil deflector placed near the valve tip to throw oil from the valve stem area.

**Undercut** - A machined groove below the normal surface.

**Undersize bearings** - Smaller diameter bearings used with re-ground crankshaft journals.

## V

**Valve grinding** - Refacing a valve in a valve-refacing machine.

**Valve train** - The valve-operating mechanism of an engine; includes all components from the camshaft to the valve.

**Vibration damper** - A cylindrical weight attached to the front of the crankshaft to minimize torsional vibration (the twist-untwist actions of the crankshaft caused by the cylinder firing impulses). Also called a harmonic balancer.

## W

**Water jacket** - The spaces around the cylinders, between the inner and outer shells of the cylinder block or head, through which coolant circulates.

**Web** - A supporting structure across a cavity.

**Woodruff key** - A key with a radiused backside (viewed from the side).

### ❋❋❋ CAUTION:

If the connecting rod caps are secured to the rods with bolts (instead of nuts), install new connecting rod cap bolts. Do NOT reuse old bolts - they have stretched and cannot be reused.

45 Slide the connecting rod back into place on the journal, install the rod cap, install the nuts or new bolts and tighten them to the torque listed in this Chapter's Specifications. Again, work up to the torque in three steps.

46 Repeat the entire procedure for the remaining pistons/connecting rods.

47 The important points to remember are:

a) Keep the back sides of the bearing inserts and the insides of the connecting rods and caps perfectly clean when assembling them.

b) Make sure you have the correct piston/rod assembly for each cylinder.

c) The mark on the piston must face the front (timing belt end) of the engine.

d) Lubricate the cylinder walls liberally with clean oil.

e) Lubricate the bearing faces when installing the rod caps after the oil clearance has been checked.

48 After all the piston/connecting rod assemblies have been correctly installed, rotate the crankshaft a number of times by hand to check for any obvious binding.

49 As a final step, check the connecting rod endplay again.

50 Compare the measured endplay to the tolerance listed in this Chapter's Specifications to make sure it's acceptable. If it was correct before disassembly and the original crankshaft and rods were reinstalled, it should still be correct. If new rods or a new crankshaft were installed, the endplay may be inadequate. If so, the rods will have to be removed and taken to an automotive machine shop for resizing.

## 10 Crankshaft - removal and installation

### REMOVAL

♦ **Refer to illustrations 10.1 and 10.3**

➡**Note:** The crankshaft can be removed only after the engine has been removed from the vehicle. It's assumed that the driveplate, crankshaft pulley, timing belt, oil pan, oil pump body, oil filter and piston/connecting rod assemblies have already been removed. The rear main oil seal retainer must be unbolted and separated from the block before proceeding with crankshaft removal.

1   Before the crankshaft is removed, measure the endplay. Mount a dial indicator with the indicator in line with the crankshaft and touching the end of the crankshaft as shown (see illustration).

2   Pry the crankshaft all the way to the rear and zero the dial indicator. Next, pry the crankshaft to the front as far as possible and check the reading on the dial indicator. The distance traveled is the endplay. A typical crankshaft endplay will fall between 0.003 to 0.010 inch (0.076 to 0.254 mm). If it is greater than that, check the crankshaft thrust surfaces for wear after it's removed. If no wear is evident, new main bearings should correct the endplay.

3   If a dial indicator isn't available, feeler gauges can be used. Gently pry the crankshaft all the way to the front of the engine. Slip feeler gauges between the crankshaft and the front face of the thrust bearing or washer to determine the clearance (see illustration).

4   Loosen the main bearing cap bolts 1/4-turn at a time each, until they can be removed by hand.

5   Gently tap the main bearing caps with a soft-face hammer. Pull the main bearing caps straight up and off the cylinder block. Try not to drop the bearing inserts if they come out with the caps.

6   Carefully lift the crankshaft out of the engine. It may be a good idea to have an assistant available, since the crankshaft is quite heavy

**10.1 Checking crankshaft endplay with a dial indicator**

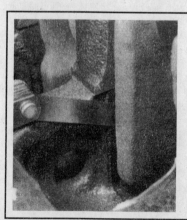

**10.3 Checking crankshaft endplay with feeler gauges at the thrust bearing journal**

**10.17 Place the Plastigage onto the crankshaft bearing journal as shown**

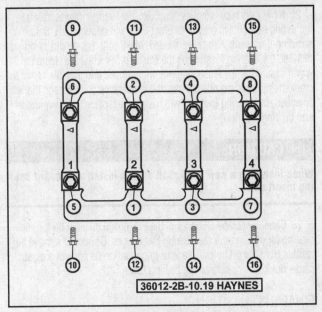

36012-2B-10.19 HAYNES

**10.19 Main bearing cap bolt tightening sequence**

and awkward to handle. With the bearing inserts in place inside the engine block and main bearing caps, reinstall the main bearing caps and tighten the bolts finger tight. Make sure you install the main bearing caps with the arrows facing the front end (timing belt) of the engine.

## INSTALLATION

7 Crankshaft installation is the first step in engine reassembly. It's assumed at this point that the engine block and crankshaft have been cleaned, inspected and repaired or reconditioned.

8 Position the engine block with the bottom facing up.

9 Remove the main bearing caps.

10 If they're still in place, remove the original bearing inserts from the block and from the main bearing caps. Wipe the bearing surfaces of the block and main bearing cap assembly with a clean, lint-free cloth. They must be kept spotlessly clean. This is critical for determining the correct bearing oil clearance.

## MAIN BEARING OIL CLEARANCE CHECK

▶ **Refer to illustrations 10.17, 10.19 and 10.21**

11 Without mixing them up, clean the back sides of the new upper main bearing inserts (with grooves and oil holes) and lay one in each main bearing saddle in the block. Each upper bearing has an oil groove and oil hole in it.

### ❊❊ CAUTION:

**The oil holes in the block must line up with the oil holes in the upper bearing inserts.**

The thrust washers must be installed in the number 3 crankshaft journal. Clean the back sides of the lower main bearing inserts and lay them in the corresponding location in the main bearing cap assembly. Make sure the tab on the bearing insert fits into the recess in the block or main bearing cap assembly. The upper bearings with the oil holes are installed into the engine block while the lower bearings without the oil holes are installed in the main bearing caps.

### ❊❊ CAUTION:

**DO NOT apply any lubrication at this time.**

12 Clean the faces of the bearing inserts in the block and the crankshaft main bearing journals with a clean, lint-free cloth.

13 Check or clean the oil holes in the crankshaft, as any dirt here can go only one way - straight through the new bearings.

14 Once you're certain the crankshaft is clean, carefully lay it in position in the cylinder block.

15 Before the crankshaft can be permanently installed, the main bearing oil clearance must be checked.

16 Cut several strips of the appropriate size of Plastigage. They must be slightly shorter than the width of the main bearing journal.

17 Place one piece on each crankshaft main bearing journal, parallel with the journal axis as shown (see illustration).

18 Clean the faces of the bearing inserts in the main bearing caps. Hold the bearing inserts in place and install the assembly onto the crankshaft and cylinder block. DO NOT disturb the Plastigage. Make sure you install the main bearing caps with the arrows facing the front (timing belt end) of the engine.

19 Apply clean engine oil to all bolt threads prior to installation, then install all bolts finger-tight. Tighten the main bearing cap bolts (the 8 main bolts followed by the 8 side bolts) in the sequence shown (see illustration) progressing in steps, to the torque listed in this Chapter's Specifications. DO NOT rotate the crankshaft at any time during this operation.

20 Remove the bolts in the reverse order of the tightening sequence and carefully lift the main bearing caps straight up and off the block. Do not disturb the Plastigage or rotate the crankshaft. If the main bearing caps are difficult to remove, tap them gently from side-to-side with a soft-face hammer to loosen it.

21 Compare the width of the crushed Plastigage on each journal to the scale printed on the Plastigage envelope to determine the main bearing oil clearance (see illustration). A typical main bearing oil clearance should fall between 0.0015 and 0.0023-inch. Check with an automotive machine shop for the oil clearance for your engine.

22 If the clearance is not as specified, the bearing inserts may be the wrong size (which means different ones will be required). Before deciding if different inserts are needed, make sure that no dirt or oil was between the bearing inserts and the cap or block when the clearance was measured. If the Plastigage was wider at one end than the other, the crankshaft journal may be tapered. If the clearance still exceeds the limit specified, the bearing insert(s) will have to be replaced with an under-size bearing insert(s).

### ❊❊ CAUTION:

**When installing a new crankshaft always install a standard bearing insert set.**

23 Carefully scrape all traces of the Plastigage material off the main bearing journals and/or the bearing insert faces. Be sure to remove all residue from the oil holes. Use your fingernail or the edge of a plastic card - don't nick or scratch the bearing faces.

## FINAL INSTALLATION

24 Carefully lift the crankshaft out of the cylinder block.

➡ **Note: On 2WD models, install the oil jets and the oil jet bolts into the engine block and tighten them to the torque listed in this Chapter's Specifications.**

25 Clean the bearing insert faces in the cylinder block, then apply a thin, uniform layer of moly-base grease or engine assembly lube to each of the bearing surfaces. Be sure to coat the thrust faces as well as the journal face of the thrust bearing.

26 Make sure the crankshaft journals are clean, then lay the crankshaft back in place in the cylinder block.

27 Clean the bearing insert faces and then apply the same lubricant to them. Clean the engine block thoroughly. The surfaces must be free of oil residue.

28 Assemble the main bearing caps and bearings and install each

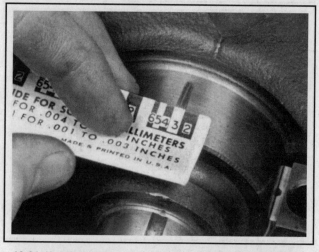

**10.21 Use the scale on the Plastigage package to determine the bearing oil clearance - be sure to measure the widest part of the Plastigage and use the correct scale; it comes with both standard and metric scales**

main bearing cap onto the crankshaft and cylinder block. Make sure the arrows face the front (timing belt) of the engine.

29 Prior to installation, apply clean engine oil to all bolt threads wiping off any excess, then install all bolts finger-tight.

30 Torque the main bearing cap bolts followed by the side bolts in the correct sequence (see illustration 10.19).

31 Recheck crankshaft endplay with a feeler gauge or a dial indicator. The endplay should be correct if the crankshaft thrust faces aren't worn or damaged and if new bearings have been installed.

32 Rotate the crankshaft a number of times by hand to check for any obvious binding. It should rotate with a running torque of 50 in-lbs or less. If the running torque is too high, correct the problem at this time.

33 Install a new rear main oil seal (see Chapter 2A).

## 11 Engine overhaul - reassembly sequence

1 Before beginning engine reassembly, make sure you have all the necessary new parts, gaskets and seals as well as the following items on hand:

*Common hand tools*
*A 1/2-inch drive torque wrench*
*New engine oil*
*Gasket sealant*
*Thread locking compound*

2 If you obtained a short block it will be necessary to install the cylinder heads, the oil pump and pick-up tube, the oil pan, the water pump, the timing belt and timing covers, and the valve covers (see Chapter 2A). In order to save time and avoid problems, the external

components must be installed in the following general order:

*Thermostat and housing cover*
*Water pump*
*Intake and exhaust manifolds*
*Fuel injection components*
*Emission control components*
*Spark plugs*
*Ignition coils*
*Oil filter*
*Engine mounts and mount brackets*
*Driveplate*

## 12  Initial start-up and break-in after overhaul

### ✳✳ WARNING:

**Have a fire extinguisher handy when starting the engine for the first time.**

1   Once the engine has been installed in the vehicle, double-check the engine oil and coolant levels.

2   With the spark plugs out of the engine and the ignition system and fuel pump disabled (see Section 3), crank the engine until oil pressure registers on the gauge or the light goes out.

3   Install the spark plugs and ignition ciols, then restore the fuel pump function.

4   Start the engine. It may take a few moments for the fuel system to build up pressure, but the engine should start without a great deal of effort.

5   After the engine starts, it should be allowed to warm up to normal operating temperature. While the engine is warming up, make a thorough check for fuel, oil and coolant leaks.

6   Shut the engine off and recheck the engine oil and coolant levels.

7   Drive the vehicle to an area with minimum traffic, accelerate from 30 to 50 mph, then allow the vehicle to slow to 30 mph with the throttle closed. Repeat the procedure 10 or 12 times. This will load the piston rings and cause them to seat properly against the cylinder walls. Check again for oil and coolant leaks.

8   Drive the vehicle gently for the first 500 miles (no sustained high speeds) and keep a constant check on the oil level. It is not unusual for an engine to use oil during the break-in period.

9   At approximately 500 to 600 miles, change the oil and filter.

10  For the next few hundred miles, drive the vehicle normally. Do not pamper it or abuse it.

11  After 2000 miles, change the oil and filter again and consider the engine broken in.

## Specifications

### General

| | |
|---|---|
| Bore | |
| 2007 Acura models | 3.54 inches (90.0 mm) |
| All other models | 3.50 inches (89.0 mm) |
| Stroke | |
| 2007 Acura models | 3.78 inches (96.0 mm) |
| All other models | 3.66 inches (93.0 mm) |
| Displacement | |
| 2007 Acura models | 224 cubic inches (3.7 liters) |
| All other models | 212 cubic inches (3.5 liters) |
| Cylinder compression pressure | 135 to 163 psi (930 to 1,130 kPa) |
| Oil pressure at 178-degrees F (80-degrees C) | |
| At curb idle | 10 psi (78 kPa) |
| At 3,000 rpm | 71 psi (490 kPa) |

## Torque specifications

| | Ft-lbs (unless otherwise indicated) | Nm |
|---|---|---|
| Connecting rod bearing cap bolts | | |
| Step 1 | 168 in-lbs | 20 |
| Step 2 | Tighten an additional 1/4-turn (90-degrees) | |
| Main bearing caps (see illustration 10.19) | | |
| Main bolts | | |
| 2001 and 2002 Acura and | | |
| 2003 and 2004 Honda models | 56 | 76 |
| All other models | 54 | 74 |
| Side bolts | 36 | 49 |
| Oil jet bolts (2WD models) | 144 in-lbs | 16 |
| Subframe mounting bolts (see illustration 7.46) | | |
| Large bolts (A) | 76 | 103 |
| Bracket bolts | | |
| Bolts B | 54 | 74 |
| Bolts C | 86 | 117 |
| Crossmember bolts | 40 | 54 |

**Section**

**Reference to other Chapters**

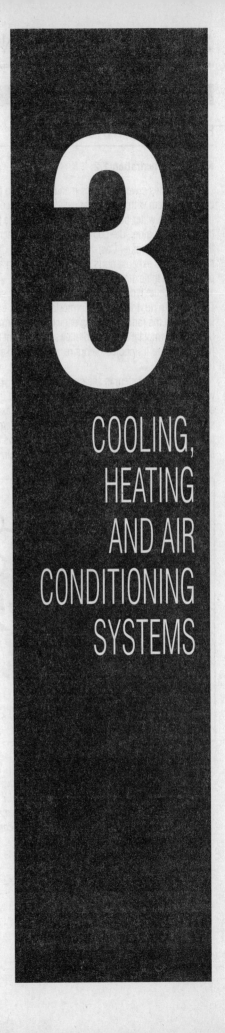

# 3

COOLING,
HEATING
AND AIR
CONDITIONING
SYSTEMS

**1    General information**

## ENGINE COOLING SYSTEM

♦ **Refer to illustration 1.2**

All vehicles covered by this manual employ a pressurized engine cooling system with thermostatically controlled coolant circulation. An impeller-type water pump mounted on the engine block pumps coolant through the engine. The coolant flows around each cylinder and toward the rear of the engine. Cast-in coolant passages direct coolant around the intake and exhaust ports, near the spark plug areas and in close proximity to the exhaust valve guides.

A wax-pellet type thermostat controls engine coolant temperature. During warm up, the closed thermostat prevents coolant from circulating through the radiator. As the engine nears normal operating temperature, the thermostat opens and allows hot coolant to travel through the radiator, where it's cooled before returning to the engine (see illustration).

The cooling system is sealed by a pressure-type radiator cap, which raises the boiling point of the coolant and increases the cooling efficiency of the radiator. If the system pressure exceeds the cap pressure relief value, the excess pressure in the system forces the spring-loaded valve inside the cap off its seat and allows the coolant to escape through the overflow tube into a coolant reservoir. When the system

cools, the excess coolant is automatically drawn from the reservoir back into the radiator.

The coolant reservoir serves as both the point at which fresh coolant is added to the cooling system to maintain the proper fluid level and as a holding tank for overheated coolant.

This type of cooling system is known as a closed design because coolant that escapes past the pressure cap is saved and reused.

## ENGINE COOLING FANS

These models are equipped with two electric cooling fans; a radiator fan and a condenser fan. The fans are controlled by relays and the main computer for the engine. The relays are located in the engine compartment. The computer uses information from various sensors and the air conditioning system to control the application of the two fans.

## HEATING SYSTEM

A typical heating system consists of a blower fan and heater core located in a housing under the dash, the hoses connecting the heater core to the engine cooling system and the heater/air conditioning control head on the dashboard. Hot engine coolant is circulated through the heater core. When the heater mode is activated, a flap door in the housing opens to expose the heater core to the passenger compartment through air ducts. A fan switch on the control head activates the blower motor, which forces air through the core, heating the air. Most models are equipped with a second housing with an additional heater core for heating the rear passenger compartment. Additional controls are placed in the interior so they can be accessed by the rear passengers.

## AIR CONDITIONING SYSTEM

The air conditioning system consists of a condenser mounted in front of the radiator, an evaporator mounted adjacent to the heater core, a compressor mounted on the engine, a receiver-drier built onto the condenser and the plumbing connecting all of the above components.

A blower fan forces the warmer air of the passenger compartment through the evaporator core (sort of a radiator-in-reverse), transferring the heat from the air to the refrigerant. The liquid refrigerant boils off into low pressure vapor, taking the heat with it when it leaves the evaporator.

Most models are equipped with a second housing with an additional evaporator for cooling the rear passenger compartment. Additional controls are placed in the interior so they can be accessed by the rear passengers.

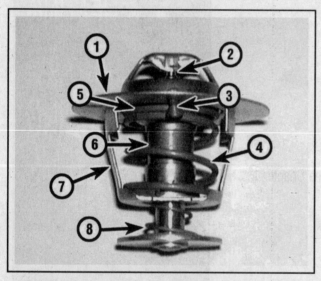

**1.2  Typical thermostat**

| | | | |
|---|---|---|---|
| 1 | Flange | 5 | Valve seat |
| 2 | Piston | 6 | Valve |
| 3 | Jiggle pin | 7 | Frame |
| 4 | Main coil spring | 8 | Secondary coil spring |

## 2    Antifreeze - general information

♦ Refer to illustration 2.5

**❄ WARNING:**

Do not allow antifreeze to come in contact with your skin or painted surfaces of the vehicle. Rinse off spills immediately with plenty of water. Antifreeze is highly toxic if ingested. Never leave antifreeze lying around in an open container or in puddles on the floor; children and pets are attracted by its sweet smell and may drink it. Check with local authorities about disposing of used antifreeze. Many communities have collection centers which will see that antifreeze is disposed of safely. Never dump used antifreeze on the ground or pour it into drains.

**❄ WARNING:**

Do not mix coolants of different colors. Doing so might damage the cooling system and/or the engine. Read the warning label in the engine compartment for additional information.

➡Note: Non-toxic antifreeze is now manufactured and available at local auto parts stores, but even this type must be disposed of properly.

The cooling system should be filled with a water/ethylene glycol based antifreeze solution, which will prevent freezing down to at least -20-degrees F (even lower in cold climates). It also provides protection against corrosion and increases the coolant boiling point. The engines in these vehicles have aluminum heads. The manufacturer recommends that the correct type of coolant be used and strongly urges that coolant types not be mixed (see the Chapter 1 Specifications).

Drain, flush and refill the cooling system at least every other year (see Chapter 1). The use of antifreeze solutions for periods of longer than two years is likely to cause damage and encourage the formation of rust and scale in the system.

Before adding antifreeze to the system, inspect all hose connections. Antifreeze can leak through very minute openings.

2.5  Use a hydrometer (available at most auto parts stores) to test the condition of your coolant

The exact mixture of antifreeze to water, which you should use, depends on the relative weather conditions. The mixture should contain at least 50-percent antifreeze, but should never contain more than 70-percent antifreeze. Consult the mixture ratio chart on the container before adding coolant.

➡Note: Premixed antifreeze, with water already added, is now commonly available at most auto parts stores. The percentage is usually a 50/50 mix of antifreeze to water. Be sure to read the label on the antifreeze container closely to be certain that you are filling the cooling system with the proper mix of antifreeze and water.

Hydrometers are available at most auto parts stores to test the coolant (see illustration). Use antifreeze that meets factory specifications for engines with aluminum heads (see Chapter 1)..

## 3    Thermostat - check and replacement

**❄ WARNING:**

Do not remove the radiator cap, drain the coolant or replace the thermostat until the engine has cooled completely.

**❄ WARNING:**

Don't drive the vehicle without a thermostat. The computer may stay in open loop and emissions and fuel economy will suffer.

## CHECK

1    Before assuming the thermostat is to blame for a cooling system problem, check the coolant level, drivebelt tension (see Chapter 1) and temperature gauge operation.

2    If the engine seems to be taking a long time to warm up, based on heater output or temperature gauge operation, the thermostat is probably stuck open. Replace the thermostat with a new one.

3    If the engine runs hot, use your hand to check the temperature of the lower radiator hose. If the hose isn't hot, but the engine is, the thermostat is probably stuck closed, preventing the coolant inside the engine from escaping to the radiator. Replace the thermostat.

4    If the lower radiator hose is hot, it means that the coolant is flowing and the thermostat is open. Consult the *Troubleshooting* Section at the front of this manual for cooling system diagnosis.

## REPLACEMENT

♦ Refer to illustrations 3.8, 3.12 and 3.13

5    Disconnect the cable from the negative battery terminal (see Chapter 5, Section 1).

6    Drain the cooling system (see Chapter 1). If the coolant is relatively new or in good condition (see Chapter 1), save it and reuse it. Read the **Warning** in Section 2.

7   Remove the air intake duct between the throttle body and the air filter housing (see Chapter 4).

8   Follow the lower radiator hose to the engine to locate the thermostat housing cover (see illustration).

9   Loosen the hose clamp, then detach the hose from the fitting. If it's stuck, grasp it near the end with a pair of adjustable pliers and twist it to break the seal, then pull it off. If the hose is old or deteriorated, cut it off and install a new one.

10   Over time, the outer surface of the hose fitting on the thermostat housing cover can become heavily corroded or pitted. Further damage can occur when the hose is removed. Install a new thermostat housing cover if necessary.

11   Remove the thermostat housing cover bolts and detach the housing cover (see illustration 3.8). If the cover is stuck, tap it with a soft-face hammer to jar it loose. Be prepared for some coolant to spill as the gasket seal is broken.

➡Note: It is not necessary to disconnect the ground wires or electrical connector to the ECT sensor unless the housing cover needs to be replaced.

12   Note how the thermostat is installed (with the jiggle pin up), then remove it (see illustration).

13   Install a new rubber seal over the thermostat making sure that the small rubber tang aligns with the jiggle pin (see illustration).

14   Install the new thermostat into the housing (without using sealant). When the small tang on the seal is matched to the notch in the housing, the jiggle pin will be located at the top (see illustration 3.12).

15   Install the housing cover and bolts. Tighten the bolts to the torque listed in this Chapter's Specifications.

16   Reattach the hose and tighten the hose clamp securely. Install all components that were removed for access.

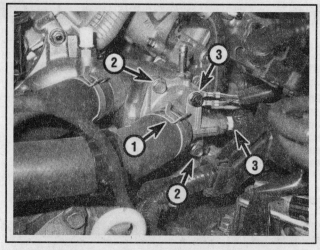

**3.8   Location of the thermostat housing and cover and mounting details (2005 Pilot model shown, other models similar):**

1   *Lower radiator hose and clamp (use pliers to squeeze the coolant hose clamp and slide the clamp away from the thermostat housing)*
2   *Thermostat housing cover mounting bolts*
3   *Electrical connections (detach only if replacing the housing cover)*

17   Refill the cooling system (see Chapter 1).

18   Reconnect the battery (see Chapter 5, Section 1).

19   Start the engine and allow it to reach normal operating temperature, then check for leaks and proper thermostat operation (as described in Steps 3 and 4).

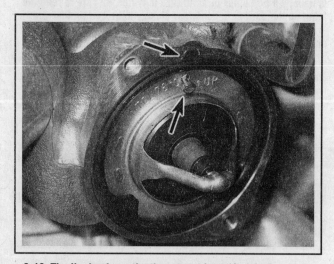

**3.12   The jiggle pin on the thermostat is at 12 o'clock . . .**

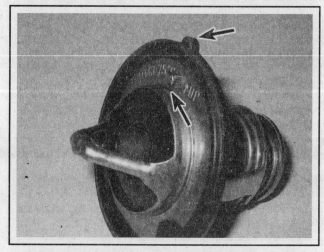

**3.13   . . .and the rubber tang on the seal is directly over the jiggle pin**

## 4  Engine cooling fans - check and replacement

To avoid possible injury or damage, DO NOT operate the engine with a damaged fan. Do not attempt to repair fan blades - replace a damaged fan with a new one.

➡Note: On 2007 Acura MDX models, remove the radiator before removing the engine cooling fans.

## CHECK

♦ Refer to illustrations 4.1a, 4.1b, 4.3a and 4.3b

1   If the engine is getting hot (or overheating) and neither of the cooling fans are coming on, check their fuses first. If the fuses are okay, unplug the electrical connector for each fan motor and apply battery voltage to each one (see illustrations). Use a fused jumper wire on terminal A and another jumper wire going to ground on terminal B. If either fan motor doesn't come on, replace it.

Do not apply battery power to the harness side of the connector. Be sure to test the cooling fan motor only.

2   If the fan motors are okay, check the fan relay(s).
3   Locate the fan relays in the engine compartment fuse/relay box and in the smaller additional relay box in front of the Powertrain Control Module (PCM) (see illustrations).
4   Test the relays (see Chapter 12).

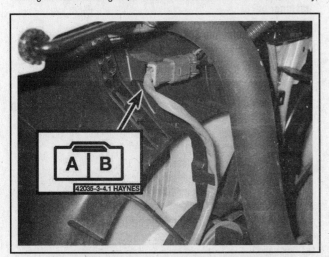

4.1a  To test either fan motor, disconnect the electrical connector and use jumper wires to connect the fan directly to the battery (A) and ground (B) - if the fan still doesn't work, replace the motor (radiator fan shown) - 2005 Honda shown, other models similar

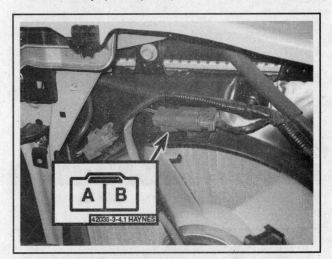

4.1b  The location of the condenser fan connector - 2005 Honda shown, other models similar

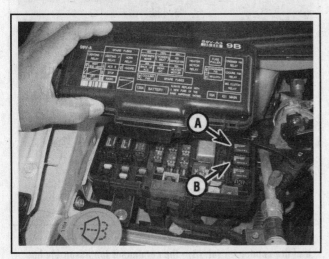

4.3a  The air conditioning condenser fan relay (A) and the radiator fan relay (B) are located in the engine compartment fuse/relay box - 2005 Honda shown, other models similar

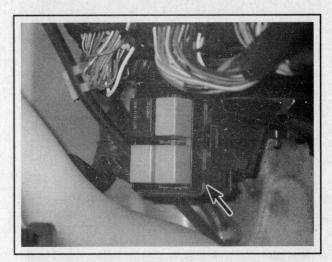

4.3b  The fan control relay is located in a small relay box in front of the Powertrain Control Module - 2005 Honda shown, other models similar

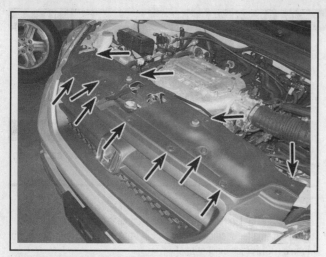

**4.7a  Location of the radiator cover fasteners**

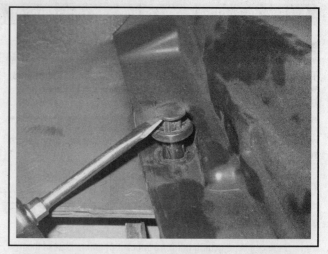

**4.7b  Lift up on the center release pin, then pull the entire fastener out**

5   If the fuses, motors and relays are functional, check all wiring and connections to the fan motors. If no obvious problems are found, have the cooling fan system and circuits diagnosed by a dealer service department or repair shop with the proper diagnostic equipment.

## REPLACEMENT

♦ **Refer to illustrations 4.7a, 4.7b, 4.14, 4.15, 4.17 and 4.18**

**❋❋ WARNING:**

**Wait until the engine is completely cool before beginning this procedure.**

6   Remove the battery and battery tray (see Chapter 5).
7   Remove the plastic cover over the radiator (see illustrations).
8   Disconnect all electrical connectors and separate the wire harnesses on the fan shroud assemblies except for the harnesses attached directly to the fan motors (see illustrations 4.1a and 4.1b).

9   Remove the ground cable attached to the radiator support, if equipped.

10  Drain the cooling system (see Chapter 1). If the coolant is relatively new or in good condition, save it and reuse it. Read the **Warning** in Section 2.

11  Detach the upper radiator hose from the radiator and position it aside for access (see Section 6).

12  Remove the hood latch (see Chapter 11).

13  Remove the lower engine splash shield (see Chapter 2A).

14  Remove the bracket for the hood latch (see illustration).

15  Remove the radiator (driver's side) fan assembly mounting bolts, pull the assembly up slightly (to release the bottom mounts) and then remove it through the opening created by the removed battery and tray (see illustration).

16  Remove the condenser fan assembly (passenger side) upper and lower mounting bolts, then remove the fan assembly through the opening mentioned in the previous step (see illustration 4.15).

**4.14  The upper fasteners for the bracket that supports the hood latch - the lower fastener is on the bottom of the bracket**

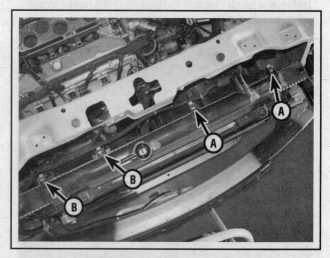

**4.15  The top mounting fasteners for the radiator fan (A) and the condenser fan (B) - the condenser fan assembly has two additional fasteners on the bottom. The bottom of the radiator fan assembly fits in mounts attached to the bottom of the radiator**

**4.17  To remove the fan, unscrew the nut in the center, then pull the fan blade from the motor shaft**

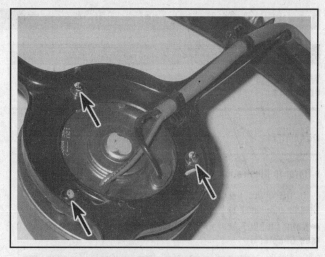

**4.18  Engine cooling fan motor mounting screws**

17  To detach the fan from the motor, remove the motor shaft nut (see illustration).

18  To detach the fan motor from the shroud, remove the mounting screws (see illustration).

19  Installation is the reverse of removal. Be sure that the hood latch is properly aligned when installed (see Chapter 11). Be sure to fill the cooling system with the proper mixture of antifreeze and water (see Chapter 1) and to check for leaks after the vehicle has reached normal operating temperature.

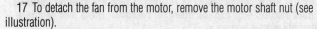

**5  Coolant reservoir - removal and installation**

▶ **Refer to illustration 5.1**

**❄❄ WARNING:**

**Wait until the engine is completely cool before beginning this procedure.**

1  Disconnect the reservoir hose and plug it to prevent leakage. Check the hose for cracks or hardness and replace it if necessary (see illustration).

2  Lift the reservoir off its bracket and out of the engine compartment.

3  Clean the inside of the tank with soapy water and a brush to remove any deposits. Inspect the reservoir carefully for cracks. If you find a crack, replace the reservoir.

4  Installation is the reverse of removal.

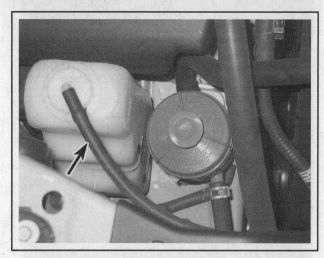

**5.1  Remove the coolant hose and then lift the coolant reservoir straight up and out of its bracket**

## 6 Radiator - removal and installation

**⁂ WARNING:**

**Wait until the engine is completely cool before beginning this procedure.**

## REMOVAL

◆ **Refer to illustration 6.7a, 6.7b, 6.9 and 6.10**

1  Disconnect the cable from the negative battery terminal (see Chapter 5, Section 1).

➡**Note: On 2007 Acura MDX models, remove the battery tray (see Chapter 5)**

2  Set the parking brake and block the rear wheels. Raise the front of the vehicle and support it securely on jackstands. Remove the lower engine splash shield (see Chapter 2A).

3  On 2007 Acura MDX models, remove the air filter housing (see

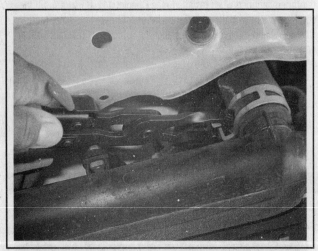

**6.7a  Use spring-clamp pliers, or regular pliers, to expand the hose clamp and slide it down the upper radiator hose and off of the radiator fitting . . .**

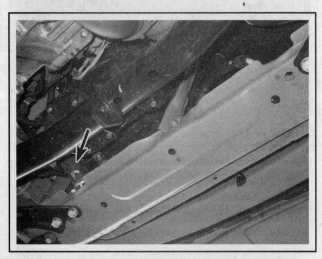

**6.7b  . . . and repeat the procedure for the lower radiator hose at the bottom of the radiator**

Chapter 4).

4  Drain the cooling system (see Chapter 1). If the coolant is relatively new or in good condition, save it and reuse it. Read the **Warning** in Section 2.

5  Remove the plastic cover over the radiator (see illustrations 4.7a and 4.7b).

6  Remove the bumper cover (see Chapter 11).

➡**Note: On 2007 Acura MDX models, remove the front grill instead of the bumper cover (see Chapter 11).**

7  Detach the upper and lower radiator hoses from the radiator. Expand the clamps and slide them down the hose away from the fitting and then detach the hoses (see illustrations). If a hose is stuck, grasp it at the end with a pair of slip-joint pliers and twist it to break the seal, then pull it off - be careful not to damage the radiator fitting! If the hoses are old or deteriorated, cut them off and install new ones. Also, disconnect the small hose to the coolant reservoir.

➡**Note: Spring-type hose clamps are commonly used from the factory for securing hoses to fittings. There are special purpose tools available to expand them for removal, but a pair of pliers usually works just as well.**

8  Remove the engine cooling fans (see Section 4).

➡**Note: On 2007 Acura MDX models, completely separate the cooling fans and lean them towards the engine compartment. They can only be removed after the radiator has been removed.**

9  Disconnect the transaxle fluid cooler hoses and related line brackets from the bottom of the radiator and plug them (see illustration). On 2007 Acura MDX models, disconnect the ECT sensor from the bottom of the radiator (see Chapter 6).

10  Remove the radiator and air conditioning condenser mounting brackets (see illustration). Check the rubber mounts in the brackets for cracks or hardness and replace them if necessary.

11  Carefully lift out the radiator, being careful not to damage the fins on the radiator or air conditioning condenser. Don't spill coolant on the vehicle or scratch the paint.

12  Inspect the radiator for leaks and damage. If it needs repair, have a radiator shop or dealer service department perform the work, as special techniques are required.

**6.9  Remove the cooler line bracket fasteners (A) and the hoses (B) - one hose is located on the right side of the radiator and hidden from view in this photo**

**6.10 Location of the radiator mounting brackets (A) and the condenser mounting brackets (B)**

13  Bugs and dirt can be removed from the radiator by spraying it with a garden hose nozzle from the back side. The radiator should be flushed out with a garden hose before reinstallation.

14  Check the rubber mounts on the bottom of the radiator for wear or deterioration and replace them if necessary.

## INSTALLATION

15  Installation is the reverse of the removal procedure. Carefully guide the radiator into position and make certain that the rubber mounts on the bottom are properly seated into the support.

16  Tighten the radiator and air conditioning condenser bracket bolts to the torque listed in this Chapter's Specifications.

17  After installation, fill the cooling system with the proper mixture of antifreeze and water (see Chapter 1).

18  Start the engine and check for leaks. Allow the engine to reach normal operating temperature, then recheck the coolant level and add more if required.

19  Check the transaxle fluid and add more as needed (see Chapter 1).

---

**7   Water pump - check**

▶ **Refer to illustration 7.3**

1   A failure in the water pump can cause serious engine damage due to overheating.

2   The water pump is driven by the timing belt and is located beneath the timing belt cover. Water pump leaks are harder to detect with this design. Look for coolant coming out the lower timing belt cover.

3   Water pumps are equipped with weep (or vent) holes (see illustration). If a failure occurs in the pump seal, coolant will leak from the hole. With the timing belt cover removed, use a flashlight and small mirror to find the hole on the water pump from underneath to check for leaks.

➡ **Note: If there is coolant on any of the timing belt components or covers, consider this evidence of a severe leak.**

4   If the water pump shaft bearings fail, there may be a howling sound at the pump while it's running. Shaft wear can be felt with the timing belt removed if the water pump pulley is rocked up and down (with the engine off). Don't mistake drivebelt slippage, which causes a squealing sound, for water pump bearing failure.

5   Even a pump that exhibits no outward signs of a problem, such as noise or leakage, can still be due for replacement. Removal for close examination is the only sure way to tell. Sometimes the fins on the back of the impeller can corrode to the point that cooling efficiency is hampered.

6   If the pump is defective, replace it with a new or rebuilt unit.

**7.3 The weep hole on the underside of the pump - you'll need a flashlight and small mirror to inspect it (with the timing belt cover removed)**

## 8    Water pump - replacement

▶ Refer to illustrations 8.5 and 8.10

**※※ WARNING:**

**Wait until the engine is completely cool before beginning this procedure.**

1    Disconnect the cable from the negative battery terminal (see Chapter 5, Section 1).

2    Drain the cooling system (see Chapter 1). If the coolant is relatively new or in good condition, save it and reuse it. Read the **Warning** in Section 2.

3    Remove the drivebelts (see Chapter 1).

4    Remove the timing belt, timing belt tensioner and adjuster assembly (adjuster and pulley) (see Chapter 2A).

5    Remove the mounting bolts and detach the water pump from the engine (see illustration).

6    Clean the bolt threads and the threaded holes in the engine to remove corrosion and sealant.

7    Compare the new pump to the old one to make sure they're identical.

8    Remove all traces of sealant or O-ring from the engine mating surface.

9    Clean the engine and new water pump mating surfaces with lacquer thinner or acetone.

10    Apply a thin layer of RTV sealant to the O-ring groove of the new pump, then carefully set a new O-ring in the groove (see illustration).

11    Carefully attach the pump to the engine and thread the bolts into the holes finger tight. Use a small amount of RTV sealant on the bolt threads, and make sure that any dowel pins are in their original locations.

12    Tighten the bolts to the torque listed in this Chapter's Specifications in 1/4-turn increments.

**※※ WARNING:**

**Don't over-tighten the bolts or the pump may become distorted.**

13    Reinstall all parts removed for access to the pump.

14    Reconnect the battery (see Chapter 5, Section 1).

15    Refill and bleed the cooling system and check the drivebelt tension (see Chapter 1). Run the engine and check for leaks.

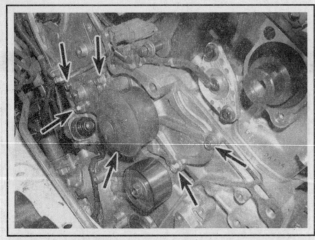

**8.5  Water pump mounting bolts - one bottom bolt isn't visible in this photo**

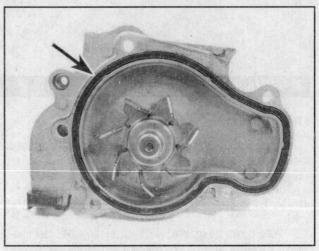

**8.10  Apply a thin layer of RTV sealant to the O-ring groove of the new pump, then carefully set a new O-ring in the groove - typical shown**

## 9    Coolant temperature indicator - check

**※※ WARNING:**

**Wait until the engine is completely cool before beginning this procedure.**

1    The coolant temperature indicator system consists of the temperature gauge (on the dash), a sensor mounted on the engine and the vehicle's main computer. The Engine Coolant Temperature (ECT) sensor provides a signal to the Powertrain Control Module (PCM - the vehicle's computer) (see Chapter 6). The PCM controls the temperature gauge.

2    If the temperature gauge goes above normal and begins to read 'hot', check the coolant level in the system (see Chapter 1). Also, check that the coolant mixture is correct (see Section 2). Finally, refer to the *Troubleshooting* section at the beginning of this book before assuming that the temperature indicator is faulty.

3    Start the engine and warm it up for 10 minutes. If the temperature gauge has not moved from the C position, check the wiring harness connections going to the instrument cluster.

4    If there is a problem with the ECT sensor, it is very likely that the CHECK ENGINE light will come on and the sensor or circuit will need repair (see Chapter 6). Due to the complexity of this system, further diagnosis and repair should be referred to a dealership service department or a qualified repair shop.

## 10 Blower motor transistor and blower motor - replacement

**✳✳ WARNING:**

The models covered by this manual are equipped with Supplemental Restraint systems (SRS), more commonly known as airbags. Always disable the airbag system before working in the vicinity of any airbag system component to avoid the possibility of accidental deployment of the airbag, which could cause personal injury (see Chapter 12).

## BLOWER MOTOR TRANSISTOR

### Front

▶ Refer to illustrations 10.1 and 10.2

1 Working in the passenger compartment under the glove box, disconnect the electrical connector from the blower motor transistor (see illustration).

2 Remove the blower motor transistor mounting screws and remove the transistor from the blower housing (see illustration).

3 Installation is the reverse of removal.

### Rear

▶ Refer to illustration 10.5

➡Note: Some models utilize a blower motor resistor for the rear heater/air conditioning system. This component mounts virtually the same as the blower motor transistor.

4 Remove the center console (see Chapter 11).

5 Disconnect the electrical connector from the blower motor transistor (see illustration).

6 Remove the blower motor transistor from the blower housing.

7 Installation is the reverse of removal.

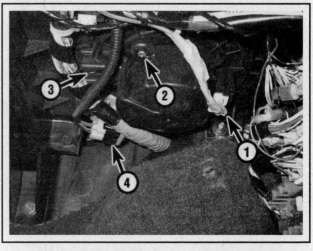

**10.1 Blower motor transistor and blower motor details:**

1 *Electrical connector (blower motor)*
2 *Blower motor cover mounting screw (one hidden)*
3 *Blower motor mounting screw (two hidden)*
4 *Electrical connector (blower motor transistor)*

## BLOWER MOTOR

### Front

▶ Refer to illustration 10.10

8 Working in the passenger compartment under the glove box, disconnect the electrical connector from the blower motor (see illustration 10.1).

9 Remove the blower motor mounting screws, then remove the blower motor assembly (see illustration 10.1).

10 Remove the blower motor fan circlip and remove the blower fan from the motor (see illustration).

11 Installation is the reverse of removal.

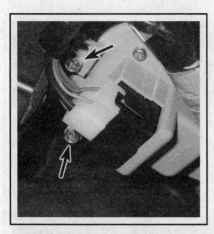

**10.2 Mounting screws for the blower motor transistor (front)**

**10.5 Rear blower motor transistor (or resistor) location - 2005 Honda shown, other models similar**

**10.10 Use pliers to remove the circlip from the motor shaft and lift the blower fan from the motor**

### Rear

▶ Refer to illustration 10.13

12  Remove the center console (see Chapter 11).

13  Disconnect the blower motor electrical connector (see illustration).

14  Remove the blower motor mounting screws and then remove the blower motor (see illustration 10.13).

15  Remove the blower motor fan circlip and remove the blower fan from the motor (see illustration 10.11).

16  Installation is the reverse of removal.

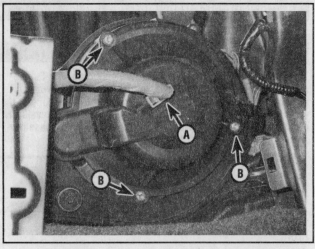

**10.13  Remove the blower motor electrical connector (A) and the mounting screws (B) - 2005 Honda shown, other models similar**

## 11  Heater/air conditioning control assembly - removal and installation

### ✳✳✳ WARNING:

**The models covered by this manual are equipped with Supplemental Restraint systems (SRS), more commonly known as airbags. Always disable the airbag system before working in the vicinity of any airbag system component to avoid the possibility of accidental deployment of the airbag, which could cause personal injury (see Chapter 12).**

1  Disconnect the cable from the negative battery terminal (see Chapter 5, Section 1).

## FRONT HEATER/AIR CONDITIONING CONTROL ASSEMBLY

▶ Refer to illustrations 11.4a, 11.4b, 11.4c, 11.4d and 11.5

2  Remove the instrument panel center bezel (see Chapter 11).

3  On 2006 and earlier Acura MDX models, remove the four heater/air conditioning control assembly mounting screws, then remove it from the center bezel

4  On all other models, remove the mounting screws for the center components in the instrument panel, disconnect all electrical connectors in the rear and then remove the components (see illustrations).

➡Note: On most models, the heater/air conditioning control assembly is mounted with other components in the instrument panel. Remove these components as an assembly and then separate the control assembly from them.

5  Remove the mounting brackets for the center components and then separate the heater/air conditioning control assembly (see illustration).

6  Installation is the reverse of removal.

**11.4a  Mounting screws for the instrument panel center components - 2005 Honda shown, other models similar**

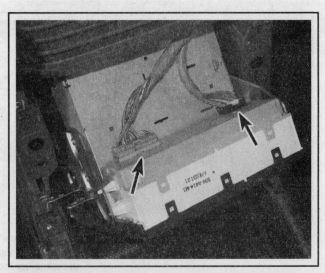

**11.4b  Electrical connectors for the heater/air conditioning control assembly - 2005 Honda shown, other models similar**

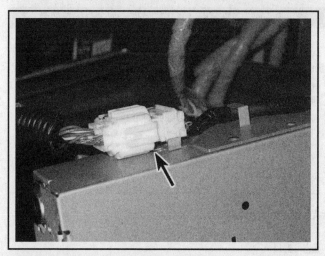

**11.4c Electrical connector for the CD changer (if equipped) - 2005 Honda shown, other models similar**

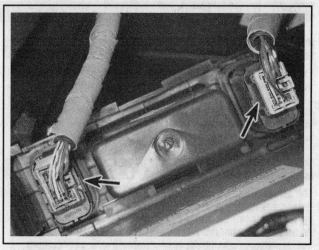

**11.4d Electrical connectors for the heated seat switches (if equipped) - 2005 Honda shown, other models similar**

## REAR HEATER/AIR CONDITIONING CONTROL ASSEMBLY

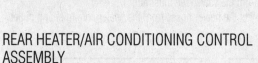

▶ **Refer to illustration 11.8**

7   Remove the rear trim panel from the center console (see Chapter 11).

8   Remove the electrical connectors from the control assembly (see illustration).

9   Separate the control assembly from the panel.

10  Installation is the reverse of the removal.

**11.5 Remove the center component mounting bracket fasteners and then separate the heater/air conditioning control assembly (one side shown) - 2005 Honda shown, other models similar**

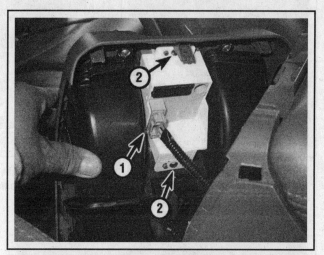

**11.8 Rear heater/air conditioning control assembly mounting details (2005 Honda shown - other models similar):**

*1   Electrical connector (blower motor)*
*2   Blower motor cover mounting screw (one hidden)*

## 12 Heater core - replacement

**✳✳ WARNING 1:**

The models covered by this manual are equipped with Supplemental Restraint systems (SRS), more commonly known as airbags. Always disable the airbag system before working in the vicinity of any airbag system component to avoid the possibility of accidental deployment of the airbag, which could cause personal injury (see Chapter 12).

**✳✳ WARNING 2:**

The air conditioning system is under high pressure. DO NOT loosen any fittings or remove any components until after the system has been discharged. Air conditioning refrigerant must be properly discharged into an EPA-approved container at a dealer service department or an automotive air conditioning repair facility. Always wear eye protection when disconnecting air conditioning system fittings.

1   If you're removing the front heater core, have the air conditioning system discharged by a licensed automotive air conditioning technician before proceeding (see the **Warning** above).

➥**Note: This step is not necessary for the rear heater core removal.**

2   Disconnect the cable from the negative battery terminal (see Chapter 5, Section 1).

3   Drain the cooling system (see Chapter 1).

## FRONT HEATER CORE

### All models except 2007 Acura MDX

▶ **Refer to illustrations 12.4, 12.5, 12.6, 12.7a, 12.7b, 12.9 and 12.11**

4   Place a reference mark on the heater control valve cable, then disconnect it from the valve (see illustration).

5   Disconnect the heater hoses from the heater core inlet and outlet

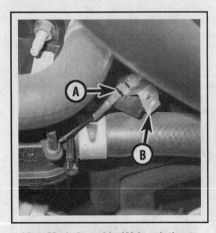

**12.4  Mark the cable (A) in relation to the clip and then pull the end of the clip (B) up to release the cable from the bracket**

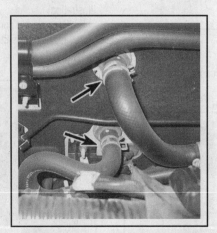

**12.5  Release the clamps and separate the heater hoses from the heater core**

**12.6  Disconnect the air conditioning lines at the firewall**

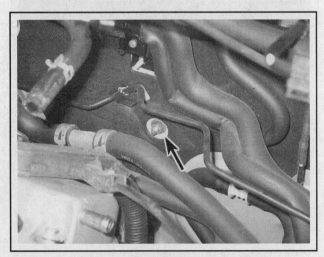

**12.7a  Remove the mounting nut for the heater housing inside the engine compartment**

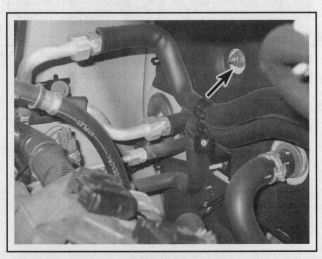

**12.7b  Remove the mounting nut for the evaporator housing inside the engine compartment**

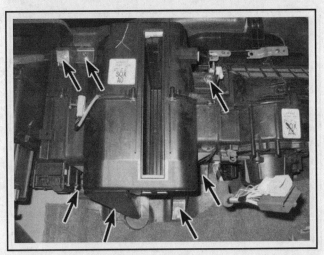

**12.9 Location of the evaporator housing mounting bolts**

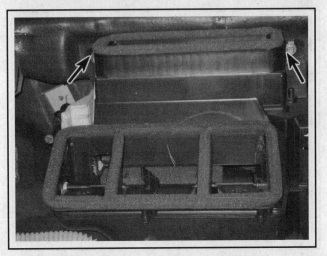

**12.11 Location of the heater housing mounting bolts**

pipes at the firewall (see illustration). Plug the heater core pipes to prevent coolant spillage when the heater housing is removed.

6  Disconnect the evaporator inlet and outlet lines at the engine compartment firewall (see illustration).

7  Remove the mounting nuts for the heater core and evaporator housing located in the engine compartment on the firewall (see illustrations).

8  Remove the instrument panel (see Chapter 11).

9  Remove the evaporator housing mounting fasteners (see illustration).

10  Remove the evaporator housing from the heater housing.

11  Remove the heater core housing mounting bolts, then carefully remove the assembly from the passenger compartment (see illustration).

12  Remove the clamps that secure the heater core pipes and then pull the heater core from the housing by carefully gripping the edges to release it from the interior seal.

13  Installation is the reverse of removal. Be sure to reconnect the heater core and evaporator inlet and outlet hoses at the firewall.

14  Reconnect the cable to the negative terminal of the battery (see Chapter 5, Section 1). Refill the cooling system (see Chapter 1). Have the air conditioning system recharged and leak tested by the shop that discharged it.

### 2007 Acura MDX models

15  Place a reference mark on the heater control valve cable and then disconnect it from the valve (see illustration 12.4).

16  Disconnect the heater hoses from the heater core inlet and outlet pipes at the firewall (see illustration 12.5).

17  Disconnect the air conditioning evaporator inlet and outlet line fittings located on the right (passenger) side of the engine compartment firewall.

➡**Note: There are two metal refrigerant lines (one larger than the other) secured by bolts. The port through the firewall where the fittings are located is round.**

18  Remove the mounting nuts for the heater core and evaporator housing located in the engine compartment on the firewall. One is below the refrigerant line fittings and the other is near the heater valve.

19  Remove the instrument panel (see Chapter 11).

20  Disconnect the electrical connector and harness from the blower fan motor and housing (below the glove compartment) (see illustration 10.1).

21  Disconnect all of the electrical connectors from the air conditioning/heater core housing.

22  Fold the carpet back to gain access to the lower heater duct, remove the wire harness clips to it and then remove the duct.

23  The air conditioning/heater housing is mounted to the firewall with six threaded-studs and six nuts. There are four for the top part of the housing and two below. Remove all mounting nuts for the housing.

24  Remove the air conditioning/heater core housing by sliding it towards the rear of the vehicle. At the same time, note the evaporator drain tube location as it is withdrawn from the firewall.

25  The heater core can be removed from the housing by removing the parts from the passenger's side of the housing that cover it. The parts are held on by self-tapping screws that screw into the plastic of the housing. Start by removing the small passenger's side duct, then the larger expansion valve cover. Remove the heater core cover that's directly over the core and then remove the clamps that hold the heater core pipes in place.

26  Remove the heater core by carefully gripping the edges to release it from the interior seal.

27  Installation is the reverse of removal.

28  Reconnect the cable to the negative terminal of the battery (see Chapter 5, Section 1). Refill the cooling system (see Chapter 1). Have the air conditioning system recharged and leak tested by the shop that discharged it.

## REAR HEATER CORE

▶ **Refer to illustrations 12.30 and 12.32**

29  Remove the center console (see Chapter 11).

30  Disconnect the heater hoses from the rear air conditioning/heating housing (see illustration).

➡**Note: Coolant will leak when the hoses are disconnected. Place a thick towel and plastic beneath the connections before disconnecting them.**

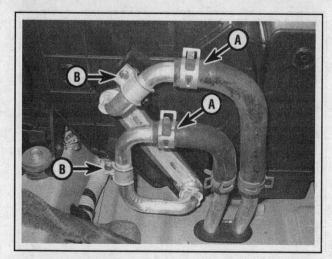

**12.30 Disconnect the heater hoses (A) and heater core pipe clamps (B)**

**12.32 Remove the rear air conditioning/heater housing mounting bolts**

31 Remove the clamps that hold the heater core pipes in place (see illustration 12.30).

32 Remove the two right air conditioning/heating housing mounting bolts (see illustration).

33 Tilt the right side of the housing up just enough to remove the heater core from the housing.

### ✳✳ WARNING:

Tilting the housing more than necessary could bend the refrigerant lines or cause a refrigerant leak at the line fittings on the other side.

➡Note: If the housing will not tilt easily, remove the housing mounting bolts on the left (driver's) side.

34 Installation is the reverse of removal.

35 Reconnect the cable to the negative terminal of the battery (see Chapter 5, Section 1). Refill the cooling system (see Chapter 1). Have the air conditioning system recharged and leak tested by the shop that discharged it.

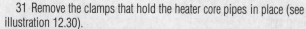

## 13  Air conditioning and heating system - check and maintenance

▶ Refer to illustrations 13.1a and 13.1b

### ✳✳ WARNING:

The air conditioning system is under high pressure. Do not loosen any hose fittings or remove any components until after the system has been discharged by a dealer service department or service station. Always wear eye protection when disconnecting air conditioning system fittings.

1   The following maintenance checks should be performed on a regular basis to ensure the air conditioner continues to operate at peak efficiency.

a)  *Check the compressor drivebelt. If it's worn or deteriorated, replace it (see Chapter 1).*

b)  *Check the drivebelt tension and, if necessary, adjust it (see Chapter 1).*

c)  *Check the system hoses. Look for cracks, bubbles, hard spots and deterioration. Inspect the hoses and all fittings for oil bubbles and seepage. If there's any evidence of wear, damage or leaks, replace the hose(s).*

d)  *Inspect the condenser fins for leaves, bugs and other debris. Use a fin comb or compressed air to clean the condenser.*

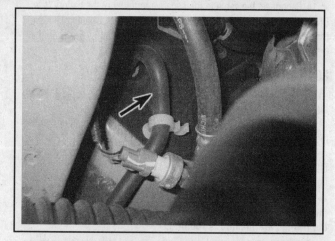

**13.1a  Look for the evaporator drain hose on the firewall - make sure it isn't clogged**

e)  *Make sure the system has the correct refrigerant charge.*

f)  *Check the evaporator housing drain tube for blockage (see illustrations).*

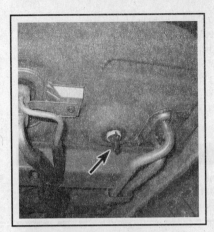

**13.1b On models with rear air conditioning, there is an additional evaporator drain hose under the vehicle**

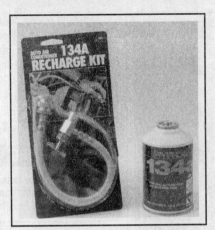

**13.9 A basic charging kit for R-134a systems is available at most auto parts stores - it must say R-134a (not R-12) and so should the can of refrigerant**

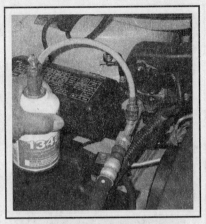

**13.12 Add R-134a to the low side port only - the procedure is easier if you wrap the can with a warm, wet towel to prevent icing**

2  It's a good idea to operate the system for about 10 minutes at least once a month, particularly during the winter. Long term non-use can cause hardening, and subsequent failure, of the seals.

3  Because of the complexity of the air conditioning system and the special equipment necessary to service it, in-depth troubleshooting and repairs are not included in this manual (refer to the *Haynes Automotive Heating and Air Conditioning Repair Manual*). However, simple checks and component replacement procedures are provided in this Chapter.

4  The most common cause of poor cooling is simply a low system refrigerant charge. If a noticeable drop in cool air output occurs, the following quick check will help you determine if the refrigerant level is low.

## CHECKING THE REFRIGERANT CHARGE

5  Warm the engine up to normal operating temperature.

6  Place the air conditioning temperature selector at the coldest setting and the blower at the highest setting. Open the vehicle doors (to make sure the air conditioning system doesn't cycle off as soon as it cools the passenger compartment).

7  With the compressor engaged - the clutch will make an audible click and the center of the clutch will rotate - feel the evaporator inlet and outlet lines at the firewall. The inlet (small diameter) line should feel warm and the outlet (large diameter) line should feel cold. If so, the system is properly charged.

8  Place a thermometer in the dashboard vent nearest the evaporator and operate the system until the indicated temperature is around 40 to 45-degrees F. If the ambient (outside) air temperature is very high, say 110-degrees F, the duct air temperature may be as high as 60-degrees F, but generally the air conditioning is 30 to 40-degrees F cooler than the ambient air.

➡**Note: Humidity of the ambient air also affects the cooling capacity of the system. Higher ambient humidity lowers the effectiveness of the air conditioning system.**

## ADDING REFRIGERANT

▶ **Refer to illustrations 13.9, 13.12, 13.13 and 13.15**

9  Buy an automotive charging kit at an auto parts store (see illus-

tration). A charging kit includes a 12 or 14-ounce can of refrigerant, a tap valve and a short section of hose that can be attached between the tap valve and the system low side service valve.

➡**Note: Leak detection kits with refrigerant dye, a UV light and special glasses are also available at most automotive supply stores. This kit can help you pinpoint leaks in your air conditioning system.**

**✳✳ WARNING:**

**There are two types of refrigerant used in automotive systems; R-12 - which has been widely used on earlier models and the more environmentally-friendly R-134a used in all models covered by this manual. These two refrigerants (and their appropriate refrigerant oils) are not compatible and must never be mixed or components will be damaged. Use only R-134a refrigerant in the models covered by this manual.**

10  Hook up the charging kit by following the manufacturer's instructions.

**✳✳ WARNING:**

**DO NOT hook the charging kit hose to the system high side! The fittings on the charging kit are designed to fit only on the low side of the system.**

11  Back off the valve handle on the charging kit and screw the kit onto the refrigerant can, making sure first that the O-ring or rubber seal inside the threaded portion of the kit is in place.

**✳✳ WARNING:**

**Wear protective eyewear when dealing with pressurized refrigerant cans.**

12  Remove the dust cap from the low-side charging connection and attach the quick-connect fitting on the kit hose (see illustration).

13  Warm up the engine and turn on the air conditioner. Keep the

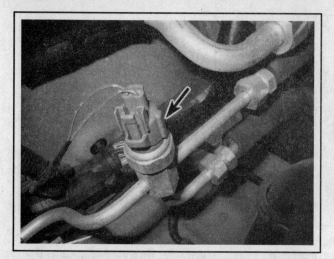

**13.13 Disconnect the A/C pressure switch, near the firewall on the right side of the engine compartment, and connect a jumper wire between the terminals on the harness connector**

charging kit hose away from the fan and other moving parts.

➡**Note: The compressor needs to be running in order to charge the system. However, if your system is very low on refrigerant, the compressor may turn off or not come on at all. If this happens, disconnect the A/C pressure switch electrical connector and use a jumper wire between the two terminals in the connector (see illustration). This will keep the compressor running.**

14 Turn the valve handle on the kit until the stem pierces the can, then back the handle out to release the refrigerant. You should be able to hear the rush of gas. Add refrigerant to the low side of the system until both the receiver-drier surface and the evaporator inlet pipe feel about the same temperature. Allow stabilization time between each addition.

15 If you have an accurate thermometer, place it in the center air conditioning vent (see illustration) and note the temperature of the air coming out of the vent. A fully-charged system which is working cor-

**13.15 Insert a thermometer in the center vent, turn on the air conditioning system and wait for it to cool down; depending on the humidity, the output air should be 30 to 40-degrees cooler than the ambient air temperature**

rectly should cool down to about 40-degrees F. Generally, an air conditioning system will put out air that is 30 to 40-degrees F cooler than the ambient air. For example, if the ambient (outside) air temperature is very high (over 100-degrees F), the temperature of air coming out of the registers should be 60 to 70-degrees F.

16 When the can is empty, turn the valve handle to the closed position and release the connection from the low-side port. Replace the dust cap.

### ✺✺ WARNING:

**Never add more than one can of refrigerant to the system. If more refrigerant than that is required, the system should be evacuated and leak tested.**

17 Remove the charging kit from the can and store the kit for future use with the piercing valve in the UP position, to prevent inadvertently piercing the can on the next use.

## HEATING SYSTEMS

18 If the carpet under the heater core is damp, or if antifreeze vapor or steam is coming through the vents, the heater core is leaking. Remove it (see Section 12) and install a new unit (most radiator shops will not repair a leaking heater core).

19 If the air coming out of the heater vents isn't hot, the problem could stem from any of the following causes:

a) *The thermostat is stuck open, preventing the engine coolant from warming up enough to carry heat to the heater core. Replace the thermostat (see Section 3).*

b) *There is a blockage in the system, preventing the flow of coolant through the heater core. Feel both heater hoses at the firewall. They should be hot. If one of them is cold, there is an obstruction in one of the hoses or in the heater core, or the heater control valve is shut. Detach the hoses and back flush the heater core with a water hose. If the heater core is clear but circulation is impeded, remove the two hoses and flush them out with a water hose.*

c) *If flushing fails to remove the blockage from the heater core, the core must be replaced (see Section 12).*

## ELIMINATING AIR CONDITIONING ODORS

▶ **Refer to illustration 13.23**

20 Unpleasant odors that often develop in air conditioning systems are caused by the growth of a fungus, usually on the surface of the evaporator core. The warm, humid environment there is a perfect breeding ground for mildew to develop.

21 The evaporator core on most vehicles is difficult to access, and factory dealerships have a lengthy, expensive process for eliminating the fungus by opening up the evaporator case and using a powerful disinfectant and rinse on the core until the fungus is gone. You can service your own system at home, but it takes something much stronger than basic household germ-killers or deodorizers.

22 Aerosol disinfectants for automotive air conditioning systems are available in most auto parts stores, but remember when shopping for them that the most effective treatments are also the most expensive. The

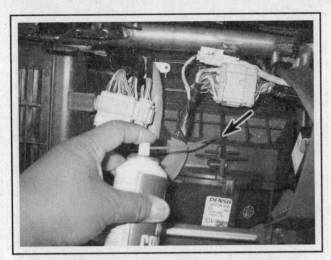

**13.23 Move the glove box down for access (see Chapter 11) and insert the nozzle of the disinfectant can into the evaporator housing by guiding it through the air recirculation door**

basic procedure for using these sprays is to start by running the system in the RECIRC mode for ten minutes with the blower on its highest speed. Use the highest heat mode to dry out the system and keep the compressor from engaging by disconnecting the wiring connector at the compressor (see Section 14).

23  Make sure that the disinfectant can comes with a long spray hose. Point the nozzle through the air recirculation door so that it protrudes inside the evaporator housing (see illustration), and then spray according to the manufacturer's recommendations. Try to cover the whole surface of the evaporator core, by aiming the spray up, down and sideways. Follow the manufacturer's recommendations for the length of spray and waiting time between applications.

24  Once the evaporator has been cleaned, the best way to prevent the mildew from coming back again is to make sure your evaporator housing drain tube is clear (see illustration 13.1).

## 14  Air conditioning compressor - removal and installation

▶ **Refer to illustrations 14.7, 14.8, 14.9 and 14.10**

❋❋ **WARNING:**

**The air conditioning system is under high pressure. Do not loosen any hose fittings or remove any components until after the system has been discharged. Air conditioning refrigerant must be properly discharged into an EPA-approved recovery/recycling unit at a dealer service department or an automotive air conditioning repair facility. Always wear eye protection when disconnecting air conditioning system fittings.**

➡**Note: The receiver-drier should be replaced whenever the compressor is replaced.**

### REMOVAL

1  Have the air conditioning system refrigerant discharged and recovered by an air conditioning technician.

➡**Note: If the compressor is being removed for reasons other than replacement and is working, turn it on for a few minutes on your way to the location that is going to discharge the system.**

2  Disconnect the cable from the negative battery terminal (see Chapter 5, Section 1).

3  Remove the drivebelt (see Chapter 1).

4  Set the parking brake, block the rear wheels and raise the front of the vehicle, supporting it securely on jackstands.

5  Remove the splash shield from under the engine compartment (see Chapter 2A).

6  Disconnect the wiring harness electrical connector for the compressor clutch.

➡**Note: On 2007 and later Acura MDX models, the connector is mounted to the compressor on the end opposite from the pulley.**

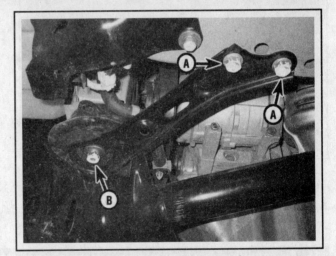

**14.7 Remove the subframe bracket bolts (A), the subframe mounting bolt (B), and remove the bracket**

On all other models, it's mounted on the fan shroud assembly in front of the alternator. Simply follow the wires from the compressor to find the connector.

7  Support the right-side of the subframe with a floor jack, then remove the subframe bracket located below the compressor (see illustration).

➡**Note: The manufacturer recommends that the subframe mounting bolt be replaced with a new one upon installation of the subframe bracket.**

8  Disconnect the refrigerant lines from the compressor. Plug the open fittings to prevent entry of dirt and moisture (see illustration).

9  Remove the compressor mounting bolts (see illustration).

10  Remove the compressor (see illustration).

**14.8 Remove the mounting bolt for the suction line fitting (low side) and the mounting nut for the discharge line fitting (high side) and detach the lines from the compressor**

**14.9 Remove the air conditioning compressor mounting bolts**

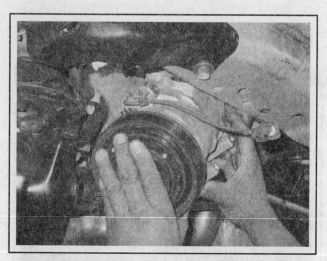

**14.10 Carefully remove the compressor through the opening between the subframe and the body of the vehicle**

11 The compressor mounting bracket mounting bolts are now accessible and the bracket can easily be removed if necessary. The lower alternator mounting bolt must be removed first (see Chapter 5).

## INSTALLATION

12 The clutch may have to be transferred from the old compressor to the new unit.

13 If a new or rebuilt compressor is being installed, follow the accompanying directions (with the compressor) to properly adjust the oil level before installing it.

14 Installation is the reverse of removal, using new O-rings where the line fittings attach to the compressor. Tighten the subframe bracket bolts and subframe mounting bolt to the torque listed in the Chapter 2B Specifications.

15 Reconnect the battery (see Chapter 5, Section 1).

16 Have the system evacuated, recharged and leak tested by the shop that discharged it.

## 15 Air conditioning receiver-drier - removal and installation

♦ Refer to illustrations 15.4, 15.5 and 15.6

❋❋ **WARNING:**

**The air conditioning system is under high pressure. Do not loosen any hose fittings or remove any components until after the system has been discharged. Air conditioning refrigerant must be properly discharged into an EPA-approved recovery/recycling unit at a dealer service department or an automotive air conditioning repair facility. Always wear eye protection when disconnecting air conditioning system fittings.**

➡Note: The receive-drier is built into the air conditioning condenser. This procedure specifically covers removal and installation of the desiccant inside the receiver-drier portion of the condenser.

1 Have the refrigerant discharged and recovered by an air conditioning technician.

2 Disconnect the cable from the negative battery terminal (see Chapter 5, Section 1).

3 Remove the condenser (see Section 16).

4 Remove the cap from the condenser (see illustration).

5 Remove the filter from the condenser (see illustration).

6 Remove the receiver-drier desiccant (see illustration).

7 Installation is the reverse of removal. Be sure to install new O-rings onto the receiver-drier cap. Apply a thin layer of refrigerant oil to the O-rings before installing them.

8 Reconnect the battery (see Chapter 5, Section 1).

9 Have the system evacuated, charged and leak tested by the shop that discharged it.

**15.4 Remove the cap from the condenser**

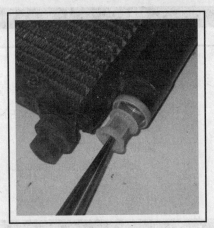

**15.5 Remove the filter from the condenser**

**15.6 Use pliers to remove the desiccant from the condenser**

## 16 Air conditioning condenser - removal and installation

### ※※ WARNING:

The air conditioning system is under high pressure. Do not loosen any hose fittings or remove any components until after the system has been discharged. Air conditioning refrigerant must be properly discharged into an EPA-approved recovery/recycling unit at a dealer service department or an automotive air conditioning repair facility. Always wear eye protection when disconnecting air conditioning system fittings.

### ※※ WARNING:

When replacing entire components, additional refrigerant oil must be added to them. Be sure to read the label on the container before adding any oil to the system; make sure it is compatible with the R-134a system.

**16.8 Remove the suction and discharge lines from the condenser**

## REMOVAL

◆ **Refer to illustration 16.8**

1   Have the refrigerant discharged and recovered by an air conditioning technician.

2   Disconnect the cable from the negative battery terminal (see Chapter 5, Section 1).

3   Remove the plastic cover over the radiator (see illustrations 4.7a and 4.7b).

4   Remove the front bumper cover (see Chapter 11).

5   Remove the hood latch (see Chapter 11).

6   On 2007 and later Acura MDX models, remove the ATF cooler bracket located in front of the condenser.

7   Remove the radiator and condenser mounting brackets (see illustration 6.10).

8   Disconnect the refrigerant lines from the condenser (see illustration). Cap the fittings on the condenser and lines to prevent entry of dirt or moisture.

9   Remove the condenser by lifting it straight up and out of the engine compartment between the radiator and power steering lines or

ATF cooler. Be careful not to damage any of the fins on it or the radiator.

10  Check the rubber mounts on the bottom of the condenser for wear or deterioration and replace them if necessary.

## INSTALLATION

11  Installation is the reverse of removal. Tighten the line fitting mounting bolts to the torque listed in this Chapter's Specifications. If a new condenser is being installed, add 1-1/6 ounces (35 ml) of fresh refrigerant oil. Assemble all connections with new O-rings, lightly lubricated with R-134a refrigerant oil.

➡**Note: On 2007 Acura MDX models, add 1-2/3 ounces (50 ml) of fresh refrigerant oil).**

12  Reconnect the battery (see Chapter 5, Section 1).

13  Have the system evacuated, charged and leak tested by the shop that discharged it.

## Specifications

### General

| | |
|---|---|
| Radiator cap pressure rating | 14 to 18 psi (93 to 123 kPa) |
| Thermostat rating (opening to fully open temperature range) | 169 to 194-degrees F (76 to 90-degrees C) |
| Cooling system capacity | See Chapter 1 |
| Refrigerant type | R-134a |
| Refrigerant capacity | Refer to HVAC specification tag |

### Torque specifications

| | Ft-lbs (unless otherwise indicated) | Nm |
|---|---|---|
| Condenser inlet and outlet bolts | 86 in-lbs | 10 |
| Condenser bracket bolts | 86 in-lbs | 10 |
| Radiator bracket bolts | 86 in-lbs | 10 |
| Thermostat housing cover bolts | 104 in-lbs | 12 |
| Water pump bolts | 104 in-lbs | 12 |

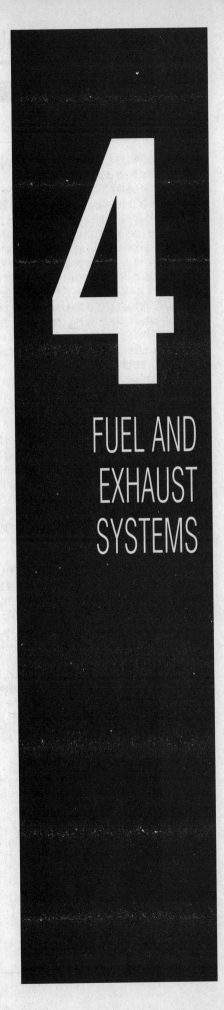

# 4

# FUEL AND EXHAUST SYSTEMS

**Section**

**Reference to other Chapters**

## 1 General information

### AIR INDUCTION SYSTEM

The air induction system consists of the air filter assembly, the air intake duct, the resonator(s), the throttle body and the intake manifold.

The throttle body contains a throttle plate, which regulates the amount of air entering the intake manifold. On 2001 and 2002 Acura and 2003 and 2004 Honda models, the throttle plate is opened and closed by the accelerator cable. The throttle body is also the location of the Throttle Position (TP) sensor, a potentiometer that monitors the opening angle of the throttle plate and sends a variable voltage signal to the Powertrain Control Module (PCM). A Manifold Absolute Pressure (MAP) sensor is located on top of the throttle body.

On 2003 through 2006 Acura and 2005 and later Honda models, the throttle plate is electronically controlled by the Powertrain Control Module (PCM). Even on these models there is an "accelerator cable," but it connects the accelerator pedal to the Accelerator Pedal Position (APP) sensor, which is located on the firewall, not to the throttle body. On these models the APP sensor relays the angle of the throttle link to the PCM, which processes this information and commands a small servo inside the throttle body to open or close the throttle plate. This setup allows the PCM to "fine tune" the position of the throttle plate in response to other inputs besides the position of the accelerator pedal, which means better fuel efficiency and lower emissions.

On 2007 Acura models, the Accelerator Pedal Position (APP) sensor is located at the top of the accelerator pedal, so there is no accelerator cable. But the APP sensor on these models functions just like earlier APP sensors: it tells the PCM the position (angle) of the accelerator pedal, and the PCM uses this data, along with data from other information sensors, to determine the optimal position of the throttle plate for the conditions.

On 2001 and 2002 Acura and 2003 and 2004 Honda models, the Intake Air Temperature (IAT) sensor is located at the left rear corner of the intake manifold. On 2003 and 2004 Acura models the IAT sensor is located on the air intake duct. On 2005 and 2006 Acura and 2005 and later Honda models, the IAT sensor is located on the front of the intake manifold plenum, right next to the throttle body. On 2007 Acura models the IAT sensor is an integral component of the Mass Air Flow (MAF) sensor, which is located on the air filter housing. All of the air induction components (resonator, air filter housing, air intake duct and throttle body) are covered in this Chapter, except for the intake manifold, which is in Chapter 2A. The information sensors (APP, IAT and MAF sensors) and the PCM are in Chapter 6.

### FUEL SYSTEM

The fuel system consists of the fuel tank, an electric fuel pump (located in the fuel tank), the fuel rail and the fuel injectors. Pro-grammed Fuel Injection (PGM-FI) is a "sequential multiport" system, which means that the fuel injectors deliver fuel directly into the intake ports of the cylinders in firing order sequence (1-4-2-5-3-6). Sequential multiport systems provide much better control of the air/fuel mixture ratio than earlier fuel injection systems, and are therefore able to produce more power, better mileage and lower emissions.

2001 and 2002 Acura and 2003 and 2004 Honda models are also equipped with a fuel pulsation damper and a fuel pressure regulator (see Fuel pump and fuel lines below). On 2003 and later Acura and 2005 and later Honda models, there is no fuel pulsation damper. And the fuel pressure regulator is an integral component of the fuel pump/ fuel level sending unit module inside the fuel tank. On these models the pressure regulator is simply spring-loaded; it is not vacuum-operated.

For more information about the PGM-FI system, see Section 11. For more information about the PCM and the information sensors, refer to Chapter 6.

### FUEL PUMP AND FUEL LINES

Fuel is circulated through metal lines located on the underside of the vehicle from the fuel tank to the fuel injection system and, on 2001 and 2002 Acura and 2003 and 2004 Honda models, back to the fuel tank. On 2003 and later Acura and 2005 and later Honda models, there is no fuel return line. An electric fuel pump module is located inside the fuel tank. The fuel level sending unit and the fuel filter are an integral part of the fuel pump assembly.

On 2001 and 2002 Acura and 2003 and 2004 Honda models, a fuel pulsation damper, which is located at the junction of the fuel supply line and the fuel rail, attenuates the hydraulic and acoustic "noise" produced by the fuel pump when it's operating. A fuel pressure regulator, which is installed on the fuel rail at the connection for the fuel return line, maintains the fuel pressure within the specified operating range.

On 2003 and later Acura and 2005 and later Honda models, the fuel pump module also includes an integral fuel pressure regulator, and there is no pulsation damper on these models.

The fuel pump/fuel filter/fuel level sending unit module can be accessed through a cover plate in the floor of the vehicle, and any of the major components can be replaced separately.

### EXHAUST SYSTEM

The exhaust system consists of the exhaust manifolds (on models so equipped - on others, warm-up catalytic converters bolt directly to the cylinder heads), the "Y" pipe that connects both manifolds (or converters) to the under-floor catalytic converter, the catalyst itself, the muffler and the tailpipe. The exhaust manifolds are covered in Chapter 2A, and the catalytic converter is covered in Chapter 6.

## 2  Fuel pressure relief procedure

◆ Refer to illustration 2.2

### ✱✱ WARNING:

Gasoline is extremely flammable, so take extra precautions when you work on any part of the fuel system. Don't smoke or allow open flames or bare light bulbs near the work area, and don't work in a garage where a gas-type appliance (such as a water heater or a clothes dryer) is present. Since gasoline is carcinogenic, wear fuel-resistant gloves when there's a possibility of being exposed to fuel, and, if you spill any fuel on your skin, rinse it off immediately with soap and water. Mop up any spills immediately and do not store fuel-soaked rags where they could ignite. The fuel system is under constant pressure, so, if any fuel lines are to be disconnected, the fuel pressure in the system must be relieved first. When you perform any kind of work on the fuel system, wear safety glasses and have a Class B type fire extinguisher on hand.

**2.2  On 2003 and later Acura and 2005 and later Honda models, the PGM-FI relay 2 is located under the instrument panel, to the right of the steering column, near the diagnostic connector**

### 2001 AND 2002 ACURA AND 2003 AND 2004 HONDA MODELS

1   Pull out the fuel pump fuse, which is located in the passenger compartment fuse and relay panel, under the left end of the dash (refer to the fuse guide in your owner's manual). Then try to start the engine, which will crank but will probably not start because the fuel pump has been disabled. The fuel pressure is now relieved, but there is still fuel in the lines, so be sure to have shop rags handy to mop up any spilled fuel when disconnecting fuel lines.

### 2003 AND LATER ACURA AND 2005 AND LATER HONDA MODELS

2   Pull the PGM-FI relay 2 (see illustration), which is located under the instrument panel, to the right of the steering column, near the diagnostic connector. Try to start the engine, which will crank but will not start because the fuel pump has been disabled. The fuel pressure is now relieved, but there is still fuel in the lines, so be sure to have shop rags handy to mop up any spilled fuel when disconnecting fuel lines.

## 3  Fuel pump/fuel pressure - check

### ✱✱ WARNING:

Gasoline is extremely flammable, so take extra precautions when you work on any part of the fuel system. See the Warning in Section 2.

### GENERAL CHECKS

1   Verify that there is fuel in the fuel tank.
2   Verify that the fuel pump actually runs. Turn the ignition switch to ON - you should hear a brief whirring noise for about two seconds as the pump comes on and pressurizes the system.

➡Note: If you can't hear the pump from inside the vehicle, open the fuel filler neck cap, then have an assistant turn the ignition switch to ON while you listen to the pump through the fuel filler neck.

### FUEL PUMP/FUEL PRESSURE TEST

#### 2001 and 2002 Acura and 2003 and 2004 Honda models
◆ Refer to illustrations 3.3, 3.5, 3.6 and 3.7

3   To measure the fuel pressure on a 2001 and 2002 Acura and a 2003 and 2004 Honda model, you'll need a fuel pressure gauge (see illustration) capable of measuring high fuel pressure. You will also need some fuel hose and a suitable double flare fitting and adapter nut.
4   Before disconnecting any fuel line fittings, relieve system fuel pressure (see Section 2), then disconnect the cable from the negative battery terminal (see Chapter 5, Section 1).
5   Disconnect the fuel supply line from the fuel rail hose at the connection located on the firewall (see illustration).
6   To tee the gauge into the fuel system at this connection, you'll need a double flare fitting and nut (see illustration).

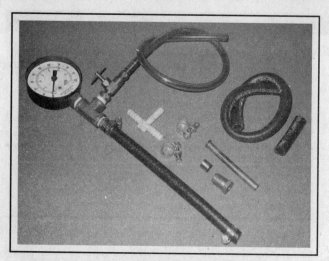

**3.3 To measure the fuel pressure on 2001 and 2002 Acura and 2003 and 2004 Honda models, you'll need a fuel pressure gauge, some extra fuel hose and a suitable double-flare fitting and adapter nut**

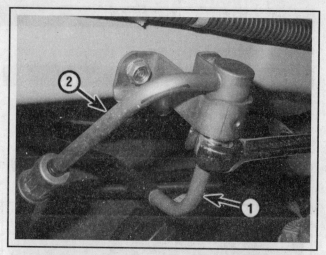

**3.5 Disconnect the fuel supply line (1) from the fuel rail hose (2) at this connection on the firewall; use a flare-nut wrench, if you have one, to protect the nut (2001 and 2002 Acura and 2003 and 2004 Honda models)**

7  Connect the fuel pressure gauge to the fuel system (see illustration).

8  Reconnect the battery.

9  Turn the ignition switch to ON (don't start the engine yet) with the air conditioning off. The fuel pump should run for about two seconds - pressure should register on the gauge and should hold steady.

10  Start the engine and let it warm up until it's idling at its normal operating temperature.

11  Note the indicated fuel pressure reading on the gauge and compare it with the operating range listed in this Chapter's Specifications. Now disconnect the vacuum hose from the fuel pressure regulator (see Section 15) - the pressure reading should increase.

12  If the indicated fuel pressure doesn't go up when you disconnect the vacuum line from the regulator, apply vacuum to the pressure regulator with a hand-held vacuum pump and note what happens.

13  If the fuel pressure drops, the regulator is okay, but there's probably a crack or tear in the vacuum hose. Replace the vacuum hose and retest.

14  If the pressure still doesn't go down with the new vacuum hose connected, check for vacuum at the hose using a vacuum gauge. If no vacuum is present, the port that the hose connects to is probably clogged.

15  If the indicated fuel pressure is higher than the specified range with the vacuum hose connected, verify that the fuel pressure regulator is receiving a good vacuum signal by putting your finger over the regulator end of the vacuum hose, or by checking it with a vacuum gauge. Vacuum should fluctuate up and down in accordance with the increase or decrease in the engine rpm (at idle the vacuum is high, but as engine speed increases the vacuum signal becomes weaker). If vacuum is pres-

**3.6 To tee into the fuel lines at this connection, you'll need a double-flare fitting and a suitable adapter nut (2001 and 2002 Acura and 2003 and 2004 Honda models)**

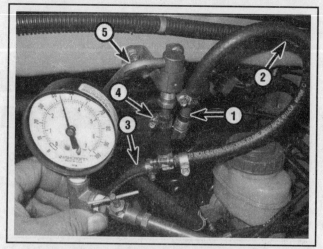

**3.7 Here's what your fuel pressure gauge test rig should look like when it's correctly hooked up (2001 and 2002 Acura and 2003 and 2004 Honda models):**

*1  This is the fuel that you disconnected in Step 5)*
*2  Clamp one end of your gauge hose to No. 1*
*3  This is the hose that connects the fuel pressure gauge to the tee fitting*
*4  Tee fitting-to-firewall connection (5) hose*
*5  Fuel line leading to the fuel rail*

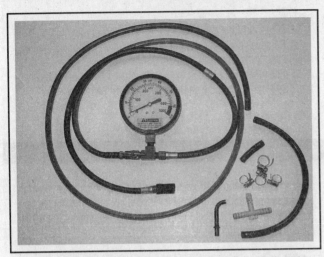

**3.21 To measure the fuel pressure on 2003 and later Acura and 2005 and later Honda models, you'll need an adapter setup that will connect the gauge between the two halves of the quick-connect fitting at the firewall**

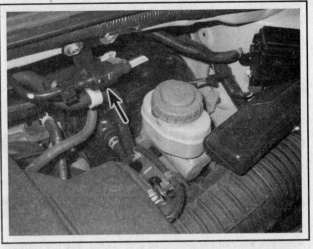

**3.23 This quick-connect fitting on the firewall is the easiest place to tee your fuel pressure gauge into the fuel system on 2003 and later Acura and 2005 and later Honda models**

ent, check for a kinked, pinched or clogged fuel return hose or line. If the return line is OK, replace the regulator.

16 If the indicated fuel pressure is lower than the specified range, a fuel line might be leaking or the fuel filter might be clogged. Inspect the fuel lines and replace any damaged lines. To rule out the possibility of a clogged fuel filter, replace the filter (see Sections 5 and 6). The fuel filter is an integral component of the fuel pump/fuel level sending unit assembly, so you must remove the fuel pump/fuel level sending unit module to replace the filter.

17 If the indicated fuel pressure is still lower than the specified range, start the engine and pinch off the return line. If the pressure now rises above the specified operating range, the regulator is not closing fully. Replace it (see Section 15).

18 If the indicated fuel pressure is still lower than the specified range even when you pinch off the fuel return line, one or more of the fuel injectors or injector O-rings might be leaking (see Section 16), or the fuel pump might be faulty (see Sections 5 and 6). Replace the defective component(s) and retest.

19 After the test is complete, relieve the system fuel pressure (see Section 2), then disconnect the cable from the negative battery terminal.

20 Remove your fuel pressure testing rig, then reconnect the fuel supply line to the connection at the firewall. Reconnect the cable to the negative battery terminal (see Chapter 5, Section 1). Start the engine and check for fuel leaks.

## 2003 and later Acura and 2005 and later Honda models

▶ **Refer to illustrations 3.21, 3.23 and 3.24**

21 To measure the fuel pressure on 2003 and later Acura and 2005 and later Honda models, you'll need a fuel pressure gauge capable of measuring high fuel pressure. To tee the gauge into the fuel system at the connection on the firewall, you'll need an adapter setup that will connect the gauge between the two halves of the quick-connect fitting (see illustration).

22 Before disconnecting any fuel line fittings, relieve system fuel pressure (see Section 2), then disconnect the cable from the negative battery terminal (see Chapter 5, Section 1).

23 Disconnect the fuel supply line quick-connect fitting on the firewall (see illustration).

**3.24 Here's what your fuel pressure test rig should look like when it's correctly hooked up (2003 and later Acura and 2005 and later Honda models)**

➡ **Note: If you're unfamiliar with quick-connect fittings, refer to Section 4.**

24 Connect the fuel pressure gauge to the fuel system (see illustration).

25 Reconnect the battery.

26 Turn the ignition switch to ON (don't start the engine yet) with the air conditioning off. The fuel pump should run for about two seconds, and pressure should register on the gauge and should hold steady.

27 Start the engine and let it warm up until it's idling at its normal operating temperature.

28 Note the indicated fuel pressure reading on the gauge and compare it with the operating range listed in this Chapter's Specifications.

29 If the indicated pressure is within the specified range, the system is operating correctly.

30 If the indicated pressure is lower than the specified range, a fuel line might be leaking or the fuel filter might be clogged. Inspect the fuel lines and replace any damaged lines. To rule out the possibility of a clogged fuel filter, replace the filter (see Sections 5 and 6). The fuel

filter is an integral component of the fuel pump/fuel level sending unit assembly, so you must remove the fuel pump/fuel level sending unit module to replace the filter.

31 If the indicated pressure is still outside the specified range, replace the fuel pressure regulator (see Section 15).

32 After the test is complete, relieve the system fuel pressure (see Section 2).

33 Disconnect the cable from the negative battery terminal.

34 Remove your fuel pressure testing rig, then reconnect the fuel supply line to the connection at the firewall.

35 Reconnect the cable to the negative battery terminal (see Chapter 5, Section 1). Start the engine and check for fuel leaks.

## 4   Fuel lines and fittings - general information

▶ **Refer to illustration 4.2**

> **⁑⁑ WARNING:**
>
> **Gasoline is extremely flammable, so take extra precautions when you work on any part of the fuel system. See the Warning in Section 2.**

1   Always relieve the fuel pressure before servicing fuel lines or fittings (see Section 2), then disconnect the cable from the negative battery terminal (see Chapter 5, Section 1) before proceeding.

2   The fuel supply and return lines connect the fuel pump in the fuel tank to the fuel rail on the engine. The Evaporative Emission (EVAP) system lines connect the fuel tank to the EVAP canister and connect the canister to the intake manifold. All lines are secured to the underbody with small metal brackets that are bolted to the vehicle floorpan. The lines are attached to these metal brackets by plastic clips that are easy to detach from the brackets (see illustration).

3   Whenever you're working under the vehicle, be sure to inspect all fuel and evaporative emission lines for leaks, kinks, dents and other damage. Always replace a damaged fuel or EVAP line immediately. Leaking fuel and EVAP lines will result in loss of fuel and excessive air pollution (the leaking raw fuel emits unburned hydrocarbon vapors into the atmosphere).

4   If you find signs of dirt in the lines during disassembly, disconnect all lines and blow them out with compressed air. Inspect the fuel strainer on the fuel pump pick-up unit (see Sections 5 and 6) for dam-

age and deterioration. And inspect the fuel filter, which is an integral component of the fuel pump/fuel level sending unit module (see Sections 5 and 6). Also inspect the fuel strainers, if equipped, in the fuel injectors (see Section 16).

### STEEL TUBING

5   Because fuel lines used on fuel-injected vehicles are under fairly high pressure, it is critical that they be replaced with lines of equivalent specification. If you have to replace a fuel or EVAP line, use only steel tubing that meets the manufacturer's specifications. Don't use copper or aluminum tubing to replace steel tubing. These materials cannot withstand normal vehicle vibration.

6   Some steel fuel lines have threaded fittings. When loosening these fittings to service or replace components:

a) *Always hold the stationary fitting with a wrench while turning the tube nut (this will prevent the line from twisting).*

b) *If you're going to replace one of these fittings, use original equipment parts or parts that meet original equipment standards.*

### PLASTIC TUBING

7   Some fuel lines - between the fuel supply and return pipes of the fuel pump and the front of the fuel tank, for example - are plastic. If you ever have to replace either line, use only the original equipment plastic tubing.

> **⁑⁑ CAUTION:**
>
> **When removing or installing plastic fuel line tubing, be careful not to bend or twist it too much, which can damage it. And damaged fuel lines MUST be replaced! Also, be aware that the plastic fuel tubing is NOT heat resistant, so keep it away from excessive heat. Nor is it acid-proof, so don't wipe it off with a shop rag that has been used to wipe off battery electrolyte. If you accidentally spill or wipe electrolyte on plastic fuel tubing, replace the tubing.**

### FLEXIBLE HOSES

> **⁑⁑ WARNING:**
>
> **Use only original equipment replacement hoses or their equivalent. Unapproved hoses might fail when subjected to the high operating pressures of the fuel system.**

**4.2  The EVAP and fuel lines are secured to the underside of the vehicle by a series of brackets and plastic clips; to release the plastic clip from the bracket, squeeze these mounting tabs together and push out the bracket, which can then be unclipped from the lines**

8   Don't route fuel hoses (or metal lines) within four inches of the exhaust system or within ten inches of the catalytic converter. Make

sure that no rubber hoses are installed directly against the vehicle, particularly in places where there is any vibration. If allowed to touch some vibrating part of the vehicle, a hose can easily become chafed and it might start leaking. A good rule of thumb is to maintain a minimum of 1/4-inch clearance around a hose (or metal line) to prevent contact with the vehicle underbody.

## DISCONNECTING AND RECONNECTING FUEL SYSTEM FITTINGS

9  Four types of fittings are used on the fuel system. There is one threaded fitting at the connection on the firewall and one banjo-type fitting at the fuel pulsation damper. These two fittings are covered in Section 3 (threaded fitting) and Section 14 (banjo fitting). The rest of the fittings in the fuel system consist of conventional spring-type hose clamps and quick-connect fittings. Spring-type hose clamps are used to connect fuel hoses on the (low-pressure) return side of the system, i.e. between the fuel pressure regulator and the fuel tank. Quick-connect fittings are used to connect lines on the (high-pressure) supply side of the system, such as the connections at the fuel pump (supply and return line connections).

### Conventional spring-type hose clamps

▸ **Refer to illustration 4.13**

10  Relieve the system fuel pressure (see Section 2), then disconnect the cable from the negative battery terminal (see Chapter 5, Section 1).

11  To disconnect a spring-type hose clamp, simply squeeze the two ends together with a pair of pliers to loosen the clamp, then slide the clamp away from the pipe to which the hose is attached.

12  If a spring-type hose clamp feels easy to squeeze open, or if it's obviously not clamping the hose tightly against the metal pipe to which the hose is connected, replace the clamp.

13  When installing spring-type hose clamps, make sure to slide the hose onto the pipe to which you're connecting it up to the second raised ridge on the pipe, then slide the hose clamp down the hose until it's centered between the two ridges (see illustration).

14  Reconnect the cable to the negative battery cable (see Chapter 5, Section 1).

15  Start the engine and verify that no fuel is leaking out at the connection you just reconnected. If there's a leak, either the clamp is weak or it's not centered correctly between the two raised ridges on the metal line or pipe to which you connected the fuel hose. Or the hose itself is leaking because it's cracked or torn where the clamp squeezes down on it.

### Quick-connect fittings

▸ **Refer to illustrations 4.16a, 4.16b and 4.16c**

> ❈❈ **CAUTION:**
>
> **When disconnecting or reconnecting quick-connect fittings, be careful not to bend or twist them excessively, or they will be damaged and will have to be replaced. Also, be aware that the quick-connect fittings are NOT heat resistant, so keep them away from excessive heat. Nor are they acid-proof, so don't wipe them off with a shop rag that has been used to wipe off battery electrolyte. If you accidentally spill or wipe electrolyte on quick-connect fittings, replace them.**

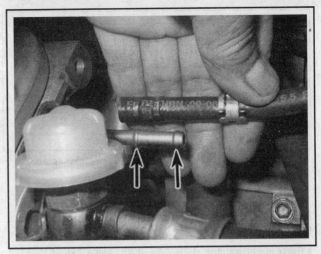

**4.13  Slide the hose onto the metal line up to the second raised ridge on the line or pipe (left arrow), then center the clamp between the two ridges**

➡Note: There are three places on the vehicle where quick-connect fittings are used: at the fuel pump, at the front of the fuel tank and in the engine compartment. There are quick-connect fittings at the supply and (on 2001 and 2002 Acura and 2003 and 2004 Honda models) the return lines at the fuel pump. Quick-connect fittings are also used at the connection(s) in front of the tank where the fuel supply line from the pump (and, if equipped, the return line to the pump) connect to the line(s) leading under the vehicle to the engine compartment (these are the connections that you must disconnect when removing the fuel tank). The third place that you will find quick-connect fittings is the engine compartment. On 2003 and later Acura and 2005 and later Honda models, you'll find a quick-connect fitting on the firewall where the fuel supply line from underneath the vehicle connects to the fuel supply hose, and at the other end of the fuel supply hose where it connects to the fuel rail crossover line. And the crossover line itself is connected to the front fuel rail by a third quick-connect fitting.

16  You must replace the quick-connect fitting retainers whenever you disconnect a quick-connect fitting. It is critical that you use the correct replacement retainer, which depends on the manufacturer of the tubing and the end of the tube (fuel pump end or "pipe" end) on which you're installing it, because the retainers are not all the same diameter. To help you distinguish the various diameter retainers, Honda color codes them (see illustrations).

| Fuel line | Manufacturer | Line color | Retainer color |
|---|---|---|---|
| **Supply line** | | | |
| Fuel pump end | Tokai | Black | Orange |
| Forward end | Tokai | Black | Blue green |
| **Return line** | | | |
| Forward end | Tokai | Black | Green |
| Fuel pump end | Tokai | Black | Blue green |

**4.16a  Quick-connect fitting color code (2002 and 2002 Acura and 2003 and 2004 Honda models)**

| Fitting location | Manufacturer | Retainer color | Line diameter |
|---|---|---|---|
| Engine compartment | Tokai | Blue green | 0.31 in (8.0 mm) |
| Fuel pump supply line | | | |
| Fuel pump end | Tokai | Orange | 0.37 in (9.5 mm) |
| Forward end | Tokai | Blue green | 0.31 in (8.0 mm) |
| EVAP purge line | Tokai | Orange | 0.37 in (9.5 mm) |

**4.16b  Quick-connect fitting color code (2003 through 2006 Acura and 2005 and later Honda models)**

| Fitting location | Manufacturer | Retainer color | Line diameter |
|---|---|---|---|
| Engine compartment | Tokai | Blue green | 0.31 in (8.0 mm) |
| Fuel pump supply line | | | |
| Fuel pump end | TI Automotive | Blue | 0.37 in (9.5 mm) |
| Forward end | TI Automotive | Gray | 0.31 in (8.0 mm) |
| Front left wheel well | | | |
| Two lower fittings | Tokai | Orange | 0.37 in (9.5 mm) |
| Upper fitting | Tokai | Natural | 0.47 in (12 mm) |
| EVAP fuel vapor tube | | | |
| Canister end | TI Automotive | Blue | 0.37 in (9.5 mm) |
| Vapor line end | TI Automotive | Natural | 0.47 in (12 mm) |

**4.16c  Quick-connect fitting color code (2007 Acura models)**

## Quick-connect fittings at the fuel pump and in front of the fuel tank

♦ Refer to illustrations, 4.20, 4.24, 4.25a and 4.25b

➡Note: You'll find quick-connect fittings like these on all models.

17 The following procedure shows how to disconnect and reconnect the quick-connect fittings at the fuel pump, but the procedure for disconnecting and reconnecting quick-connect fittings at the front of the fuel tank is identical. The second procedure here shows how to disconnect a typical quick-connect fitting at the fuel rail on 2003 and later Acura and 2005 and later Honda models.

18 Relieve the system fuel pressure (see Section 2), then disconnect the cable from the negative battery terminal (see Chapter 5, Section 1).

19 To disconnect the fuel line quick-connect fittings at the fuel pump, you'll have to remove the second-row seats, the carpet (see Chapter 11) and the fuel pump access cover (see Section 5). To access the quick-connect fittings at the front of the fuel tank, raise the vehicle and place it securely on jackstands.

20 Holding the black side of the fitting with one hand, squeeze the retainer tabs on the white part of the fitting with your other hand to release the tabs (see illustration), then pull the two halves of the fitting apart.

21 Inspect the contact surface of the line for dirt and damage.

22 Cover the disconnected ends of the fitting with plastic bags to keep out dirt and moisture.

23 Remove the old retainer from the fitting.

24 Inspect the O-ring inside the bore of the fitting (see illustration).

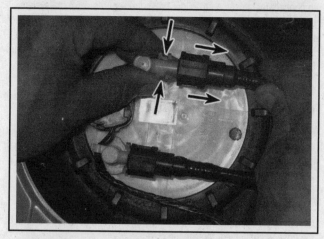

**4.20  To disconnect a quick-connect fitting, squeeze the retainer tabs on the white part of the fitting and pull on the black part of the fitting until the two halves are separated (2001 and 2002 Acura and 2003 and 2004 Honda models)**

If it's cracked, torn or otherwise damaged, replace it.

25 Install a new retainer in the female side of the fitting (see illustration). Be sure to align the locking pawls of the retainer with the grooves in the side of the connector (see illustration).

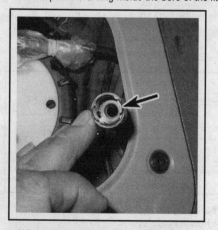

**4.24  Inspect this O-ring inside the fitting; if it's cracked, torn or damaged, replace it (2001 and 2002 Acura and 2003 and 2004 Honda models)**

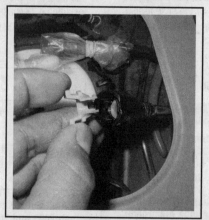

**4.25a  Install a new retainer in the female side of the fitting . . .**

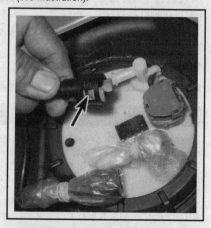

**4.25b  . . . and align the retainer locking pawls with the grooves in the connector (2001 and 2002 Acura and 2003 and 2004 Honda models)**

**4.33a Squeeze these two retainer tangs . . .**

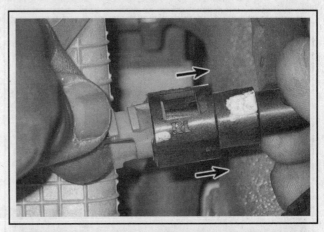

**4.33b . . . and pull the quick-connect fitting off the fuel pipe (2003 and later Acura and 2005 and later Honda models)**

26 Press the two halves of the quick-connect fitting together until both retainer tabs lock with a clicking sound.

27 Verify that the quick-connect fitting is correctly reconnected by trying to pull the two halves of the connector apart.

28 Reconnect the cable to the negative battery terminal (see Chapter 5, Section 1).

29 Start the engine and check for leaks.

30 If you're servicing the quick-connect fittings at the fuel pump, reinstall the access cover (see Section 5), install the carpet (see Chapter 11) and install the second-row seats. If you're servicing the fittings in front of the tank, lower the vehicle.

**Quick-connect fittings in the engine compartment**

◆ Refer to illustrations 4.33a, 4.33b and 4.34

➡Note: You'll find these quick-connect fittings on 2003 and later Acura and 2005 and later Honda models. The photos accompanying this section depict the quick-connect fitting used to connect the forward end of the fuel rail crossover line to the front fuel rail, but the fittings used to connect the fuel supply hose to the fuel supply line at the firewall and to the fuel rail crossover line are identical.

31 Relieve the system fuel pressure (see Section 2), then disconnect the cable from the negative battery terminal (see Chapter 5, Section 1).

32 Remove the protective cover from the quick connect fitting by pulling it straight off.

33 Squeeze the two retainer tangs toward the fuel pipe and pull the quick-connect fitting off the fuel pipe (see illustrations).

34 Before reconnecting a quick-connect fitting, always inspect the

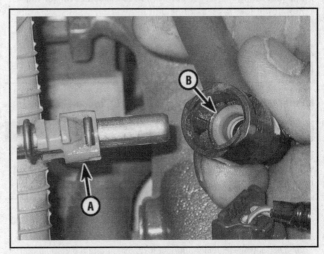

**4.34 Before reconnecting a quick-connect fitting, always inspect the condition of the retainer (A) and the O-ring (B) inside the fitting. If either part is cracked, torn or otherwise deteriorated, replace it**

condition of the retainer and the O-ring inside the fitting (see illustration). If either part is cracked, torn or otherwise deteriorated, replace it (and it's a good idea to just replace these two parts even if they look in good shape)

35 Reconnection is the reverse of disconnection. Refer to Steps 21 through 29.

---

## 5   Fuel pump/fuel level sending unit module - removal and installation

◆ Refer to illustration 5.3

1 Detach the cable from the negative battery terminal (see Chapter 5, Section 1).

2 Relieve the fuel system pressure (see Section 2).

3 Remove the driver's side second-row seat (see Chapter 11), then

remove the carpet from the indicated area underneath. There are two sets of perforations in the carpeting under the seat. The smaller one (which might already be cut), is the flap for accessing the electrical connector for the fuel pump/fuel level sending unit. The larger perforation is for removing the fuel pump/fuel level sending unit. Cut along the larger perforation (see illustration) and peel back the flap.

**5.3  Cut along the larger perforation to access cover for the fuel pump/fuel level sending unit module**

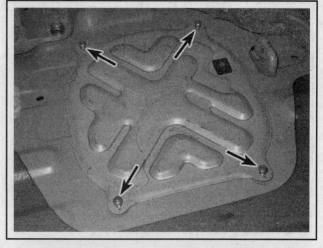

**5.4  To detach the fuel pump access cover, remove these screws (2001 and 2002 Acura and 2003 and 2004 models)**

## 2001 AND 2002 ACURA AND 2003 AND 2004 HONDA MODELS

▶ Refer to illustrations 5.4, 5.5, 5.7a, 5.7b, 5.8 and 5.9

### ✳✳ WARNING:

Gasoline is extremely flammable, so take extra precautions when you work on any part of the fuel system. See the Warning in Section 2.

4   Remove the fuel pump access cover screws (see illustration) and remove the fuel pump access cover.

5   Disconnect the fuel pump/fuel level sending unit electrical connector (see illustration).

6   Disconnect the quick-connect fittings for the fuel supply and return lines (see Section 4) and set the fuel lines aside. Be sure to cover the ends of the fittings with plastic bags to prevent dirt and moisture from entering the system.

**5.5  Disconnect the electrical connector from the fuel pump/fuel level sending unit (2001 and 2002 Acura and 2003 and 2004 models)**

**5.7a  This is the special Honda tool (available through dealer parts departments, specialty tool manufacturers and some auto parts stores) for loosening and tightening the fuel pump/fuel level sending unit locknut; if you can obtain one, this is the way to go because it won't damage the plastic locknut**

**5.7b  If you're unable to obtain the special Honda tool, you can use a large pair of pliers as shown (we don't recommend this method because it can tear up the locknut) (2001 and 2002 Acura and 2003 and 2004 Honda models)**

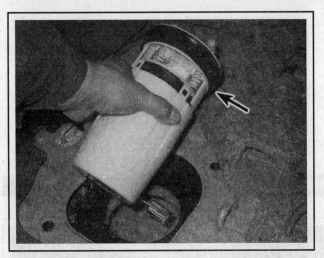

**5.8 Carefully remove the fuel pump/fuel level sending unit module from the tank, then inspect the condition of the seal around the top of the module; if the seal is cracked, torn or deteriorated, replace it (2001 and 2002 Acura and 2003 and 2004 Honda models)**

**5.9 Install the seal into the hole for the fuel pump/fuel level sending module before installing the module; if you try to install the seal by putting it on the module, it might become pinched or distorted when you try to push the module down into the hole (2001 and 2002 Acura and 2003 and 2004 Honda models)**

7   Remove the fuel pump/fuel level sending unit locknut (see illustrations).

8   Remove the fuel pump/fuel level sending unit module from the tank (see illustration). Be sure to inspect the seal at the top of the module for cracks, tears and deterioration. If it's damaged, replace it.

9   When installing the fuel pump/fuel level sending unit module, install the seal in the hole first (see illustration). Don't try to install it

with the module, which might cause it to become pinched or distorted.

10  Installation is the reverse of removal.

11  Before installing the access plate, carpeting and seat, reconnect the cable to the negative terminal of the battery (see Chapter 5, Section 1), start the engine and check for fuel leaks.

## 2003 AND LATER ACURA AND 2005 AND LATER HONDA MODELS

▶ **Refer to illustrations 5.12a, 5.12b and 5.13**

12  Peel off the rubber weather seal grommet from the fuel pump access cover and disconnect the electrical connector from the fuel pump/fuel level sending unit (see illustrations).

13  Remove the fuel pump access cover screws (see illustration), then remove the access cover.

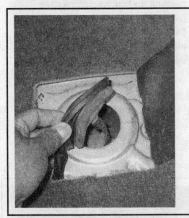

**5.12a  Peel out the rubber weather seal grommet . . .**

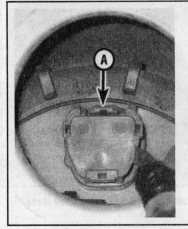

**5.12b  . . . depress this release tab (A) and disconnect the electrical connector from the fuel pump/ fuel level sending unit (2003 and later Acura and 2005 and later Honda models)**

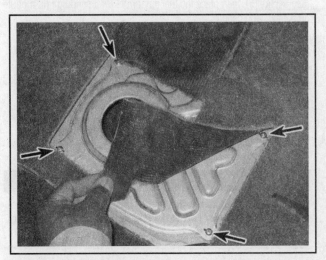

**5.13  Remove the fuel pump access cover screws and remove the access cover (2003 and later Acura and 2005 and later Honda models)**

14 Disconnect the fuel line quick-connect fitting from the fuel pump (see Section 4). Be sure to cover the ends of the fitting with plastic bags to prevent dirt and moisture from entering the system.

15 Unscrew the big locknut that secures the fuel pump to the tank (see illustrations 5.7a and 5.7b).

16 Place some clean shop rags around the access hole, then remove the fuel pump/fuel level sending unit module from the fuel tank.

17 Installation is the reverse of removal. When installing the fuel pump/fuel level sending unit module, install the seal in the hole first (see illustration 5.9). Don't try to install it with the module, which might cause it to become pinched or distorted.

18 Before installing the access plate, carpeting and seat, reconnect the cable to the negative terminal of the battery (see Chapter 5, Section 1), start the engine and check for fuel leaks.

## 6   Fuel pump/fuel filter/fuel level sending unit module - replacement

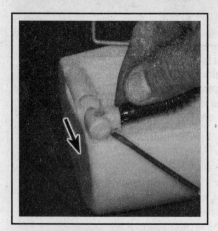

6.4  To disconnect the return hose from the case, release the locking tab with a small screwdriver and pull off the hose fitting (2001 and 2002 Acura and 2003 and 2004 Honda models)

6.5a  To disconnect the fuel pump electrical connector, release this locking tab with a small screwdriver and pull out the connector (2001 and 2002 Acura and 2003 and 2004 Honda models)

6.5b  To disconnect the fuel level sending unit connector, release this locking tab, then pull out the connector with a pair of needle-nose pliers (2001 and 2002 Acura and 2003 and 2004 Honda models)

1   Relieve the system fuel pressure (see Section 2).

2   Disconnect the cable from the negative battery terminal (see Chapter 5, Section 1).

3   Remove the fuel pump/fuel level sending unit from the fuel tank (see Section 5), then place the fuel pump/fuel level sending unit module on a clean workbench.

### 2001 AND 2002 ACURA AND 2003 AND 2004 HONDA MODELS

#### Disassembly

▶ Refer to illustrations 6.4, 6.5a, 6.5b, 6.6a, 6.6b, 6.6c, 6.7, 6.8, 6.9, 6.10, 6.11a, 6.11b, 6.12 and 6.13

### ❇❇ WARNING:

Gasoline is extremely flammable, so take extra precautions when you work on any part of the fuel system. See the Warning in Section 2.

4   Disconnect the return hose from the case (see illustration).

5   Disconnect the electrical connectors for the fuel pump and for the fuel level sending unit (see illustrations).

6   Separate the bracket and the case (see illustrations).

7   Disconnect the ground wire from its terminal on the side of the fuel filter housing (see illustration).

8   Disconnect the fuel filter outlet tube from the fuel filter housing (see illustration).

6.6a  To separate the bracket from the case, release these two locking tabs . . .

6.6b . . . disengage the fuel pump wiring harness from the wire harness guide and release this locking tab . . .

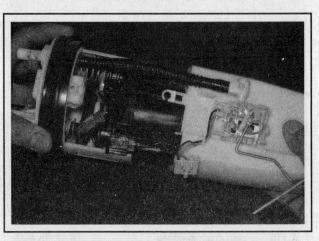

6.6c . . . and pull the bracket and case apart (2001 and 2002 Acura and 2003 and 2004 Honda models)

6.7 To disconnect the ground wire from its terminal on the side of the fuel filter housing, push down the locking tab on the end of the ground wire with a small screwdriver and carefully pull out the ground wire (2001 and 2002 Acura and 2003 and 2004 Honda models)

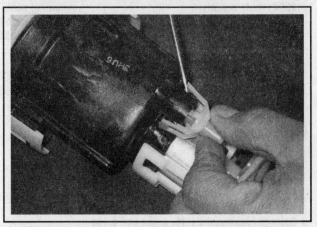

6.8 To detach the outlet tube from the fuel filter housing, pry the locking tabs loose and pull it off (2001 and 2002 Acura and 2003 and 2004 Honda models)

9  Remove the pump retainer (see illustration).

10  Remove the rubber isolator (see illustration).

11  Separate the fuel pump from the fuel filter housing (see illustrations). If you're simply replacing the fuel filter, no further disassembly is

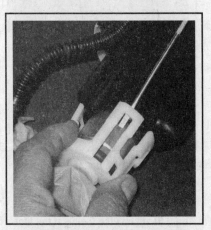

6.9 To detach the pump retainer, pry the locking tabs loose and pull it off (2001 and 2002 Acura and 2003 and 2004 Honda models)

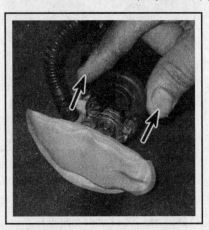

6.10 To remove the rubber isolator, simply pull it off (2001 and 2002 Acura and 2003 and 2004 Honda models)

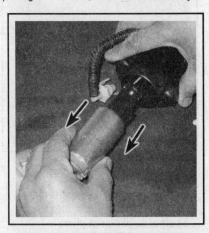

6.11a To remove the fuel pump from the fuel filter housing, pull it out . . .

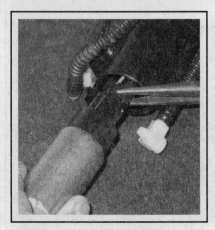

**6.11b** . . . and disconnect the electrical connector from the pump (2001 and 2002 Acura and 2003 and 2004 Honda models)

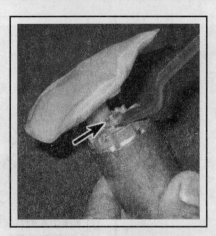

**6.12** To detach the fuel inlet "sock" (strainer) from the fuel pump, pry it off right here, at the flange for the mounting stud. Use a new retainer clip for installation (2001 and 2002 Acura and 2003 and 2004 Honda models)

**6.13** To detach the fuel level sending unit from the case, depress the locking tang with a small screwdriver and slide the sending unit to the left as indicated (2001 and 2002 Acura and 2003 and 2004 Honda models)

necessary. (The fuel filter is an integral component of the filter housing; the filter and housing are not available separately.) However, we strongly recommend cleaning the fuel inlet strainer (see Steps 14 and 15) and replacing the fuel filter inlet and outlet O-rings (see Step 16).

12 Remove the fuel inlet "sock" (strainer) from the fuel pump (see illustration).

13 Remove the fuel level sending unit from the case (see illustration).

## Reassembly

▶ **Refer to illustrations 6.15, 6.16a and 6.16b**

14 Before reassembling the fuel pump, fuel filter and fuel level sending unit, wash the fuel strainer thoroughly in clean solvent. If it's impossible to clean, replace it.

15 When installing the strainer on the fuel pump (see illustration), use a new retainer and make sure that it's firmly seated.

16 Before installing the fuel pump in the fuel filter housing, inspect the condition of the fuel filter inlet and outlet O-rings (see illustration). If either O-ring is cracked, torn or deteriorated, replace it. Also make sure that the spacer at the top of the pump is in place (see illustration). This spacer insures a tight fit between the pump outlet pipe and the fuel filter inlet O-ring. If the spacer is damaged or missing, replace it.

17 Reassembly is otherwise the reverse of disassembly, but stop when you're done installing the pump. Before installing the fuel pump access cover, reconnect the cable to the negative battery terminal (see Chapter 5, Section 1), start the engine and check for fuel leaks at the pump fuel line connections. If there are no leaks, install the access cover, the carpet and the second-row seat.

**6.15** To install the strainer on the fuel pump, align the hole in the strainer mounting flange with the locator pin on the pump, then use a pair of needle-nose pliers to push against these lugs to push the strainer into the pump (2001 and 2002 Acura and 2003 and 2004 Honda models)

**6.16a** Inspect the O-rings for the fuel filter inlet and outlet; if either O-ring is cracked, torn or deteriorated, replace it (2001 and 2002 Acura and 2003 and 2004 Honda models)

**6.16b** Make sure that the spacer at the top of the pump is in place and in good condition; without this spacer, the pump outlet pipe will not be a tight fit against the O-ring at the fuel filter inlet (2001 and 2002 Acura and 2003 and 2004 Honda models)

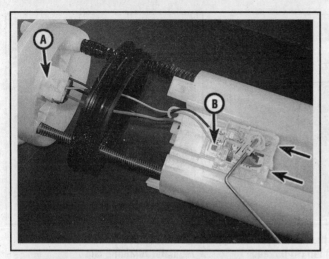

6.18  Depress the release tab (A) and disconnect the electrical connector, then depress the locking lug (B) with the screwdriver and push the sending unit toward the upper end of the housing with your thumbs (2003 and later Acura and 2005 and later Honda models)

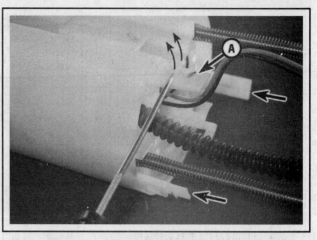

6.19  The case is secured to the fuel pump/fuel filter housing by three slotted lock tabs. To disengage each lock tab from its locking lug (A), carefully pry the tab off the lug. When all three lock tabs are freed from their lugs, pull off the case (2003 and later Acura and 2005 and later Honda models)

## 2003 AND LATER ACURA AND 2005 AND LATER HONDA MODELS

▶ Refer to illustrations 6.18, 6.19, 6.20a, 6.20b, 6.21, 6.22a, 6.22b, 6.23a, 6.23b, 6.25a, 6.25b and 6.27

18  Disconnect the electrical connector for the fuel level sending unit, then detach the fuel level sending unit from the fuel filter housing (see illustration).

19  Remove the case from the fuel pump/fuel filter housing (see illustration).

20  Disconnect the fuel supply line fitting from the fuel pump/fuel filter housing (see illustration). Remove and discard the O-ring for the fuel supply line fitting (see illustration). This O-ring must be replaced when reassembling the pump module.

21  Disconnect the electrical connectors for the fuel pump wiring harness and detach the pump ground wire from the fuel pump/fuel filter housing (see illustration).

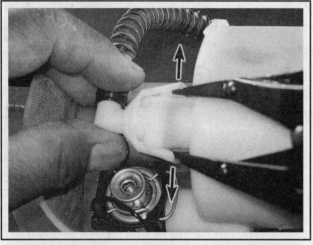

6.20a  To disconnect the fuel supply line fitting from the fuel pump/fuel filter housing, spread these two locking tangs apart and pull off the fitting (2003 and later Acura and 2005 and later Honda models)

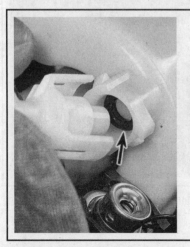

6.20b  Inspect the fuel supply line fitting O-ring. Replace it if it's cracked, torn or deteriorated (2003 and later Acura and 2005 and later Honda models)

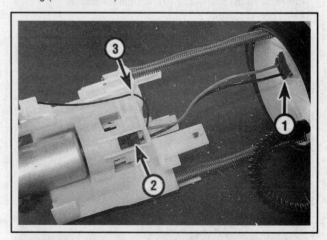

6.21  Disconnect the fuel pump electrical connectors from the underside of the pump module mounting flange (1) and from the upper end of the pump/filter housing (2), then detach pump ground wire from the clip (3) on the pump/filter housing (2003 and later Acura and 2005 and later Honda models)

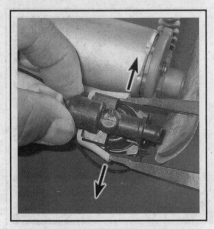

6.22a To remove the fuel pressure regulator housing from the fuel pump/ fuel filter housing, spread these two locking tangs apart . . .

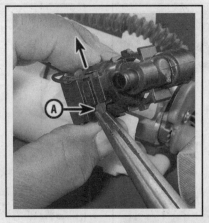

6.22b . . . pull out the housing, squeeze the locking tab (A) flat and push the fuel pump ground wire up and out of the regulator housing

6.23a Remove the fuel pressure regulator retaining clip . . .

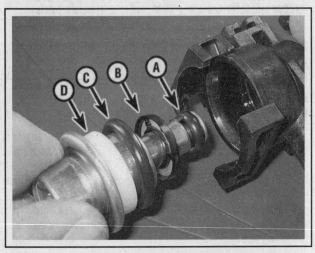

6.23b . . . and remove the fuel pressure regulator from the housing. Be sure to use new O-rings (A and C) when installing the regulator. Inspect the condition of the mesh filter screen (B) and spacer (D). If either of them is damaged, replace it

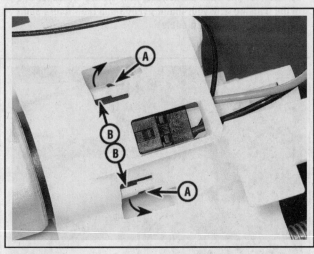

6.25a The fuel pump is secured to the pump/filter housing by a pair of locking lugs (A). To disengage the two slotted lock tabs (B) from the lugs, carefully pry them away from the pump . . .

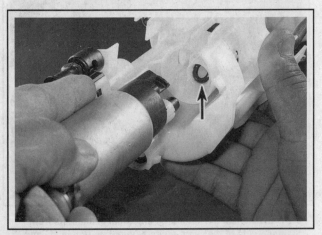

6.25b . . . and pull the pump out of the housing. Remove and discard the pump O-ring inside the upper end of the pump recess. This O-ring must be replaced

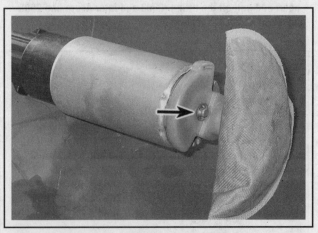

6.27 To detach the suction filter, carefully pry off this retainer clip

22 Remove the fuel pressure regulator housing (see illustration), then disconnect the fuel pump ground wire from the regulator housing (see illustration).

23 Remove the fuel pressure regulator retaining clip (see illustration) and pull the regulator out of the housing (see illustration).

24 Remove and discard the fuel pressure regulator O-rings (see illustration 6.23b). This O-ring must be replaced when reassembling the pump module. Inspect the condition of the spacer and the mesh filter screen. If either of these parts is damaged, replace it.

25 Remove the fuel pump (see illustrations).

26 Remove and discard the fuel pump O-ring inside the upper end of the pump recess (see illustration 6.25b). This O-ring must be replaced when reassembling the pump module.

27 Remove the suction filter retainer clip (see illustration) and remove the suction filter from the fuel pump.

28 Before reassembling the fuel pump, fuel filter and fuel level sending unit, wash the fuel strainer thoroughly in clean solvent. If it's impossible to clean, replace it.

29 Reassembly is the reverse of disassembly. Be sure to use new O-rings and a new retainer clip on the strainer during reassembly.

30 When you're done installing the pump, STOP! Before installing the fuel pump access cover, reconnect the cable to the negative battery terminal (see Chapter 5, Section 1), start the engine and check for fuel leaks at the pump fuel line connections. If there are no leaks, install the access cover, the carpet and the second-row seat.

## 7   Fuel tank - removal and installation

▶ Refer to illustrations 7.9, 7.10a, 7.10b, 7.11, 7.12, 7.13 and 7.15

### ❄❄ WARNING 1:

Gasoline is extremely flammable, so take extra precautions when you work on any part of the fuel system. See the Warning in Section 2.

### ❄❄ WARNING 2:

The following procedure is much easier to perform if the fuel tank is empty. The tank has no drain plug, so the fuel must be siphoned from the tank with a siphoning kit, which is available at most auto parts stores. NEVER try to start the siphoning action with your mouth!

1   Remove the fuel tank filler cap to relieve fuel tank pressure.

2   Relieve the fuel system pressure (see Section 2).

3   Disconnect the cable from the negative battery terminal (see Chapter 5, Section 1).

4   Disconnect the electrical connector from the fuel pump/fuel level sending unit module (see Section 5).

5   If the fuel tank is empty or nearly empty, it's not necessary to siphon the remaining fuel from the tank. But if there is a lot of fuel in the tank, remove the fuel pump/fuel level sending unit (see Section 5) and siphon out the remaining fuel through the fuel pump mounting hole in the tank.

### ❄❄ WARNING:

Always siphon fuel into an approved gasoline container.

6   Raise the vehicle and place it securely on jackstands.

7   Remove the rear part of the exhaust system (see Section 17).

8   On 4WD models, remove the driveshaft (see Chapter 8).

9   Remove the fuel tank rock guard mounting bolts and/or nuts (see illustration) and remove the rock guard. (The fuel tank on 2007 Acura models has two rock guards.)

10   On 2001 and 2002 Acura and 2003 and 2004 Honda models, disconnect the quick-connect fittings for the fuel supply and return lines (see illustration). Be sure to cover the ends of the fuel line fitting(s) with

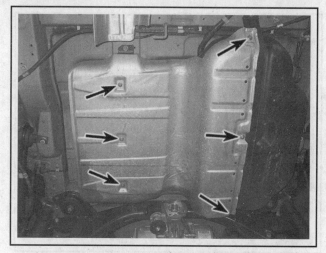

7.9  To detach the fuel tank rock guard, remove these nuts

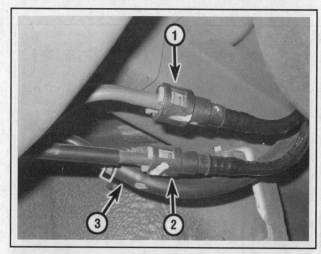

7.10a  On 2001 and 2002 Acura and 2003 and 2004 Honda models, disconnect the fuel supply line (1), the fuel return line (2) and the EVAP hose (3) at these quick-connect fittings at the front of the fuel tank

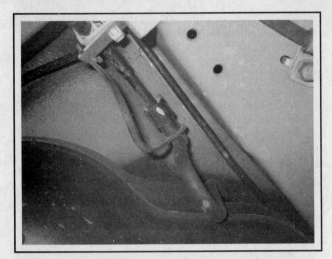

**7.10b** On 2003 and later Acura and 2005 and later Honda models, disconnect the quick-connect fitting for the fuel supply line and cover the open ends with plastic bags

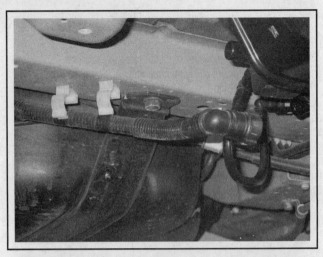

**7.11** Disconnect the EVAP hose that connects the fuel tank to the EVAP canister

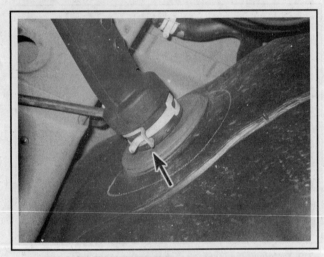

**7.12** To disconnect the fuel filler neck hose, loosen and slide back this spring-type hose clamp and pull off the hose

plastic bags to prevent dirt and moisture from contaminating the fuel system. On 2003 and later Acura and 2005 and later Honda models, disconnect the fuel supply line quick-connect fitting (see illustration). (There is no return line on these later models.)

11 Disconnect the EVAP hose that connects the fuel tank to the EVAP canister (see illustration).

12 Disconnect the fuel filler neck hose (see illustration).

13 Disconnect the EVAP hose (breather hose for the fuel filler neck hose) located above the filler neck hose (see illustration).

14 Support the fuel tank.

15 Remove the fuel tank retaining strap bolts (see illustration) and remove the straps.

16 Carefully lower the fuel tank.

17 If you're going to clean the fuel tank, refer to Section 8.

18 If you're cleaning the fuel tank, this would be a good time to inspect and clean the inlet strainer for the fuel pump/fuel level sending unit module (see Section 6).

19 Installation is the reverse of removal. Be sure to tighten the fuel tank strap bolts securely.

20 When you're done, reconnect the cable to the negative battery terminal (see Chapter 5, Section 1), then start the engine and check for fuel leaks.

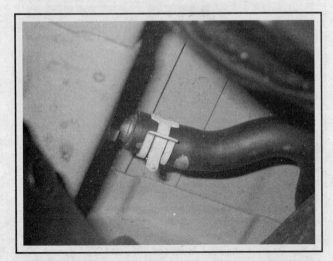

**7.13** To disconnect the EVAP hose (breather hose for the fuel filler neck hose) right above the filler neck hose, loosen and slide back this spring-type hose clamp and pull off the hose

**7.15** Fuel tank strap bolts

## 8 Fuel tank cleaning and repair - general information

1   The fuel tanks installed in the vehicles covered by this manual are made of plastic and are not repairable. If the fuel tank has been removed for cleaning, this is a job that should be left to a professional who has experience in this critical and potentially dangerous work. Even after cleaning and flushing of the fuel tank, explosive fumes can remain.

2   If the fuel tank is removed from the vehicle, it should not be placed in an area where sparks or open flames could ignite the fumes coming out of the tank. Be especially careful inside garages where a gas-type appliance is located, because it could cause an explosion.

## 9 Air filter housing and intake duct - removal and installation

### AIR INTAKE DUCT

▶ **Refer to illustrations 9.1, 9.2a, 9.2b and 9.4**

1   Disconnect the PCV fresh air inlet hose (see illustration) from the air intake duct. Clearly label any other cables and hoses that are attached or connected to the air intake duct, then detach or disconnect them and set them aside.

2   Disconnect the left end of the air intake duct from the air filter housing (see illustration). Loosen the hose clamp that secures the air intake duct to the throttle body (see illustration).

3   Remove the air intake duct.

4   If you removed the air intake duct just to access some other component(s), skip this step. But if you're planning to replace the air intake duct itself, or either of the small resonators attached to the duct, loosen the hose clamp(s) and remove the resonator(s) (see illustration).

5   Installation is the reverse of removal.

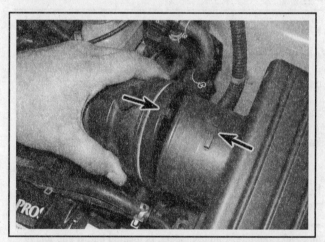

9.2a  The left end of the air intake duct uses a spring to secure it to the air filter housing, so all you have to do is pull it off; when installing the air intake duct, be sure align the locator tab on the duct between the two ridges on the air filter housing

9.1  Disconnect the PCV fresh air inlet hose from the air intake duct

9.2b  To detach the air intake duct from the throttle body, loosen this hose clamp screw

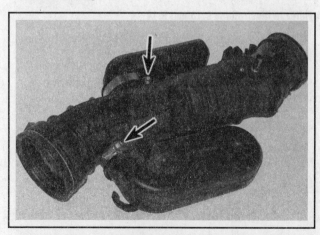

9.4  If you're replacing the air intake duct, loosen these hose clamp screws and detach the resonators (you can also replace either of the resonators separately)

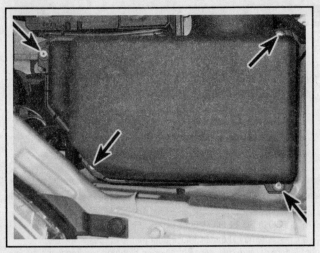

9.8 To detach the air filter housing, unscrew these four bolts

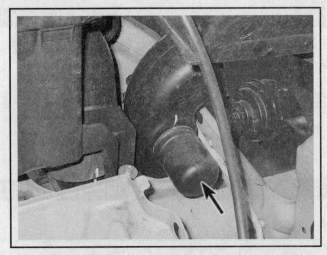

9.13 Remove the side branch tube by pulling it straight off

## AIR FILTER HOUSING

▶ Refer to illustration 9.8

6   Remove the air intake duct (see Steps 1 through 4).

7   On 2001 and 2002 Acura and 2003 and 2004 Honda models, detach the cruise control cable clip from the air filter housing.

8   Remove the air filter housing mounting bolts (see illustration) and remove the air filter housing.

9   Inspect the condition of the air filter housing insulator(s). If an insulator is cracked, torn or otherwise deteriorated, replace it.

10  Installation is the reverse of removal.

## RESONATOR

➡Note: The resonator, which is used on 2003 and later Acura and 2005 and later Honda models, is located below and ahead of the air filter housing, in the void behind the left corner of the front bumper cover and in front of the left front wheel well.

### 2003 through 2006 Acura and 2005 and later Honda models

▶ Refer to illustrations 9.13 and 9.14

11  Raise the front of the vehicle and place it securely on jackstands.

12  Remove the front bumper cover (see Chapter 11).

13  Remove the side branch tube from the resonator (see illustration).

14  Remove the resonator mounting bolts (see illustration) and remove the resonator.

15  Installation is the reverse of removal.

9.14 To detach the resonator, remove these two mounting bolts

### 2007 Acura models

16  Remove the air filter housing (see Steps 6 through 9).

17  Remove the battery (see Chapter 5).

18  Remove the front bumper cover (see Chapter 11).

19  Remove the left headlight housing (see Chapter 12).

20  Remove the two clips that secure the small plastic cover and remove the cover.

21  Remove the two resonator mounting bolts and remove the resonator.

22  Installation is the reverse of removal.

## 10 Accelerator cable - removal, installation and adjustment

### 2001 AND 2002 ACURA AND 2003 AND 2004 HONDA MODELS

#### Removal and installation

▶ **Refer to illustrations 10.2, 10.3, 10.4, 10.5a, 10.5b, 10.6a and 10.6b**

1   Disconnect the cable from the negative battery terminal (see Chapter 5, Section 1).

2   Rotate the throttle lever cam until the cable is lined up with the slot in the cam, then disengage the cable from the cam (see illustration).

3   Using a pair of wrenches, loosen the accelerator cable locknut at the cable bracket (see illustration) and disengage the accelerator cable from its bracket.

4   Tracing the cable from the cable bracket back to the firewall, detach or disengage it from any clamps, clips or cable guides (see illustration).

5   Using a flashlight so that you can see underneath the dash, locate the cable connection at the top of the accelerator pedal (see illustration), push the upper end of the pedal forward and disengage the cable from the pedal arm (see illustration).

6   Remove the two nuts (see illustration) that secure the accelerator cable grommet and mounting flange to the firewall, then pull the cable assembly through the firewall from the passenger compartment side (see illustration).

7   Installation is the reverse of removal.

**10.2   To disengage the accelerator cable from the throttle lever cam, rotate the cam until the cable is aligned with the slot in the cam, then pull out the cable (2001 and 2002 Acura and 2003 and 2004 Honda models)**

**10.3   Loosen the accelerator cable locknut and disengage the cable from the cable bracket (2001 and 2002 Acura and 2003 and 2004 Honda models)**

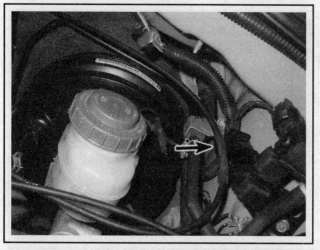

**10.4   Trace the accelerator cable back from its cable bracket to the firewall and disengage it from any clamps, clips or cable guides (other models might have slightly different cable routing) (2001 and 2002 Acura and 2003 and 2004 Honda models)**

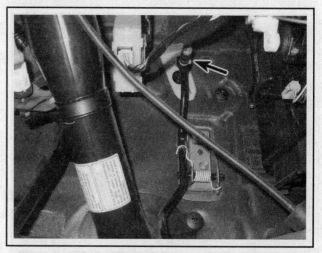

**10.5a   The accelerator cable is connected to the top end of the accelerator pedal arm (2001 and 2002 Acura and 2003 and 2004 Honda models)**

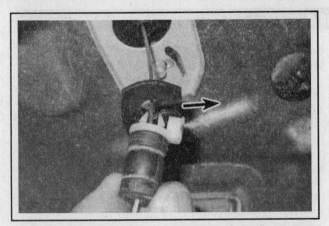

**10.5b** To disengage the accelerator cable from the accelerator pedal arm, push the upper end of the arm forward, pull back on the cable end plug and pull out the cable through the slot in the pedal arm (2001 and 2002 Acura and 2003 and 2004 Honda models)

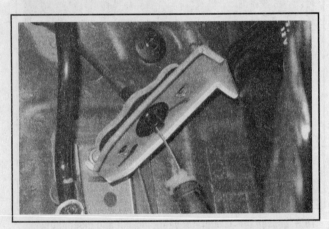

**10.6b** . . . then pull the cable through the firewall from the passenger compartment side (2001 and 2002 Acura and 2003 and 2004 Honda models)

**10.8a** To adjust the accelerator cable, rotate the throttle cam (A) toward the cable bracket until the lever on the cam contacts the throttle stop tang (C); there should be no clearance at the point of contact (B) (2001 and 2002 Acura and 2003 and 2004 Honda models)

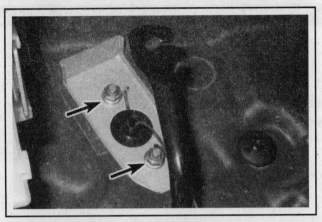

**10.6a** To detach the accelerator cable grommet and mounting flange from the firewall, remove these two nuts . . .

## Adjustment

▶ **Refer to illustrations 10.8a, 10.8b and 10.8c**

8   Rotate the accelerator cable throttle cam toward the cable bracket until the small lever on the bottom of the cam contacts the throttle stop bracket (see illustrations), then measure the cable deflection (see illustration) and compare your measurement to the cable deflection listed in this Chapter's Specifications.

9   If the cable deflection is incorrect, loosen the cable locknut (see illustration 10.8c) and turn the adjustment nut until the deflection is within the specified range.

## 2003 THROUGH 2006 ACURA AND 2005 AND LATER HONDA MODELS

10   These models are equipped with an electronic throttle body that doesn't use an accelerator cable. Instead, the throttle plate is opened and closed by an electric servo motor that is controlled by the Powertrain Control Module (PCM). However, these models are still

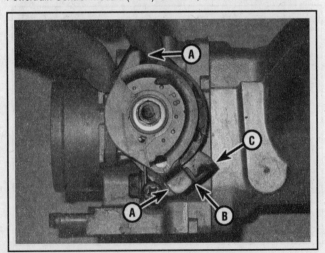

**10.8b** Here's a better view of the lever on the throttle cam (A) contacting the throttle stop bracket (C), with zero clearance at the point of contact (B) (throttle body removed for clarity) (2001 and 2002 Acura and 2003 and 2004 Honda models)

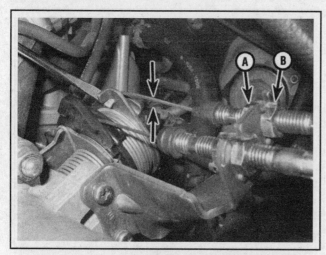

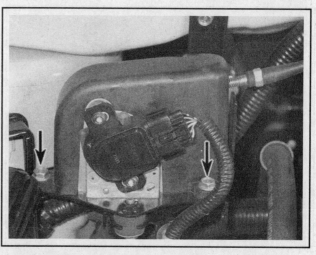

10.8c Measure the cable deflection where indicated and compare your measurement to the deflection listed in this Chapter's Specifications; if the cable deflection is out of range, adjust it by loosening the locknut (A) and turning the adjustment nut (B) until the deflection is within the specified range (2001 and 2002 Acura and 2003 and 2004 Honda models)

10.12 To detach the cover from the APP sensor assembly, remove these two bolts (2003 through 2006 Acura and 2005 and later Honda models)

equipped with an "accelerator cable," though it isn't an accelerator cable in the conventional sense. Instead, this cable connects the accelerator pedal to the Accelerator Pedal Position (APP) sensor, which is located on the firewall. The APP sensor produces an analog voltage output that the PCM uses to determine the position (angle) of the accelerator pedal. The PCM processes this information continuously, and commands the servo inside the throttle body to open and close the throttle plate accordingly. For more information about the electronic control system and the APP sensor, refer to Chapter 6.

## Removal and installation

▶ Refer to illustrations 10.12, 10.13, 10.14 and 10.16

11 Disconnect the cable from the negative battery terminal (see

Chapter 5, Section 1).

12 Remove the APP sensor cover bolts (see illustration) and remove the cover.

13 Rotate the throttle lever cam counterclockwise to its fully open position so that the cable is lined up with the slot in the cam, then disengage the cable from the cam (see illustration).

14 Loosen the accelerator cable locknut at the cable bracket (see illustration) and disengage the accelerator cable from its bracket.

15 Using a flashlight so that you can see underneath the dash, locate the cable connection at the top of the accelerator pedal (see illustration 10.5a), push the upper end of the pedal forward and disengage the cable from the pedal arm (see illustration 10.5b).

16 Trace the cable forward to the hole in the firewall. To disengage the retainer, rotate it counterclockwise 90-degrees (see illustration), then pull the cable assembly through the firewall and into the passenger compartment.

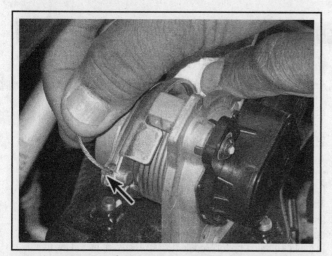

10.13 To disconnect the accelerator cable from the throttle cam, rotate the cam counterclockwise until the cable is lined up with the slot in the cam, then slide out the cable end plug from its mounting hole in the cam (2003 through 2006 Acura and 2005 and later Honda models)

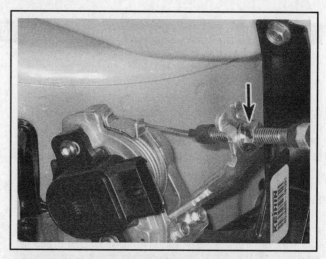

10.14 Loosen the accelerator cable locknut at the cable bracket and disengage the cable from the cable bracket (2003 through 2006 Acura and 2005 and later Honda models)

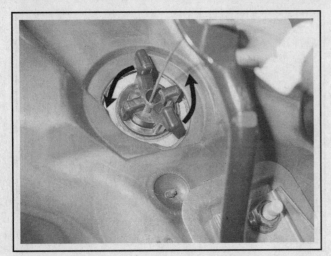

**10.16 To disengage the accelerator cable retainer from the firewall, rotate it 1/4-turn counterclockwise**

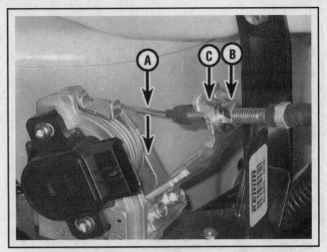

**10.18 To check accelerator cable freeplay, deflect the cable downward at point A and measure the deflection. If the deflection is incorrect, loosen the cable locknut (B) and turn the adjuster nut (C) until the deflection is correct. Tighten the locknut when you're done (2003 through 2006 Acura and 2005 and later Honda models)**

17 Installation is the reverse of removal. Be sure to check and, if necessary, adjust the accelerator cable before installing the cover.

## Adjustment

▶ **Refer to illustration 10.18**

18 With the throttle cam in its closed position, deflect the accelerator cable between the cable bracket and the throttle cam and measure the amount of cable deflection (see illustration). Compare your measurement to the cable deflection listed in this Chapter's Specifications.

19 If the cable deflection is incorrect, loosen the cable locknut (see illustration 10.18) and turn the adjustment nut until the deflection is within the specified range.

20 Once you have adjusted the cable, have an assistant depress the accelerator pedal all the way until it stops while you verify that the throttle cam is opening fully. Then have your assistant release the accelerator pedal while you verify that the throttle cam returns to its idle (closed) position. If the throttle cam doesn't open all the way and close fully, readjust the cable. Install the cover when you're done.

## 11 Programmed Fuel Injection (PGM-FI) system - general information

The Programmed Fuel Injection (PGM-FI) system is a "sequential multiport" system. This means that there is a fuel injector in each intake port, and that these fuel injectors inject fuel into the intake ports in the cylinder firing order (1-4-2-5-3-6). The injectors are turned on and off by the Powertrain Control Module (PCM). When the engine is running, the PCM constantly monitors engine operating conditions with an array of information sensors, calculates the correct amount of fuel, then varies the interval of time during which the injectors are open. Sequential multiport systems provide much better control of the air/fuel mixture ratio than earlier fuel injection systems, and are therefore able to produce more power, better mileage and lower emissions.

The PGM-FI system uses the PCM and an array of information sensors to determine and deliver the correct air/fuel ratio under all operating conditions. The PGM-FI system consists of three sub-systems: air induction, electronic control and fuel delivery. The PGM-FI system is also closely interrelated with PCM-controlled emission control systems. For additional information about the PCM, the information sensors and the emission control systems, refer to Chapter 6.

### AIR INDUCTION SYSTEM

The air induction system consists of the resonator, the air filter assembly, the air intake duct, the throttle body and the intake manifold.

### 2001 and 2002 Acura and 2003 and 2004 Honda models

The single-barrel, side-draft, cast aluminum throttle body contains a throttle plate that regulates the amount of air entering the intake manifold. The throttle plate is opened and closed by the accelerator cable. The Throttle Position (TP) sensor is located on one end of the shaft for the throttle plate. A TP sensor is a potentiometer that monitors the opening angle of the throttle plate and sends a variable voltage signal to the Powertrain Control Module (PCM). The lower part of the throttle body is heated by engine coolant to prevent icing in cold weather.

A Manifold Absolute Pressure (MAP) sensor is located on top of the throttle body. The MAP sensor measures intake manifold pressure and vacuum and generates a variable voltage signal that's proportionate to the pressure or vacuum. The PCM uses this data to calculate the load on the engine. Another information sensor, the Intake Air Temperature (IAT) sensor, is located at the left rear corner of the intake manifold. The IAT sensor relays a voltage signal to the PCM that varies in accordance with the temperature of the incoming air in the manifold. The PCM uses this data to calculate how rich or lean the air/fuel mixture should be. All of the air induction components (air filter housing, air intake duct and throttle body) are covered in this Chapter, except for the intake manifold, which is covered in Chapter 2A, and the information sensors, which are covered in Chapter 6.

When the engine is idling, the Idle Air Control (IAC) system maintains the correct idle speed by regulating the amount of air that bypasses the (closed) throttle plate in response to a command from the Powertrain Control Module (PCM). The IAC system consists of the IAC valve (located on the throttle body), the PCM, and several information sensors, including the Engine Coolant Temperature (ECT) sensor, the Intake Air Temperature (IAT) sensor and the Manifold Absolute Pressure (MAP) sensor. The IAC valve is activated and controlled by the PCM in response to the running conditions of the engine (cold or warm running, power steering pressure high or low, air conditioning system on or off, etc.). As the PCM receives data from the information sensors (vehicle speed, coolant temperature, air conditioning and/or power steering load, etc.) it adjusts the idle according to the demands of the engine and driver.

### 2003 and later Acura and 2005 and later Honda models

These models are equipped with an electronic throttle control system, which consists of the throttle actuator, the throttle actuator control module, the throttle actuator control relay, two Throttle Position (TP) sensors, the Accelerator Pedal Position (APP) sensor and the Powertrain Control Module (PCM). The single-barrel, side-draft, cast aluminum electronic throttle body contains a throttle plate that regulates the amount of air entering the intake manifold. The throttle plate is opened and closed by the integral throttle actuator (electric motor). The PCM-controlled throttle actuator opens and closes the throttle plate in response to the position of the accelerator pedal. The position (angle) of the accelerator pedal is determined by the Accelerator Pedal Position (APP) sensor, which is located on the firewall on all models except the 2007 Acura, on which it's located at the top of the accelerator pedal. On all models except the 2007 Acura, the accelerator pedal is connected to the APP sensor by an "accelerator cable." On 2007 Acura models, there is no cable because the APP sensor is an integral component of the accelerator pedal assembly. The throttle body is also the location of two Throttle Position (TP) sensors. A TP sensor is a potentiometer that monitors the opening angle of the throttle plate and sends a variable voltage signal to the Powertrain Control Module (PCM). Both TP sensors are integral components of the electronic throttle body and cannot be serviced separately. The lower part of the electronic throttle body is heated by engine coolant to prevent icing in cold weather.

A Manifold Absolute Pressure (MAP) sensor is located on top of the throttle body. The MAP sensor measures intake manifold pressure and vacuum and generates a variable voltage signal that's proportionate to the pressure or vacuum. The PCM uses this data to calculate the load on the engine. Another information sensor, the Intake Air Temperature (IAT) sensor, is located on the air intake duct (2003 and 2004 Acura models) or on the front of the intake manifold (2005 and 2006 Acura and 2005 and later Honda models). On 2007 Acura models the IAT sensor is an integral component of the Mass Air Flow (MAF) sensor, which is located on the air filter housing. The IAT sensor relays a voltage signal to the PCM that varies in accordance with the temperature of the incoming air in the manifold. The PCM uses this data to calculate how rich or lean the air/fuel mixture should be. All of the air induction com-

ponents (resonator, air filter housing, air intake duct and throttle body) are covered in this Chapter, except for the intake manifold, which is covered in Chapter 2A, and the information sensors, which are covered in Chapter 6.

These models are also equipped with an electronic idle control system. When the engine is idling, the PCM controls the idle speed by opening and closing the throttle plate as necessary in response to inputs from several information sensors, including the Engine Coolant Temperature (ECT) sensor, the Intake Air Temperature (IAT) sensor, the Manifold Absolute Pressure (MAP) sensor, the Power Steering Pressure (PSP) switch and the air conditioning ON switch.

## ELECTRONIC CONTROL SYSTEM

For more information about the electronic control system, i.e. the PCM, its information sensors and output actuators, refer to Chapter 6.

## FUEL DELIVERY SYSTEM

The fuel delivery system consists of the fuel pump, the fuel filter, the fuel pressure regulator the fuel rail and fuel injectors, and the lines and fittings that carry fuel between all of these components. Earlier models are also equipped with a fuel pulsation damper (see below).

### Fuel pump/fuel level sending unit module

The fuel pump module is an in-tank design, and it can be removed from the top of the fuel tank without removing the tank. Fuel is drawn through a "sock" (or strainer) at the pump inlet, then pumped out the other end of the pump into an integral fuel filter (located in the same housing as the pump). After the pressurized fuel has been filtered, it's pumped through a supply line up to the fuel rail, which is located between the cylinder heads on the engine. The fuel pump module also includes a fuel level sending unit, which uses a float on the end of a float arm to operate a variable potentiometer, which sends a voltage signal to the PCM and to the fuel level gauge on the instrument cluster.

### 2001 and 2002 Acura and 2003 and 2004 Honda models

Right before the fuel reaches the fuel rail, it's pumped through a fuel pulsation damper, which is located at the rear end of the left fuel rail, at a junction block connection for the fuel return line. The pulsation damper attenuates the hydraulic and acoustic "noise" produced by the fuel pump when it's operating. A fuel pressure regulator, which is installed on the fuel rail at the connection for the fuel return line, maintains the fuel pressure within the specified operating range.

### 2003 and later Acura and 2005 and later Honda models

These models do not use a pulsation damper or a fuel return line. They have a pressure regulator, but it's an integral component of the fuel pump/fuel level sending unit module and is spring-loaded but not vacuum-controlled. When the fuel pressure rises beyond its normal operating range during deceleration or idle, the pressure regulator opens and fuel is diverted out of the fuel pump module and dumped directly back into the fuel tank. A returnless system has one major advantage over a conventional fuel system with supply and return lines. Because fuel isn't being pumped to the hot fuel rail on top of the engine, then - if it isn't used - returned to the fuel tank at an elevated temperature, there is less heat buildup of the fuel inside the tank, which means less fuel vapors inside the fuel tank. This in turn reduces the likelihood of leakage of evaporative emissions from the fuel tank, EVAP canister and EVAP hoses.

### Fuel rail and fuel injector assembly (all models)

The fuel rail assembly is simply a pair of parallel, identical tubes that are bolted to the lower intake manifold alongside the inner wall of each cylinder head. The fuel rail houses the upper end of each fuel injector, and the lower end of each injector is inserted into the intake manifold. Each fuel injector is a solenoid-actuated, pintle-type design consisting of a solenoid, plunger, needle valve and housing. When the engine is running, there is always voltage on the "hot" side of each injector terminal. The PCM turns the injectors on and off by switching their ground paths on and off. When the ground path for an injector is closed by the PCM, current flows through the solenoid coil, the needle valve raises and pressurized fuel inside the injector housing squirts out the nozzle. The quantity of fuel injected each time an injector opens is determined by the "pulse width," which is the interval of time during which the valve is open.

### 12  Programmed Fuel Injection (PGM-FI) system - check

▸ **Refer to illustration 12.7**

✳✳ **WARNING:**

**Gasoline is extremely flammable, so take extra precautions when you work on any part of the fuel system. See the Warning in Section 2.**

➡**Note: The following procedure is based on the assumption that the fuel pump is working and the fuel pressure is adequate (see Section 3).**

1   Check all electrical connectors that are related to the system. Check the ground wire connections for tightness. Loose connectors and poor grounds can cause many problems that resemble more serious malfunctions.

2   Verify that the battery is fully charged. The Powertrain Control Module (PCM), information sensors and output actuators (the fuel injectors are output actuators) depend on a stable voltage supply in order to meter fuel correctly.

3   Inspect the air filter element (see Chapter 1). A dirty or partially blocked filter will severely impede performance and economy.

4   Check all fuses related to the fuel system (see Chapter 12). If you find a blown fuse, replace it and see if it blows again. If it does, look for a wire shorted to ground in the circuit(s) protected by that fuse.

5   Check the air induction system between the throttle body and the intake manifold for air leaks, which will cause a lean air/fuel mixture ratio. (When the mixture ratio becomes excessively lean, the engine will begin misfiring.) Also inspect the condition of all vacuum hoses connected to the intake manifold and to the throttle body. A loose or broken vacuum hose will allow "false (unmetered) air" into the intake manifold. The Manifold Absolute Pressure (MAP) sensor and the PCM can compensate for some false air, but if it's excessive, especially at idle and during other high-intake-manifold-vacuum conditions, the engine will misfire.

6   Remove the air intake duct from the throttle body and look for dirt, carbon, varnish, or other residue in the throttle body, particularly around the throttle plate. If it's dirty, clean it with carb cleaner, a toothbrush and a clean shop towel.

7   With the engine running, place an automotive stethoscope against each injector, one at a time, and listen for a clicking sound that indicates operation (see illustration).

➡**Note: This is a difficult task on this engine, especially on the rear cylinder bank. The injectors for cylinders 1, 3, 4 and 6 can be reached from the ends of the engine, but the injectors for cylinders 2 and 5 have to be accessed from between the upper intake manifold and the valve covers.**

✳✳ **WARNING:**

**Stay clear of the drivebelt and any rotating components.**

8   If you can hear the injectors operating, but the engine is misfiring, then the electrical circuits are functioning correctly, but the injectors might be dirty or clogged. Try a commercial injector cleaning product (available at auto parts stores). If cleaning the injectors doesn't help, the injectors probably need to be replaced.

9   If an injector is not operating, i.e. it makes no sound, remove the upper intake manifold (see Chapter 2A), disconnect the injector electrical connector and measure the resistance across the injector terminals with an ohmmeter. Compare your measurement with the resistance values of the other injectors. If the resistance of the non-operational injector is well outside the range of resistance of the other injectors, replace it.

10  If the injector is not operating, but the resistance reading is within the range of resistance of the other injectors, the PCM or the circuit between the PCM and the injector might be faulty.

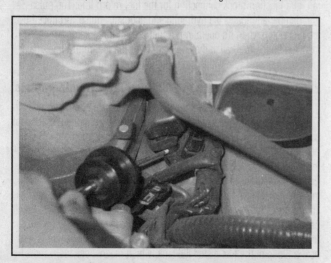

**12.7  Use a stethoscope to listen to each injector; it should make a clicking sound that rises and falls with engine speed**

## 13 Throttle body - removal and installation

**13.4 To detach the accelerator cable and cruise control cable bracket from the throttle body, remove these two screws (2001 and 2002 Acura and 2003 and 2004 Honda models)**

**13.5 Disconnect the electrical connector from the Manifold Absolute Pressure (MAP) sensor (2001 and 2002 Acura and 2003 and 2004 Honda models)**

**13.6 Disconnect the electrical connector from the Throttle Position (TP) sensor (2001 and 2002 Acura and 2003 and 2004 Honda models)**

### ❊❊❊ WARNING:

**Wait until the engine is completely cool before beginning this procedure.**

1  Disconnect the cable from the negative battery terminal (see Chapter 5, Section 1).

2  Pinch off the two coolant hoses to the throttle body. If you don't have tools suitable for doing this, drain the engine coolant until the level in the cooling system is lower than the throttle body (see Chapter 1).

3  Remove the air intake duct (see Section 9).

## 2001 AND 2002 ACURA AND 2003 AND 2004 HONDA MODELS

▶ **Refer to illustrations 13.4, 13.5, 13.6, 13.7, 13.8, 13.9 and 13.10**

4  Detach the cable bracket (see illustration) from the throttle body. (By detaching the cable bracket from the throttle body, but leaving the accelerator and cruise control cables attached to the cable bracket, you won't disturb the adjustment of either cable.) Then disconnect the accelerator cable and the cruise control cable from the throttle lever cam as described in Section 10.

5  Disconnect the electrical connector from the Manifold Absolute Pressure (MAP) sensor (see illustration).

6  Disconnect the electrical connector from the Throttle Position (TP) sensor (see illustration).

7  Loosen and slide back the hose clamps and disconnect the coolant hoses from the throttle body (see illustration). Be prepared to mop up any coolant still in the hoses or in the throttle body.

8  Disconnect the Evaporative Emissions (EVAP) purge valve hose from the throttle body (see illustration).

**13.8 Loosen the hose clamp, slide it back and disconnect the Evaporative Emissions (EVAP) system purge valve hose from the throttle body (2001 and 2002 Acura and 2003 and 2004 Honda models)**

**13.7 Pinch off the two coolant hoses (A) connected to the throttle body, then loosen the hose clamps (B), slide them back and disconnect both coolant hoses from the throttle body (2001 and 2002 Acura and 2003 and 2004 Honda models)**

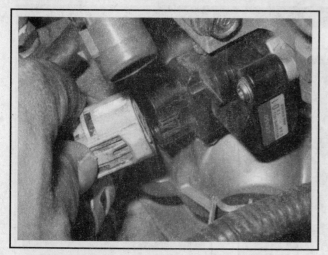

**13.9 Disconnect the electrical connector from the Idle Air Control (IAC) valve, which is located underneath the throttle body (2001 and 2002 Acura and 2003 and 2004 Honda models)**

**13.10 To detach the throttle body from the intake manifold, remove the two upper mounting nuts and the two lower mounting bolts (2001 and 2002 Acura and 2003 and 2004 Honda models)**

**13.16 To disconnect the electrical connector from the MAP sensor, depress this release tab and pull off the connector (2003 and later Acura and 2005 and later Honda models)**

9  Disconnect the electrical connector from the Idle Air Control (IAC) valve (see illustration).

10  Remove the two bolts and two nuts that attach the throttle body to the intake manifold (see illustration) and remove the throttle body, the spacer and the two gaskets.

11  Remove all traces of old gasket material from the throttle body, the spacer and the intake manifold.

12  Installation is the reverse of removal. Be sure to use new gaskets and tighten the throttle body mounting bolts and nuts to the torque listed in this Chapter's Specifications.

13  When you're done, check the coolant level and add some, as necessary, to bring it to the appropriate level (see Chapter 1).

14  Check the accelerator cable slack and adjust it if necessary (see Section 10).

15  Reconnect the cable to the negative battery terminal (see Chapter 5, Section 1), then start the engine and check for air and coolant leaks.

**13.17 To disconnect the throttle body electrical connector, depress this release tab and pull off the connector (2003 and later Acura and 2005 and later Honda models)**

**13.18 To disconnect the two coolant bypass hoses from these pipes on the underside of the throttle body, clamp-off the hoses, loosen the spring-type hose clamps, slide them back and pull off the hoses (2003 and later Acura and 2005 and later Honda models)**

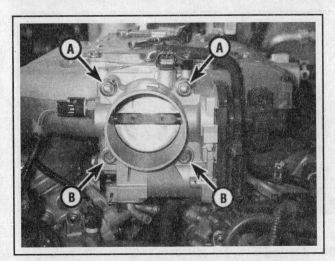

**13.19  Remove the two nuts (A) and two bolts (B) securing the throttle body to the air intake plenum (2003 and later Acura and 2005 and later Honda models)**

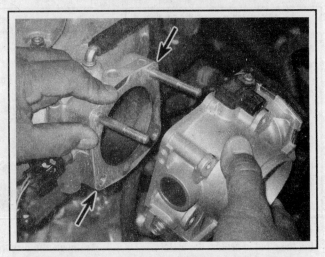

**13.20  Remove the throttle body and remove the throttle body gasket (2003 and later Acura and 2005 and later Honda models)**

## 2003 AND LATER ACURA AND 2005 AND LATER HONDA MODELS

♦ **Refer to illustrations 13.16, 13.17, 13.18, 13.19 and 13.20**

16  Disconnect the electrical connector from the MAP sensor (see illustration).

17  Disconnect the throttle body electrical connector (see illustration).

18  Disconnect the two coolant bypass hoses from the throttle body (see illustration). Be prepared to mop up any coolant still in the hoses or in the throttle body.

19  Remove the two bolts and two nuts securing the throttle body to

the upper intake manifold (see illustration).

20  Remove the throttle body and remove the throttle body gasket (see illustration).

21  Installation is the reverse of removal. Be sure to tighten the throttle body mounting bolts and nuts to the torque listed in this Chapter's Specifications.

22  Reconnect the cable to the negative battery terminal (see Chapter 5, Section 1), then start the engine and check for air and coolant leaks.

23  When you're done, check the coolant level and add some, as necessary, to bring it to the appropriate level (see Chapter 1).

## 14  Fuel pulsation damper - removal and installation

♦ **Refer to illustrations 14.4, 14.5a, 14.5b and 14.6**

### ❊❊ WARNING:

**Gasoline is extremely flammable, so take extra precautions when you work on any part of the fuel system. See the Warning in Section 2.**

➠**Note: The pulsation damper, which is used on 2001 and 2002 Acura and 2003 and 2004 Honda models, is located on a junction block at the left end of the engine.**

1  Relieve the system fuel pressure (see Section 2).

2  Disconnect the cable from the negative battery terminal (see Chapter 5, Section 1).

3  Remove the engine cover (see *Intake manifold - removal and installation* in Chapter 2A).

4  Remove the small black plastic ring from the fuel pulsation damper (see illustration).

**14.4  Remove this small black plastic ring from the fuel pulsation damper (2001 and 2002 Acura and 2003 and 2004 Honda models)**

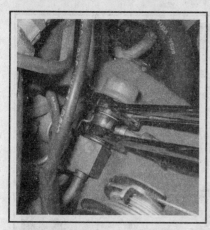

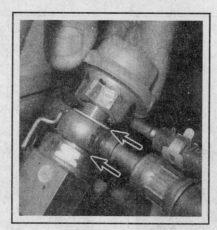

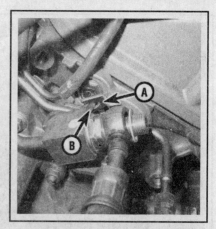

**14.5a  Using a back-up wrench on the fixed nut to protect the metal fuel line from kinking, loosen the fuel pulsation damper with another wrench . . .**

**14.5b  . . . remove the damper and remove and discard the old sealing washers on each side of the banjo fitting (2001 and 2002 Acura and 2003 and 2004 Honda models)**

**14.6  When installing the fuel pulsation damper, be sure to align the slot (A) in the banjo fitting bracket with the locator pin (B) on the junction block (2001 and 2002 Acura and 2003 and 2004 Honda models)**

5   Remove the pulsation damper (see illustrations).

6   Use new sealing washers when installing the pulsation damper, and be sure to align the slot in the banjo fitting bracket with the locator pin on the junction block (see illustration).

7   Tighten the fuel pulsation damper to the torque listed in this Chapter's Specifications.

8   Install the black plastic ring on the fixed nut. Make sure that the ridge on the inner bore of the ring is aligned with the notches in the nut.

9   Reconnect the cable to the negative battery terminal (see Chapter 5, Section 1).

10  Start the engine and check for leaks around the pulsation damper.

## 15  Fuel pressure regulator - removal and installation

### ※ WARNING:

**Gasoline is extremely flammable, so take extra precautions when you work on any part of the fuel system. See the Warning in Section 2.**

➡**Note: The pressure regulator, which is used on 2001 and 2002 Acura and 2003 and 2004 Honda models, is located on a junction block at the left end of the engine.**

1   Relieve the system fuel pressure (see Section 2).

2   Disconnect the cable from the negative battery terminal (see Chapter 5, Section 1).

3   Remove the engine cover (see *Intake manifold - removal and installation* in Chapter 2A).

4   Disconnect the vacuum hose from the fuel pressure regulator. Squeeze the clamp on the fuel return hose and slide it back, then detach the fuel return hose from the pressure regulator. Be prepared for some fuel to spill out.

5   Unscrew the fuel pressure regulator from the junction block.

6   Be sure to use a new O-ring when installing the new pressure regulator. Even if you're planning to reinstall the old pressure regulator, be sure to remove and discard the old O-ring, then install a new O-ring and coat it with a little clean engine oil. Make sure that you don't damage the new O-ring during installation or reassembly, or it might leak when subjected to operating fuel pressure.

7   When installing the fuel pressure regulator, screw it in by hand until it stops, then turn it counterclockwise until it is properly oriented. Orient the regulator so that the vacuum hose pipe is facing straight back (toward the firewall).

8   Installation is otherwise the reverse of removal. Be sure to tighten the fuel pressure regulator locking nut to the torque listed in this Chapter's Specifications.

9   When you're done, reconnect the cable to the negative battery terminal (see Chapter 5, Section 1), then start the engine and check for fuel leaks around the fuel pressure regulator.

## 16 Fuel rail and injectors - removal and installation

**Gasoline is extremely flammable, so take extra precautions when you work on any part of the fuel system. See the Warning in Section 2.**

1   Relieve the system fuel pressure (see Section 2).
2   Disconnect the cable from the negative battery terminal (see Chapter 5, Section 1).
3   Remove the engine cover (see Chapter 2A).

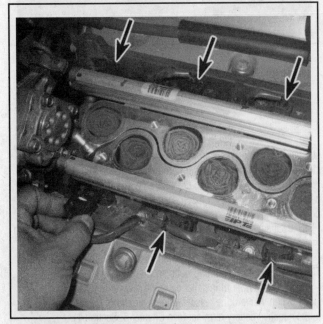

**16.4  Disconnect the electrical connectors from all six fuel injectors (2001 and 2002 Acura and 2003 and 2004 Honda models)**

### 2001 AND 2002 ACURA AND 2003 AND 2004 HONDA MODELS

#### Removal

▶ **Refer to illustrations 16.4, 16.7a, 16.7b, 16.8, 16.9a, 16.9b, 16.9c and 16.10**

4   Disconnect the electrical connectors from the fuel injectors (see illustration).
5   Disconnect the vacuum hose from the fuel pressure regulator (see Section 15).
6   Remove the fuel pulsation damper (see Section 14) and disconnect the fuel supply line banjo fitting from the junction block. Remove and discard the old fuel line banjo fitting sealing washers. Then slide back the hose clamp and disconnect the fuel return hose from the fuel pressure regulator (see Section 15).
7   Disconnect the fuel supply hose from the front fuel rail (see illustration), then remove and discard the old O-ring (see illustration). There's another similar hose that connects the right ends of the two fuel rails. This is the crossover hose. It's not necessary to disconnect the fuel crossover hose to remove the fuel rail and injectors. However, if the engine has a lot of miles on it, it's a good idea to disconnect the crossover hose and replace the O-rings where the hose connects to the fuel rails.

➡**Note: It's not absolutely necessary to disconnect the fuel supply hose from the fuel rails, since you have already disconnected the fuel supply hose banjo fitting from the junction block where the pressure regulator and fuel pulsation damper are installed, but it's easier to work the fuel rails and injectors free from the intake manifold when you disconnect the fuel supply hose from the front fuel rail because it will allow you to work each fuel rail out independently of the other rail.**

8   Remove the fuel rail mounting bolts (see illustration 16.7b), then remove each fuel rail and its three injectors as a single assembly (see illustration). If any of the injectors are difficult to extract from their bores, carefully pry them loose as shown.

**16.7a  To disconnect the fuel supply hose from the front fuel rail on 2001 and 2002 Acura and 2003 and 2004 Honda models, remove this nut**

**16.7b  After disconnecting the fuel supply hose from the front fuel rail, replace this O-ring (A). To detach the fuel rail assembly, remove all four mounting bolts: two bolts on the front rail B) and two (not shown) on the rear rail (2001 and 2002 Acura and 2003 and 2004 Honda models)**

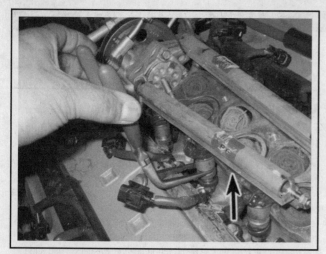

**16.8  To remove the fuel rails and the injectors, grasp each fuel rail firmly and pull up on the rails. If any of the injectors are difficult to extricate from their mounting bores in the intake manifold, carefully pry them out (2001 and 2002 Acura and 2003 and 2004 Honda models)**

**16.9a  To remove each injector from its bore in the fuel rail on 2001 and 2002 Acura and 2003 and 2004 Honda models, simply wiggle it from side to side and pull on it simultaneously**

9  Remove each injector from its bore in the fuel rail (see illustration). Remove the fuel strainer from each injector (see illustration), wash it thoroughly in clean solvent and set it aside. (If a strainer proves impossible to clean, replace it.). Remove and discard the upper O-ring, the cushion ring and the lower O-ring (see illustrations). Repeat this procedure for each injector.

➡**Note: Even if you only removed the fuel rail assembly to replace a single injector or a leaking O-ring, it's a good idea to remove all of the injectors from the fuel rail and replace all of the O-rings at the same time.**

10  Remove and discard the seal ring from the each injector bore in the cylinder head (see illustration).

### Installation

11  Coat the new cushion rings and upper O-rings with clean engine oil and slide them into place on each of the fuel injectors. Insert the fuel strainer into the top of each injector. Coat the new lower O-rings with clean engine oil and install them on the lower ends of the injectors.

12  Coat the outside surface of each upper O-ring and cushion ring with clean engine oil, then insert each injector into its corresponding bore in the fuel rail.

13  Coat each new seal ring with clean engine oil and press it into an injector bore in the intake manifold.

14  Install the injectors and fuel rail assembly on the intake manifold. Tighten the fuel rail mounting bolts securely.

15  The remainder of installation is the reverse of removal.

16  When you're done reassembling everything, reconnect the cable to the negative battery terminal (see Chapter 5, Section 1).

17  Turn the ignition switch to ON (but don't operate the starter). This activates the fuel pump for about two seconds, which builds up fuel pressure in the fuel lines and the fuel rail. Repeat this step two or three times, then check the fuel lines, fuel rails and injectors for fuel leaks.

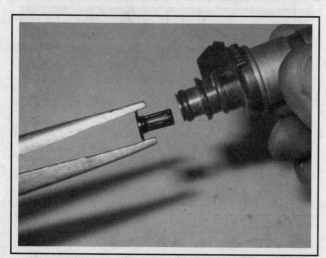

**16.9b  Carefully remove the fuel strainer from the top of each fuel injector, wash it in clean solvent, then install it (2001 and 2002 Acura and 2003 and 2004 Honda models)**

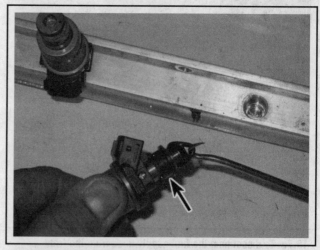

**16.9c  Carefully remove the upper and lower O-rings and the cushion ring and discard them (2001 and 2002 Acura and 2003 and 2004 Honda models)**

16.18 To disconnect the electrical connector from a fuel injector, depress these two release tabs and pull off the connector (2003 and later Acura and 2005 and later Honda models)

16.10 Carefully pry the seal ring from each of the six injector bores; be extremely careful not to damage the injector bores (2001 and 2002 Acura and 2003 and 2004 Honda models)

16.19b Remove and discard the old O-ring from the fuel rail crossover hose (2003 and later Acura and 2005 and later Honda models)

16.19a To disconnect the crossover hose from the fuel rail on 2003 and later Acura and 2005 and later Honda models:

1   Remove the fuel supply line bracket mounting nut and pull the bracket off the stud on the rear cylinder head

2   Remove the nut from the stud on the rear fuel rail and pull off the fitting

3   Disconnect the quick-connect fitting from the front fuel rail (see Section 4)

## 2003 AND LATER ACURA AND 2005 AND LATER HONDA MODELS

### Removal

▶ Refer to illustrations 16.18, 16.19a, 16.19b, 16.20a, 16.20b and 16.21

18 Disconnect the electrical connectors from the fuel injectors (see illustration).

19 Disconnect the crossover hose from the front and rear fuel rails (see illustrations) and set it aside.

20 Remove the four fuel rail mounting bolts (see illustration), then remove each of the fuel rails and its three injectors as a single assembly

16.20a To detach the fuel rail assembly from the intake manifold, remove the four mounting bolts: two on the front rail and two on the rear rail (2003 and later Acura and 2005 and later Honda models)

(see illustration). If one of the injectors is difficult to extract from its bore in the intake manifold, carefully wriggle the fuel rail back and forth and side to side to work it loose.

**16.20b Remove each fuel rail and its three injectors as a single assembly (2003 and later Acura and 2005 and later Honda models)**

21 To remove each injector from its bore in the fuel rail, remove the retainer, then carefully pull the injector straight out of the fuel rail (see illustration).

22 Remove and discard the upper and lower injector O-rings and discard them. Repeat this procedure for each injector.

➡**Note: Even if you only removed the fuel rail assembly to replace a single injector or a leaking O-ring, it's a good idea to remove all of the injectors from the fuel rail and replace all the O-rings at the same time.**

### Installation

23 Coat the new upper and lower O-rings with clean engine oil and slide them into place on each of the fuel injectors.

**16.21 To remove an injector from the fuel rail on a 2003 and later Acura and a 2005 and later Honda model, pull off the injector retainer, then carefully pull the injector straight out of its bore in the fuel rail**

24 Coat the outside surface of each upper and lower O-ring with clean engine oil, then insert each injector into its corresponding bore in the fuel rail.

25 Install the injectors and fuel rail assembly on the intake manifold. Tighten the fuel rail mounting bolts securely.

26 The remainder of installation is the reverse of removal.

27 When you're done reassembling everything, reconnect the cable to the negative battery terminal (see Chapter 5, Section 1).

28 Turn the ignition switch to ON (but don't operate the starter). This activates the fuel pump for about two seconds, which builds up fuel pressure in the fuel lines and the fuel rail. Repeat this step two or three times, then check the fuel lines, fuel rails and injectors for fuel leaks.

## 17 Exhaust system servicing - general information

♦ Refer to illustrations 17.1a and 17.1b

❋❋❋ **WARNING:**

Inspect and repair exhaust system components only after enough time has elapsed after driving the vehicle to allow the system components to cool completely. Also, when working under the vehicle, make sure it is securely supported on jackstands.

1 The exhaust system consists of the exhaust manifolds, the catalytic converter, the muffler, the tailpipe and all connecting pipes, flanges and clamps. The exhaust system is isolated from the vehicle body and from chassis components by a series of rubber hangers (see illustrations). Periodically inspect these hangers for cracks or other signs of deterioration, replacing them as necessary.

2 Conduct regular inspections of the exhaust system to keep it safe and quiet. Look for any damaged or bent parts, open seams, holes, loose connections, excessive corrosion or other defects which could allow exhaust fumes to enter the vehicle. Do not repair deteriorated exhaust system components; replace them with new parts.

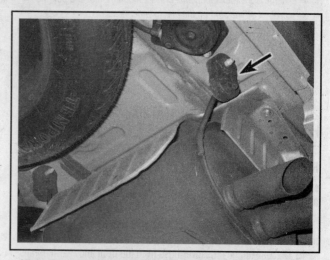

**17.1a Most exhaust system hangers look this one; to replace one of them, simply disengage it from the hook on the vehicle and from the hook on the exhaust bracket**

**17.1b  If the exhaust hanger is bolted to the underside of the vehicle, remove the mounting bolts to detach it**

remove them. The convenient strategy at this point is to have a muffler repair shop remove the corroded sections with a cutting torch. If you want to save money by doing it yourself, but you don't have a welding outfit and cutting torch, simply cut off the old components with a hacksaw. If you have compressed air, there are special pneumatic cutting chisels (available from specialty tool manufacturers) that can also be used. If you decide to tackle the job at home, be sure to wear safety goggles to protect your eyes from metal chips and wear work gloves to protect your hands.

4   Here are some simple guidelines to follow when repairing the exhaust system:

   a)  *Work from the back to the front when removing exhaust system components.*

   b)  *Apply penetrating oil to the exhaust system component fasteners to make them easier to remove.*

   c)  *Use new gaskets, hangers and clamps when installing exhaust systems components.*

   d)  *Apply anti-seize compound to the threads of all exhaust system fasteners during reassembly.*

   e)  *Be sure to allow sufficient clearance between newly installed parts and all points on the underbody to avoid overheating the floor pan and possibly damaging the interior carpet and insulation. Pay particularly close attention to the catalytic converter and heat shield.*

3   If the exhaust system components are extremely corroded, or rusted together, you'll need welding equipment and a cutting torch to

## Specifications

| | |
|---|---|
| Accelerator cable deflection | 3/8 to 1/2-inch (10 to 12 mm) |
| Fuel system pressure | |
|   Acura models | |
|     2001 and 2002 | 48 to 56 psi (330 to 382 kPa) |
|     2003 on | 57 to 64 psi (390 to 440 kPa) |
|   Honda models | |
|     2003 and 2004 | 48 to 56 psi (330 to 382 kPa) |
|     2005 | 57 to 64 psi (390 to 440 kPa) |
|     2006 on | 55 to 63 psi (380 to 430 kPa) |

## Torque specifications

| | Ft-lbs (unless otherwise indicated) | Nm |
|---|---|---|
| 2001 and 2002 Acura and 2003 and 2004 Honda models | | |
|   Fuel pressure regulator | 22 | 29 |
|   Fuel pulsation damper | 16 | 22 |
| Throttle body mounting bolts/nuts (all models) | 16 | 22 |

**Notes**

## Section

**Reference to other Chapters**
CHECK ENGINE light on - See Chapter 6

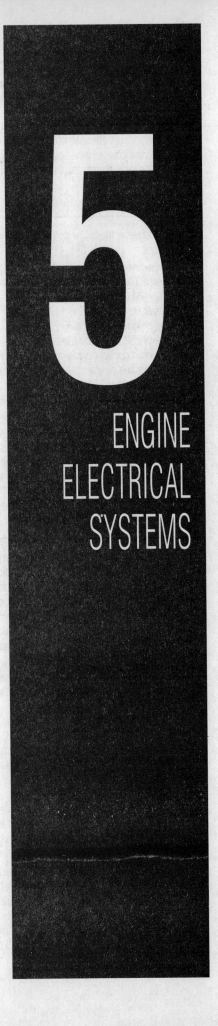

# 5

# ENGINE ELECTRICAL SYSTEMS

The engine electrical systems include all ignition, charging and starting components. Because of their engine-related functions, these components are covered separately from body electrical devices such as the lights, the instruments, etc. (which you'll find in Chapter 12).

## PRECAUTIONS

Always observe the following precautions when working on the electrical system:

a) *Be extremely careful when servicing engine electrical components. They are easily damaged if checked, connected or handled improperly.*

b) *Never leave the ignition switched on for long periods of time when the engine is not running.*

c) *Never disconnect the battery cables while the engine is running.*

d) *Maintain correct polarity when connecting battery cables from another vehicle during jump starting - see the "Booster battery (jump) starting" Section at the front of this manual.*

e) *Always disconnect the cable from the negative battery terminal before working on the electrical system, but read the following battery disconnection procedure first.*

It's also a good idea to review the safety-related information regarding the engine electrical systems located in the "Safety first!" Section at the front of this manual, before beginning any operation included in this Chapter.

## BATTERY DISCONNECTION

Some systems on the vehicle require battery power to be available at all times, either to maintain continuous operation (alarm system, power door locks, etc.), or to maintain control unit memory (radio station presets, Powertrain Control Module and other control units). When the battery is disconnected, the power that maintains these systems is cut. So, before you disconnect the battery, please note the following points to ensure that there are no unforeseen consequences of this action:

a) *The radio in some models is equipped with an anti-theft system; make sure you have the correct anti-theft codes for the radio and for the navigation system, if equipped, before disconnecting the battery.*

b) *When the battery is disconnected, the engine management system's Powertrain Control Module (PCM) will lose some data from its memory regarding the engine idle characteristics. It is imperative that you perform the "PCM idle learn procedure" (see procedure below) after disconnecting any of the components listed below.*

c) *On a vehicle with power door locks, it's a wise precaution to remove the key from the ignition and to keep it with you, so that it does not get locked inside if the power door locks should engage accidentally when the battery is reconnected!*

Devices known as "memory-savers" can be used to avoid some of these problems. Precise details vary according to the device used. The typical memory saver is plugged into the cigarette lighter and is connected to a spare battery. Then the vehicle battery can be disconnected from the electrical system. The memory saver will provide sufficient current to maintain audio unit security codes, PCM memory, etc. and will provide power to "always hot" circuits such as the clock and radio memory circuits.

**Some memory savers deliver a considerable amount of current in order to keep vehicle systems operational after the main battery is disconnected. If you're using a memory saver, make sure that the circuit concerned is actually open before servicing it.**

**⁂ WARNING 2:**

**If you're going to work near any of the airbag system components, the battery MUST be disconnected and a memory saver must NOT be used. If a memory saver is used, power will be supplied to the airbag, which means that it could accidentally deploy and cause serious personal injury.**

To disconnect the battery for service procedures requiring power to be cut from the vehicle, loosen the cable clamp nut and disconnect the cable from the negative battery post. Isolate the cable end to prevent it from coming into accidental contact with the battery post.

## BATTERY RECONNECTION

After reconnecting the battery, you must:

a) *Enter the anti-theft code for the radio and navigation system (see your owner's manual)*

b) *Enter the radio station presets (see your owner's manual)*

c) *Reset the clock (see your owner's manual)*

d) *On models with an electronic throttle body, perform a PCM idle learn procedure. (This procedure must also be performed after the PCM is replaced, updated or reset or after the throttle body is replaced or cleaned.)*

e) *Reset the power window control unit*

## POWERTRAIN CONTROL MODULE (PCM) IDLE LEARN PROCEDURE

Make sure that the PCM "learns" the engine idle characteristics after you do any of the following procedures:
Disconnect the battery
Replace, reset or update the PCM.

**➡Note: Erasing Diagnostic Trouble Codes (DTCs) does NOT require that you do the idle learn procedure.**

Remove or replace the throttle body

1   Make sure that all electrical components (air conditioning system, lights, rear window defogger, sound system, etc.) are turned OFF.

2   Start the engine, bring it up to 3000 rpm and hold it there, with no load, i.e. in PARK or NEUTRAL, until the radiator fan comes on or until the engine coolant temperature reaches 194-degrees F.

3   Allow the engine to idle for at least five minutes with no load on it.

**➡Note: If the radiator fan comes on during this five-minute period, don't include the time during which the fan runs as part of the five minutes.**

## RESETTING THE POWER WINDOW CONTROL UNIT

You must reset the power window control unit after you do any of the following procedures:

Disconnect the battery

Remove the No. 1 (20-amp) fuse from the under-dash fuse and relay box)

Disconnect the 18-pin connector from the power window control unit

Remove the window regulator, the window glass or the glass run channel

Disconnect the driver's door wiring harness

4  Turn the ignition switch to OFF, then turn it to ON.

5  Fully open the driver's window by holding the driver's switch in the AUTO DOWN position. When the window reaches its fully open position, hold the driver's switch in the AUTO DOWN position for two seconds.

6  Fully close the driver's window, without stopping, by holding the driver's switch in the AUTO UP position. When the window reaches its fully closed position, hold the driver's switch in the AUTO UP position for two seconds.

7  The power window control unit should now operate correctly.

8  If the window doesn't operate in AUTO, repeat this procedure.

## 2  Battery - emergency jump starting

Refer to the *Booster battery (jump) starting* procedure at the front of this manual.

## 3  Battery - check and replacement

### ✳✳ CAUTION 1:

**Always disconnect the cable from the negative battery terminal FIRST and hook it up LAST or the battery may be shorted by the tool being used to loosen the cable clamps.**

### ✳✳ CAUTION 2:

**The radio in some models is equipped with an anti-theft system; make sure you have the correct anti-theft codes for the radio and for the navigation system, if equipped, before disconnecting the battery.**

## CHECK

◆ **Refer to illustrations 3.2 and 3.3**

1  Disconnect the negative battery cable, then the positive cable from the battery.

2  Check the battery state of charge. Visually inspect the indicator eye on the top of the battery; if the indicator eye is black in color charge the battery as described in Chapter 1. Next perform an open voltage circuit test using a digital voltmeter.

➡**Note: The battery's surface charge must be removed before accurate voltage measurements can be made. Turn on the high beams for ten seconds, then turn them off and let the vehicle stand for two minutes. With the engine and all accessories Off, touch the negative probe of the voltmeter to the negative terminal of the battery and the positive probe to the positive terminal of the battery (see illustration). The battery voltage should be 12.5 volts or slightly above. If the battery is less than the specified voltage, charge the battery before proceeding to the next test. Do not proceed with the battery load test unless the battery charge is correct.**

3  Perform a battery load test. An accurate check of the battery condition can only be performed with a load tester (available at most auto

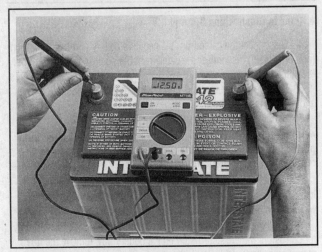

**3.2  To test the open circuit voltage of the battery, touch the black probe of the voltmeter to the negative terminal and the red probe to the positive terminal of the battery; a fully charged battery should be about 12.5 volts**

parts stores). This test evaluates the ability of the battery to operate the starter and other accessories during periods of high current draw. Connect the load tester to the battery terminals (see illustration). Load test the battery according to the tool manufacturer's instructions. This tool increases the load demand (current draw) on the battery. Maintain the load on the battery for 15 seconds or less and observe that the battery voltage does not drop below 9.6 volts. If the battery condition is weak or defective, the tool will indicate this condition immediately.

➡**Note: Cold temperatures will cause the minimum voltage reading to drop slightly. Follow the chart given in the manufacturer's instructions to compensate for cold climates. Minimum load voltage for freezing temperatures (32 degrees F) should be approximately 9.1 volts.**

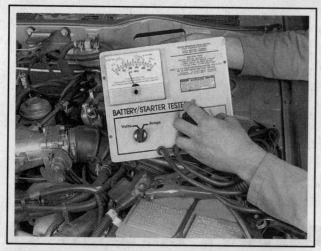

**3.3 Some battery load testers (like this one) are equipped with an ammeter that allows you to vary the amount of the load on the battery (less expensive testers only have a load switch that puts the battery under a fixed load)**

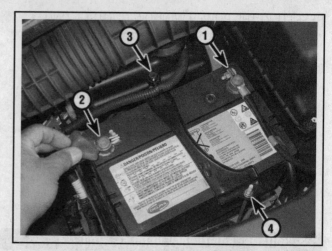

**3.4 First, disconnect the cable from the negative terminal (1), then disconnect the cable from the positive terminal (2). To remove the battery, pull off the harness retainer (3) and unscrew the nut underneath, then unscrew the other nut (4) and remove the hold-down clamp**

## REPLACEMENT

▶ **Refer to illustrations 3.4 and 3.8**

4   Disconnect the cable from the negative battery terminal first, then (and only then!) disconnect the cable from the positive battery terminal (see illustration).

5   Remove the battery hold-down clamp nuts (see illustration 3.4) and remove the hold-down clamp.

6   Lift out the battery. Be careful - it's heavy.

➡**Note: Battery straps and handlers are available at most auto parts stores for a reasonable price. They make it easier to remove and carry the battery.**

7   While the battery is out, remove the plastic battery box and inspect it for corrosion. If there's corrosion on the plastic battery box, wash it with soap and water and rinse it off thoroughly.

8   While the plastic battery box is out, inspect the metal battery tray for corrosion. If there's corrosion on the battery tray, remove the tray's mounting bolts (see illustration) and remove the tray from the engine compartment. Clean the deposits from the metal to prevent the battery tray from further corrosion.

9   If you are replacing the battery, make sure you get one that's iden-

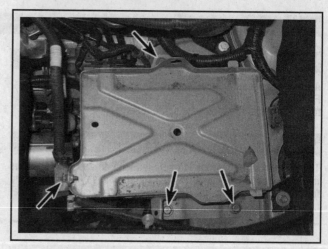

**3.8 To remove the battery tray, remove these bolts**

tical, with the same dimensions, amperage rating, cold cranking rating, etc.

10  Installation is the reverse of removal. Be sure to connect the positive cable first and the negative cable last (see Section 1).

## 4  Battery cables - check and replacement

▶ **Refer to illustrations 4.4a, 4.4b, 4.4c, 4.4d, 4.4e and 4.4f**

1   Periodically inspect the entire length of each battery cable for damage, cracked or burned insulation and corrosion. Poor battery cable connections can cause starting problems and decreased engine performance.

2   Inspect the cable-to-terminal connections at the ends of the cables for cracks, loose wire strands and corrosion. The presence of white, fluffy deposits under the insulation at the cable terminal connection means that the cable is corroded and should be replaced. Also inspect the battery posts for distortion and corrosion. If they're corroded, clean them.

3   When removing the cables, always disconnect the cable from the negative battery terminal first and hook it up last, or you might accidentally short out the battery with the tool you're using to loosen the cable clamps. Even if you're only replacing the cable for the positive terminal, be sure to disconnect the negative cable from the battery first.

### ❋❋ CAUTION:

**The radio on some models and, if equipped, the navigation system, have an anti-theft system. Make sure you have the correct anti-theft codes before disconnecting the battery. You'll also want to write down the frequencies for the radio's preset buttons.**

4   Disconnect the old cables from the battery, then trace each of them to their opposite ends and disconnect them (see illustrations). Be sure to note the routing of each cable before disconnecting it to ensure

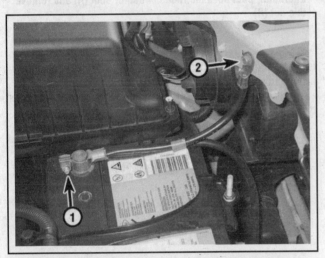

**4.4a  To remove the ground cable, loosen the nut (1) at the negative terminal and slide the cable clamp off the negative battery terminal, remove the bolt (2) from the upper radiator crossmember . . .**

**4.4b  . . . then raise the front of the vehicle, place it securely on jackstands, remove this bolt (3) and disconnect the ground cable from this bracket on the front of the transaxle**

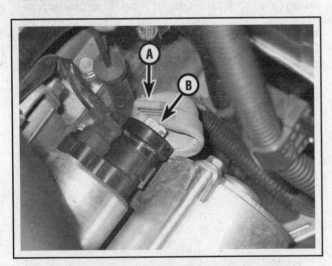

**4.4c  To detach the positive cable from the starter solenoid, raise the vehicle and place it securely on jackstands, then peel back the weather boot (A) and remove this nut (B)**

**4.4d  To detach the cable between the battery positive terminal and the engine compartment fuse and relay box, trace the routing of the cable across the top of the firewall to the fuse box at the right rear corner of the engine compartment, and detach each of the harness clips from the firewall by carefully pulling them out**

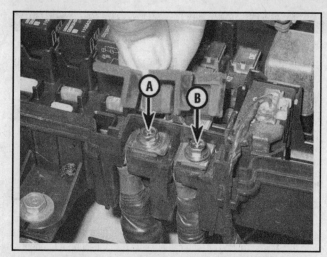

**4.4e** To disconnect the positive battery cable from the engine compartment fuse and relay box, remove the fuse box cover and the rubber weather seal from the two positive battery terminals, then remove bolt A. If you're going to replace the third positive cable, which goes to the alternator, remove bolt B

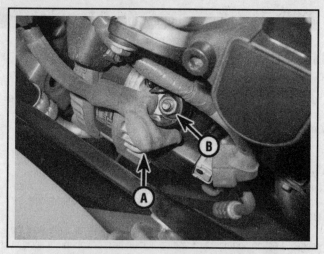

**4.4f** To disconnect the third positive battery cable from the alternator, peel back the rubber weather boot (A) and remove this nut (B)

correct installation.

5   If you are replacing any of the old cables, take them with you when buying new cables. It is vitally important that you replace the cables with identical parts.

6   Clean the threads of the solenoid or ground connection with a wire brush to remove rust and corrosion. Apply a light coat of battery terminal corrosion inhibitor or petroleum jelly to the threads to prevent future corrosion.

7   Attach the cable to the solenoid or ground connection and tighten the mounting nut/bolt securely.

8   Before connecting a new cable to the battery make sure that it reaches the battery post without having to be stretched.

9   Connect the cable to the positive battery terminal first, then connect the ground cables to the negative battery terminal (see Section 1).

## 5   Ignition system - general information

1   The electronic ignition system consists of the Powertrain Control Module (PCM), the ignition switch, the battery, the six ignition coils and the spark plugs.

2   The PCM alters ignition timing during warm-up, idle and warm running conditions. It controls ignition timing in accordance with the engine speed, the manifold absolute pressure and the engine coolant temperature. The PCM uses data from the Camshaft Position (Top Dead Center) [CMP (TDC)] sensors to determine ignition timing during start-ups, and anytime that the crank angle is abnormal. The PCM calculates engine speed based on the data that it receives from the Crankshaft Position (CKP) sensor. It uses a Manifold Absolute Pressure (MAP) sensor to determine manifold absolute pressure. For more information about the CMP (TDC), CKP and MAP sensors, refer to Chapter 6.

## 6  Ignition system - check

♦ **Refer to illustration 6.2**

### ✳✳ WARNING:

**Because of the high voltage generated by the ignition system, use extreme care when performing a procedure involving ignition components.**

1   If a malfunction occurs in the ignition system, do not immediately assume that the distributor is causing the problem. First, check the following items:

    *a)  Make sure that the cable clamps at the battery terminals are clean and tight.*

    *b)  Test the condition of the battery (see Section 3). If it doesn't pass all the tests, replace it.*

    *c)  Check the ignition coil connections.*

    *d)  Check any relevant fuses in the engine compartment fuse and relay box (see Chapter 12). If they're burned, determine the cause and repair the circuit.*

2   Check the ignition spark at the plugs. If the engine turns over but won't start, disconnect an ignition coil from a spark plug and attach a calibrated spark tester between the ignition coil high-tension terminal and the spark plug (see illustration). Spark testers are available at most auto parts stores. Then crank the engine and note whether or not the tester flashes.

3   If the tester flashes during cranking, sufficient voltage is reaching the plug to fire it. Repeat this test for each cylinder to verify that the other coils are OK.

4   If the tester doesn't flash during cranking at some cylinder(s), you cannot rule out the possibility that the spark plug for that cylinder is fouled. So before you condemn the coil, remove the spark plug and clean it thoroughly (see Chapter 1), then retest.

5   If, even after cleaning the plug, the tester doesn't flash during

**6.2  To use a calibrated spark tester, remove a coil and install the tester between the coil high-tension terminal and the spark plug. Crank the engine. If the coil is generating enough voltage to fire the plug, the tester will flash**

cranking, inspect the primary wire connector at the coil. Make sure that it's clean and tight.

6   If the spark plug is in good shape, the coil might be defective.

7   If the tester doesn't flash or flashes intermittently at all cylinders during cranking, the PCM is probably defective. Have the PCM checked out by a dealer service department or other qualified repair shop (testing the PCM is beyond the scope of the do-it-yourselfer because it requires expensive special tools).

8   Any additional testing of the ignition system must be done by a dealer service department or other qualified repair shop.

## 7  Ignition coils - replacement

♦ **Refer to illustration 7.2**

1   Remove the engine cover (see Chapter 2A).

2   Disconnect the electrical connector from the ignition coil (see illustration).

3   Remove the ignition coil mounting bolt.

4   Remove the ignition coil from the spark plug.

5   Installation is the reverse of removal.

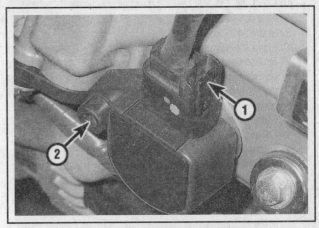

**7.2  To disconnect the electrical connector from the ignition coil, depress the release tab (1) on the side of the connector and pull off the connector. To detach an ignition coil from the valve cover, remove the bolt (2)**

## 8    Charging system - general information and precautions

The charging system includes the alternator (with an integral voltage regulator), a charge indicator light on the dash, the battery, an Electrical Load Detector (ELD), a 120-amp fuse and the wiring connecting all of these components. The charging system supplies electrical power for the ignition system, the lights, the radio, etc. The alternator is driven by a drivebelt at the one end of the engine. The alternator's voltage output is controlled by a conventional internal voltage regulator, which keeps charging output within a range of about 13.5 to 14.5 volts. The ELD, which is located in the engine compartment fuse and relay box, sends a variable voltage signal to the Powertrain Control Module (PCM) that varies in accordance with the total power demand imposed on the charging system by the electrical devices and systems in operation. The PCM uses this variable voltage signal to calculate the actual level of charging voltage needed and alters the charging voltage output accordingly.

The charging system doesn't ordinarily require periodic maintenance. However, the accessory drivebelt, battery and wires and connections should be inspected at the intervals outlined in Chapter 1.

The dashboard warning light should come on when the ignition key is turned to ON, but it should go off immediately after the engine is started. If it remains on, there is a malfunction in the charging system (see Section 9).

Be very careful when making electrical circuit connections to a vehicle equipped with an alternator and note the following:

a) *When reconnecting wires to the alternator from the battery, be sure to note the polarity.*

b) *Before using arc-welding equipment to repair any part of the vehicle, disconnect the wires from the alternator and the battery terminals.*

c) *Never start the engine with a battery charger connected.*

d) *Always disconnect both battery leads before using a battery charger.*

e) *The alternator is turned by an engine drivebelt that could cause serious injury if your hands, hair or clothes become entangled in it with the engine running.*

f) *Because the alternator is connected directly to the battery, it could arc or cause a fire if overloaded or shorted out.*

g) *Wrap a plastic bag over the alternator and secure it with rubber bands before steam cleaning the engine.*

## 9    Charging system - check

▶ **Refer to illustration 9.3**

1    If a malfunction occurs in the charging circuit, do not immediately assume that the alternator is causing the problem. First, check the following items:

a) *Make sure the battery cable clamps, where they connect to the battery, are clean and tight.*

b) *Test the condition of the battery (see Section 3). If it does not pass all the tests, replace it with a new battery.*

c) *Check the external alternator wiring and connections.*

d) *Check the drivebelt condition and tension (see Chapter 1).*

e) *Check the alternator mounting bolts for tightness.*

f) *Run the engine and check the alternator for abnormal noise.*

g) *Check the 120-amp fuse in the engine compartment fuse and relay box (see Chapter 12). If it's burned, determine the cause and repair the circuit.*

h) *Check the charge light on the dash. It should illuminate when the ignition key is turned ON (engine not running). If it doesn't come on, disconnect the electrical connector and the ground wire from the alternator. The charge light should now come on (because by opening the charging circuit, you have eliminated all charging voltage. If the light still doesn't illuminate, check fuse number 6 (15 amp), which is located in the left (driver's side) passenger compartment fuse and relay box. If the fuse No. 6 is blown, troubleshoot and repair the charge light circuit and then replace the fuse. If the charge light still doesn't come on, check the bulb (see Chapter 12). If it's blown, replace it.*

i) *Make sure that the PCM hasn't stored any diagnostic trouble codes for the Electrical Load Detector (ELD) system (see Chapter 6 for more information about the ELD).*

2    With the ignition key turned to the OFF position, check battery voltage with all electrical accessories (blower fan, radio, cigarette lighter, cooling fan, etc.) turned off. It should be about 12.5 volts (it

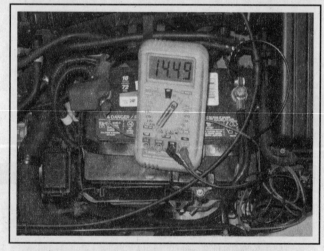

**9.3  To check charging voltage, hook up a multimeter to the battery terminals and note the indicated voltage with the engine running, which should be 13.8 to 14.8 volts**

might be slightly higher if the engine has been turned off for less than an hour).

3    Check the charging voltage with the engine running. Start the engine, raise the engine rpm to 1500 and check the battery voltage again. It should now be approximately 13.8 to 14.8 volts (see illustration).

4    Load the battery and observe the charging voltage. Turn on the high beam headlights, the A/C blower on HIGH, the windshield wipers and the radio. The voltage should drop and then come back up as each accessory is selected. If the charging system is working properly the voltage should stay above 13.5 volts. If the voltage drops below 13 volts, the charging system is defective.

5   Lower the engine rpm back to idle and observe the charging voltage. The charging voltage should not drop below 13 volts with the decrease in engine rpm. Apply the brakes and observe the charging voltage at idle. It should remain above 13 volts.

6   Turn off all the electrical loads (high beam headlights, the A/C blower on HIGH, the windshield wipers and the radio), run the engine at 1600 rpm and watch the charging voltage rise. It should not rise above 15 volts.

7   If the charging voltage does not exhibit distinct changes when engine rpm increases and accessory loads are added, the voltage regulator is defective. If the charging voltages are low and the drivebelts and battery are all in good condition, the alternator is defective. In this situation, replace the alternator and voltage regulator as a single unit.

## 10  Alternator - removal and installation

◆ **Refer to illustrations 10.4, 10.5 and 10.8**

1   Disconnect the cable from the negative battery terminal (see Section 1).

### ✳✳ CAUTION:

**The radio on some models and the optional navigation system are equipped with anti-theft systems. So make sure that you have the correct anti-theft codes before disconnecting the battery. You'll also want to write down the frequencies for the radio's preset buttons.**

2   Remove the engine cover (see Chapter 2A).
3   Remove the drivebelt (see Chapter 1).
4   Remove the nut and disconnect the battery cable from the B+ terminal and disconnect the four-pin electrical connector (see illustration).
5   Remove the alternator upper mounting bolt (see illustration). On 2001 and 2002 Acura models and 2003 and 2004 Honda models, remove the harness clamp bolt and set the harness aside.
6   Raise the vehicle and place it securely on jackstands.
7   Remove the engine splash shield (see Chapter 2A).
8   Remove the lower mounting bolt (see illustration) and remove the alternator.

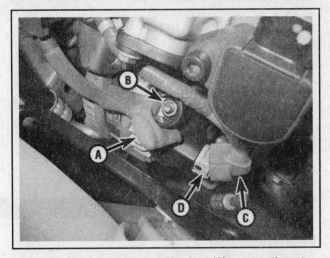

**10.4  Peel back the rubber weather boot (A), remove the nut (B) from the B+ stud-type terminal and disconnect the output cable from the alternator, then peel back the other rubber weather boot (C) and disconnect the four-pin electrical connector (D) from the alternator**

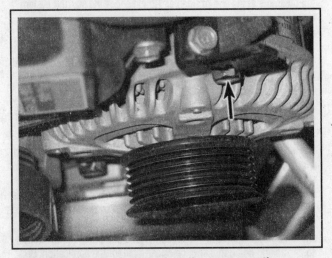

**10.5  To detach the alternator from the upper mounting bracket, remove this bolt**

**10.8  To detach the alternator from the lower mounting bracket, remove this bolt**

9 If you're replacing the alternator, take the old one with you when purchasing the replacement unit. Make sure that the new/rebuilt unit looks identical to the old alternator. Look at the electrical terminals on the backside of the alternator. They should be the same in number, size and location as the terminals on the old alternator. Finally, look at the identification numbers. They will be stamped into the housing or printed on a tag attached to the housing. Make sure that the I.D. numbers are the same on both alternators.

10 Many new/rebuilt alternators DO NOT have a pulley installed, so you might have to swap the pulley from the old unit to the new/rebuilt

one. When buying an alternator, find out the store's policy regarding pulley swaps. Some stores perform this service free of charge. If your local auto parts store doesn't offer this service, you'll have to purchase a puller for removing the pulley and do it yourself.

11 Installation is the reverse of removal. Be sure to tighten the alternator mounting bolts securely.

12 Reconnect the cable to the negative terminal of the battery (see Section 1). Check the charging voltage (see Section 9) to verify that the alternator is operating correctly.

## 11　Starting system - general information and precautions

The starting system consists of the battery, the starter motor, the starter solenoid and the wires connecting them. The solenoid is mounted directly on the starter motor. The solenoid/starter motor assembly is installed on the front of the transaxle bellhousing.

When the ignition key is turned to the START position, the starter solenoid is actuated through the starter control circuit. The starter solenoid then connects the battery to the starter. The battery supplies the electrical energy to the starter motor, which does the actual work of cranking the engine.

The starter can only be operated when the shift lever is in the PARK or NEUTRAL position.

Always observe the following precautions when working on the starting system:

a) *Excessive cranking of the starter motor can overheat it and cause serious damage. Never operate the starter motor for more than 15 seconds at a time without pausing to allow it to cool for at least two minutes.*

b) *The starter is connected directly to the battery and could arc or cause a fire if mishandled, overloaded or shorted out.*

c) *Always detach the cable from the negative terminal of the battery before working on the starting system.*

## 12　Starter motor and circuit - check

▶ **Refer to illustrations 12.3 and 12.4**

1 If a malfunction occurs in the starting circuit, do not immediately assume that the starter is causing the problem. First, check the following items:

a) *Make sure the battery cable clamps, where they connect to the battery, are clean and tight.*

b) *Check the condition of the battery cables (see Section 4). Replace any defective battery cables with new parts.*

c) *Test the condition of the battery (see Section 3). If it does not pass all the tests, replace it with a new battery.*

d) *Check the starter solenoid wiring and connections. Refer to the wiring diagrams at the end of Chapter 12.*

e) *Check the starter mounting bolts for tightness.*

f) *Check the fuses in the engine compartment fuse and relay box (see Chapter 12). If they're burned, determine the cause and repair the circuit. Also, check the ignition switch circuit for correct operation (see the wiring diagrams at the end of Chapter 12).*

g) *Check the operation of the gear position switch (automatic transaxle) or clutch start circuit (manual transaxle). Make sure the shift lever is in PARK or NEUTRAL (automatic transaxle) or the clutch pedal is pressed (manual transaxle). Refer to Chapter 7 for the gear position switch check and adjustment procedure. Refer to the Chapter 12 wiring diagrams for the necessary circuit checks for the clutch activation system. These systems must operate correctly to provide battery voltage to the starter solenoid.*

h) *Check the operation of the starter cut relay. The starter cut relay is located in the fuse/relay box under the dash on the driver's side.*

*Refer to Chapter 12 for the testing procedure.*

2 If the starter does not activate when the ignition switch is turned to the start position, check for battery voltage to the solenoid. This will determine if the solenoid is receiving the correct voltage signal from the ignition switch. Connect a voltmeter to the starter solenoid "S" terminal. Then note the indicated voltage when an assistant turns the ignition switch to the START position. It should be about the same as battery voltage. If there's no voltage at the S terminal, refer to the wiring diagrams at the end of Chapter 12 and check the starring system fuses. The two starting system fuses, which are located inside the engine compartment fuse and relay box, are No. 41 (120-amp) and No. 42 (50-amp). Also check the starter cut relay for correct operation. The starter cut relay is located inside the left (driver's side) fuse/relay panel. Refer to Chapter 12 for help with testing relays. If voltage is available but the starter motor doesn't engage and spin the driveplate ring gear, remove the starter from the engine (see Section 13) and bench test the starter (see Step 4).

3 If the starter turns over slowly, check the starter cranking voltage and the current draw from the battery. This test must be performed with the starter assembly on the engine. Crank the engine over (for 10 seconds or less) and observe the battery voltage. It should not drop below 8.5 volts. Also, observe the current draw using an ammeter (see illustration). It should not exceed 380 amps. If the starter motor exceeds these values, replace it. Several conditions might affect the starter's cranking power. The battery must be in good condition and the battery cold-cranking rating must not be under-rated for the application. Be sure to check the battery specifications carefully. The battery terminals and cables must be clean and not corroded. Also, in cases of extremely

**12.3 To use an inductive ammeter, simply hold the ammeter over the positive or negative battery cable (whichever cable has better clearance)**

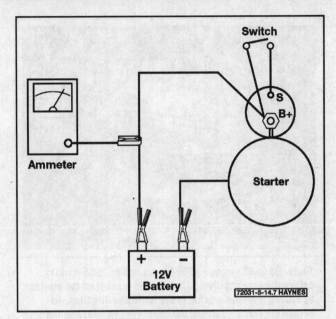

**12.4 Starter motor bench testing details**

cold temperatures, make sure the battery and/or engine block is warmed before performing the tests.

4  If the starter is receiving voltage but does not activate, remove and check the starter/solenoid assembly on the bench. Most likely the solenoid is defective. In some rare cases, the engine may be seized so be sure to try and rotate the crankshaft pulley (see Chapter 2A) before proceeding. With the starter/solenoid assembly mounted in a vise on the workbench, connect one jumper cable from the negative terminal (-) to the body of the starter (see illustration). Install another jumper cable from the positive terminal (+) on the battery to the B+ terminal on the

starter. Install a starter switch and apply battery voltage to the solenoid S terminal (for 10 seconds or less) and observe the solenoid plunger, shift lever and overrunning clutch extend and rotate the pinion drive. If the pinion drive extends but does not rotate, the solenoid is operating but the starter motor is defective. If there is no movement but the solenoid clicks, the solenoid and/or the starter motor is defective. If the solenoid plunger extends and rotates the pinion drive, the starter/solenoid assembly is working properly.

## 13  Starter motor - removal and installation

▶ Refer to illustrations 13.2a, 13.2b, 13.3a, 13.3b and 13.4

1  Detach the cable from the negative terminal of the battery (see Section 1).

### ⁂ CAUTION:

**The radio on some models and, if equipped, the navigation system, are equipped with an anti-theft system. Make sure that you have the correct anti-theft codes before disconnecting the battery. You'll also want to write down the frequencies for the radio's preset buttons.**

2  On 2001 and 2002 Acura models and 2003 and 2004 Honda models, unlatch the clamp for the automatic transmission fluid cooler hose (see illustration) and set the hose aside. On 2003 through 2006 Acura models and 2005 Honda models, detach the harness clamp from the bracket on the starter (see illustration). On 2007 Acura models, remove the air filter housing (see Chapter 4), the battery (see Section 3) and the dipstick for the automatic transaxle (see Chapter 2A).

**13.2a  Before removing the starter on 2001 and 2002 Acuras and 2003 and 2004 Hondas, pry this clamp (A) open with a small screwdriver and pull the ATF cooler hose out of the way. To detach the starter, remove the upper (not visible) and lower (B) mounting bolts**

**13.2b** On 2003 through 2006 Acuras and on 2005 Hondas, detach the harness clamp (A) from the bracket on the starter by sliding it off the bracket in the indicated direction. To detach the starter, remove the upper (not visible) and the lower (B) mounting bolts

**13.3a  Starter motor details (2001 and 2002 Acura and 2003 and 2004 Honda models)**

1   S terminal
2   B terminal (starter cable)

3   Starter mounting bolts (lower bolt not visible in this photo)

**13.3b  On 2003 and later Acura and 2005 and later Honda models, peel back the rubber boot (A) and pull off the electrical connector (B), then peel back the rubber boot (C), remove the nut (D) and remove the starter cable**

**13.4  Upper (A) and lower (B) starter mounting bolts (2003 and later Acura and 2005 and later Honda models)**

3   Disconnect the wires from the terminals on the starter motor solenoid (see illustrations). Also disconnect any clips that attach the wiring to the starter assembly.

4   Unscrew the starter mounting bolts and remove the starter.

5   Installation is the reverse of removal. Be sure to tighten the starter mounting bolts to the torque listed in this Chapter's Specifications, then reconnect the cable to the negative terminal of the battery (see Section 1).

## Specifications

### General

Battery voltage
    Engine off               12 to 12.5 volts
    Engine running       13.5 to 14.5 volts
Firing order             1-4-2-5-3-6

| Torque specifications | Ft-lbs (unless otherwise indicated) | Nm |
| --- | --- | --- |
| Alternator mounting bolts | | |
|    Upper bolt | 192 in-lbs | 22 |
|    Lower bolt | 33 | 44 |
| Starter motor mounting bolts | | |
|    Upper bolt | 33 | 44 |
|    Lower bolt | 47 | 64 |

**Notes**

# 6

## EMISSIONS AND ENGINE CONTROL SYSTEMS

**Section**

## 1 General information

♦ **Refer to illustration 1.4**

To prevent pollution of the atmosphere from incompletely burned and evaporating gases, and to maintain good driveability and fuel economy, a number of emission control systems are incorporated. They include the:

> Catalytic converter
> Electrical Load Detector (ELD)
> Evaporative Emissions Control (EVAP) system
> Exhaust Gas Recirculation (EGR) system
> On-Board Diagnostic-II (OBD-II) system
> Positive Crankcase Ventilation (PCV) system
> Programmed Fuel Injection (PGM-FI) system (electronic engine control system)
> Variable Cylinder Management (VCM) system (2WD models)
> Variable Valve Timing and Lift Electronic Control (VTEC) system (AWD models)

This Chapter includes general descriptions of these any other emissions-related devices and component replacement procedures (when possible) for each of the systems listed above. Before assuming that an emissions control system is malfunctioning, check the fuel and ignition systems carefully. The diagnosis of some emission control devices requires specialized tools, equipment and training. If a procedure is beyond your ability, consult a dealer service department or other repair shop. Remember, the most frequent cause of emissions problems is simply a loose or broken wire or vacuum hose, so always check all hose and wiring connections first.

➡**Note: Because of a Federally mandated extended warranty which covers the emissions control system components, check with your dealer about warranty coverage before working on any emissions-related systems. Once the warranty has expired, you may wish to perform some of the component checks and/or replacement procedures in this Chapter to save money.**

Pay close attention to any special precautions outlined in this Chapter. It should be noted that the illustrations of the various systems

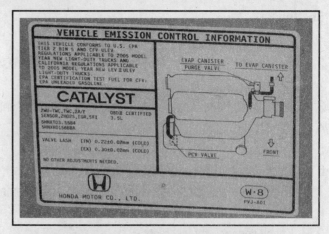

**1.4 The Vehicle Emission Control Information (VECI) label is located in the engine compartment; the VECI label specifies the emission-control systems on your vehicle, and includes important tune-up specifications and a vacuum hose routing diagram**

might not exactly match the system installed on your vehicle because of annual changes made by the manufacturer during production and because of running changes made during a model year.

A Vehicle Emissions Control Information (VECI) label is attached to the underside of the hood (see illustration). This label specifies the important emissions systems on the vehicle and it provides the important specifications for tune-ups. Part of the VECI label, the Vacuum Hose Routing Diagram, provides a vacuum hose schematic with emissions components identified. If there's a discrepancy between the information in this manual and the information on the VECI label, defer to the information on the VECI label. It contains the most up-to-date information about your vehicle, and might reflect some running change made to the vehicle after the manual was published.

## 2 On Board Diagnosis (OBD) system and trouble codes

### SCAN TOOL INFORMATION

♦ **Refer to illustrations 2.1 and 2.2**

1   Hand-held scanners are handy for analyzing the engine management systems used on late-model vehicles. Because extracting the Diagnostic Trouble Codes (DTCs) from an engine management system is now the first step in troubleshooting many computer-controlled systems and components, even the most basic generic code readers are capable of accessing a computer's DTCs (see illustration). More powerful scan tools can also perform many of the diagnostics once associated with expensive factory scan tools. If you're planning to obtain a generic scan tool for your vehicle, make sure that it's compatible with OBD-II systems. If you don't plan to purchase a code reader or scan tool and don't have access to one, you can have the codes extracted by a dealer service department or by an independent repair shop.

2   With the advent of the Federally mandated emission control system known as On-Board Diagnostics-II (OBD-II), specially designed

**2.1 Simple code readers are an economical way to extract trouble codes when the CHECK ENGINE light comes on**

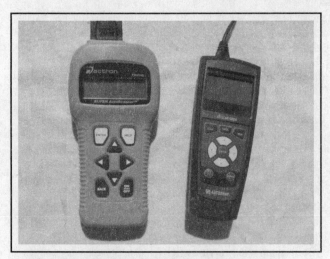

**2.2 Scanners like these from Actron and AutoXray are powerful diagnostic aids - they can tell you just about anything that you want to know about your engine management system**

scanners were developed. Several tool manufacturers have released OBD-II scan tools for the home mechanic (see illustration).

➡**Note: An aftermarket generic scanner should work with any model covered by this manual. Before purchasing a generic scan tool, verify that it will work properly with the OBD-II system you want to scan. If necessary, of course, you can always have the codes extracted by a dealer service department or an independent repair shop with a professional scan tool. Some auto parts stores even provide this service.**

## OBD SYSTEM GENERAL DESCRIPTION

3    All models are equipped with the second generation OBD-II system. This system consists of an on-board computer known as the Powertrain Control Module (PCM), and information sensors, which monitor various functions of the engine and send data to the PCM. This system incorporates a series of diagnostic monitors that detect and identify fuel injection and emissions control systems faults and store the information in the computer memory. This updated system also tests sensors and output actuators, diagnoses drive cycles, freezes data and clears codes.

4    This powerful diagnostic computer must be accessed using an OBD-II scan tool, or OBD-II code reader, plugged into the 16-pin Data Link Connector (DLC) located under the driver's dash area. The PCM is located below the center of the instrument panel, mounted to the firewall. The PCM is the "brain" of the electronically controlled fuel and emissions system. It receives data from a number of sensors and other electronic components (switches, relays, etc.). Based on the information it receives, the PCM generates output signals to control various relays, solenoids (i.e. fuel injectors) and other actuators. The PCM is specifically calibrated to optimize the emissions, fuel economy and driveability of the vehicle.

5    It isn't a good idea to attempt diagnosis or replacement of the PCM or emission control components at home while the vehicle is under warranty. Because of a Federally mandated warranty which covers the emissions system components and because any owner-induced damage to the PCM, the sensors and/or the control devices may void this warranty, take the vehicle to a dealer service department if the PCM or a system component malfunctions.

## INFORMATION SENSORS

6    **Accelerator Pedal Position (APP) sensor** - The APP sensor, which is part of the electronic throttle control system, is located at the right rear corner of the engine compartment (2003 through 2006 Acura and 2005 and later Honda models), or at the top of the accelerator pedal (2007 Acura models). All of these models are equipped with an Electronic Throttle Control (ETC) system, which uses an electronic throttle body, i.e. there is no accelerator cable. The throttle plate inside the throttle body is electronically controlled by the PCM. The APP sensor is a potentiometer that receives a constant voltage input from the PCM and sends back a voltage signal that varies in relation to the position (angle) of the accelerator pedal. As you press the accelerator pedal, the APP sensor alters its voltage signal to the PCM in proportion to the angle of the pedal, and the PCM commands a motor inside the throttle body to open or close the throttle plate accordingly.

7    **Camshaft Position (CMP) sensor** - The CMP sensor produces a signal that the PCM uses to identify the number 1 cylinder and to time the firing sequence of the fuel injectors. The CMP sensor is located on the right end of the front cylinder head.

8    **Crankshaft Position (CKP) sensor** - The CKP sensor produces a signal that the PCM uses to determine the position of the crankshaft. The CKP sensor is located on the right end of the engine, down near the crankshaft pulley.

9    **Electrical Load Detector (ELD)** - The ELD monitors the electrical load on the system and keeps the PCM informed. The PCM controls the voltage output of the alternator in response to the data conveyed by this signal. The ELD is located inside the engine compartment fuse and relay box.

10    **Engine Coolant Temperature (ECT) sensor** - The ECT sensor is a thermistor (temperature-sensitive variable resistor) that sends a voltage signal to the PCM, which uses this data to determine the temperature of the engine coolant. The ECT sensor helps the PCM control the air/fuel mixture ratio and ignition timing, and it also helps the PCM determine when to turn the Exhaust Gas Recirculation (EGR) system on and off. The ECT sensor is located below the left end of the upper intake manifold, on top of the coolant crossover housing. There are two ECT sensors on 2003 through 2006 Acura and 2005 and later Honda models. They're located on the same coolant housing as on earlier models.

11    **Fuel tank pressure sensor** - The fuel tank pressure sensor measures the fuel tank pressure when the PCM tests the EVAP system, and it's also used to control fuel tank pressure by signaling the EVAP system to purge the fuel tank vapors when the pressure becomes excessive. The fuel tank pressure sensor is located on top of the EVAP canister.

12    **Input shaft (mainshaft) speed sensor** - The input shaft (or mainshaft) speed sensor is a magnetic pick-up coil located on the front of the transaxle.

13    **Intake Air Temperature (IAT) sensor** - The IAT sensor monitors the temperature of the air entering the engine and sends a signal to the PCM. On 2001 and 2002 Acura and 2003 and 2004 Honda models, the IAT sensor is located at the left rear corner of the intake manifold. On 2003 and 2004 Acura models, the IAT sensor is located on the air intake duct. On 2005 and 2006 Acura and on 2005 and later Honda models, the IAT sensor is located on the front of the intake manifold. On 2007 Acura models the IAT sensor is an integral component of the Mass Air Flow (MAF) sensor, which is located on the air filter housing.

14    **Knock sensor** - The knock sensor is a "piezoelectric" crystal that oscillates in proportion to engine vibration. (The term piezoelectric refers to the property of certain crystals that produce a voltage when

subjected to a mechanical stress.) The oscillation of the piezoelectric crystal produces a voltage output that is monitored by the PCM, which retards the ignition timing when the oscillation exceeds a certain threshold. When the engine is operating normally, the knock sensor oscillates consistently and its voltage signal is steady. When detonation occurs, engine vibration increases, and the oscillation of the knock sensor exceeds a design threshold. (Detonation is an uncontrolled explosion, after the spark occurs at the spark plug, which spontaneously combusts the remaining air/fuel mixture, resulting in a "pinging" or "slapping" sound.) If allowed to continue, the engine could be damaged. The knock sensor is located below the intake manifold, in the valley between the cylinder heads, on top of the engine block. You have to remove the intake manifold to access the knock sensor.

15 **Manifold Absolute Pressure (MAP) sensor** - The MAP sensor, which is located on top of the throttle body, monitors the pressure or vacuum downstream from the throttle plate, inside the intake manifold. The MAP sensor measures intake manifold pressure and vacuum on the absolute scale, i.e. from zero instead of from sea-level atmospheric pressure (14.7 psi). The MAP sensor converts the absolute pressure into a variable voltage signal that changes with the pressure. The PCM uses this data to determine engine load so that it can alter the ignition advance and fuel enrichment.

16 **Mass Air Flow/Intake Air Temperature (MAF/IAT) sensor** - The MAF/IAT sensor is used only on 2007 Acura models. The MAF sensor is the means by which the PCM measures the amount of intake air drawn into the engine. It uses a hot-wire sensing element to measure the amount of air entering the engine. The wire is constantly maintained at a specified temperature above the ambient temperature of the incoming air by electrical current. As intake air passes through the MAF sensor and over the hot wire, it cools the wire, and the control system immediately corrects the temperature back to its constant value. The current required to maintain the constant value is used by the PCM to determine the amount of air flowing through the MAF sensor. The MAF sensor also includes an integral Intake Air Temperature (IAT) sensor. The two components cannot be serviced separately; if either sensor is defective, replace the MAF/IAT sensor. The MAF/IAT sensor is located on top of the air filter housing.

17 **Output shaft (countershaft) speed sensor** - The output shaft (or countershaft) speed sensor is a magnetic pick-up coil, which is located on top of the transaxle. The output shaft speed sensor provides the Powertrain Control Module (PCM) with information about the rotational speed of the output shaft in the transmission. The PCM uses this information to control the torque converter and to calculate speed scheduling and the correct operating pressure for the transaxle.

18 **Oxygen sensors** - An oxygen sensor is a galvanic battery that generates a small variable voltage signal in proportion to the difference between the oxygen content in the exhaust stream and the oxygen content in the ambient air. The PCM uses the voltage signal from the upstream oxygen sensor to maintain a "stoichiometric" air/fuel ratio of 14.7:1 by constantly adjusting the "on-time" of the fuel injectors. On 2001 and 2002 Acura and 2003 and 2004 Honda models, there are two oxygen sensors: one upstream sensor (ahead of the catalytic converter) and a downstream oxygen sensor (on the catalyst). On 2003 and later Acura and 2005 and later Honda models, there are three catalytic converters, one for each cylinder head (warm-up catalysts) and one underfloor catalyst, so there are four oxygen sensors, one upstream and one downstream for each warm-up catalyst.

19 **Power Steering Pressure (PSP) switch** - The PSP switch monitors the pressure inside the power steering system. When the pressure exceeds a certain threshold at idle or during low speed maneuvers, the switch sends a voltage signal to the PCM, which raises the idle slightly to compensate for the extra load on the engine. The PSP switch is located on the power steering pressure line, at the right end of the steering rack, right above the rack.

20 **Throttle Position (TP) sensor** - 2001 and 2002 Acura and 2003 and 2004 Honda models use a conventional, cable-actuated throttle body, which is equipped with a TP sensor. The TP sensor is a potentiometer that receives a constant voltage input from the PCM and sends back a voltage signal that varies in relation to the opening angle of the throttle plate inside the throttle body. This voltage signal tells the PCM when the throttle is closed, half-open, wide open or anywhere in between. The PCM uses this data, along with information from other sensors, to calculate injector "pulse width" (the interval of time during which an injector solenoid is energized by the PCM). The TP sensor is located on the throttle body, on the end of the throttle plate shaft. If the TP sensor is defective on any of these models you must replace the throttle body. The TP sensor cannot be replaced separately.

21 **Transmission range switch** - The transmission range switch is located at the manual lever on the left side of the transaxle. The transmission range switch functions like a conventional Park/Neutral Position (PNP) switch: it prevents the engine from starting in any gear other than Park or Neutral, and it closes the circuit for the back-up lights when the shift lever is moved to Reverse. The PCM also sends a voltage signal to the transmission range switch, which uses a series of step-down resistors that act as a voltage divider. The PCM monitors the voltage output signal from the switch, which corresponds to the position of the manual lever. Thus the PCM is able to determine the gear selected and is able to determine the correct pressure for the electronic pressure control system of the transaxle.

## OUTPUT ACTUATORS

22 **EVAP canister purge valve** - The EVAP canister purge valve is located in the engine compartment, at the left rear corner of the intake manifold. The purge valve is normally closed, but when ordered to do so by the PCM, it allows the fuel vapors that are stored in the EVAP canister to be drawn into the intake manifold, where they're mixed with intake air, then burned along with the normal air/fuel mixture, under certain operating conditions. The PCM-controlled purge valve also controls this vapor flow.

23 **EVAP canister vent shut valve** - The EVAP canister vent shut valve is located underneath the vehicle, on the left end of the EVAP canister. The canister vent shut valve is normally open, but it closes and seals off the EVAP system for inspection and maintenance tests and for OBD-II leak and pressure tests.

24 **Exhaust Gas Recirculation (EGR) valve** - When the engine is put under a load (hard acceleration, passing, going up a steep hill, pulling a trailer, etc.), combustion chamber temperature increases. When combustion chamber temperature exceeds 2500 degrees, excessive amounts of oxides of nitrogen (NOx) are produced. NOx is a precursor of photochemical smog. When combined with hydrocarbons (HC), other "reactive organic compounds" (ROCs) and sunlight, it forms ozone, nitrogen dioxide and nitrogen nitrate and other nasty stuff. The PCM-controlled EGR valve allows exhaust gases to be recirculated back to the intake manifold where they dilute the incoming air/fuel mixture, which lowers the combustion chamber temperature and decreases the amount of NOx produced during high-load conditions. The EGR valve is located at the left front corner of the engine.

25 **Fuel injectors** - The fuel injectors, which spray a fine mist of fuel into the intake ports, where it is mixed with incoming air, are inductive coils under PCM control. For more information about the injectors, see Chapter 4.

26 **Idle Air Control (IAC) valve** - 2001 and 2002 Acura and 2003 and 2004 Honda models use a conventional, cable-operated throttle body, which is equipped with an Idle Air Control (IAC) valve. The IAC valve controls the amount of air allowed to bypass the throttle plate when the throttle plate is at its (nearly closed) idle position. The IAC valve is controlled by the PCM. When the engine is placed under an additional load at idle (high power steering pressure or running the air conditioning compressor during low-speed maneuvers, for example), the engine can run roughly, stumble and even stall. To prevent this from happening, the PCM opens the IAC valve to increase the idle speed enough to overcome the extra load imposed on the engine. The IAC valve is mounted on the underside of the throttle body. On later models, the Powertrain Control Module and various information sensors such as the Power Steering Pressure (PSP) switch and the Brake Pedal Position (BPP) switch handle the idle function.

27 **Ignition coils** - The ignition coils are under the control of the Powertrain Control Module (PCM). There is no separate ignition control module. Instead, "coil drivers" inside the PCM turn the primary side of the coils on and off. For more information about the ignition coils, see Chapter 5.

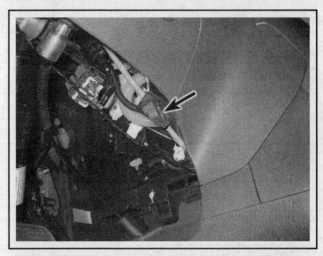

**2.30  The Data Link Connector (DLC) is located under the lower edge of the dash, between the steering column and the center console**

## OBTAINING AND CLEARING DIAGNOSTIC TROUBLE CODES (DTCS)

28 All models covered by this manual are equipped with on-board diagnostics. When the PCM recognizes a malfunction in a monitored emission control system, component or circuit, it turns on the Malfunction Indicator Light (MIL) on the dash. The PCM will continue to display the MIL until the problem is fixed and the Diagnostic Trouble Code (DTC) is cleared from the PCM's memory. You'll need a scan tool to access any DTCs stored in the PCM.

29 Before outputting any DTCs stored in the PCM, thoroughly inspect ALL electrical connectors and hoses. Make sure that all electrical connections are tight, clean and free of corrosion. And make sure that all hoses are correctly connected, fit tightly and are in good condition (no cracks or tears).

### Accessing the DTCs

▶ **Refer to illustration 2.30**

30 On these models, all of which are equipped with On-Board Diagnostic II (OBD-II) systems, the Diagnostic Trouble Codes (DTCs) can only be accessed with a scan tool. Professional scan tools are expensive, but relatively inexpensive generic scan tools (see illustrations 2.1 and 2.2) are available at most auto parts stores. Simply plug the connector of the scan tool into the diagnostic connector (see illustration),

which is located under the lower edge of the dash, just to the right of the steering column. Then follow the instructions included with the scan tool to extract the DTCs.

31 Once you have outputted all of the stored DTCs, look them up on the accompanying DTC chart.

32 After troubleshooting the source of each DTC make any necessary repairs or replace the defective component(s).

### Clearing the DTCs

33 Clear the DTCs with the scan tool in accordance with the instructions provided by the scan tool's manufacturer.

## DIAGNOSTIC TROUBLE CODES

34 The accompanying tables are a list of the Diagnostic Trouble Codes (DTCs) that can be accessed by a do-it-yourselfer working at home (there are many, many more DTCs available to professional mechanics with proprietary scan tools and software, but those codes cannot be accessed by a generic scan tool). If, after you have checked and repaired the connectors, wire harness and vacuum hoses (if applicable) for an emission-related system, component or circuit, the problem persists, have the vehicle checked by a dealer service department or other qualified repair shop.

## OBD-II TROUBLE CODES

➡**Note: Not all trouble codes apply to all models.**

| Code | Probable cause |
| --- | --- |
| P0036 | Downstream oxygen sensor (rear cylinder head), heater circuit malfunction |
| P0056 | Downstream oxygen sensor (front cylinder head, heater circuit malfunction |
| P0097 | Intake Air Temperature (IAT) sensor 2 circuit, low voltage |
| P0098 | Intake Air Temperature (IAT) sensor 2 circuit, high voltage |
| P0101 | Mass Air Flow (MAF) sensor circuit, range or performance problem |
| P0102 | Mass Air Flow (MAF) sensor circuit, low voltage |
| P0103 | Mass Air Flow (MAF) sensor circuit, high voltage |
| P0107 | Manifold Absolute Pressure (MAP) sensor circuit, low voltage |
| P0108 | Manifold Absolute Pressure (MAP) sensor circuit, high voltage |
| P0111 | Intake Air Temperature (IAT) sensor circuit, range or performance problem |
| P0112 | Intake Air Temperature (IAT) sensor circuit, low voltage |
| P0112 | Intake Air Temperature (IAT) sensor 1 circuit, low voltage |
| P0113 | Intake Air Temperature (IAT) sensor circuit, high voltage |
| P0113 | Intake Air Temperature (IAT) sensor 1 circuit, high voltage |
| P0116 | Engine Coolant Temperature (ECT) sensor circuit, range or performance problem |
| P0116 | Engine Coolant Temperature (ECT) sensor 1 circuit, range or performance problem |
| P0117 | Engine Coolant Temperature (ECT) sensor circuit, low voltage |
| P0117 | Engine Coolant Temperature (ECT) sensor 1 circuit, low voltage |
| P0118 | Engine Coolant Temperature (ECT) sensor circuit, high voltage |
| P0118 | Engine Coolant Temperature (ECT) sensor 1 circuit, high voltage |
| P0122 | Throttle Position (TP) sensor circuit, low voltage |
| P0122 | Throttle Position (TP) sensor A circuit, low voltage |
| P0123 | Throttle Position (TP) sensor circuit, high voltage |
| P0123 | Throttle Position (TP) sensor A circuit, high voltage |
| P0125 | Engine Coolant Temperature (ECT) sensor, malfunction or slow response |
| P0125 | Engine Coolant Temperature (ECT) sensor 1, malfunction or slow response |
| P0128 | Cooling system malfunction |
| P0131 | Upstream oxygen sensor circuit, low voltage |
| P0132 | Upstream oxygen sensor circuit, high voltage |
| P0133 | Upstream oxygen sensor circuit, slow response |
| P0133 | Upstream oxygen sensor circuit (rear cylinder head), slow response |
| P0134 | Upstream oxygen sensor (rear cylinder head), heater system malfunction |

| Code | Probable cause |
| --- | --- |
| P0135 | Upstream oxygen sensor circuit, heater circuit malfunction |
| P0135 | Upstream oxygen sensor circuit (rear cylinder head), heater circuit malfunction |
| P0137 | Downstream oxygen sensor circuit, low voltage |
| P0137 | Downstream oxygen sensor circuit (rear cylinder head), low voltage |
| P0138 | Downstream oxygen sensor circuit, high voltage |
| P0138 | Downstream oxygen sensor circuit (rear cylinder head), high voltage |
| P0139 | Downstream oxygen sensor circuit, slow response |
| P0139 | Downstream oxygen sensor circuit (rear cylinder head), slow response |
| P0141 | Downstream oxygen sensor, heater circuit malfunction |
| P0141 | Downstream oxygen sensor (rear cylinder head), heater circuit malfunction |
| P0153 | Upstream oxygen sensor (front cylinder head), slow response |
| P0154 | Upstream oxygen sensor (front cylinder head), heater system malfunction |
| P0155 | Upstream oxygen sensor (front cylinder head), heater circuit malfunction |
| P0157 | Downstream oxygen sensor circuit (front cylinder head), low voltage |
| P0158 | Downstream oxygen sensor circuit (front cylinder head), high voltage |
| P0159 | Downstream oxygen sensor circuit (front cylinder head), slow response |
| P0161 | Downstream oxygen sensor circuit (front cylinder head), heater circuit malfunction |
| P0171 | Fuel system too lean |
| P0171 | Fuel system too lean (rear cylinder head) |
| P0172 | Fuel system too rich |
| P0172 | Fuel system too rich (rear cylinder head) |
| P0174 | Fuel system too lean (front cylinder head) |
| P0175 | Fuel system too rich (front cylinder head) |
| P0201 | No. 1 injector circuit malfunction |
| P0202 | No. 2 injector circuit malfunction |
| P0203 | No. 3 injector circuit malfunction |
| P0204 | No. 4 injector circuit malfunction |
| P0205 | No. 5 injector circuit malfunction |
| P0206 | No. 6 injector circuit malfunction |
| P0222 | Throttle Position (TP) sensor B circuit, low voltage |
| P0223 | Throttle Position (TP) sensor B circuit, high voltage |
| P0300 | Random misfire detected |
| P0301 | Cylinder no. 1 misfire detected |
| P0302 | Cylinder no. 2 misfire detected |

## OBD-II TROUBLE CODES (CONTINUED)

→Note: Not all trouble codes apply to all models.

| Code | Probable cause |
|------|----------------|
| P0303 | Cylinder no. 3 misfire detected |
| P0304 | Cylinder no. 4 misfire detected |
| P0305 | Cylinder No. 5 misfire detected |
| P0306 | Cylinder No. 6 misfire detected |
| P0325 | Knock sensor circuit malfunction |
| P0335 | Crankshaft Position (CKP) sensor, no signal |
| P0335 | Crankshaft Position (CKP) sensor A, no signal |
| P0336 | Crankshaft Position (CKP) sensor, intermittent interruption |
| P0339 | Crankshaft Position (CKP) sensor A, intermittent interruption |
| P0340 | Camshaft Position (CMP) sensor, no signal |
| P0340 | Camshaft Position (CMP) sensor A, no signal |
| P0341 | Camshaft Position (CMP) sensor A, intermittent interruption |
| P0344 | Camshaft Position (CMP) sensor, intermittent interruption |
| P0365 | Camshaft Position (CMP) sensor B, no signal |
| P0366 | Camshaft Position (CMP) sensor B, intermittent interruption |
| P0385 | Crankshaft Position (CKP) sensor B, no signal |
| P0389 | Crankshaft Position (CKP) sensor B, intermittent interruption |
| P0401 | Exhaust Gas Recirculation (EGR) system, insufficient flow |
| P0404 | Exhaust Gas Recirculation (EGR) control circuit, range or performance problem |
| P0406 | Exhaust Gas Recirculation (EGR) valve position sensor circuit, high voltage |
| P0420 | Catalyst system efficiency below threshold |
| P0420 | Catalyst system efficiency below threshold (rear cylinder head) |
| P0430 | Catalyst system efficiency below threshold (front cylinder head) |
| P0443 | Evaporative Emission Control (EVAP) canister purge valve, circuit malfunction |
| P0451 | Fuel Tank Pressure (FTP) sensor circuit, range or performance problem |
| P0452 | Fuel Tank Pressure (FTP) sensor circuit, low voltage |
| P0453 | Fuel Tank Pressure (FTP) sensor circuit, high voltage |
| P0455 | Evaporative Emission Control (EVAP) system, very large leak detected |
| P0456 | Evaporative Emission Control (EVAP) system, very small leak detected |
| P0457 | Evaporative Emission Control (EVAP) system, leak detected/fuel cap loose or missing |
| P0461 | Fuel level sensor (fuel gauge sending unit) circuit, range or performance problem |
| P0462 | Fuel level sensor (fuel gauge sending unit) circuit, low voltage |

| Code | Probable cause |
|---|---|
| P0463 | Fuel level sensor (fuel gauge sending unit) circuit, high voltage |
| P0496 | Evaporative Emission Control (EVAP), high purge flow |
| P0497 | Evaporative Emission Control (EVAP), low purge flow |
| P0498 | Evaporative Emission Control (EVAP) canister vent shut valve control circuit, low voltage |
| P0499 | Evaporative Emission Control (EVAP) canister vent shut valve control circuit, high voltage |
| P0505 | Idle control system malfunction |
| P0506 | Idle control system, rpm lower than expected |
| P0507 | Idle control system, rpm higher than expected |
| P0562 | Charging system low voltage |
| P0563 | Powertrain Control Module (PCM) power source circuit, unexpected voltage |
| P0602 | Powertrain Control Module (PCM) programming error |
| P0603 | Powertrain Control Module (PCM), Keep Alive Memory (KAM) error |
| P0607 | Powertrain Control Module (PCM), internal circuit malfunction |
| P0607 | Lost communication with Electronic Throttle Control System (ECTS) |
| P060A | Powertrain Control Module (PCM) (automatic transaxle system) internal control module malfunction |
| P0615 | Starter cut relay STRLD circuit malfunction |
| P0627 | PGM-FI main relay 2 (fuel pump) circuit malfunction |
| P0627 | Fuel pump control module system malfunction |
| P061F | Electronic Throttle Control System (ETCS) malfunction |
| P062F | Powertrain Control Module (PCM) internal control module Keep Alive Memory (KAM) error |
| P0630 | VIN not programmed or mismatch |
| P0641 | Sensor reference voltage A malfunction |
| P0651 | Sensor reference voltage B malfunction |
| P0657 | Oxygen sensor relay circuit malfunction |
| P0685 | Powertrain Control Module (PCM), power control circuit or internal circuit malfunction |

## AUTOMATIC TRANSAXLE DIAGNOSTIC TROUBLE CODES

| Code | Probable cause |
|---|---|
| P0700 | Automatic transmission control system malfunction |
| P0705 | Transmission Range (TR) switch, multiple shift position input |
| P0706 | Transmission Range (TR) switch, open circuit |
| P0710 | Automatic Transmission Fluid temperature sensor |
| P0711 | ATF temperature sensor, range or performance problem |
| P0712 | ATF temperature sensor, short circuit |

## AUTOMATIC TRANSAXLE DIAGNOSTIC TROUBLE CODES (CONTINUED)

| Code | Probable cause |
|---|---|
| P0713 | ATF temperature sensor, open circuit |
| P0715 | Input shaft (mainshaft) speed sensor |
| P0716 | Input shaft (mainshaft) speed sensor, range or performance problem |
| P0717 | Input shaft (mainshaft) speed sensor, no signal input |
| P0718 | Input shaft (mainshaft) speed sensor, intermittent failure |
| P0720 | Output shaft (countershaft) speed sensor |
| P0721 | Output shaft (countershaft) speed sensor, range or performance problem |
| P0722 | Output shaft (countershaft) speed sensor, no signal input |
| P0723 | Output shaft (countershaft) speed sensor, intermittent failure |
| P0730 | Shift control system |
| P0731 | 1st gear, incorrect ratio |
| P0732 | 2nd gear, incorrect ratio |
| P0733 | 3rd gear, incorrect ratio |
| P0734 | 4th gear, incorrect ratio |
| P0735 | 5th gear, incorrect ratio |
| P0740 | Lock-up control system |
| P0741 | Torque converter clutch circuit, performance or stuck off |
| P0743 | Torque converter clutch solenoid valve |
| P0746 | Automatic transaxle clutch pressure control solenoid valve A, stuck off |
| P0747 | Automatic transaxle clutch pressure control solenoid valve A, stuck on |
| P0748 | Automatic transaxle clutch pressure control solenoid valve A |
| P0751 | Shift solenoid valve A stuck off |
| P0752 | Shift solenoid valve A stuck on |
| P0753 | Shift solenoid valve A |
| P0756 | Shift solenoid valve B stuck off |
| P0757 | Shift solenoid valve B stuck on |
| P0758 | Shift solenoid valve B |
| P0761 | Shift solenoid valve C stuck off |
| P0762 | Shift solenoid valve C stuck on |
| P0763 | Shift solenoid valve C |
| P0766 | Shift solenoid valve D, stuck off |
| P0767 | Shift solenoid valve D, stuck on |
| P0776 | Automatic transaxle clutch pressure control solenoid valve B, stuck off |

| Code | Probable cause |
|------|----------------|
| P0777 | Automatic transaxle clutch pressure control solenoid valve B, stuck on |
| P0778 | Automatic transaxle clutch pressure control solenoid valve B |
| P0780 | Shift control system or mechanical problem in hydraulic system |
| P0780 | Shift control system |
| P0796 | Automatic transaxle clutch pressure control solenoid valve C stuck off |
| P0797 | Automatic transaxle clutch pressure control solenoid valve C stuck on |
| P0798 | Automatic transaxle clutch pressure control solenoid valve C |
| P0812 | Transmission Range (TR) switch ATP R switch |
| P0815 | Transmission gear selection switch upshift switch, short or stuck on |
| P0816 | Transmission gear selection switch downshift switch, short or stuck on |
| P0842 | 2nd clutch transmission fluid pressure switch, short or stuck on |
| P0843 | 2nd clutch transmission fluid pressure switch, open or stuck off |
| P0845 | Third clutch transaxle fluid pressure switch |
| P0847 | 3rd clutch transmission fluid pressure switch, shorted or stuck on |
| P0848 | 3rd clutch transmission fluid pressure switch, open or stuck off |
| P0872 | 4th clutch transmission fluid pressure switch, shorted or stuck on |
| P0873 | 4th clutch transmission fluid pressure switch, open or stuck off |
| P0957 | Transmission gear selection switch, shorted or stuck on |
| P0958 | Transmission gear selection switch, shorted or stuck off |
| P0962 | Automatic transaxle clutch pressure control solenoid valve A, short |
| P0963 | Automatic transaxle clutch pressure control solenoid valve A, open |
| P0966 | Automatic transaxle clutch pressure control solenoid valve B, open or short |
| P0967 | Automatic transaxle clutch pressure control solenoid valve B |
| P0970 | Automatic transaxle clutch pressure control solenoid valve C, open or short |
| P0971 | Automatic transaxle clutch pressure control solenoid valve C |
| P0973 | Shift solenoid valve A, short |
| P0974 | Shift solenoid valve A, open |
| P0976 | Shift solenoid valve B, short |
| P0977 | Shift solenoid valve B, open |
| P0979 | Shift solenoid valve C, short |
| P0980 | Shift solenoid valve C, open |
| P0982 | Shift solenoid valve D, short |
| P0983 | Shift solenoid valve D open |

## 3 Accelerator Pedal Position (APP) sensor - replacement

### 2003 THROUGH 2006 ACURA AND 2005 AND LATER HONDA MODELS

▶ Refer to illustrations 3.1, 3.4 and 3.6

➡ Note: The APP sensor is located on the firewall, and is connected to the accelerator pedal by a cable.

1  Remove the APP sensor cover bolts (see illustration) and remove the sensor cover.

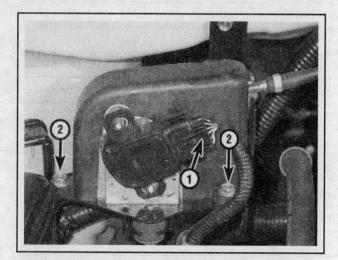

3.1  To disconnect the electrical connector from the APP sensor, depress the release tab (1). To detach the APP sensor cover, remove these two bolts (2) (2001 through 2006 Acura and 2005 and later Honda models)

2  Disconnect the electrical connector from the APP sensor (see illustration 3.1).

3  Disconnect the accelerator cable from the APP sensor cam (see *Accelerator cable - removal, installation and adjustment* in Chapter 4).

➡ Note: It isn't necessary to detach the cable from the cable bracket; just disconnect the cable from the cam. If you DO disconnect the cable from the cable bracket you will have to adjust the cable when you're done.

4  Detach the accelerator cable bracket from the APP sensor (see illustration).

5  Remove the APP sensor mounting bracket bolts (see illustration 3.4) and remove the sensor and bracket as a single assembly.

6  Remove the two APP sensor mounting bolts (see illustration) and remove the APP sensor from the mounting bracket.

7  Installation is the reverse of removal. If you disconnected the accelerator cable from the cable bracket (instead of simply unbolting the cable bracket from the APP sensor), be sure to check and, if necessary, adjust the accelerator cable (see Chapter 4) before installing the APP sensor cover.

### 2007 ACURA MODELS

➡ Note: The APP sensor is located at the top of the accelerator pedal and is an integral component of the accelerator pedal module (you cannot separate the APP sensor from the module). There is no accelerator cable.

8  Disconnect the electrical connector from the APP sensor.

9  Remove the APP sensor module mounting nuts and remove the sensor module.

10  Installation is the reverse of removal.

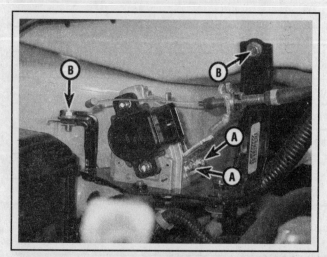

3.4  To detach the accelerator cable bracket from the APP sensor, remove these two bolts (A). To detach the APP sensor mounting bracket from the firewall, remove these two bolts (B) (2001 through 2006 Acura and 2005 and later Honda models)

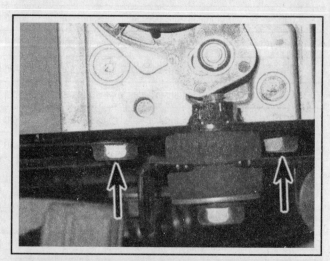

3.6 To detach the APP sensor assembly from its mounting bracket, remove these two bolts (2001 through 2006 Acura and 2005 and later Honda models)

### 4   Camshaft Position (CMP) sensor - replacement

#### 2001 AND 2002 ACURA AND 2003 AND 2004 HONDA MODELS

⬧ **Refer to illustrations 4.1a, 4.1b, 4.3 and 4.4**

➡**Note: The CMP sensor is located at the right end of the front cylinder head.**

1   Disconnect the CMP sensor electrical connector (see illustrations).

2   Remove the timing belt cover and the timing belt, then remove the camshaft sprocket from the front cylinder head (see Chapter 2A).

3   Remove the rear timing belt cover mounting bolts (see illustration) and remove the cover.

4   Remove the CMP sensor mounting bolts (see illustration) and remove the CMP sensor.

5   Installation is the reverse of removal. Be sure to tighten the CMP sensor mounting bolts to the torque listed in this Chapter's Specifications.

#### 2003 AND LATER ACURA AND 2005 AND LATER HONDA MODELS

⬧ **Refer to illustrations 4.6, 4.8 and 4.9**

➡**Note: The CMP sensor is located at the right end of the front cylinder head.**

6   Disconnect the electrical connector from the CMP sensor (see illustration).

7   Remove the timing belt cover, the timing belt and the camshaft sprocket (see Chapter 2A).

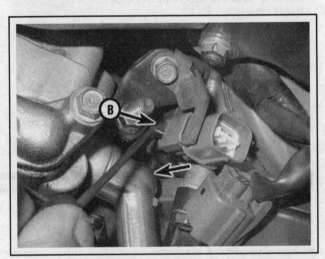

4.1a  To disconnect the CMP sensor electrical connector, depress the release button (A) and pull the upper half of the connector (the harness side) straight up . . .

4.1b  . . . and to disengage the lower half of the connector (the CMP sensor side) from its mounting bracket, depress this release button (B) and push the connector straight down (2001 and 2002 Acura and 2003 and 2004 Honda models)

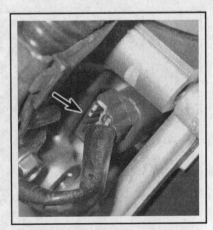

4.3  To detach the rear timing belt cover from the cylinder head, remove these two bolts (2001 and 2002 Acura and 2003 and 2004 Honda models)

4.4  To detach the CMP sensor from the rear timing belt cover, remove these mounting bolts (2001 and 2002 Acura and 2003 and 2004 Honda models)

4.6  To disconnect the electrical connector from the CMP sensor, depress the release tab and pull off the connector (2003 and later Acura and 2005 and later Honda models)

**4.8 To detach the rear timing belt cover, remove these two bolts (2003 and later Acura and 2005 and later Honda models)**

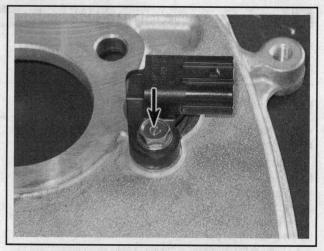

**4.9 To detach the CMP sensor from the rear timing belt cover, remove this mounting bolt (2003 and later Acura and 2005 and later Honda models)**

8   Remove the rear timing belt cover mounting bolts (see illustration), then remove the cover.

9   Remove the CMP sensor mounting bolt (see illustration) and remove the CMP sensor from the rear part of the timing belt cover.

10  Installation is the reverse of removal.

## 5   Crankshaft Position (CKP) sensor - replacement

### 2001 AND 2002 ACURA AND 2003 AND 2004 HONDA MODELS

▶ **Refer to illustrations 5.2 and 5.4**

1   Raise the front of the vehicle and place it securely on jackstands. Remove the engine cover (see Chapter 2A).

2   Disconnect the CKP sensor electrical connector (see illustration).

3   Remove the timing belt cover and the timing belt (see Chapter 2A).

4   Remove the CKP sensor mounting bolt (see illustration) and remove the CKP sensor.

5   Installation is the reverse of removal. Be sure to tighten the CKP sensor mounting bolt to the torque listed in this Chapter's Specifications.

**5.2 The CKP sensor electrical connector is located behind the right end of the engine, above the timing belt tensioner (2001 and 2002 Acura and 2003 and 2004 Honda models)**

**5.4 To detach the CKP sensor from the engine, remove this mounting bolt (2001 and 2002 Acura and 2003 and 2004 Honda models)**

**5.8  Remove the two nuts that secure the shield for the CKP sensor wiring harness shield, then remove the shield (2003 and later Acura and 2005 and later Honda models)**

**5.9  To detach the CKP sensor from the engine block, remove the sensor mounting bolt (1), pull off the CKP sensor, depress the electrical connector release tab (2) and disconnect the connector from the sensor (2003 and later Acura and 2005 and later Honda models)**

## 2003 AND LATER ACURA AND 2005 AND LATER HONDA MODELS

▶ **Refer to illustrations 5.8 and 5.9**

➡**Note: The CMP sensor is located at the right end of the front cylinder head.**

6  Raise the front of the vehicle and place it securely on jackstands. Remove the engine cover (see Chapter 2A).

7  Remove the crankshaft pulley and the upper and lower timing belt covers (see Chapter 2A).

8  Remove the two nuts that secure the shield for the CKP sensor wiring harness (see illustration) and remove the CKP sensor and the harness shield.

9  Remove the CKP sensor mounting bolt (see illustration), remove the sensor from the engine block, disconnect the electrical connector from the sensor and remove the sensor.

10  Installation is the reverse of removal.

## 6  Electrical Load Detector (ELD) - replacement

▶ **Refer to illustrations 6.3, 6.6 and 6.7**

1  Disconnect the cable from the negative battery terminal (see Chapter 5, Section 1).

2  Remove the cover from the engine compartment fuse and relay box (see Chapter 12 if necessary).

3  Locate the ELD (see illustration) in the fuse and relay box.

4  Remove the mounting screws for the 120-amp fuse and remove the fuse, then remove the mounting screws for the 50-amp fuse and remove it too.

5  Disconnect the electrical connector from the top of the ELD.

6  Remove the ELD (see illustration).

7  Remove the contact plate from the ELD (see illustration), inspect it for corrosion, clean it off as necessary, then install it in the new ELD. Note that the contact plate must be oriented exactly the same way it was in the old ELD. It won't fit into the fuse and relay box if it's incorrectly oriented.

8  Installation is the reverse of removal. Reconnect the cable to the negative battery terminal (see Chapter 5, Section 1).

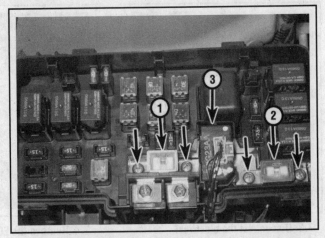

**6.3  The Electrical Load Detector (ELD) is located inside the engine compartment fuse and relay box**

1   120-amp fuse        2   50-amp fuse        3   ELD module

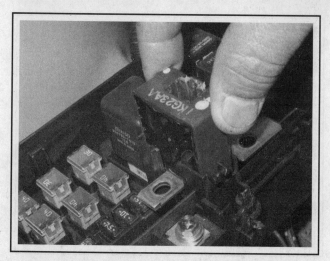

6.6 Remove the ELD from the fuse and relay box

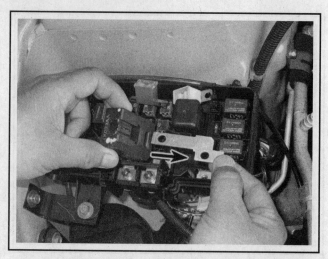

6.7 Before removing the contact plate from the old ELD, note how it's oriented in relation to the ELD and to the fuse and relay box; be sure to install it exactly the same way in the new unit

## 7 Engine Coolant Temperature (ECT) sensor - replacement

### ✳✳ WARNING:

Wait until the engine has cooled completely before beginning this procedure.

### 2001 AND 2002 ACURA AND 2003 AND 2004 HONDA MODELS

▶ Refer to illustrations 7.3, 7.4 and 7.5

1   Remove the engine cover.
2   Drain the engine coolant (see Chapter 1). (It is possible to replace the sensor without draining the coolant. If you don't drain the coolant, some coolant will run out of the coolant crossover when you remove the ECT sensor, so install the new sensor as quickly as possible.)
3   Disconnect the electrical connector from the ECT sensor (see illustration).
4   Unscrew the ECT sensor with a wrench (see illustration). (Most deep sockets won't fit over the ECT sensor.)

### ✳✳ CAUTION:

If you're planning to reuse the old ECT sensor, handle it with care. Damage to the ECT sensor will adversely affect the operation of the PGM-FI system.

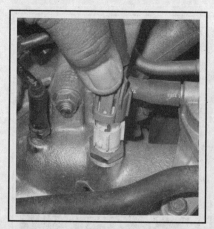

7.3 Disconnect the electrical connector from the ECT sensor (2001 and 2002 Acura and 2003 and 2004 Honda models)

7.4 Remove the ECT sensor with a wrench (most deep sockets are too small to fit over the sensor) (2001 and 2002 Acura and 2003 and 2004 Honda models)

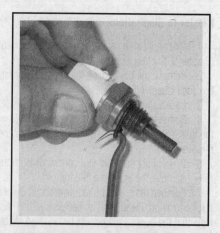

7.5 Be sure to remove and discard the old O-ring; always use a new O-ring when installing the sensor (2001 and 2002 Acura and 2003 and 2004 Honda models)

**7.9a ECT sensor location (2003 through 2006 Acura and 2005 and later Honda models)**

1   ECT sensor 1          2   ECT sensor 2

5   Remove and discard the old ECT sensor O-ring (see illustration). Whether you're planning to reuse the old ECT sensor or install a new unit, be sure to use a new O-ring.

6   Installation is the reverse of removal. Be sure to tighten the ECT sensor to the torque listed in this Chapter's Specifications. Refill the cooling system (or, if you didn't drain the coolant, check the coolant level, adding as necessary) (see Chapter 1).

## 2003 THROUGH 2006 ACURA AND 2005 AND LATER HONDA MODELS

▶ **Refer to illustrations 7.9a, 7.9b and 7.11**

➡**Note: There are two ECT sensors on the water passage casting that houses the thermostat. This casting is located under the throttle body, and is bolted to the engine block and to the left ends of the two cylinder heads.**

7   Remove the engine cover (see Chapter 2A).

8   Drain the engine coolant (see Chapter 1). (It is possible to replace the sensor without draining the coolant. If you don't drain the coolant, some coolant will run out of the coolant crossover when you remove the ECT sensor, so install the new sensor as quickly as possible.)

9   Disconnect the electrical connector from the ECT sensor (see illustrations).

10  Unscrew the ECT sensor with a wrench. (Most deep sockets won't fit over the ECT sensor.)

### ❉❉ CAUTION:

**If you're planning to reuse the old ECT sensor, handle it with care. Damage to the ECT sensor will adversely affect the operation of the PGM-FI system.**

11  Remove and discard the old ECT sensor O-ring (see illustration).

12  Install a new O-ring whether you're installing the old ECT sensor or a new unit. Do NOT re-use the old O-ring.

13  Installation is the reverse of removal. Be sure to tighten the ECT sensor to the torque listed in this Chapter's Specifications.

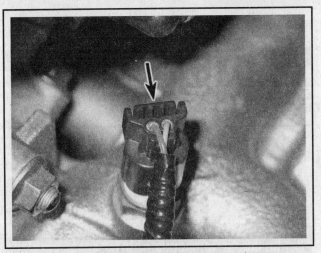

**7.9b To disconnect the electrical connector from an ECT sensor, depress this release tab and pull off the connector (ECT sensor 1 connector shown, ECT sensor 2 connector identical) (2003 through 2006 Acura and 2005 and later Honda models)**

**7.11 Always remove and discard the old ECT sensor O-ring and install a new O-ring when installing the sensor (O-ring for ECT sensor 1 shown)**

## 2007 ACURA MODELS

➡**Note: There are two ECT sensors on these models. ECT sensor 1 is in the same location as on 2003 through 2006 Acura models (on the water passage). ECT sensor 2 is located on the front of the engine block.**

### ECT sensor 1

14  Refer to Steps 7 through 13.

### ECT sensor 2

15  Raise the front of the vehicle and place it securely on jackstands.

16  Remove the engine splash shield (see Chapter 2A, Section 7).

17  Drain the engine coolant (see Chapter 1).

18  Disconnect the electrical connector from the ECT sensor.

19 Unscrew the ECT sensor with a wrench. (Most deep sockets won't fit over the ECT sensor.)

### ✻✻ CAUTION:

If you're planning to reuse the old ECT sensor, handle it with care. Damage to the ECT sensor will adversely affect the operation of the PGM-FI system.

20 Remove and discard the old ECT sensor O-ring.
21 Install a new O-ring on the ECT sensor whether you're installing the old ECT sensor or a new unit. Do NOT re-use the old O-ring.
22 Installation is the reverse of removal. Be sure to tighten the ECT sensor to the torque listed in this Chapter's Specifications. Refill the cooling system (see Chapter 1).

## 8   Intake Air Temperature (IAT) sensor - replacement

### 2001 AND 2002 ACURA AND 2003 AND 2004 HONDA MODELS

▶ Refer to illustration 8.3

➡Note: The IAT sensor is located at the left rear corner of the intake manifold.

1   Remove the key from the ignition key lock cylinder.
2   Remove the engine cover (see Chapter 2A).
3   Disconnect the electrical connector from the IAT sensor (see illustration).
4   Unscrew and remove the IAT sensor.
5   Remove and discard the old IAT sensor O-ring (see illustration 7.5). Be sure to use a new O-ring, even if you're planning to reuse the old IAT sensor.
6   Installation is the reverse of removal. Be sure to use a new O-ring, and tighten the IAT sensor to the torque listed in this Chapter's Specifications.

### 2003 AND 2004 ACURA MODELS

➡Note: The IAT sensor is located on the air intake duct.

7   Disconnect the electrical connector from the IAT sensor.
8   Remove the retainer clip and pull the IAT sensor out of the air intake duct.
9   Installation is the reverse of removal.

### 2005 AND 2006 ACURA AND 2005 AND LATER HONDA MODELS

▶ Refer to illustrations 8.11 and 8.13

➡Note: The IAT sensor is located on the front of the intake manifold, right next to the throttle body mounting flange.

10  Remove the engine cover (see Chapter 2A).
11  Disconnect the electrical connector from the IAT sensor (see illustration).

8.3  To disconnect the electrical connector from the IAT sensor, depress the locking tab on the bottom of the connector, then pull the connector straight back (2001 and 2002 Acura and 2003 and 2004 Honda models)

8.11  To disconnect the electrical connector from the IAT sensor, depress this release tab and pull off the connector

8.13  The IAT sensor O-ring is countersunk into the intake manifold. When removing it, be careful not to scratch the walls of the countersink or the sensor bore

12 Unscrew the IAT sensor from the intake manifold.

13 Remove and discard the old IAT sensor O-ring (see illustration).

14 Be sure to use a new O-ring, even if you're planning to reuse the old IAT sensor.

15 Installation is the reverse of removal. Be sure to use a new O-ring, and tighten the IAT sensor to the torque listed in this Chapter's Specifications.

## 2007 ACURA MODELS

The IAT sensor is an integral component of the Mass Air Flow (MAF) sensor. To replace the IAT sensor or the MAF sensor, refer to Section 11.

---

## 9  Knock sensor - replacement

➡Note: The knock sensor is located under the intake manifold, on top of the engine block.

1 Remove the upper and lower intake manifolds (see Chapter 2A).

2 Remove the fuel rail assembly (see Chapter 4).

3 Disconnect the electrical connector from the knock sensor.

4 Remove the knock sensor.

5 Installation is the reverse of removal. Be sure to use a new O-ring, and tighten the knock sensor to the torque listed in this Chapter's Specifications.

---

## 10  Manifold Absolute Pressure (MAP) sensor - replacement

▶ Refer to illustration 10.2

➡Note: The MAP sensor is located on top of the throttle body.

1 Remove the engine cover (see Chapter 2A).

2 Disconnect the electrical connector from the MAP sensor (see illustration).

3 Remove the MAP sensor retaining screw and remove the MAP sensor from the throttle body.

4 Remove the old MAP sensor O-ring and discard it.

5 Installation is otherwise the reverse of removal. Be sure to use a new O-ring and tighten the MAP sensor retaining bolt securely.

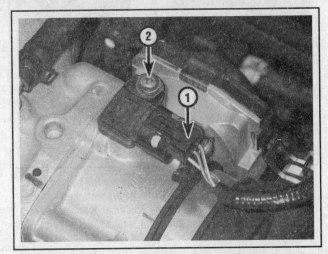

10.2  To disconnect the electrical connector from the MAP sensor, depress this release tab (1) and pull off the connector. To detach the MAP sensor from the throttle body, remove this screw (2)

---

## 11  Mass Air Flow/Intake Air Temperature (MAF/IAT) sensor - replacement

➡Note: The MAF/IAT sensor, which is used only on 2007 Acura models, is located on top of the air filter housing.

1 Disconnect the electrical connector from the MAF/IAT sensor.

2 Remove the MAF/IAT sensor retaining screw and remove the

MAF/IAT sensor.

3 Remove the old O-ring from the MAF/IAT sensor.

4 Installation is the reverse of removal. Be sure to use a new O-ring.

## 12 Oxygen sensors - replacement

### GENERAL PRECAUTIONS

➡ Note: Because it is installed in the exhaust manifold or pipe, both of which contract when cool, an oxygen sensor might be very difficult to loosen when the engine is cold. Rather than risk damage to the sensor or its mounting threads, start and run the engine for a minute or two, then shut it off. Be careful not to burn yourself during the following procedure.

1   Be particularly careful when servicing an oxygen sensor:

a) *Oxygen sensors have a permanently attached pigtail and an electrical connector that cannot be removed. Damaging or removing the pigtail or electrical connector will render the sensor useless.*

b) *Keep grease, dirt and other contaminants away from the electrical connector and the louvered end of the sensor.*

c) *Do not use cleaning solvents of any kind on an oxygen sensor.*

d) *Oxygen sensors are extremely delicate. Do not drop a sensor or throw it around or handle it roughly.*

e) *Make sure that the silicone boot on the sensor is installed in the correct position. Otherwise, the boot might melt and it might prevent the sensor from operating correctly.*

### REPLACEMENT

#### 2001 and 2002 Acura and 2003 and 2004 Honda models

➡ Note: There are two oxygen sensors, one upstream and one downstream. Both oxygen sensors are located under the vehicle. The upstream oxygen sensor is located right behind the exhaust pipe "Y" junction and ahead of the catalytic converter. The downstream sensor is screwed into the catalyst. You'll have to raise the vehicle to replace either sensor.

2   Raise the vehicle and support it securely on jackstands.

**Upstream oxygen sensor**

▶ Refer to illustrations 12.3 and 12.4

3   Detach the wire harness clip and disconnect the upstream oxygen sensor electrical connector (see illustration).

4   Remove the upstream oxygen sensor (see illustration).

5   If you're going to install the old sensor, apply anti-seize compound to the threads of the sensor to facilitate future removal. If you're going to install a new oxygen sensor, it's not necessary to apply anti-seize compound to the threads. The threads on new sensors already have anti-seize compound on them.

6   Installation is the reverse of removal. Be sure to tighten the oxygen sensor securely.

**Downstream oxygen sensor**

▶ Refer to illustrations 12.7 and 12.8

7   Detach the wire harness clip and disconnect the downstream oxygen sensor electrical connector (see illustration).

8   Remove the downstream oxygen sensor (see illustration).

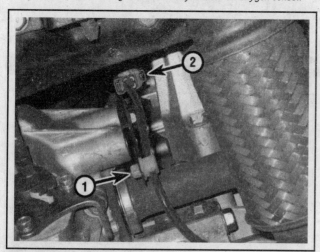

**12.3  To detach this wiring clip (1), squeeze the two locator pins together and pull the clip out of its bracket; then depress the locking tab and disconnect the electrical connector (2) (2001 and 2002 Acura and 2003 and 2004 Honda models)**

**12.4  Use a wrench to remove the upstream oxygen sensor (there isn't room for an oxygen sensor socket) (2001 and 2002 Acura and 2003 and 2004 Honda models)**

**12.7  Disconnect the downstream oxygen sensor electrical connector (2001 and 2002 Acura and 2003 and 2004 Honda models)**

**12.8  Use an oxygen sensor socket to remove the downstream oxygen sensor (use a wrench if you don't have an oxygen sensor socket) (2001 and 2002 Acura and 2003 and 2004 Honda models)**

**12.12a  Locations of upstream oxygen sensor electrical connector (A) and upstream oxygen sensor (B), front cylinder head**

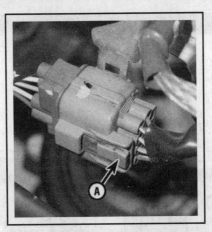

**12.12b  To disconnect an oxygen sensor electrical connector, depress this release tab (A) and pull off the connector**

**12.13  Use an oxygen sensor socket to remove the upstream oxygen sensor**

9   If you're going to install the old sensor, apply anti-seize compound to the threads of the sensor to facilitate future removal. If you're going to install a new oxygen sensor, it's not necessary to apply anti-seize compound to the threads. The threads on new sensors already have anti-seize compound on them.

10  Installation is the reverse of removal. Be sure to tighten the oxygen sensor securely.

### 2003 and later Acura and 2005 and later Honda models

➡ Note: There are three catalytic converters on these models, one under the vehicle and one for each cylinder bank (it's these "warm-up" converters that contain the oxygen sensors), so there are four oxygen sensors, one upstream and one downstream for each warm-up catalyst. It's not necessary to raise the vehicle to replace the upstream oxygen sensor for the front cylinder head, and you might be able to reach the upstream sensor for the rear cylinder head from above, though you'll need a mirror to see it. You can also reach the rear upstream sensor by raising the vehicle and working from below, to the right of the catalyst for the rear head. You'll also have to raise the vehicle to replace either downstream sensor.

**Upstream oxygen sensors**

▶ **Refer to illustrations 12.12a, 12.12b and 12.13**

11  Remove the engine cover (see Chapter 2A).

12  Disconnect the upstream oxygen sensor electrical connector (see illustrations).

13  Remove the upstream oxygen sensor (see illustration).

14  If you're going to install the old sensor, apply anti-seize compound to the threads of the sensor to facilitate future removal. If you're going to install a new oxygen sensor, it's not necessary to apply anti-seize compound to the threads. The threads on new sensors already have anti-seize compound on them.

15  Installation is the reverse of removal. Be sure to tighten the oxygen sensor securely.

**Downstream oxygen sensors**

▶ **Refer to illustration 12.17**

16  Raise the vehicle and support it securely on jackstands.

17  Locate the downstream oxygen sensor (see illustration), then trace the lead up to the electrical connector and disconnect the connector.

18  Remove the upstream oxygen sensor with an oxygen sensor socket.

19  If you're going to install the old sensor, apply anti-seize compound to the threads of the sensor to facilitate future removal. If you're going to install a new oxygen sensor, it's not necessary to apply anti-seize compound to the threads. The threads on new sensors already have anti-seize compound on them.

20  Installation is the reverse of removal. Be sure to tighten the oxygen sensor securely.

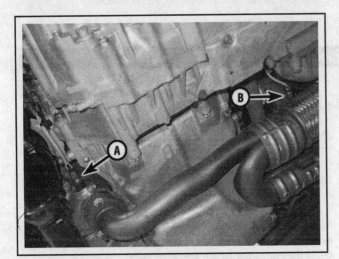

**12.17  Downstream oxygen sensor locations**

*A   Front catalyst sensor*        *B   Rear catalyst sensor*

## 13  Power Steering Pressure (PSP) switch - replacement

♦ **Refer to illustrations 13.2 and 13.3**

➡**Note: The PSP switch is located above the right end of the steering gear assembly.**

1  Raise the front of the vehicle and place it securely on jackstands.
2  Disconnect the electrical connector from the PSP switch (see illustration).

3  Unscrew the PSP switch (see illustration). Be prepared for some fluid spillage.
4  Installation is the reverse of removal. Be sure to tighten the PSP switch securely.
5  When you're done, lower the vehicle and check the power steering fluid level, adding fluid of the proper type if necessary.

**13.2  To release the PSP switch electrical connector, depress this locking tab, then pull off the connector**

**13.3  Use a wrench to remove the PSP switch; be sure to use a back-up wrench on the power steering fluid line to prevent the line from kinking**

## 14  Throttle Position (TP) sensor - replacement

2001 and 2002 Acura and 2003 and 2004 Honda models are equipped with a conventional, cable-operated throttle body that uses an externally mounted Throttle Position (TP) sensor. But the TP sensor is not available separately. If it's defective, you must replace the throttle body (see Chapter 4). On later models, which are equipped with electronic throttle bodies, the TP sensor is an integral component of the throttle body housing and is housed inside the throttle body. Again, a defective TP sensor means throttle body replacement.

## 15  Transmission range switch - replacement and adjustment

1  Place the shift lever in NEUTRAL. Apply the parking brake and block the rear wheels.
2  Raise the vehicle and place it securely on jackstands.

### 2001 AND 2002 ACURA AND 2003 AND 2004 HONDA MODELS

♦ **Refer to illustrations 15.3a, 15.3b, 15.4, 15.5, 15.6, 15.7a and 15.7b**

3  Detach the transmission range switch electrical connector from its mounting bracket, then disconnect it (see illustrations).
4  Detach the wiring harness for the transmission range switch from the transaxle (see illustration).
5  Remove the transmission range switch cover bolts (see illustration) and remove the cover.
6  Remove the transmission range switch mounting bolts (see illustration) and remove the switch.

7  Before installing the transmission range switch, make sure that the switch is in the Neutral position (see illustration). (You'll hear/feel a click when you put the switch into Neutral.) Also make sure that the control shaft is in the Neutral position before installing the transmission range switch. If it isn't, rotate the control shaft in a clockwise direction until it stops. As you rotate the shaft, it clicks into each gear position. Rotate it counterclockwise to the third gear position (third click), which is Neutral (see illustration).
8  The remainder of installation is the reverse of removal. Be sure to tighten the transmission range switch mounting bolts securely.

➡**Note: Be careful not to move the transmission range switch while tightening the switch mounting bolts.**

9  Turn the ignition switch to ON, move the shift lever through all the gears and verify that the transmission range switch is correctly synchronized with the gear position indicator on the instrument cluster.
10  Verify that the engine will NOT start in any gear position other than Park or Neutral, and that the back-up lights come on when the shift lever is in the Reverse position.

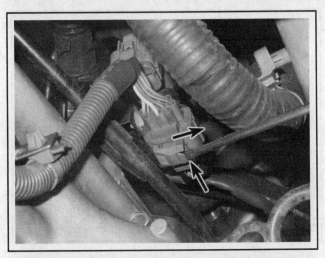

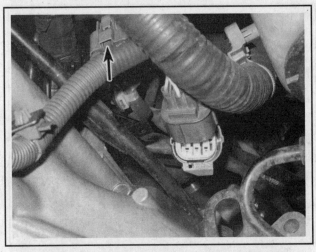

15.3a  The electrical connector for the transmission range switch is secured to - and locked together by - a small metal bracket. To detach the connector from the bracket, insert a thin slotted screwdriver blade between the release lever and the connector, pry the release lever down and pull the connector off the bracket

15.3b  To disconnect the electrical connector, depress the release tab on top of the connector and pull the two halves of the connector apart. The release tab for the transmission range switch connector isn't visible in this photo, but the arrow indicates the release tab on a nearby connector of the same design

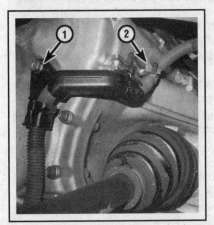

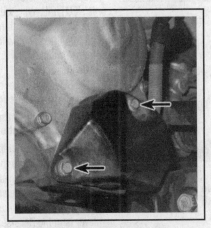

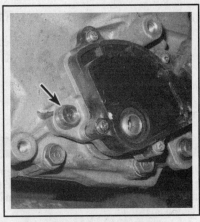

15.4  To detach the wiring harness from the transaxle, remove this bolt (1), then squeeze the locator pins (2) together and push this clip out of its metal bracket

15.5  To detach the transmission range switch cover, remove these two bolts

15.6  To detach the transmission range switch from the transaxle, remove these two bolts

15.7a  Before installing the transmission range switch, make sure that the switch is in the Neutral position: Rotate the moving part of the switch so that its longer inside diameter is aligned with the stationary Neutral index mark located on the upper part of the switch

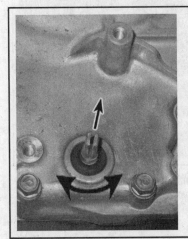

15.7b  If for some reason the control shaft is not in the Neutral position, rotate the shaft in a clockwise direction until it stops. As you rotate the shaft, it clicks into each gear position. Rotate it counterclockwise to the third gear position (third click), which is Neutral

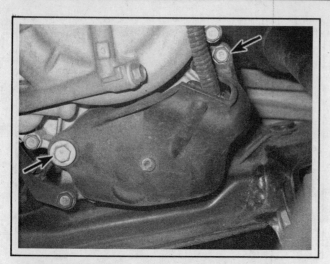

**15.11 To detach the transmission range switch cover, remove these two bolts**

**15.12 To disconnect the electrical connector from the transmission range switch, depress this release tab and pull off the connector**

## 2003 AND LATER ACURA AND 2005 AND LATER HONDA MODELS

▶ **Refer to illustrations 15.11, 15.12, 15.13 and 15.14**

11 Remove the transmission range switch cover bolts (see illustration) and remove the cover.

12 Disconnect the electrical connector from the transmission range switch (see illustration).

13 Remove the transmission range switch mounting bolts (see illustration) and remove the switch.

### ❉✴❉ CAUTION:

**While the transmission range switch is removed, do NOT rotate the transaxle control shaft. If you do, you'll have to put it back into the NEUTRAL position before you can install the transmission range switch.**

14 Before installing the transmission range switch, make sure that the switch is in the NEUTRAL position. You'll hear/feel a click when you put the switch into NEUTRAL. Also make sure that the transaxle control shaft is in the NEUTRAL position before installing the transmission range switch. If it isn't, rotate the control shaft in a clockwise direction until it stops. As you rotate the shaft, it clicks into each gear position. Rotate it counterclockwise to the third gear position (third click), which is NEUTRAL. With the transmission range switch and control shaft in the NEUTRAL position, install a small, straight length of wire or a drill bit into the range switch alignment slots as shown, then install the range switch on the control shaft and install the switch mounting bolts (see illustration).

15 The remainder of installation is the reverse of removal. Be sure to tighten the transmission range switch mounting bolts securely.

➡**Note: Be careful not to move the transmission range switch while tightening the switch mounting bolts.**

16 Turn the ignition switch to ON, move the shift lever through all the gears and verify that the transmission range switch is correctly synchronized with the gear position indicator on the instrument cluster.

17 Verify that the engine will NOT start in any gear position other than Park or Neutral, and that the back-up lights come on when the shift lever is in the Reverse position.

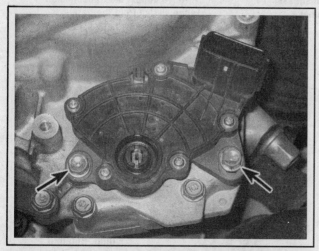

**15.13 To detach the transmission range switch from the transaxle, remove these two bolts**

**15.14 Install a short length of wire or a drill bit into the slots in the switch as shown to hold it in NEUTRAL, then, with the transaxle control shaft in the NEUTRAL position, install the range switch on the control shaft and install the bolts**

## 16  Transmission speed sensors - replacement

### 2001 AND 2002 ACURA AND 2003 THROUGH 2005 HONDA MODELS

#### Input shaft (mainshaft) speed sensor

▶ Refer to illustration 16.2

➡Note: The input shaft (mainshaft) speed sensor is located on the front left corner of the transaxle.

1   Loosen the lug nuts for the left front wheel. Raise the vehicle and place it securely on jackstands. Remove the left front wheel.

2   Disconnect the electrical connector from the input shaft speed sensor (see illustration).

3   Remove the input shaft speed sensor mounting bolt and remove the sensor.

4   Remove and discard the sensor O-ring.

5   Installation is the reverse of removal. Be sure to use a new O-ring and to tighten the sensor mounting bolt securely.

#### Output shaft (countershaft) speed sensor

▶ Refer to illustration 16.6

➡Note: The output shaft (countershaft) speed sensor is located on top of the transaxle.

6   Disconnect the electrical connector from the output shaft (countershaft) speed sensor (see illustration).

7   Remove the output shaft sensor mounting bolt and remove the sensor by pulling it straight up.

8   Remove and discard the sensor O-ring.

9   Installation is the reverse of removal. Be sure to use a new O-ring and to tighten the sensor mounting bolt securely.

### 2003 AND LATER ACURA AND 2006 AND LATER HONDA MODELS

#### Input shaft (mainshaft) speed sensor

➡Note: The input shaft (mainshaft) speed sensor is located on the front of the transaxle.

10  Raise the vehicle and place it securely on jackstands.

11  Remove the engine splash shield (see Chapter 2A).

12  Disconnect the electrical connector from the input shaft speed sensor.

13  Remove the input shaft speed sensor mounting bolt and remove the sensor.

14  Remove and discard the sensor O-ring.

15  Installation is the reverse of removal. Be sure to use a new O-ring and to tighten the sensor mounting bolt securely.

#### Output shaft (countershaft) speed sensor

➡Note: The output shaft (countershaft) speed sensor is located on top of the transaxle.

16  Remove the air intake duct (see *Air filter housing - removal and installation* in Chapter 4).

17  Disconnect the electrical connector from the output shaft (countershaft) speed sensor.

18  Remove the output shaft sensor mounting bolt and remove the sensor by pulling it straight up.

19  Remove and discard the sensor O-ring.

20  Installation is the reverse of removal. Be sure to use a new O-ring and to tighten the sensor mounting bolt securely.

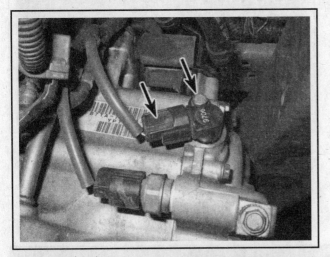

16.2  The input shaft (mainshaft) speed sensor is located at the left front corner of the transaxle. To remove it, depress the release tab and disconnect the electrical connector, then remove this bolt (2001 and 2002 Acura and 2003 and 2004 Honda models)

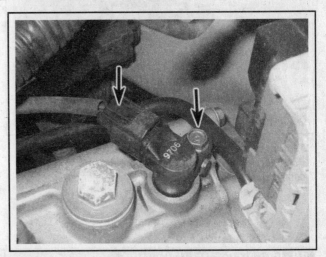

16.6  The output shaft (countershaft) speed sensor is located on top of the transaxle. To remove it, depress the release tab and disconnect the electrical connector, then remove the sensor mounting bolt (2001 and 2002 Acura and 2003 and 2004 Honda models)

## 17 Powertrain Control Module (PCM) - removal and installation

### GENERAL INFORMATION

1   The Powertrain Control Module (PCM) is the brain of the engine management system. It also controls a wide variety of other vehicle systems, including the "immobilizer" (vehicle security) system. If the PCM fails, and you have to replace it with a new PCM unit, the new immobilizer code must be programmed into the new PCM by a dealership service department before the engine will start. In order to program the new PCM, the dealer needs the vehicle, the new PCM unit and all of the vehicle keys. So if you're planning to replace the old PCM with a new unit, there is no point in trying to do so at home because you won't be able to program it yourself.

### REMOVAL AND INSTALLATION

♦ **Refer to illustrations 17.3, 17.4 and 17.5**

➡**Note: The PCM is located in the right front corner of the engine compartment.**

2   Disconnect the cable from the negative terminal of the battery (see Chapter 5, Section 1).
3   Remove the cover from the PCM (see illustration).
4   Unplug the electrical connectors from the PCM (see illustration).

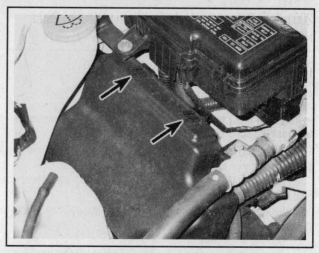

**17.3  Unclip the cover from the PCM and remove it**

5   Unscrew the mounting bolts and remove the PCM from the engine compartment (see illustration).
6   Installation is the reverse of removal.

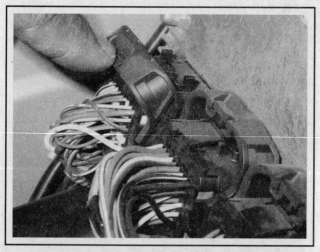

**17.4  To disconnect the electrical connectors from the PCM, depress the button on top of the connector, swing the connector lock forward, then pull the connector out**

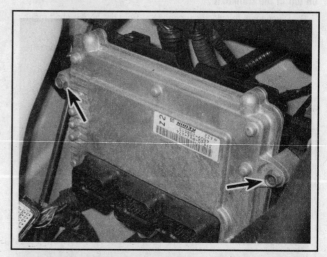

**17.5  PCM mounting bolts**

## 18 Idle Air Control (IAC) valve - replacement

♦ **Refer to illustrations 18.2 and 18.3**

➡**Note: On 2001 and 2002 Acura and 2003 and 2004 Honda models, the IAC valve is located on the underside of the throttle body. (2003 and later Acura and 2005 and later Honda models are equipped with an electronic throttle body, which doesn't have an IAC valve.)**

1   Remove the throttle body from the intake manifold (see Chapter 4).
2   Remove the IAC valve mounting screws (see illustration) and remove the IAC valve.
3   Remove the old IAC valve gasket (see illustration) and discard it.
4   When installing the IAC valve, be sure to use a new gasket and tighten the IAC valve mounting screws securely.
5   Installation is otherwise the reverse of removal.

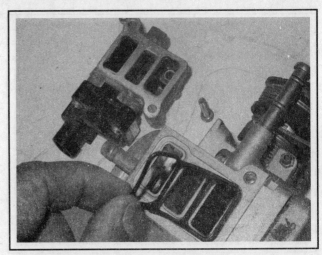

**18.2  To detach the IAC valve from the throttle body, remove these two screws**

**18.3  Remove and discard the old IAC valve gasket, and be sure to use a new gasket when installing the IAC valve**

## 19  Catalytic converter - description, check and replacement

➡️**Note: Because of a Federally mandated extended warranty which covers emissions-related components like the catalytic converter, check with a dealer service department before replacing the converter at your own expense.**

### DESCRIPTION

1   A catalytic converter (or catalyst) is an emission control device in the exhaust system that reduces certain pollutants in the exhaust gas stream. There are two types of converters: oxidation converters and reduction converters.

2   Oxidation converters contain a "monolithic substrate" (a ceramic honeycomb) coated with the semi-precious metals platinum and palladium. An oxidation catalyst reduces unburned hydrocarbons (HC) and carbon monoxide (CO) by adding oxygen to the exhaust stream as it passes through the substrate, which, in the presence of high temperature and the catalyst materials, converts the HC and CO to water vapor ($H_2O$) and carbon dioxide ($CO_2$).

3   Reduction converters contain a monolithic substrate coated with platinum and rhodium. A reduction catalyst reduces oxides of nitrogen (NOx) by removing oxygen, which in the presence of high temperature and the catalyst material produces nitrogen (N) and carbon dioxide ($CO_2$).

4   Catalytic converters that combine both types of catalysts in one assembly are known as "three-way catalysts" or TWCs. A TWC can reduce all three pollutants. All models covered by this manual are equipped with three-way catalysts.

5   On 2001 and 2002 Acura and 2003 and 2004 Honda models, the catalytic converter is located in the exhaust pipe behind the junction of the outlet pipes of the exhaust manifolds. On 2003 and later Acura and 2005 and later Honda models, there are three catalytic converters, one bolted to each cylinder head and one under the vehicle. (There are no separate exhaust manifolds; the "manifolds" are integral with the cylinder head castings.)

### CHECK

6   The test equipment for a catalytic converter (a "loaded-mode" dynamometer and a 5-gas analyzer) is expensive. If you suspect that the converter on your vehicle is malfunctioning, take it to a dealer or authorized emission inspection facility for diagnosis.

7   Whenever you raise the vehicle to service underbody components, inspect the converter assembly for leaks, corrosion, dents and other damage. Carefully inspect the welds and/or flange bolts and nuts that attach the front and rear ends of the converter to the exhaust system. If you note any damage, replace the converter.

### ✳✳ WARNING:

**Inspect catalytic converters only after enough time has elapsed after driving the vehicle to allow the system components to cool completely. Also, when working under the vehicle, make sure that it is securely supported on jackstands.**

8   Although catalytic converters don't break too often, they can become clogged or even plugged up. The easiest way to check for a restricted converter is to use a vacuum gauge to diagnose the effect of a blocked exhaust on intake vacuum.

  a) *Connect a vacuum gauge to any intake manifold vacuum source (any pipe on the intake manifold with a vacuum hose connected to it will provide the necessary intake manifold vacuum).*

  b) *Warm the engine to operating temperature, place the transaxle in*

**19.11a  To detach the front catalyst mounting flange from the exhaust system, remove these three nuts (2001 and 2002 Acura and 2003 and 2004 Honda models)**

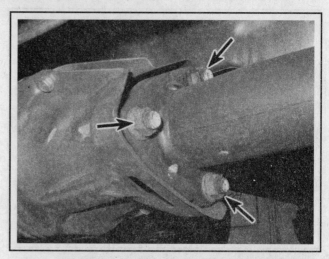

**19.11b  To detach the rear catalyst mounting flange from the exhaust system, remove these three nuts (2001 and 2002 Acura and 2003 and 2004 Honda models)**

*Park and apply the parking brake.*
c) *Note the vacuum reading at idle and write it down.*
d) *Quickly open the throttle to near its wide-open position and then quickly get off the throttle and allow it to close. Note the vacuum reading and write it down.*
e) *Do this test three more times, recording your measurement after each test.*
f) *If your fourth reading is more than one in-Hg lower than the reading that you noted at idle, the exhaust system might be restricted (the catalytic converter could be plugged, or an exhaust pipe or muffler could be restricted).*

## REPLACEMENT

### ✳✳ WARNING:

Replace catalytic converters only after enough time has elapsed after driving the vehicle to allow the system components to cool completely. Also, when working under the vehicle, make sure it is securely supported on jackstands.

**19.16  To detach the upper end of the front catalytic converter from the front cylinder head, remove these nuts (2003 and later Acura and 2005 and later Honda models)**

## 2001 and 2002 Acura and 2003 and 2004 Honda models

▶ **Refer to illustrations 19.11a and 19.11b**

➡**Note: The catalytic converter is located under the vehicle.**

9   Raise the vehicle and place it securely on jackstands.
10  Disconnect the electrical connector from the downstream oxygen sensor and remove the sensor (see Section 12).
11  Remove the retaining nuts from the front and rear catalyst mounting flanges (see illustrations).
12  Installation is the reverse of removal. Be sure to replace any rusted or damaged fasteners and to tighten all fasteners to the torque listed in this Chapter's Specifications.

## 2003 and later Acura and 2005 and later Honda models

▶ **Refer to illustrations 19.16, 19.19 and 19.21**

➡**Note: There are three catalytic converters, one bolted to each cylinder head and one under the vehicle.**

### Warm-up catalytic converter

13  On all models except 2007 Acura models, remove the condenser fan/shroud assembly (see Chapter 3).
14  On 2007 Acura models, remove the radiator fan and air conditioning fan/shroud assemblies (see Chapter 3).
15  Disconnect the electrical connector for the upstream oxygen sensor and remove the sensor (see Section 12).
16  Remove the nuts from the catalytic converter's upper mounting flange (see illustration).
17  Raise the vehicle and support it securely on jackstands.
18  Remove the engine splash shield (see Chapter 2A).
19  Remove the transaxle crossmember (see illustration).
20  Disconnect the electrical connector for the downstream oxygen sensor and remove the sensor (see Section 12).
21  Remove the nuts from the lower mounting flanges of both catalytic converters, remove the nuts from the exhaust pipe's rear flange (see illustration) and remove the exhaust pipe.
22  If you're removing the rear catalyst, remove the intermediate axleshaft (see Chapter 8).

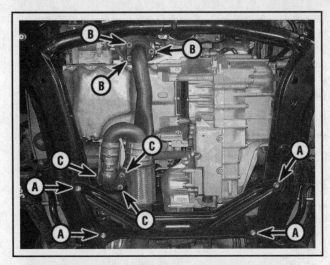

**19.19  To disconnect the front exhaust pipe from the front and rear catalysts (2003 and later Acura and 2005 and later Honda models):**

A   Remove the four crossmember bolts and remove the crossmember
B   Remove the three nuts from the lower end of the front catalytic converter
C   Remove the three nuts from the lower end of the rear catalytic converter

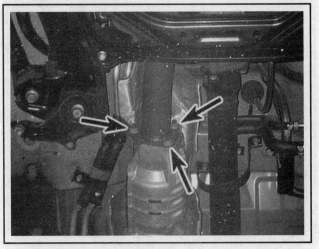

**19.21  To disconnect the front exhaust pipe from the rear exhaust pipe, remove these three nuts**

23  Remove the catalytic converter and discard the old mounting flange gaskets.

24  Installation is the reverse of removal. Be sure to use new gaskets at both catalyst mounting flanges and tighten the flange nuts securely.

**Under-vehicle catalytic converter**

25  Refer to Steps 9 through 12.

## 20  Evaporative Emissions Control (EVAP) system - description and component replacement

### GENERAL DESCRIPTION

1   The Evaporative Emissions Control (EVAP) system prevents fuel system vapors (which contain unburned hydrocarbons) from escaping into the atmosphere. On warm days, vapors trapped inside the fuel tank expand until the pressure reaches a certain threshold. Then the fuel vapors are routed from the fuel tank through the fuel vapor vent valve and the fuel vapor control valve to the EVAP canister, where they're stored temporarily until the next time the vehicle is operated. When the conditions are right (engine warmed up, vehicle up to speed, moderate or heavy load on the engine, etc.) the PCM opens the canister purge valve, which allows fuel vapors to be drawn from the canister into the intake manifold. Once in the intake manifold, the fuel vapors mix with incoming air before being drawn through the intake ports into the combustion chambers where they're burned up with the rest of the air/fuel mixture. The EVAP system is complex and virtually impossible to troubleshoot without the right tools and training. However, the following description should give you a good idea of how it works:

2   The EVAP canister is located under the vehicle, ahead of the fuel tank. The canister, which contains activated carbon, is a repository for storing fuel vapors. You'll have to raise the vehicle to inspect or replace the canister, or any other part of the EVAP system, except for the canister purge valve (which is located in the engine compartment). But the canister is designed to be maintenance-free and should last the life of the vehicle. There are several other important components located on or near the canister: the canister filter, the canister vent shut valve, the two-way valve, the bypass solenoid valve and the fuel tank pressure sensor.

3   The EVAP canister filter is located on the front side of the EVAP canister. When the canister is purged, fresh air is drawn through the filter before passing through the canister. The filter prevents dust and dirt particles from entering the EVAP canister and the EVAP system.

4   The canister vent shut valve is located on the left end of EVAP canister. The canister vent shut valve is normally closed, but it opens to allow fresh air from the filter to enter the EVAP canister when the canister is being purged.

5   The fuel tank pressure sensor is located behind the upper rear edge of the EVAP canister, above the EVAP bypass solenoid valve. The fuel tank pressure sensor monitors the pressure inside the fuel tank, converts fuel tank absolute pressure into a variable voltage signal and transmits this data to the PCM.

6   The EVAP two-way valve is located at the left rear corner of the EVAP canister. When the pressure of the fuel vapors inside the fuel tank exceeds the preset value of the two-way valve, the valve opens and regulates the flow of excess vapors to the canister. The two-way valve also prevents excessive vacuum in the fuel tank by drawing in fresh air through the EVAP canister.

7   The EVAP bypass solenoid valve is located behind the EVAP canister, below the fuel tank pressure sensor, to the right of the EVAP two-way valve. The bypass solenoid valve opens to bypass the two-way valve when the PCM does an EVAP system leak check.

8   The EVAP canister purge control solenoid valve, which is under the control of the Powertrain Control Module (PCM), regulates the flow of vapors being purged from the EVAP canister into the intake manifold. The canister purge valve is always closed when engine coolant temperature is below 147-degrees F (64-degrees C), which cuts off intake

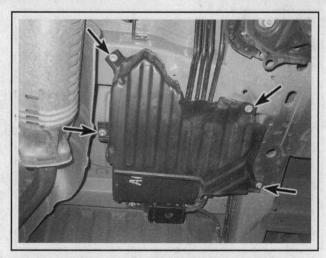

20.17 To detach the EVAP system rock guard, remove these four bolts

manifold vacuum to the EVAP canister. Above that threshold, the PCM opens or closes the purge solenoid valve in accordance with data from various information sensor inputs. The interval of time during which the purge valve is opened by the PCM is known as its "duty cycle." The purge valve is located at the left end of the intake manifold.

## General system checks

9　The most common symptom of a faulty EVAP system is a strong fuel odor (particularly during hot weather). If you smell fuel while driving or (more likely) right after you park the vehicle and turn off the engine, check the fuel filler cap first. Make sure that it's screwed onto the fuel filler neck all the way. If the odor persists, inspect all EVAP hose connections, both in the engine compartment and under the vehicle. You'll have to raise the vehicle and place it securely on jackstands to inspect most of the EVAP system, since it's located under the vehicle. Be sure to inspect each hose attached to the canister for damage and leakage along its entire length. Repair or replace as necessary. Inspect the canister for damage and look for fuel leaking from the bottom. If fuel is leaking or the canister is otherwise damaged, replace it.

10　Poor idle, stalling, and poor driveability can be caused by a defective fuel vapor vent valve or canister purge valve, a damaged canister, cracked hoses, or hoses connected to the wrong tubes. Fuel loss or fuel odor can be caused by fuel leaking from fuel lines or hoses, a cracked or damaged canister, or a defective vapor valve.

20.19 To detach the air filter from its mounting bracket, squeeze the two-halves of each locator pin together and pull the canister away from the bracket

11　A complete test can only be done with a proprietary OBD-II scan tool (see Section 2), which will run a series of checks using the fuel tank pressure sensor and other output actuators to detect excessive pressure. You'll have to take the vehicle to a dealer service department or other qualified repair shop to have the EVAP system professionally diagnosed.

## COMPONENT REPLACEMENT

### 2004 and earlier models

#### EVAP purge control solenoid valve

➥Note: The EVAP purge control solenoid valve is located at the left end of the intake manifold.

12　Disconnect the electrical connector from the purge control solenoid valve.
13　Disconnect the vacuum hoses from the purge control solenoid valve.
14　Remove the purge control solenoid valve.
15　Installation is the reverse of removal.

#### EVAP canister air filter

▶ Refer to illustrations 20.17 and 20.19

➥Note: The canister air filter is located under the vehicle on a bracket next to the EVAP canister.

16　Raise the vehicle and place it securely on jackstands.
17　Remove the EVAP system rock guard (see illustration).
18　Clearly label the three hoses connected to the EVAP canister air filter, then disconnect them.
19　The canister air filter is secured to its mounting bracket by a pair of split-type locator pins. To detach the air filter from its mounting bracket, squeeze the two-halves of each locator pin together and pull the canister away from the bracket (see illustration).
20　Installation is the reverse of removal.

#### EVAP canister vent shut valve

▶ Refer to illustration 20.26

21　Raise the vehicle and place it securely on jackstands.
22　Remove the EVAP system rock guard (see illustration 20.17).
23　Disconnect the electrical connector from the EVAP canister vent shut valve.
24　Disconnect the hose that connects the EVAP canister air filter to the vent shut valve.
25　Remove the EVAP canister retaining bolt and lower the canister. (It's not necessary to disconnect anything else, but the canister must be lowered before you can remove the upper vent shut valve retaining screw.)
26　Remove the vent shut valve from the EVAP canister (see illustration).
27　Remove the old O-ring from the vent shut valve.
28　Installation is the reverse of removal. Be sure to use a new O-ring

#### EVAP two-way valve/bypass solenoid valve/fuel tank pressure sensor assembly

▶ Refer to illustrations 20.31 and 20.35

29　Raise the vehicle and place it securely on jackstands.
30　Remove the EVAP system rock guard (see illustration 20.17).
31　Detach the mounting bracket for the two-way valve/bypass sole-

**20.26  To detach the EVAP canister vent shut valve from the canister, remove these two screws**

**20.31  To detach the mounting bracket for the two-way valve, bypass solenoid and fuel tank pressure sensor, remove this bolt**

noid valve/fuel tank pressure sensor assembly from the EVAP canister mounting bracket (see illustration).

32  Swing the mounting bracket down and disconnect the four vacuum hoses from the two-way valve.

33  Disconnect the electrical connectors from the bypass solenoid valve and from the fuel tank pressure sensor.

34  Separate the two-way valve/bypass solenoid valve/fuel tank pressure sensor assembly from the mounting bracket.

35  If you're replacing the two-way valve or the bypass solenoid valve, separate them from each other (see illustration).

36  If you're replacing the fuel tank pressure sensor, disconnect it from the two vacuum hoses. Be sure to inspect both vacuum hoses for cracks, tears and deterioration. If either hose is damaged or deteriorated, replace it.

37  If you've separated the bypass solenoid valve from the two-way valve, be sure to remove and discard the old O-rings. Be sure to use new O-rings when reattaching the two-way valve and the bypass solenoid valve.

38  Reassembly is the reverse of disassembly.

39  Installation is the reverse of removal.

### EVAP canister

▶ **Refer to illustrations 20.41 and 20.45**

40  Raise the vehicle and place it securely on jackstands.

41  Disconnect the hose that connects the air filter to the vent shut valve and disconnect the vacuum hose that connects the EVAP canister to the purge control solenoid valve (see illustration).

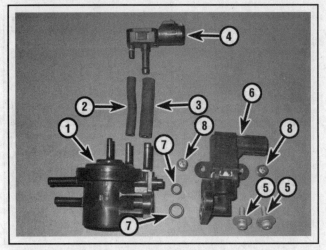

**20.35  Two-way check valve/bypass solenoid valve/fuel tank pressure sensor assembly details**

*1   Two-way valve*
*2   Hose connecting fuel tank pressure sensor and two-way valve*
*3   Hose connecting fuel tank pressure sensor and bypass solenoid (tees into line between two-way valve and bypass solenoid valve)*
*4   Fuel tank pressure sensor*
*5   Bypass solenoid valve-to-two-way check valve retaining screws*
*6   Bypass solenoid valve*
*7   O-rings*
*8   Two-way check valve/bypass solenoid valve/fuel tank pressure sensor assembly retaining screws*

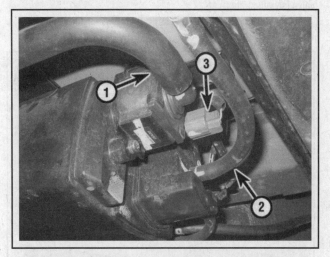

**20.41  Before removing the EVAP canister, disconnect the:**

*1   Hose from air filter to vent shut valve*
*2   Hose from EVAP canister to purge control solenoid valve*
*3   Vent shut valve electrical connector*

**20.45 EVAP canister mounting bolt**

42 Clearly label then disconnect any other vacuum hoses that connect any components attached to the EVAP canister with components located elsewhere (see illustration 20.32).

43 Disconnect the electrical connectors from the bypass solenoid valve and from the fuel tank pressure sensor.

44 Disconnect the electrical connector from the canister vent shut valve.

45 Remove the EVAP canister mounting bolt (see illustration), then lower the rear end of the canister and disengage the slot in the front end from the mounting bracket.

46 Installation is the reverse of removal.

## 2005 and later Acura and Honda models

### EVAP canister purge valve

▶ Refer to illustration 20.47

➡**Note: The EVAP canister purge valve is located in the engine compartment, at the left rear corner of the intake manifold.**

47 Disconnect the electrical connector from the EVAP canister purge valve (see illustration).

48 Disconnect the vacuum hoses from the EVAP canister purge valve.

**20.52 To detach the EVAP canister cover, remove these five bolts and remove the cover**

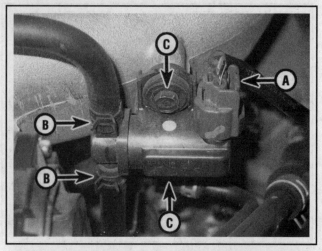

**20.47 EVAP canister purge valve details (2005 and 2006 Acura and 2005 and later Honda models):**

A   Purge valve electrical connector
B   Purge valve hoses
C   Purge valve mounting bolts

49 On 2005 and 2006 Acura and 2005 and later Honda models, remove the EVAP canister purge valve mounting bolts and remove the purge valve. On 2007 Acura models, remove the EVAP canister purge valve mounting bracket nuts and remove the purge valve and mounting bracket as a single assembly, then remove the canister purge valve mounting bolts and separate the purge valve from its mounting bracket.

50 Installation is the reverse of removal.

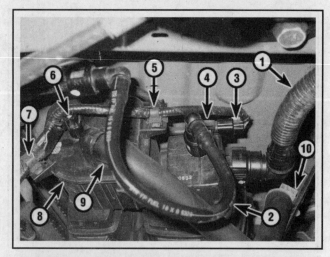

**20.53 EVAP canister assembly details (2005 and 2006 Acura and 2005 and later Honda models):**

1   Hose from the fuel tank
2   Purge line going to the EVAP canister purge valve
3   Fuel Tank Pressure (FTP) sensor electrical connector
4   Fuel Tank Pressure (FTP) sensor
5   FTP sensor wiring harness clip
6   Canister vent shut valve electrical connector
7   Canister vent shut valve harness clip
8   Canister vent shut valve location
9   Fresh air inlet hose from the inlet air filter
10  Fresh air inlet hose clip

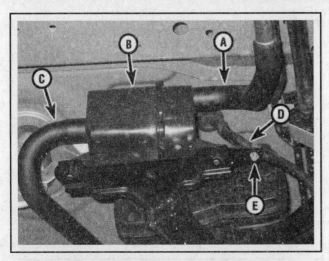

**20.55  Disconnect the hoses from the air filter (2005 and 2006 Acura and 2005 and later Honda models)**

- A  *Disconnect the fresh air inlet hose coming from the engine compartment*
- B  *Fresh air inlet filter location*
- C  *Disconnect the filter outlet hose going to the EVAP canister*
- D  *Fuel Tank Pressure (FTP) sensor and EVAP canister vent shut valve electrical wiring harness*
- E  *Detach the clip for the FTP sensor and vent shut valve wiring harness*

## EVAP canister assembly

▶ **Refer to illustrations 20.52, 20.53, 20.55 and 20.56**

➡**Note: The EVAP canister assembly is located under the left side of the vehicle, in front of the fuel tank. The EVAP canister assembly includes the canister vent shut valve, the Fuel Tank Pressure (FTP) sensor and the canister itself, all of which are located under the left side of the vehicle, in front of the fuel tank.**

51  Raise the vehicle and place it securely on jackstands.
52  Remove the EVAP canister cover bolts (see illustration) and remove the cover.
53  Disconnect the EVAP hoses that connect the fuel tank to the EVAP

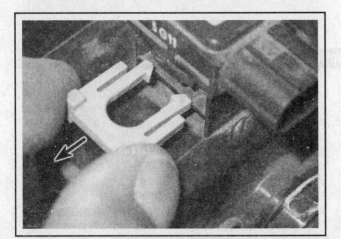

**20.60  To remove the FTP sensor from the EVAP canister assembly, spread the two ends of the retainer apart and pull off the retainer . . .**

**20.56  Remove the three EVAP canister mounting bracket bolts and remove the canister, air filter and mounting bracket as a single assembly (2005 and 2006 Acura and 2005 and later Honda models)**

canister and the canister to the purge valve (see illustration).
54  Disconnect the electrical connectors from the Fuel Tank Pressure (FTP) sensor and from the EVAP canister vent shut valve and detach the wiring harness clips.
55  Disconnect the fresh air filter inlet and outlet hoses and detach the wiring harness clip for FTP sensor and EVAP canister vent shut valve (see illustration).
56  Remove the three EVAP canister mounting bracket bolts (see illustration) and remove the canister and mounting bracket as a single assembly.
57  Remove the two EVAP canister mounting nuts and separate the canister from its mounting bracket.
58  Installation is the reverse of removal.

## Fuel Tank Pressure (FTP) sensor

▶ **Refer to illustrations 20.60 and 20.61**

➡**Note: The FTP sensor is mounted on top of the EVAP canister.**

59  Remove the EVAP canister assembly (see Steps 51 through 57).
60  Remove the FTP sensor retainer (see illustration).
61  Pull the FTP sensor straight up, then remove and discard the old FTP sensor O-ring (see illustration).

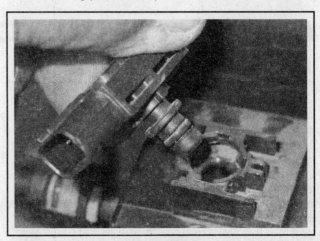

**20.61  . . . then pull out the FTP sensor**

62 Installation is the reverse of removal. Be sure to use a new O-ring and, when installing the sensor retainer, push it in until the lugs on the ends of the retainer click into place.

**EVAP canister vent shut valve**

▶ **Refer to illustration 20.64**

➡ **Note: The EVAP canister vent shut valve is mounted on the end of the EVAP canister.**

63 Remove the EVAP canister assembly (see Steps 51 through 57).
64 Pry open the four (two upper and two lower) lock tabs (see illustration) and pull out the canister vent shut valve.
65 Remove and discard the old vent shut valve O-ring.
66 Installation is the reverse of removal.

**EVAP canister air filter (2005 and 2006 Acura and 2005 and later Honda models)**

▶ **Refer to illustration 20.68**

➡ **Note: The EVAP canister filter is mounted on the same mounting bracket as the EVAP canister.**

67 Remove the EVAP canister assembly (see Steps 51 through 56).
68 Disconnect the air outlet hose from the filter (see illustration).
69 Remove the air filter mounting bolts and remove the filter from the EVAP canister mounting bracket.
70 Installation is the reverse of removal.

**EVAP canister air filter (2007 Acura models)**

➡ **Note: The EVAP canister filter is located ahead of the EVAP canister assembly and is mounted on its own mounting bracket, so you can replace it without removing the EVAP canister assembly.**

71 Raise the vehicle and place it securely on jackstands.
72 Disconnect the hoses from the filter.
73 Remove the air filter mounting bracket bolt and remove the filter and bracket as a single assembly.
74 Remove the air filter mounting bolts and separate the filter from its mounting bracket.
75 Installation is the reverse of removal.

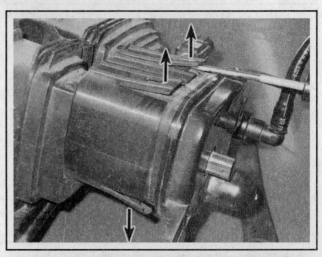

20.64 Pry open the four (two upper and two lower) lock tabs and pull out the canister vent shut valve

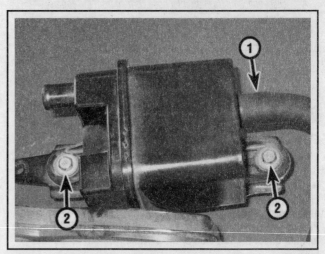

20.68 To detach the filter from the EVAP canister mounting bracket, disconnect the air filter outlet hose (1) and the air filter mounting bolts (2) (2005 and 2006 Acura and 2005 and later Honda models)

## 21 Exhaust Gas Recirculation (EGR) system - description and component replacement

### DESCRIPTION

1 Oxides of nitrogen (or simply NOx) is a compound that is formed in the combustion chambers when the oxygen and nitrogen in the incoming air mix together. NOx is a natural byproduct of high combustion chamber temperatures. When NOx is emitted from the tailpipe, it mixes with reactive organic compounds (ROCs), hydrocarbons (HC) and sunlight to form ozone and photochemical smog. The EGR system reduces oxides of nitrogen by recirculating exhaust gases from the exhaust manifold, through the EGR valve and intake manifold, then back to the combustion chambers, where it mixes with the incoming air/fuel mixture before being consumed. These recirculated exhaust gases "dilute" the incoming air/fuel mixture, which cools the combustion chambers, thereby reducing NOx emissions.

2 The EGR system consists of the Powertrain Control Module (PCM), the EGR valve, the EGR valve position sensor and various other information sensors that the PCM uses to determine when to open the EGR valve. The degree to which the EGR valve is opened is referred to as "EGR valve lift." The PCM is programmed to produce the ideal EGR valve lift for varying operating conditions. The EGR valve position sensor, which is an integral part of the EGR valve, detects the amount of EGR valve lift and sends this information to the PCM. The PCM then compares it with the appropriate EGR valve lift for the operating conditions. The PCM increases current flow to the EGR valve to increase valve lift and reduces the current to reduce the amount of lift. If EGR flow is inappropriate to the operating conditions (idle, cold engine, etc.) the PCM simply cuts the current to the EGR valve and the valve closes.

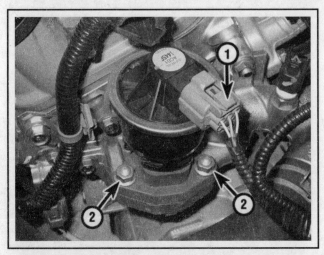

21.4  To remove the EGR valve, depress this release tab (1) and disconnect the electrical connector from the EGR valve, then remove these two mounting nuts (2)

21.6  Be sure to remove all traces of old gasket material with a gasket scraper, and be extremely careful not to scratch or gouge the surfaces

## EGR VALVE REPLACEMENT

▶ **Refer to illustrations 21.4 and 21.6**

3   Remove the engine cover (see Chapter 2A).

4   Disconnect the electrical connector from the EGR valve (see illustration).

5   Remove the EGR valve mounting nuts and remove the EGR valve.

6   Remove and discard the old EGR valve gasket (see illustration).

7   Installation is the reverse of removal. Be sure to use a new EGR valve gasket, and tighten the EGR valve mounting nuts securely.

---

**22  Positive Crankcase Ventilation (PCV) system - description, check and component replacement**

## DESCRIPTION

1   The Positive Crankcase Ventilation (PCV) system reduces hydrocarbon emissions by scavenging crankcase vapors. It does this by circulating fresh air from the air intake duct into and through the crankcase, where it mixes with blow-by gases before being drawn by intake manifold vacuum through a PCV valve to the intake manifold. The PCV valve maintains idle quality by restricting the flow of crankcase vapors into the intake manifold when intake manifold vacuum is high, and allows full flow when intake manifold decreases. The main components of the PCV system are the PCV valve and a pair of vacuum hoses.

### 2001 and 2002 Acura and 2003 and 2004 Honda models

2   The fresh air inlet hose connects the air intake duct to the left end of the front valve cover. The fresh air inlet hose draws fresh air from the air intake duct into the crankcase (via the valve cover). This fresh air combines with blow-by gases in the crankcase. This mixture of fresh air and crankcase vapors is drawn into the intake manifold by intake manifold vacuum through the PCV valve and the "crankcase ventilation hose," which connects the crankcase (via the rear valve cover) to the intake manifold.

### 2003 and later Acura and 2005 and later Honda models

3   The fresh air inlet hose connects the air intake duct to the left end of the rear valve cover. The fresh air inlet hose draws fresh air from the air intake duct into the crankcase (via the valve cover). This fresh air combines with blow-by gases in the crankcase. This mixture of fresh air and crankcase vapors is drawn into the intake manifold by intake manifold vacuum through the PCV valve and the crankcase ventilation hose, which connects the crankcase (via the front valve cover) to the intake manifold.

## CHECK

### 2001 and 2003 Acura and 2003 and 2004 Honda models

▶ **Refer to illustration 22.6**

4   Remove the engine cover (see Chapter 2A) and the rear ignition coil harness cover (see illustration 22.17a).

5   Inspect the two PCV system hoses for cracks, tears or deterioration. If either hose is damaged or worn, replace it.

6   Start the engine and allow it to warm up. With the engine idling, pull out the PCV valve and cover the open end of the valve with your

22.6 To check the PCV valve, plug it with your finger while the engine is idling and see if you can feel vacuum; if you can't, either the crankcase ventilation hose or the PCV valve is damaged or defective (2001 and 2002 Acura and 2003 and 2004 Honda models)

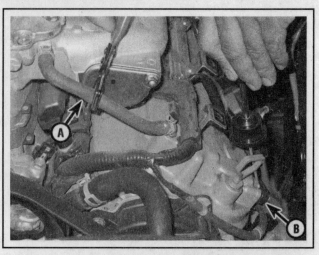

22.13 To check the PCV valve on a 2003 and later Acura or 2005 or later Honda model, pinch the PCV hose (A) while listening to the PCV valve (B) with a stethoscope. It should make a clicking sound each time you pinch the hose

finger (see illustration). You should feel intake vacuum at the PCV valve.

7   If there is no vacuum at the valve, the crankcase ventilation hose is either clogged or it has a hole in it. Remove the crankcase ventilation hose (see Steps 11 through 15), blow it out with compressed air, then inspect it for damage.

8   If the hose is damaged or clogged, replace it, then retest the valve. If there is still no intake vacuum at the PCV valve, replace the valve.

9   While the PCV valve is removed, inspect the PCV valve grommet for cracks, tears or deterioration. If the grommet is worn or damaged, replace it.

10  If you're not going to replace anything, install the rear ignition coil harness cover and the engine cover.

### 2003 and later Acura and 2005 and later Honda models

▶ Refer to illustration 22.13

11  Remove the engine cover (see Chapter 2A).

12  Inspect the two PCV system hoses for cracks, tears or deterioration. If either hose is damaged or worn, replace it.

13  Start the engine and allow it to warm up. With the engine idling, pinch the PCV hose with your fingers or with pliers and listen to the PCV valve with a stethoscope (see illustration). You should hear a clicking sound inside the PCV valve. Repeat this test several times. You should hear the clicking sound each time that you pinch the PCV hose.

14  If there is no clicking sound, inspect the PCV valve grommet for cracks, tears or deterioration. If the grommet is damaged, replace it and retest.

15  If the grommet is okay, replace the PCV valve, then retest.

22.16 The PCV crankcase ventilation hose is connected to this pipe at the right rear corner of the intake manifold; to disconnect the crankcase ventilation hose, loosen the hose clamp, slide it back and pull off the hose (2001 and 2002 Acura and 2003 and 2004 Honda models)

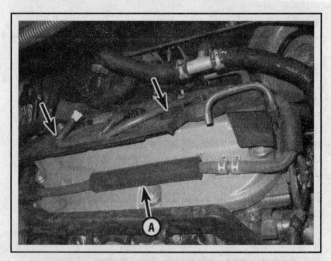

22.17a Remove the two bolts securing the ignition coil harness cover to the valve cover and detach the cover. The intake manifold is removed for clarity only; it's not necessary to actually remove the intake manifold to replace the crankcase ventilation hose (A) (2001 and 2002 Acura and 2003 and 2004 Honda models)

22.17b To disconnect the crankcase ventilation hose from the PCV valve (1), loosen the hose clamp (2), slide back the clamp and pull off the hose (2001 and 2002 Acura and 2003 and 2004 Honda models)

## COMPONENT REPLACEMENT

### 2001 and 2002 Acura and 2003 and 2004 Honda models

#### Crankcase ventilation hose

▶ Refer to illustrations 22.16, 22.17a and 22.17b

16 Remove the engine cover (see Chapter 2A), then disconnect the hose from the intake manifold (see illustration).

17 Remove the ignition coil harness cover, then disconnect the crankcase ventilation hose from the PCV valve (see illustrations).

18 Pull the crankcase ventilation hose out from under the intake manifold.

19 Installation is the reverse of removal.

#### PCV valve

20 Remove the engine cover (see Chapter 2A), then disconnect the crankcase ventilation hose from the PCV valve (see illustration 22.17b).

21 Remove the PCV valve (see illustration 22.6a).

22.28 To detach the MAF sensor wiring harness clips (1) from the bracket on the PCV fresh air inlet pipe, squeeze the split pins underneath and push the clips out of the bracket. Then loosen and slide back the spring type hose clamps for the fresh air inlet pipe (2) and for the coolant pipe (3) (2003 and later Acura and 2005 and later Honda models)

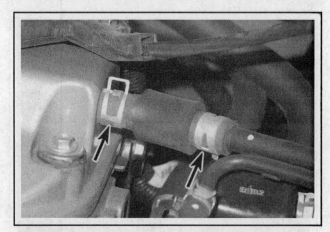

22.25 To remove the fresh air inlet hose, loosen these two spring-type clamps and slide them back, then pull off the hose (2003 and later Acura and 2005 and later Honda models)

22 Inspect the PCV valve grommet for cracks, tears and other deterioration. If the grommet is worn or damaged, replace it.

23 Installation is the reverse of removal.

### 2003 and later Acura and 2005 and later Honda models

24 Remove the engine cover (see Chapter 2A).

#### PCV fresh air inlet pipe and hose

➡Note: The PCV fresh air inlet pipe connects the air intake duct to the left end of the rear valve cover. The smaller diameter pipe that's integral with the fresh air inlet pipe is a coolant pipe that carries coolant from the coolant passage between the heads to the throttle body. The metal part of the fresh air inlet pipe should never need replacement, but the short rubber hose that connects the pipe to the rear valve cover can crack, tear or deteriorate. If you need to remove the metal air inlet pipe you'll have to drain the coolant because the coolant pipe is an integral part of the air inlet pipe assembly.

#### Fresh air inlet hose

▶ Refer to illustration 22.25

➡Note: This section applies only to the short rubber hose that connects the fresh air inlet pipe to the rear valve cover. If you're removing the metal fresh air inlet pipe, go to Step 27.

25 Loosen and slide back the spring type clamps at both ends of the fresh air inlet hose (see illustration) and remove the air inlet hose.

26 Installation is the reverse of removal

#### Fresh air inlet pipe

▶ Refer to illustration 22.28

### ✳✳ WARNING:

Wait until the engine is completely cool before beginning this procedure.

27 Drain the engine coolant (see Chapter 1) and remove the air intake duct (see Chapter 4).

28 Detach the two clips that secure the Mass Air Flow (MAF) sensor wire harness from the bracket on the air inlet pipe (see illustration).

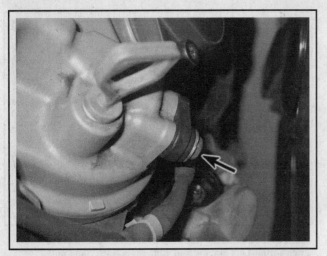

**22.31 To remove the PCV valve, remove this bolt (2003 and later Acura and 2005 and later Honda models)**

29 Loosen and slide back the spring-type clamps at each end of the air inlet pipe and at each end of the coolant pipe.

30 Installation is the reverse of removal. Refill the cooling system (see Chapter 1).

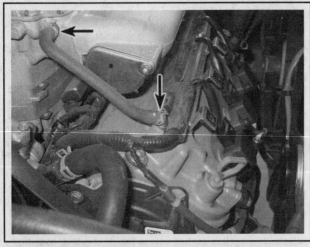

**22.34 To remove the crankcase ventilation hose (PCV hose), loosen and slide back the two spring-type clamps and pull off the hose (2003 and later Acura and 2005 and later Honda models)**

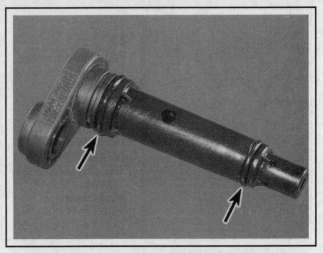

**22.32 Remove and discard the two old PCV O-rings (2003 and later Acura and 2005 and later Honda models)**

**PCV valve**

▶ **Refer to illustrations 22.31 and 22.32**

✳✳ **WARNING:**

If the vehicle has been driven recently, make sure that the engine is cool before beginning this procedure.

➡**Note: The PCV valve is located in the right end of the front valve cover.**

31 Remove the PCV valve retaining bolt (see illustration) and pull the PCV valve out of the valve cover.

32 Remove and discard the two old PCV O-rings (see illustration).

33 Installation is the reverse of removal. Be sure to use new O-rings and tighten the PCV retaining bolt to the torque listed in this Chapter's Specifications.

**Crankcase ventilation hose (PCV hose)**

▶ **Refer to illustration 22.34**

34 Loosen and slide back the two spring-type clamps (see illustration) and pull off the PCV hose.

35 Installation is the reverse of removal.

## 23  Variable Valve Timing and Lift Electronic Control (VTEC) system - description and component replacement

### DESCRIPTION

1   A low-lift, short-duration camshaft intake lobe produces good torque, quick response, good fuel economy and low emissions at lower engine speeds, but can't deliver sufficient air/fuel mixture to the combustion chamber at higher engine speeds. A high-lift, long-duration intake cam lobe produces good power at high engine speeds, but produces a lumpy idle and poor driveability, wastes fuel and produces unacceptable emissions at lower engine speeds. That's why camshaft intake lobe profiles are always a compromise between economy and performance. But Honda's Variable Valve Timing and Lift Electronic Control (VTEC) system allows an engine to operate economically and make good power at the same time.

2   The VTEC system is used on all models covered in this manual except 2WD Honda models. The principal differences between VTEC and non-VTEC engines are in the cylinder head, the camshaft(s) and the rocker arms. The block, the lubrication and cooling systems and most other components are identical on VTEC and non-VTEC engines. For more information about the cylinder head, the camshaft(s) and the rocker arms, see Chapter 2. This Section is intended to familiarize you with how VTEC works and to show you how to replace the PCM-controlled components such as the VTEC solenoid valve and the VTC oil control solenoid valve.

3   There are two cam lobes for each pair of intake valves on a VTEC engine. These "primary" and "secondary" lobe profiles differ in lift and duration: the secondary lobe has lower lift and less duration (it opens later and closes sooner), while the primary lobe has higher lift and more duration (opens sooner and closes later). Each lobe operates its own rocker arm, which in turn pushes on its own valve. At low speeds, the secondary camshaft lobe operates one intake valve and the primary cam lobe operates the other valve. The low-lift, short-duration lobe produces good low-end torque and responsiveness.

4   When more power is needed at higher engine speeds, the PCM activates the VTEC solenoid valve, which allows higher oil pressure to a

hydraulically-operated, spring-loaded pin inside the primary rocker arm. When hydraulic pressure overcomes spring pressure, the pin slides sideways and locks the secondary rocker arm to the primary rocker arm. The two rocker arms are both activated by the primary cam lobe; the secondary rocker arm no longer contacts its own camshaft lobe again until the system is disengaged. So both valves are now opened by the primary camshaft lobe with its higher lift and longer duration, increasing performance.

5   The PCM turns the VTEC solenoid valve on and off in accordance with engine rpm, vehicle speed, throttle opening angle, engine load and coolant temperature. Although diagnosis of the VTEC system is beyond the scope of the home mechanic, it's not difficult to replace the VTEC solenoid valve or to clean the filter for the system, both of which are outlined below.

### COMPONENT REPLACEMENT

#### VTEC solenoid valve

▶ Refer to illustrations 23.7a and 23.7b

➡ Note: The VTEC solenoid valve is located at the lower right corner of the backside of the engine block at the upper end of the oil filter housing, above the VTEC oil pressure switch.

6   Raise the front of the vehicle and place it securely on jackstands.

7   Locate the VTEC solenoid valve (see illustration), then trace the electrical lead up to the electrical connector (see illustration) and disconnect it.

8   Remove the two VTEC solenoid valve mounting bolts (see illustration 23.7a) and remove the solenoid valve.

9   Remove and discard the VTEC solenoid valve O-ring.

10  Installation is the reverse of removal. Be sure to use a new O-ring and tighten the VTEC solenoid valve mounting bolts to the torque listed in this Chapter's Specifications.

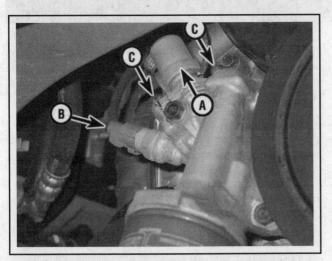

23.7a  The VTEC solenoid valve (A) is located at the lower right rear corner of the engine, right above the VTEC oil pressure switch (B). To detach the solenoid valve, simply remove the two mounting bolts (C)

23.7b  To find the electrical connector for the VTEC solenoid valve, trace the electrical lead up to the connector. Depress the release tab (A) and pull the lower half of the connector out of the upper half

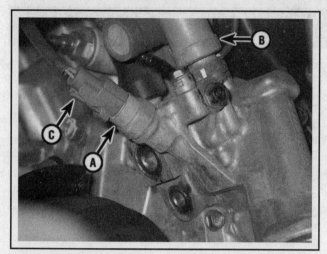

23.12 The VTEC oil pressure switch (A) is located below the VTEC solenoid valve (B). To disconnect the electrical connector from the oil pressure switch, depress the release tab (C) and pull off the connector

### VTEC oil pressure switch

▶ Refer to illustrations 23.12 and 23.14

➡Note: The VTEC oil pressure switch is located at the lower right corner of the backside of the engine block, at the upper end of the oil filter housing, below the VTEC solenoid valve.

11 Raise the front of the vehicle and place it securely on jackstands.

23.14 Always remove and discard the old VTEC oil pressure switch O-ring and install a new O-ring

12 Disconnect the electrical connector from the VTEC oil pressure switch (see illustration).

13 Unscrew and remove the VTEC oil pressure switch.

14 Remove and discard the old VTEC oil pressure switch O-ring (see illustration).

15 Installation is the reverse of removal. Be sure to use a new O-ring and tighten the oil pressure switch to the torque listed in this Chapter's Specifications.

## 24 Intake Manifold Runner Control (IMRC) system - description, adjustment and component replacement

### DESCRIPTION

1 The Intake Manifold Runner Control (IMRC) system is used on 2001 and 2002 Acura models. The IMRC system consists of the control module, the control actuator, the control cable and the two IMRC valves inside the intake manifold. When commanded to do so by the Powertrain Control Module (PCM), the control actuator opens or closes the IMRC valves via a short cable connected to a spring-loaded link on the right end of the shaft to which the valves are attached. You'll find the cable connection to this link at the right end of the intake manifold.

2 Basically, the control module closes the IMRC valves at low speed and opens them at high speed. When the IMRC valves are closed, they increase the effective length of the intake runners, which improves torque at low speed. When the valves are open, they shorten the effective length of the intake runners, which improves power at high speed. Here's why: When intake air is drawn into the cylinders at idle or at low engine speeds, less air is needed because the cylinders don't need to be filled so often or so quickly. So at idle and at low engine speeds, the air drawn into an engine with longer intake runners will have a higher velocity than one with shorter intake runners. However, at

higher engine speeds, longer intake runners would prevent the cylinders from filling quickly enough and would therefore limit power. Most intake manifold designs are a compromise between the conflicting demands of low and high engine speeds.

3 The IMRC system uses a specially designed intake manifold. Inside the manifold are a pair of long, rectangular-shaped valves mounted on a shaft that is controlled by the actuator. When the engine is idling or operating below a specified rpm, the two valves inside the manifold direct incoming air through a longer path. Directing incoming air through a longer intake path at low engine speeds promotes higher intake air velocities because the incoming air can move more quickly through the intake manifold to fill the cylinders. When engine speed reaches the specified rpm, the PCM energizes the actuator, which turns the shaft and the two valves, altering the intake pathway through the intake manifold. When the valves turn, they send the incoming air through a shorter intake path designed to handle a larger volume of air. At that point, the volume of air drawn into the cylinders is sufficient to promote good velocity even through the shorter intake path. And the shorter intake path enhances performance during heavy acceleration or high cruising speeds.

## CONTROL CABLE ADJUSTMENT

4   Remove the engine cover (see Chapter 2A).

5   The IMRC valves are opened and closed by a short cable coming from the control actuator. The control cable is connected to a spring-loaded linkage cam on the right end of the intake manifold. When the IMRC valves are closed, there should be no clearance between the adjuster screw and the stop. Verify that there is no clearance here. If there is any clearance, adjust the control cable as follows.

6   Trace the cable to its other end at the control actuator on the backside of the intake manifold. The cable is connected to another cam link on the actuator. Freeplay is determined by the position of the adjuster nut and locknut on the threaded adjuster barrel at the end of the cable sheath. Check the cable freeplay between the cable bracket and the actuator cam and compare your measurement to the cable freeplay listed in this Chapter's Specifications. If the cable freeplay is outside the specified range, loosen the locknut and adjuster nut at the cable bracket and adjust the cable as necessary. When the freeplay is satisfactory, tighten the locknut and adjuster nut securely, then check the clearance again between the adjuster screw and the stop at the other end of the cable. Repeat, if necessary, until the cable freeplay produces zero clearance between the adjuster screw and the stop.

## COMPONENT REPLACEMENT

7   Remove the engine cover (see Chapter 2A).

### IMRC control actuator

➡Note: The IMRC control actuator is located on the backside of the intake manifold.

8   Disconnect the electrical connector from the IMRC control actuator.

9   Remove the actuator mounting bolts and remove the actuator from the intake manifold.

10  Loosen the control cable locknut and adjuster nut and detach the cable from the cable bracket. To disengage the cable end plug from the cam link on the actuator, rotate the spring-loaded link cam counterclockwise and slide the end plug out of its slot in the cam.

11  Installation is the reverse of removal. Be sure to adjust control cable freeplay when you're done.

### IMRC control cable

12  Remove the control actuator and disconnect the control cable from the actuator (see Steps 7 through 9).

13  At the IMRC valve end of the cable, loosen the control cable locknut and adjuster nut and detach the cable from the cable bracket. To disengage the cable end plug from the cam link on the IMRC valve shaft, rotate the spring-loaded link cam counterclockwise and slide the end plug out of its slot in the cam.

14  Installation is the reverse of removal

15  Be sure to adjust the control cable when you're done (see Steps 4 and 5).

### IMRC control module

➡Note: The IMRC control module is located under the instrument panel, on top of the center tunnel.

16  Remove the passenger side center console trim (see Chapter 11).

17  Remove the IMRC control module retaining bolt.

18  Remove the IMRC control module from its mounting bracket, flip it upside down and disconnect the electrical connector from the module.

19  Installation is the reverse of removal.

### Intake manifold

20  Refer to Chapter 2A.

## 25 Intake Manifold Tuning (IMT) system - description and component replacement

## DESCRIPTION

1   The Intake Manifold Tuning (IMT) system, which is used on 2003 and later Acura models and on 2006 and later 2WD Honda models, is a new and improved version of the previous Intake Manifold Runner Control (IMRC) system used on 2001 and 2002 Acura models. The IMT system consists of the Powertrain Control Module (PCM), a tuning valve actuator with an integral position sensor, which is bolted onto the intake manifold, and the two IMT valves, which are located inside the intake manifold. The PCM uses the position sensor to monitor the position (angle) of the IMT valves. When the valves are closed, they improve torque at low speed by increasing the effective length of the intake runners. When the valve are open, they improve power at high speed by decreasing the effective length of the intake runners. Here's why: When intake air is drawn into the cylinders at idle or at low engine speeds, less air is needed because the cylinders don't need to be filled so often or so quickly. So at idle and at low engine speeds, the air drawn into

an engine with longer intake runners will have a higher velocity than one with shorter intake runners. However, at higher engine speeds, longer intake runners would prevent the cylinders from filling quickly enough and would therefore limit power. Most intake manifold designs are a compromise between the conflicting demands of low and high engine speeds.

2   The IMT system helps to maintain a uniformly higher intake air velocity throughout the engine's operating range. Higher intake air velocity promotes better vaporization of the fuel sprayed into the stream of incoming air by the fuel injectors, which means more complete combustion, more power, better fuel economy and less emissions.

3   The IMT system uses a specially designed intake manifold. Inside the manifold are a pair of long, rectangular-shaped valves mounted on a shaft that is controlled by the actuator. When the engine is idling or operating below a specified rpm, the two valves inside the manifold direct incoming air through a longer path. Directing incoming air through a longer intake path at low engine speeds promotes higher

intake air velocities because the incoming air can move more quickly through the intake manifold to fill the cylinders. When engine speed reaches the specified rpm, the PCM energizes the actuator, which turns the shaft and the two valves, altering the intake pathway through the intake manifold. When the valves turn, they send the incoming air through a shorter intake path designed to handle a larger volume of air. At that point, the volume of air drawn into the cylinders is sufficient to promote good velocity even through the shorter intake path. The shorter intake path enhances performance during heavy acceleration or high cruising speeds.

## COMPONENT REPLACEMENT

### IMT actuator

4   Remove the engine cover (see Chapter 2A).
5   Disconnect the electrical connector from the IMT actuator.
6   Remove the actuator mounting bolts and remove the actuator.
7   Remove and discard the actuator O-ring.
8   Installation is the reverse of removal. Be sure to use a new O-ring and tighten the actuator mounting bolts to the torque listed in this Chapter's Specifications.

### Intake manifold

9   Refer to Chapter 2A.

## 26  Variable Cylinder Management (VCM) system - description and component replacement

## DESCRIPTION

1   The Variable Cylinder Management (VCM) system is used only on 2006 and later 2WD models. Under certain conditions (such as light-load cruising and deceleration) the VCM system saves fuel by cutting the spark and fuel to the rear cylinders and deactivating the intake and exhaust valves. Because the valves are not being actuated, friction from valve spring compression is reduced. Piston drag is also reduced because no air is compressed as the pistons come up.

## COMPONENT REPLACEMENT

### Engine Oil Pressure (EOP) sensor

➡**Note: The EOP sensor is screwed into the rocker arm oil control solenoid valve, which is located on the left end of the rear cylinder head.**

2   Remove the engine cover (see Chapter 2A).
3   Disconnect the EOP sensor electrical connector.

4   Unscrew the sensor from the rocker arm oil control solenoid valve.
5   Remove and discard the old EOP sensor O-ring.
6   Installation is the reverse of removal. Be sure to use a new O-ring and tighten the EOP sensor to the torque listed in this Chapter's Specifications.

### Rocker arm oil control solenoid valve and filter

➡**Note: The rocker arm oil control solenoid valve is located on the left end of the rear cylinder head.**

7   Remove the engine cover (see Chapter 2A).
8   Disconnect the EOP sensor electrical connector.
9   Remove the rocker arm oil control solenoid mounting bolts and remove the rocker arm oil control solenoid valve.
10  Remove the rocker arm oil control solenoid valve O-ring and filter.
11  Inspect the filter for clogging. If it's clogged, replace the filer/O-ring, and replace the engine oil and the oil filter (see Chapter 1).
12  Installation is the reverse of removal. Be sure to tighten the mounting bolts to the torque listed in this Chapter's Specifications.

## Specifications

| Torque specifications | Ft-lbs (unless otherwise indicated) | Nm |
| --- | --- | --- |
| Engine Coolant Temperature (ECT) sensor | 156 in-lbs | 18 |
| Intake Manifold Tuning (IMT) actuator | | |
|     mounting bolts | 86 in-lbs | 10 |
| Knock sensor | 23 | 31 |
| Positive Crankcase Ventilation (PCV) | | |
|     valve retaining bolt | 104 in-lbs | 12 |
| Variable Cylinder Management (VCM) system | | |
|     Engine Oil Pressure (EOP) sensor | 192 in-lbs | 22 |
|     Rocker arm oil control solenoid valve | | |
|         mounting bolts | 192 in-lbs | 22 |
| Variable Valve Timing and Lift Electronic | | |
|     Control (VTEC) system | | |
|     VTEC oil pressure switch | 192 in-lbs | 22 |
|     VTEC solenoid valve mounting bolts | 104 in-lbs | 12 |

**Notes**

## Section

7

AUTOMATIC
TRANSAXLE

## 1  General information

The automatic transaxle is an electronically controlled, 5-speed unit. The automatic transaxles are designated according to the model and type:

**Honda Pilot**

BVLA - 2WD models
BVGA - 4WD models

**Acura MDX**

BGHA - 2001 and 2002 models
MGHA - 2001 and 2002 models
MDKA - 2003 through 2006 models
BDKA - 2006 models
BYFA - 2007 models

The transaxle model number is stamped onto a plate on the transaxle. Refer to *Vehicle identification numbers* at the front of this manual for the location of the plate.

Due to the complexity of the clutches and the hydraulic control system, and because of the special tools and expertise required to perform an automatic transaxle overhaul, it should not be undertaken by the home mechanic. Therefore, the procedures in this Chapter are limited to general diagnosis, shift cable adjustment, certain component replacement procedures and transaxle removal and installation.

If the transaxle requires major repair work, it should be left to a dealer service department or an automotive or transaxle repair shop. You can, however, remove and install the transaxle yourself and save the expense, even if the repair work is done by a transaxle shop (but be sure a proper diagnosis has been made before removing the transaxle).

## 2  Diagnosis - general

1  Automatic transaxle malfunctions may be caused by five general conditions:

a) *Poor engine performance*
b) *Improper adjustments*
c) *Hydraulic malfunctions*
d) *Mechanical malfunctions*
e) *Malfunctions in the computer or its signal network*

2  Diagnosis of these problems should always begin with a check of the easily repaired items: fluid level and condition (see Chapter 1), shift cable adjustment and shift lever installation. Next, perform a road test to determine if the problem has been corrected or if more diagnosis is necessary. If the problem persists after the preliminary tests and corrections are completed, additional diagnosis should be performed by a dealer service department or other qualified transmission repair shop. Refer to the *Troubleshooting* section at the front of this manual for information on symptoms of transaxle problems.

### PRELIMINARY CHECKS

3  Drive the vehicle to warm the transaxle to normal operating temperature.

4  Check the fluid level as described in Chapter 1:

a) *If the fluid level is unusually low, add enough fluid to bring the level within the designated area of the dipstick, then check for external leaks (see below).*
b) *If the fluid level is abnormally high, drain off the excess, then check the drained fluid for contamination by coolant. The presence of engine coolant in the automatic transmission fluid indicates that a failure has occurred in the internal radiator walls that separate the coolant from the transmission fluid (see Chapter 3).*
c) *If the fluid is foaming, drain it and refill the transaxle, then check for coolant in the fluid, or a high fluid level.*

5  Make sure the engine idle speed is correct. If the idle speed is incorrect, have it adjusted by a dealer service department or other qualified repair shop before proceeding.

6  Inspect the shift cable. Make sure that it's properly adjusted and operates smoothly (see Section 3).

### FLUID LEAK DIAGNOSIS

7  Most fluid leaks are easy to locate visually. Repair usually consists of replacing a seal or gasket. If a leak is difficult to find, the following procedure may help.

8  Identify the fluid. Make sure it's transmission fluid and not engine oil or brake fluid (automatic transmission fluid is a deep red color).

9  Try to pinpoint the source of the leak. Drive the vehicle several miles, then park it over a large sheet of cardboard. After a minute or two, you should be able to locate the leak by determining the source of the fluid dripping onto the cardboard.

10  Make a careful visual inspection of the suspected component and the area immediately around it. Pay particular attention to gasket mating surfaces. A mirror is often helpful for finding leaks in areas that are hard to see.

11  If the leak still cannot be found, clean the suspected area thoroughly with a degreaser or solvent, then dry it.

12  Drive the vehicle for several miles at normal operating temperature and varying speeds. After driving the vehicle, visually inspect the suspected component again.

13  Once the leak has been located, the cause must be determined before it can be properly repaired. If a gasket is replaced but the sealing flange is bent, the new gasket will not stop the leak. The bent flange must be straightened.

14  Before attempting to repair a leak, check to make sure that the following conditions are corrected or they may cause another leak.

→**Note: Some of the following conditions cannot be fixed without highly specialized tools and expertise. Such problems must be referred to a transmission shop or a dealer service department.**

### Seal leaks

15  If a transaxle seal is leaking, the fluid level or pressure may be too high, the vent may be plugged, the seal bore may be damaged, the seal itself may be damaged or improperly installed, the surface of the shaft protruding through the seal may be damaged or a loose bearing may be causing excessive shaft movement.

16  Make sure the dipstick tube seal is in good condition and the

tube is properly seated. Periodically check the area around the speedometer gear or sensor for leakage. If transmission fluid is evident, check the O-ring for damage.

## Case leaks

17 If the case itself appears to be leaking, the casting is porous and will have to be repaired or replaced.

18 Make sure the oil cooler hose fittings are tight and in good condition.

## Fluid comes out vent pipe or fill tube

19 If this condition occurs, the transaxle is overfilled, there is coolant in the fluid, the case is porous, the dipstick is incorrect, the vent is plugged or the drain-back holes are plugged.

## 3  Shift cable - replacement and adjustment

### ❈❈ WARNING:

The models covered by this manual are equipped with a Supplemental Restraint System (SRS), more commonly known as airbags. Always disable the airbag system before working in the vicinity of any airbag system component to avoid the possibility of accidental deployment of the airbag(s), which could cause personal injury (see Chapter 12). Do not use a memory saving device to preserve the PCM or radio memory when working on or near airbag system components.

## HONDA MODELS

### Replacement

♦ Refer to illustration 3.4

1  Set the parking brake and block the rear wheels. Disconnect the cable from the negative terminal of the battery (see Chapter 5, Section 1).

2  Remove the steering column covers (see Chapter 11).

3  Place the shift lever in the Neutral position.

4  Remove the locking nut from the cable adjuster, then rotate the grommet counterclockwise a 1/4 turn and slide the grommet and cable from the bracket (see illustration).

3.4  Remove the locking nut from the shift cable (A), then rotate the grommet (B) 90-degrees to detach the cable from the steering column

### 2003 through 2005 models

♦ Refer to illustrations 3.6a, 3.6b, 3.7 and 3.8

5  Raise the vehicle and support it securely on jackstands.

6  Working at the transaxle, remove the shift cable cover (see illustration) and the mounting bolts for the shift cable holder (see illustration).

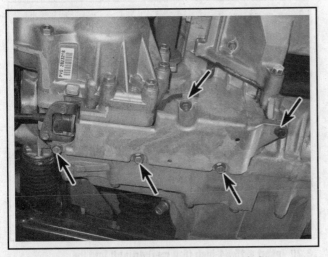

3.6a  Location of the shift cable cover mounting bolts

3.6b  Remove the two shift cable holder mounting bolts

**3.7 First remove the lock bolt (A) securing the shift lever, then remove the shift lever pin (B) to separate the assembly from the transaxle**

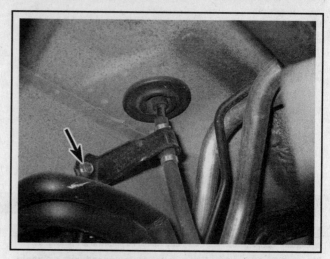

**3.8 Remove the shift cable guide bracket bolt, separate the shift cable from the bracket and pry the shift cable body grommet from the firewall**

7  Remove the lock bolt securing the shift lever (see illustration) and slide the shift lever pin and shift lever from the transaxle.

8  Working at the firewall, remove the shift cable guide bracket bolt and separate the shift cable from the bracket (see illustration).

9  Disengage the rubber grommet and pull the shift cable through the firewall.

### 2006 and later models

10  Remove the air intake duct and the air filter housing (see Chapter 4).

11  Remove the battery and the battery tray (see Chapter 5).

12  Remove the shift cable bracket nuts retaining the shift cable to the transaxle.

13  Remove the spring clip/washer and control pin and detach the shift cable end from the lever at the transaxle.

14  Remove the shift cable guide bracket nuts and separate the shift cable from the firewall.

15  Disengage the rubber grommet and pull the shift cable through the firewall.

### All models

16  Installation is the reverse of the removal procedure:

17  Be sure to adjust the cable before reattaching it to the shift lever (see Steps 19 through 25).

### Adjustment

♦ Refer to illustrations 3.19, 3.20 and 3.21

18  Position the shift lever to the Neutral position, then working under the steering column, remove the locknut from the shift cable and disconnect it from the mounting bracket (see Step 4).

19  Push the shift cable until it stops and release your hand. Pull back two clicks until the cable stops (locks-in) in position. This is the NEUTRAL position (see illustration).

20  With the ignition key OFF, insert a 15/64-inch (6.0 mm) pin into the positioning hole on the shift lever bracket base (see illustration). Once the pin is slid through the positioning hole on the shift lever bracket base, align the shift lever and slide the pin into the shift lever positioning hole to lock the assembly into place. This is the NEUTRAL position.

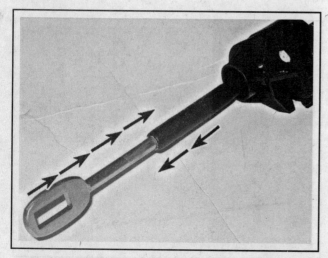

**3.19 Push the shift cable until it stops and pull back two clicks to set the cable in the NEUTRAL position**

**3.20 Insert a 15/64-inch (6.0 mm) drill bit into the positioning hole**

**3.21  Make sure the cable end fits over the square shank on the pin**

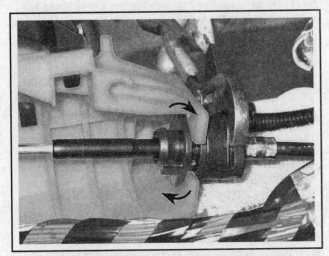

**3.28  Rotate the socket holder 1/4-turn until the flattened edge of the cable grommet guide aligns with the base**

**3.32  Remove the shift cable guide bracket bolt and separate the cable from the body**

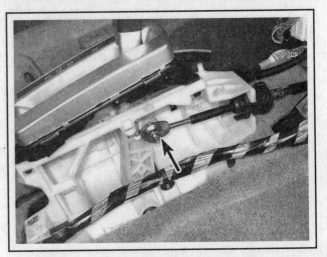

**3.27  Remove the locking nut from the threaded stud on the cable end**

21  Install the shift cable into the mounting bracket, then install the cable end to the shift lever mounting bolt and align the square surface with the alignment casting on the mounting bolt (see illustration).

22  Install the locknut and tighten it securely.

23  Remove the alignment pin (drill bit) from the shift lever bracket base.

24  Start the engine and check the shift lever in all gears. If the engine won't start, or will start in any range other than Park or Neutral, check the adjustment of the Transmission Range switch (see Chapter 6).

## ACURA MODELS

### Replacement

25  Disconnect the cable from the negative terminal of the battery (see Chapter 5, Section 1).

26  Remove the center console (see Chapter 11).

#### 2001 and 2002 models

▶ **Refer to illustrations 3.27, 3.28 and 3.32**

27  Position the shift lever in Reverse. Remove the locking nut from the threaded stud on the shift lever assembly (see illustration).

28  Rotate the grommet counterclockwise a 1/4-turn and slide the grommet along with the cable from the bracket (see illustration).

29  Raise the vehicle and support it securely on jackstands.

30  Working at the transaxle, remove the shift cable cover (see illustration 3.6a) and the mounting bolts for the shift cable holder (see illustration 3.6b).

31  Remove the lock bolt securing the shift lever (see illustration 3.7) and slide the shift lever pin and shift lever from the transaxle.

32  Working in the engine compartment, remove the shift cable guide bracket nut and separate the shift cable from the body (see illustration).

33  Disengage the rubber grommet and pull the shift cable through the firewall.

#### 2003 and later models

▶ **Refer to illustrations 3.34 and 3.36**

34  Working in the passenger compartment, position the shift lever in Reverse. Remove the locking nut from the threaded stud on the shift

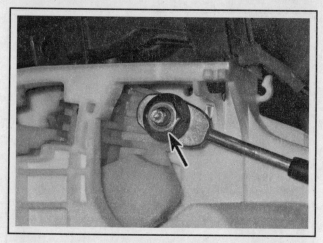

**3.34 Remove the nut from the threaded stud on the shift cable end**

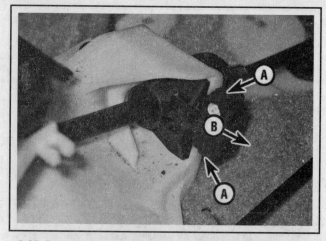

**3.36 Press the holder lock release mechanism tabs (A) and pull the socket holder (B) away from the shift lever bracket base**

lever assembly (see illustration).

35 On 2003 through 2006 models, rotate the grommet counterclockwise a 1/4-turn and slide the grommet along with the cable from the bracket (see illustration 3.28).

36 On 2007 models, press the holder lock release mechanism and pull the socket holder from the shift lever bracket base (see illustration).

37 Working in the engine compartment, remove the air intake duct and the air filter housing (see Chapter 4).

38 Disconnect the cable from the negative terminal of the battery (see Chapter 5, Section 1).

39 Remove the battery and the battery tray (see Chapter 5, Section 1).

40 Remove the fuse/relay box from the bracket and remove the bracket from the battery base.

41 Remove the shift cable bracket nuts and separate the shift cable from the transaxle.

42 Remove the spring washer and control pin from the shift cable stud at the cable end.

43 On 2007 models, remove the heat shield from under the shift cable grommet.

44 Remove the mounting nuts from the shift cable guide bracket.

**➡Note: On 2007 models, first remove the mounting nuts from**

the shift cable bracket and separate the drain hose clamp and guide bracket from the body.

45 Disengage the rubber grommet and pull the shift cable through the firewall.

46 Installation is the reverse of the removal procedure:

47 Be sure to adjust the cable before reattaching it to the shift lever (see Steps 48 through 57).

### Adjustment

▶ **Refer to illustrations 3.50 and 3.51**

48 Remove the center console (see Chapter 11).

49 Make sure the shift lever is in the Reverse position.

50 Push the shift cable all the way in until it stops and then back one click into the reverse position (see illustration).

**➡Note: Turn the ignition key to ON (engine not running) and observe that the R position indicator illuminates on the instrument cluster. After checking, turn the ignition key to OFF.**

51 Install a 0.24 inch pin (6 mm) into the positioning hole on the shift lever bracket base and into the alignment hole on the shift lever (see illustration). A drill bit of the same diameter will also work.

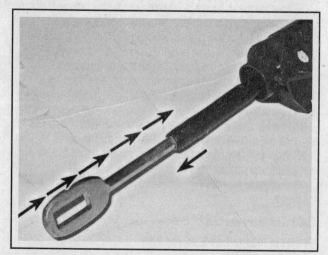

**3.50 Push the shift cable until it stops and pull back one click until the cable stops (locks-in) in the REVERSE position**

**3.51 Install a 0.24 inch (6.0 mm) pin (drill bit) into the alignment hole on the shift lever bracket base and into the alignment hole in the shift lever - early models shown, late models similar**

52 Align the socket holder on the shift cable with the slot on the bracket base. Slide the holder onto the bracket base until it snaps into place.

53 Install the shift cable end onto the shift lever pin, making sure it fits over the square shank on the pin (see illustration 3.21).

54 Install the nut on the shift lever pin and tighten it securely.

55 Remove the alignment pin or drill bit from the alignment hole.

56 Turn the ignition key to On (don't start the engine), move the shift lever to each gear position and verify that the gear position indicator light comes on in each position. Make sure the engine only starts in Park and Neutral.

57 The remainder of installation is the reverse of removal.

## 4  Shift lever assembly - replacement

**✳✳ WARNING:**

**The models covered by this manual are equipped with a Supplemental Restraint System (SRS), more commonly known as airbags. Always disable the airbag system before working in the vicinity of any airbag system component to avoid the possibility of accidental deployment of the airbag(s), which could cause personal injury (see Chapter 12). Do not use a memory saving device to preserve the PCM or radio memory when working on or near airbag system components.**

## HONDA MODELS

▶ **Refer to illustration 4.6**

1  Remove the steering column covers (see Chapter 11).

2  Set the parking brake, then place the shift lever in the Neutral position.

3  Detach the shift cable from the shift lever and bracket (see Section 3).

4  Disconnect the anti-theft system connector, if equipped.

5  Disconnect the shift lock solenoid and the park pin switch connector (see illustration 5.5).

6  Remove the shift lever mounting bolts (see illustration), then remove the shift lever.

7  Installation is the reverse of the removal. Be sure to adjust the shift cable (see Section 3).

## ACURA MODELS

▶ **Refer to illustration 4.12**

8  Remove the center console (see Chapter 11).

9  Set the parking brake, then place the shift lever in the Reverse position.

10 Disconnect the shift cable from the shift lever assembly (see Section 3).

11 Disconnect the shift interlock solenoid connector and the park pin switch connector (see Section 5).

12 Remove the four mounting bolts from the shift lever bracket base (see illustration).

13 Installation is the reverse of removal. Be sure to adjust the shift cable (see Section 3).

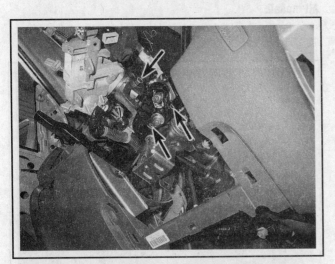

**4.6  Shift lever mounting bolts - Honda models**

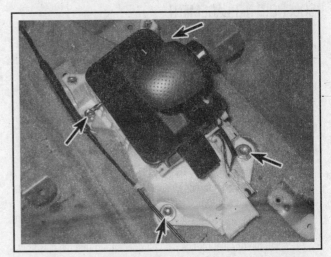

**4.12  Shift lever mounting bolts - Acura models**

## 5 Shift interlock system - description and solenoid replacement

**☀☀ WARNING:**

**The models covered by this manual are equipped with Supplemental Restraint systems (SRS), more commonly known as airbags. Always disable the airbag system before working in the vicinity of any airbag system component to avoid the possibility of accidental deployment of the airbag, which could cause personal injury (see Chapter 12). Do not use a memory saving device to preserve the PCM's memory when working on or near airbag system components.**

## DESCRIPTION

1   Vehicles equipped with an automatic transaxle have an interlock system to prevent the shifter from being moved out of the Park position unless the brake is applied. It also prevents the key from being removed from the ignition lock cylinder unless the shifter is placed in the Park position. The interlock system consists of two subsystems: a shift lock system and a key interlock system.

### Key interlock system

2   The key interlock system prevents the ignition key from being removed from the ignition switch unless the shift lever is in the Park position. If the key interlock solenoid fails, the ignition switch/key lock cylinder must be replaced (see Chapter 12).

### Shift lock system

3   The shift lock system prevents the shift lever from moving from the Park position unless the brake pedal is depressed. Nor can the shift lever be shifted when the brake pedal and the accelerator pedal are depressed at the same time. In the event of a system malfunction, an override feature allows you to release the shift lever by inserting the ignition key or a screwdriver into the release slot near the shift lever (Honda models) or in the center console (Acura models) (see Steps 20 through 22).

## SOLENOID REPLACEMENT

➡Note: The following procedure pertains only to the shift lock solenoid. For information on how to replace the key interlock solenoid, refer to the "Ignition switch/key lock cylinder assembly - replacement" Section in Chapter 12. The key interlock solenoid isn't available separately.

### Honda models

▸ Refer to illustrations 5.5 and 5.6

4   Remove the shift lever assembly (see Section 4).
5   Disconnect the shift lock solenoid and park pin switch electrical connectors (see illustration).
6   Remove the shift lock solenoid mounting screws (see illustration) and separate the shift lock solenoid from the shift lever assembly.
7   Install the original plunger and plunger spring into the new shift lock solenoid.
8   Engage the joint in the end of the plunger with the tip of the shift lock extension.
9   Connect the shift lock solenoid electrical connector.
10   The remainder of installation is the reverse of removal.

5.5  Disconnect the shift lock solenoid connector and park pin switch connectors from the steering column assembly

### Acura models

11 Remove the shift lever assembly (see Section 4).
12 Disconnect the shift interlock solenoid connector.

### 2001 through 2006 models

13 Remove the set screws from the shift lever knob, lift the knob from the shift lever and remove the gear position indicator bracket assembly from the shift lever assembly.
14 Remove the four bolts from the detent bracket and the shift lever bracket base. Separate the two assemblies to access the shift lock solenoid.

### 2007 models

15 Detach the shift lock release arm from the shift linkage on the shift lever assembly. The shift lock release arm is mounted on the left side of the shift lever assembly.

### All models

16 Remove the shift lock solenoid from the detent bracket and from the shift lever assembly.

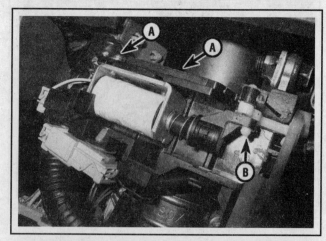

5.6  Remove the shift lock solenoid mounting screws (A) (one hidden from view) and separate the shift lock solenoid from the linkage (B)

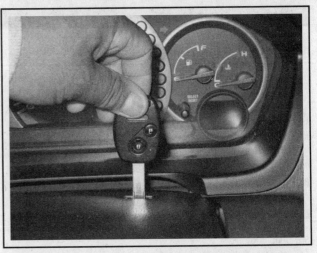

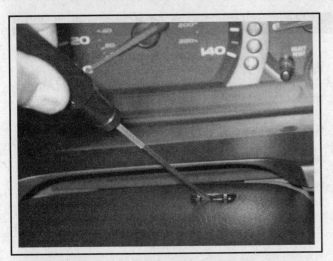

**5.21a Carefully pry the access cover from the upper steering column cover . . .**

**5.21b . . . and insert a screwdriver or ignition key to depress the release lever**

17 Install the plunger and plunger spring into the new shift lock solenoid.

18 Engage the shift lock solenoid plunger with the pin of the shift lock stop. Make sure the shift lock solenoid engages the bracket base securely.

19 The remainder of installation is the reverse of removal.

## SHIFT LOCK OVERRIDE FEATURE

▶ **Refer to illustrations 5.21a and 5.21b**

**✳✳ WARNING:**

**Set the parking brake before performing this procedure.**

20 In the event the shift interlock system fails and the shift lever cannot be moved out of gear when the brake is depressed, the system is equipped with an override feature which allows the shifter to be moved out of the Park position.

21 On Honda models, remove the access cover (see illustration), insert the ignition key or a flat-bladed screwdriver into the slot and press down to release the shift lever (see illustration).

22 On Acura models, remove the access cover alongside the shift lever, insert the ignition key or a flat-bladed screwdriver into the slot and press down to release the shift lever.

23 Move the shift lever into Neutral, depress the brake pedal and start the engine.

24 Repair the shift interlock system as soon as possible.

## 6 Automatic transmission fluid cooler - removal and installation

▶ **Refer to illustration 6.2**

➥**Note: 2007 Acura MDX models are equipped with an external transmission fluid cooler. On all other models, the automatic transmission fluid cooler is an integral component of the radiator.**

1  Raise the vehicle and secure it on jackstands.

2  Remove the engine splash shield (see illustration).

3  Remove the front bumper (see Chapter 11).

4  Position a drain pan underneath the cooler, then remove the clamps and separate the transmission fluid cooler hoses from the cooler.

5  Remove the power steering hose bracket from the transmission cooler mounting bracket.

6  Unscrew the mounting bolts and remove the transmission cooler.

7  Installation is the reverse of removal. Check the automatic transaxle fluid level, adding as necessary (see Chapter 1).

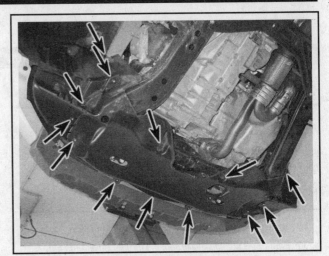

**6.2 Location of the engine splash shield fasteners - some hidden from view**

## 7 Driveaxle oil seals - replacement

### REMOVAL

▶ **Refer to illustrations 7.5 and 7.9**

1   Oil leaks may occur due to wear of the driveaxle oil seals. Replacement of these seals is relatively easy, since the repairs can be performed without removing the transaxle from the vehicle.

2   The driveaxle oil seals are located in the sides of the transaxle, where the driveaxles are attached. If leakage at the seal is suspected, raise the vehicle and support it securely on jackstands. If the seal is leaking, fluid will be found on the sides of the transaxle.

3   Remove the driveaxle(s) (see Chapter 8).

4   Remove the intermediate shaft from the right side of the transaxle (see Chapter 8).

5   Use a screwdriver or prybar to carefully pry the oil seal out of the transaxle bore (see illustration).

6   If the oil seal cannot be removed with a screwdriver or prybar, a special oil seal removal tool (available at auto parts stores) is required.

7   Compare the old seal to the new one to be sure it's the correct one.

8   Coat the outside and inside diameters of the new seal with a small amount of transmission fluid.

9   Using a seal driver or a large deep socket (slightly smaller than the outside diameter of the seal) as a drift, install the new oil seal (see illustration). Drive it into the bore squarely and make sure it is completely seated. Coat the seal lip with transmission fluid.

10  Install the intermediate shaft and the driveaxles (see Chapter 8).

11  Installation is the reverse of removal.

**7.5  Insert the tip of a large screwdriver or prybar behind the oil seal and very carefully pry the seal out**

**7.9  Using a seal driver or a large socket, drive the new seal squarely into the bore**

## 8 Automatic transaxle - removal and installation

### REMOVAL

1   Drain the transaxle fluid (see Chapter 1).

2   Refer to Chapter 2B, Section 7 to remove the engine/transaxle assembly, then separate the transaxle from the engine as described in that Section.

### INSTALLATION

3   Installation is the reverse of removal, noting the following points:

a)  *Prior to installation, make sure the torque converter is fully engaged in the transaxle. To do this, rotate the converter while pushing it towards the transaxle. If it wasn't already fully in place,* you'll feel it "clunk" into position as it engages with the input shaft and front pump. It may even "clunk" more than once. Lubricate the torque converter hub with multi-purpose grease.

b)  *Move the transaxle forward carefully until the dowel pins and the torque converter are engaged. Make sure the marks on the torque converter and driveplate are in alignment.*

c)  *Install the transaxle-to-engine bolts. Tighten the bolts to the torque listed in this Chapter's Specifications.*

d)  *Install the engine/transaxle assembly (see Chapter 2B). Once in place, tighten the driveplate-to-torque converter bolts to the torque listed in this Chapter's Specifications.*

e)  *Install and adjust the shift cable (see Section 4).*

f)  *Fill the transaxle with the recommended type and amount of fluid (see Chapter 1), run the vehicle and check for fluid leaks.*

## 9   Automatic transaxle overhaul - general information

In the event of a problem occurring, it will be necessary to establish whether the fault is electrical, mechanical or hydraulic in nature, before repair work can be contemplated. Diagnosis requires detailed knowledge of the transaxle's operation and construction, as well as access to specialized test equipment, and so is deemed to be beyond the scope of this manual. It is therefore essential that problems with the automatic transaxle are referred to a dealer service department or other qualified repair facility for assessment.

Note that a faulty transaxle should not be removed before the vehicle has been diagnosed by a knowledgeable technician equipped with the proper tools, as troubleshooting must be performed with the transaxle installed in the vehicle.

## Specifications

### General

| | |
|---|---|
| Fluid type and capacity | See Chapter 1 |

| Torque specifications | Ft-lbs (unless otherwise indicated) | Nm |
|---|---|---|
| Torque converter-to-driveplate bolts | 104 in-lbs | 12 |
| Oil pan-to-transaxle bolts | | |
| 2001 and 2002 Acura and | | |
| 2003 through 2005 Honda models | 28 | 38 |
| All other models | 54 | 74 |
| Transaxle-to-engine bolts | | |
| 2001 and 2002 Acura and 2003 | | |
| through 2005 Honda models | 40 | 54 |
| All other models | 47 | 64 |

**Notes**

# 8

## DRIVELINE

**Section**

## 1 Driveaxles - removal and installation

### FRONT

### Removal

▶ **Refer to illustrations 1.1, 1.2, 1.8 and 1.9**

1  Set the parking brake. Remove the wheel cover or hubcap. If the driveaxle/hub nut is staked, unstake it with a center punch or chisel (see illustration).

2  Loosen the driveaxle/hub nut with a large socket and breaker bar, but don't remove it yet (see illustration).

3  Loosen the front wheel lug nuts, raise the vehicle and support it securely on jackstands. Remove the wheel.

4  If you're removing the left driveaxle, drain the transaxle lubricant (see Chapter 1).

5  Remove the driveaxle/hub nut.

6  Disconnect the upper end of the stabilizer bar link (see Chapter 10).

7  Separate the control arm from the steering knuckle (see Chapter 10).

8  To loosen the driveaxle from the hub splines, tap the end of the driveaxle with a hammer and brass punch (see illustration). If the drive-axle is stuck in the hub splines and won't move, it may be necessary to push it from the hub with a puller.

9  Pull out on the steering knuckle and detach the driveaxle from the hub (see illustration). Suspend the outer end of the driveaxle on a bungee cord or piece of wire.

10  Before you remove the driveaxle, look for lubricant leakage in the area around the differential seal. If there's evidence of a leak, you'll want to replace the seal after removing the driveaxle (see Section 4).

11  To remove a right (passenger's side) driveaxle, tap the inboard joint off the intermediate shaft using a long drift. To remove a left-side (driver's side) driveaxle, position the prybar against the inner joint and carefully pry the joint off the transaxle side gear. Do not use the drive-axle to pull on the inner joint. Doing so might damage the inner joint components. Remove the driveaxle assembly, being careful not to over-extend the inner joint or damage the axleshaft boots.

12  Should it become necessary to move the vehicle while the drive-axle is out, place a large bolt with two large washers (one on each side of the hub) through the hub and tighten the nut securely.

**1.1  If the driveaxle is "staked," use a center punch or chisel to unstake it**

**1.2  Loosen the driveaxle/hub nut with a long breaker bar**

**1.8  To loosen the driveaxle from the hub splines, tap the end of the driveaxle with a hammer and brass punch**

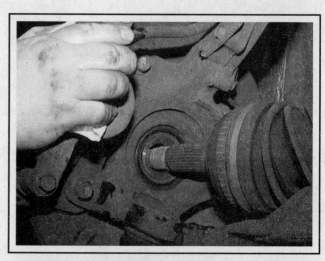

**1.9  Swing the hub/knuckle out (away from the vehicle) and pull the driveaxle from the hub**

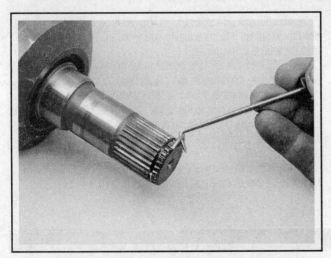

**1.13a  Pry the old set-ring from the inner end of the driveaxle (or the outer end of the intermediate shaft) with a small screwdriver or awl**

**1.13b  To install the new set-ring, start one end in the groove and work the ring over the shaft end, into the groove**

## Installation

▶ Refer to illustrations 1.13a and 1.13b

13 Installation is the reverse of removal, but with the following additional points:

a) *Remove the old set-ring from the inner CV joint (left driveaxle) or from the end of the intermediate shaft (right driveaxle) and install a new one (see illustrations).*

b) *Apply a film of multi-purpose grease around the splines of the joints.*

c) *When installing the driveaxle, hold the driveaxle straight out, push it in sharply to seat the driveaxle set-ring into the groove in the transaxle side gear or center support bearing. To make sure the set-ring is properly seated in the gear groove, attempt to pull the driveaxle out of the transaxle by hand. If the set-ring is properly seated the inner joint will not move out.*

d) *Clean all foreign matter from the driveaxle outer CV joint threads. Install the new driveaxle/hub nut. Tighten the nut securely but not to the specified torque at this time.*

e) *Tighten the suspension fasteners to the torque listed in the Chapter 10 Specifications.*

f) *Install the wheel and lug nuts, then lower the vehicle.*

g) *Install a new driveaxle/hub nut and tighten it to the torque listed in this Chapter's Specifications. Stake the nut to the groove in the driveaxle.*

h) *Tighten the wheel lug nuts to the torque listed in the Chapter 1 Specifications.*

i) *Add transaxle lubricant if it was drained, or if any fluid spilled out (see Chapter 1).*

## REAR (AWD MODELS)

## Removal

▶ Refer to illustration 1.23

14 Remove the wheel cover or hub cap. Unstake the nut with a punch or chisel (see illustration 1.1).

15 Break the hub nut loose with a socket and large breaker bar (see illustration 1.2).

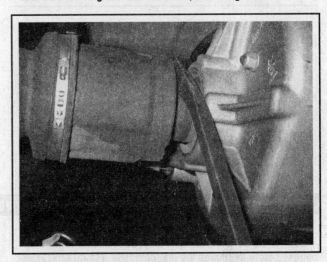

**1.23  Carefully pry the inner CV joint out of the differential**

16 Loosen the wheel lug nuts, raise the vehicle and support it securely on jackstands. Remove the wheel.

17 Drain the differential lubricant (see Chapter 1).

18 Remove the pivot bolt securing the upper arm to the rear crossmember (see Chapter 10).

19 Remove the rear shock absorber (see Chapter 10).

20 Remove the bolts that secure lower arm B to the rear knuckle (see Chapter 10).

21 Remove the ABS sensor bracket from lower arm B.

22 Remove the driveaxle nut, then pull the driveaxle assembly out of the rear knuckle. Make sure you don't damage the lip of the inner rear knuckle seal. If the splines on the outer CV joint spindle hang up on the splines in the hub, knock them loose with a hammer and punch.

### ❋ CAUTION:

**Don't let the driveaxle hang by the inner CV joint.**

23 Carefully pry the inner end of the driveaxle from the differential using a large screwdriver or prybar positioned between the differential and the CV joint housing (see illustration). Support the CV joints and carefully remove the driveaxle from the vehicle.

## Installation

24 Pry the old spring clip from the end of the differential stub shaft and install a new one (see illustrations 1.13a and 1.13b). Lubricate the differential stub shaft seal with multi-purpose grease and raise the driveaxle into position while supporting the CV joints.

25 Insert the end of the inner CV joint onto the differential stub shaft and make sure the spring clip locks in its groove.

26 Apply a light coat of multi-purpose grease to the outer CV joint splines, pull out on the rear knuckle assembly and install the stub axle into the hub.

27 Reconnect the control arms to the rear knuckle and the crossmember (see the torque specifications in Chapter 10).

28 Install a new driveaxle/hub nut. Tighten the hub nut securely, but don't try to tighten it to the actual torque specification until you've lowered the vehicle to the ground.

29 Grasp the inner CV joint housing (not the driveaxle), and pull it out to make sure the driveaxle has seated securely in the differential.

30 Install the wheel and lug nuts, then lower the vehicle.

31 Tighten the lug nuts to the torque listed in the Chapter 1 Specifications. Tighten the hub nut to the torque listed in this Chapter's Specifications. Stake the nut to the groove in the driveaxle, using a hammer and punch.

32 Refill the transaxle with the recommended type and amount of lubricant if it was drained (see Chapter 1).

## 2 Intermediate shaft - removal and installation

### REMOVAL

1 Raise the front of the vehicle and support it securely on jackstands.

2 Drain the transaxle lubricant (see Chapter 1).

3 Remove the right driveaxle (see Section 1).

4 Remove the exhaust pipe bracket and bearing support-to-engine block bolts and slide the intermediate shaft out of the transaxle. Be careful not to damage the differential seal when pulling the shaft out.

5 Check the support bearing for smooth operation by turning the shaft while holding the bearing. If it feels rough or sticky it should be replaced. Take it to a dealer service department or other repair shop, as special tools are needed to perform this job.

### INSTALLATION

6 Lubricate the lips of the transaxle seal with multi-purpose grease. Carefully guide the intermediate shaft into the transaxle side gear then install the mounting bolts through the bearing support. Tighten the bolts to the torque listed in this Chapter's Specifications.

7 Reinstall the driveaxle (see Section 1).

8 Refill the transaxle with the proper type and amount of lubricant (see Chapter 1).

## 3 Driveaxle boot replacement and CV joint inspection

➡Note: If the CV joints or boots must be replaced, explore all options before beginning the job. Complete, rebuilt driveaxles are available on an exchange basis, eliminating much time and work. Whichever route you choose to take, check on the cost and availability of parts before disassembling the vehicle.

### FRONT DRIVEAXLE

#### Inner CV joint

1 Remove the driveaxle (see Section 1).

2 Mount the driveaxle in a vise with wood-lined jaws, to prevent damage to the axleshaft. Check the CV joints for excessive play in the radial direction, which indicates worn parts. Check for smooth operation throughout the full range of motion for each CV joint. If a boot is torn, the recommended procedure is to disassemble the joint, clean the components and inspect for damage due to loss of lubrication and possible contamination by foreign matter. If the CV joint is in good condition, lubricate it with CV joint grease and install a new boot.

#### Disassembly

▶ **Refer to illustrations 3.4a, 3.4b, 3.5, 3.6 and 3.7**

3 Cut the boot clamps with side-cutters, then remove and discard them.

4 Using a screwdriver, carefully pry up on the edge of the CV boot, pull it off the CV joint housing and slide it down the axleshaft, exposing the tri-pot assembly. Mark the relationship of the joint housing to the

**3.4a Mark the relationship of the tri-pot to the housing**

tri-pot (see illustration). To separate the axleshaft and tri-pot assembly from the inner joint housing, simply pull the housing straight off (see illustration).

➡Note: When removing the housing, hold the rollers in place on the tri-pot to prevent the rollers and the needle bearings from falling free.

5 Remove the tri-pot assembly snap-ring with a pair of snap-ring pliers (see illustration).

6 Mark the tri-pot to the axleshaft to ensure that they are reassembled properly (see illustration).

3.4b  Slide the joint housing from the tri-pot

3.5  Remove the snap-ring with a pair of snap-ring pliers

7   Use a hammer and a brass drift to drive the tri-pot assembly from the axleshaft (see illustration).

8   Slide the boot off the shaft.

### Inspection

9   Thoroughly clean all components with solvent until the old CV joint grease is completely removed. Inspect the bearing surfaces of the tri-pot and housing for cracks, pitting, scoring and other signs of wear. If any part of the inner CV joint is worn, you must replace the entire joint. Depending on the availability of parts, you may even have to purchase a complete driveaxle assembly.

➡️**Note: If you're working on a right-side driveaxle, check the center bearing for smooth operation. If it feels rough or is noisy when rotated, take the intermediate shaft to an automotive machine shop to have the old bearing pressed out and a new one pressed in.**

### Reassembly

▶ **Refer to illustrations 3.10a, 3.10b, 3.10c, 3.13, 3.15a, 3.15b, 3.15c, 3.15d and 3.15e**

10  Wrap the splines on the inner end of the axleshaft with electrical or duct tape to protect the boots from the sharp edges of the splines

3.6  Use a center-punch to place marks on the tri-pot and the driveaxle to ensure that they are reassembled properly

and slide the clamps and boot onto the axleshaft (see illustration 3.18g). Remove the tape and place the tri-pot on the axleshaft with the recessed portion of the splines toward the shaft (see illustration). Tap the tri-pot onto the shaft with a brass drift until it's seated and install the snap-ring. Apply grease to the tri-pot assembly and inside the

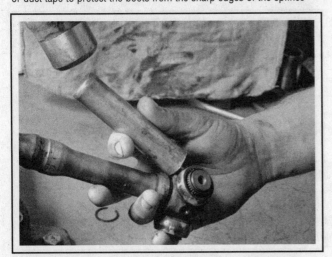

3.7  Drive the tri-pot joint from the driveaxle with a brass punch and hammer (be careful not to damage the bearing surfaces or the splines on the shaft)

3.10a  Install the tri-pot with the recessed portion of the splines facing the axleshaft

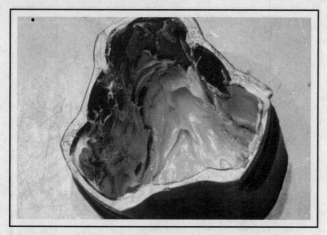

**3.10b  Place grease at the bottom of the CV joint housing**

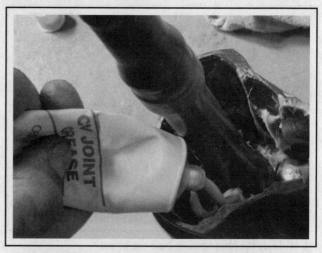

**3.10c  Install the boot and clamps onto the axleshaft, then insert the tri-pot into the housing, followed by the rest of the grease**

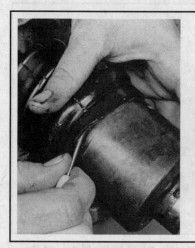

**3.13  With the CV joint positioned midway through its travel, equalize the pressure inside the boot by inserting a small, dull screwdriver between the boot and the outer race**

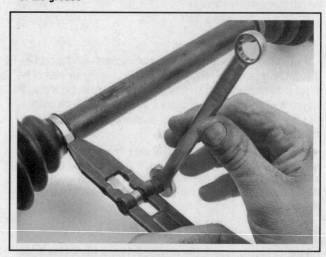

**3.15a  You'll need a special tightening tool to install "band" type boot clamps. Install the band with its end pointing in the direction of axle rotation and tighten it securely . . .**

housing (see illustration). Insert the tri-pot into the housing and pack the remainder of the grease around the tri-pot (see illustration).

11  Slide the boot into place, making sure the raised bead on the inside of the seal boot is positioned in the groove on the interconnecting shaft. If the driveaxle has multiple locating grooves on the shaft, position the boot so only one of the grooves (the thinnest) is exposed.

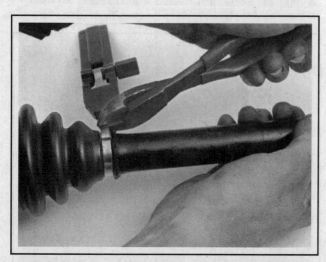

**3.15b  . . . then bend the end of the clamp back and cut off the excess**

**3.15c  If you're installing crimp-type boot clamps, you'll need a pair of special crimping pliers (available at most auto parts stores)**

**3.15d  To install fold-over type boot clamps, bend the tang down . . .**

**3.15e  . . . then tap the tabs over to hold it in place**

Position the sealing boot into the groove on the housing retaining groove.

12  Position the CV joint mid-way through its travel.

13  Equalize the pressure inside the boot by inserting a small, dull, flat screwdriver tip between the boot and the CV joint housing (see illustration).

14  Make sure each end of the boot is seated properly, and the boot is not distorted.

15  Install the boot clamps. There are three types of clamps you're likely to encounter: the band type, which requires a special tightening tool, the crimp type (which also requires a special tool), or the fold-over type (see illustrations).

16  The driveaxle is now ready for installation (see Section 1).

### Outer CV joint

▶ **Refer to illustrations 3.18a through 3.18l**

17  Remove the driveaxle (see Section 1).

18  Refer to the accompanying illustrations and perform the outer CV joint boot replacement procedure (see illustrations 3.18a through 3.18l).

**3.18a  Cut off the band retaining the boot to the shaft, then slide the boot toward the center of the shaft**

**3.18b  Clean all grease off the axleshaft and paint a mark on the shaft, then measure the distance from your mark to the face of the inner race and record this measurement; the inner race must be installed on the axleshaft in exactly the same position in which it was installed prior to removal**

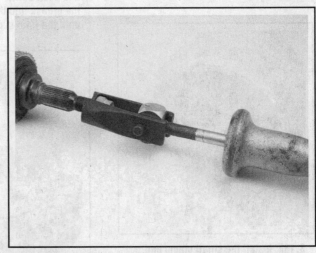

**3.18c  Outer CV joints can be removed with a slide hammer; you'll need an adapter and a slide hammer setup such as the one shown here**

**3.18d With the axleshaft firmly clamped down in a bench vise and the adapter gripping the driveaxle/hub nut, carefully extract the outer CV joint from the axleshaft**

## REAR DRIVEAXLE

### Disassembly

▶ **Refer to illustrations 3.20, 3.21, 3.22, 3.24, 3.26, 3.27 and 3.28**

19 Remove the driveaxle (see Section 1).

20 Pry open the locking tabs on the boot clamps, remove the clamps from the boot and discard them (see illustration).

21 Slide the boot back on the axleshaft and pry the wire ring ball retainer from the outer race (see illustration).

22 Pull the outer race off the inner bearing assembly (see illustration).

23 Wipe as much grease as possible off the inner bearing.

24 Remove the snap-ring from the end of the axleshaft (see illustration).

25 Slide the inner bearing assembly off the axleshaft.

26 Mark the inner race and cage to ensure that they are reassembled with the correct sides facing out (see illustration).

**3.18e After the old grease has been rinsed away, move the inner race through its full range of motion and inspect the bearing surfaces for wear or damage**

**3.18f Apply CV joint grease through the splined hole, then insert a wooden dowel (slightly smaller in diameter than the hole) into the hole and push down - the dowel will force the grease into the joint. Repeat this until the joint is packed**

**3.18g Wrap the splined area of the axleshaft with tape to prevent damage to the boot when installing it**

**3.18h Install the small clamp and the boot on the driveaxle and apply grease to the inside of the axle boot until . . .**

**3.18i . . . the level is up to the end of axle**

**3.18j Install a new circlip into the groove at the end of the driveaxle. Position the CV joint assembly on the driveaxle, aligning the splines . . .**

3.18k . . . then use a hammer and brass punch to carefully drive the joint onto the driveaxle to the same spot it was in before disassembly (see illustration 3.18b)

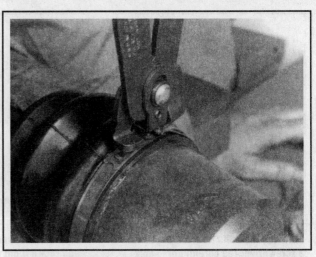

3.18l Seat the inner end of the boot in the groove and install the retaining clamp, then do the same on the other end of the boot - tighten boot clamps with the special tool

3.20 To remove the boot clamps, pry open the locking tabs

3.21 Pry the wire retainer ring from the CV joint housing with a small screwdriver

3.22 With the retainer removed, the outer race can be pulled off the bearing assembly

3.24 Remove the snap-ring from the end of the axleshaft

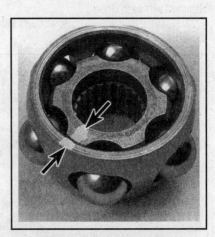

3.26 Make index marks on the inner race and cage so they'll both be facing the same direction when reassembled

**3.27 Pry the balls from the cage with a screwdriver (be careful not to nick or scratch them)**

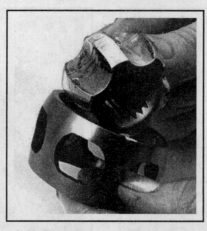

**3.28 Tilt the inner race 90-degrees and rotate it out of the cage**

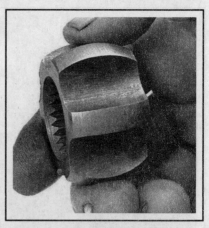

**3.29a Inspect the inner race lands and grooves for pitting and score marks**

27 Using a screwdriver or piece of wood, pry the balls from the cage (see illustration). Be careful not to scratch the inner race, the balls or the cage.

28 Rotate the inner race 90-degrees, align the inner race lands with the cage windows and rotate the race out of the cage (see illustration).

## Inspection

▶ **Refer to illustrations 3.29a and 3.29b**

29 Clean the components with solvent to remove all traces of grease. Inspect the cage and races for pitting, score marks, cracks and other signs of wear and damage. Shiny, polished spots are normal and will not adversely affect CV joint performance (see illustrations). If the outer CV joint boot is torn or damaged, now is the time to set aside the inner CV joint parts, remove the outer boot, and clean and inspect the outer CV joint.

## Reassembly

▶ **Refer to illustrations 3.31, 3.34, 3.37, 3.41a, 3.41b, and 3.41c**

30 Insert the inner race into the cage. Verify that the matchmarks are on the same side. However, it's not necessary for them to be in direct alignment with each other.

31 Press the balls into the cage windows with your thumbs (see illustration).

**3.29b Inspect the cage for cracks, pitting and score marks (shiny spots are normal and don't affect operation)**

32 Wrap the axleshaft splines with tape to avoid damaging the boot (see illustration 3.18g).

33 Slide the small boot clamp and boot onto the axleshaft, then remove the tape.

34 Install the inner race and cage assembly on the axleshaft with the larger diameter side or "bulge" of the cage facing the axleshaft end (see illustration).

**3.31 Press the balls into the cage through the windows**

**3.34 Install the inner race and cage assembly with the large diameter end toward the splined end of the axleshaft**

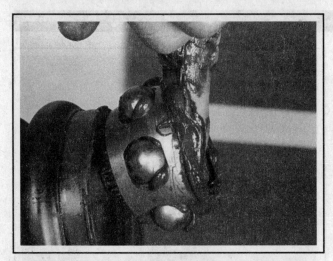

**3.37 Pack grease into the bearing until it's completely full**

35 Install the snap-ring (see illustration 3.24).
36 Fill the boot with CV joint grease (normally included with the new boot kit).
37 Pack the inner race and cage assembly with grease, by hand, until grease is worked completely into the assembly (see illustration).
38 Slide the outer race down onto the inner race and install the wire ring retainer.
39 Wipe any excess grease from the axle boot groove on the outer race. Seat the small diameter of the boot in the recessed area on the axleshaft and install the clamp. Push the other end of the boot onto the outer CV joint housing and seat it into the recessed area on the housing.

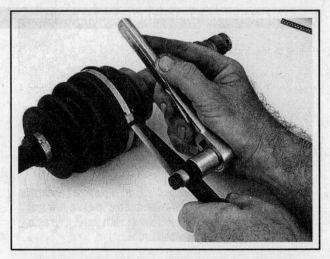

**3.41a Secure the boot clamps with a special banding tool such as the one shown here (available at most auto parts stores); install the clamp, thread it onto the tool, pull the clamp tight . . .**

40 Position the CV joint mid-way through its travel, then equalize the pressure in the boot by inserting a dull screwdriver between the boot and the outer race (see illustration 8.13). Don't damage the boot with the tool.
41 Install the boot clamps (see illustrations). A special clamp installation tool is needed. The tool is available at most auto parts stores.
42 Install the driveaxle assembly (see Section 1).

**3.41b . . . peen over the locking tabs . . .**

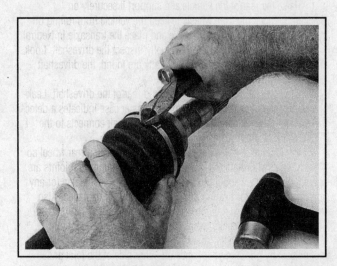

**3.41c . . . and cut off the excess**

### 4  Differential oil seals - replacement

▶ **Refer to illustration 4.4**

1  Raise the rear of the vehicle and support it securely on jackstands. Place the transaxle in Neutral with the parking brake off. Block the front wheels to prevent the vehicle from rolling.

2  Remove the driveaxle(s) (see Section 1).

3  Pry the seal from the differential housing.

4  Using a seal installer or a large deep socket as a drift, install the new oil seal. Drive it into the bore squarely and make sure it's completely seated (see illustration).

5  Lubricate the lip of the new seal with multi-purpose grease, then install the driveaxle. Be careful not to damage the lip of the new seal.

6  Check the differential lubricant level and add some, if necessary, to bring it to the appropriate level (see Chapter 1).

**4.4  Using a seal installer, drive the new seal squarely into the bore and make sure that it's completely seated**

### 5  Driveshaft - check, removal and installation

## CHECK

1  Raise the rear of the vehicle and support it securely on jackstands. Block the front wheels to keep the vehicle from rolling off the stands. Release the parking brake and place the transaxle in Neutral.

2  Crawl under the vehicle and visually inspect the driveshaft. Look for any dents or cracks in the tubing. If any are found, the driveshaft must be replaced.

3  Check for oil leakage at the front and rear of the driveshaft. Leakage where the driveshaft connects to the transfer case indicates a defective transfer case seal. Leakage where the driveshaft connects to the differential indicates a defective pinion seal.

4  While under the vehicle, have an assistant rotate a rear wheel so the driveshaft will rotate. As it does, make sure the universal joints are operating properly without binding, noise or looseness. Listen for any noise from the center bearing, indicating it's worn or damaged. Also check the rubber portion of the center bearing for cracking or separation, which will necessitate replacement of the driveshaft assembly.

5  The universal joints can also be checked with the driveshaft motionless, by gripping your hands on either side of the joint and attempting to twist the joint. Any movement at all in the joint is a sign of considerable wear. Lifting up on the shaft will also indicate movement in the universal joints. If the joints are worn, the driveshaft must be replaced as an assembly.

6  Mount a dial indicator with its plunger touching the center of either the front or rear driveshaft section. Slowly turn the driveshaft and measure the runout, comparing your findings with the runout limit listed in this Chapter's Specifications. Repeat the check on the other driveshaft section. If runout exceeds the maximum allowable limit on either shaft section, replace the driveshaft as an assembly.

7  Finally, check the driveshaft mounting bolts at the ends to make sure they're tight.

**5.9  Mark the relationship of the driveshaft to the differential pinion flange and the transfer case flange**

## REMOVAL AND INSTALLATION

▶ **Refer to illustrations 5.9, 5.10, 5.11 and 5.12**

8  Raise the rear of the vehicle and support it securely on jackstands. Place the transaxle in Neutral with the parking brake off. Block the front wheels to prevent the vehicle from rolling.

9  Make reference marks on the driveshaft flanges, the differential pinion flange and the transfer case pinion flange in line with each other (see illustration). This is to make sure the driveshaft is reinstalled in the same position to preserve the balance.

**5.10 Immobilize the driveshaft by placing a screwdriver into the universal joint while loosening the bolts**

10 Remove the rear universal joint bolts. Turn the driveshaft (or wheels) as necessary to bring the bolts into the most accessible position. Insert a screwdriver into the joint while loosening the bolts to prevent the shaft from turning (see illustration).

11 Unbolt the driveshaft safety loops from the floorpan (see illustration).

12 Unbolt the center support bearing from the floorpan (see illustration).

13 Unbolt the front of the driveshaft from the transfer case flange and remove the driveshaft assembly.

14 Installation is the reverse of the removal procedure. Be sure to align the marks on the flanges and tighten all fasteners to the torque values listed in this Chapter's Specifications.

**5.11 Remove the fasteners securing the driveshaft safety loops**

**5.12 The driveshaft center support bearing is retained by two bolts**

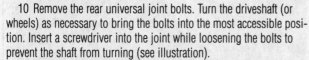

**6    Differential - removal and installation**

▶ **Refer to illustration 6.6**

1    Raise the rear of the vehicle and support it securely on jackstands. Place the transaxle in Neutral with the parking brake off. Block the front wheels to prevent the vehicle from rolling.

2    Drain the differential lubricant (see Chapter 1).

3    Remove the driveaxles (see Section 1).

4    Mark the relationship of the driveshaft to the pinion flange, then unbolt the driveshaft from the flange (see Section 5). Suspend the driveshaft with a piece of wire (don't let it hang by the center support bearing).

5    Unbolt the damper weight from the differential.

6    Support the differential with a floor jack, then remove the differential mounting bolts (see illustration).

7    Slowly lower the jack and detach the breather tube from the differential, then remove the differential out from under the vehicle.

8    Installation is the reverse of the removal procedure. Tighten all fasteners to the torque values listed in this Chapter's Specifications. Fill the differential with the proper lubricant (see Chapter 1).

**6.6 Remove the differential mounting fasteners**

## 7 Transfer case (AWD models) - removal and installation

▶ **Refer to illustrations 7.4 and 7.6**

1 Raise the front of the vehicle and support it securely on jackstands.

2 Mark the relationship of the driveshaft to the transfer case flange, then unbolt the driveshaft from the flange (see Section 5). Suspend the driveshaft with a piece of wire (don't let it hang by the center support bearing).

3 Drain the transaxle lubricant (see Chapter 1).

4 Remove the subframe stiffener (see illustration).

5 Remove the front exhaust pipe (see Chapter 4).

6 Remove the bolts securing the transfer case to the transaxle (see illustration), then carefully remove the transfer case from the transaxle.

7 Installation is the reverse of removal, noting the following points:

a) Install a new O-ring to the case.

b) Tighten the mounting bolts to the torque listed in this Chapter's Specifications.

c) Refill the transaxle with the proper type and amount of lubricant (see Chapter 1).

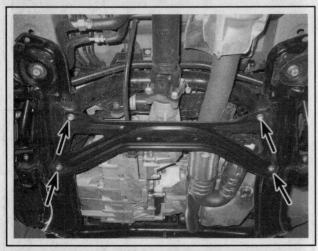

**7.4 Remove the fasteners securing the subframe stiffener**

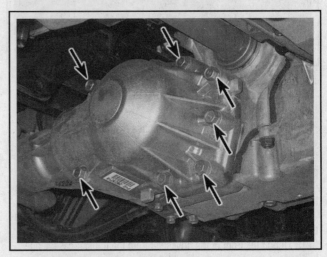

**7.6 Transfer case mounting bolts**

## Specifications

| Torque specifications | Ft-lbs | Nm |
|---|---|---|
| Driveaxle/hub nut | | |
|   Honda models | | |
|     2003 and 2004 | 181 | 245 |
|     2005 and later | 210 | 284 |
|   Acura models | | |
|     2001 and 2002 | 181 | 245 |
|     2003 through 2006 | 210 | 284 |
|     2007 | 242 | 328 |
| Driveshaft-to-differential pinion flange | | |
|   mounting bolts | 53 | 72 |
| Driveshaft-to-transfer case pinion flange | | |
|   mounting bolts | 53 | 72 |
| Driveshaft center support bearing mounting bolts | 29 | 39 |
| Intermediate shaft bearing support bolts | 29 | 39 |
| Rear differential mounting bolts | | |
|   Horizontal bolts | 63 | 85 |
|   Vertical bolt(s) | | |
|     All except 2007 Acura models | 41 | 55 |
|     2007 Acura models | 38 | 28 |
| Transfer case mounting bolts | | |
|   Honda models | | |
|     2003 through 2005 | 33 | 44 |
|     2006 and later | 38 | 51 |
|   Acura models | | |
|     2001 and 2002 | 33 | 44 |
|     2003 and later | 38 | 51 |
| Wheel lug nuts | See Chapter 1 | |

**Notes**

## Section

## Reference to other Chapters

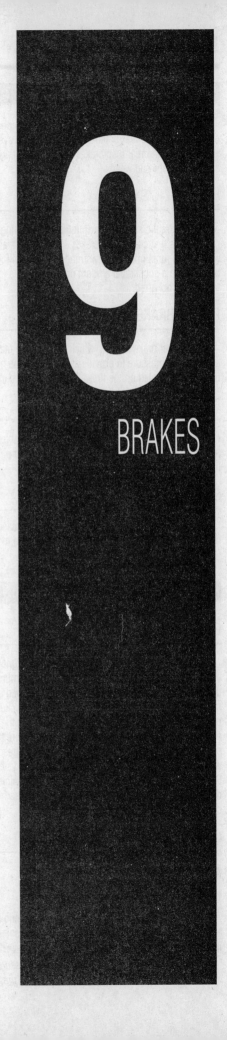

# 9

## BRAKES

## 1  General information

The vehicles covered by this manual are equipped with hydraulically operated front and rear brake systems. All brake systems are disc type.

The front and rear disc brakes are self-adjusting and automatically compensate for pad wear.

### HYDRAULIC SYSTEM

The hydraulic system is a split design, meaning there are two separate circuits that control the brakes. If one circuit fails, the other circuit will remain functional and a warning indicator will light up on the dashboard when a substantial amount of brake fluid is lost, showing that a failure has occurred.

### POWER BRAKE BOOSTER

The power brake booster, which uses engine manifold vacuum and atmospheric pressure to provide assistance to the hydraulically operated brakes, is mounted on the firewall in the engine compartment.

### PARKING BRAKE

A parking brake pedal operates a series of cables attached to each rear brake. The cables pull on levers that expand parking brake shoes in the center portion (drum) of the rear brake disc.

### SERVICE

After completing any operation involving disassembly of any part of the brake system, always test drive the vehicle to check for proper braking performance before resuming normal driving. When testing the brakes, perform the tests on a clean, dry, flat surface. Conditions other than these can lead to inaccurate test results.

Test the brakes at various speeds with both light and heavy pedal pressure. The vehicle should stop evenly without pulling to one side or the other. Avoid locking the brakes, because this slides the tires and diminishes braking efficiency and control of the vehicle.

Tires, vehicle load and wheel alignment are factors which also affect braking performance.

### PRECAUTIONS

There are some general cautions and warnings involving the brake system on these vehicles:

a) *Use only brake fluid conforming to DOT 3 specifications.*

b) *The brake pads and linings may contain materials which are hazardous to your health. Whenever you work on brake system components, clean all parts with brake system cleaner. Do not allow the fine dust to become airborne, and wear a filter/mask over your nose and mouth when cleaning or servicing brakes.*

c) *Safety should be the primary concern when performing any brake service. Do not use parts or fasteners which are not in perfect condition, and be sure that all clearances and torque specifications are adhered to. If you are unsure about a certain procedure, seek professional advice. Upon completion of any brake system work, test the brakes carefully in a controlled area before putting the vehicle into normal service.*

d) *If a problem is suspected in the brake system, don't drive the vehicle until it's fixed.*

## 2  Anti-lock Brake System (ABS) - general information

### GENERAL INFORMATION

1   The Anti-lock Brake System (ABS) is designed to help maintain vehicle steerability, directional stability and optimum deceleration under severe braking conditions and on most road surfaces. The ABS system is primarily designed to prevent wheel lockup during heavy or panic braking situations. It works by monitoring the rotational speed of each wheel and controlling the brake line pressure to each wheel when engaged. The data provided by the ABS wheel speed sensors is shared with another system closely related to the ABS system called Vehicle Stability Assist (VSA). This system enhances vehicle control and handling by utilizing traction control, over/under-steering and acceleration control when the system is engaged.

### COMPONENTS

**Actuator assembly**

▸ **Refer to illustration 2.2**

2   The actuator assembly is mounted in the engine compartment and consists of an electric hydraulic pump and solenoid valves (see illustration).

a) *The electric pump provides hydraulic pressure to charge the reservoirs in the actuator, which supplies pressure to the brak-*

**2.2  The ABS hydraulic unit (air intake duct removed for clarity)**

*ing system. The pump and reservoirs are housed in the actuator assembly.*

b) *The solenoid valves modulate brake line pressure during ABS operation.*

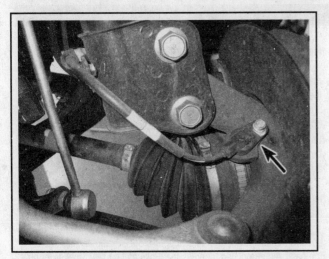

**2.4 Front wheel speed sensor**

**2.5 Rear wheel speed sensor (4WD model shown, 2WD similar)**

## Wheel speed sensors

▶ **Refer to illustrations 2.4 and 2.5**

3    These sensors are located at each wheel and generate small electrical pulsations when the toothed sensor rings are turning, sending a signal to the electronic controller indicating wheel rotational speed.

4    The front speed sensors are mounted to the front steering knuckle in close relationship to the toothed sensor rings, which are integral with the front driveaxle outer CV joints (see illustration).

5    The rear wheel sensors are mounted to the rear suspension knuckles (see illustration).

## ABS/VSA computer

6    The ABS/VSA computer is mounted with the actuator and is the brain for the ABS/VSA system. One function of the computer is to accept and process information received from the wheel speed sensors to control the hydraulic line pressure to the brakes, avoiding wheel lock up. There are many other sensors utilized by the computer for the VSA part of the system. The computer also constantly monitors these systems for proper operation.

## DIAGNOSIS AND REPAIR

7    If a dashboard warning light comes on and stays on while the vehicle is in operation, the ABS/VSA system requires attention. Although special electronic diagnostic testing tools are necessary to properly diagnose the system, you can perform a few preliminary checks before taking the vehicle to a dealer service department.

*a) Check the brake fluid level in the reservoir.*
*b) Verify that the computer electrical connectors are securely connected.*
*c) Check the electrical connectors at the hydraulic control unit.*
*d) Check the fuses.*
*e) Follow the wiring harness to each wheel and verify that all connections are secure and that the wiring is undamaged.*

8    If the above preliminary checks do not rectify the problem, the

vehicle should be diagnosed by a dealer service department or other qualified repair shop. Due to the complexity of this system, all actual repair work must be done by a qualified automotive technician.

### ❊❊ WARNING:

**Do NOT try to repair an ABS wiring harness. The ABS system is sensitive to even the smallest changes in resistance. Repairing the harness could alter resistance values and cause the system to malfunction. If the ABS wiring harness is damaged in any way, it must be replaced.**

### ❊❊ CAUTION:

**Make sure the ignition is turned off before unplugging or reattaching any electrical connections.**

## WHEEL SPEED SENSOR - REMOVAL AND INSTALLATION

9    Loosen the wheel lug nuts, raise the vehicle and support it securely on jackstands. Remove the wheel.

10   Make sure the ignition key is in the Off position.

11   Trace the wiring back from the sensor, detaching all brackets and clips while noting its correct routing, then disconnect the electrical connector.

12   Remove the mounting bolt and carefully pull the sensor out from the knuckle (see illustrations 2.4 and 2.5).

13   Installation is the reverse of the removal procedure. Tighten the mounting bolt securely.

14   Install the wheel and lug nuts, tightening them securely. Lower the vehicle and tighten the lug nuts to the torque listed in the Chapter 1 Specifications.

## 3 Disc brake pads - replacement

▶ Refer to illustrations 3.5, 3.6a through 3.6o

### ✳✳ WARNING:

**Disc brake pads must be replaced on both front or both rear wheels at the same time - never replace the pads on only one wheel. Also, the dust created by the brake system is harmful to your health. Never blow it out with compressed air and don't inhale any of it. An approved filtering mask should be worn when working on the brakes. Do not, under any circumstances, use petroleum-based solvents to clean brake parts. Use brake system cleaner only!**

➡Note: This procedure applies to both front and rear disc brakes.

1   Remove the cap from the brake fluid reservoir.
2   Loosen the wheel lug nuts, raise the front or rear of the vehicle and support it securely on jackstands. Block the wheels at the opposite end.
3   Remove the wheels. Work on one brake assembly at a time, using the assembled brake for reference if necessary.
4   Inspect the brake disc carefully as outlined in Section 5. If machining is necessary, follow the information in that Section to remove the disc, at which time the pads are removed as well.
5   Push the piston back into its bore to provide room for the new brake pads. A C-clamp can be used to accomplish this (see illustration). As the piston is depressed to the bottom of the caliper bore, the fluid in the master cylinder will rise. Make sure that it doesn't overflow. If necessary, remove some of the fluid.
6   Follow the accompanying photos beginning with illustration 3.6a for the actual pad replacement procedure. Be sure to stay in order and read the caption under each illustration.
7   When reinstalling the caliper, be sure to tighten the mounting bolts to the torque listed in this Chapter's Specifications. After the job has been completed, depress the brake pedal a few times to bring the pads into contact with the disc. Check the level of the brake fluid, adding some if necessary. Check the operation of the brakes carefully before placing the vehicle into normal service.

3.5  Before removing the caliper, slowly depress the piston in the caliper bore by using a large C-clamp between the outer brake pad and the back of the caliper

3.6a  Before removing anything, clean the brake assembly with brake cleaner and allow it to dry - position a drain pan under the brake assembly to catch the residue - DO NOT USE COMPRESSED AIR TO BLOW BRAKE DUST OFF THE PARTS!

3.6b  Remove the lower caliper bolt. To detach the caliper completely, remove both caliper bolts but do not let the caliper hang by the brake hose

3.6c  Pivot the caliper up (be careful not to damage the boot for the upper slide pin) . . .

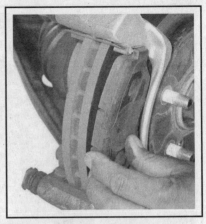

3.6d . . . and secure it with a piece of wire; do not allow the caliper to hang by the flexible brake hose

3.6e  Remove the inner pad and shim(s) . . .

3.6f . . . and the outer pad and shim(s) and note the position of any small metal wear indicators that may be attached to either pad

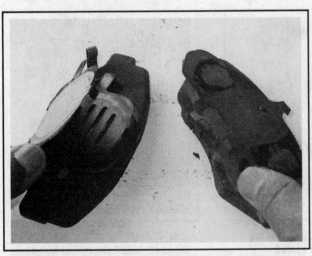

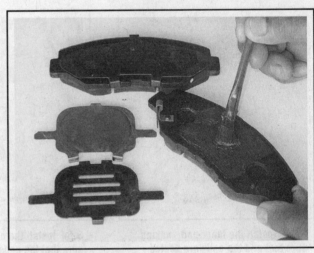

3.6g  Remove the shim(s) from each brake pad, noting the order and position

3.6h  Apply a thin film of disc brake grease in between the shim(s) and the back of each brake pad

3.6i  Place the shims on the pads in the correct order and position as they were originally. If necessary, refer to the installed pads on the other side of the vehicle if there is any question about shim placement

3.6j  Remove the upper and lower pad support plates; make sure they are a tight fit and aren't worn. If necessary, replace them

**3.6k Install the upper and lower pad support plates**

**3.6l Pull out the upper and lower sliding pins and clean them. Apply a coat of high-temperature grease to the pins and reinstall them. Be careful not to damage the pin boots; replace any boots that are worn or damaged**

**3.6m Install the inner pad, making sure that and the ends are seated correctly on the pad support plates and any wear indicators are in their original positions**

**3.6n Install the outer pad, making sure that the ends are seated correctly on the pad support plates**

**3.6o Position the caliper back over the pads, install the caliper bolt(s) and tighten them to the torque listed in this Chapter's Specifications**

## 4  Disc brake caliper - removal and installation

### ✳✳ WARNING:

**Dust created by the brake system is harmful to your health. Never blow it out with compressed air and don't inhale any of it. An approved filtering mask should be worn when working on the brakes. Do not, under any circumstances, use petroleum-based solvents to clean brake parts. Use brake system cleaner only!**

➡Note: Always replace the calipers in pairs - never replace just one of them.

### REMOVAL

▸ **Refer to illustrations 4.2a and 4.2b**

1   Loosen the wheel lug nuts, raise the vehicle and support it securely on jackstands. Remove the wheels.

2   Remove the brake hose banjo bolt and disconnect the hose from the caliper. Plug the hose to keep contaminants out of the brake system and to prevent losing any more brake fluid than is necessary (see illustrations).

➡Note: If you're just removing the caliper for access to other components, don't detach the hose.

3   Remove the caliper mounting bolts.

4   Remove the caliper. If necessary, remove the caliper bracket from the steering knuckle or rear knuckle (see illustration 5.2).

### INSTALLATION

5   Install the caliper by reversing the removal procedure. Tighten the caliper mounting bolts (and bracket bolts, if removed) to the torque listed in this Chapter's Specifications. Install new sealing washers on either side of the brake hose banjo fitting, then tighten the banjo bolt to

**4.2a Caliper mounting details:**

1    *Caliper mounting bolts*       2    *Banjo bolt and hose fitting*

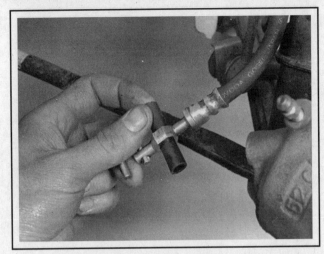

**4.2b Using a short piece of rubber hose of the appropriate diameter, plug the brake line banjo fitting**

the torque listed in this Chapter's Specifications.

6   Bleed the brake system (see Section 10).

7   Install the wheels and lug nuts. Lower the vehicle and tighten the lug nuts to the torque listed in the Chapter 1 Specifications.

---

## 5   Brake disc - inspection, removal and installation

### ✳✳ WARNING:

**The dust created by the brake system is harmful to your health. Never blow it out with compressed air and don't inhale any of it. An approved filtering mask should be worn when working on the brakes. Do not, under any circumstances, use petroleum-based solvents to clean brake parts. Use brake system cleaner only!**

### INSPECTION

▶ *Refer to illustrations 5.2, 5.3, 5.4a, 5.4b, 5.5a and 5.5b*

1   Loosen the wheel lug nuts, raise the vehicle and support it securely on jackstands. If you're checking the rear discs, release the

parking brake.

2   Remove the brake caliper as outlined in Section 4. It isn't necessary to disconnect the brake hose. After removing the caliper bolts, suspend the caliper out of the way with a piece of wire. Remove the two caliper mounting bracket-to-steering knuckle bolts (see illustration) or, on rear calipers, the bracket-to-knuckle bolts and remove the mounting bracket.

3   Visually check the disc surface for score marks, cracks and other damage. Light scratches and shallow grooves are normal after use and may not always be detrimental to brake operation. Deep score marks or cracks may require disc refinishing by an automotive machine shop or disc replacement (see illustration). Be sure to check both sides of

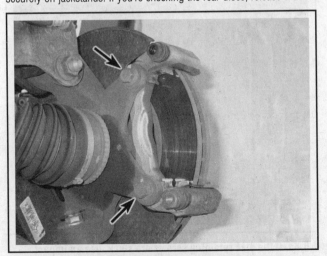

**5.2 The caliper mounting bracket is retained by two bolts**

**5.3 The brake pads on this vehicle were obviously neglected, as they wore down completely and cut deep grooves into the disc - wear this severe means the disc must be replaced**

5.4a To check disc runout, mount a dial indicator as shown and rotate the disc

the disc. If pulsating has been noticed during application of the brakes, suspect disc runout.

➡️**Note: The most common symptoms of damaged or worn brake discs are pulsation in the brake pedal when the brakes**

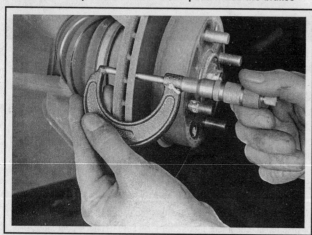

5.5a Use a micrometer to measure disc thickness

5.5b The minimum thickness specification is cast in the disc (A). For rear discs (shown) the maximum diameter specification for the drum portion is provided also (B)

5.4b Using a swirling motion, remove the glaze from the disc surface with sandpaper or emery cloth

are applied or loud grinding noises caused from severely worn brake pads. If these symptoms are extreme, it is very likely that the discs will need to be replaced.

4   To check disc runout, place a dial indicator at a point about 1/2-inch from the outer edge of the disc (see illustration). Set the indicator to zero and turn the disc. The indicator reading should not exceed the specified allowable runout limit. If it does, the disc should be refinished by an automotive machine shop.

➡️**Note: If disc refinishing or replacement is not necessary, you can deglaze the brake pad surface on the disc with emery cloth or sandpaper (use a swirling motion to ensure a non-directional finish) (see illustration).**

5   It's absolutely critical that the disc not be machined to a thickness under the specified minimum thickness. The minimum (or discard) thickness is cast or stamped into the disc. The disc thickness can be checked with a micrometer (see illustrations).

## REMOVAL

▶ **Refer to illustrations 5.6a, 5.6b and 5.7**

6   Remove the two disc retaining screws (see illustration) and remove the disc from the hub. If the disc is stuck to the hub and won't come off, thread two bolts into the holes provided and tighten them (see illustration). Alternate turning between the bolts; a couple of turns at a

5.6a If the disc retaining screws are stuck, use an impact screwdriver to loosen them

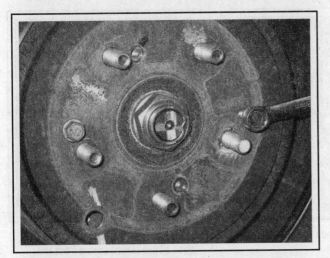

**5.6b If the disc is stuck on the hub flange, thread two bolts into the disc and tighten them evenly to force the disc off**

**5.7 Remove the rubber plug covering the access hole to the parking brake adjuster and rotate the disc to the six o'clock position. Use a flat-blade screwdriver and turn the star adjuster by rotating it up or down**

time will eventually separate the disc from the hub evenly and the disc will become loose. Remove the disc from the hub.

➥**Note: On rear discs, you may need to move the parking brake shoes away from the drum portion of the disc before installing the bolts that push the disc off the flange - see the procedure below.**

7   On rear discs, make sure that the parking brake is released. If necessary, move the parking brake shoes away from the drum portion of the disc by turning the star-wheel adjuster (see illustration).

## INSTALLATION

8   Place the disc onto the flange. Install the disc retaining screws and tighten them securely.

➥**Note: If there is any rust on the face of the hub flange or on the disc where it mounts to the flange, clean these surfaces and lightly coat them with anti-seize lubricant before installing the disc.**

9   On rear discs, adjust the parking brake shoes (see Section 7).

10  Install the caliper mounting bracket and caliper, tightening the bolts to the torque values listed in this Chapter's Specifications.

11  Install the wheels and then lower the vehicle to the ground. Tighten the lug nuts to the torque listed in the Chapter 1 Specifications. Depress the brake pedal a few times to bring the brake pads into contact with the disc. Bleeding won't be necessary unless the brake hose was disconnected from the caliper. Check the operation of the brakes carefully before driving the vehicle.

## 6   Parking brake shoes - replacement

**6.4 Before removing anything, clean the brake assembly with brake cleaner and allow it to dry - position a drain pan under the brake assembly to catch the residue - DO NOT USE COMPRESSED AIR TO BLOW BRAKE DUST OFF THE PARTS!**

◆ **Refer to illustrations 6.4 and 6.5a through 6.5x**

### ❋❋ WARNING 1:

Dust created by the brake system is hazardous to your health. Never blow it out with compressed air and don't inhale any of it. An approved filtering mask should be worn when working on the brakes. Do not, under any circumstances, use petroleum-based solvents to clean brake parts. Use brake system cleaner only!

### ❋❋ WARNING 2:

Parking brake shoes must be replaced on both wheels at the same time - never replace the shoes on only one wheel.

1   Remove the brake disc (see Section 5).

2   Measure the thickness of the lining material on the shoes. If the lining has worn down to 1 mm or less, the shoes must be replaced.

3   Inspect the drum portion of the disc for scoring, grooves or cracks due to heat. If any of these conditions exist or there is significant wear to the drum, the disc must be replaced.

4   Wash off the brake parts with brake system cleaner (see illustration).

**6.5a Remove the rear parking brake shoe upper return spring from the anchor pin . . .**

**6.5b . . . and unhook it from the rear shoe**

**6.5c Remove the front parking brake shoe upper return spring from the anchor pin . . .**

**6.5d . . . and unhook it from the front shoe**

**6.5e Remove the rod and spring from between the shoes**

5  Follow the accompanying illustrations for the brake shoe replacement procedure (see illustrations 6.5a through 6.5x). Be sure to stay in order and read the caption under each illustration.

6  Install the brake disc and the disc retaining screws.

7  Adjust the rear parking brake shoes (see Section 7).

8  Install the caliper bracket (see illustration 5.2b) and brake caliper (see Section 4). Be sure to tighten the bolts to the torque listed in this Chapter's Specifications.

9  Install the wheel and tighten the lug nuts to the torque specified in Chapter 1.

**6.5f Remove the shoe guide from the anchor pin**

**6.5g Remove the front shoe hold-down spring and pin**

**6.5h Remove the adjuster assembly**

6.5i Remove the lower return spring and front shoe

6.5j Remove the rear shoe hold-down spring and pin

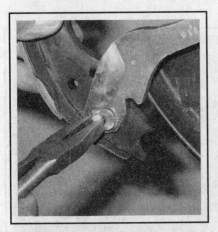

6.5k Pop the U-clip off the pivot pin on the back of the rear shoe . . .

6.5l . . . be careful not to lose or damage the wave washer beneath it . . .

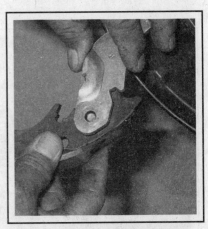

6.5m . . . and pull the parking brake lever off the pivot pin

6.5n Apply a thin coat of high-temperature grease to the contact surfaces of the backing plate and where the shoes meet the anchor pin

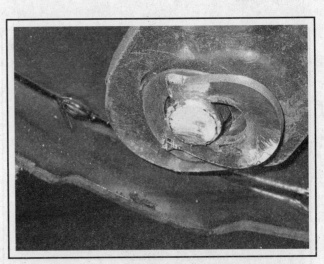

6.5o Apply a very small amount of high-temperature grease to the pivot pin on the new brake shoe and then slide the parking brake lever onto the pin. Install the wave washer and a new U-clip

6.5p Lubricate these areas of the adjuster with high-temperature grease

6.5q Install the rear shoe hold-down spring and pin

6.5r Install the lower return spring while holding the front shoe

6.5s Install the adjuster while holding the front shoe

6.5t Install the front shoe hold-down spring and pin

6.5u Lubricate the ends of the rod where it contacts the shoes with high-temperature grease and then install the rod and spring

**6.5v  Install the shoe guide to the anchor pin**

**6.5w  Install the front shoe upper return spring . . .**

**6.5x  . . . and then the rear shoe upper return spring**

10  Break in the new shoes by performing the following procedure:

a)  *Set and release the parking brake a few times.*

b)  *Set the parking brake at two to four clicks.*

c)  *Drive the vehicle one-quarter mile and do not exceed 30 miles per hour.*

d)  *Stop the vehicle and then RELEASE THE PARKING BRAKE IMME-*

*DIATELY. Allow the parking brake shoes and disc/drum to cool for 10 minutes.*

11  Set the parking brake and count the number of clicks that it travels. It should be between about four to six clicks - if it's not, check the parking brake adjustment at the shoes and then adjust the parking brake cable (see Section 7).

---

## 7  Parking brake - adjustment

▶ **Refer to illustration 7.6**

➡**Note: If the parking brake shoe clearance or cable adjusting nut require a significant amount of adjustment, it is advisable to inspect the brake shoe lining thickness (see Section 6).**

1   The parking brake pedal, when properly adjusted, should travel four to six clicks when set. If it travels less than specified, there's a chance the parking brake might not be releasing completely and the parking brake shoes might be dragging on the drum. If the pedal travels more than specified, the parking brake may not hold the vehicle adequately on an incline; allowing the car to roll.

2   There are two areas of adjustment for the parking brake: the star-wheel adjuster at the bottom of the shoes for each rear wheel and the adjusting nut on the brake cable at the parking brake pedal assembly. Adjustment at the shoes is performed first.

3   Block the front wheels, raise the rear of the vehicle and support it securely on jackstands. Remove the rear wheels.

4   Use the access hole in the disc to adjust the parking brake shoe clearance (see illustration 5.7). Turn the star-wheel adjuster until the disc cannot be rotated and then reverse the adjuster ten notches. Reinstall the rubber plug that covers the access hole.

5   Set the parking brake and count the number of clicks that it travels. It should be between about four to six clicks - if it's not, move on to the next adjustment at the parking brake pedal assembly.

6   Locate the adjusting nut at the pedal assembly and either tighten or loosen it to achieve the proper number of clicks when the parking brake pedal is set (see illustration). Tightening the nut (turning it clock-

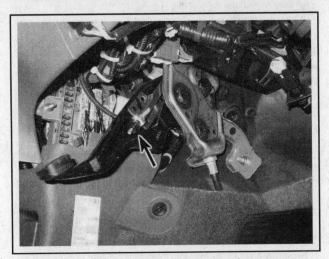

**7.6  Remove the small plastic cover (if equipped) from the adjusting nut and turn the nut to achieve the proper pedal travel for the parking brake**

wise) decreases the number of clicks, while the opposite is achieved by loosening the nut (turning it counterclockwise).

7   Release the parking brake and confirm that the brakes don't drag when the rear wheels are turned. Again, the travel on the parking brake pedal should be four to six clicks when it is properly adjusted.

## 8 Master cylinder - removal and installation

### HONDA PILOT AND 2006 AND EARLIER ACURA MDX MODELS

### Removal

◆ **Refer to illustration 8.2**

1  Remove the air intake duct (see Chapter 4).

2  Disconnect the electrical connectors for the fluid level sensor and remove as much fluid as you can from the reservoir with a syringe, such as an old turkey baster (see illustration).

### ✳✳ WARNING:

**If a baster is used, never again use it for the preparation of food.**

3  Place rags under the fluid fittings and prepare caps or plastic bags to cover the ends of the lines once they are disconnected.

### ✳✳ CAUTION:

**Brake fluid will damage paint. Cover all body parts and be careful not to spill fluid during this procedure.**

4  Use a flare nut wrench to loosen the fittings at the ends of the brake lines where they enter the master cylinder (see illustration 8.2). Pull the brake lines slightly away from the master cylinder and plug the ends to prevent contamination.

5  Remove the master cylinder mounting nuts and pull the master cylinder off the studs and out of the engine compartment. Again, be careful not to spill the fluid as this is done.

6  If a new master cylinder is being installed, remove the reservoir from the master cylinder and transfer it to the new master cylinder, if necessary.

➡Note: **Be sure to use new reservoir-to-master cylinder seals when transferring the reservoir.**

### Installation

◆ **Refer to illustration 8.8**

7  Bench bleed the new master cylinder before installing it. Mount the master cylinder in a vise, with the jaws of the vise clamping on the mounting flange.

8  Attach a pair of master cylinder bleeder tubes to the outlet ports of the master cylinder (see illustration).

9  Fill the reservoir with brake fluid of the recommended type (see Chapter 1).

10  Slowly push the pistons into the master cylinder (a large Phillips screwdriver can be used for this) - air will be expelled from the pressure chambers and into the reservoir. Because the tubes are submerged in fluid, air can't be drawn back into the master cylinder when you release the pistons.

11  Repeat the procedure until no more air bubbles are present.

12  Remove the bleed tubes, one at a time, and install plugs in the open ports to prevent fluid leakage and air from entering. Install the reservoir cap.

13  Install the master cylinder over the studs on the power brake booster and tighten the attaching nuts only finger tight at this time.

**8.2  Master cylinder mounting details:**

1  Brake line fittings
2  Mounting nuts
3  Fluid level sensor electrical connectors

➡Note: **Be sure to install a new O-ring into the sleeve of the master cylinder.**

14  Thread the brake line fittings into the master cylinder. Since the master cylinder is still a bit loose, it can be moved slightly in order for the fittings to thread in easily. Do not strip the threads as the fittings are tightened.

15  Fully tighten the mounting nuts, then the brake line fittings. Tighten the nuts to the torque listed in this Chapter's Specifications.

16  Fill the master cylinder reservoir with fluid, then bleed the master cylinder and the brake system as described in Section 10. To bleed the cylinder on the vehicle, have an assistant depress the brake pedal and hold the pedal to the floor. Loosen the fitting to allow air and fluid to escape. Repeat this procedure on both fittings until the fluid is clear of air bubbles.

**8.8  The best way to bleed air from the master cylinder before installing it on the vehicle is with a pair of bleeder tubes that direct brake fluid into the reservoir during bleeding**

**Have plenty of rags on hand to catch the fluid - brake fluid will ruin painted surfaces. After the bleeding procedure is completed, rinse the area under the master cylinder with plenty of clean water.**

17 Install the air intake duct. If the accelerator and cruise control cables were disconnected, reattach and adjust them as described in Chapter 4.

18 Test the operation of the brake system carefully before placing the vehicle into normal service.

**Do not operate the vehicle if you are in doubt about the effec-**

tiveness of the brake system. It is possible for air to become trapped in the anti-lock brake system hydraulic control unit, so, if the pedal continues to feel spongy after repeated bleedings or the BRAKE or ANTI-LOCK light stays on, have the vehicle towed to a dealer service department or other qualified shop for service.

## 2007 ACURA MDX MODELS

19 The power brake booster pushrod length on these models must be checked and adjusted for proper installation of the master cylinder. Because the pushrod is recessed in the booster, special tools are required for this procedure. It is recommended that the vehicle be towed to a dealer service department or other qualified repair for replacement of the master cylinder.

## 9    Brake hoses and lines - inspection and replacement

1    About every six months, with the vehicle raised and placed securely on jackstands, the flexible hoses which connect the steel brake lines with the front and rear brake assemblies should be inspected for cracks, chafing of the outer cover, leaks, blisters and other damage. These are important and vulnerable parts of the brake system and inspection should be complete. A light and mirror will be needed for a thorough check. If a hose exhibits any of the above defects, replace it with a new one.

### FLEXIBLE HOSES

▶ **Refer to illustrations 9.3a and 9 3b**

2    Clean all dirt away from the ends of the hose.
3    Disconnect the brake hose from the brake line (see illustrations).
4    Disconnect the hose from the caliper, discarding the sealing washers on either side of the fitting.

5    Using new sealing washers, attach the new brake hose to the caliper.
6    To reattach a brake hose to the metal line, insert the end of the hose through the frame bracket, make sure the hose isn't twisted, then attach the metal line by tightening the tube nut fitting securely. Install the U-clip at the frame bracket.
7    Carefully check to make sure the suspension or steering components don't make contact with the hose. Have an assistant push down on the vehicle and also turn the steering wheel lock-to-lock during inspection.
8    Bleed the brake system (see Section 10).

### METAL BRAKE LINES

9    When replacing brake lines, be sure to use the correct parts. Don't use copper tubing for any brake system components. Purchase steel brake lines from a dealer parts department or auto parts store.

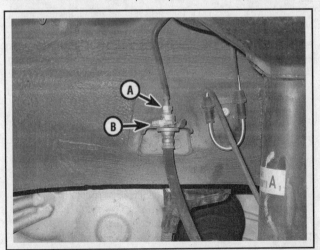

**9.3a  Front brake hose mounting details (rear brake hose similar):**

| | | | |
|---|---|---|---|
| 1 | Banjo bolt/hose fitting | 3 | Brake line-to-brake hose fitting |
| 2 | Hose-to-strut bracket | | |

**9.3b  Unscrew the brake line threaded fitting with a flare-nut wrench to protect the fitting corners from being rounded off (A), then pull off the U-clip (B)**

10 Prefabricated brake line, with the tube ends already flared and fittings installed, is available at auto parts stores and dealer parts departments. These lines can be bent to the proper shapes using a tubing bender.

11 When installing the new line, make sure it's well supported in the brackets and has plenty of clearance between moving or hot components.

12 After installation, check the master cylinder fluid level and add fluid as necessary. Bleed the brake system as outlined in Section 10 and test the brakes carefully before placing the vehicle into normal operation.

## 10 Brake hydraulic system - bleeding

▶ **Refer to illustration 10.8**

### ✳✳ WARNING:

**Wear eye protection when bleeding the brake system. If the fluid comes in contact with your eyes, immediately rinse them with water and seek medical attention.**

➡️**Note: Bleeding the brake system is necessary to remove any air that's trapped in the system when it's opened during removal and installation of a hose, line, caliper, wheel cylinder or master cylinder.**

1 It will probably be necessary to bleed the system at all four brakes if air has entered the system due to low fluid level, or if the brake lines have been disconnected at the master cylinder.

2 If a brake line was disconnected only at a wheel, then only that caliper or wheel cylinder must be bled.

3 If a brake line is disconnected at a fitting located between the master cylinder and any of the brakes, that part of the system served by the disconnected line must be bled.

4 Remove any residual vacuum (or hydraulic pressure) from the brake power booster by applying the brake several times with the engine off.

5 Remove the master cylinder reservoir cap and fill the reservoir with brake fluid. Reinstall the cap.

➡️**Note: Check the fluid level often during the bleeding operation and add fluid as necessary to prevent the fluid level from falling low enough to allow air bubbles into the master cylinder.**

6 Have an assistant on hand, as well as a supply of new brake fluid, an empty clear plastic container, a length of plastic, rubber or vinyl tubing to fit over the bleeder valve and a wrench to open and close the bleeder valve.

7 Beginning at the front left wheel, loosen the bleeder screw slightly, then tighten it to a point where it's snug but can still be loosened quickly and easily.

8 Place one end of the tubing over the bleeder screw fitting and submerge the other end in brake fluid in the container (see illustration).

9 Have the assistant slowly depress the brake pedal and hold it in the depressed position.

10 While the pedal is held depressed, open the bleeder screw just enough to allow a flow of fluid to leave the valve. Watch for air bubbles to exit the submerged end of the tube. When the fluid flow slows after a couple of seconds, tighten the screw and have your assistant release the pedal.

**10.8 When bleeding the brakes, a hose is connected to the bleed screw at the caliper and submerged in brake fluid - air will be seen as bubbles in the tube and container (all air must be expelled before moving to the next wheel)**

11 Repeat Steps 9 and 10 until no more air is seen leaving the tube, then tighten the bleeder screw and proceed to the right front wheel, the right rear wheel and the left rear wheel, in that order, and perform the same procedure. Be sure to check the fluid in the master cylinder reservoir frequently.

12 Never use old brake fluid. It contains moisture which can boil, rendering the brake system inoperative.

13 Refill the master cylinder with fluid at the end of the operation.

14 Check the operation of the brakes. The pedal should feel solid when depressed, with no sponginess. If necessary, repeat the entire process.

### ✳✳ WARNING:

**Do not operate the vehicle if you are in doubt about the effectiveness of the brake system. It is possible for air to become trapped in the anti-lock brake system hydraulic control unit, so, if the pedal continues to feel spongy after repeated bleedings or the BRAKE or ANTI-LOCK light stays on, have the vehicle towed to a dealer service department or other qualified shop for service.**

## 11 Power brake booster - removal and installation

### OPERATING CHECK

1   Depress the brake pedal several times with the engine off and make sure that there is no change in the pedal reserve distance.

2   Depress the pedal and start the engine. If the pedal goes down slightly, operation is normal.

### AIRTIGHTNESS CHECK

3   Start the engine and turn it off after one or two minutes. Depress the brake pedal several times slowly. If the pedal goes down farther the first time but gradually rises after the second or third depression, the booster is airtight.

4   Depress the brake pedal while the engine is running, then stop the engine with the pedal depressed. If there is no change in the pedal reserve travel after holding the pedal for 30 seconds, the booster is airtight.

### REMOVAL AND INSTALLATION

#### Honda Pilot and 2006 and earlier Acura MDX models

▶ Refer to illustrations 11.8 and 11.9

5   Disassembly of the power unit requires special tools and is not ordinarily performed by the home mechanic. If a problem develops, it's recommended that a new or factory rebuilt unit be installed.

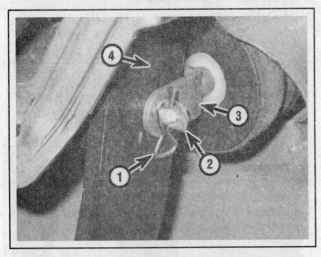

**11.8  Booster pushrod mounting details:**

| | | | |
|---|---|---|---|
| 1 | Lock pin | 3 | Pushrod clevis |
| 2 | Joint pin | 4 | Brake pedal arm |

6   Remove the master cylinder (see Section 8). On 2004 and earlier Honda models and 2001 and 2002 Acura models, disconnect the accelerator cable and cruise control cable from the throttle body (see Chapter 4).

7   Disconnect the large vacuum hose from the power brake booster.

8   In the passenger compartment, remove the joint pin and then disconnect the pushrod clevis from the brake pedal arm (see illustration).

9   Remove the nuts attaching the booster to the firewall (see illustration).

10   Carefully lift the booster unit away from the firewall and out of the engine compartment being especially careful not to bend the hydraulic brakes lines that are in front of the booster.

11   To install the booster, place it into position and tighten the retaining nuts to the torque listed in this Chapter's Specifications. Connect the pushrod to the brake pedal.

➡**Note: The manufacturer states to use a new lock pin for the pushrod joint pin when installing the brake booster.**

12   Install the master cylinder. Reconnect the vacuum hose. Bleed the brakes (see Section 10).

13   Carefully test the operation of the brakes before placing the vehicle in normal service.

#### 2007 Acura MDX models

14   The pushrod length on these models must be adjusted for proper installation of the brake booster. Special tools are required for this procedure. It is recommended that the vehicle be towed to a dealer service department or other qualified repair shop for replacement of the power brake booster.

**11.9  To detach the power brake booster from the firewall, remove the four mounting nuts (two nuts not visible in photo)**

## 12  Brake Pedal Position (BPP) switch - replacement

▶ Refer to illustration 12.1

➡Note: There are two different designs used for these models: one design uses a locknut to secure the switch, while the other uses a locking mount. They are distinguished by the metal or plastic threaded section on the switch - the metal type is equipped with the locknut.

1   Disconnect the electrical connector from the brake pedal position (BPP) switch (see illustration).

### MODELS WITHOUT A LOCKNUT

▶ Refer to illustration 12.3

2   Rotate the switch counterclockwise until it unlocks from its mount. With the switch loose, it can be pulled straight out.

3   To install the switch, insert it into its mount until the switch's plunger is compressed and the threaded barrel section of the switch is against the rubber pad on the brake pedal arm. Lightly lift up on the brake pedal to make sure it's fully released (up). Rotate the switch 45-degrees clockwise to lock it into place. With the switch secured in place, the proper gap between the switch and the pedal arm is automatically set (see illustration).

➡Note: Make certain that the brake pedal arm is fully released (up) while installing the BPP switch.

### MODELS WITH A LOCKNUT

▶ Refer to illustration 12.5

4   Check the pedal height and adjust if necessary (see Section 13).

5   Loosen the locknut and unscrew the switch from the pedal bracket (see illustration).

**12.1  Brake pedal position (BPP) switch location**

6   Installation is the reverse of removal noting the following points:

a)  *Adjust the switch by screwing it in until the threaded barrel section just contacts the rubber pad on the pedal arm and the plunger in the switch is compressed. Then, back the switch out by a three-quarter turn. This should create the proper gap between the switch and the rubber pad on the pedal arm.*

➡Note: Make certain that the brake pedal arm is fully released (up) while installing the BPP switch.

b)  *Tighten the locknut securely.*

### ALL MODELS

7   Plug the electrical connector into the switch.

8   Confirm proper operation of the brake lights when the pedal is depressed and released. If necessary, adjust the switch again until the proper adjustment is achieved.

**12.3  BPP switch details:**

1   *Threaded barrel section*
2   *Rubber pad*
3   *Clearance between switch and rubber pad on the brake pedal arm*
4   *Switch mount*

**12.5  Loosen the locknut on the switch, then unscrew the switch to remove it**

## 13  Brake pedal - adjustment

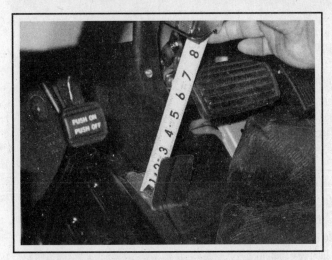

**13.2  With the brake pedal fully released (up), from the middle of the pedal on the left side, measure the distance from the bottom edge of the pedal pad to the floor**

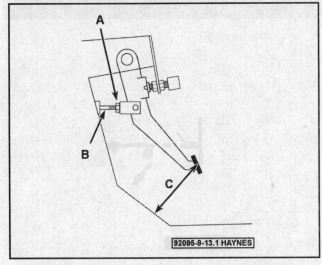

**13.3  Brake pedal height measuring and adjustment (2007 Acura MDX models):**

A   *Pushrod/clevis locknut*
B   *Brake power booster push rod (turn this rod to raise or lower the pedal)*
C   *Pedal height measurement points*

▶ **Refer to illustrations 13.2, 13.3 and 13.5**

➡**Note: The brake pedal height and freeplay are not adjustable on all models but can be inspected to rule out damage or wear to any of the related components.**

1   Remove the brake pedal position (BPP) switch (see Section 12).

2   Pull the carpet back and find the insulator cutout, then with the brake pedal fully released (up), measure the distance from the brake pedal pad to the floor (see illustration).

3   The height should be within the Specifications listed at the beginning of this Chapter. If it is not, inspect the brake pedal arm and linkage for wear and damage. On models that are adjustable, perform a pedal adjustment by loosening the locknut on the pushrod and then turning the pushrod with a pair of pliers to raise of lower the pedal (see illustration).

4   Install the BPP switch and check the brake pedal freeplay.

➡**Note: The 2007 Acura MDX models are the only models that have an adjustable pedal height.**

5   Press down lightly on the brake pedal to measure the freeplay (see illustration). This distance should be very small and within the Specifications listed at the beginning of this Chapter. If it isn't, check the brake booster pushrod clevis, lock pin and the hole in the brake pedal arm for excessive wear. Also make sure the BPP switch is properly installed (see Section 12).

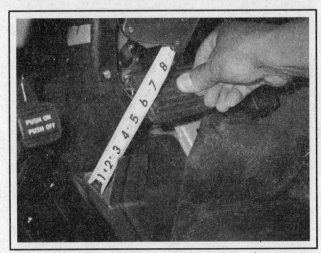

**13.5  To measure brake pedal freeplay, lightly press down on the pedal and measure the distance that it moves freely before resistance is felt**

## Specifications

### General

| | |
|---|---|
| Brake fluid type | See Chapter 1 |
| Brake pedal height | |
|     Honda Pilot | 6-1/8 inches (155 mm) |
|     Acura MDX | |
|         2007 | 7 inches (178 mm) |
|         2006 and earlier | 6-7/16 inches (164 mm) |
| Brake pedal freeplay | 1/16 to 3/16 inch (1 to 5 mm) |

### Disc brakes

| | |
|---|---|
| Brake pad minimum thickness | See Chapter 1 |
| Disc lateral runout limit | 0.004 inch (0.10 mm) |
| Disc minimum thickness | Cast into disc |
| Parallelism (thickness variation) limit | 0.0006 inch (0.015 mm) |

## Torque specifications

| | Ft-lbs | Nm |
|---|---|---|
| Caliper mounting bracket bolts | | |
|     Acura MDX 2007 | | |
|         Front | 101 | 137 |
|         Rear | 65 | 88 |
|     All others | | |
|         Front | 80 | 108 |
|         Rear | 41 | 55 |
| Caliper mounting bolts | | |
|     All except 2007 Acura front caliper | 27 | 37 |
|     2007 Acura front caliper | 53 | 72 |
| Master cylinder mounting nuts | 18 | 25 |
| Power brake booster mounting nuts | 18 | 25 |
| Wheel lug nuts | See Chapter 1 | |

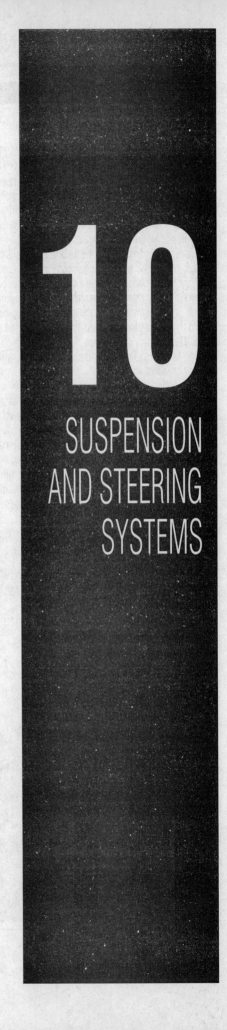

# 10

## SUSPENSION AND STEERING SYSTEMS

♦ **Refer to illustrations 1.1 and 1.2**

The front suspension is a MacPherson strut/coil spring design. The upper end of each strut is attached to the vehicle's body strut support. The lower end of the strut is connected to the upper end of the steering knuckle. The steering knuckle is attached to a balljoint mounted on the outer end of the suspension control arm. A stabilizer bar connected to each control arm and mounted to the suspension crossmember reduces body roll during cornering (see illustration).

The rear suspension utilizes trailing arms, shock absorbers, coil springs, one upper and two lower control arms (see illustration). A stabilizer bar is clamped to the top of the rear suspension subframe and connected to the rear lower control arms by two links.

The power-assisted rack-and-pinion steering gear, which is located behind the engine/transaxle assembly, is mounted on the front subframe. The steering gear moves the tie-rods, which are attached to the steering knuckles. The steering column is designed to collapse in the event of an accident.

Frequently, when working on the suspension or steering system components, you may come across fasteners that seem impossible to loosen. These fasteners on the underside of the vehicle are continually subjected to water, road grime, mud, etc., and can become rusted or "frozen," making them extremely difficult to remove. In order to unscrew these stubborn fasteners without damaging them (or other components), be sure to use lots of penetrating oil and allow it to soak in for a while. Using a wire brush to clean exposed threads will also ease removal of the nut or bolt and prevent damage to the threads.

Sometimes a sharp blow with a hammer and punch will break the bond between a nut and bolt threads, but care must be taken to prevent the punch from slipping off the fastener and ruining the threads. Heating the stuck fastener and surrounding area with a torch sometimes helps too, but isn't recommended because of the obvious dangers associated with fire. Long breaker bars and extension, or "cheater," pipes will increase leverage, but never use an extension pipe on a ratchet - the ratcheting mechanism could be damaged. Sometimes tightening the nut or bolt first will help to break it loose. Fasteners that require drastic measures to remove should always be replaced with new ones.

Since most of the procedures dealt with in this Chapter involve jacking up the vehicle and working underneath it, a good pair of jackstands will be needed. A hydraulic floor jack is the preferred type of jack to lift the vehicle, and it can also be used to support certain components during various operations.

### ✳✳ WARNING:

**Never, under any circumstances, rely on a jack to support the vehicle while working on it. Whenever any of the suspension or steering fasteners are loosened or removed they must be inspected and, if necessary, replaced with new ones of the same part number or of original equipment quality and design. Torque specifications must be followed for proper reassembly and component retention. Never attempt to heat or straighten any suspension or steering components. Instead, replace any bent or damaged part with a new one.**

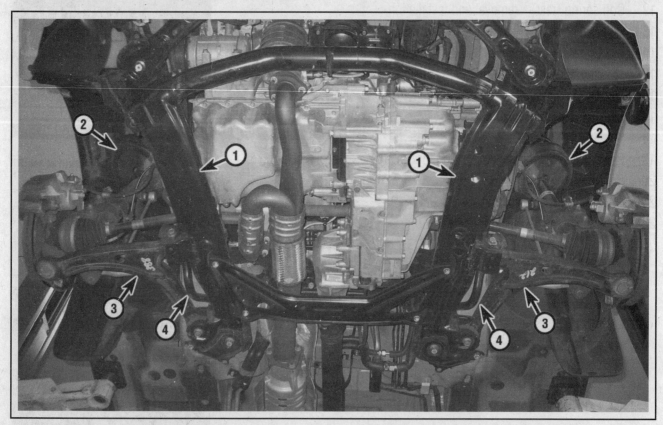

**1.1 Front suspension components**

| 1 | Subframe | 2 | Strut/coil spring assembly | 3 | Control arm | 4 | Stabilizer bar |

**1.2  Rear suspension components**

| | | | |
|---|---|---|---|
| 1 | Subframe | 3 | Trailing arm |
| 2 | Shock absorber | 4 | Lower arm A |

| | | | |
|---|---|---|---|
| 5 | Rear knuckle | 6 | Lower arm B |

## 2  Stabilizer bar, bushings and links (front) - removal and installation

### BUSHINGS AND LINKS

▶ **Refer to illustrations 2.2 and 2.3**

1   Loosen the front wheel lug nuts. Raise the front of the vehicle and support it securely on jackstands. Apply the parking brake and block the rear wheels to keep the vehicle from rolling off the stands. Remove the front wheels.

2   Remove the bolts from the stabilizer bar bushing retainers (see illustration). Remove the retainers from the bushings, prying them off, if necessary.

3   Remove the nuts that attach the upper and lower ends of the stabilizer links to the strut/coil spring assembly and to the stabilizer bar (see illustration). Detach the links.

➡**Note: If the stud on the link turns while attempting to remove the nut, hold it with an Allen wrench placed in the center of the stud.**

**2.2  Remove the bolts attaching the stabilizer bar bracket to the subframe**

4   Inspect the retainer bushings for cracks and tears. If either bushing is broken, damaged, distorted or worn, replace both of them. If the ballstuds on the links are loose or otherwise worn, replace the links.

5   Install the links, tightening the link nuts to the torque listed in this Chapter's Specifications.

6   Install the retainer bushings. Clean the areas on the stabilizer bar where the bushings are located. Lubricate the inside and outside of the new bushings with vegetable oil (used in cooking) to simplify reassembly.

### ❊❊ CAUTION:

**Don't use petroleum or mineral-based lubricants or brake fluid - they will lead to deterioration of the bushings. These bushings are split so that you can install them without having to slide them onto the ends of the stabilizer bar. Install the bushings with the slit in each bushing facing forward.**

7   Install the retainers and bolts, tightening the bolts to the torque listed in this Chapter's Specifications.

8   Install the wheels and lug nuts. Lower the vehicle and tighten the lug nuts to the torque listed in the Chapter 1 Specifications.

## STABILIZER BAR

### All models except 2007 Acura MDX

9   Stabilizer bar removal involves removing the subframe from under the vehicle while supporting the engine from above. This is an extensive procedure and important safety precautions must be observed. Refer to Chapter 2B, *Engine - removal and installation*, for

**2.3  Stabilizer bar link mounting nuts**

instructions on subframe removal. It is important to note that the need to remove the stabilizer bar from the vehicle is usually due to damage from an accident. If this is the case, it is highly likely that other major components (such as the subframe itself) have also been damaged. We recommend having the vehicle inspected by a qualified body repair shop before replacing the stabilizer bar.

### 2007 Acura MDX

10   On these models it isn't necessary to remove the subframe to remove the stabilizer bar. Simply remove the links and bushings (see Steps 2 and 3) and remove the bar from one side of the vehicle.

## 3   Strut assembly - removal, inspection and installation

### REMOVAL

▶ **Refer to illustrations 3.4 and 3.6**

### ❊❊ WARNING:

**On 2007 Acura MDX models with active damper control, refer to an authorized dealership or qualified repair facility regarding front strut assembly replacement. A proprietary scan tool is required to check for proper function of the damper units after installation.**

➡**Note: The manufacturer recommends the use of new lower strut fasteners upon installation.**

1   Loosen the wheel lug nuts, raise the vehicle and support it securely on jackstands. Remove the wheel.

2   Disconnect the stabilizer bar link from the strut, then remove the brake hose bracket from the strut.

3   Detach the ABS speed sensor wiring harness from the strut by removing the clamp bracket bolt.

4   Mark the relationship of the strut to the knuckle (these marks will be used during installation to ensure the camber is returned to its original setting). Remove the strut-to-knuckle nuts and knock the bolts out with a hammer and punch (see illustration). Discard the fasteners.

**3.4  After making reference marks, remove the strut-to-steering knuckle nuts and bolts**

5   Separate the strut from the steering knuckle. Be careful not to overextend the inner CV joint. Also, don't let the steering knuckle fall outward, as the brake hose could be damaged.

6   Remove the access covers from the cowl cover. Mark the stud that is closest to the front of the vehicle so the strut can be installed back in the same position upon reassembly. Support the strut and

spring assembly and remove the three strut upper mounting nuts (see illustration). Remove the assembly from the fenderwell. Make certain that the struts are marked left or right if both are being removed.

## INSPECTION

7   Check the strut body for leaking fluid, dents, cracks and other obvious damage that would warrant repair or replacement.

8   Check the coil spring for chips or cracks in the spring coating (this can cause premature spring failure due to corrosion). Inspect the spring seat for cuts, hardness and general deterioration.

9   If any undesirable conditions exist, proceed to the strut disassembly procedure (see Section 4).

## INSTALLATION

10   Guide the strut assembly up into the fenderwell and insert the three upper mounting studs through the holes in the shock tower placing the marked stud closest towards the front of the vehicle. Once the three studs protrude from the shock tower, install the nuts so the strut won't fall back through. It's best to use an assistant with this step because the strut is heavy and awkward.

11   Slide the steering knuckle into the strut flange and insert two new mounting bolts. Install the new nuts and tighten them to the torque listed in this Chapter's Specifications.

12   Reattach the brake hose bracket to the strut. Install the speed

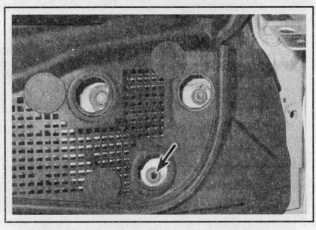

**3.6  Mark the stud closest to the front, then remove the three strut upper mounting nuts while supporting it from underneath**

sensor wiring harness bracket, and reconnect the stabilizer link.

13   Install the wheel and lug nuts, then lower the vehicle and tighten the lug nuts to the torque listed in the Chapter 1 Specifications.

14   Tighten the three upper mounting nuts to the torque listed in this Chapter's Specifications.

15   Have the front wheel alignment checked and, if necessary, adjusted.

## 4   Strut/coil spring assembly - replacement

### ※ WARNING:

**Struts and/or coil springs must be replaced in pairs - never replace just one of them.**

1   If the struts or coil springs exhibit the telltale signs of wear (leaking fluid, loss of damping capability, chipped, sagging or cracked coil springs) explore all options before beginning any work. The strut/shock absorber assemblies are not serviceable and must be replaced if a problem develops. However, strut assemblies complete with springs may be available on an exchange basis, which eliminates much time and work. Whichever route you choose to take, check on the cost and availability of parts before disassembling your vehicle.

### ※ WARNING:

**Disassembling a strut is potentially dangerous and utmost attention must be directed to the job, or serious injury may result. Use only a high-quality spring compressor and carefully follow the manufacturer's instructions furnished with the tool. After removing the coil spring from the strut assembly, set it aside in a safe, isolated area.**

## DISASSEMBLY

♦ **Refer to illustrations 4.3, 4.5, 4.6 and 4.7**

2   Remove the strut and spring assembly (see Section 3). Mount the strut assembly in a vise. Line the vise jaws with wood or rags to prevent

**4.3  Install the spring compressor following the tool manufacturer's instructions; compress the spring until all pressure is relieved from the upper spring seat (you can verify the spring is loose by wiggling it)**

damage to the unit and don't tighten the vise excessively.

3   Following the tool manufacturer's instructions, install the spring compressor (which can be obtained at most auto parts stores or equipment yards on a daily rental basis) on the spring and compress it sufficiently to relieve all pressure from the upper spring seat (see illustration). This can be verified by wiggling the spring.

**4.5  Lift the upper mount off the damper rod**

**4.6  Remove the upper spring seat and the upper pad from the damper rod**

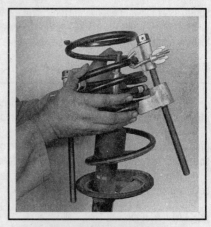

**4.7  Remove the compressed spring from the strut/shock absorber assembly - keep the ends of the spring pointed away from your body**

4   Hold the strut piston rod with an Allen wrench, and unscrew the thrust bearing retaining nut with a box-end wrench.

5   Remove the nut and upper mount (see illustration). Lay the parts out in the exact order in which they are removed. Inspect the bearing in the suspension support for smooth operation. If it doesn't turn smoothly, replace the upper mount. Check the rubber portion of the upper mount for cracking and general deterioration. If there is any separation of the rubber, replace it.

6   Remove the upper spring seat from the damper shaft (see illustration). Check the spring seat for cracking and hardness; replace it if necessary. Remove the upper insulator from the damper shaft.

**4.11  When installing the spring, make sure the end fits into the recessed portion of the lower seat**

7   Carefully lift the compressed spring from the assembly (see illustration) and set it in a safe place.

## ✳✳ WARNING:

**When removing the compressed spring, lift it off carefully and set it in a safe place. Keep the ends of the spring away from your body.**

➡**Note: If you are disassembling both struts, mark the springs LEFT and RIGHT so you don't mix them up (they're different).**

8   Remove the dust cover plate and dust cover.

9   Slide the rubber bump stop off the damper shaft. Check the bump stop for cracking and general deterioration. If there is any deterioration of the rubber, replace it.

## REASSEMBLY

▸ **Refer to illustration 4.11**

10  Extend the damper rod to its full length and install the rubber bump stop, dust cover and dust cover plate.

11  Carefully place the compressed coil spring onto the lower seat of the damper, with the end of the spring resting in the lowest part of the seat (see illustration).

12  Install the upper insulator and spring seat.

13  Install the bearing and suspension support.

14  Install the washer and nut and tighten it to the torque listed in this Chapter's Specifications. Remove the spring compressor tool.

15  Install the strut/spring assembly (see Section 3).

## 5  Control arm - removal, inspection and installation

### REMOVAL

▶ Refer to illustrations 5.2, 5.3 and 5.5

**❋❋ WARNING:**

**The manufacturer recommends using new mounting fasteners during installation.**

➡Note: A special tool, available at most auto parts stores, is necessary to separate the lower control arm balljoint from the steering knuckle.

1  Loosen the wheel lug nuts on the side to be disassembled, apply the parking brake, raise the front of the vehicle, support it securely on jackstands and remove the wheel.

2  Remove the lock pin from the castle nut (see illustration). Loosen the nut until there is a small gap between the knuckle and the nut.

3  Install the balljoint separating tool, being careful not to tear the balljoint grease seal (see illustration).

➡Note: Apply grease to the portion of the tool that contacts the balljoint grease seal and to the threads of the bolt on the tool.

Once the balljoint stud has been released from the steering knuckle, remove the castle nut and separate the balljoint from the steering knuckle completely.

**❋❋ CAUTION:**

**Be careful not to overextend the inner C/V joint and do not attempt to pry the lower balljoint from the steering knuckle.**

4  On 2007 Acura MDX models equipped with the active damper system option, remove the small arm linked to the system sensor from the control arm.

5  On all except 2007 Acura models, remove the two bolts that attach the control arm to the subframe (see illustration). On 2007 Acura models, remove the pivot bolt and the two bolts securing the bushing to the subframe. Remove the control arm.

5.2  Lower control arm-to-steering knuckle nut and lock pin

### INSPECTION

6  Make sure the control arm is straight. If it's bent, replace it. Do not attempt to straighten a bent control arm.

7  Inspect the bushings. If they're cracked, torn or worn out, replace the control arm.

8  On 2007 Acura models, the rear bushing can be replaced by removing the nut and sliding the bushing off the shaft. When installing the new bushing, use a new nut and tighten it to the torque listed in this Chapter's Specifications.

### INSTALLATION

9  Installation is the reverse of removal, noting the following points:

a) Tighten the balljoint stud castle nut to the lower torque figure listed in this Chapter's Specifications, then, if necessary, tighten it a little more to line up the slots in the nut with the hole in the stud.

b) Install a new lock pin and use new mounting fasteners for the control arm.

5.3  Use the balljoint separator tool to separate the steering knuckle from the balljoint stud

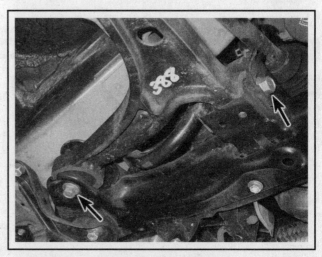

5.5  Control arm-to-subframe mounting bolts

c) On 2007 Acura MDX models, make sure that the round slotted 'stops' on each side of the control arm bushing are aligned correctly. The rubber bushing has two small raised areas on each side; one on the top and one on the bottom. The round 'stops' have slots that match up with the raised areas on the bushing.

d) Raise the outer end of the control arm with a floor jack (to simulate normal ride height), then tighten the control arm-to-subframe bolts to the torque listed in this Chapter's Specifications.

10  Install the wheel and lug nuts, lower the vehicle and tighten the lug nuts to the torque listed in the Chapter 1 Specifications.

11  It's a good idea to have the front wheel alignment checked, and if necessary, adjusted after this job has been performed. On 2007 Acura MDX models equipped with the active damper system, it may be necessary to have the vehicle checked by an authorized dealer service department if there are any dash warning lights (related to that system) that stay on after the control arm has been installed.

## 6  Balljoints - check and replacement

### CHECK

1  Raise the front of the vehicle and support it securely on jackstands. Apply the parking brake and block the rear wheels to keep the vehicle from rolling off the jackstands.

2  Place a large prybar under the balljoint and resting on the wheel, then try to pry the balljoint up while feeling for movement between the balljoint and steering knuckle. Now, pry between the control arm and the steering knuckle and try to lever the control arm down while feeling for movement between the balljoint and steering knuckle. If any movement is evident in either check, the balljoint is worn.

3  Have an assistant grasp the tire at the top and bottom and move the top of the tire in-and-out. Touch the balljoint stud nut. If any looseness is felt, suspect a worn balljoint stud or a widened hole in the steering knuckle boss. If the latter problem exists, the steering knuckle should be replaced as well as the balljoint/control arm.

4  Separate the control arm from the steering knuckle (see Section 5). Using your fingers (don't use pliers), try to twist the stud in the socket. If the stud turns, replace the balljoint.

### REPLACEMENT

5  The balljoints on these models are not replaceable; the entire control arm must be replaced if the balljoint has failed.

6  The balljoint dust boot can be replaced if it is damaged. You should not replace the dust boot if it has been cracked or damaged while the vehicle was in use because dirt and other contaminants have probably gotten into the balljoint. However, if the dust boot was damaged during removal of the control arm, replace it. To do this, pry off the old dust boot and remove the retaining clip from it. Place grease at the base of the balljoint stud (the area that is normally covered by the dust boot). Push the new dust boot onto the balljoint until it seats into the groove at the base of the balljoint. A special tool is available to place the retaining clip into the groove on the boot, but with some effort, you can place the clip in position with your fingers while being careful not to damage the new boot with the clip in the process.

7  Clean any excess grease off the tapered portion of the balljoint stud that seats into the steering knuckle, then reattach the balljoint to the knuckle.

8  Tighten the balljoint stud castle nut to the lower torque figure listed in this Chapter's Specifications, then, if necessary, tighten it a little more to line up the slots in the nut with the hole in the stud.

9  Install a new lock clip.

10  Install the wheel and lug nuts (if removed) and lower the vehicle. Tighten the lug nuts to the torque listed in the Chapter 1 Specifications.

## 7  Steering knuckle and hub (front) - removal and installation

### ✳✳ WARNING:

**Dust created by the brake system is harmful to your health. Never blow it out with compressed air and don't inhale any of it. Do not, under any circumstances, use petroleum-based solvents to clean brake parts. Use brake system cleaner only.**

### REMOVAL

1  Loosen the driveaxle/hub nut (see Chapter 8). Loosen the wheel lug nuts, raise the vehicle and support it securely on jackstands. Remove the wheel.

2  Remove the brake disc from the hub, the ABS wheel speed sensor from the knuckle and the brake hose from the strut (see Chapter 9).

3  Loosen, but do not remove the strut-to-steering knuckle fasteners (see Section 3) (see illustration 3.4).

➡**Note: Be sure to mark the relationship between the strut and the knuckle before loosening any fasteners.**

4  Separate the tie-rod end from the steering knuckle arm (see Section 15).

5  Remove the lock pin for the balljoint castle nut, loosen the castle nut and then separate the balljoint from the knuckle (see illustrations 5.2 and 5.3).

6  Remove the strut-to-knuckle fasteners and discard them.

7  Remove and discard the driveaxle/hub nut, then push the driveaxle from the hub and support the end with a piece of wire as described in Chapter 8. Separate the steering knuckle from the strut.

## INSTALLATION

8   Guide the knuckle and hub assembly into position, inserting the driveaxle into the hub.

9   Push the knuckle into the strut flange and install new fasteners, but don't tighten them yet.

10  Connect the balljoint to the steering knuckle and install the nut, but don't tighten it yet.

11  Attach the tie-rod to the steering knuckle arm (see Section 15). Tighten the strut fasteners, the balljoint castle nut and the tie-rod nut to the torque values listed in this Chapter's Specifications. Install new cotter and lock pins.

12  Place the brake disc on the hub and install the caliper as outlined in Chapter 9.

13  Install a new driveaxle/hub nut and tighten it securely (final tightening will be carried out when the vehicle is lowered).

14  Install the wheel and lug nuts.

15  Lower the vehicle and tighten the lug nuts to the torque listed in the Chapter 1 Specifications. Tighten the driveaxle/hub nut to the torque listed in the Chapter 8 Specifications.

16  Have the front wheel alignment checked and, if necessary, adjusted.

---

## 8   Hub and bearing assembly (front) - replacement

### 2007 ACURA MDX MODELS

### Removal

▶ **Refer to illustration 8.5**

> ✳✳ **WARNING:**
>
> **The manufacturer recommends replacing the driveaxle/hub nut with a new one whenever it is removed.**

1   Loosen the driveaxle/hub nut (see Chapter 8).

2   Loosen the wheel lug nuts, raise the front of the vehicle and support it securely on jackstands and remove the wheel.

3   Remove the brake caliper, the caliper mounting bracket and the brake disc from the hub (see Chapter 9).

➡ **Note: Be sure to support the brake caliper as described in Chapter 9.**

4   Remove the driveaxle/hub nut.

5   Remove the hub/bearing assembly mounting bolts from the rear of the steering knuckle (see illustration).

6   Remove the hub/bearing assembly from the steering knuckle.

➡ **Note: If the driveaxle splines stick in the hub, push the driveaxle out of the hub with a two-jaw puller.**

### Installation

7   Make sure that the mounting surface inside the steering knuckle and on the driveaxle splines is smooth and free of burrs and nicks prior to installing the hub/bearing assembly.

8   Lubricate the driveaxle splines with multi-purpose grease. Install the hub/bearing assembly onto the driveaxle and into the steering knuckle until it is seated on the steering knuckle.

9   Install the hub/bearing assembly-to-steering knuckle bolts. Tighten the bolts equally in a criss-cross pattern until the hub/bearing assembly is seated securely against the steering knuckle. Tighten the bolts to the torque listed in this Chapter's Specifications.

10  Install a new driveaxle/hub nut. Do not tighten the nut yet.

11  Install the brake disc, the caliper mounting bracket and the caliper; tighten the fasteners to the torque values listed in the Chapter 9 Specifications.

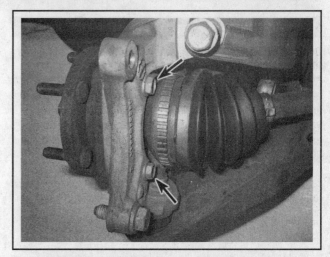

**8.5  Hub and bearing assembly mounting bolts (2007 Acura models only) - two hidden from view (typical shown)**

12  Install the wheel and lug nuts, remove the jackstands, and lower the vehicle.

13  Tighten the driveaxle/hub nut to the torque listed in the Chapter 8 Specifications.

➡ **Note: Have an assistant apply the brakes while tightening the driveaxle/hub nut.**

14  Tighten the lug nuts to the torque listed in the Chapter 1 Specifications.

### ALL OTHER MODELS

Due to the special tools and expertise required to press the hub and bearing from the steering knuckle, this job should be left to a professional mechanic. However, the steering knuckle and hub may be removed and the assembly taken to an automotive machine shop or other qualified repair facility equipped with the necessary tools. See Section 7 for the steering knuckle and hub removal procedure.

## 9 Shock absorber (rear) - removal, inspection and installation

▶ Refer to illustration 9.4

**⁜ WARNING:**

**Always replace the shock absorbers in pairs - never replace just one of them.**

➡Note: On 2007 Acura MDX models with active damper control, refer to an authorized dealership or qualified repair facility regarding rear shock absorber replacement. A proprietary scan tool is required to check for proper function of the shock absorbers after installation.

1   Loosen the rear wheel lug nuts. Chock the front wheels to keep the vehicle from rolling, then raise the rear of the vehicle and support it securely on jackstands placed underneath the rear jacking points. Remove the rear wheels.

2   Support the lower arm B with a floor jack placed under the coil spring pocket (see illustration 10.2).

**⁜ WARNING:**

**Do not move the jack while it is supporting the lower arm B and the coil spring tension.**

3   On 2007 Acura MDX models, remove the stabilizer link from the lower arm B (see Section 11) and remove the ABS speed sensor and wire harness from the lower arm B and move it aside.

4   Remove the shock absorber upper mounting bolt (see illustration).

5   Remove the shock absorber lower mounting nut and washer and remove the shock absorber. On 2007 Acura MDX models, remove the lower mounting bolt and the bolt attaching the rear knuckle to the lower arm B.

6   Compress the shock, if necessary, and remove it. On 2007 Acura

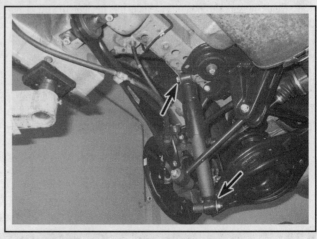

**9.4  Rear shock absorber mounting fasteners**

MDX models, use the floor jack to slowly lower the lower arm B and then remove the shock.

7   To install the shock absorber, reverse the removal procedure. On all but 2007 Acura MDX models, be sure to install the washer on the lower mounting stud with the concave side facing away from the shock absorber.

8   Raise lower arm B with the jack to simulate normal ride height, then tighten the upper and lower mounting fasteners to the torque listed in this Chapter's Specifications. On 2007 Acura MDX models, tighten the lower arm B-to-knuckle bolt to the torque listed in this Chapter's Specifications.

9   Repeat the procedure to replace the other rear shock absorber.

10  Install the wheels and lug nuts and lower the vehicle. Tighten the lug nuts to the torque listed in the Chapter 1 Specifications.

## 10 Suspension arms (rear) and rear knuckle - removal and installation

**⁜ WARNING:**

**The manufacturer recommends replacing the mounting fasteners for these components with new ones whenever they are removed.**

1   Loosen the rear wheel lug nuts. Raise the rear of the vehicle and support it securely on jackstands. Block the front wheels to prevent the vehicle from rolling. Remove the wheel.

➡Note: If you are removing the rear knuckle, loosen the drive-axle/hub nut (see Chapter 8).

### UPPER ARM

▶ Refer to illustrations 10.2, 10.3 and 10.4

➡Note: A special tool, available at most auto parts stores, is necessary to separate the upper arm balljoint from the rear knuckle.

2   Support the lower arm B with a floor jack placed under the coil spring pocket (see illustration).

**10.2  Support the lower arm B with a floor jack placed beneath the coil spring pocket**

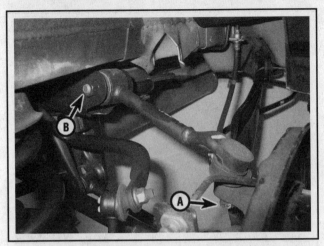

**10.3  Upper arm balljoint castle nut (A) and arm-to-subframe mounting bolt (B) (remove it from the other side)**

## ✳✳ WARNING:

**Do not move the jack while it is supporting the lower arm B and the coil spring tension.**

3  Remove the lock pin from the castle nut on the balljoint stud (see illustration). Loosen the nut until there is a small gap between the knuckle and the nut.

4  Install the balljoint separating tool, being careful not to tear the balljoint grease seal (see illustration).

➡**Note: Apply grease to the portion of the tool that contacts the balljoint grease seal and to the threads of the bolt on the tool.**

Once the balljoint stud has been released from the knuckle, remove the castle nut and separate the arm from the knuckle completely.

5  Remove the upper arm-to-subframe mounting bolt, then remove the arm.

6  Installation is the reverse of removal, noting the following points:

a) *Tighten the balljoint stud castle nut to the lower torque figure listed in this Chapter's Specifications, then, if necessary, tighten it a little more to line up the slots in the nut with the hole in the stud.*

**10.8  Lower arm A mounting fasteners**

**10.4  Use a balljoint separating tool to release the lower arm B balljoint from the rear knuckle**

b) *Install a new lock pin.*
c) *Raise the lower arm B with a floor jack to simulate normal ride height, then tighten the arm-to-subframe bolt to the torque listed in this Chapter's Specifications.*
d) *Tighten the wheel lug nuts to the torque listed in the Chapter 1 Specifications.*

## LOWER ARM A

▶ **Refer to illustration 10.8**

7  Support the lower arm B with a floor jack placed under the coil spring pocket (see illustration 10.2).

## ✳✳ WARNING:

**Do not move the jack while it is supporting the lower arm B and the coil spring tension.**

8  Remove the lower arm-to-subframe mounting bolt and the lower arm-to-knuckle mounting nut and washer (see illustration). On 2007 Acura MDX models, remove the front trailing arm mounting bolts (see illustration 10.20).

9  Remove the arm from the vehicle.

10  Installation is the reverse of the removal procedure. Be sure to install the washer on the arm-to-knuckle mounting stud with the concave side facing away from the arm. Before tightening the fasteners to the torque listed in this Chapter's Specifications, raise the rear suspension with the floor jack to simulate normal ride height. Tighten the wheel lug nuts to the torque listed in the Chapter 1 Specifications.

## LOWER ARM B

▶ **Refer to illustrations 10.12, 10.14 and 10.15**

11  Support the lower arm B with a floor jack placed under the coil spring pocket (see illustration 10.2).

## ✳✳ WARNING:

**Do not move the jack while it is supporting the lower arm B and the coil spring tension.**

**10.12  Lower arm B mounting fasteners (A) and the ABS wheel speed harness brackets (B)**

**10.14  With a floor jack supporting the lower arm B, slowly lower the jack until the coil spring can be removed**

12  Remove the ABS wheel speed sensor harness from the lower arm (see illustration).

13  Remove the bolt securing the arm to the knuckle (see illustration 10.12).

14  Slowly lower the floor jack until the coil spring is extended, then remove the coil spring (see illustration) (see Section 12).

15  Mark the relationship of the toe adjuster cam to the subframe, then remove the pivot bolt and nut from the inner end of the arm (see illustration). Remove the arm from the vehicle.

16  Installation is the reverse of removal, noting the following points:

a)  Align the mark you made on the toe adjuster cam with the mark on the subframe.

b)  Raise the outer end of lower arm B with a floor jack to simulate normal ride height, then tighten the fasteners to the torque listed in this Chapter's Specifications.

c)  Tighten the wheel lug nuts to the torque listed in the Chapter 1 Specifications.

d)  Have the rear wheel alignment checked and, if necessary, adjusted.

## TRAILING ARM

▶ **Refer to illustration 10.20**

17  Remove the parking brake shoe assembly (see Chapter 9).

18  Unbolt the brake hose and brake line brackets from the trailing arm. Unbolt the parking brake cable brackets.

19  Support the lower arm B with a floor jack placed under the coil spring pocket (see illustration 10.2).

**✳✳ WARNING:**

**Do not move the jack while it is supporting the lower arm B and the coil spring tension.**

20  Remove the trailing arm-to-knuckle bolts, then remove the trailing arm-to-chassis mounting bolts (see illustration).

21  Remove the trailing arm.

22  Installation is the reverse of removal, noting the following points:

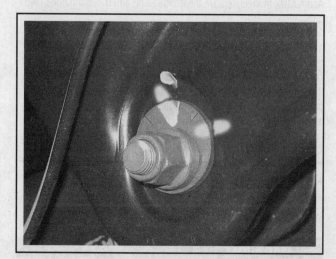

**10.15  Place an alignment mark on the toe adjuster cam and the subframe, then unscrew the nut and remove the pivot bolt**

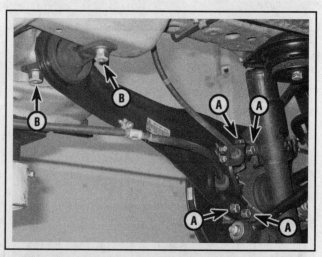

**10.20  Remove the trailing arm-to-knuckle bolts (A) and the trailing arm-to-chassis mounting bolts (B)**

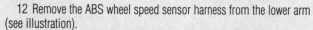

a) *Tighten all fasteners to the proper torque specifications.*
b) *It won't be necessary to bleed the brakes unless a hydraulic fitting was loosened (if a fitting was loosened, refer to Chapter 9 for the brake bleeding procedure).*
c) *Have the rear wheel alignment checked and, if necessary, adjusted.*

## REAR KNUCKLE

▶ **Refer to illustration 10.26**

23  Remove the parking brake shoe assembly (see Chapter 9).
24  On 4WD models, remove the driveaxle/hub nut and discard it. On 2WD models, remove the axle shaft from the hub.
25  On 2007 Acura MDX models, remove the hub and bearing assembly (see Section 13).
26  Unbolt the brake hose bracket from the trailing arm and the brake line bracket from the knuckle (see illustration).
27  Remove the ABS wheel speed sensor and harness from the knuckle, then carefully place it aside (see Chapter 9).

➡**Note: There is no need to disconnect the electrical connector for the sensor.**

28  Support the lower arm B with a floor jack placed under the coil spring pocket (see illustration 10.2).

### ❋❋ WARNING:

**Do not move the jack while it is supporting the lower arm B and the coil spring tension.**

29  Detach the upper arm from the knuckle (see Step 2).
30  Detach lower arm A from the knuckle (see Step 7).
31  Detach the trailing arm from the knuckle (see Step 17).
32  Detach the lower arm B from the knuckle (see Step 11).
33  On 4WD models, carefully push the driveaxle while removing the knuckle. Use a puller if the driveaxle is stuck in the hub (see Chapter 8).

**10.26  Unbolt the brake hose bracket from the rear knuckle**

### ❋❋ CAUTION:

**Do not pull on the driveaxle because the inner CV joint could separate.**

34  Installation is the reverse of removal, noting the following points:
a) *Tighten the balljoint stud castle nut to the lower torque figure listed in this Chapter's Specifications, then, if necessary, tighten it a little more to line up the slots in the nut with the hole in the stud. Install a new lock pin.*
b) *Install a new driveaxle/hub nut.*
c) *Raise the lower arm B with a floor jack, then tighten the fasteners to the torque listed in this Chapter's Specifications.*
d) *Tighten the wheel lug nuts to the torque listed in the Chapter 1 Specifications.*
e) *Tighten the driveaxle/hub nut to the torque listed in the Chapter 8 Specifications.*

## 11  Stabilizer bar, bushings and links (rear) - removal and installation

## ALL MODELS EXCEPT 2007 ACURA MDX

1  Stabilizer bar removal involves removing the rear subframe. It is important to note that the need to remove the stabilizer bar from the vehicle is usually due to damage from an accident. If this is the case, it is highly likely that other major components (such as the subframe itself) have also been damaged. We recommend having the vehicle inspected by a qualified body repair shop before replacing the stabilizer bar.
2  The rear stabilizer bar link replacement procedure is similar to the front stabilizer bar link procedure (see Section 2).

### 2007 Acura MDX

3  On these models it isn't necessary to remove the subframe to remove the stabilizer bar. The links and bushings can be removed following the procedure described in Section 2.

## 12 Coil spring (rear) - removal and installation

### ✳✳ WARNING:

**Always replace the springs as a set - never replace just one of them.**

1 Loosen the wheel lug nuts, raise the vehicle and support it securely on jackstands. Block the front wheels to prevent the vehicle from rolling. Remove the wheel.

2 On 2007 Acura MDX models, remove the rubber hangers from the each side of the muffler (see Chapter 4).

3 Remove the stabilizer bar link from the lower arm B (see Section 11).

4 Support the lower arm B with a floor jack placed under the coil spring pocket (see illustration 10.2).

### ✳✳ WARNING:

**Do not move the jack while it is supporting the lower arm B and the coil spring tension.**

5 Remove the ABS wheel speed sensor harness from the lower arm B (see illustration 10.12).

6 Mark the position of the spring to the spring insulators.

7 On 2007 Acura MDX models, remove the lower shock absorber mounting bolt (see Section 9).

8 Remove the bolt securing the lower arm B to the knuckle (see illustration 10.12).

9 Slowly lower the floor jack and remove the coil spring (see illustration 10.14).

10 Check the spring for cracks and chips, replacing the springs as a set if any defects are found. Also check the upper insulator for damage and deterioration, replacing it if necessary.

11 Installation is the reverse of removal, noting the following points:

a) Be sure to position the lower end of the coil spring in the depressed area of the trailing arm.

b) Raise the outer end of lower arm B with a floor jack to simulate normal ride height, then tighten the control arm-to-knuckle bolt to the torque listed in this Chapter's Specifications.

c) Tighten the wheel lug nuts to the torque listed in the Chapter 1 Specifications.

## 13 Hub and bearing assembly (rear) - removal and installation

### 2007 ACURA MDX MODELS

#### Removal

##### ✳✳ WARNING:

**The manufacturer recommends replacing the driveaxle/hub nut with a new one whenever it is removed.**

1 Loosen the driveaxle/hub nut (see Chapter 8).

2 Loosen the wheel lug nuts, raise the rear of the vehicle and support it securely on jackstands and remove the wheel.

3 Remove the brake caliper, the caliper mounting bracket and the brake disc from the hub (see Chapter 9).

➡Note: Be sure to support the brake caliper as described in Chapter 9.

4 Remove the driveaxle/hub nut and discard it.

5 Remove the four hub/bearing assembly mounting bolts from the rear of the rear knuckle.

6 Remove the hub/bearing assembly from the rear knuckle.

➡Note: If the driveaxle splines stick in the hub, push the driveaxle out of the hub with a two-jaw puller.

##### ✳✳ CAUTION:

**Do not pull on the driveaxle because the inner CV joint could separate.**

#### Installation

7 Make sure that the mounting surface inside the rear knuckle and on the driveaxle splines is smooth and free of burrs and nicks prior to installing the hub/bearing assembly.

8 Lubricate the driveaxle splines with multi-purpose grease. Install the hub/bearing assembly onto the driveaxle and into the rear knuckle until it is seated on the rear knuckle.

9 Install the hub/bearing assembly-to-knuckle bolts. Tighten the bolts equally in a criss-cross pattern until the hub/bearing assembly is seated securely against the rear knuckle, then tighten the bolts to the torque listed in this Chapter's Specifications.

10 Install a new driveaxle/hub nut. Do not tighten the nut yet.

11 Install the brake disc, the caliper mounting bracket and the caliper; tighten the fasteners to the torque values listed in the Chapter 9 Specifications.

12 Install the wheel and lug nuts, remove the jackstands, and lower the vehicle.

13 Tighten the driveaxle/hub nut to the torque listed in the Chapter 8 Specifications.

➡Note: Have an assistant apply the brakes while tightening the driveaxle/hub nut.

14 Tighten the lug nuts to the torque listed in the Chapter 1 Specifications.

### ALL OTHER MODELS

Due to the special tools and expertise required to press the hub and bearing from the steering knuckle, this job should be left to a professional mechanic. However, the rear knuckle and hub may be removed and the assembly taken to an automotive machine shop or other qualified repair facility equipped with the necessary tools. See Section 10 for the rear knuckle and hub removal procedure.

## 14 Steering wheel - removal and installation

### ✳✳ WARNING 1:

These models are equipped with a Supplemental Restraint System (SRS), more commonly known as airbags. Always disable the airbag system before working in the vicinity of any airbag system component to avoid the possibility of accidental deployment of the airbag(s), which could cause personal injury (see Chapter 12).

### ✳✳ WARNING 2:

Do not use a memory saving device to preserve the PCM or radio memory when working on or near airbag system components

## REMOVAL

▶ Refer to illustrations 14.2, 14.3, 14.4, 14.6, 14.8 and 14.10

1  Make sure the front wheels are pointed straight ahead, then disconnect the cable from the negative terminal of the battery (see Chapter 5, Section 1). Wait at least three minutes before proceeding.

2  Remove the airbag connector access panel from the bottom of the steering wheel (see illustration).

3  Disconnect the airbag module electrical connector to disable the airbag module (see illustration). On 2007 Acura MDX models, disconnect the small additional electrical connector for the horn that is in the same area.

4  Remove airbag module mounting fasteners from each side of the steering wheel (see illustration).

5  Pull off the airbag module, then carefully set it in a safe location.

### ✳✳ WARNING:

Carry the airbag module with the trim side facing away from you, and set the airbag module down with the trim side facing up. Don't place anything on top of the airbag module.

6  Disconnect the connectors for the radio remote switch and the cruise control switch (see illustration).

7  Remove the steering wheel retaining nut or, if you're working on a 2007 Acura MDX model, remove the steering wheel retaining bolt. Mark the relationship of the steering wheel hub to the steering shaft and then replace the nut or bolt loosely (threads showing) for the next step.

8  Install a steering wheel puller. The puller screw must contact the steering wheel bolt or shaft only (see illustration).

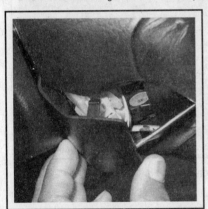

14.2  Remove the panel at the bottom of the steering wheel to gain access to the airbag module electrical connector

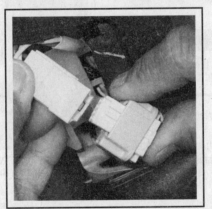

14.3  Disconnect the electrical connector for the airbag module

14.4  Remove the mounting fasteners for the airbag module on each side of the steering wheel

14.6  Disconnect the electrical connectors for the switches on the steering wheel

14.8  Use a steering wheel puller to break the steering wheel from the shaft

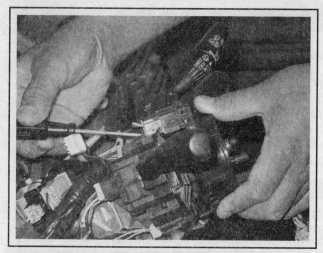

**14.10 The clockspring can be separated from the combination switch by releasing its retaining clips and disconnecting the electrical connectors on top**

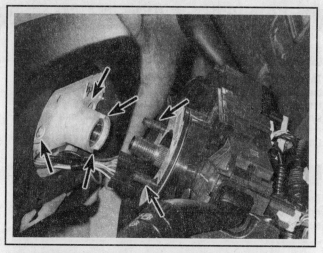

**14.12a Match the locating pins and notches to properly install the steering wheel**

---

✳ **CAUTION 1:**

**Don't thread the bolts of the puller into the steering wheel more than five turns, as they could contact the airbag clockspring and damage it.**

---

✳ **CAUTION 2:**

**While the steering wheel is removed, DO NOT turn the steering shaft. If you do so, the airbag clockspring could be damaged.**

---

9  If it is necessary to remove the clockspring, remove the steering column covers (see Chapter 11).

10  Unplug the clockspring electrical connectors from the top of the clockspring, then release the clockspring from the three retaining clips that attach it to the combination switch (see illustration).

## INSTALLATION

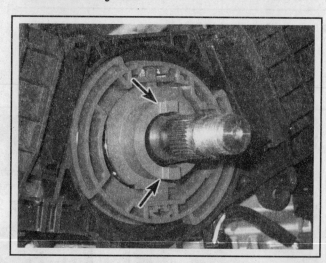

**14.12b Lugs on the signal canceling cam**

◆ **Refer to illustrations 14.12a and 14.12b**

11  With the front wheels are pointed straight ahead, make sure that the airbag clockspring is centered with the arrow on the clockspring pointing up. This shouldn't be a problem as long as you have not turned the steering shaft while the wheel was removed. If for some reason the shaft was turned, center the clockspring as follows:

  a) *Rotate the clockspring clockwise until it stops.*
  b) *Rotate the clockspring counterclockwise about 2-1/2 turns until the arrow on the clockspring points straight up.*

12  When placing the steering wheel back on the steering shaft, align the steering wheel hub with the shaft using the index mark that was made in step 7. Also, make sure the locating pins on the clockspring engage the holes in the backside of the steering wheel, and the notches in the steering wheel hub engage the tabs on the turn signal canceling cam (see illustrations). Install the steering wheel bolt/nut and tighten it to the torque listed in this Chapter's Specifications.

13  Connect the radio remote switch and the cruise control switch connectors.

14  Reattach the airbag module using NEW fasteners and tighten them to the torque listed in this Chapter's Specifications.

15  Plug in the electrical connector for the airbag module and horn, if equipped.

16  Reconnect the negative battery cable (see Chapter 5, Section 1).

## 15 Steering column - removal and installation

### ※※ WARNING 1:

These models are equipped with a Supplemental Restraint System (SRS), more commonly known as airbags. Always disable the airbag system before working in the vicinity of any airbag system component to avoid the possibility of accidental deployment of the airbag(s), which could cause personal injury (see Chapter 12).

### ※※ WARNING 2:

Do not use a memory saving device to preserve the PCM or radio memory when working on or near airbag system components.

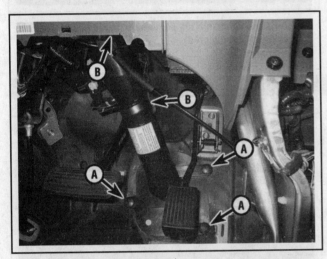

**15.9  Remove the cover over the steering column shaft by removing the push-pin fasteners (A) and the spring clips (B), if equipped.**

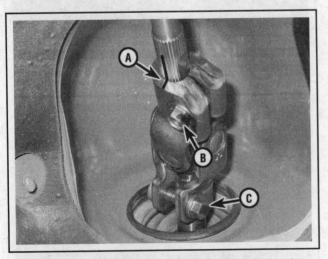

**15.10  Mark the relationship of the intermediate shaft to the steering gear U-joint (A), then remove the pinch bolt (B). C is the U-joint to steering gear input shaft pinch bolt**

## REMOVAL

▶ **Refer to illustrations 15.9, 15.10, 15.11 and 15.12**

1   Park the vehicle with the wheels pointing straight ahead. Disconnect the cable from the negative terminal of the battery (see Chapter 5, Section 1).

2   Adjust the steering wheel tilt option to the Neutral position, approximately 8 mm down from the uppermost position. On 2007 Acura MDX models, adjust the column to its fully down and (telescopically adjusted) out position.

3   Remove the steering wheel (see Section 14). Prevent the steering shaft from turning.

### ※※ CAUTION:

If this is not done, the airbag clockspring could be damaged.

4   Remove the steering column covers (see Chapter 11).

5   On 2007 Acura MDX models, remove the panel below the instrument panel on the driver's side by pulling the edge closest to you down to release its clips. Disconnect any related electrical connectors.

6   Remove the clockspring (see Section 14).

7   Remove the steering column switches (see Chapter 12).

8   Remove the shift cable from the shift lever and cable mounting bracket (see Chapter 7).

9   Remove the steering shaft cover, if equipped (see illustration).

10  Mark the relationship of the U-joint to the intermediate shaft, then remove the pinch bolt (see illustration).

11  Detach the clip that holds the main wiring harness to the steering column. Follow the harness and disconnect any remaining electrical connectors (see illustration).

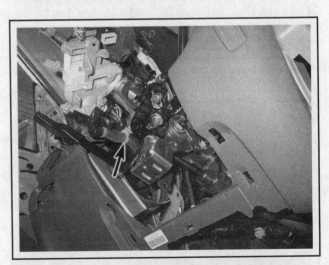

**15.11  The main wiring harness for the steering column**

12 Remove the steering column mounting fasteners (see illustration), lower the column and pull it to the rear, making sure nothing is still connected, then remove the column.

## INSTALLATION

13 Guide the steering column into position while connecting the intermediate shaft with the U-joint at the bottom - noting the alignment marks made previously.

14 Install the steering column mounting fasteners and tighten them to the torque listed in this Chapter's Specifications.

15 Install the intermediate shaft pinch bolt and nut, tightening it to the torque listed in this Chapter's Specifications.

16 The remainder of installation is the reverse of removal. Reconnect the negative battery cable (see Chapter 5, Section 1).

**15.12  Remove the steering column mounting fasteners (one fastener not pictured)**

## 16  Tie-rod ends - removal and installation

### REMOVAL

▶ **Refer to illustrations 16.2, 16.3 and 16.4**

1   Loosen the wheel lug nuts, raise the front of the vehicle and support it securely on jackstands. Apply the parking brake and block the rear wheels to keep the vehicle from rolling off the jackstands. Remove the wheel.

2   Loosen the tie-rod end jam nut (see illustration).

3   Mark the relationship of the tie-rod end to the threaded portion of the tie-rod. This will ensure that the toe-in setting is restored when reassembled (see illustration).

4   Remove the cotter pin and loosen the nut from the tie-rod end ballstud a few turns.  Disconnect the tie-rod end ballstud from the steering knuckle arm with a balljoint separator tool or equivalent (see illustration).

5   Remove the nut from the ballstud, separate the tie-rod end from the steering knuckle, and then unscrew the tie-rod end from the tie-rod.

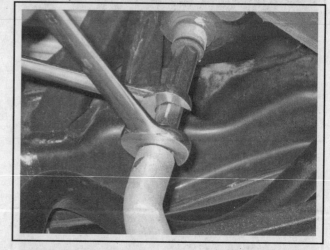

**16.2  Back off the jam nut . . .**

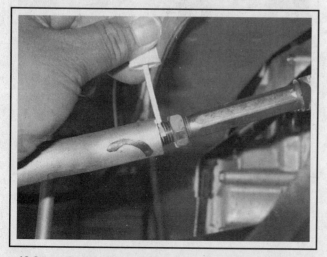

**16.3  . . . then mark the exposed threads so that the new tie-rod end is threaded on with the same number of turns**

**16.4  A balljoint separator tool, or equivalent, can be used to push the tie-rod end stud out of the steering knuckle**

## INSTALLATION

6    Thread the tie-rod end onto the tie-rod to the marked position and connect the tie-rod end to the steering arm. Install the nut on the ballstud and tighten it to the torque listed in this Chapter's Specifications. Install a new cotter pin.

➡**Note: If necessary, tighten the nut a little more to allow insertion of the cotter pin. Never loosen the nut to align the cotter pin holes.**

7    Tighten the jam nut securely and install the wheel. Lower the vehicle and tighten the lug nuts to the torque listed in the Chapter 1 Specifications.

8    Have the front end alignment checked and, if necessary, adjusted.

## 17  Steering gear boots - replacement

◆ **Refer to illustration 17.3**

1    Loosen the lug nuts, raise the front of the vehicle and support it securely on jackstands. Remove the wheel.

2    Remove the tie-rod end and jam nut (see Section 16).

3    Remove the steering gear boot clamps (see illustration) and slide the boot off.

4    Before installing the new boot, wrap the threads and serrations on the end of the steering rod with a layer of tape so the small end of the new boot isn't damaged.

5    Slide the new boot into position on the steering gear until it seats in the groove in the steering rod and install new clamps.

6    Remove the tape and install the tie-rod end (see Section 16).

7    Install the wheel and lug nuts. Lower the vehicle and tighten the lug nuts to the torque listed in the Chapter 1 Specifications.

**17.3  Steering gear boot clamps (the outer one can be removed with pliers; the inner one must be cut off)**

## 18  Steering gear - removal and installation

### ※※ WARNING:

**Make sure the steering wheel (shaft) is not turned while the steering gear is removed or you could damage the airbag system. To prevent the shaft from turning, place the ignition key in the LOCK position or thread the seat belt through the steering wheel and clip it into place.**

## REMOVAL

1    Disconnect the cable from the negative battery terminal (see Chapter 5, Section 1).

2    Drain the power steering fluid from the remote power steering reservoir. This can be accomplished with a suction gun or large syringe, or by disconnecting the fluid hose and draining the fluid into a container.

3    From inside the vehicle under the dashboard, remove the steering shaft cover, if equipped (see illustration 15.9), mark the relationship of both shafts at the U-joint and then remove the lower pinch bolt (see illustration 15.10).

➡**Note: Discard the small part between the U-joint and steering gear input shaft, if equipped; it is used for manufacturing purposes only.**

4    Loosen the front wheel lug nuts, raise the vehicle and support it securely on jackstands. Remove both front wheels.

➡**Note: The jackstands must be behind the front suspension subframe, not supporting the vehicle by the subframe.**

### 2007 Acura MDX models

5    Remove the panel that is under the driver's side of the instrument panel.

6    Remove the air filter housing (see Chapter 4).

7    Secure the engine using an engine support brace that is fitted above the engine compartment. If an engine support brace is not available, install an engine hoist and a lifting chain assembly (see Chapter 2B).

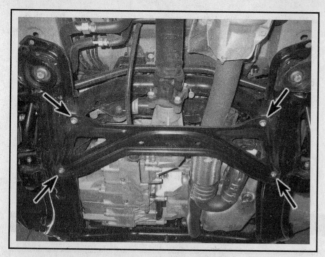

**18.34 The power steering pressure switch electrical connector**

**18.32 Subframe stiffener plate mounting bolts**

8   Remove the hose and line fittings at the steering gear. Use a flare nut wrench for the line fitting.

9   Detach the tie-rod ends from the steering knuckles (see Section 16).

10  Disconnect the stabilizer bar links from the lower control arm (see Section 2).

11  Remove the engine splash shield(s) (see Chapter 2B)

12  Remove the mounting bolts securing the subframe stiffener plate and remove the plate.

13  Remove the exhaust system from the under-floor catalytic converter to the tailpipe(s).

14  Remove the driveshaft (see Chapter 8).

15  Remove the pressure line brackets from the subframe that are on each side of the rear engine mount.

16  Remove all components of the rear engine mount (see Chapter 2A).

17  Detach the ground cable and bracket from the transmission (see Chapter 7).

18  Mark the relationship of the subframe and brackets to the chassis.

19  Using two floor jacks, support the subframe. Position one jack on

each side of the subframe, midway between the front and rear mounting points.

20  Loosen the four subframe-to-chassis mounting bolts. Loosen the bolts approximately 1-3/16 inch (40 mm) from the mounting surface. Do not remove the bolts.

21  Remove the front subframe-to-chassis bracket mounting bolts.

22  Remove the rear subframe-to-chassis bracket mounting bolts.

23  Slowly and carefully lower the floor jacks until the subframe meets the mounting bolts that were loosened. Leave the jacks in place to support the subframe.

24  Remove the steering gear mounting bolts on the left side of the gear.

25  Remove the steering gear stiffener bracket from the subframe.

26  Remove the steering gear mounting clamp on the right side of the gear.

27  Pass the steering gear assembly through the left wheel opening and remove it from the vehicle.

### All other models

▶ **Refer to illustrations 18.32, 18.34, 18.37, 18.38, 18.44, 18.45 and 18.48**

28  Remove the power steering pump pressure line from the pump (see Section 19). Follow the line and remove the bracket that secures it to the engine.

29  Remove the two engine bracket bolts at the right engine mount (see Chapter 2A).

30  Secure the engine using an engine support brace that is fitted above the engine compartment. If an engine support brace is not available, install an engine hoist and a lifting chain assembly (see Chapter 2B).

31  Detach the tie-rod ends from the steering knuckles (see Section 16).

32  Remove the mounting bolts securing the subframe stiffener plate and remove the plate (see illustration).

33  Remove the exhaust hanger located in front of the under-floor catalytic converter. Disconnect the catalytic converter from the pipes leading to the muffler (see Chapter 4).

34  Disconnect the electrical connector for the power steering pressure switch (see illustration).

35  Remove the driveshaft center support bearing and safety loops from the floor pan (see Chapter 8).

36  Remove the engine splash shield (see Chapter 2B).

37  Mark the relationship of the subframe and brackets to the chassis (see illustration).

**18.37 Use the reference marks (A) and the alignment hole (B) along with your own reference marks (C) to install the subframe back to its original position**

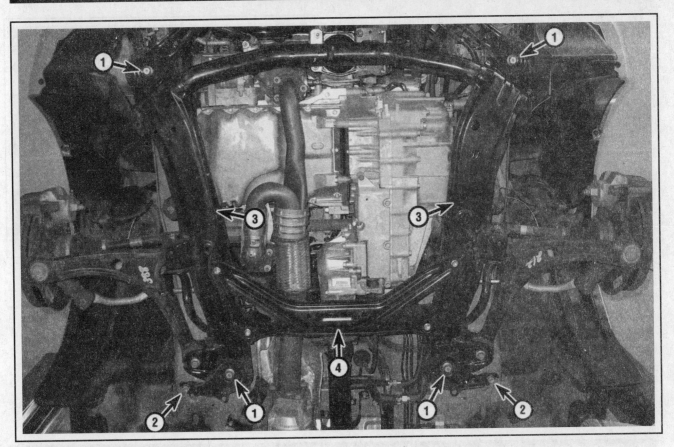

**18.38 Subframe mounting details:**

*1  Subframe-to-chassis mounting bolts*
*2  Subframe-to-chassis mounting bracket bolts*
*3  Midpoint of subframe where floor jacks are placed*
*4  Subframe stiffener plate*

38  Using two floor jacks, support the subframe. Position one jack on each side of the subframe, midway between the front and rear mounting points (see illustration).

39  Loosen the four subframe-to-chassis mounting bolts). Loosen the bolts approximately 1-15/16 inch (50 mm) from the mounting surface. Do not remove the bolts.

40  Remove the front subframe-to-chassis bracket mounting bolt.

41  Remove the rear subframe-to-chassis bracket mounting bolts.

42  Slowly and carefully lower the floor jacks until the subframe meets the mounting bolts that were loosened. Leave the jacks in place to support the subframe and to lower the subframe further in the follow-

ing procedures.

43  Remove the brackets securing the return line to the subframe.

44  Place a drain pan or tray under the vehicle, positioned beneath the steering gear. Using a flare-nut wrench, disconnect the pressure and return lines from the steering gear (see illustration). Plug the lines to prevent excessive fluid loss.

45  Remove the steering gear stiffener bracket from the subframe (see illustration).

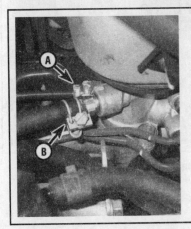

**18.44  Using a flare-nut wrench, disconnect the pressure line (A); also remove the hose clamp for the return line (B)**

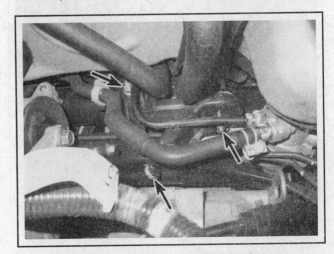

**18.45  Locations for the steering gear stiffener fasteners**

46 Loosen the four main subframe mounting bolts another 2 inches (50mm) approximately.

47 Slowly and carefully lower the floor jacks until the subframe meets the mounting bolts that were loosened. Leave the jacks in place to support the subframe.

48 Remove the steering gear mounting clamp on the right side (see illustration) and the mounting fasteners on left side near the line fittings.

49 Pass the steering gear assembly through the left wheel opening and remove it from the vehicle.

## INSTALLATION

50 Installation is the reverse of removal, noting the following points:

a) Tighten the steering gear mounting fasteners and stiffener bracket bolts to the torque listed in this Chapter's Specifications.

b) Use the reference marks and alignment holes in the subframe brackets and chassis to position the subframe into its original position. Tighten the subframe mounting bolts to the torque listed in this Chapter 2B.

c) Reconnect the negative battery cable (see Chapter 5, Section 1).

d) Fill the power steering pump with the recommended fluid (see Chapter 1), bleed the system (see Section 20) and recheck the fluid level. Check for leaks.

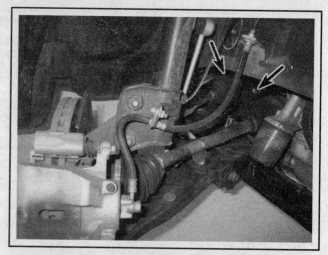

**18.48 Locations for the steering gear mounting clamp fasteners**

e) Run the engine and check for proper operation and leaks. Shut off the engine and recheck fluid levels.

f) Have the front end alignment checked and, if necessary, adjusted.

## 19  Power steering pump - removal and installation

♦ **Refer to illustrations 19.2 and 19.4**

1 Remove the drivebelt (see Chapter 1).

2 Clamp the power steering feed hose shut so fluid loss will be minimized when the hose is disconnected, then disconnect the feed hose and pressure line at the pump (see illustration).

3 Cap or plug all openings (line, hose and pump) to prevent leakage or contamination.

4 Remove the pump mounting fasteners and remove the pump (see illustration).

5 Installation is the reverse of removal. Install a new O-ring on the end of the pressure line. On models with a separate power steering belt, be sure that the drivebelt tension is correct (see Chapter 1), check the power steering fluid level and add some, if necessary (see Chapter 1), then bleed the power steering system (see Section 20).

**19.2  Power steering pump details**

1   Mounting bolt (one of two)        3   Pressure line fitting bolts
2   Feed hose and clamp

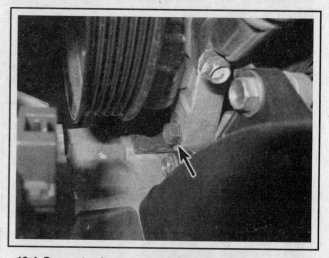

**19.4  Power steering pump lower mounting bolt**

## 20 Power steering system - bleeding

1   Following any operation in which the power steering fluid lines have been disconnected, the power steering system must be bled to remove all air and obtain proper steering performance.

2   With the front wheels in the straight ahead position, check the power steering fluid level and, if low, add fluid until it reaches the MIN mark on the reservoir.

3   Start the engine and allow it to run at fast idle. Recheck the fluid level and add more if necessary to reach the MIN mark on the reservoir.

4   Bleed the system by turning the wheels from side to side, without hitting the stops. This will work the air out of the system. Keep the res-ervoir full of fluid as this is done.

5   When the air is worked out of the system, return the wheels to the straight ahead position and leave the vehicle running for several more minutes before shutting it off.

6   Road test the vehicle to be sure the steering system is function-ing normally and noise free.

7   Recheck the fluid level to be sure it is up to the MAX mark on the reservoir while the engine is at normal operating temperature. Add fluid if necessary (see Chapter 1).

## 21 Wheels and tires - general information

▶ **Refer to illustration 21.1**

1   All vehicles covered by this manual are equipped with metric-sized steel belted radial tires (see illustration). Use of other size or type of tires may affect the ride and handling of the vehicle. Don't mix different types of tires, such as radials and bias belted, on the same vehicle as handling may be seriously affected. It's recommended that tires be replaced in pairs on the same axle, but if only one tire is being replaced, be sure it's the same size, structure and tread design as the other.

2   Because tire pressure has a substantial effect on handling and wear, the pressure on all tires should be checked at least once a month or before any extended trips (see Chapter 1).

3   Wheels must be replaced if they are bent, dented, leak air, have elongated bolt holes, are heavily rusted, out of vertical symmetry or if the lug nuts won't stay tight. Wheel repairs that use welding or peening are not recommended.

4   Tire and wheel balance is important in the overall handling, brak-ing and performance of the vehicle. Unbalanced wheels can adversely affect handling and ride characteristics as well as tire life. Whenever a tire is installed on a wheel, the tire and wheel should be balanced by a shop with the proper equipment.

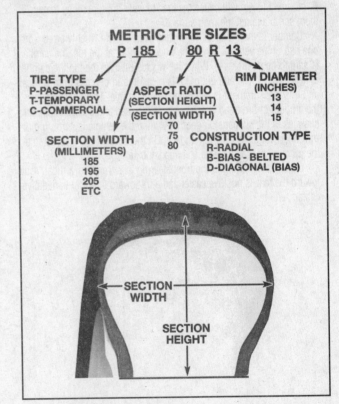

**21.1  Metric tire size codes**

## 22 Wheel alignment - general information

▶ **Refer to illustration 22.1**

A wheel alignment refers to the adjustments made to the wheels so they are in proper angular relationship to the suspension and the ground. Wheels that are out of proper alignment not only affect vehicle control, but also increase tire wear. The front end angles normally measured are camber, caster and toe-in (see illustration). Toe-in and camber are adjustable in the front. If the caster is not correct, check for bent components. Toe-in is adjustable in the rear.

Getting the proper wheel alignment is a very exacting process, one in which complcated and expensive machines are necessary to perform the job properly. Because of this, you should have a technician with the proper equipment perform these tasks. We will, however, use this space to give you a basic idea of what is involved with a wheel alignment so you can better understand the process and deal intelligently with the shop that does the work.

Toe-in is the turning in of the wheels. The purpose of a toe specification is to ensure parallel rolling of the wheels. In a vehicle with zero toe-in, the distance between the front edges of the wheels will be the same as the distance between the rear edges of the wheels. The actual amount of toe-in is normally only a fraction of an inch. At the front, toe-in is controlled by the tie-rod end position on the tie-rod. At the rear it is adjusted by turning the cam bolt at the inner end of lower arm B. Incorrect toe-in will cause the tires to wear improperly by making them scrub against the road surface.

Camber is the tilting of the wheels from vertical when viewed from one end of the vehicle. When the wheels tilt out at the top, the camber is said to be positive (+). When the wheels tilt in at the top the camber is negative (-). The amount of tilt is measured in degrees from vertical and this measurement is called the camber angle. This angle affects the amount of tire tread which contacts the road and compensates for changes in the suspension geometry when the vehicle is cornering or traveling over an undulating surface. On the front end it is adjusted at the juncture of the strut and steering knuckle.

Caster is the tilting of the front steering axis from the vertical. A tilt toward the rear is positive caster and a tilt toward the front is negative caster.

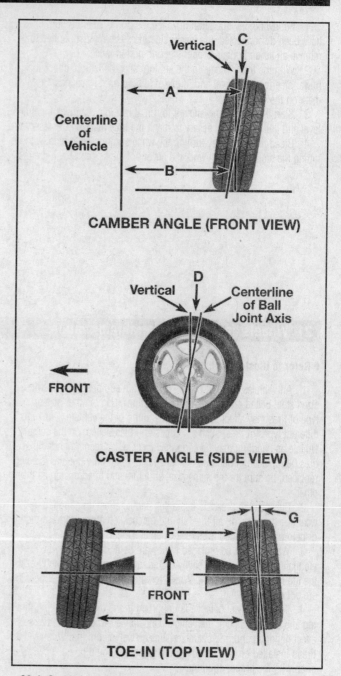

**CAMBER ANGLE (FRONT VIEW)**

**CASTER ANGLE (SIDE VIEW)**

**TOE-IN (TOP VIEW)**

22.1 Camber, caster and toe-in angles

*A minus B = C (degrees camber)*
*D = degrees caster*
*E minus F = toe-in (measured in inches)*
*G = toe-in (expressed in degrees)*

## Specifications

| Torque specifications | Ft-lbs (unless otherwise indicated) | Nm |
|---|---|---|
| **Front suspension** | | |
| Control arm | | |
| Arm-to-subframe bolts | | |
| All except 2007 Acura | 69 | 93 |
| 2007 Acura | | |
| Front pivot bolt | 119 | 162 |
| Rear bushing-to-subframe bolts | 69 | 93 |
| Rear bushing-to-control arm nut | 119 | 162 |
| Balljoint-to-steering knuckle nut | | |
| All except 2007 Acura | 43 to 51 | 59 to 69 |
| 2007 Acura | 76 to 83 | 103 to 113 |
| Hub and bearing-to-steering knuckle bolts | | |
| (2007 Acura only) | 72.3 | 98 |
| Strut | | |
| Strut upper mounting nuts | 43 | 59 |
| Strut-to-steering knuckle bolts/nuts | | |
| All except 2007 Acura | 116 | 157 |
| 2007 Acura | 156 | 211 |
| Stabilizer bar | | |
| Stabilizer bar link nuts | 58 | 78 |
| Stabilizer bar retainer bolts | 29 | 39 |
| Driveaxle/hub nut | See Chapter 8 | |
| **Rear suspension** | | |
| Hub and bearing-to-rear knuckle bolts | | |
| (2007 Acura only) | 72.3 | 98 |
| Lower arm B-to-subframe mounting bolt/nut | | |
| All except 2007 Acura | 61 | 83 |
| 2007 Acura | 97.5 | 132 |
| Lower arm B-to-knuckle bolt | | |
| All except 2007 Acura | 54 | 74 |
| 2007 Acura | 83 | 113 |
| Lower arm A-to-subframe mounting bolt | | |
| All except 2007 Acura | 105 | 142 |
| 2007 Acura | 69 | 93 |
| Lower arm A-to-knuckle mounting nut | | |
| All except 2007 Acura | 47 | 64 |
| 2007 Acura | 90 | 123 |
| Rear hub nut (2WD models) | 181 | 245 |
| Shock absorber mounting nuts | 47 | 64 |

**Torque specifications (continued)**  Ft-lbs (unless otherwise indicated)    Nm

| | Ft-lbs | Nm |
|---|---|---|
| Stabilizer bar link nuts | | |
|   Honda | | |
|     2003 and 2004 models | | |
|       (upper and lower) | 29 | 39 |
|     2005 and later models | | |
|       Upper | 29 | 39 |
|       Lower | 36 | 49 |
|   Acura | | |
|     2001 through 2006 (upper and lower) | 29 | 39 |
|     2007 | | |
|       Upper | 27 | 37 |
|       Lower | 36 | 49 |
| Stabilizer bar retainer bolts | 16 | 22 |
| Trailing arm-to-chassis mounting bolts | 76 | 103 |
| Trailing arm-to-knuckle mounting bolts | 47 | 64 |
| Upper control arm-to-subframe bolt | | |
|   Honda | | |
|     2003 and 2004 models | 47 | 64 |
|     2005 and later models | 69 | 93 |
|   Acura | | |
|     2001 through 2006 models | 47 | 64 |
|     2007 models | 69 | 93 |
| Upper control arm balljoint-to-knuckle nut | | |
|   All except 2007 Acura | 36 to 43 | 49 to 59 |
|   2007 Acura | 43 to 51 | 59 to 69 |

## Steering

| | Ft-lbs | Nm |
|---|---|---|
| Airbag module-to-steering wheel bolts | 86 in-lbs | 9.8 |
| Power steering pump mounting nut/bolt | 17 | 24 |
| Steering gear mounting bolts/nuts | | |
|   Left side | | |
|     All except 2007 Acura | 43 | 58 |
|     2007 Acura | 37 | 50 |
|   Right side | 29 | 39 |
| Steering gear stiffener bracket bolts | 28 | 38 |
| Tie-rod end-to-steering knuckle nut | 40 | 54 |
| Intermediate shaft pinch-bolt | | |
|   All except 2007 Acura | 16 | 22 |
|   2007 Acura | 21 | 28 |
| Steering column mounting nuts | 144 in-lbs | 16 |
| Steering wheel mounting bolt/nut | | |
|   All except 2007 Acura | 36 | 49 |
|   2007 Acura | 29 | 39 |

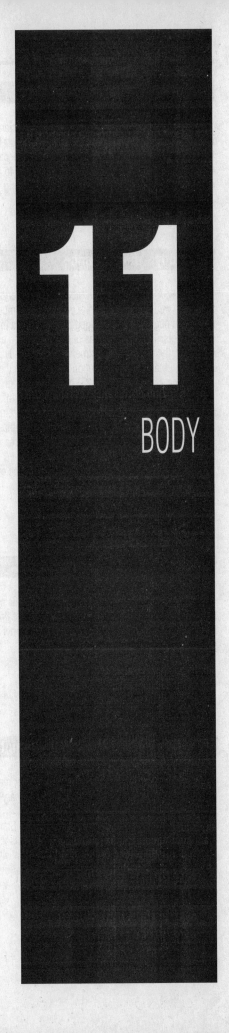

11

BODY

**Section**

## 1 General information

These models feature a "unibody" construction, using a floor pan with front and rear frame side rails which support the body components, front and rear suspension systems and other mechanical components. Certain components are particularly vulnerable to accident damage and can be unbolted and repaired or replaced. Among these parts are the body moldings, front fenders, bumpers, hood, doors, trunk lid and all glass.

Only general body maintenance practices and body panel repair procedures within the scope of the do-it-yourselfer are included in this Chapter.

## 2 Body - maintenance

1   The condition of your vehicle's body is very important, because the resale value depends a great deal on it. It's much more difficult to repair a neglected or damaged body than it is to repair mechanical components. The hidden areas of the body, such as the wheel wells, the frame and the engine compartment, are equally important, although they don't require as frequent attention as the rest of the body.

2   Once a year, or every 12,000 miles, it's a good idea to have the underside of the body steam cleaned. All traces of dirt and oil will be removed and the area can then be inspected carefully for rust, damaged brake lines, frayed electrical wires, damaged cables and other problems. The front suspension components should be greased after completion of this job.

3   At the same time, clean the engine and the engine compartment with a steam cleaner or water soluble degreaser.

4   The wheel wells should be given close attention, since undercoating can peel away and stones and dirt thrown up by the tires can cause the paint to chip and flake, allowing rust to set in. If rust is found, clean down to the bare metal and apply an anti-rust paint.

5   The body should be washed about once a week. Wet the vehicle thoroughly to soften the dirt, then wash it down with a soft sponge and plenty of clean soapy water. If the surplus dirt is not washed off very carefully, it can wear down the paint.

6   Spots of tar or asphalt thrown up from the road should be removed with a cloth soaked in solvent.

7   Once every six months, wax the body and chrome trim. If a chrome cleaner is used to remove rust from any of the vehicle's plated parts, remember that the cleaner also removes part of the chrome, so use it sparingly.

## 3 Vinyl trim - maintenance

Don't clean vinyl trim with detergents, caustic soap or petroleum-based cleaners. Plain soap and water works just fine, with a soft brush to clean dirt that may be ingrained. Wash the vinyl as frequently as the rest of the vehicle.

After cleaning, application of a high quality rubber and vinyl protectant will help prevent oxidation and cracks. The protectant can also be applied to weatherstripping, vacuum lines and rubber hoses (which often fail as a result of chemical degradation) and to the tires.

## 4 Upholstery and carpets - maintenance

1   Every three months remove the carpets or mats and clean the interior of the vehicle (more frequently if necessary). Vacuum the upholstery and carpets to remove loose dirt and dust.

2   Leather upholstery requires special care. Stains should be removed with warm water and a very mild soap solution. Use a clean, damp cloth to remove the soap, then wipe again with a dry cloth. Never use alcohol, gasoline, nail polish remover or thinner to clean leather upholstery.

3   After cleaning, regularly treat leather upholstery with a leather wax. Never use car wax on leather upholstery.

4   In areas where the interior of the vehicle is subject to bright sunlight, cover leather seats with a sheet if the vehicle is to be left out for any length of time.

## 5 Body repair - minor damage

♦ **See photo sequence**

### REPAIR OF MINOR SCRATCHES

1  If the scratch is superficial and does not penetrate to the metal of the body, repair is very simple. Lightly rub the scratched area with a fine rubbing compound to remove loose paint and built-up wax. Rinse the area with clean water.

2  Apply touch-up paint to the scratch, using a small brush. Continue to apply thin layers of paint until the surface of the paint in the scratch is level with the surrounding paint. Allow the new paint at least two weeks to harden, then blend it into the surrounding paint by rubbing with a very fine rubbing compound. Finally, apply a coat of wax to the scratch area.

3  If the scratch has penetrated the paint and exposed the metal of the body, causing the metal to rust, a different repair technique is required. Remove all loose rust from the bottom of the scratch with a pocket knife, then apply rust inhibiting paint to prevent the formation of rust in the future. Using a rubber or nylon applicator, coat the scratched area with glaze-type filler. If required, the filler can be mixed with thinner to provide a very thin paste, which is ideal for filling narrow scratches. Before the glaze filler in the scratch hardens, wrap a piece of smooth cotton cloth around the tip of a finger. Dip the cloth in thinner and then quickly wipe it along the surface of the scratch. This will ensure that the surface of the filler is slightly hollow. The scratch can now be painted over as described earlier in this Section.

### REPAIR OF DENTS

4  When repairing dents, the first job is to pull the dent out until the affected area is as close as possible to its original shape. There is no point in trying to restore the original shape completely as the metal in the damaged area will have stretched on impact and cannot be restored to its original contours. It is better to bring the level of the dent up to a point which is about 1/8-inch below the level of the surrounding metal. In cases where the dent is very shallow, it is not worth trying to pull it out at all.

5  If the back side of the dent is accessible, it can be hammered out gently from behind using a soft-face hammer. While doing this, hold a block of wood firmly against the opposite side of the metal to absorb the hammer blows and prevent the metal from being stretched.

6  If the dent is in a section of the body which has double layers, or some other factor makes it inaccessible from behind, a different technique is required. Drill several small holes through the metal inside the damaged area, particularly in the deeper sections. Screw long, self-tapping screws into the holes just enough for them to get a good grip in the metal. Now the dent can be pulled out by pulling on the protruding heads of the screws with locking pliers.

7  The next stage of repair is the removal of paint from the damaged area and from an inch or so of the surrounding metal. This is done with a wire brush or sanding disk in a drill motor, although it can be done just as effectively by hand with sandpaper. To complete the preparation for filling, score the surface of the bare metal with a screwdriver or the tang of a file, or drill small holes in the affected area. This will provide a good grip for the filler material. To complete the repair, see the subsection on filling and painting later in this Section.

### REPAIR OF RUST HOLES OR GASHES

8  Remove all paint from the affected area and from an inch or so of the surrounding metal using a sanding disk or wire brush mounted in a drill motor. If these are not available, a few sheets of sandpaper will do the job just as effectively.

9  With the paint removed, you will be able to determine the severity of the corrosion and decide whether to replace the whole panel, if possible, or repair the affected area. New body panels are not as expensive as most people think and it is often quicker to install a new panel than to repair large areas of rust.

10  Remove all trim pieces from the affected area except those which will act as a guide to the original shape of the damaged body, such as headlight shells, etc. Using metal snips or a hacksaw blade, remove all loose metal and any other metal that is badly affected by rust. Hammer the edges of the hole in to create a slight depression for the filler material.

11  Wire brush the affected area to remove the powdery rust from the surface of the metal. If the back of the rusted area is accessible, treat it with rust inhibiting paint.

12  Before filling is done, block the hole in some way. This can be done with sheet metal riveted or screwed into place, or by stuffing the hole with wire mesh.

13  Once the hole is blocked off, the affected area can be filled and painted. See the following subsection on filling and painting.

### FILLING AND PAINTING

14  Many types of body fillers are available, but generally speaking, body repair kits which contain filler paste and a tube of resin hardener are best for this type of repair work. A wide, flexible plastic or nylon applicator will be necessary for imparting a smooth and contoured finish to the surface of the filler material. Mix up a small amount of filler on a clean piece of wood or cardboard (use the hardener sparingly). Follow the manufacturer's instructions on the package, otherwise the filler will set incorrectly.

15  Using the applicator, apply the filler paste to the prepared area. Draw the applicator across the surface of the filler to achieve the desired contour and to level the filler surface. As soon as a contour that approximates the original one is achieved, stop working the paste. If you continue, the paste will begin to stick to the applicator. Continue to add thin layers of paste at 20-minute intervals until the level of the filler is just above the surrounding metal.

16  Once the filler has hardened, the excess can be removed with a body file. From then on, progressively finer grades of sandpaper should be used, starting with a 180-grit paper and finishing with a 600-grit wet-or-dry paper. Always wrap the sandpaper around a flat rubber or wooden block, otherwise the surface of the filler will not be completely flat. During the sanding of the filler surface, the wet-or-dry paper should be periodically rinsed in water. This will ensure that a very smooth finish is produced in the final stage.

17  At this point, the repair area should be surrounded by a ring of bare metal, which in turn should be encircled by the finely feathered edge of good paint. Rinse the repair area with clean water until all of the dust produced by the sanding operation is gone.

18  Spray the entire area with a light coat of primer. This will reveal any imperfections in the surface of the filler. Repair the imperfections

These photos illustrate a method of repairing simple dents. They are intended to supplement Body repair - minor damage in this Chapter and should not be used as the sole instructions for body repair on these vehicles.

1  If you can't access the backside of the body panel to hammer out the dent, pull it out with a slide-hammer-type dent puller. In the deepest portion of the dent or along the crease line, drill or punch hole(s) at least one inch apart . . .

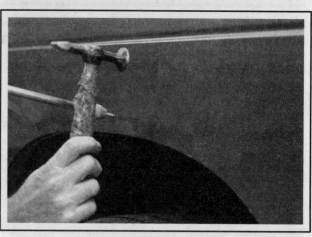

2  . . . then screw the slide-hammer into the hole and operate it. Tap with a hammer near the edge of the dent to help 'pop' the metal back to its original shape. When you're finished, the dent area should be close to its original contour and about 1/8-inch below the surface of the surrounding metal

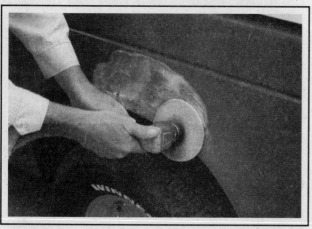

3  Using coarse-grit sandpaper, remove the paint down to the bare metal. Hand sanding works fine, but the disc sander shown here makes the job faster. Use finer (about 320-grit) sandpaper to feather-edge the paint at least one inch around the dent area

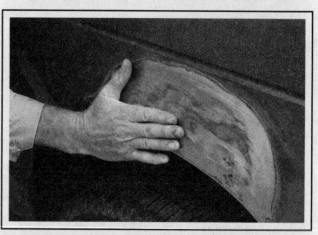

4  When the paint is removed, touch will probably be more helpful than sight for telling if the metal is straight. Hammer down the high spots or raise the low spots as necessary. Clean the repair area with wax/silicone remover

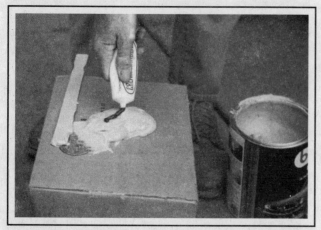

5  Following label instructions, mix up a batch of plastic filler and hardener. The ratio of filler to hardener is critical, and, if you mix it incorrectly, it will either not cure properly or cure too quickly (you won't have time to file and sand it into shape)

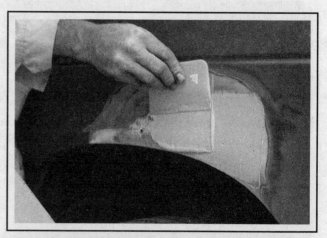

6  Working quickly so the filler doesn't harden, use a plastic applicator to press the body filler firmly into the metal, assuring it bonds completely. Work the filler until it matches the original contour and is slightly above the surrounding metal

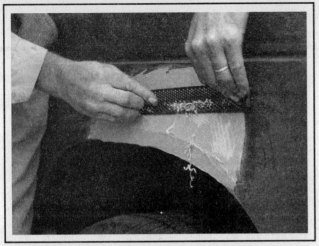

7  Let the filler harden until you can just dent it with your fingernail. Use a body file or Surform tool (shown here) to rough-shape the filler

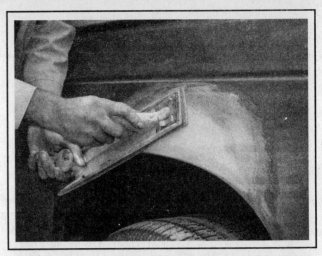

8  Use coarse-grit sandpaper and a sanding board or block to work the filler down until it's smooth and even. Work down to finer grits of sandpaper - always using a board or block - ending up with 360 or 400 grit

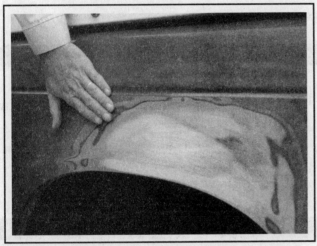

9  You shouldn't be able to feel any ridge at the transition from the filler to the bare metal or from the bare metal to the old paint. As soon as the repair is flat and uniform, remove the dust and mask off the adjacent panels or trim pieces

10  Apply several layers of primer to the area. Don't spray the primer on too heavy, so it sags or runs, and make sure each coat is dry before you spray on the next one. A professional-type spray gun is being used here, but aerosol spray primer is available inexpensively from auto parts stores

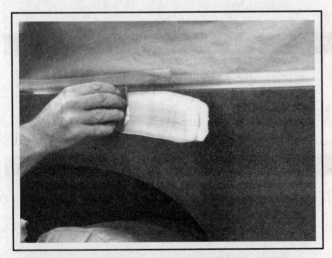

11  The primer will help reveal imperfections or scratches. Fill these with glazing compound. Follow the label instructions and sand it with 360 or 400-grit sandpaper until it's smooth. Repeat the glazing, sanding and respraying until the primer reveals a perfectly smooth surface

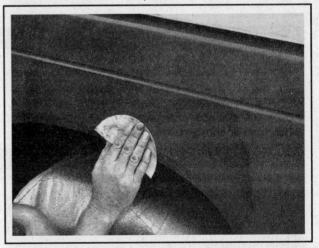

12  Finish sand the primer with very fine sandpaper (400 or 600-grit) to remove the primer overspray. Clean the area with water and allow it to dry. Use a tack rag to remove any dust, then apply the finish coat. Don't attempt to rub out or wax the repair area until the paint has dried completely (at least two weeks)

with fresh filler paste or glaze filler and once more smooth the surface with sandpaper. Repeat this spray-and-repair procedure until you are satisfied that the surface of the filler and the feathered edge of the paint are perfect. Rinse the area with clean water and allow it to dry completely.

19 The repair area is now ready for painting. Spray painting must be carried out in a warm, dry, windless and dust free atmosphere. These conditions can be created if you have access to a large indoor work area, but if you are forced to work in the open, you will have to pick the day very carefully. If you are working indoors, dousing the floor in the work area with water will help settle the dust which would otherwise be in the air. If the repair area is confined to one body panel, mask off the surrounding panels. This will help minimize the effects of a slight mismatch in paint color. Trim pieces such as chrome strips, door handles, etc., will also need to be masked off or removed. Use masking tape and several thickness of newspaper for the masking operations.

20 Before spraying, shake the paint can thoroughly, then spray a test area until the spray painting technique is mastered. Cover the repair area with a thick coat of primer. The thickness should be built up using several thin layers of primer rather than one thick one. Using 600-grit wet-or-dry sandpaper, rub down the surface of the primer until it is very smooth. While doing this, the work area should be thoroughly rinsed with water and the wet-or-dry sandpaper periodically rinsed as well. Allow the primer to dry before spraying additional coats.

21 Spray on the top coat, again building up the thickness by using several thin layers of paint. Begin spraying in the center of the repair area and then, using a circular motion, work out until the whole repair area and about two inches of the surrounding original paint is covered. Remove all masking material 10 to 15 minutes after spraying on the final coat of paint. Allow the new paint at least two weeks to harden, then use a very fine rubbing compound to blend the edges of the new paint into the existing paint. Finally, apply a coat of wax.

## 6 Body repair - major damage

1 Major damage must be repaired by an auto body shop specifically equipped to perform these repairs. Most shops have the specialized equipment required to do the job properly.

2 If the damage is extensive, the body must be checked for proper alignment or the vehicle's handling characteristics may be adversely affected and other components may wear at an accelerated rate.

3 Due to the fact that all of the major body components (hood, fenders, etc.) are separate and replaceable units, any seriously damaged components should be replaced rather than repaired. Sometimes the components can be found in a wrecking yard that specializes in used vehicle components, often at considerable savings over the cost of new parts.

## 7 Hinges and locks - maintenance

Once every 3000 miles, or every three months, the hinges and latch assemblies on the doors, hood and trunk should be given a few drops of light oil or lock lubricant. The door latch strikers should also be lubricated with a thin coat of grease to reduce wear and ensure free movement. Lubricate the door and trunk locks with spray-on graphite lubricant.

## 8 Windshield and fixed glass - replacement

Replacement of the windshield and fixed glass requires the use of special fast-setting adhesive/caulk materials and some specialized tools. It is recommended that these operations be left to a dealer or a shop specializing in glass work.

## 9 Hood - removal, installation and adjustment

➡️**Note: The hood is heavy and somewhat awkward to remove and install - at least two people should perform this procedure.**

### REMOVAL AND INSTALLATION

▶ **Refer to illustrations 9.2 and 9.4**

1 Use blankets or pads to cover the cowl area of the body and fenders. This will protect the body and paint as the hood is lifted off.

2 Make marks or scribe a line around the hood hinge to ensure proper alignment during installation (see illustration).

3 Disconnect the windshield washer hose and any cables or wires that will interfere with removal.

4 Have an assistant support one side of the hood while you support the other. Simultaneously remove the hinge-to-hood bolts (see illustration).

5 Lift off the hood.

6 Installation is the reverse of removal.

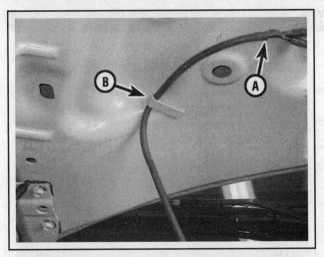

**9.2  Before removing the hood, draw a mark around the hinge plate. Also detach the windshield washer hose from the fitting (A) and the clip (B)**

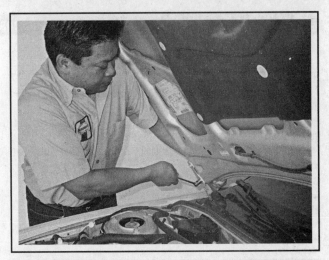

**9.4  Support the hood with your shoulder while removing the hood bolts**

## ADJUSTMENT

▶ **Refer to illustrations 9.10 and 9.11**

7    Fore-and-aft and side-to-side adjustment of the hood is done by moving the hinge plate slot after loosening the bolts or nuts.

8    Mark around the each hinge plate so you can determine the amount of movement (see illustration 9.2).

9    Loosen the bolts or nuts and move the hood into correct alignment. Move it only a little at a time. Tighten the hinge bolts and carefully lower the hood to check the position.

10   If necessary after installation, the hood latch can be adjusted up-and-down as well as from side-to-side on the radiator support so the hood closes securely and flush with the fenders. To make the adjustment, scribe a line or mark around the hood latch mounting bolts to provide a reference point, then loosen them and reposition the latch, as necessary (see illustration). Following adjustment, retighten the mounting bolts.

11   Finally, adjust the hood bumpers on the radiator support so the hood, when closed, is flush with the fenders (see illustration).

12   The hood latch assembly, as well as the hinges, should be periodically lubricated with white, lithium-base grease to prevent binding and wear.

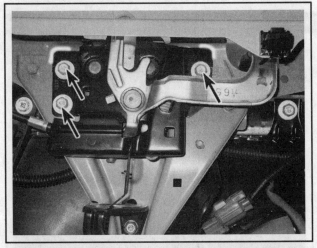

**9.10  Make a mark around the latch to use as a reference point. To adjust the hood latch, loosen the retaining bolts, move the latch and retighten bolts, then close the hood to check the fit**

**9.11  Adjust the hood closing height by turning the hood bumpers in or out**

## 10 Hood latch and release cable - removal and installation

### LATCH

1   Scribe a line around the latch to aid alignment when reinstalling the latch assembly.

2   Remove the latch retaining bolts securing the latch to the radiator support (see illustration 9.10) and remove the latch.

3   Disconnect the hood release cable by disengaging the cable from the back of the latch assembly.

4   Installation is the reverse of the removal procedure.

➥Note: Adjust the latch so the hood engages securely when closed and the hood bumpers are slightly compressed.

### CABLE

▶ Refer to illustration 10.9

5   Remove the hood latch as described earlier in this Section, then detach the cable from the latch.

6   Remove the left-side inner fender splash shield (see illustration 13.2).

7   Attach a length of wire to the end of the cable (in the engine compartment). This will be used to pull the new cable back into the engine compartment.

8   Working in the engine compartment, detach the cable from all of its retaining clips. It may be necessary to cut some of the clips to free the cable.

9   Working under the instrument panel, remove the left-side kick panel (see illustration).

10.9  Remove the fastener, then detach the kick panel

10  Remove the screws and detach the hood release handle. Dislodge the grommet and pull the cable through the firewall and into the cab.

11  Detach the wire from the old cable, then attach it to the end of the new cable.

➥Note: Make sure the new cable is equipped with a grommet.

12  Pull the new cable through the firewall and into the engine compartment. Seat the grommet in the firewall.

13  The remainder of installation is the reverse of removal.

## 11 Radiator grille - removal and installation

▶ Refer to illustration 11.2

1   Remove the bumper cover (see Section 12).

2   Remove the fasteners securing the grille to the bumper cover (see illustration).

3   Installation is the reverse of removal.

11.2  Radiator grille mounting fasteners

## 12  Bumper covers - removal and installation

1   Bumpers on all models are composed of a plastic fascia, or bumper cover, fascia support and a structural beam.

### FRONT BUMPER COVER

▶ **Refer to illustrations 12.3, 12.4 and 12.5**

2   Raise the vehicle and support it securely on jackstands.
3   Working in the front wheelwell, remove the fastener securing the end of the bumper to the fender (see illustration).
4   Remove the upper radiator cover (see illustration).
5   Remove the bumper cover lower mounting fasteners and remove the bumper cover (see illustration).
6   Disconnect the fog lamps, if equipped, then carefully remove the bumper cover from the vehicle.
7   Installation is the reverse of removal.

### REAR BUMPER COVER

▶ **Refer to illustrations 12.9 and 12.10**

8   Raise the vehicle and support it securely on jackstands.

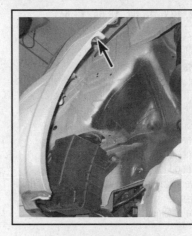

**12.3  Remove the fastener securing the end of the bumper cover to the fender**

9   Working in the rear wheelwell, remove the fasteners securing the bumper cover to the rear quarter panel and inner fender splash shield (see illustration).
10  Remove the remaining bumper cover mounting fasteners and remove the bumper cover (see illustration).
11  Installation is the reverse of removal.

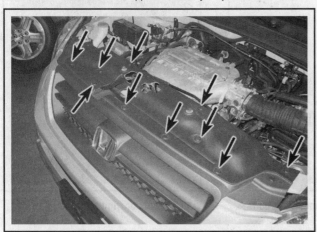

**12.4  Remove the fasteners securing the radiator cover**

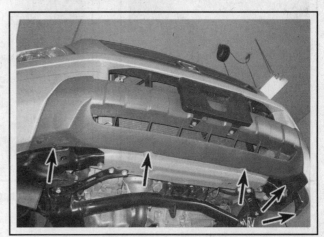

**12.5  Remove the bumper cover lower mounting fasteners**

**12.9  Remove the fasteners securing the bumper cover to the rear quarter panel and inner fender splash shield**

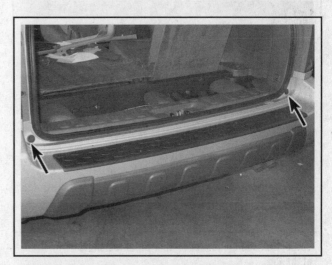

**12.10  Bumper cover upper mounting fasteners**

## 13 Front fender - removal and installation

▸ **Refer to illustrations 13.2, 13.5, 13.6a, 13.6b, 13.6c and 13.6d**

1    Loosen the wheel lug nuts, then raise the vehicle and support it securely on jackstands. Remove the front wheel.

2    Remove the fasteners retaining the fender inner splash shield (see illustration).

3    Remove the front bumper cover (see Section 12).

4    Remove the headlight housing (see Chapter 12).

5    Remove the A-pillar corner trim (see illustration).

6    Remove the fender mounting bolts (see illustrations).

7    Detach the fender. It's a good idea to have an assistant support the fender while it's being moved away from the vehicle to prevent damage to the surrounding body panels.

8    Installation is the reverse of removal.

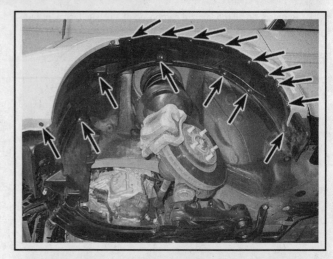

**13.2  Remove the fender inner splash shield mounting fasteners**

**13.5  Remove the fastener securing the A-pillar corner trim, then remove the trim piece**

**13.6a  Fender upper mounting bolts**

**13.6b  Fender front mounting bolt**

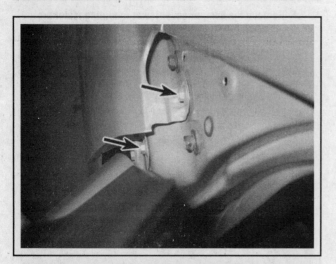

**13.6c  Remove the fender-to-door pillar fasteners at the top . . .**

**13.6d  . . . and at the bottom**

## 14  Door trim panels - removal and installation

**Refer to illustrations 14.1a, 14.1b, 14.3, 14.4, 14.5, 14.6 and 14.8**

1   Remove the inside door handle trim cover. Remove the mounting screw, then disconnect the electrical connector and detach the handle rod (see illustrations).

2   If you're working on a 1996 or earlier Acura model, use a trim stick and carefully pry off the door speaker cover, then remove the three screws securing the door panel.

3   Carefully pry off and remove the power window control switch (see illustration).

4   Remove the mirror fastener trim cover (see illustration).

5   Remove the remaining door trim panel retaining fastener (see illustration).

6   Remove the door trim panel using a door panel removal tool (see illustration). Start from the bottom of the trim panel and work around the perimeter until all the fasteners have been released from the door.

### ❋❋ CAUTION:

**To avoid damaging the trim panel or the fasteners, pry only at the fastener locations. The fastener locations can be detected by sliding the tool between the door and the door panel.**

7   Lift the trim panel up to disengage the panel from the door ridge, unplug any electrical connectors, and remove the panel.

8   For access to the inner door, carefully peel back the plastic watershield (see illustration).

9   Installation is the reverse of removal.

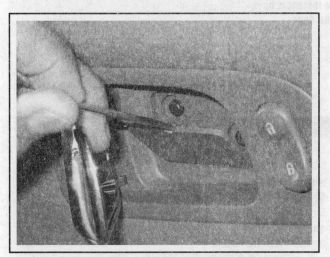

**14.1a  Pry back the cover and remove the handle retaining screw . . .**

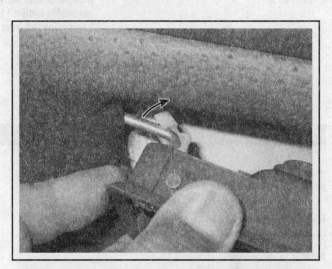

**14.1b  . . . then unclip the retainer and detach the handle rod**

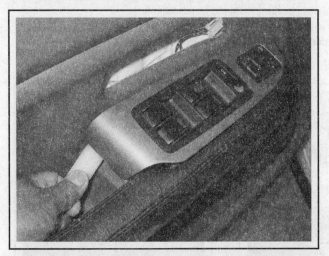

**14.3  Using a trim stick, carefully pry up the power window control switch to release the clips**

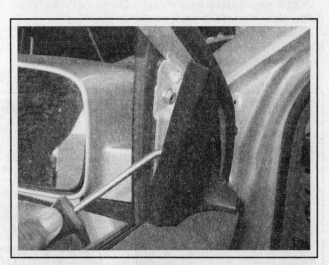

**14.4  Pry off the mirror fastener trim cover**

**14.5 Door trim panel retaining fastener**

**14.6 Start from the bottom of the trim panel and work around the perimeter until all the fasteners have been released from the door**

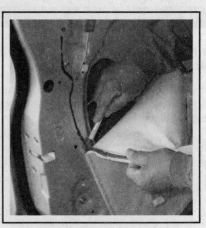

**14.8 From the corner, carefully peel back the plastic watershield**

## 15 Door - removal, installation and adjustment

➡ Note: The door is heavy and somewhat awkward to remove and install - at least two people should perform this procedure.

### REMOVAL AND INSTALLATION

▸ **Refer to illustrations 15.6 and 15.8**

1  Raise the window completely in the door, then disconnect the cable from the negative battery terminal (see Chapter 5, Section 1).
2  Open the door all the way and support it from the ground on jacks or blocks covered with rags to prevent damaging the paint.
3  Remove the door trim panel and watershield as described in Section 14.
4  Disconnect all electrical connections, ground wires and harness retaining clips from the door.

➡ Note: It is a good idea to label all connections to aid the reassembly process.

5  From the door side, detach the rubber conduit between the body and the door. Then pull the wiring harness through the conduit hole and remove it from the door.
6  Remove the door stop strut bolt (see illustration).
7  Mark around the door hinges with a pen or a scribe to facilitate realignment during reassembly.
8  With an assistant holding the door, remove the hinge-to-door bolts (see illustration) and lift the door off.

➡ Note: Draw a reference line around the hinges before removing the bolts.

9  Installation is the reverse of removal.

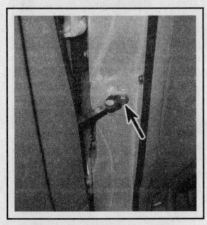

**15.6 Remove the door stop strut mounting bolt**

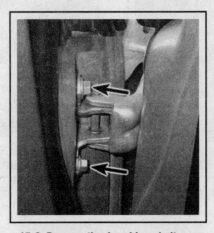

**15.8 Remove the door hinge bolts**

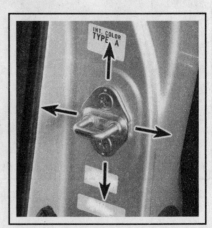

**15.13 The latch striker on the door jamb can be adjusted slightly up/ down or in/out**

## ADJUSTMENT

▶ **Refer to illustration 15.13**

10  Having proper door-to-body alignment is a critical part of a well-functioning door assembly. First check the door hinge pins for excessive play. Fully open the door and lift up and down on the door without lifting the body. If a door has 1/16-inch or more excessive play, the hinges should be replaced.

11  Door-to-body alignment adjustments are made by loosening the hinge-to-body bolts or hinge-to-door bolts and moving the door. Proper body alignment is achieved when the top of the doors are parallel with the roof section, the front door is flush with the fender, the rear door is flush with the rear quarter panel and the bottom of the doors are aligned with the lower rocker panel. If these goals can't be reached by adjusting the hinge-to-body or hinge-to-door bolts, body alignment shims may have to be purchased and inserted behind the hinges to achieve correct alignment.

12  To adjust the door-closed position, scribe a line or mark around the striker plate to provide a reference point, then check that the door latch is contacting the center of the latch striker. If not, adjust the up and down position first.

13  Finally adjust the latch striker sideways position, so that the door panel is flush with the center pillar or rear quarter panel and provides positive engagement with the latch mechanism (see illustration).

---

## 16  Door latch, lock cylinder and handle - removal and installation

### ❇❇ WARNING:

**The sheetmetal edges of the openings in the door (as well as certain components within the door) are sharp. It's a good idea to wear long gloves to protect your hands and forearms.**

1  Raise the window completely and remove the door trim panel and watershield (see Section 14).

## LATCH

▶ **Refer to illustrations 16.2, 16.3, 16.4 and 16.5**

2  Remove the fastener at the center glass run channel and move the channel away from the latch (see illustration). This provides a little extra working room in the latch area inside the door.

3  Remove the lock rod protector (see illustration).

4  Rotate the plastic retaining clips off the lock and outside handle rods, then detach the latch links (see illustration).

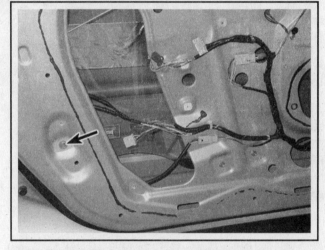

**16.2  Remove this fastener at the center glass run channel then move the channel away from the latch**

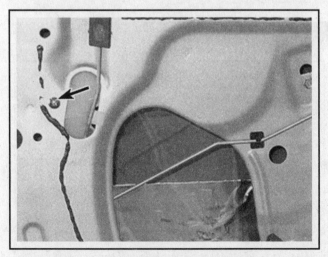

**16.3  Remove this fastener, then remove the lock rod protector**

**16.4  Rotate the plastic retaining clips off the lock (A) and outside handle rods (B)**

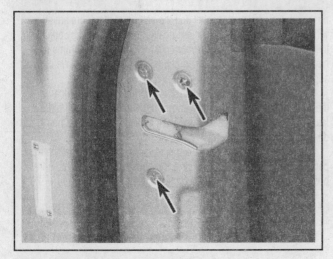

**16.5 Remove the latch mounting screws**

**16.11 Remove the lock cylinder retainer clip**

5   Disconnect the electrical connectors at the latch. Remove the three mounting screws (it may be necessary to use an impact-type screwdriver to loosen them), then remove the latch from the door (see illustration).

6   Place the latch in position and install the screws. Tighten the screws securely.

7   Connect the link rods and electrical connector to the latch.

8   The remainder of installation is the reverse of removal.

## LOCK CYLINDER

▶ **Refer to illustration 16.11**

9   Remove the fastener at the center glass run channel and move the channel away from the latch (see illustration 16.2).

10  Remove the lock rod protector (see illustration 16.3).

11  With a hook shaped tool, remove the lock cylinder retainer clip

(see illustration).

12  Remove the screw securing the lock switch to the lock cylinder.

13  Installation is the reverse of removal.

## OUTSIDE HANDLE

14  Remove the fastener at the center glass run channel and move the channel away from the latch (see illustration 16.2).

15  Remove the lock rod protector (see illustration 16.3).

16  Remove the lock cylinder (see Steps 10 thru 13).

17  Disconnect the link rods from the outside handle, remove the mounting fasteners and detach the handle from the door.

18  Place the handle in position, attach the link and install the fasteners, tightening them securely.

19  The remainder of installation is the reverse of removal.

## 17  Door window glass - removal and installation

### ❊❊ WARNING:

The sheetmetal edges of the openings in the door (as well as certain components within the door) are sharp. It's a good idea to wear long gloves to protect your hands and forearms.

## FRONT

▶ **Refer to illustrations 17.2 and 17.3**

1   Remove the door trim panel and watershield (see Section 14).

2   If you're working the driver's door, remove the power window control unit (see illustration).

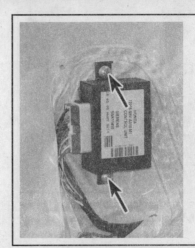

**17.2 Remove fasteners securing the power window control unit**

3  Lower the window to access the glass retaining fasteners, then remove the fasteners (see illustration).

4  Remove the window by tilting it forward, then lifting it out of the door.

5  To install, lower the glass into the door, slide it into position and install the bolts.

6  The remainder of installation is the reverse of removal.

## REAR

7  The rear doors are serviced similarly to the front doors.

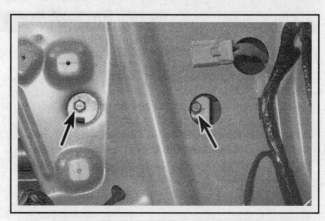

**17.3  Align the window so that the fasteners can be removed from the glass track**

## 18  Door window glass regulator - removal and installation

▶ **Refer to illustration 18.3**

### ✳✳ WARNING:

**The sheetmetal edges of the openings in the door (as well as certain components within the door) are sharp. It's a good idea to wear long gloves to protect your hands and forearms.**

1  Remove the door trim panel and watershield (see Section 14).

2  Unbolt the window glass from the regulator (see Section 17). Push the glass all the way up and tape it to the door frame.

3  Remove the window regulator-to-door and track mounting fasteners (see illustration).

4  Unplug the electrical connector from the motor.

5  Remove the regulator from the door.

6  Installation is the reverse of removal.

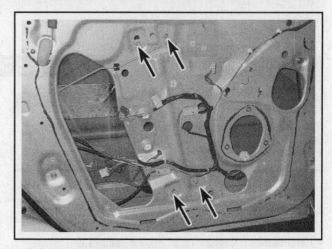

**18.3  Door window regulator mounting bolt locations**

## 19  Mirrors - removal and installation

## OUTSIDE MIRRORS

▶ **Refer to illustration 19.2**

1  Remove the mirror cover (see illustration 14.4).

2  On power mirrors, unplug the electrical connector, then remove the fasteners and detach the mirror from the door (see illustration).

3  Installation is the reverse of removal.

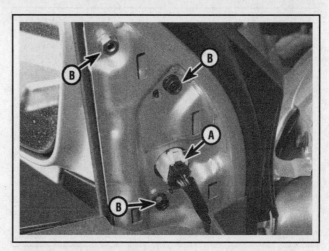

**19.2  Disconnect the electrical connector (A), then remove the mirror mounting fasteners (B)**

## 20  Liftgate - removal and installation

▶ Refer to illustration 20.5

1   Open the liftgate and cover the upper body area around the opening with pads or cloths to protect the painted surfaces when the liftgate is removed.

2   Using a trim stick, remove the liftgate trim panels (see Section 21), then disconnect the body-to-liftgate electrical connectors.

3   Paint or scribe alignment marks around the liftgate hinge flanges.

4   While an assistant supports the liftgate, detach the support struts (see Section 21).

5   Remove the hinge bolts and detach the liftgate from the vehicle (see illustration).

6   Installation is the reverse of removal.

7   After installation, close the liftgate and make sure it's in proper alignment with the surrounding body panels.

8   If the liftgate needs to be adjusted, loosen the hinge bolts slightly, gently close the liftgate and verify that it's centered (the striker should center it). Then carefully open the liftgate and retighten the hinge bolts.

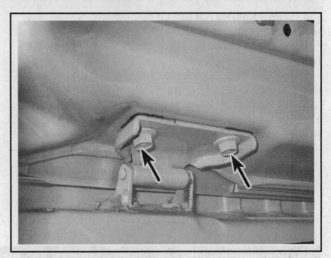

20.5  Remove the hinge bolts

## 21  Liftgate panels, outside handle, latch, lock cylinder and support struts - removal and installation

❋❋ WARNING:

The sheetmetal edges of the openings in the liftgate are sharp. It's a good idea to wear long gloves to protect your hands and forearms.

### LIFTGATE TRIM PANELS

▶ Refer to illustrations 21.1a, 21.1b, 21.2 and 21.3

1   Using a trim stick, carefully pry around the upper and side trim panels to release the clips securing them (see illustrations).

2   Remove the fasteners securing the lower trim panel inside the pull handle (see illustration).

3   Using a trim stick, carefully pry around the lower trim panel to release the clips securing the trim panel (see illustration).

4   With the lower panel pulled away from the liftgate, disconnect the electrical connectors at the courtesy lights.

5   Installation is the reverse of the removal procedure.

### OUTSIDE HANDLE

▶ Refer to illustration 21.7

6   Remove the liftgate trim panels.

7   Working through the liftgate access hole, disconnect the latch cable, then remove the handle mounting fasteners (see illustration).

8   Installation is the reverse of the removal procedure.

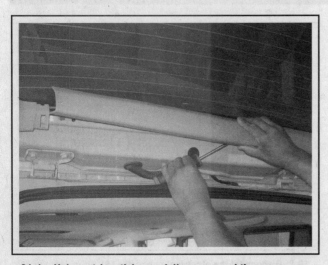

21.1a  Using a trim stick, carefully pry around the upper . . .

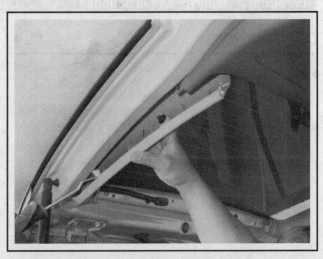

21.1b  . . . and side trim panels to release the clips securing them

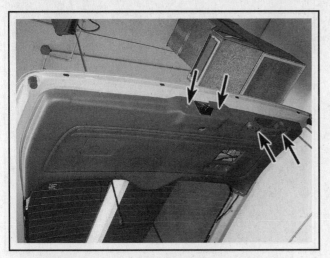

21.2 Remove the fasteners securing the lower trim panel

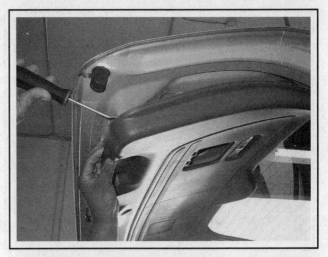

21.3 Carefully pry around the lower trim panel to release the clips securing the trim panel

## LATCH

▶ **Refer to illustrations 21.10 and 21.11**

9  Remove the liftgate trim panels.

10 Working through the liftgate access hole, disconnect the latch electrical connector and handle cable (see illustration).

11 Remove the latch mounting fasteners (see illustration).

12 Installation is the reverse of the removal procedure.

## LOCK CYLINDER

▶ **Refer to illustration 21.14**

13 Remove the liftgate trim panels.

14 Working through the liftgate access hole, disconnect the latch rod and the lock cylinder electrical connector, then remove the lock cylinder mounting fasteners (see illustration).

15 Installation is the reverse of the removal procedure.

21.7 Disconnect the latch cable (A), then remove the handle mounting fasteners (B)

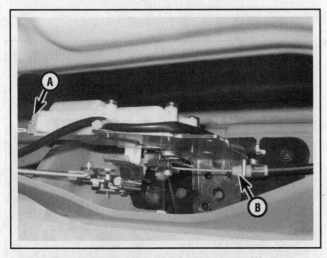

21.10 Disconnect the latch electrical connector (A) and handle cable (B)

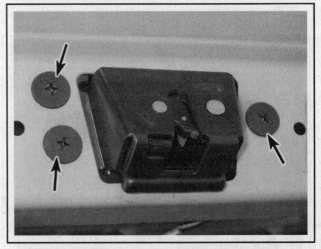

21.11 Remove the latch mounting fasteners

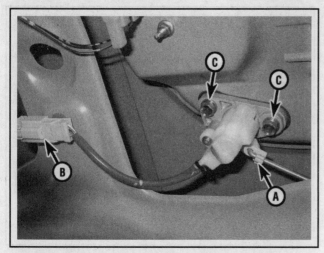

**21.14 Disconnect the latch rod (A) and the lock cylinder electrical connector (B), then remove the lock cylinder mounting fasteners (C)**

## SUPPORT STRUTS

▶ **Refer to illustration 21.17**

16 Open the liftgate and prop it securely in the full open position.

**21.17 Detach the retaining clip using a small screwdriver**

17 Using a small screwdriver, detach the retaining clip at the ends of the support struts (see illustration). Then pry or pull sharply to detach it from the vehicle.

18 Installation is the reverse of the removal procedure.

---

## 22 Cowl cover - removal and installation

▶ **Refer to illustrations 22.2 and 22.3**

1 Remove the windshield wiper arms (see Chapter 12).
2 Remove the hood seal (see illustration).

3 Detach the cowl cover clips by pulling upward on the cover (see illustration), then remove the cover.
4 Disconnect the windshield washer hose.
5 Installation is the reverse of removal.

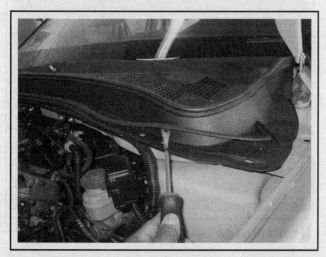

**22.2 Carefully pry off the hood seal**

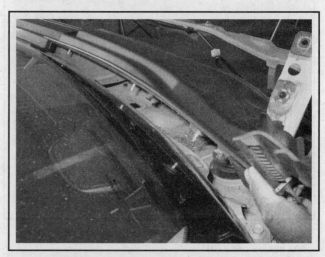

**22.3 Carefully pull upward on the cover to release the clips**

## 23 Center console - removal and installation

▶ Refer to illustrations 23.2, 23.3 and 23.4

### ❂❂ WARNING:

The models covered by this manual are equipped with Supplemental Restraint Systems (SRS), more commonly known as airbags. Always disable the airbag system before working in the vicinity of any airbag system components to avoid the possibility of accidental deployment of the airbags, which could cause personal injury (see Chapter 12).

23.2  Carefully pry off the panel on the rear of the console

1   If you're working on a Pilot model, remove the lower center trim panel (see Section 25).

2   Using a trim removal tool, carefully pry off the panel on the rear of the console (see illustration). Unplug any electrical connectors and remove the panel.

3   Remove the console side trim (see illustration).

4   Remove the center console mounting fasteners (see illustrations).

5   Unplug any electrical connectors and remove the console from the vehicle.

6   Installation is the reverse of removal.

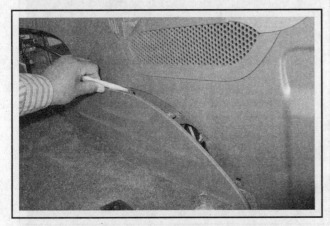

23.3  Carefully detach the center console side panels by prying outwards to release the clips

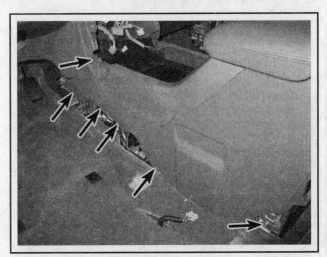

23.4  Center console mounting fasteners (left side shown, right side similar)

## 24 Steering column covers - removal and installation

▶ Refer to illustration 24.2

### ❂❂ WARNING:

The models covered by this manual are equipped with Supplemental Restraint Systems (SRS), more commonly known as airbags. Always disable the airbag system before working in the vicinity of any airbag system component to avoid the possibility of accidental deployment of the airbags, which could cause personal injury (see Chapter 12).

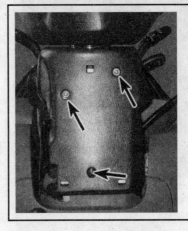

24.2  Remove the screws securing the upper cover to the lower cover

1   Remove the screws securing the upper cover to the lower cover (see illustration).

2   Remove the lower cover.

3   Tilt the column to its lowest position, then remove the top cover.

4   Installation is the reverse of the removal procedure.

## 25 Dashboard trim panels - removal and installation

### ⁕⁕ WARNING:

The models covered by this manual are equipped with Supplemental Restraint Systems (SRS), more commonly known as airbags. Always disable the airbag system before working in the vicinity of any airbag system component to avoid the possibility of accidental deployment of the airbags, which could cause personal injury (see Chapter 12).

### INSTRUMENT CLUSTER BEZEL

▶ **Refer to illustration 25.1**

1  Tilt the steering column to its lowest position. Remove the screws above the instrument cluster (see illustration).

2  Grasp the bezel securely and gently pull it out to detach the retaining clips from the instrument panel.

3  Installation is the reverse of removal.

### DRIVER'S DASHBOARD LOWER COVER

▶ **Refer to illustration 25.4**

4  Remove the fastener securing the cover (see illustration).

5  Pull out then down to remove the lower cover.

6  Installation is the reverse of removal.

### CENTER LOWER COVER

▶ **Refer to illustrations 25.7, 25.8a and 25.8b**

7  Remove the center front covers (see illustration).

8  Remove the fasteners securing the lower cover (see illustrations).

9  Grasp the lower cover securely and gently pull it out to detach the retaining clips from the instrument panel. Unplug any electrical connectors and remove the panel.

10  Installation is the reverse of removal.

**25.1  Remove the screws at the top of the instrument cluster bezel**

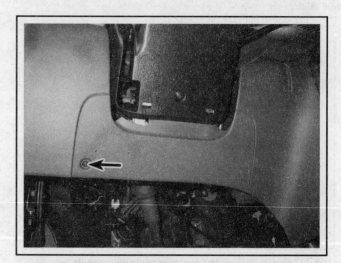

**25.4  Remove the fastener securing the cover**

**25.7  Using a trim stick, carefully pry off the center front covers**

**25.8a  Remove these four fasteners . . .**

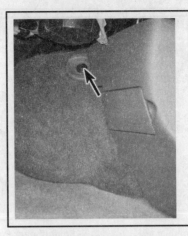

**25.11 Remove the fastener, then detach the kick panel**

**25.8b . . . and the fasteners located in the coin pocket**

## GLOVE BOX

▶ **Refer to illustrations 25.11 and 25.12**

11 Remove the right side kick panel (see illustration).
12 Open the glove box door and pry the glove box stops out to allow the compartment to drop (see illustration).
13 With the door closed, remove the mounting fasteners at the bottom of the glove box door.
14 Installation is the reverse of removal.

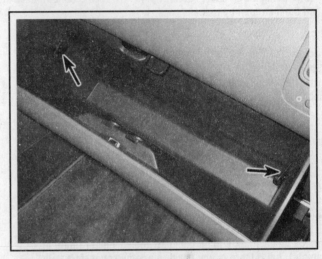

**25.12 Pull out the stop from each side of the glove box**

## 26 Instrument panel - removal and installation

▶ **Refer to illustrations 26.3, 26.5a, 26.5b, 26.10, 26.13a and 26.13b**

### ☼ WARNING:

The models covered by this manual are equipped with Supplemental Restraint Systems (SRS), more commonly known as airbags. Always disable the airbag system before working in the vicinity of any airbag system components to avoid the possibility of accidental deployment of the airbags, which could cause personal injury (see Chapter 12).

➡Note 1: This is a difficult procedure for the home mechanic. There are many hidden fasteners, difficult angles to work in and many electrical connectors to tag and disconnect/connect. We recommend that this procedure be done at a dealership or qualified shop.

➡Note 2: During removal of the instrument panel, make careful notes of how each piece comes off, where it fits in relation to other pieces and what holds it in place. If you note how each part is installed before removing it, getting the instrument panel back together again will be much easier.

➡Note 3: It is not necessary, but it is suggested to remove both front seats to allow additional working space and lessen the chance of damage to the seats during this procedure.

1 Turn the front wheels to the straight-ahead position and lock the steering column. Disconnect the cable from the negative battery terminal (see Chapter 5, Section 1).
2 Remove the right and left side kick panels (see illustrations 10.9 and 25.11).
3 Remove the instrument panel end caps (see illustration).
4 Remove the center console (see Section 23).

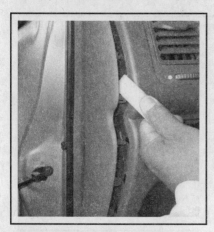

**26.3  Using a trim stick, carefully pry off the instrument panel end caps**

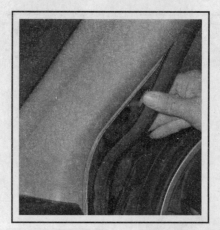

**26.5a  Pull back the door seal . . .**

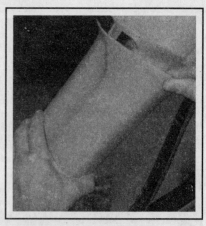

**26.5b  . . . then pry off the A-pillar trim**

5    Remove the A-pillar trim from both sides of the instrument panel (see illustrations).

6    Remove all of the dashboard trim panels as described in Section 25.

7    Remove the instrument cluster (see Chapter 12).

8    Remove the audio unit (see Chapter 12) and the air conditioning control panel (see Chapter 3).

9    Refer to Chapter 10 and remove the steering column.

10   Disconnect the harness connector from the Occupant Restraint Controller (see illustration).

11   Disconnect the instrument panel electrical connectors.

→**Note: A number of electrical connectors must be disconnected in order to remove the instrument panel. Most are designed so that they will only fit on the matching connector (male or female), but if there is any doubt, mark the connectors with masking tape and a marking pen before disconnecting them.**

12   Remove the bolt securing the fuse/relay box.

13   Disconnect any remaining electrical connectors, then remove the instrument panel retaining fasteners (see illustrations).

14   Remove the instrument panel from the vehicle.

15   Installation is the reverse of removal.

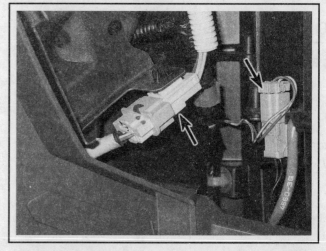

**26.10  Disconnect the harness connectors from the Occupant Restraint Controller**

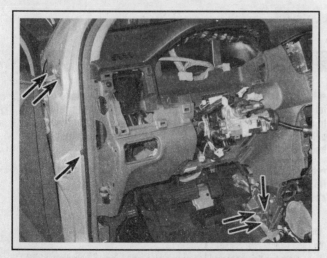

**26.13a  Remove the fasteners from the left-side (three fasteners not visible above steering column) . . .**

**26.13b  . . . and right-side of the instrument panel**

## 27 Seats - removal and installation

※※ **WARNING:**

Some models are equipped with seat belt pre-tensioners, which are pyrotechnic (explosive) devices that tighten the seat belts during an impact of sufficient force. Always disable the airbag system before working in the vicinity of any restraint system component to avoid the possibility of accidental deployment of the airbag(s) and seat belt pre-tensioners, which could cause personal injury (see Chapter 12).

### FRONT SEAT

▶ **Refer to illustrations 27.2a, 27.2b, 27.2c and 27.2c**

1   Disconnect the cable from the negative battery terminal (see Chapter 5, Section 1).

2   Remove the plastic covers, then remove the seat track-to-floor bolts and remove the front seat assembly (see illustrations).

➡**Note: This is a job for two people.**

Disconnect any electrical connectors.

3   Installation is the reverse of removal.

### SECOND ROW SEATS

4   Disconnect the cable from the negative battery terminal (see Chapter 5, Section 1).

5   Remove the plastic covers, then remove the seat track-to-floor bolts and remove the seat assembly.

➡**Note: This is a job for two people.**

6   Installation is the reverse of removal.

### THIRD ROW SEATS

7   Remove the plastic covers, then remove the seat front mounting bolts. Lift the seat cushion up and remove the rear mounting bolts. Remove the seat assembly.

➡**Note: This is a job for two people.**

8   Installation is the reverse of removal.

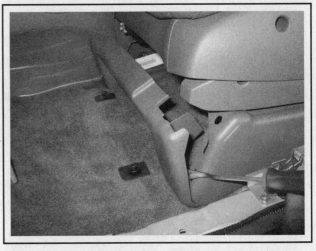

**27.2a  Pry off the plastic covers at the front . . .**

**27.2b  . . . and rear of the seat**

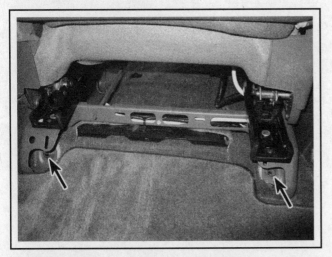

**27.2c  Remove the rear bolts from the front seat . . .**

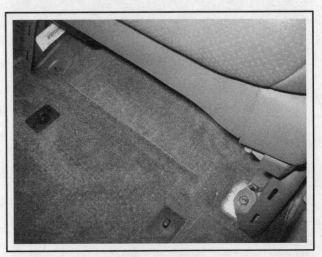

**27.2d  . . . then remove the front bolts**

**Notes**

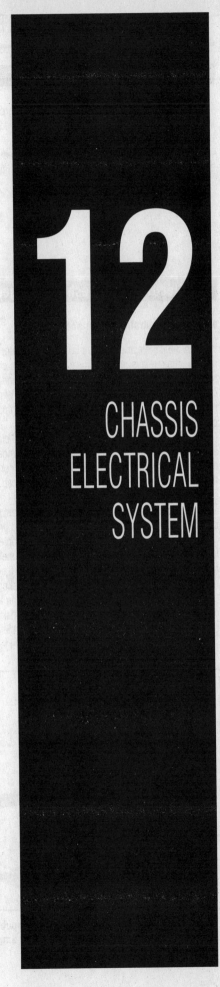

**12**

CHASSIS
ELECTRICAL
SYSTEM

**Section**

## 1  General information

The electrical system is a 12-volt, negative ground type. Power for the lights and all electrical accessories is supplied by a lead/acid-type battery, which is charged by the alternator.

This Chapter covers repair and service procedures for the various electrical components not associated with the engine. Information on the battery, ignition system, alternator and starter motor can be found in Chapter 5.

It should be noted that when portions of the electrical system are serviced, the negative battery cable should be disconnected from the battery to prevent electrical shorts and/or fires.

## 2  Electrical troubleshooting - general information

**▶ Refer to illustrations 2.5a and 2.5b**

1   A typical electrical circuit consists of an electrical component, any switches, relays, motors, fuses, fusible links or circuit breakers related to that component and the wiring and connectors that link the component to both the battery and the chassis. Wiring diagrams are included at the end of this Chapter to help you pinpoint an electrical circuit problem.

2   Before tackling any troublesome electrical circuit, study the appropriate wiring diagrams to get a complete understanding of what makes up that individual circuit. Noting if other components related to the circuit are operating correctly, for instance, can often narrow trouble spots down. If several components or circuits fail at one time, chances are the problem is in a fuse or ground connection, because several circuits are often routed through the same fuse and ground connections.

3   Electrical problems usually stem from simple causes, such as loose or corroded connections, a blown fuse, a melted fusible link or a failed relay. Visually inspect the condition of all fuses, wires and connections in a problem circuit before troubleshooting the circuit.

4   If test equipment and instruments are going to be utilized, use the diagrams to plan ahead of time where you will make the necessary connections in order to accurately pinpoint the trouble spot.

5   Basic electrical troubleshooting tools include a circuit tester, test light or voltmeter, a continuity tester, a set of test leads and a jumper wire (preferably with a circuit breaker), which can be used to bypass electrical components (see illustrations). Before attempting to locate a problem with test instruments, use the wiring diagram(s) to decide where to make the connections.

## VOLTAGE CHECKS

**▶ Refer to illustration 2.6**

6   Voltage checks should be performed if a circuit is not functioning correctly. Connect one lead of a circuit tester to either the negative battery terminal or a known good ground. Connect the other lead to a connector in the circuit being tested, preferably nearest to the battery or fuse (see illustration). If the bulb of the tester lights, voltage is present, which means that the part of the circuit between the connector and the battery is problem free. Continue checking the rest of the circuit in the same fashion. When you reach a point at which no voltage is present, the problem lies between that point and the last test point with voltage. Most of the time the problem can be traced to a loose connection.

**➡Note: Keep in mind that some circuits receive voltage only when the ignition key is in the ACC or ON position.**

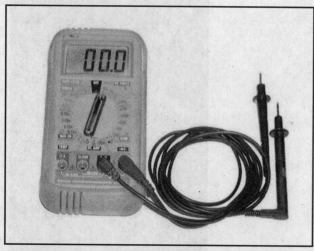

**2.5a  The most useful tool for electrical troubleshooting is a digital multimeter that can check volts, amps, and test continuity**

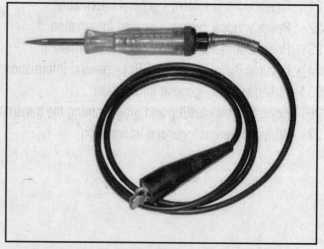

**2.5b  A simple test light is a very handy tool for testing voltage**

2.6 In use, a basic test light's lead is clipped to a known good ground, then the pointed probe can test connectors, wires or electrical sockets - if the bulb lights, the circuit being tested has battery voltage

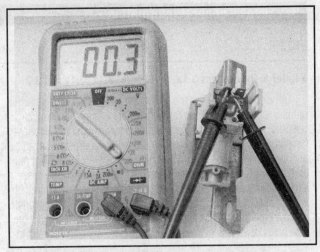

2.9 With a multimeter set to the ohm scale, resistance can be checked across two terminals - when checking for continuity, a low reading indicates continuity, a high reading or infinity indicates high resistance or lack of continuity

## FINDING A SHORT

7   One method of finding shorts in a live circuit is to remove the fuse and connect a test light in place of the fuse terminals (fabricate two jumper wires with small spade terminals, plug the jumper wires into the fuse box and connect the test light). There will be voltage present in the circuit if the circuit is shorted. Move the suspected wiring harness from side-to-side while watching the test light. If the bulb goes off, there is a short to ground somewhere in that area, probably where the insulation has rubbed through.

## GROUND CHECK

8   Perform a ground test to check whether a component is correctly grounded. Disconnect the battery and connect one lead of a continuity tester or multimeter (set to the ohm scale), to a known good ground. Connect the other lead to the wire or ground connection being tested. If the resistance is low (less than 5 ohms), the ground is good. If the bulb on a self-powered test light does not go on, the ground is not good.

## CONTINUITY CHECK

▶ **Refer to illustration 2.9**

9   Do a continuity check to verify that there are no opens in a circuit. With the circuit off (no power in the circuit), a self-powered continuity tester or multimeter can be used to check the circuit. Connect the test leads to both ends of the circuit (or to the "power" end and a good ground), and if the test light comes on the circuit is passing current correctly (see illustration). If the resistance is low (less than 5 ohms), there is continuity; if the reading is 10,000 ohms or higher, there is a break somewhere in the circuit. The same procedure can be used to test a switch, by connecting the continuity tester to the switch terminals. With the switch turned to ON, the test light should come on (or low resistance should be indicated on a meter).

## FINDING AN OPEN CIRCUIT

10 When diagnosing for possible open circuits, it is often difficult to locate them by sight because the connectors hide oxidation or terminal misalignment. Merely wiggling a connector on a sensor or in the wiring harness may correct the open circuit condition. Remember this when an open circuit is indicated when troubleshooting a circuit. Intermittent problems may also be caused by oxidized or loose connections.

11 Electrical troubleshooting is simple if you keep in mind that all electrical circuits are basically electricity running from the battery, through the wires, switches, relays, fuses and fusible links to each electrical component (light bulb, motor, etc.) and to ground, from which it is passed back to the battery. Any electrical problem is an interruption in the flow of electricity to and from the battery.

## CONNECTORS

12 Most electrical connections on these vehicles are made with multi-wire plastic connectors. The mating halves of many connectors are secured with locking clips molded into the plastic connector shells. The mating halves of large connectors, such as some of those under the instrument panel, are held together by a bolt through the center of the connector.

13 To separate a connector with locking clips, use a small screwdriver to pry the clips apart carefully, then separate the connector halves. Pull only on the shell, never pull on the wiring harness as you may damage the individual wires and terminals inside the connectors. Look at the connector closely before trying to separate the halves. Often the locking clips are engaged in a way that is not immediately clear. Additionally, many connectors have more than one set of clips.

14 Each pair of connector terminals has a male half and a female half. When you look at the end view of a connector in a diagram, be sure to understand whether the view shows the harness side or the component side of the connector. Connector halves are mirror images of each other, and a terminal that is shown on the right side end-view of one half will be on the left side end view of the other half.

## 3   Fuses - general information

### FUSES

♦ **Refer to illustrations 3.1a, 3.1b, 3.1c, 3.1d, 3,1e and 3.2**

The electrical circuits of the vehicle are protected by a combination of fuses, circuit breakers and relays (for more information about circuit breakers, refer to Section 4; for more information about relays, refer to Section 5). Fuse and relay boxes are located in the engine compartment and underneath the dashboard (see illustrations). A wide array of mini and maxi-style fuses is used to protect various circuits. These fuses, which employ a blade terminal design, can be removed and installed without special tools. Each fuse protects a specific circuit or circuits, and the protected circuits are identified on the fuse panel cover. If the fuse panel cover is difficult to read, or missing, you can also refer to your owner's manual, which includes a complete guide to all fuses and relays in all three fuse/relay boxes.

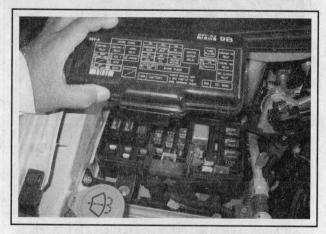

**3.1a  The engine compartment fuse/relay box is located on the right side of the engine compartment. The fuses and relays are listed by location and function on the fuse/relay box cover**

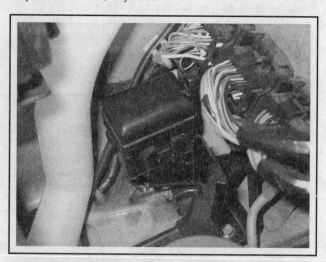

**3.1b  The auxiliary relay box is also located in the engine compartment, in front of and below the PCM. Typically, the auxiliary relay box contains four relays, such as the windshield intermittent wiper relay, the rear window intermittent wiper relay, the fan control relay and the seat heater relay**

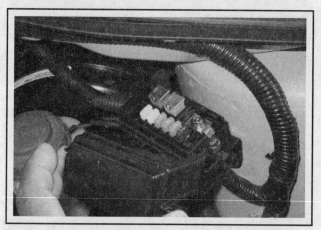

**3.1c  Another auxiliary fuse and relay box is located on the firewall, to the left of the brake master cylinder reservoir. There's a guide to the fuses and relays on the underside of the lid**

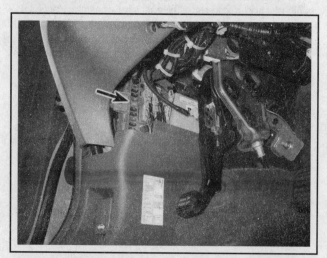

**3.1d  Inside the vehicle, there's a fuse box under the left end of the instrument panel, above the kick panel . . .**

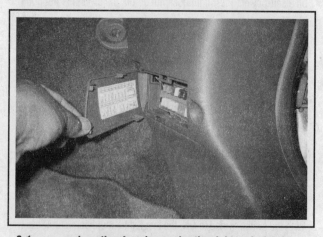

**3.1e  . . . and another fuse box under the right end of the instrument panel, behind the right kick panel. This panel is behind a small access door with a fuse guide on the inside**

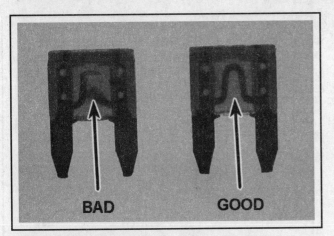

**3.2 When a fuse blows, the element between the terminals melts**

If an electrical component fails, always check the fuse first. The best way to check a fuse is with a test light. Check for power at the exposed terminal tips of each fuse. If power is present on one side of the fuse but not the other, the fuse is blown. A blown fuse can also be confirmed by visually inspecting it (see illustration).

Be sure to replace blown fuses with the correct type. Fuses of different ratings are physically interchangeable, but only fuses of the correct rating should be used. Replacing a fuse with one of a higher or lower value than specified is not recommended. Each electrical circuit needs a specific amount of protection. The amperage value of each fuse is molded into the fuse body.

If the replacement fuse immediately fails, don't replace it again until the cause of the problem is isolated and corrected. In most cases, this will be a short circuit in the wiring caused by a broken or deteriorated wire.

## 4   Circuit breakers - general information

Circuit breakers protect certain circuits, such as the power windows or heated seats. The number of circuit breakers employed on your vehicle depends on its electrical accessories. Some circuit breakers are located in a fuse/relay box; others are located as stand-alone units under the dash and in other locations throughout the vehicle.

Because a circuit breaker resets automatically, a temporary or intermittent electrical overload in a circuit-breaker-protected system will cause the circuit to open momentarily, then close again. If a circuit-breaker-protected circuit does not close, or constantly opens and closes, check it immediately. There's probably an intermittent short or ground somewhere in the circuit that's causing the current overload, which causes the circuit breaker to cycle the circuit on and off.

For a basic check, pull the circuit breaker up out of its socket on the fuse panel, but just far enough to probe with a voltmeter. The breaker should still contact the sockets.

With the voltmeter negative lead on a good chassis ground, touch each end prong of the circuit breaker with the positive meter probe. There should be battery voltage at each end. If there is battery voltage only at one end, the circuit breaker must be replaced.

Some circuit breakers must be reset manually.

## 5   Relays - general information and testing

### GENERAL INFORMATION

1   Several electrical accessories in the vehicle, such as the fuel injection system, horns, starter, and fog lamps use relays to transmit the electrical signal to the component. A relay allows a low-current circuit (the control circuit) to be used to open and close a high-current circuit (the power circuit). If a relay is defective, the component(s) powered by the high-current circuit controlled by the relay will not operate. Relays are located in the engine compartment fuse/relay box and in or near the fuse and relay boxes under the dash (see illustrations 3.1a through 3.1c). If a relay is suspect, test it using the procedure below, or have it tested by a dealer service department or a repair shop. Defective relays must be replaced, because they cannot be repaired.

### TESTING

2   There are three basic types of relays used in these vehicles: normally-open Type A, normally-open Type B and the five-terminal type. Type A and Type B relays have similar internal circuitry, but their external spade terminals are arranged differently and they're numbered differently. Five-terminal relays have different internal circuitry and one more external spade terminal than Type A and Type B relays. To test a relay, remove it from the vehicle and use an ohmmeter to check for continuity.

#### Normally-open Type A relays

▶ **Refer to illustration 5.4**

3   Normally-open type A relays are used for:

*Air-conditioning clutch relay*
*Air/fuel (A/F) ratio sensor relay*
*Condenser fan relay*
*Headlight relay No. 1 (2001 models)*
*Headlight relay No. 2 (2001 models)*
*Headlight relay (2002 and later models)*
*Horn relay*
*Power window relay*
*Radiator fan relay*
*Reverse relay*
*Starter cut relay*
*Taillight relay*
*Daytime Running Lights (DRL) relay (Canadian models)*
*PGM-FI main relay No. 1*
*PGM-FI main relay No. 2*

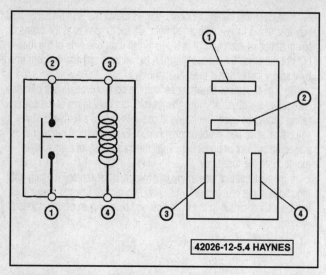

**5.4  Normally-open Type A relay**

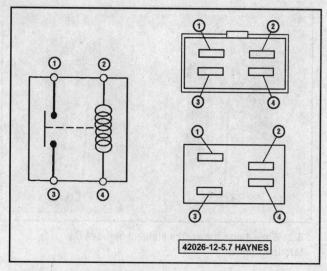

**5.7  Normally-open Type B relay**

4   Type A relays (see illustration) have four external spade terminals: two horizontal terminals, one on top of the other, with two vertical terminals, side-by-side, below them.

5   To test a normally-open Type A relay verify that there is no continuity between terminal No. 1 and No. 2 when the power is disconnected. Then verify that there is continuity between terminal No. 1 and No. 2 when the No. 3 and No. 4 terminals are connected to power and ground, respectively.

## Normally-open Type B relays

▶ **Refer to illustration 5.7**

6   Normally-open Type B relays are used for:
   *Blower motor relay*
   *Rear window defogger relay*

7   Type B relays also have four external spade terminals (see illustration), but they're arranged in two parallel rows, with two terminals per row.

8   To test a normally-open Type B relay, verify that there is no continuity between terminal No. 1 and No. 3 when the power is disconnected. Then verify that there is continuity between terminal No. 1 and No. 3 when the No. 2 and No. 4 terminals are connected to power and ground, respectively.

## Five-terminal type relays

▶ **Refer to illustration 5.10**

9   Five-terminal relays are used for:
   *Moonroof-closing relay*
   *Moonroof-opening relay*
   *Low-beam cut relay (Canadian models)*

10  To test a five-terminal relay verify that there is continuity between terminal No. 1 and No. 4 when the power is disconnected (see illustration). Then verify that there is continuity between terminal No. 1 and No. 2 when power and ground are connected to the No. 3 and No. 5 terminals.

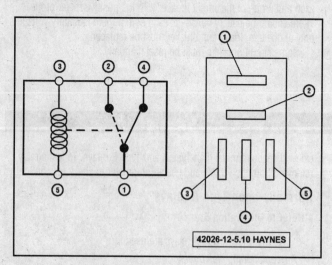

**5.10  Five-terminal relay**

## 6   Turn signal and hazard flasher - check and replacement

▶ Refer to illustrations 6.4a, 6.4b and 6.4c

1   The turn signal and hazard flashers are controlled from a single electronic flasher unit, which is located on the backside of the fuse/relay box under the left end of the dash.

2   If the flasher unit is functioning correctly, you can hear an audible click when it's operating. If one of the turn signal indicators on the instrument cluster flashes more rapidly than normal, a turn signal bulb for that side has a blown filament.

3   If neither turn signal indicator blinks, the problem might be a blown fuse, a faulty flasher unit, a broken switch or a loose or open connection. If the left or right turn signal fuse has blown, check the wiring for a short before installing a new fuse.

4   To replace the flasher unit, remove the driver's side fuse and relay box (see illustrations). Then remove the flasher (see illustration) from the backside of the fuse and relay box.

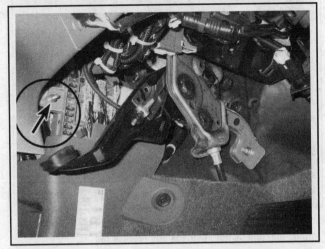

**6.4a  To access the turn signal and hazard flasher unit, remove this nut . . .**

5   Make sure that the replacement unit is identical to the original. Compare the old one to the new one before installing it.

6   Installation is the reverse of removal.

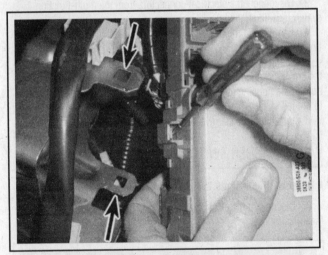

**6.4b  . . . release the two locking tabs from the upper and lower mounting brackets and remove the fuse and relay box**

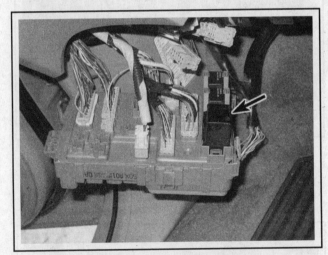

**6.4c  To remove the turn signal and hazard flasher unit, simply pull it out of the fuse and relay box**

## 7   Steering column switches - replacement

1   Disconnect the cable from the negative battery terminal (see Chapter 5, Section 1), then wait at least three minutes before proceeding.

2   Remove the knee bolster and the upper and lower steering column covers (see Chapter 11).

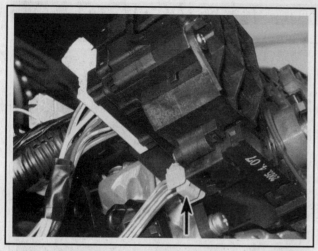

**7.3a  To disconnect the lower electrical connector from the multi-function switch, depress this release tab**

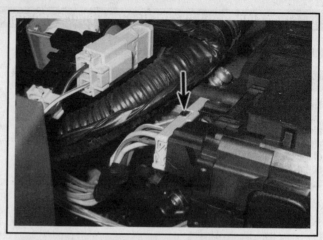

**7.3b  To disconnect the upper electrical connector from the multi-function switch, depress this release tab**

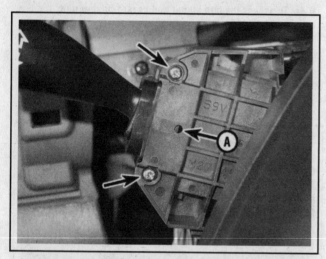

**7.4  To detach the multi-function switch from its housing, remove these two screws. Note the small lug (A) that protrudes through this hole in the housing; this lug also secures the multi-function switch to the housing**

## MULTI-FUNCTION SWITCH

▶ **Refer to illustrations 7.3a, 7.3b, 7.4 and 7.5**

➥**Note: The multi-function switch includes the headlight switch, high beam/low beam switch (dimmer switch) and turn signal switch.**

3   Disconnect the electrical connectors from the multi-function switch (see illustrations).

4   Remove the multi-function switch retaining screws (see illustration).

5   Using a small screwdriver, carefully pry the housing away from the small lug on the switch which locks the switch into place through a hole in the housing (see illustration), then carefully pull out the switch to the left.

6   Installation is the reverse of removal.

## WIPER/WASHER SWITCH

▶ **Refer to illustrations 7.7, 7.8 and 7.9**

7   Disconnect the electrical connector from the wiper/washer switch (see illustration).

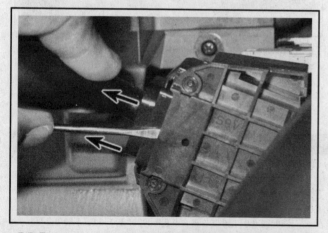

**7.5  To remove the multi-function switch from its housing in the combination switch assembly, carefully pry the housing off the lug that locks the switch into the housing, then pull out the switch**

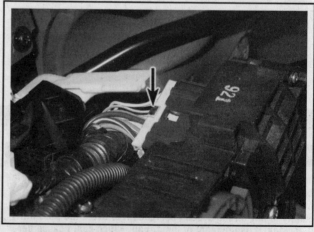

**7.7  To disconnect the electrical connector from the windshield wiper/washer switch, depress this release tab**

**7.8 To detach the windshield wiper/washer switch, remove these two screws. Note the small lug (A) that protrudes through this hole in the housing; this lug also secures the multi-function switch to the housing**

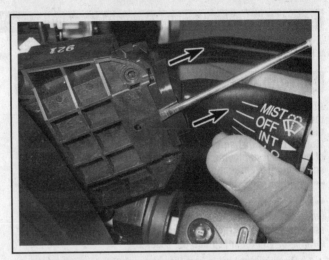

**7.9 To remove the windshield wiper/washer switch from its housing in the combination switch assembly, carefully pry the housing off the lug that locks the switch into the housing, then pull out the switch**

8    Remove the wiper/washer switch retaining screws (see illustration) and remove the switch.

9    Using a small screwdriver, carefully pry the housing away from the small lug on the switch which locks the switch into place through a hole in the housing (see illustration), then carefully pull out the switch to the right.

10    Installation is the reverse of removal.

## COMBINATION SWITCH ASSEMBLY

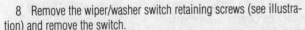

▶ **Refer to illustrations 7.12, 7.13 and 7.14**

➡**Note: The combination switch assembly houses the multi-function and wiper/washer switches and the connection between the clockspring and the airbag electrical harness. It's not nec-**essary to remove the combination switch assembly to replace either of the above switches, but you do have to remove it to remove the steering column.

11    Remove the steering wheel and the airbag clockspring (see Chapter 10).

12    Disconnect the electrical connectors from the multi-function and windshield wiper/washer switches (see illustrations 7.3a, 7.3b and 7.7) and from the combination switch (see illustration).

13    Detach the clip for the airbag electrical harness from the small bracket on the key lock cylinder/ignition switch housing, then disconnect the big yellow connector for the airbag harness (see illustration).

14    Remove the three combination switch mounting screws (see illustration) and remove the switch assembly from the steering column.

15    Installation is the reverse of removal.

**7.12 To disconnect the electrical connector from the combination switch assembly, depress this release tab**

**7.13 Detach the clip (1) that secures the airbag electrical harness to this small bracket, then disconnect the airbag harness electrical connector (2)**

**7.14 To detach the combination switch assembly from the steering column, remove these three screws (upper screw not visible)**

## 8 Key lock cylinder/ignition switch assembly- replacement

▶ Refer to illustration 8.4, 8.6, 8.7a and 8.7b

### ✳ WARNING:

**All models covered by this manual are equipped with a Supplemental Restraint System (SRS), more commonly known as airbags. Always disable the airbag system before working in the vicinity of any airbag system component to avoid the possibility of accidental deployment of the airbag, which could cause personal injury (see Section 25).**

➡Note: The key lock cylinder and ignition switch assembly (which Honda refers to as the "steering lock") is a one-piece assembly. If either the key lock cylinder or the ignition switch is defective, you must replace the assembly.

1   Disconnect the cable from the negative battery terminal (see Chapter 5, Section 1), then wait at least three minutes before proceeding.

2   Remove the knee bolster and the upper and lower steering column covers (see Chapter 11).

3   Detach the driver's side fuse and relay box (see Section 3) and turn it over so that you can access the backside of the panel.

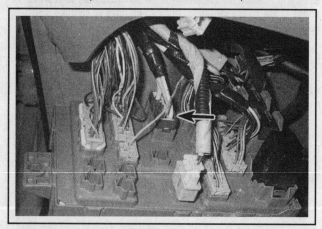

**8.4 Detach the fuse box above the left kick panel, turn it over and disconnect the ignition switch electrical connector from the backside of the box**

4   Trace the electrical harness down from the key lock cylinder/ignition switch assembly to the driver's side fuse and relay box and detach any harness clips, then disconnect the ignition switch electrical connector from the fuse and relay box (see illustration).

5   Detach the clip for the driver's side airbag wiring harness from the bracket on the key lock cylinder/ignition switch assembly (see illustration 7.13).

6   Disconnect the small electrical connector from the key lock cylinder/ignition switch assembly (see illustration).

7   Center-punch the two shear-head bolts that secure the mounting clamp for the key lock cylinder/ignition switch assembly, then drill out the center of each bolt (see illustrations) and remove the bolts with a screw extractor.

➡Note: An alternative method which may work would be to use a hammer and chisel to knock the bolts in a counterclockwise direction.

Remove the bracket and detach the lock cylinder/ignition switch assembly from the steering column.

8   Installation is the reverse of removal. Tighten the new shear-head bolts until the heads break off.

9   When you're done, reconnect the cable to the negative battery terminal (see Chapter 5, Section 1).

10  Verify that the key lock cylinder/ignition switch assembly works correctly.

**8.6 Disconnect this small electrical connector from the key lock cylinder/ ignition switch assembly**

**8.7a To detach the key lock cylinder/ignition switch assembly from the steering column, center punch . . .**

**8.7b . . . then drill out these two shear bolts, remove the mounting clamp and pull off the lock cylinder/switch assembly**

## 9  Dashboard switches - replacement

### ⁂ WARNING:

The models covered by this manual are equipped with a Supplemental Restraint System (SRS), more commonly known as airbags. Always disable the airbag system before working in the vicinity of any airbag system component to avoid the possibility of accidental deployment of the airbag, which could cause personal injury (see Section 25).

### SWITCHES ON DRIVER'S SWITCH PANEL

▶ Refer to illustrations 9.1, 9.2 and 9.3

➡Note: The driver's switch panel houses various switches, including Vehicle Stability Assist (VSA) OFF switch, the cruise control switch, the interior lighting switch and the moonroof switch. To replace any of these switches you must first remove the switch panel.

1  Using a trim panel removal tool or a screwdriver, carefully pry the switch trim panel loose (see illustration).

2  Pull out the switch panel and disconnect the electrical connectors from the switches (see illustration).

3  Remove the switch that you want to replace (see illustration).

4  Installation is the reverse of removal.

### HAZARD FLASHER SWITCH, VTM-4 LOCK SWITCH AND PASSENGER AIRBAG SWITCH

▶ Refer to illustrations 9.5a, 9.5b and 9.6

➡Note: These switches are located in the radio trim panel.

5  Using a trim panel removal tool, carefully pry the radio trim panel loose (see illustration). Pull out the radio trim panel and disconnect the electrical connectors from the switches (see illustration).

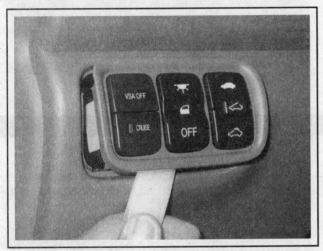

9.1  Carefully pry the dashboard switch trim panel loose with a trim panel removal tool

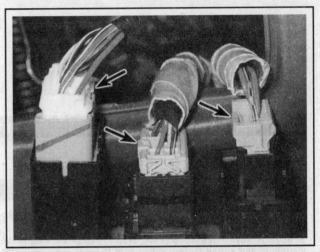

9.2  To disconnect the electrical connectors from the switches, depress the release tab on each connector and pull off the connector

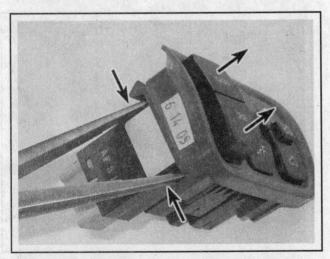

9.3  To release any of the switches located on this switch panel, squeeze the locking tabs and push out the switch through the front side of the panel

9.5a  Carefully pry the radio trim panel loose with a trim panel removal tool

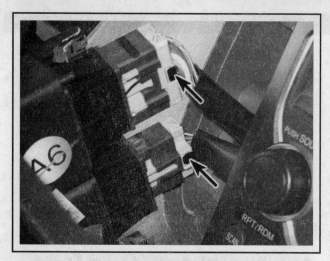

**9.5b Pull out the radio trim panel, depress the release tab on each electrical connector and disconnect the connectors from the switches**

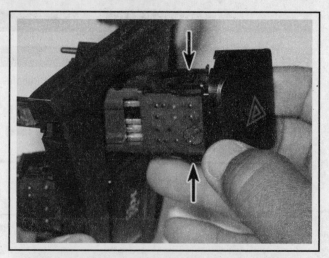

**9.6 To remove a switch from the radio trim panel, depress the two lock tabs and pull the switch out the front side of the panel**

6   Remove the switch that you want to replace (see illustration).

7   Installation is the reverse of removal.

8   When you're done, reconnect the cable to the negative battery terminal (see Chapter 5, Section 1).

## 10  Instrument cluster - removal and installation

▶ **Refer to illustrations 10.2a and 10.2b**

**✳✳ WARNING:**

**The models covered by this manual are equipped with a Supplemental Restraint System (SRS), more commonly known as airbags. Always disable the airbag system before working in the vicinity of any airbag system component to avoid the possibility of accidental deployment of the airbag, which could cause personal injury (see Section 25).**

1   Remove the instrument cluster bezel (see Chapter 11).

2   Remove the instrument cluster retaining screws (see illustration), then pull out the cluster and disconnect the electrical connectors from the backside (see illustration).

3   Installation is the reverse of removal.

**10.2a To detach the instrument cluster from the dashboard, remove these four screws (two lower screws not visible) . . .**

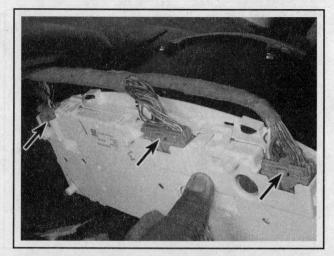

**10.2b . . . then pull out the cluster and disconnect the three electrical connectors**

## 11 Wiper motors - check and replacement

### WIPER MOTOR CIRCUIT CHECK

➡**Note: Refer to the wiring diagrams for wire colors in the following checks. When checking for voltage, probe a grounded 12-volt test light to each terminal at a connector until it lights; this verifies voltage (power) at the terminal. If the following checks fail to locate the problem, have the system diagnosed by a dealer service department or other properly equipped repair facility.**

1   If the wipers work slowly, make sure the battery is fully charged and in good condition (see Chapter 5). If the battery is in good shape, remove the wiper motor (see below) and operate the wiper arms by hand. Check for binding linkage and pivots. Lubricate or repair the linkage or pivots as necessary. Reinstall the wiper motor. If the wipers still operate slowly, check for loose or corroded connections, especially the ground connection. If all connections look OK, replace the motor.

2   If the wipers fail to operate when activated, check the fuse (see Section 3). If the fuse is OK, connect a jumper wire between the wiper motor's ground terminal and ground, then retest. If the motor works

now, repair the ground connection. If the motor still doesn't work, turn the wiper switch to the HI position and check for voltage at the motor.

➡**Note: The cowl cover will have to be removed to access the electrical connector (see Steps 7 and 8).**

3   If there's voltage at the connector, remove the motor and check it off the vehicle with fused jumper wires from the battery. If the motor now works, check for binding linkage (see Step 1). If the motor still doesn't work, replace it. If there's no voltage to the motor, check for voltage at the wiper control relays. If there's voltage at the wiper control relays and no voltage at the wiper motor, have the switch tested. If the switch is OK, the wiper control relay is probably bad. See Section 5 for relay testing.

4   If the interval (delay) function is inoperative, check the continuity of all the wiring between the switch and the wiper control module.

5   If the wipers fail to "park" (if they stop at the position that they're in when the switch is turned off instead of returning to their normal "off" position), turn the wiper switch to OFF and the ignition switch to ON, then check for voltage at the park feed wire of the wiper motor connector. If no voltage is present, check for an open circuit between the wiper motor and the fuse panel.

### WIPER MOTOR REPLACEMENT

#### Windshield wiper motor

▸ **Refer to illustrations 11.7, 11.9, 11.10, 11.11 and 11.12**

6   Open the hood, then pull off the protective cap from each windshield wiper arm retaining nut (see illustration).

7   Remove the windshield wiper arm retaining nuts. Be sure to mark the position of each wiper arm in relation to its splined shaft (see illustration), then remove the wiper arms.

8   Remove the cowl cover (see Chapter 11).

9   Disconnect the electrical connector from the windshield wiper motor (see illustration).

10  Remove the four mounting bolts for the windshield wiper linkage/motor assembly (see illustration), then remove the linkage/motor assembly from the cowl.

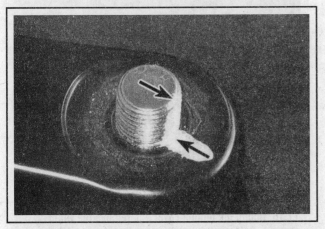

**11.7  Be sure to mark each windshield wiper arm in relation to the splined shaft to ensure that the arm is installed in the same position**

**11.9  Depress the release tab and disconnect the electrical connector from the windshield wiper motor**

**11.10  To detach the windshield wiper linkage/motor assembly, remove these four bolts**

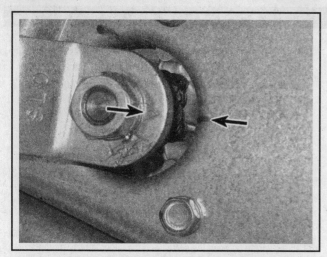

**11.11 To separate the windshield wiper linkage from the wiper motor, mark the relationship of the link to the wiper motor mounting bracket, then holding one end of the link with a pair of pliers, remove the nut and carefully pry the link off the wiper motor shaft**

11 Separate the windshield wiper linkage from the wiper motor (see illustration).

12 Remove the windshield wiper motor mounting bolts (see illustration) and separate the motor from its mounting bracket.

13 Before installing the windshield wiper linkage (especially if you're installing the old linkage), grease the moving parts.

14 Installation is otherwise the reverse of removal. Be sure to align the marks you made between the link and the motor mounting bracket and between the windshield wiper arms and the wiper arm shafts.

### Rear window wiper motor

▶ **Refer to illustrations 11.15, 11.16, 11.18 and 11.19**

15 Remove the protective cover for the rear window wiper motor shaft nut (see illustration), then remove the nut, mark the relationship of the wiper arm to the wiper motor shaft (see illustration 11.7) and remove the rear window wiper arm.

**11.12 To detach the windshield wiper motor from its mounting bracket, remove these three bolts**

**11.15 Unclip the hinged cover and remove the wiper arm nut. Before removing the arm, be sure to mark the relationship of the arm to the wiper motor shaft (see illustration 11.7)**

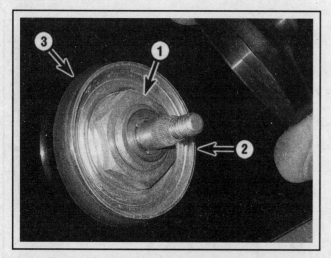

**11.16 Remove the protective cover and the wiper motor shaft nut (1), the spacer (2) and the rubber seal (3)**

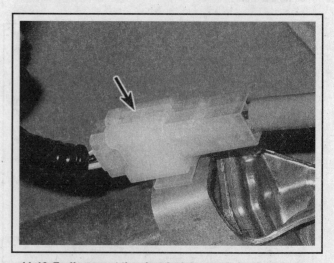

**11.18 To disconnect the electrical connector for the rear window wiper motor, depress the release tab and pull off the connector**

16 Remove the protective cover for the wiper motor shaft retaining nut (see illustration), remove the shaft retaining nut, the spacer and the rubber seal.

17 Remove the tailgate trim panel (see Chapter 11).

18 Disconnect the wiper motor electrical connector (see illustration).

19 Remove the rear window wiper motor mounting bolts (see illustration) and remove the motor.

20 Installation is the reverse of removal.

11.19 To detach the rear window wiper motor from the tailgate, remove these three mounting bolts

## 12 Radio and speakers - removal and installation

### ⁂ WARNING:

The models covered by this manual are equipped with a Supplemental Restraint System (SRS), more commonly known as airbags. Always disable the airbag system before working in the vicinity of any airbag system component to avoid the possibility of accidental deployment of the airbag, which could cause personal injury (see Section 25).

### RADIO

#### Without navigation

♦ Refer to illustration 12.2a, 12.2b and 12.3

1 Remove the radio trim panel (see illustrations 9.5a and 9.5b).

2 Remove the radio mounting screws (see illustration), then pull out the radio far enough to disconnect the antenna and the electrical connector from the back of the unit (see illustration).

3 If you're replacing the old radio, remove the radio mounting brackets (see illustration).

12.2a To detach the radio from the dash, remove these four mounting screws . . .

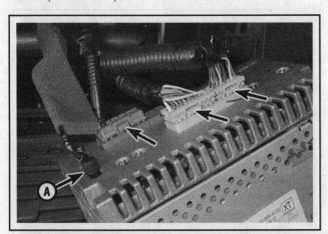

12.2b . . . then pull out the radio far enough to disconnect the electrical connectors and the antenna cable (A) from the back of the unit (typical model without navigation)

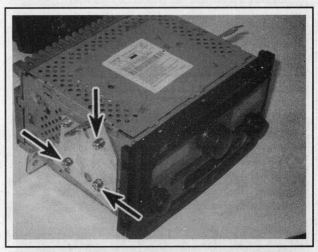

12.3 Remove the three screws from each radio mounting bracket and remove both brackets and install them on the new radio unit

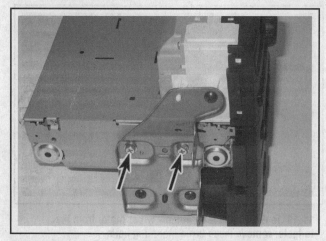

**12.12 To detach the CD changer from the heater/air conditioning control assembly mounting brackets, remove these two screws from each bracket**

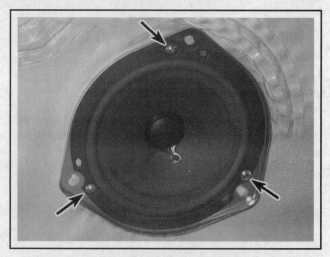

**12.21 To detach a door speaker, remove the mounting screws**

4   If you're replacing the old radio, install the radio mounting bracket on the new radio unit.

5   Installation is the reverse of removal.

## With navigation

6   Remove the center lower trim panel (see Chapter 11).

7   Remove the heater/air conditioning control assembly (see Chapter 3). (On these models you have to remove the heater/air conditioning controls and the radio as a single assembly.)

8   The radio and the heater/air conditioning control assembly share their two mounting brackets. Remove the four radio mounting screws from each mounting bracket and remove the radio.

9   Installation is the reverse of removal.

## CD CHANGER

### Without navigation

▶ **Refer to illustration 12.12**

10   Remove the center lower trim panel (see Chapter 11).

11   Remove the heater/air conditioning control assembly (see Chapter 3). (On these models you have to remove the heater/air conditioning controls and the CD changer as a single assembly.)

12   The heater/air conditioning control assembly, the CD changer and the seat heater switches share their two mounting brackets. Remove the two CD changer mounting screws from each mounting bracket (see illustration) and remove the CD changer.

13   Installation is the reverse of removal.

### With navigation

14   Slide back the driver's seat.

15   Remove the four CD changer mounting nuts and lift up the changer unit.

16   Disconnect the CD changer electrical connector and remove the changer unit.

17   If you're replacing the old CD changer unit, remove the four screws from each mounting bracket and remove the mounting brackets.

18   If you're replacing the old CD changer unit, install the mounting brackets on the new CD changer unit.

19   Installation is the reverse of removal.

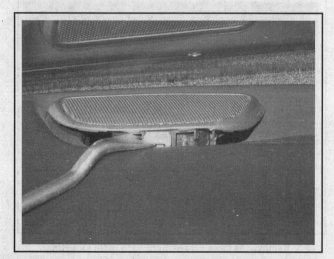

**12.23 Pry the tweeter out of the dash with a trim removal tool**

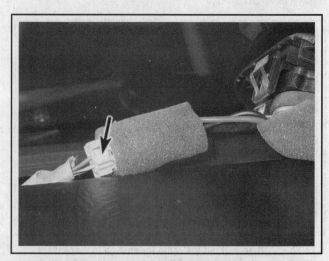

**12.24 Pull the tweeter out of the dash, depress the release tab and disconnect the electrical connector**

## SPEAKERS

### Door speakers

▸ **Refer to illustration 12.21**

20  On Acura models, use a trim removal tool to pry off the speaker grille. On Honda models, remove the door trim panel (see Chapter 11).

21  Remove the speaker mounting screws (see illustration), remove the speaker from the door and disconnect the electrical connector.

22  Installation is the reverse of removal.

### Tweeters

▸ **Refer to illustrations 12.23 and 12.24**

➡**Note: The tweeters are located on the top of the dash.**

23  Using a trim removal tool, pry the tweeter out of the dash (see illustration).

24  Disconnect the electrical connector from the tweeter (see illustration).

25  Installation is the reverse of removal.

### Woofer

➡**Note: The woofer is located on the right side of the cargo area.**

26  On Acura models, remove the speaker grille. On Honda models, remove the right rear trim panel (see Chapter 11).

27  Remove the speaker mounting screws and pull the speaker out of its receptacle.

28  Disconnect the electrical connector and remove the speaker from the vehicle.

29  Installation is the reverse of removal.

## 13  Antenna - removal and installation

### ACURA MODELS

#### 2001 through 2006 models

➡**Note: The antenna is located on the roof, near the tailgate. You can replace the mast itself by simply unscrewing it. But to replace the antenna mount you must pull down the rear part of the headliner.**

1  Unscrew the antenna mast from its mounting base.

2  If you're simply replacing the antenna mast, stop here. Screw on a new mast and you're done. If you're replacing the antenna mount, proceed to the next step.

3  Pull down the rear part of the headliner.

4  Disconnect the antenna lead and the electrical connector from the antenna.

5  Remove the antenna mounting nut and remove the antenna mount.

6  Installation is the reverse of removal.

#### 2007 models

➡**Note: The antenna is an integral component of the tailgate spoiler trim. To replace the antenna you must replace the tailgate spoiler trim.**

7  Remove the tailgate spoiler trim (see Chapter 11).

8  Installation is the reverse of removal.

### HONDA MODELS

➡**Note: The antenna grid is an integral component of the left rear window, between the C-pillar and the D-pillar.**

9  To replace the antenna grid you must replace the left rear window.

10  You can repair the antenna grid using the same procedure that you would use to repair the rear window heater grid. You'll find this procedure in the next section.

## 14  Rear window defogger - check and repair

1  The rear window defogger consists of a number of horizontal elements baked onto the glass surface.

2  Small breaks in the element can be repaired without removing the rear window.

### CHECK

▸ **Refer to illustrations 14.4, 14.5 and 14.7**

3  Turn the ignition switch and defogger system switches to the ON position. Using a voltmeter, place the positive probe against the defogger grid positive terminal and the negative probe against the ground terminal. If battery voltage is not indicated, check the fuse, defogger switch and related wiring. If voltage is indicated, but all or part of the defogger doesn't heat, proceed with the following tests.

4  When measuring voltage during the next two tests, wrap a piece of aluminum foil around the tip of the voltmeter positive probe and press the foil against the heating element with your finger (see illustration). Place the negative probe on the defogger grid ground terminal.

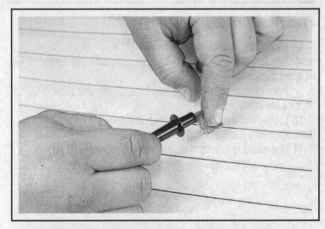

**14.4  When measuring the voltage at the rear window defogger grid, wrap a piece of aluminum foil around the positive probe of the voltmeter and press the foil against the wire with your finger**

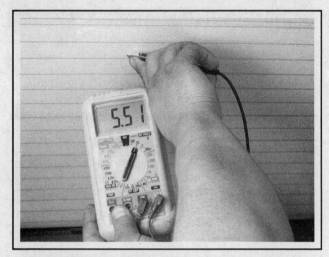

**14.5 To determine whether a wire has broken, check the voltage at the center of each wire. If the voltage is five to six volts, the wire is unbroken; if the voltage is 10 to 12 volts, the wire is broken between the center of the wire and the ground side; if the voltage is zero, the wire is broken between the center of the wire and the power side**

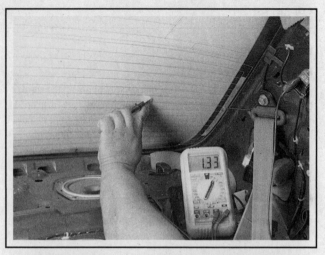

**14.7 To find the break, place the voltmeter negative lead against the ground terminal, place the voltmeter positive lead with the foil strip against the heat wire at the positive terminal end and slide it toward the negative terminal end; the point at which the voltmeter deflects from several volts to zero volts is the point at which the wire is broken**

5    Check the voltage at the center of each heating element (see illustration). If the voltage is 5 or 6-volts, the element is okay (there is no break). If the voltage is zero, the element is broken between the center of the element and the positive end. If the voltage is 10 to 12-volts the element is broken between the center of the element and ground. Check each heating element.

6    Connect the negative lead to a good body ground. The reading should stay the same. If it doesn't, the ground connection is bad.

7    To find the break, place the voltmeter negative probe against the defogger ground terminal. Place the voltmeter positive probe with the foil strip against the heating element at the positive terminal end and slide it toward the negative terminal end. The point at which the voltmeter deflects from several volts to zero is the point at which the heating element is broken (see illustration).

## REPAIR

▶ **Refer to illustration 14.13**

8    Repair the break in the element using a repair kit for this purpose (available at most auto parts stores). Make sure that the repair kit includes plastic conductive epoxy.

9    Prior to repairing a break, turn off the system and allow it to cool off for a few minutes.

10    Lightly buff the element area with fine steel wool, then clean it thoroughly with rubbing alcohol.

11    Use masking tape to mask off the area being repaired.

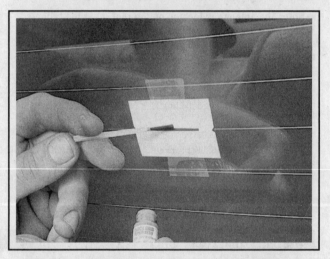

**14.13 To use a defogger repair kit, apply masking to the inside of the window at the damaged area, then brush on the special conductive coating**

12 Thoroughly mix the epoxy, following the instructions provided with the repair kit.

13 Apply the epoxy material to the slit in the masking tape, overlapping the undamaged area about 3/4-inch on either end (see illustration).

14 Allow the repair to cure for 24 hours before removing the tape and using the system.

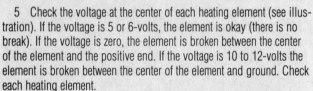

## 15  Headlight bulb - replacement

▶ Refer to illustrations 15.2, 15.3, 15.4a, 15.4b, 15.5 and 15.7

### ✳✳ WARNING:

**Halogen gas filled bulbs are under pressure and can shatter if the surface is scratched or the bulb is dropped. Wear eye protection and handle the bulbs carefully, grasping only the base whenever possible. Do not touch the surface of the bulb with your fingers because the oil from your skin could cause it to overheat and fail prematurely. If you do touch the bulb surface, clean it with rubbing alcohol.**

1   Make sure that the ignition switch and the headlight switch are both turned off, then open the hood.
2   Disconnect the electrical connector from the headlight bulb (see illustration).

3   If equipped, remove the rubber weather seal from the headlight housing (see illustration).
4   Disengage the bulb retainer wire, then remove the bulb from the headlight housing (see illustrations).
5   Without touching the glass part of the new bulb with your bare fingers, insert the bulb into the headlight assembly. Make sure that the three metal tabs on the bulb are aligned with the three slots in the plastic mounting base and that the bulb mounting flange is fully seated against the base (see illustration).
6   Swing the bulb retainer wire back into place and engage the end with its slot.
7   On models so equipped, install the rubber weather seal on the back of the headlight assembly (see illustration).
8   Plug in the electrical connector.

**15.2  Disconnect the electrical connector from the headlight**

**15.3  To remove the rubber weather seal from the headlight housing, simply pull on one of the tabs**

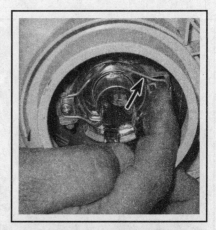

**15.4a  To release the headlight bulb retainer wire, push the end of the wire forward until it's disengaged from its slot, then push it up until it clears the slot and pull it back . . .**

**15.4b  . . . then simply pull out the headlight bulb**

**15.5  When installing a headlight bulb, make sure that the three tabs on the headlight bulb flange are aligned with their respective slots in the plastic mounting base**

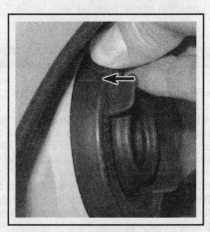

**15.7  When installing the rubber weather seal on the back of the headlight housing, make sure that an arrow, or the word "TOP," is at the 12 o'clock position**

## 16  Headlight housing - replacement

▶ **Refer to illustrations 16.2, 16.3a and 16.3b**

1   Remove the front bumper cover (see Chapter 11).

2   Remove the upper headlight housing pop fastener and mounting bolt (see illustration).

3   Remove the pop fastener that secures the black plastic "side stiffener" and the headlight housing mounting bracket to the vehicle, then remove the three mounting bracket bolts (see illustration), pull out the headlight housing and disconnect the electrical connectors (see illustration).

4   After removing the headlight housing and the mounting bracket, detach the bracket from the headlight housing by removing the bolt from the underside of the bracket.

5   Installation is the reverse of removal.

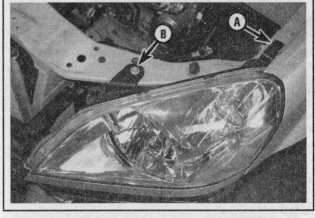

16.2  To detach the upper part of the headlight housing, remove the pop fastener (A) and the mounting bolt (B)

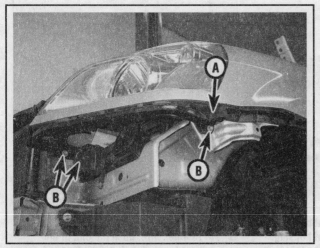

16.3a  To detach the lower part of the headlight housing, remove the pop fastener (A) that secures the side stiffener to the headlight housing bracket, then remove the headlight mounting bracket bolts (B)

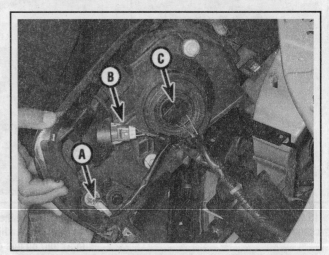

16.3b  Pull out the headlight housing and disconnect the electrical connectors from the front side marker light (A), the front turn signal/parking light (B) and the headlight (C)

## 17  Headlights - adjustment

▶ **Refer to illustrations 17.1a, 17.1b and 17.3**

➡**Note: The headlights must be aimed correctly. If adjusted incorrectly they could blind the driver of an oncoming vehicle and cause a serious accident or seriously reduce your ability to see the road. The headlights should be checked for correct aim every 12 months and any time a new headlight is installed or front end body work is performed. It should be emphasized that the following procedure is only an interim step that will provide temporary adjustment until the headlights can be adjusted by a properly equipped shop.**

1   The vertical adjuster is located on the backside of each headlight housing (see illustration). Use a Phillips screwdriver to turn the adjuster (see illustration).

➡**Note: These headlights are not equipped with horizontal adjusters.**

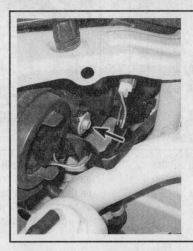

17.1a  The vertical headlight adjuster is located on the back of each headlight housing

**17.1b Use a Phillips screwdriver to turn the headlight adjuster**

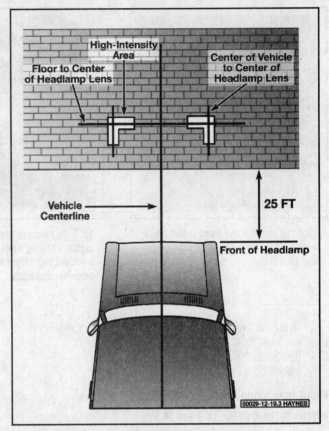

**17.3 Headlight adjustment details**

2    There are several methods for adjusting the headlights. The simplest method requires masking tape, a blank wall and a level floor.

3    Position masking tape vertically on the wall in relation to the vehicle centerline and in relation to the centerlines of both headlights (see illustration).

4    Position a horizontal tape line in reference to the centerline of all the headlights.

➡**Note: It might be easier to position the tape on the wall with the vehicle parked only a few inches away.**

5    Adjustment should be made with the vehicle parked 25 feet from the wall, sitting level, the gas tank half-full and no heavy load in the vehicle.

6    With the low beams turned on, position the high intensity zone so it is two inches below the horizontal line.

---

## 18  Bulb replacement

### EXTERIOR LIGHT BULBS

### Front sidemarker light bulbs

◗ **Refer to illustrations 18.2 and 18.3**

➡**Note: This procedure applies to either front sidemarker light bulb.**

1    Loosen the front wheel lug nuts. Raise the vehicle and place it securely on jackstands, then remove the wheel. Remove the inner fender splash shield (see Chapter 11).

2    Locate the front sidemarker light bulb socket; it's the socket at the outer end of the headlight housing (see illustration 16.3b). To disconnect the electrical connector from the bulb holder, depress the release tab on the bottom of the connector (see illustration) and pull off the connector.

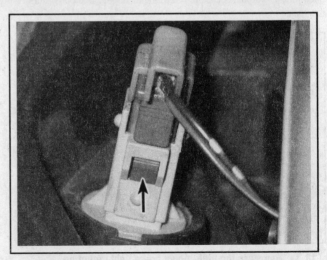

**18.2 To disconnect the electrical connector from the front sidemarker bulb holder, depress this release tab and pull off the connector**

**18.3  To remove the front sidemarker bulb holder, turn it counterclockwise and pull it out**

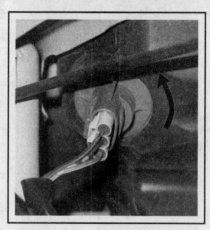

**18.7  To remove the front turn signal/parking light bulb socket from the headlight housing, turn it counterclockwise**

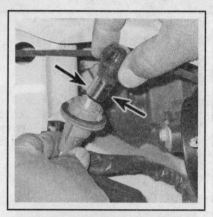

**18.9  When installing a front turn signal/parking light bulb, align the pegs on the bulb with the slots in the socket. Note how the pegs are offset (the slots in the socket are of differing lengths)**

3   To remove the bulb holder, simply turn it counterclockwise (see illustration) and pull it out of the housing.

4   Remove the bulb from the bulb holder.

5   Installation is the reverse of removal.

### Front turn signal/parking light bulbs

▶ **Refer to illustrations 18.7 and 18.9**

➡ **Note: This procedure applies to either front turn signal/parking light bulb.**

6   Locate the front turn signal/parking light bulb holder (see illustration 16.3b).

➡ **Note: You don't have to remove the headlight housing to access this bulb.**

7   To remove the bulb holder, turn it counterclockwise (see illustration) and pull it out of the housing. (It's not necessary to disconnect the electrical connector from the bulb holder.)

8   To remove the front turn signal/parking light bulb from its holder, push it down into the socket, turn it counterclockwise and pull it out of the socket.

9   To install a new bulb in the holder, insert the bulb into the socket, aligning the pegs on the bulb with the slots in the socket (see illustration), push down and turn it clockwise to lock it into place.

10  Installation is the reverse of removal.

### High-mount brake light bulb

▶ **Refer to illustration 18.11**

11  Carefully pry off the two small trim caps at each end of the high-mount brake light assembly (see illustration).

12  Remove the two mounting screws and pull out the high-mount brake light housing.

13  To remove the bulb holder from the high-mount brake light housing, rotate the bulb holder counterclockwise and pull it out of the housing.

14  To remove the old bulb from the bulb holder, simply pull it straight out of the holder. To install a new bulb, push it straight into the bulb holder.

15  Installation is the reverse of removal.

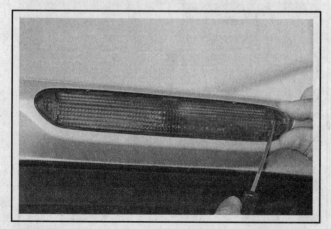

**18.11  To access the high-mount brake light mounting screws, carefully pry out the trim caps from each end of the lens, then remove both mounting screws and pull off the high-mount lens**

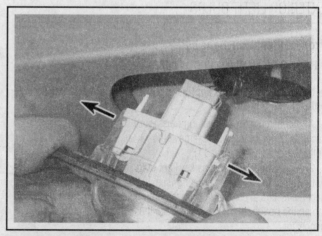

**18.16  Carefully pry the license plate light assembly from the liftgate, then spread the two lens retaining tabs apart and remove the lens from the bulb holder**

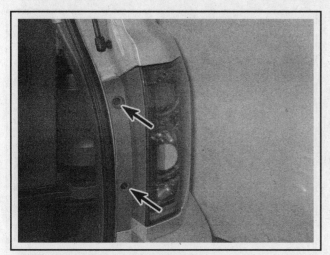

**18.21  To detach the taillight housing from the vehicle, remove these two mounting bolts**

**18.22  Taillight bulb arrangement:**

| A | Running light/turn signal light | B | Sidemarker light |
| | | C | Running light/brake light |

## License plate light bulbs

▶ **Refer to illustration 18.16**

➡**Note: This procedure applies to either license plate light bulb.**

16  Carefully pry the license plate light assembly from the liftgate (see illustration).

17  To remove the lens from the license plate bulb holder, spread the two lens locking tabs apart and pull the lens off the holder (see illustration 18.16).

18  To remove the bulb from the holder, pull it straight out of the socket.

19  To install a new bulb in the holder, push it into the socket until it's seated.

20  Installation is the reverse of removal.

## Taillight bulbs (brake lights, sidemarker lights and turn signal lights)

▶ **Refer to illustrations 18.21, 18.22 and 18.23**

➡**Note: This procedure applies to either taillight assembly**

21  Open the liftgate and remove the two taillight mounting bolts (see illustration).

22  Pull out the taillight assembly and locate the bulb that you want to replace (see illustration).

23  To remove one of the three bulb holders, turn it counterclockwise (see illustration) and pull it out.

24  To remove a bulb from its socket, pull it straight out.

25  Installation is the reverse of removal.

## Back-up light bulbs

▶ **Refer to illustrations 18.26 and 18.27**

26  Open the liftgate and carefully pry open the back-up light access panel in the liftgate trim panel (see illustration).

27  To remove a back-up light bulb holder, rotate it counterclockwise and pull it out (see illustration).

28  To remove the bulb from its socket, pull it straight out.

29  Installation is the reverse of removal.

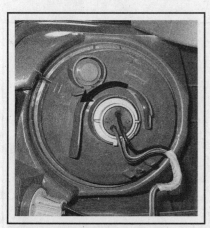

**18.23  To remove a bulb holder from the taillight housing, turn it counterclockwise and pull it out**

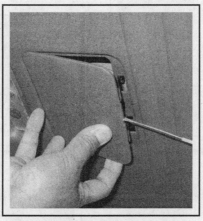

**18.26  To access a back-up light bulb, remove this small access panel in the liftgate trim panel**

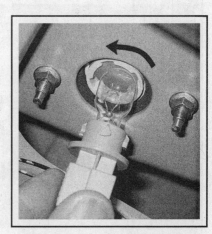

**18.27  To remove a back-up light bulb holder, turn it counterclockwise and pull it out**

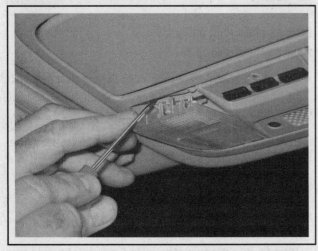

**18.30a Use a small screwdriver to carefully pry off the rear edge of the lens for the map reading light . . .**

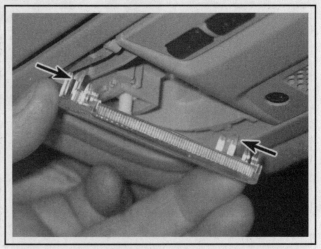

**18.30b . . . then carefully work the front edge of the lens loose and remove the lens. The two hooked tabs are fragile, so don't try to force them loose or you'll break them!**

## INTERIOR LIGHT BULBS

### Front map light bulbs

▶ **Refer to illustrations 18.30a and 18.30b**

30  Carefully pry off the lens (see illustrations).
31  To replace a bulb, simply pull it out from its terminals.
32  To install a new bulb, push it into place between the terminals until it snaps into place.
33  When installing the lens, make sure that you don't break the engagement tabs at each end.

### Rear individual map light bulbs

▶ **Refer to illustrations 18.34, 18.35 and 18.36**

34  Pry off the lens from the rear individual map light assembly with a small screwdriver (see illustration).
35  Remove the heat shield (see illustration).
36  Remove the old bulb from the rear individual map light assembly (see illustration).

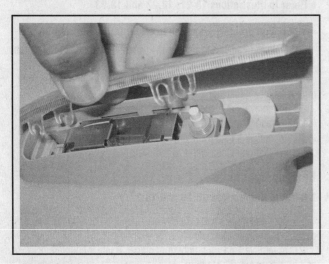

**18.34 Carefully pry off the rear individual map light lens with a small screwdriver. Make sure that you don't damage any of the four retaining tabs**

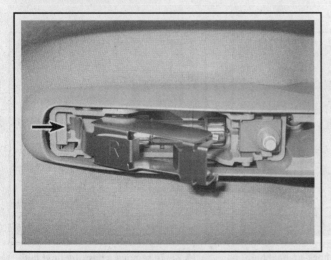

**18.35 Note how it's installed, then remove the heat shield from the rear individual map light. When installing the heat shield, be sure to insert this little tab into its slot in the map light housing**

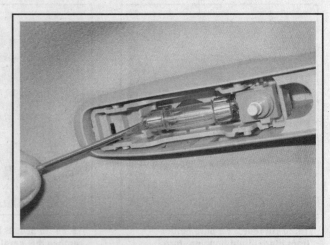

**18.36 Carefully remove the old bulb from the rear individual map light with a small screwdriver. Pry only on the metal ends of the bulb**

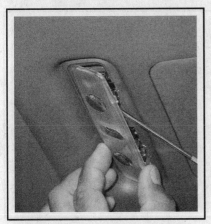

**18.38 Using a small screwdriver, carefully pry off the liftgate lens**

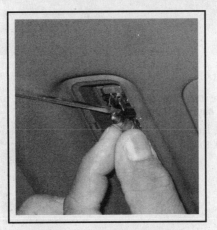

**18.39 Using a small screwdriver, carefully pry out the liftgate light bulb. Pry only on the metal ends of the bulb**

**18.41 Using a small screwdriver, carefully pry out the old glove box light bulb. Pry only on the metal ends of the bulb**

37 When installing the heat shield, make sure that you insert the tab into its mounting hole (see illustration 18.35). Installation is otherwise the reverse of removal.

### Liftgate light bulbs

▶ **Refer to illustrations 18.38 and 18.39**

38 Carefully pry off the liftgate light lens (see illustration).
39 Remove the liftgate light bulb (see illustration).
40 Installation is the reverse of removal.

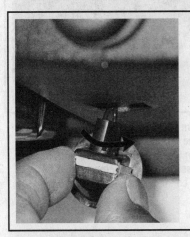

**18.43 Carefully pry out the front console light housing, then rotate the bulb holder counterclockwise 1/4-turn and pull it out of the housing**

### Glove box light bulb

▶ **Refer to illustration 18.41**

41 Open the glove box and remove the light bulb (see illustration).
42 Installation is the reverse of removal.

### Front console light bulb

▶ **Refer to illustration 18.43**

➡**Note: The front console light bulb is located to the right of the change drawer.**

43 Carefully pry out the front console light housing, then turn the bulb holder counterclockwise and remove it from the housing (see illustration).
44 Remove the front console light bulb from its bulb holder.
45 Installation is the reverse of removal.

### Vanity mirror light bulbs

▶ **Refer to illustrations 18.46 and 18.47**

46 Carefully pry off the lens from the vanity mirror light (see illustration).
47 Remove the old bulb from the vanity mirror light assembly (see illustration).
48 Installation is the reverse of removal.

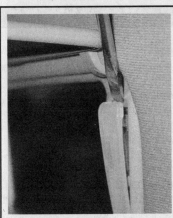

**18.46 Carefully pry off the vanity light lens with a small screwdriver**

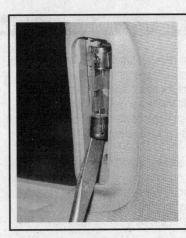

**18.47 Remove the old vanity light bulb with a small screwdriver, prying only on the metal ends**

### Courtesy light bulbs

▶ **Refer to illustration 18.49**

➡ **Note: The courtesy lights are located in the lower part of the front doors. This procedure applies to either courtesy light.**

49 Carefully pry off the courtesy light lens (see illustration).
50 Remove the courtesy light bulb by pulling it straight out of its socket.
51 Installation is the reverse of removal.

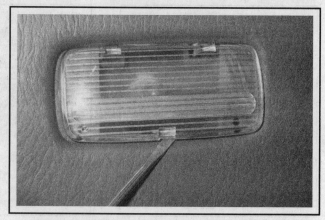

**18.49 Carefully pry off the courtesy light lens with a small screwdriver**

## 19 Horns - replacement

▶ **Refer to illustration 19.2**

➡ **Note: There are two horns. They're located at the front of the vehicle, behind the bumper cover and below the headlight housings.**

1 Raise the front of the vehicle and place it securely on jackstands. Remove the engine splash shield (see Chapter 2A).
2 Using a flashlight, locate the horn that you want to replace (see illustration).
3 Disconnect the electrical connector from the horn.
4 Remove the horn mounting bracket bolt and remove the horn.
5 Installation is the reverse of removal.

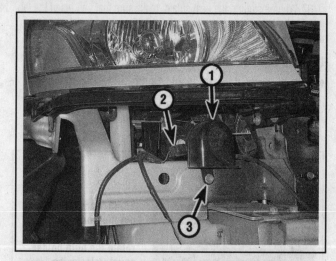

**19.2 This is the right horn (1). The left horn is located in the same place, under the left headlight housing (bumper cover removed for clarity; you can access either horn by removing the engine splash shield). To remove the a horn, disconnect the electrical connector (2), then remove the horn mounting bolt (3)**

## 20 Electric side view mirrors - general information

1 Most electric rear view mirrors use two motors to move the glass; one for up and down adjustments and one for left-right adjustments.
2 During mirror adjustment, the power mirror adjustment switch sends voltage to the left or right side mirror. With the ignition key turned to ON (engine not running), operate the mirror adjustment switch through all of its functions (left-right and up-down) for both the left and right side mirrors.
3 Listen carefully for the sound of the electric motors running in the mirrors.
4 If you can hear the motors but the mirror glass doesn't move, there's a problem with the drive mechanism inside the mirror.
5 If the mirrors do not operate and no sound comes from the mir-

rors, check the fuse (see Section 3).
6 If the fuse is OK, remove the power mirror adjustment switch (see *Door trim panels – removal and installation* in Chapter 11). Have the switch continuity checked by a dealership service department or other qualified automobile repair facility.
7 Test the ground connections.
8 If the mirror still doesn't work, remove the mirror and check the wires at the mirror for voltage.
9 If there is no voltage in any switch position, check the circuit between the mirror and the adjustment switch for opens and shorts.
10 If there's voltage, remove the mirror and test it off the vehicle with jumper wires. Replace the mirror if it fails this test.

## 21 Cruise control system - general information

### 2001 AND 2002 ACURA AND 2003 AND 2004 HONDA MODELS

1   The cruise control system maintains vehicle speed with an electrically-operated motor located in the engine compartment, which is connected to the throttle body by a cable. The system consists of the cruise control module, the cruise control switches, the cruise control cable, the Powertrain Control Module (PCM) and the brake light switch. The cruise control system requires diagnostic procedures that are beyond the scope of this manual. Listed below are some general procedures that may be used to locate common problems.

2   Check the fuses (see Section 3).

3   Have an assistant operate the brake pedal while you check the operation of the brake lights (voltage from the brake light switch deactivates the cruise control).

4   If the brake lights don't come on, or if they stay on all the time, correct the problem and retest the cruise control system.

5   Visually inspect the control cable between the cruise control motor and the throttle body for free movement. Replace it if necessary.

6   Test drive the vehicle to determine if the cruise control is now working. If it isn't, take it to a dealer service department or an automotive electrical specialist for further diagnosis.

### 2003 AND LATER ACURA AND 2005 AND LATER HONDA MODELS

7   These models have an electrically controlled throttle body. The accelerator pedal communicates with the throttle body through the Powertrain Control Module (PCM). (See Chapters 4 and 6 for more information about the electronic throttle control system.) The PCM also controls the cruise control system, which is now an integral function of the electronic throttle control system. If the system malfunctions, take it to a dealer service department or other qualified repair shop for further diagnosis.

## 22 Power window system - general information

1   The power window system operates electric motors, mounted in the doors, which lower and raise the windows. The system consists of the control switches, the motors, regulators, glass mechanisms and associated wiring.

2   The power windows can be lowered and raised from the master control switch by the driver or by remote switches located at the individual windows. Each window has a separate motor, which is reversible. The position of the control switch determines the polarity and therefore the direction of operation.

3   The circuit is protected by a fuse and a circuit breaker. Each motor is also equipped with an internal circuit breaker, this prevents one stuck window from disabling the whole system.

4   The power window system will only operate when the ignition switch is turned to ON. There's also a main switch at the master power window control panel (in the driver's door) which, when activated, disables the switches at the rear windows and the switch at the passenger's window. So if there's a problem with the passenger window or with either of the rear windows, make sure that it's not simply a matter of flipping the main switch before proceeding.

5   The procedures listed below are general in nature, so if you can't find the problem using them, take the vehicle to a dealer service department.

6   If the power windows won't operate, always check the fuses and relays first (see Sections 3 and 5, respectively). Also verify that there's voltage to the relay and that the relay is well grounded.

7   If only the rear windows are inoperative, or if the windows only operate from the master control switch, check the main switch for continuity in the unlocked position. Replace it if it doesn't have continuity (see *Door trim panel - removal and installation* in Chapter 11).

8   Check the wiring between the switches and the fuse and relay box for continuity. Repair the wiring, if necessary.

9   If only one window is inoperative from the main switch, try the other control switch at the window.

➡**Note: This doesn't apply to the driver's door window.**

10   If the same window works from one switch, but not the other, check the switch for continuity.

11   If the switch tests OK, check for a short or open in the circuit between the affected switch and the window motor.

12   If one window is inoperative from both switches, remove the trim panel from the affected door (see *Door trim panel - removal and installation* in Chapter 11) and check for voltage at the switch and at the motor while the switch is operated.

13   If voltage is reaching the motor, disconnect the glass from the regulator (see Chapter 11). Move the window up and down by hand while checking for binding and damage. Also check for binding and damage to the regulator. If the regulator is not damaged and the window moves up and down smoothly, replace the motor. If there's binding or damage, lubricate, repair or replace parts, as necessary.

14   If voltage isn't reaching the motor, check the wiring in the circuit for continuity between the switches and motors. You'll need to consult the wiring diagram for the vehicle.

### RESETTING THE POWER WINDOW CONTROL UNIT

15   The power window control unit might have to be reset after any of these procedures:

*The battery has been disconnected*
*The No. 79 (20-amp) fuse has been removed from the engine compartment fuse and relay box*
*The 18-pin electrical connector has been disconnected from the power window control unit*
*The window regulator, glass or glass run channel has been removed*
*The driver's door wiring harness has been disconnected*

16   Turn the ignition switch to OFF, then turn it to ON.

17   Fully open the driver's window by depressing the AUTO DOWN part of the driver's door power window switch. When the window is fully open, hold the switch in the AUTO DOWN position for two seconds.

18   Fully close the driver's window without stopping by holding the switch in the UP position. When the window is fully closed, hold the switch in the UP position for two seconds.

19   If the window still doesn't work, repeat this procedure.

## 23 Power door lock system - general information

1   A power door lock system operates the door lock actuators mounted in each door. The system consists of the switches, actuators, a control unit and associated wiring. On some models, the power door lock system is part of the security alarm system. On these models, the power door lock system is more complex, and more difficult to diagnose. Therefore, home troubleshooting is limited to simple checks of the wiring connections and actuators for minor faults that can be easily repaired.

2   Power door lock systems are operated by bi-directional solenoids located in the doors. The lock switches have two operating positions: LOCK and UNLOCK. When activated, the switch sends a ground signal to the door lock control unit to lock or unlock the doors. Depending on which way the switch is activated, the control unit reverses polarity to the solenoids, allowing the two sides of the circuit to be used alternately as the feed (positive) and ground side.

3   The following general guidelines should help you quickly identify and repair typical problems. If you're unable to locate the trouble using these guidelines, consult a dealer service department.

4   Always check the fuses first (see Section 3 and your owners' manual).

5   Operate the door lock switches in both directions (LOCK and UNLOCK) with the engine off. Listen for the click of the solenoids operating.

6   Test the switches for continuity. Remove the switches and have them checked by a dealer service department.

7   Check the wiring between the switches, control unit and solenoids for continuity. Repair the wiring if there's no continuity.

8   Check for a bad ground at the switches and at the control unit.

9   If only one lock solenoid doesn't operate, remove the trim panel from the door with the bad solenoid (see "Door trim panel - removal and installation" in Chapter 11) and check for voltage at the solenoid while the lock switch is operated. One of the wires should have voltage in the Lock position; the other should have voltage in the Unlock position.

10  If the inoperative solenoid is receiving voltage, replace the solenoid.

11  If the inoperative solenoid isn't receiving voltage, check for an open or short in the wire between the lock solenoid and the control unit.

➡**Note: Wire harnesses typically break between the body and door, because repeatedly opening and closing the door fatigues and eventually breaks the wires.**

## 24 Daytime Running Lights (DRL) - general information

The Daytime Running Lights (DRL) system illuminates the headlights whenever the engine is running. The only exception is with the engine running and the parking brake engaged. Once the parking brake is released, the lights will remain on as long as the ignition switch is on, even if the parking brake is later applied. The DRL system supplies reduced power to the headlights so they won't be too bright for daytime use, while prolonging headlight life.

If one of the headlight low beams is out, the low-beam filament is probably burned out, but check the DRL relay first (see Section 3). The DRL relay is located in the engine compartment fuse and relay box. If the relay is okay, replace the bad headlight bulb (see Section 15).

## 25 Airbag system - general information

## GENERAL INFORMATION

1   All models are equipped with a Supplemental Restraint System (SRS), more commonly known as airbags. This system is designed to protect the driver, and the front seat passenger, from serious injury in the event of a head-on or frontal collision. It uses a single crash sensor built into the SRS control unit on 2001 and 2002 Acura and 2003 and 2004 Honda models, or a pair of crash sensors mounted behind the front bumper (2003 and later Acura and 2005 and later Honda models). The airbag assemblies are mounted on the steering wheel and inside the passenger's end of the dash. All models are also equipped with side-impact airbags mounted in the backs of the front seats.

Some models are also equipped with seat belt pre-tensioners. These are pyrotechnic (explosive) devices that reduce the slack in the seat belts during an impact of sufficient force to trigger the airbags.

## AIRBAG MODULE

### Driver's side airbag

2   The airbag inflator module contains a housing incorporating the cushion (airbag) and inflator unit, mounted in the center of the steering wheel. The inflator assembly is mounted on the back of the housing over a hole through which gas is expelled, inflating the bag almost instantaneously when an electrical signal is sent from the system. A "clockspring" on the steering column under the steering wheel carries this signal to the module. This clockspring assembly can transmit an electrical signal regardless of steering wheel position. The igniter in the airbag converts the electrical signal to heat and ignites the powder, which inflates the bag.

3   For information on how to remove and install the driver's side airbag, refer to "Steering wheel - removal and installation" in Chapter 10.

## Passenger's side airbag

4   The airbag is mounted at the top of the passenger's side of the instrument panel. It consists of an inflator containing an igniter, a reaction housing/airbag assembly and a trim cover.

5   The passenger's side airbag is considerably larger than the steering wheel-mounted unit and is mounted inside the dash, near the glove box. The airbag trim cover on top of the dash is textured and painted to match the instrument panel and has a molded seam, which splits when the bag inflates.

## SRS CONTROL UNIT

6   This unit supplies the current to the airbag system (and seat belt pre-tensioners, on models so equipped) in the event of the collision, even if battery power is cut off. It checks this system every time the vehicle is started, causing the "SRS" light to go on, then off, if the system is operating correctly. If there is a fault in the system, the light will go on and stay on, or it will flash or the dash will make a beeping sound. If this happens, take the vehicle to your dealer immediately for service.

## DISARMING THE SYSTEM AND OTHER PRECAUTIONS

### ❊❊ WARNING:

**Failure to follow these precautions could result in accidental deployment of the airbag and personal injury.**

7   Whenever working in the vicinity of the steering wheel, instrument panel or any of the other SRS system components, the system must be disarmed. To disarm the system:

a)  *Point the wheels straight ahead and turn the key to the Lock position.*

b)  *Disconnect the cable from the negative battery terminal(s). Refer to Chapter 5, Section 1 for the disconnecting procedure.*

c)  *Wait at least three minutes for the back-up power supply to be depleted.*

8   Whenever handling an airbag module, always keep the airbag opening side pointed away from your body. Never place the airbag module on a bench or other surface with the airbag opening facing the surface. Always place the airbag module in a safe location with the airbag opening facing up.

9   Never measure the resistance of any SRS component or use any electrical test equipment on any of the wiring or components. An ohmmeter has a built-in battery supply that could accidentally deploy the airbag.

10  Never use electrical welding equipment on a vehicle equipped with an airbag without first disconnecting the airbag electrical connectors. The connector for the driver's side airbag is located near the bottom of the steering column (see *Steering wheel - removal and installation* in Chapter 10); the connector for the passenger's side airbag is located inside the dash, near the glove box (see below). The seat belt pre-tensioner electrical connectors are located behind the B-pillar trim panels. The electrical connectors for the side impact airbags, on models so equipped, are located under the front seats.

11  Never dispose of a live airbag module or seat belt pre-tensioner. Return it to a dealer service department or other qualified repair shop for safe deployment and disposal.

## AIRBAG MODULE REMOVAL AND INSTALLATION

### Driver's side airbag module and clockspring

12  Refer to Chapter 10, *Steering wheel - removal and installation*, for the driver's side airbag module and clockspring removal and installation procedures.

### Passenger's side airbag module

13  It's not necessary to remove the passenger's side airbag for any procedure covered in this manual. Therefore, we don't recommend that you attempt to do so. You will have to disconnect three electrical connectors to remove the instrument panel (dashboard) in order to replace the conditioning/heating housing. But disconnecting those connectors is part of the procedure for removing the instrument panel (see Chapter 11).

### Side-impact airbag

14  Under normal circumstances there would never be a reason to remove a side-impact airbag. However, if it has been determined that there is a problem with the side-impact airbag module, the work must be left to a dealer service department or other qualified repair shop.

---

### 26  Keyless entry - testing and programming the transmitter

1   Here's how the transmitter should work:

*If a door or the liftgate is open, you can't lock the doors and tailgate with the transmitter.*

*If you unlock the doors with the transmitter, but don't open a door within 30 seconds, all the doors automatically relock.*

*If the ignition key is inserted into the ignition switch key lock cylinder, the transmitter will neither lock nor unlock the doors.*

2   If the doors lock or unlock with the transmitter, but the LED on the transmitter doesn't come on, replace the transmitter.

### TESTING THE TRANSMITTER

▶ **Refer to illustrations 26.4a, 26.4b, 26.5a, 26.5b, 26.5c and 26.5d**

3   Press the LOCK or UNLOCK button five or six times to reset the transmitter.

*If the locks now work, the transmitter is okay.*

*If the locks don't work, go to the next step.*

**26.4a  To open the transmitter housing, remove this screw . . .**

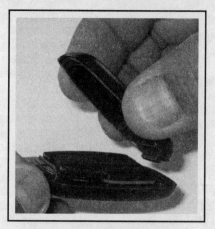

**26.4b  . . . and separate the two halves of the transmitter housing**

**26.5a  To replace the battery, remove the transmitter from the transmitter housing . . .**

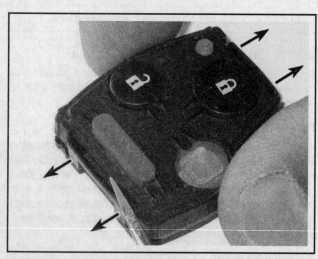

**26.5b  . . . then pry open the retainers on both ends of the transmitter . . .**

4   Open the transmitter (see illustrations) and inspect it for water damage.

*If you see water damage, replace the transmitter.*
*If there is no water damage, go to the next step.*

5   Replace the transmitter battery with a new battery (see illustrations), then try to lock and unlock the doors with the transmitter by pressing the LOCK or UNLOCK button five or six times.

*If the doors lock and unlock, the transmitter is okay.*
*If the doors don't lock and unlock go to the next step.*

6   Reprogram the transmitter (see Step 7), then try to lock and unlock the doors.

*If the doors lock and unlock, the transmitter is okay.*
*If the doors still don't lock and unlock, replace the transmitter.*

**26.5c  . . . and carefully remove the battery**

**26.5d  When installing the new battery, make sure that the positive side faces down (toward the transmitter)**

## PROGRAMMING THE TRANSMITTER

**→Note 1: Make sure that all the doors, the hood and the tailgate are closed.**

**→Note 2: It is essential that you perform each step of the programming procedure within one to four seconds of the previous step.**

**→Note 3: You can store up to three transmitter codes in the keyless receiver unit's memory. If you exceed this number, the first code that you stored will be erased.**

7  Turn the ignition switch to ON, then within one to four seconds, aim the transmitter at the keyless receiver (near the right kick panel) and press the transmitter LOCK or UNLOCK button

8  Within another one to four seconds, turn the ignition switch to OFF.

9  Within another one to four seconds, turn the ignition switch to ON.

10  Within another one to our seconds, aim the transmitter at the keyless receiver and press the transmitter LOCK or UNLOCK button.

11  Within another one to four seconds, turn the ignition switch to OFF.

12  Within another one to four seconds, turn the ignition switch to ON.

13  Within another one to four seconds, aim the transmitter at the keyless receiver and press the transmitter LOCK or UNLOCK button.

14  Within another one to four seconds, turn the ignition switch to OFF.

15  Within another one to four seconds, turn the ignition switch to ON.

16  Within another one to four seconds, aim the transmitter at the keyless receiver and press the transmitter LOCK or UNLOCK button.

17  Verify that you can hear the door lock actuators operating, then within four seconds, press the transmitter LOCK or UNLOCK button again.

18  Within 10 seconds, aim the transmitter at the keyless receiver unit, then press the LOCK or UNLOCK button. Verify that you can hear the door lock actuators operating after the transmitter code is stored.

19  Turn the ignition switch to OFF and pull out the ignition key.

20  Verify that the vehicle's keyless entry system operates correctly with each transmitter code.

## 27  Wiring diagrams - general information

Since it isn't possible to include all wiring diagrams for every year covered by this manual, the following diagrams are those that are typical and most commonly needed.

Prior to troubleshooting any circuits, check the fuses and relays to ensure that they're in good condition. Make sure that the battery is correctly charged and check the cable connections (see Chapters 1 and 5).

When checking a circuit, make sure that all connections are clean and tight, with no broken or loose terminals. If an electrical connector is difficult to disconnect, it's probably because the two halves of the connector are locked together on one or two sides of the connector. So stop and look for the locks, which are usually small plastic tabs that must either be depressed to unlock them, or must be released with a small screwdriver. If you have a problem finding the lock(s), clean off the connector with electronic parts cleaner, then look again. If you're trying to unplug a connector that's located in a dark area, use a flashlight to find the locks. When disconnecting an electrical connector, do NOT pull on the wires; pull on the two halves of the connector itself.

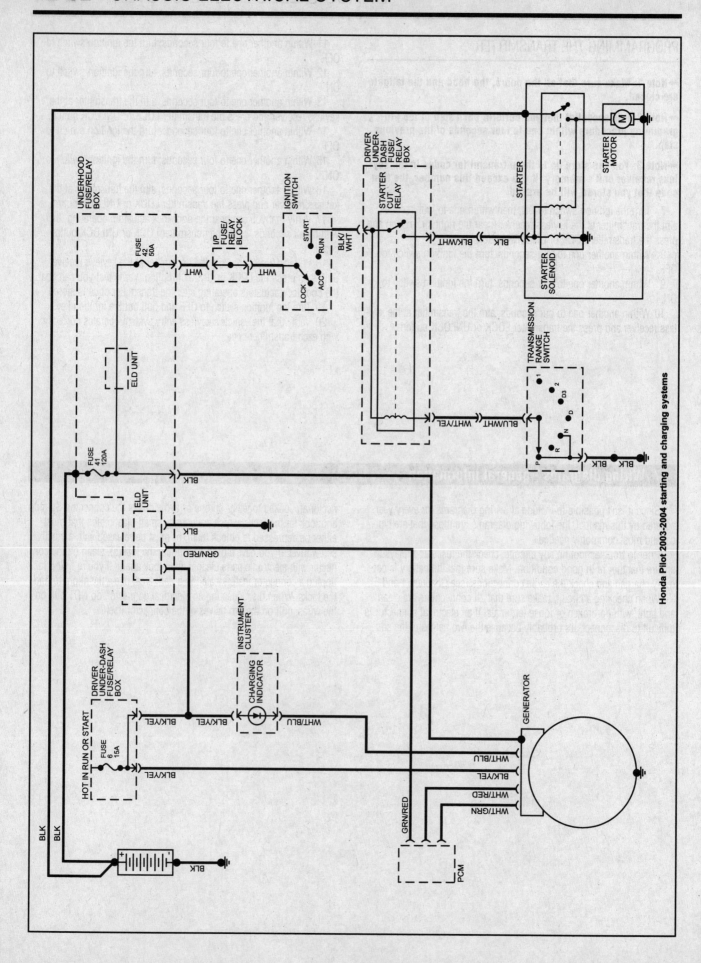

**Honda Pilot 2003-2004 starting and charging systems**

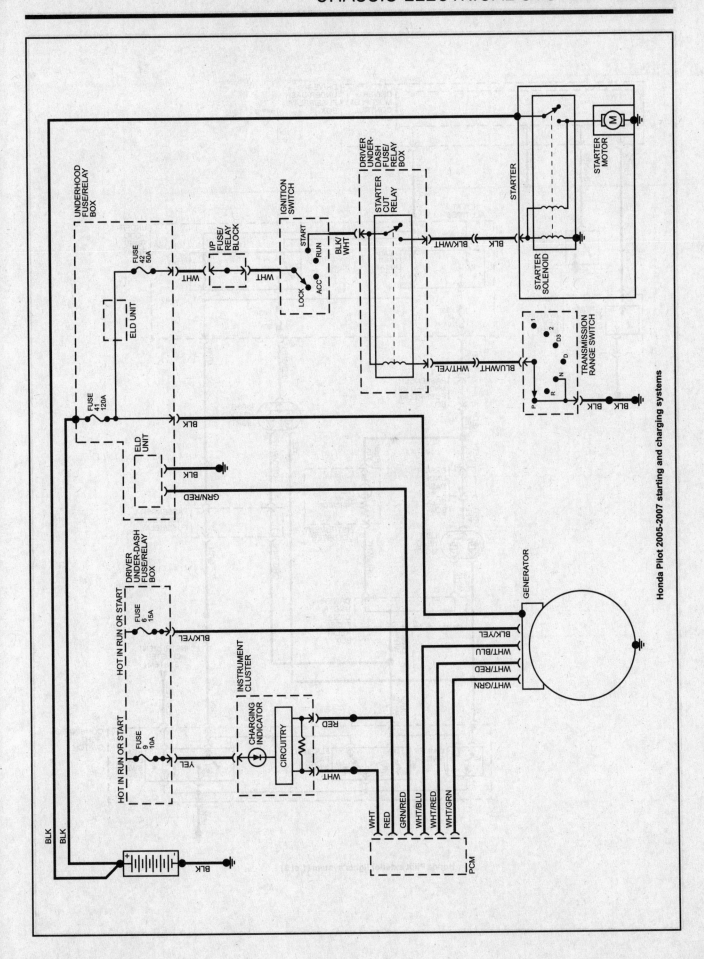

Honda Pilot 2005-2007 starting and charging systems

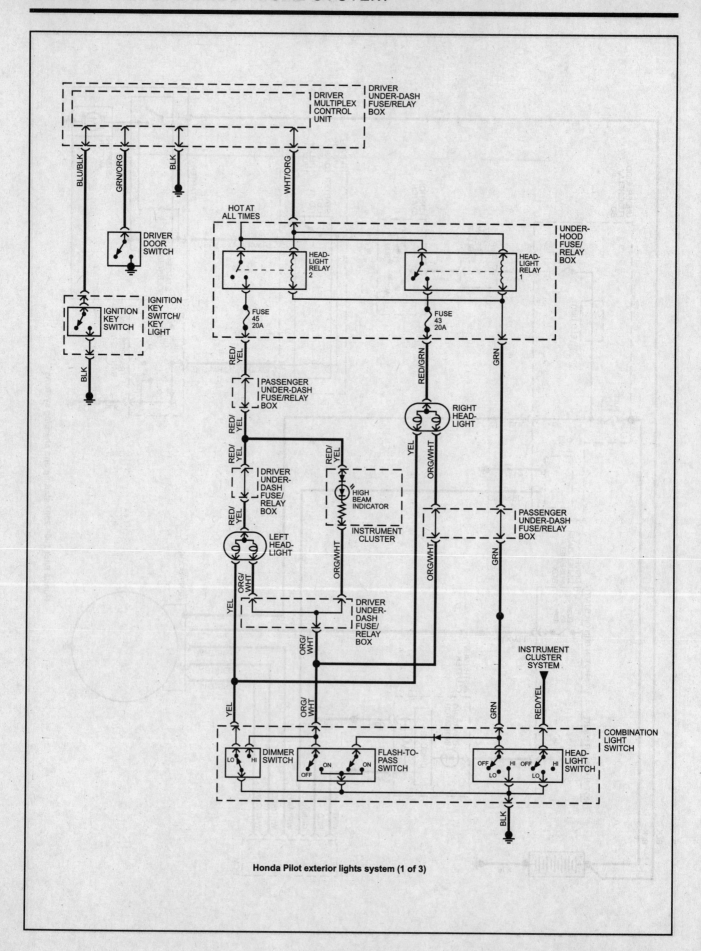

**Honda Pilot exterior lights system (1 of 3)**

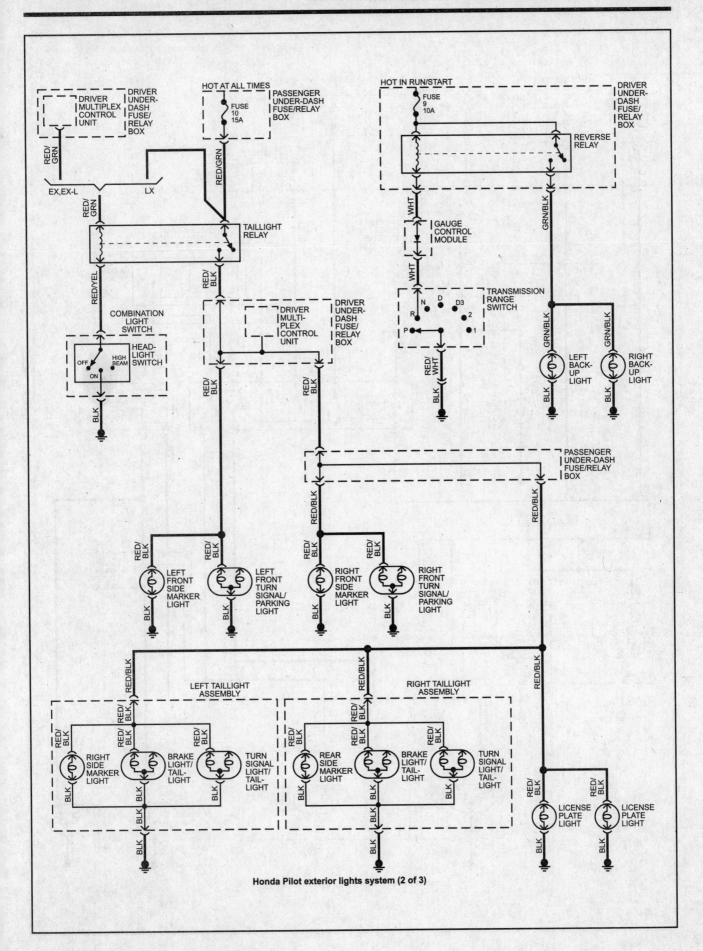

**Honda Pilot exterior lights system (2 of 3)**

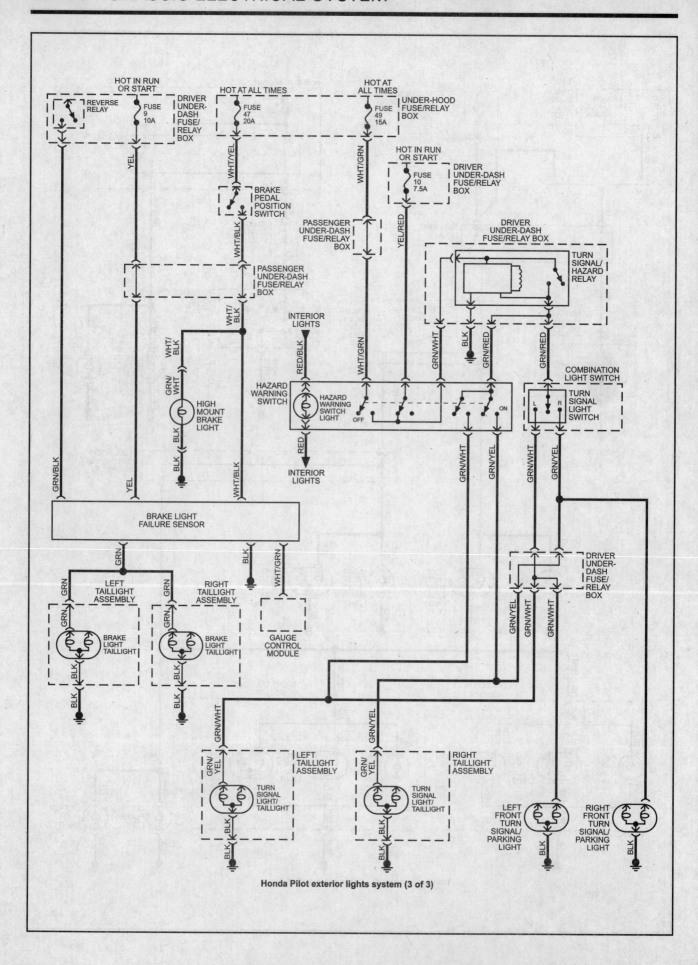

Honda Pilot exterior lights system (3 of 3)

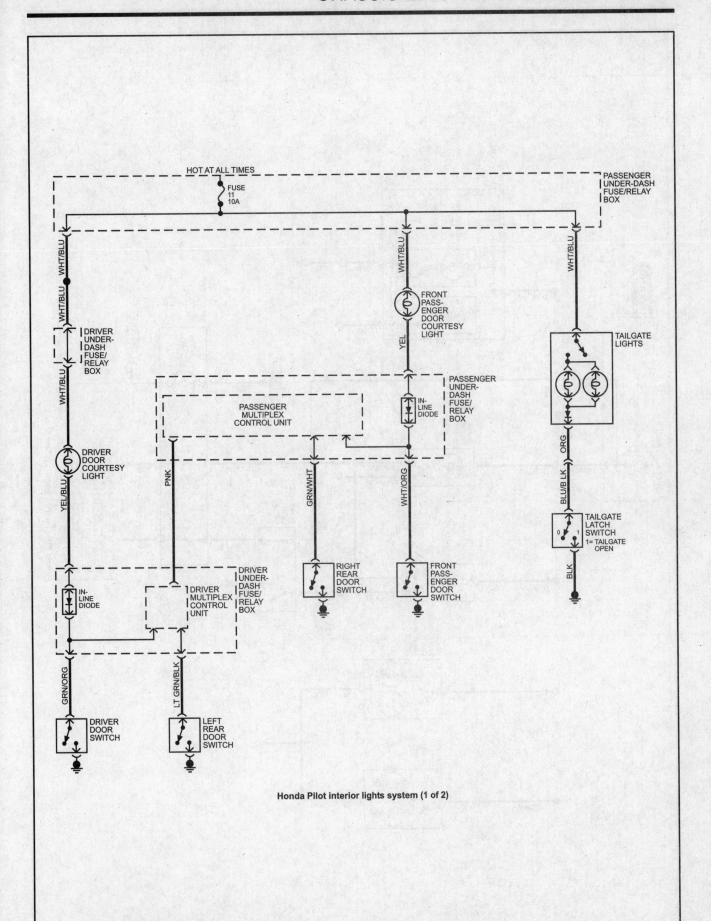

**Honda Pilot interior lights system (1 of 2)**

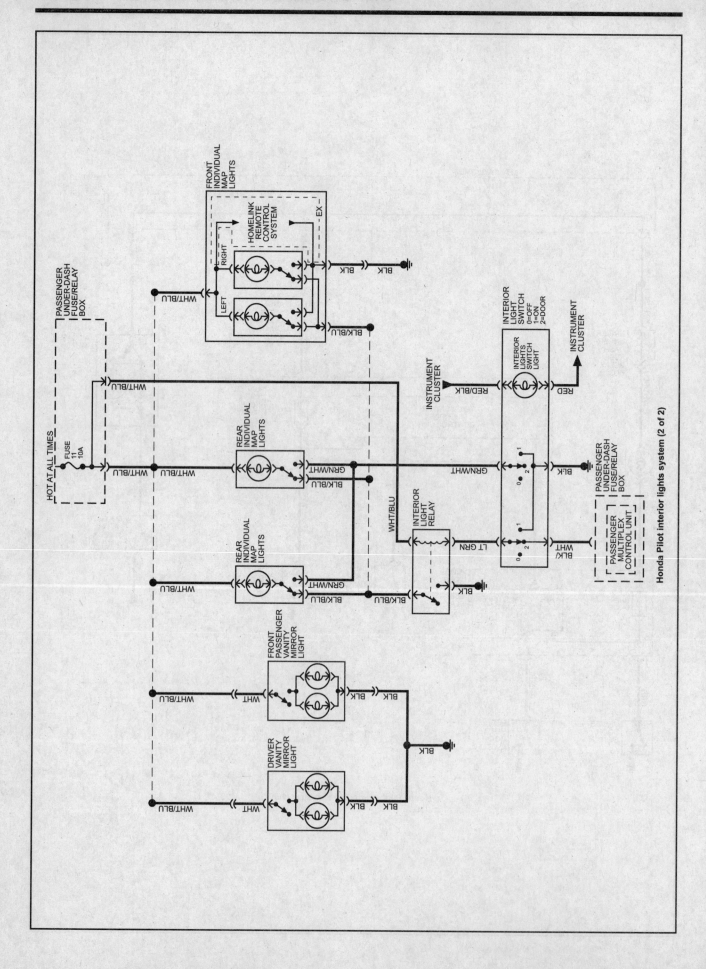

Honda Pilot interior lights system (2 of 2)

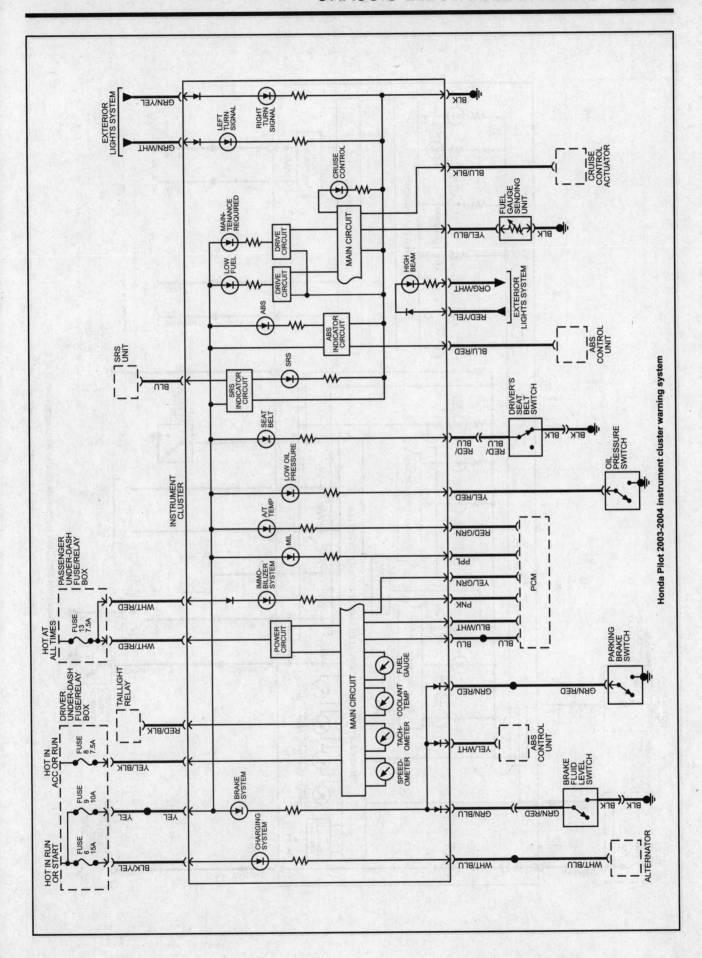

Honda Pilot 2003-2004 instrument cluster warning system

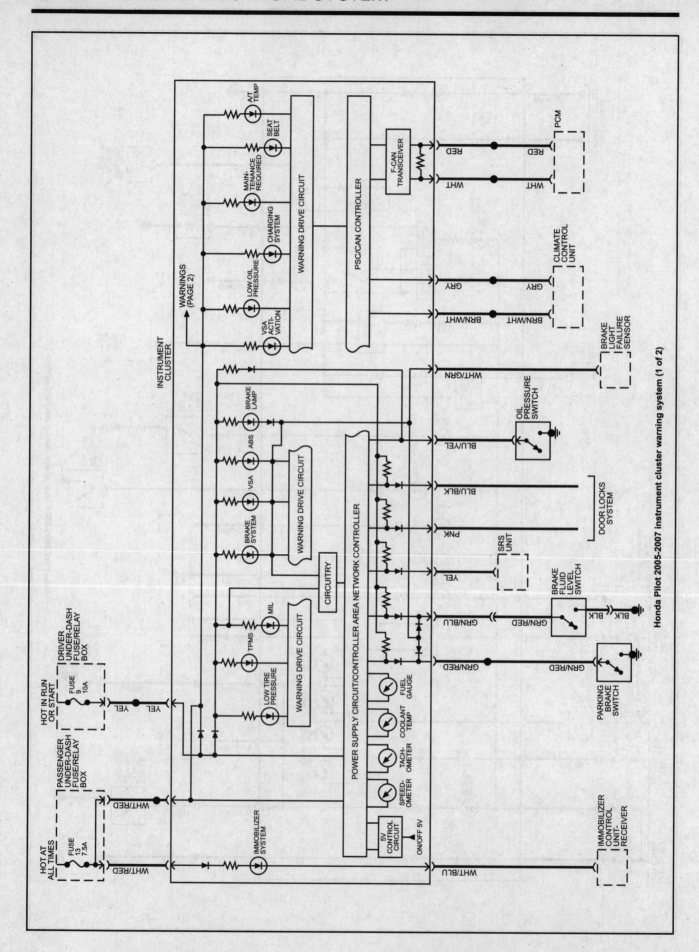

**Honda Pilot 2005-2007 instrument cluster warning system (1 of 2)**

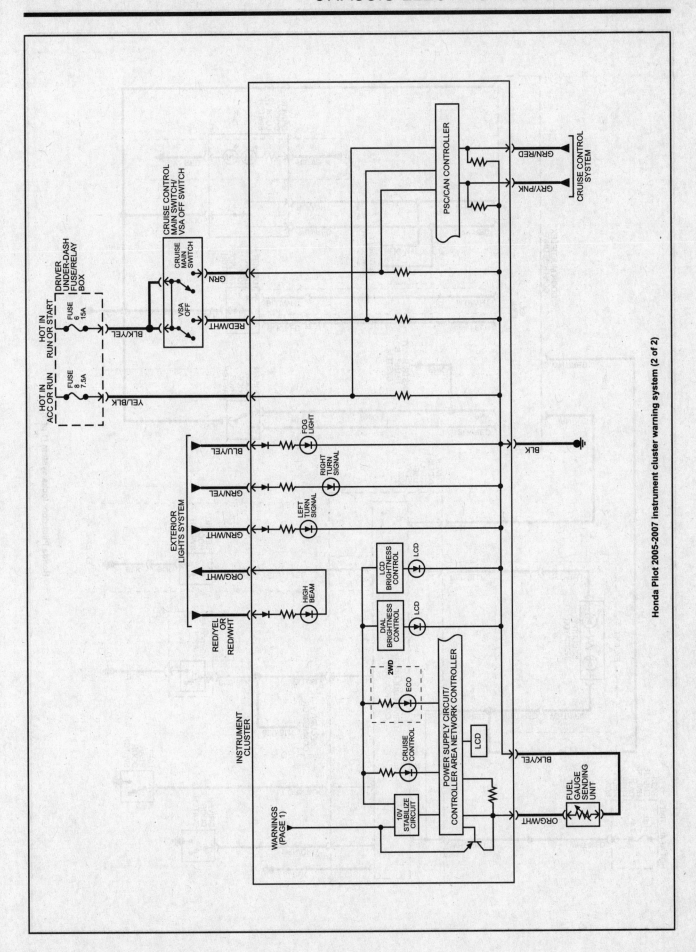

**Honda Pilot 2005-2007 instrument cluster warning system (2 of 2)**

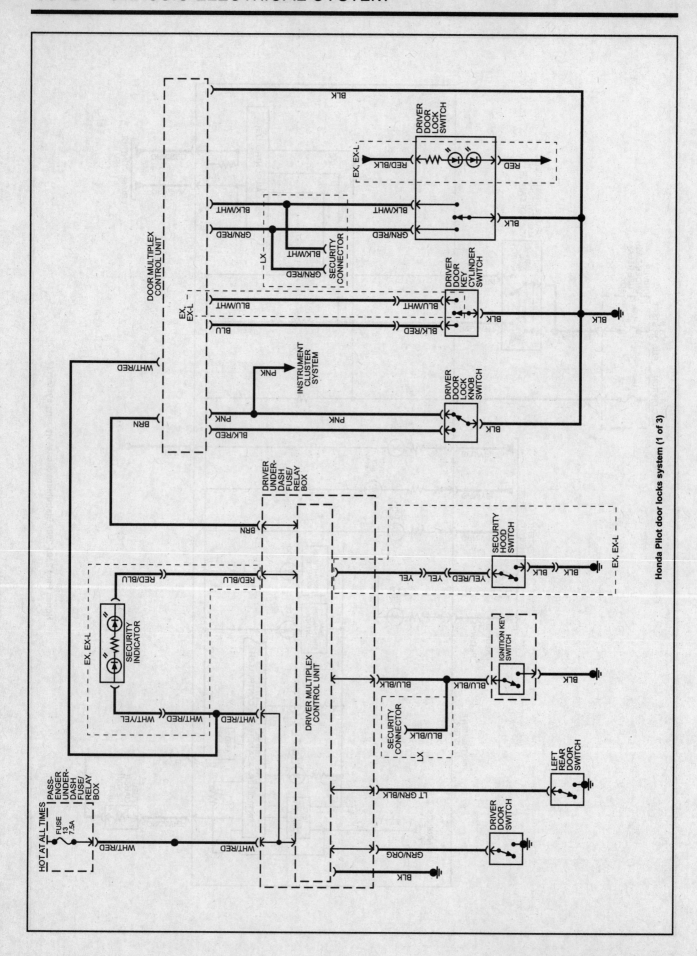

Honda Pilot door locks system (1 of 3)

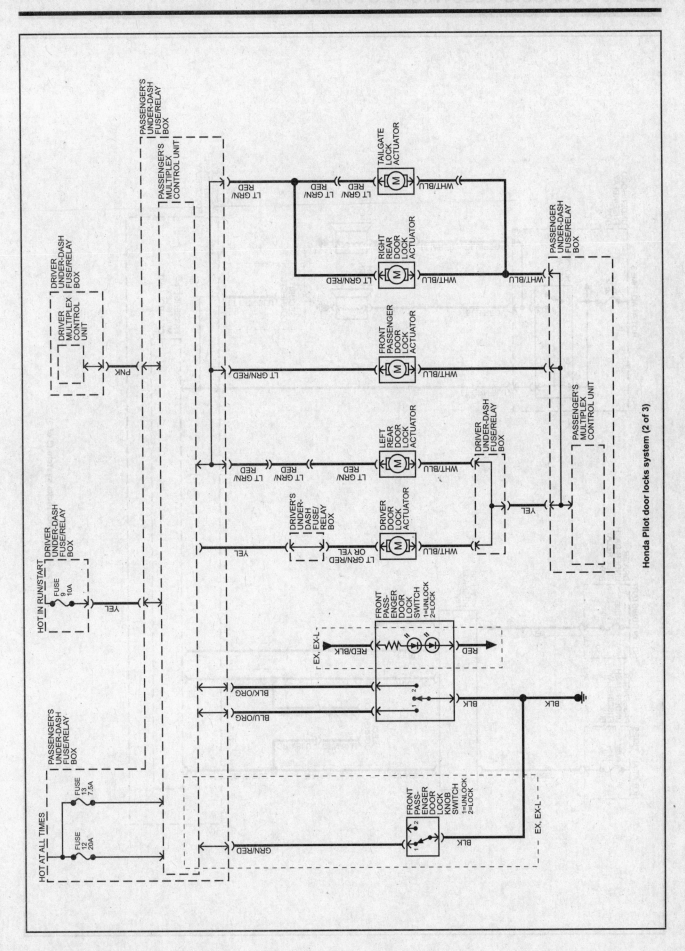

Honda Pilot door locks system (2 of 3)

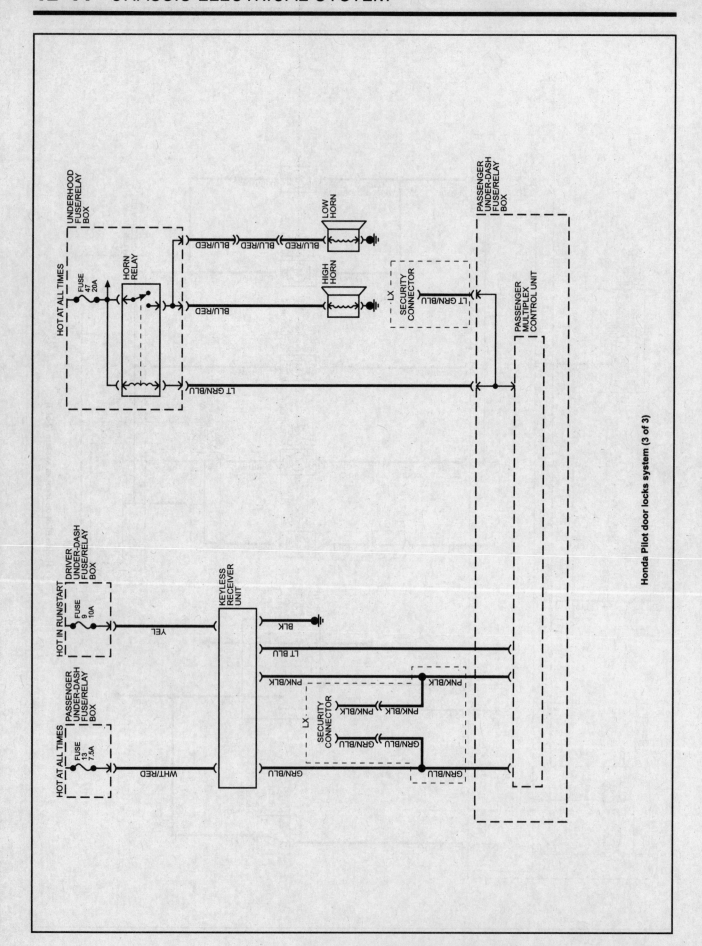

**Honda Pilot door locks system (3 of 3)**

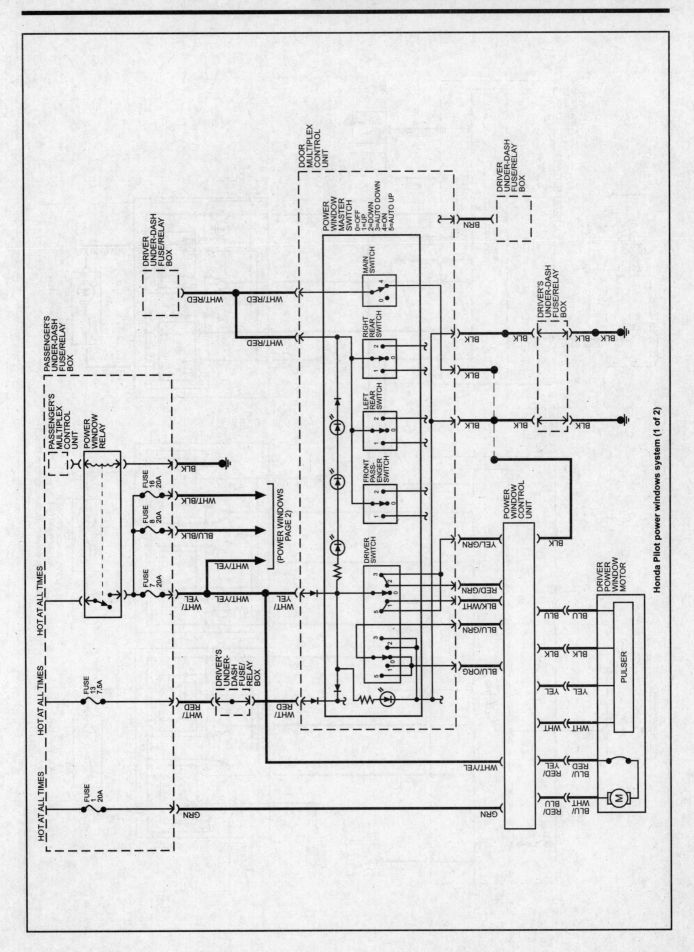

Honda Pilot power windows system (1 of 2)

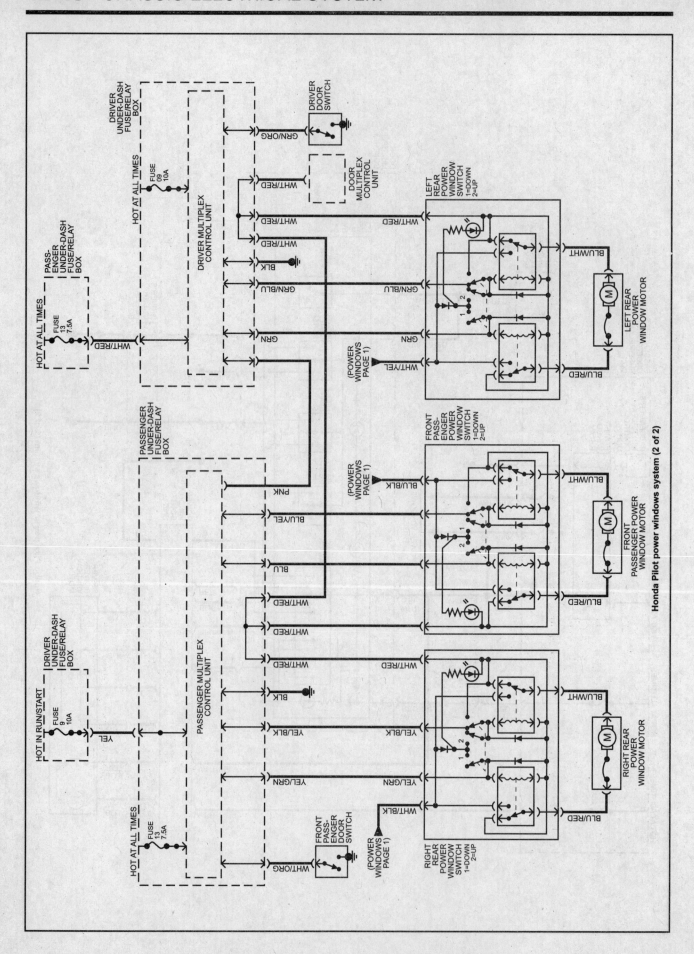

Honda Pilot power windows system (2 of 2)

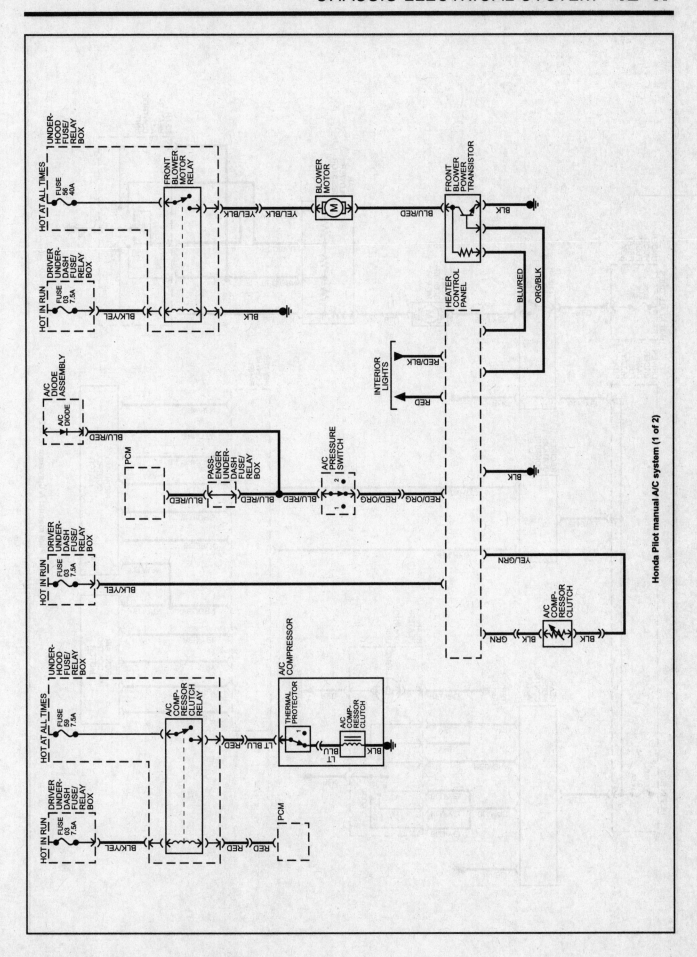

Honda Pilot manual A/C system (1 of 2)

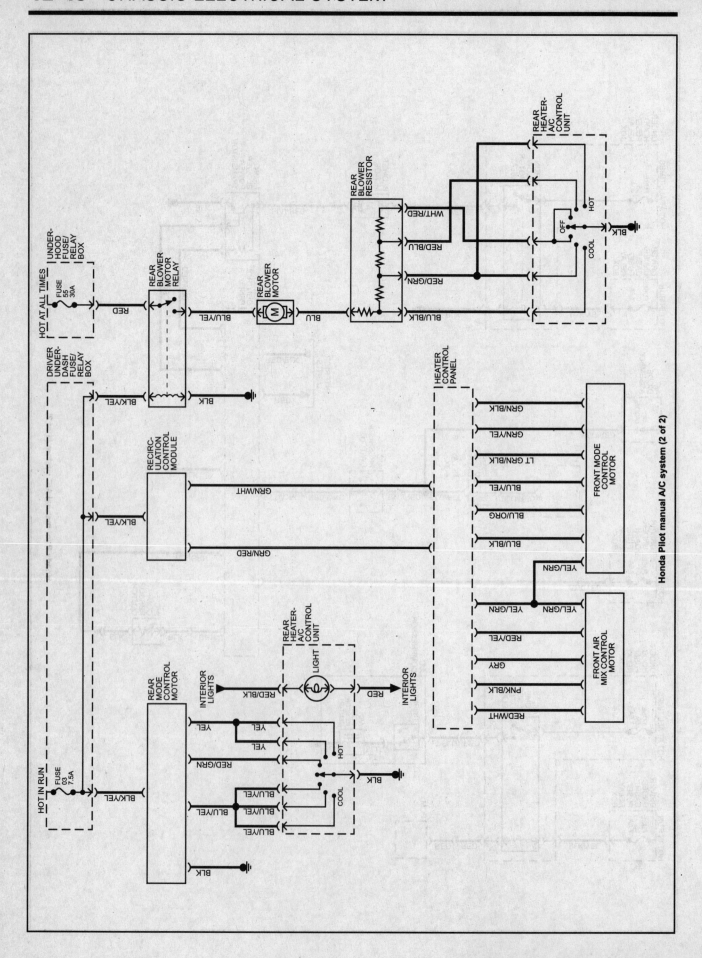

**Honda Pilot manual A/C system (2 of 2)**

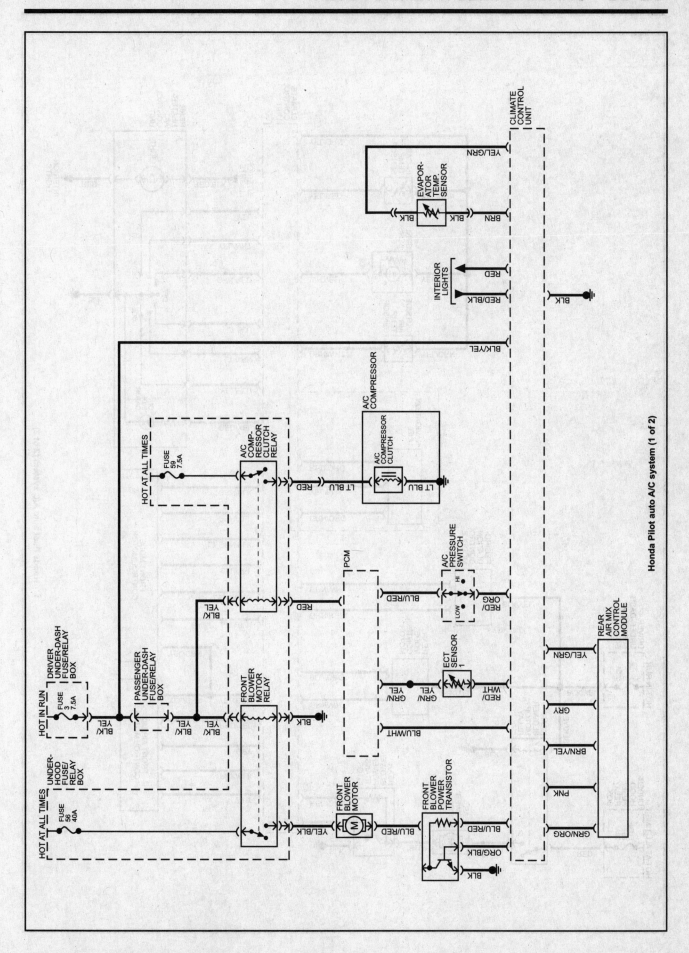

Honda Pilot auto A/C system (1 of 2)

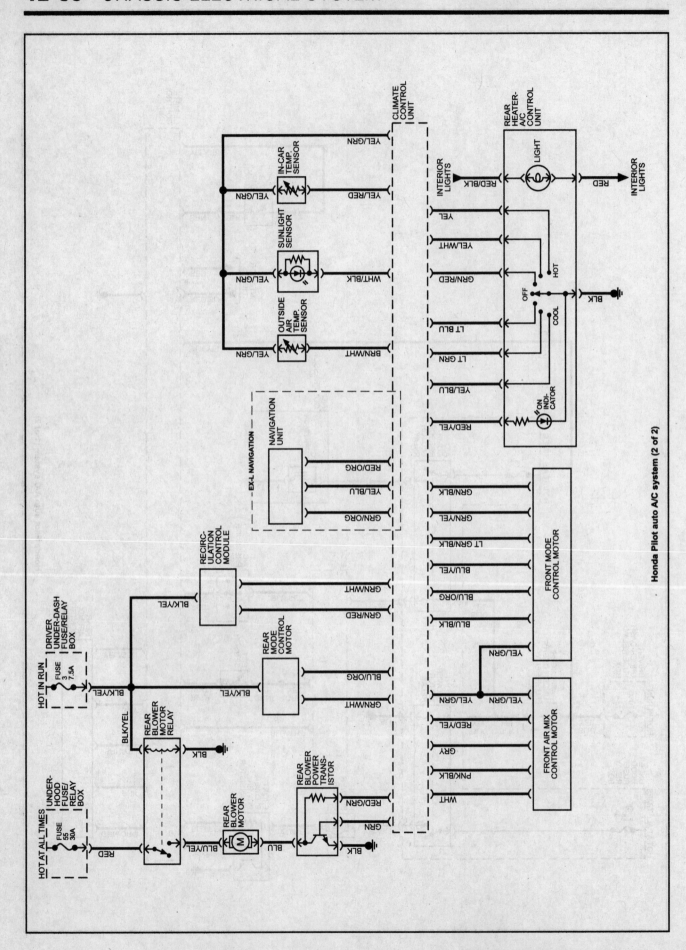

Honda Pilot auto A/C system (2 of 2)

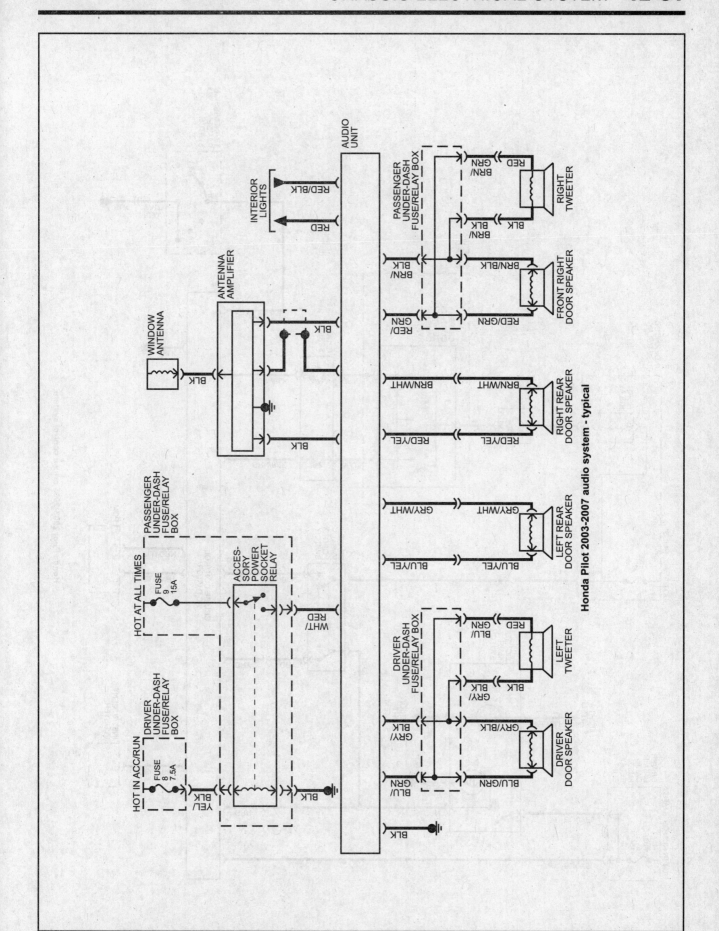

Honda Pilot 2003-2007 audio system - typical

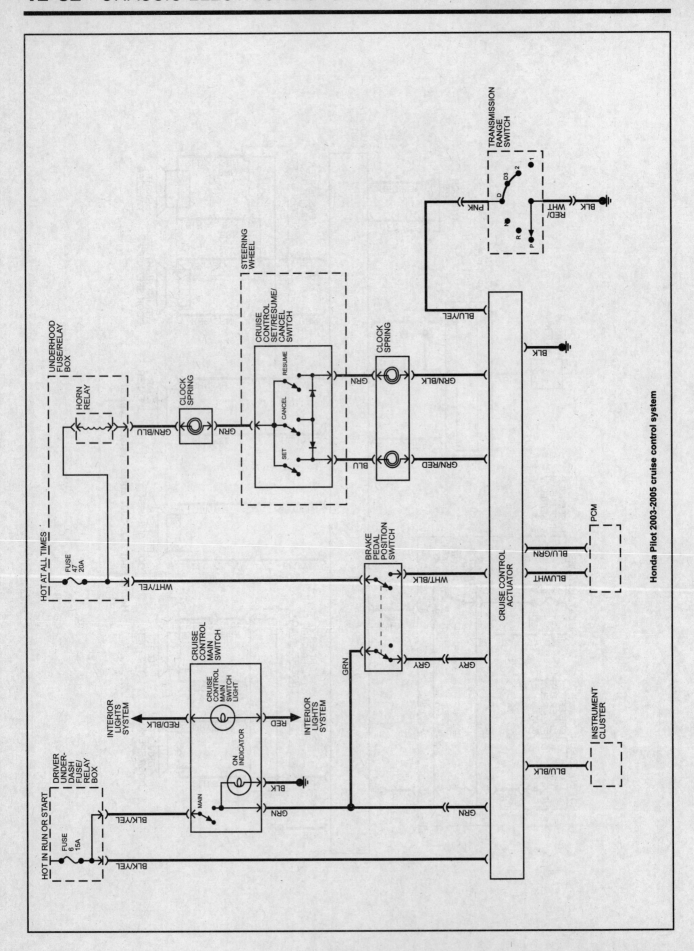

Honda Pilot 2003-2005 cruise control system

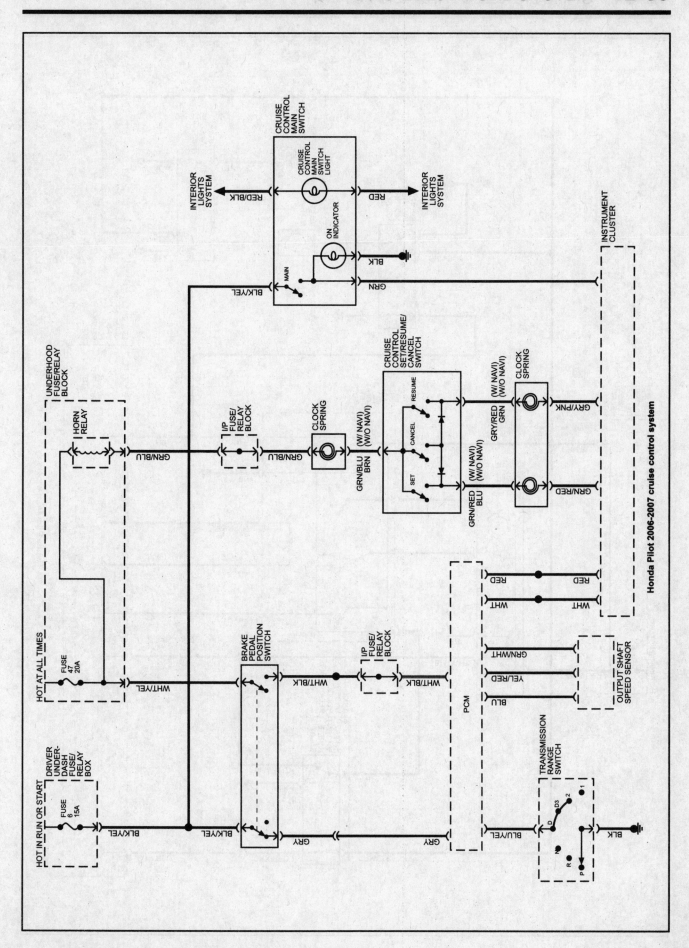

Honda Pilot 2006-2007 cruise control system

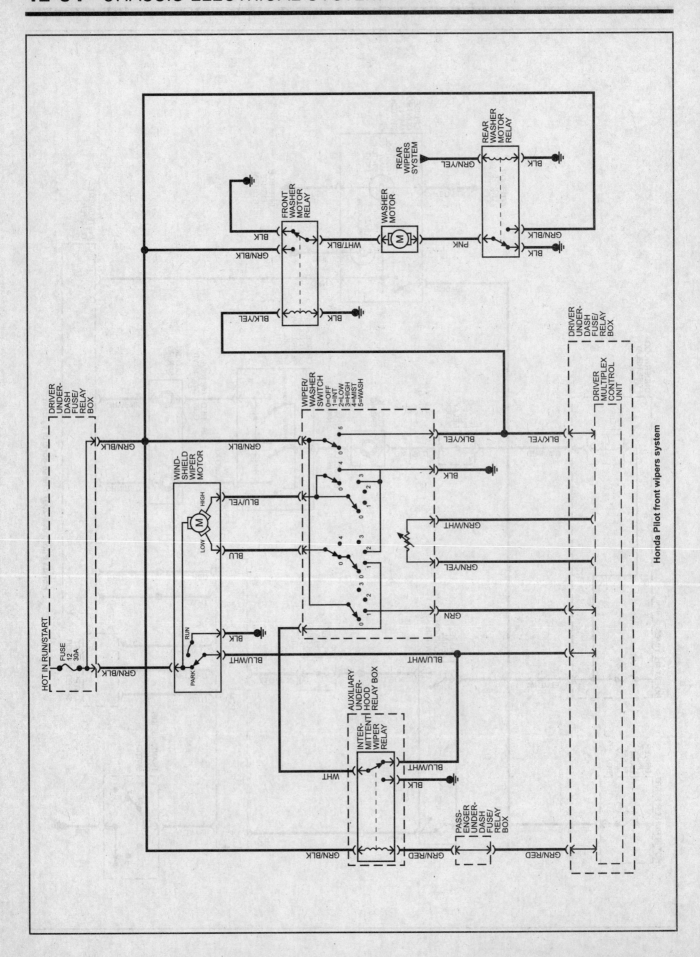

Honda Pilot front wipers system

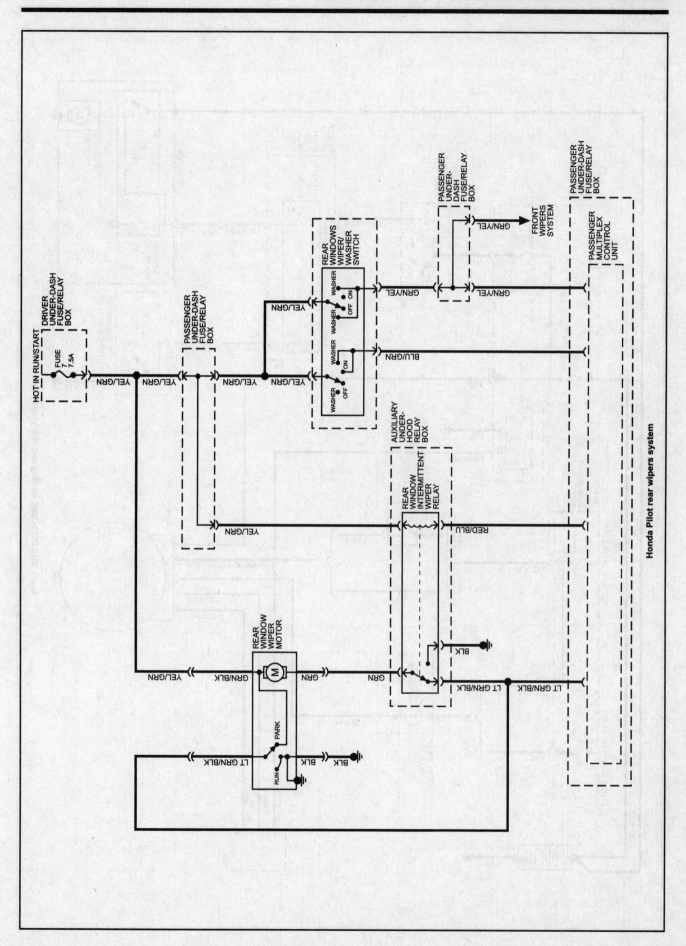

Honda Pilot rear wipers system

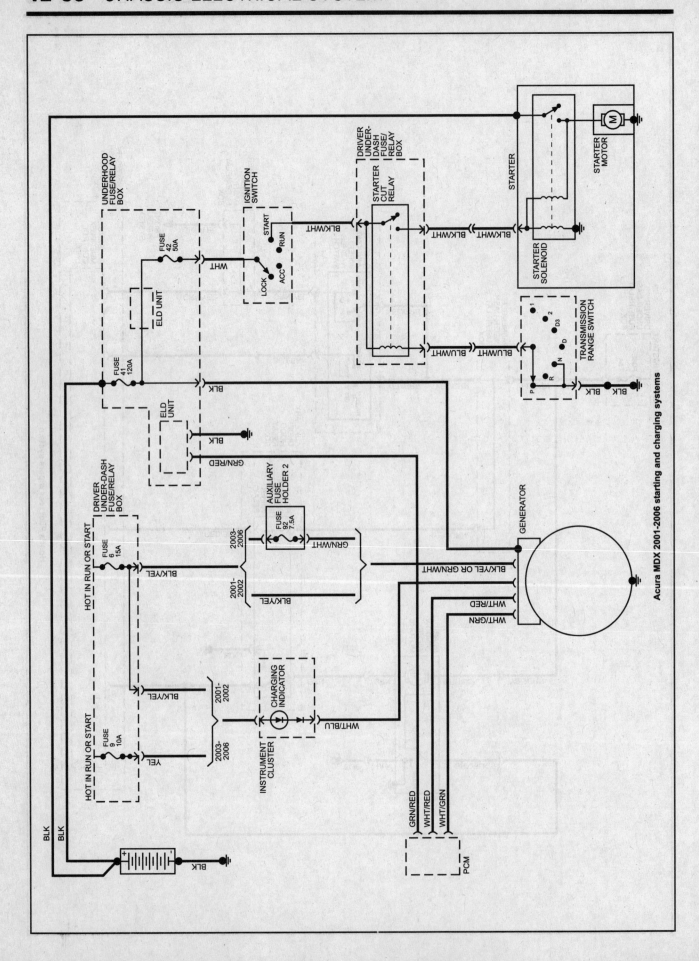

Acura MDX 2001-2006 starting and charging systems

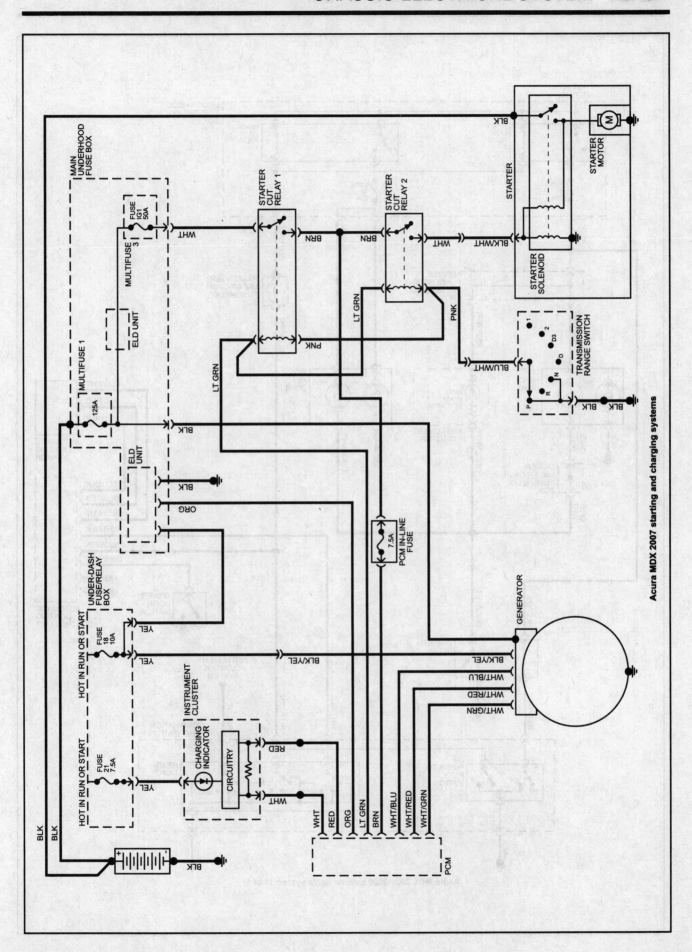

Acura MDX 2007 starting and charging systems

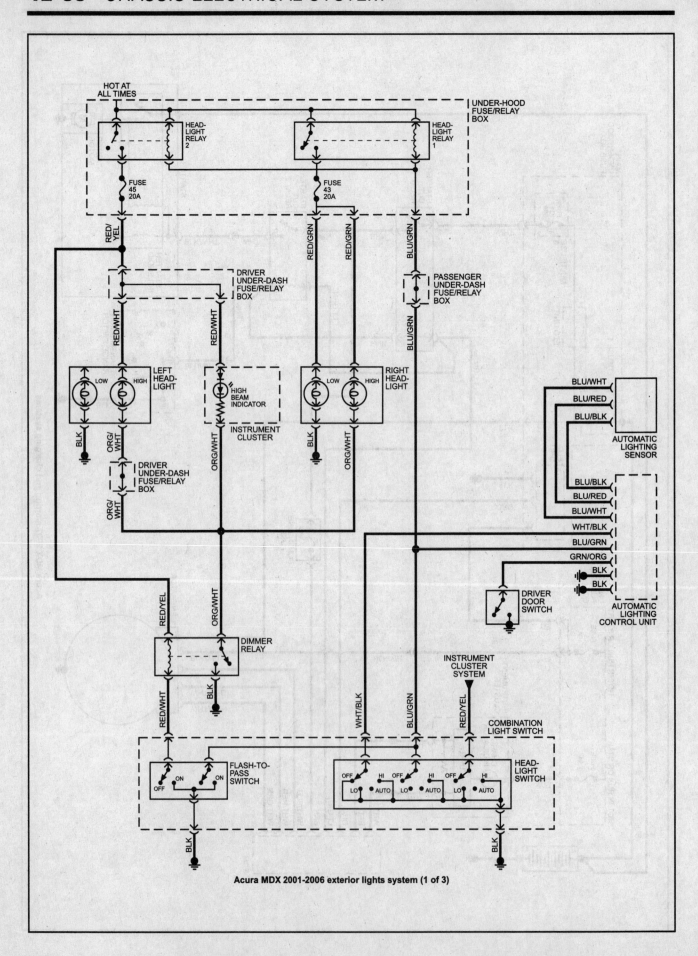

**Acura MDX 2001-2006 exterior lights system (1 of 3)**

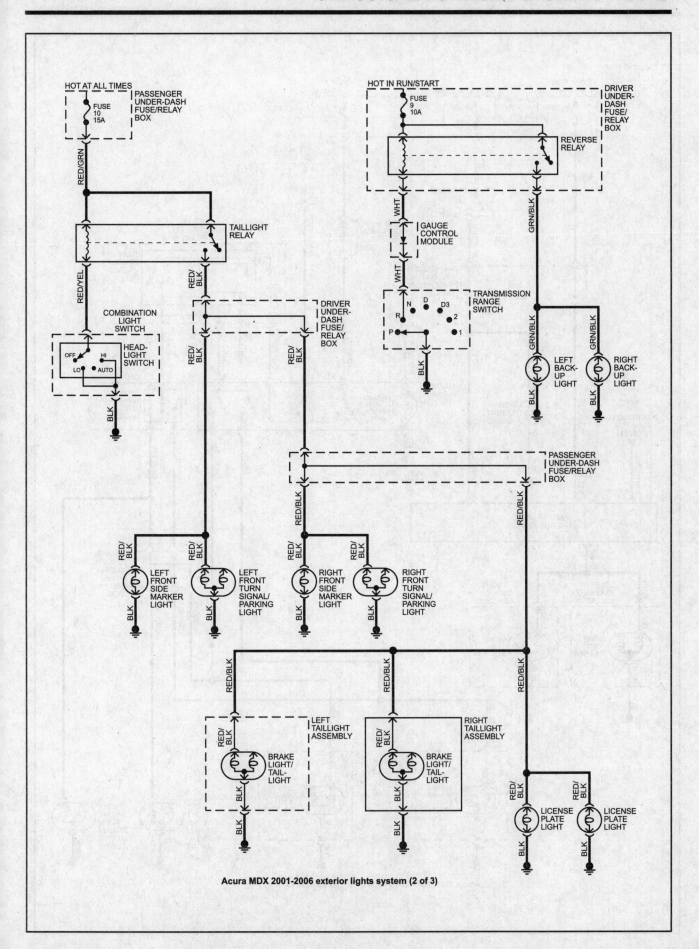

**Acura MDX 2001-2006 exterior lights system (2 of 3)**

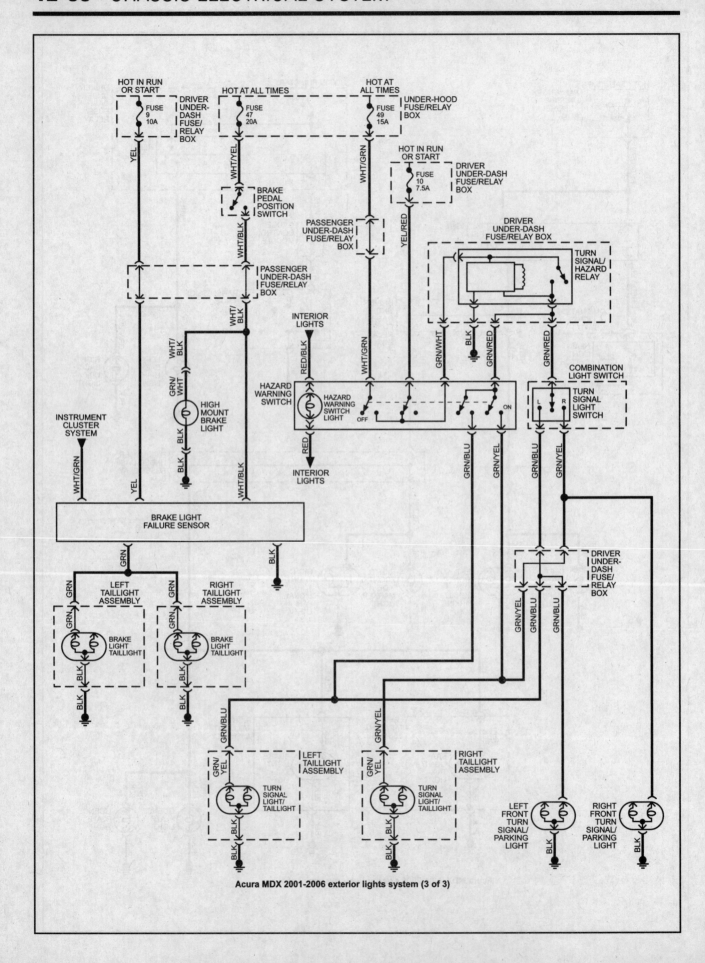

Acura MDX 2001-2006 exterior lights system (3 of 3)

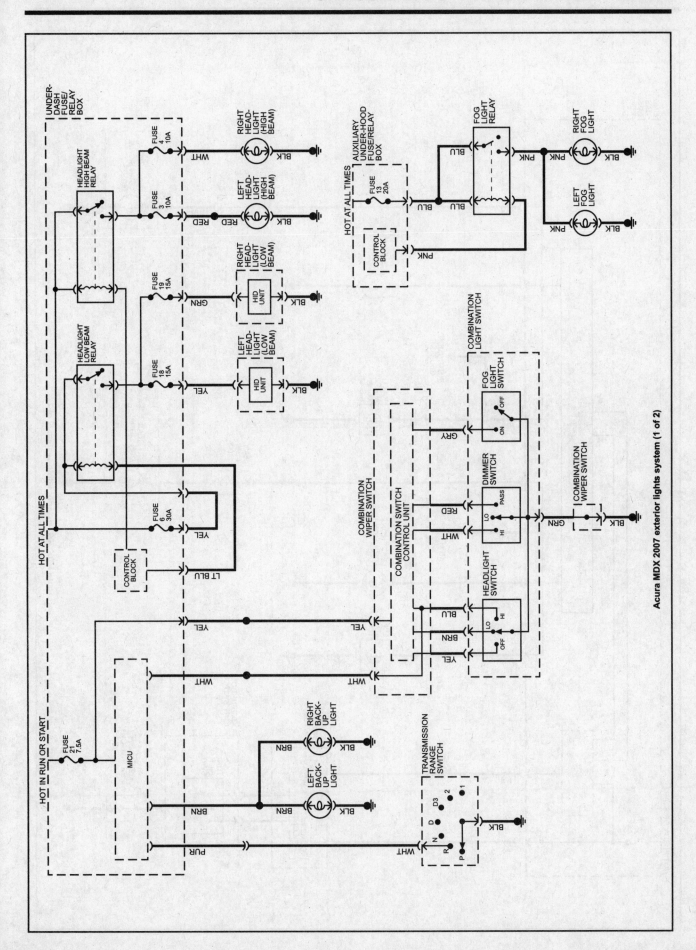

**Acura MDX 2007 exterior lights system (1 of 2)**

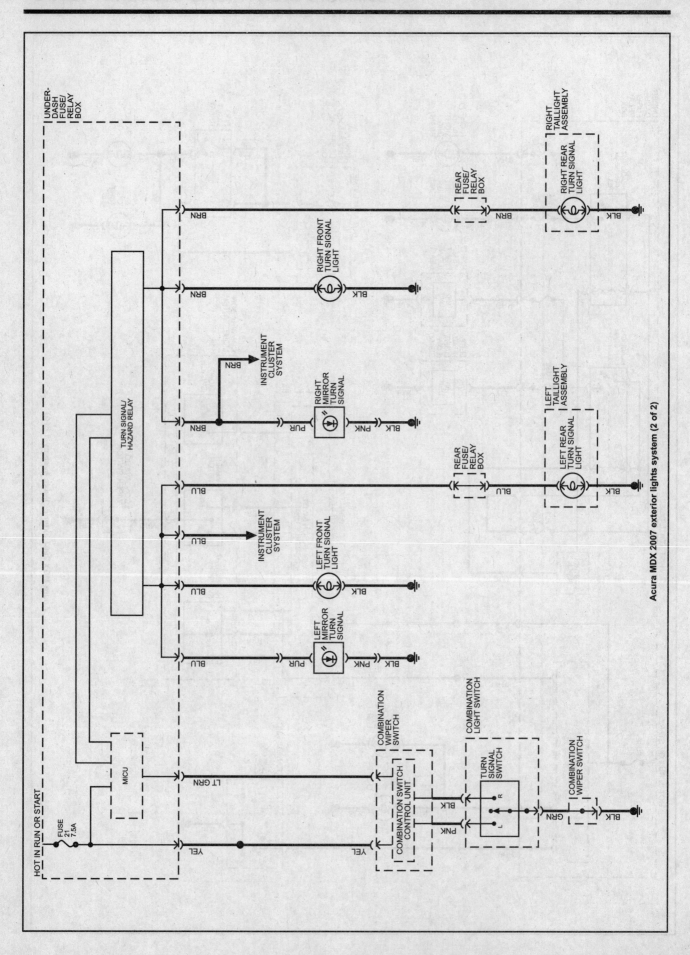

Acura MDX 2007 exterior lights system (2 of 2)

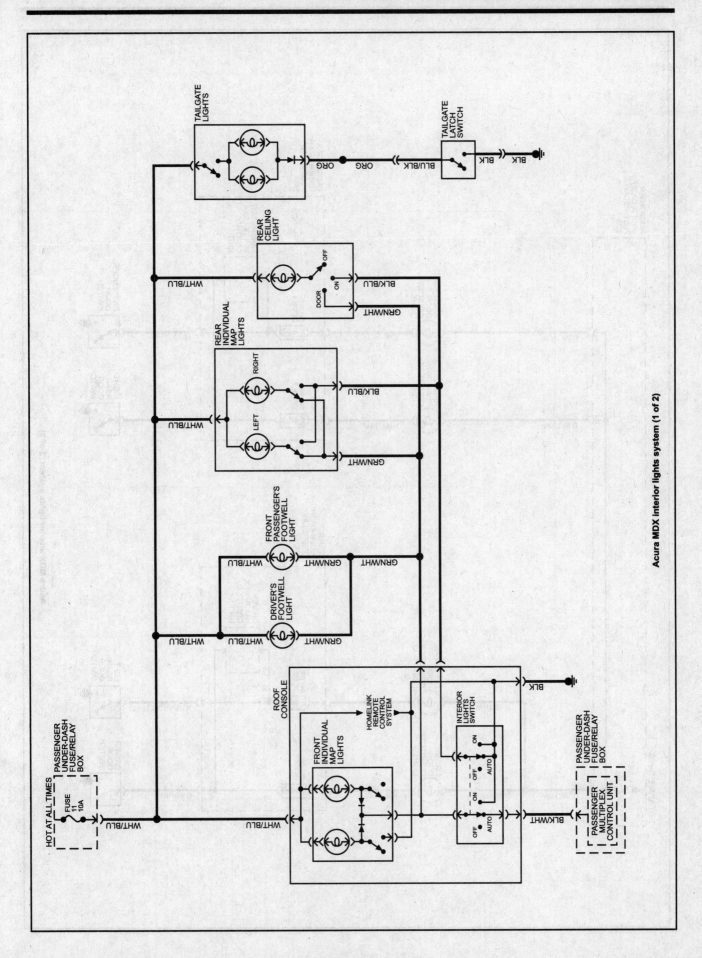

Acura MDX interior lights system (1 of 2)

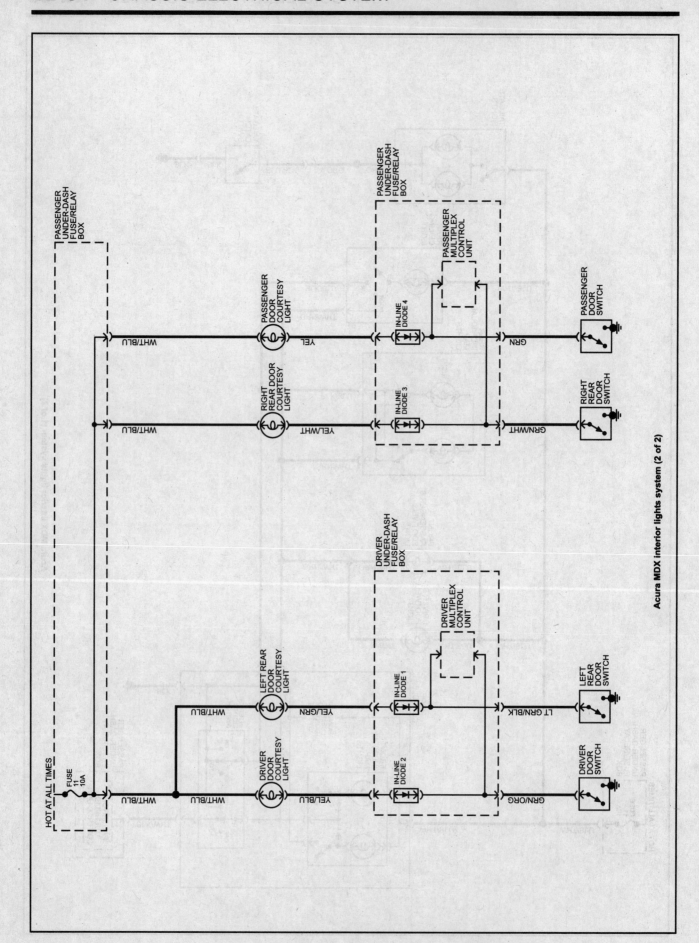

Acura MDX interior lights system (2 of 2)

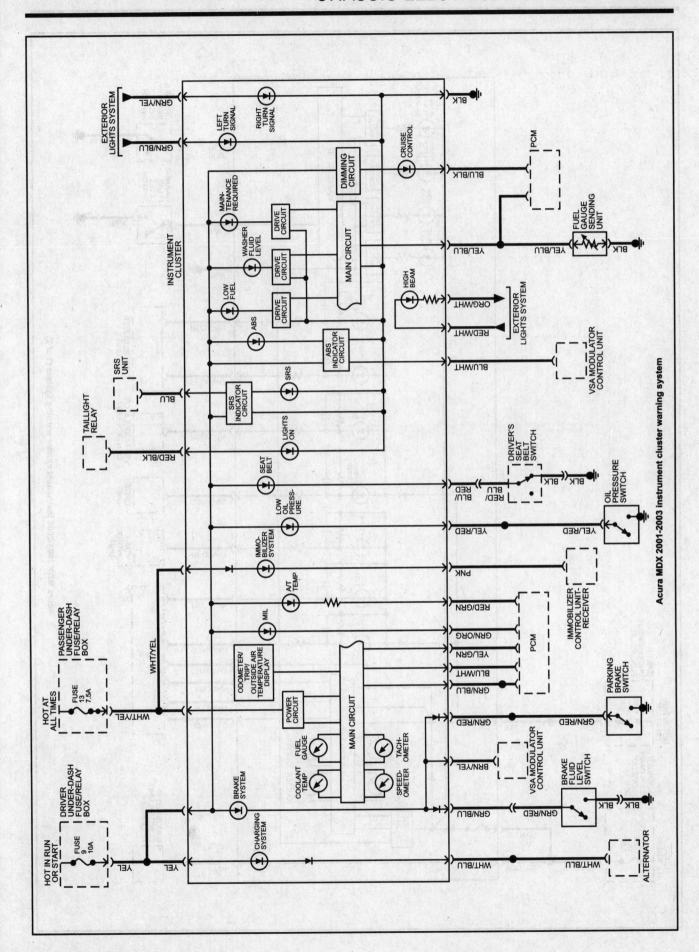

Acura MDX 2001-2003 instrument cluster warning system

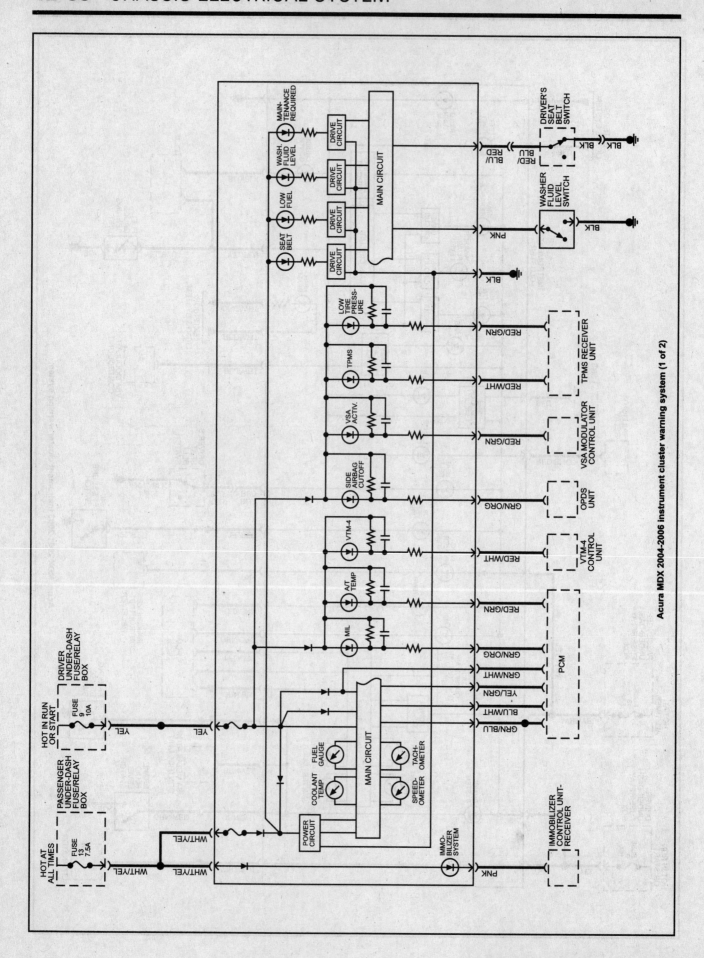

Acura MDX 2004-2006 instrument cluster warning system (1 of 2)

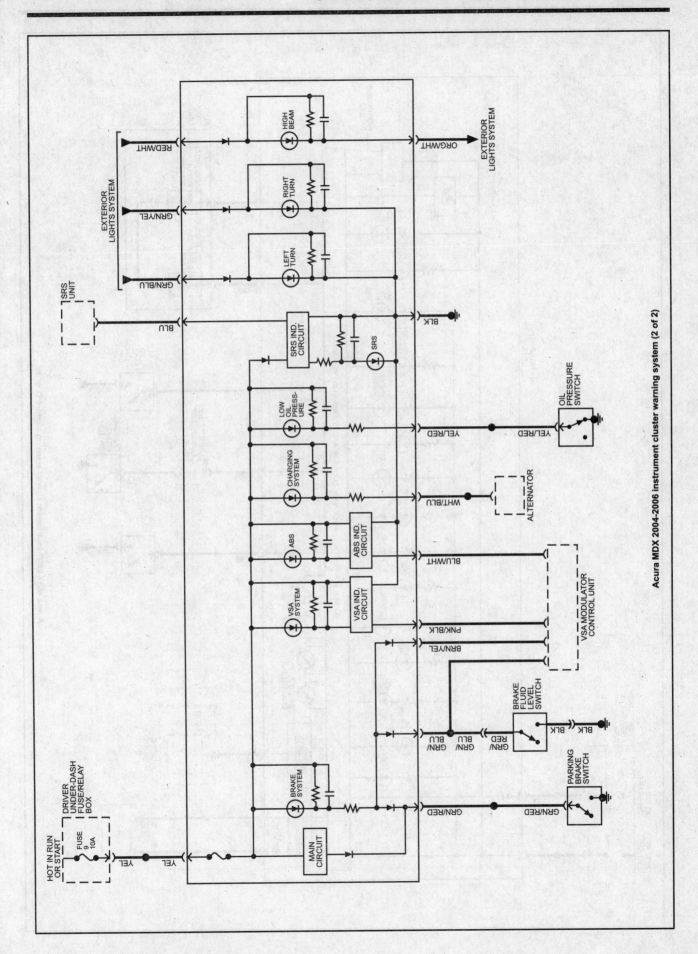

Acura MDX 2004-2006 instrument cluster warning system (2 of 2)

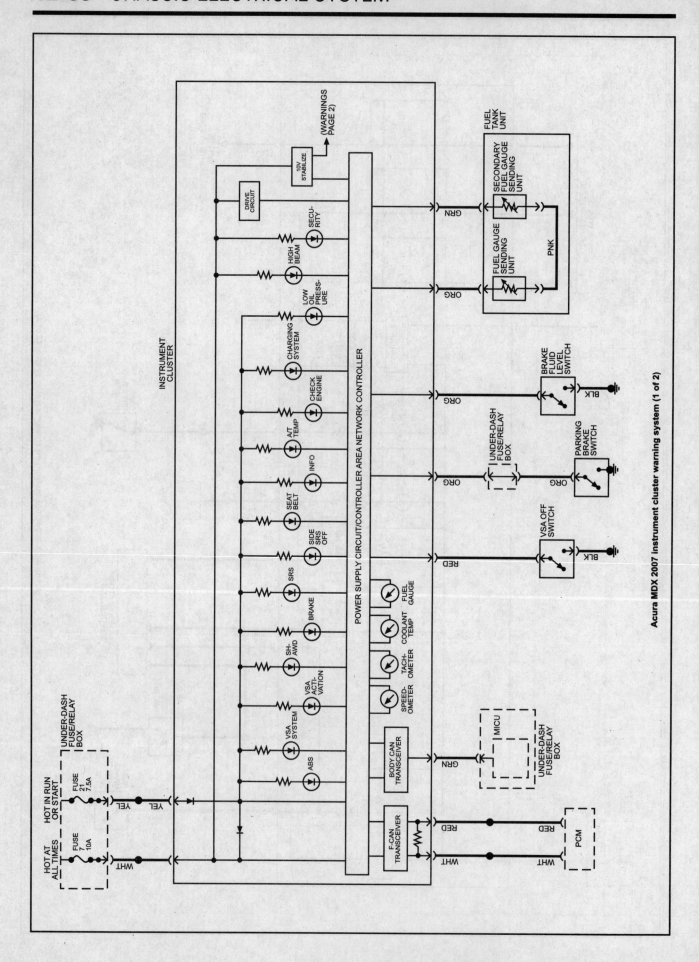

Acura MDX 2007 instrument cluster warning system (1 of 2)

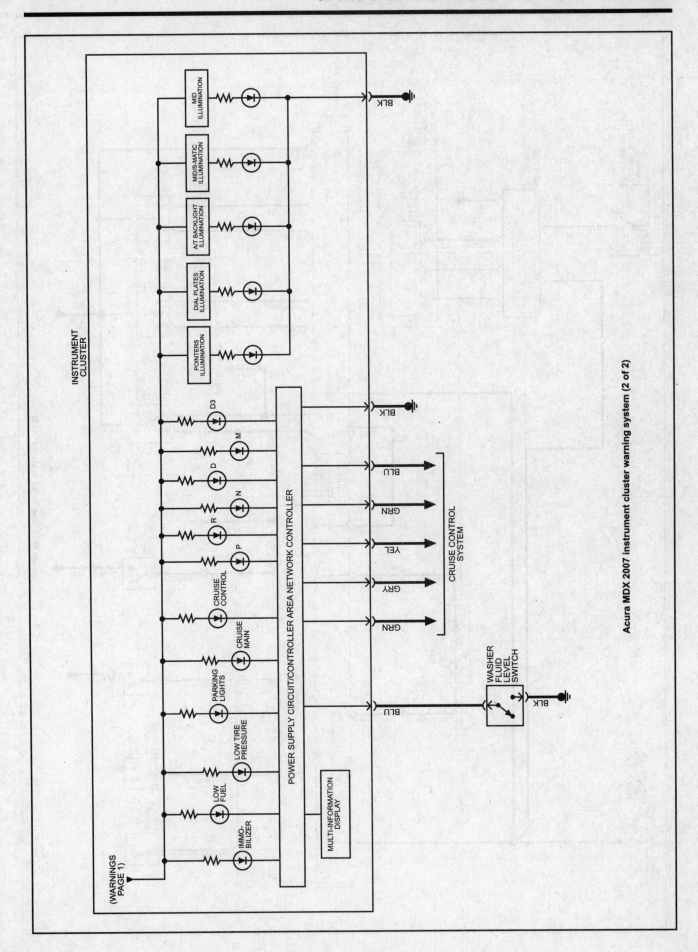

Acura MDX 2007 instrument cluster warning system (2 of 2)

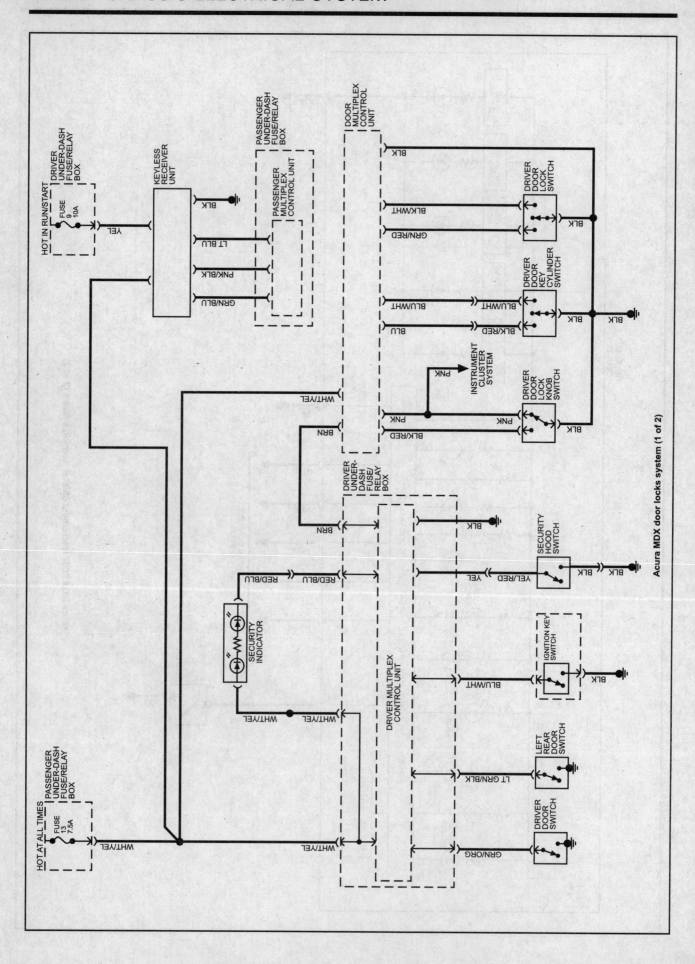

Acura MDX door locks system (1 of 2)

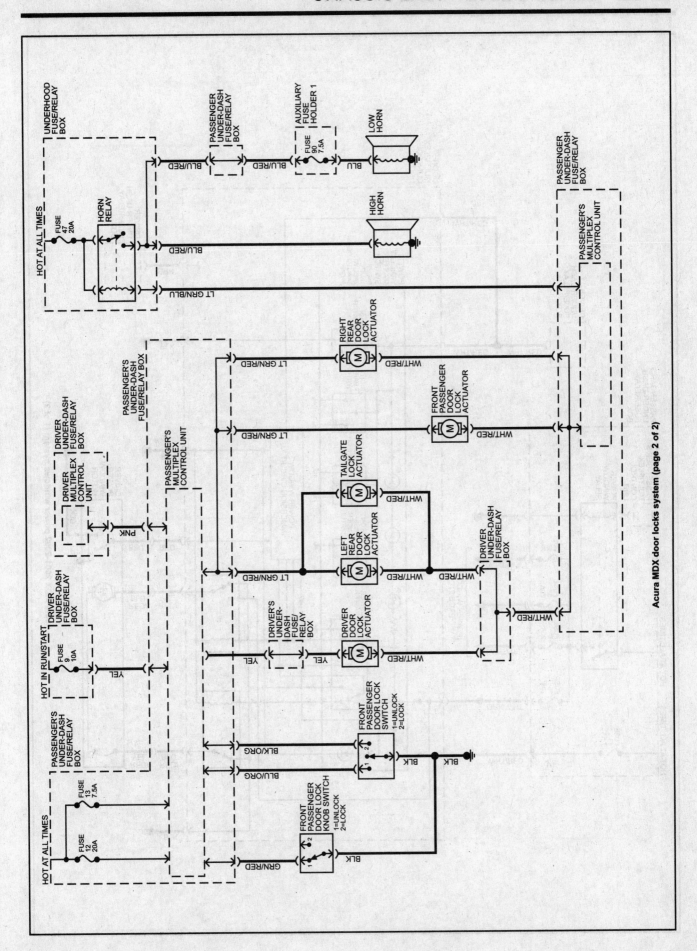

Acura MDX door locks system (page 2 of 2)

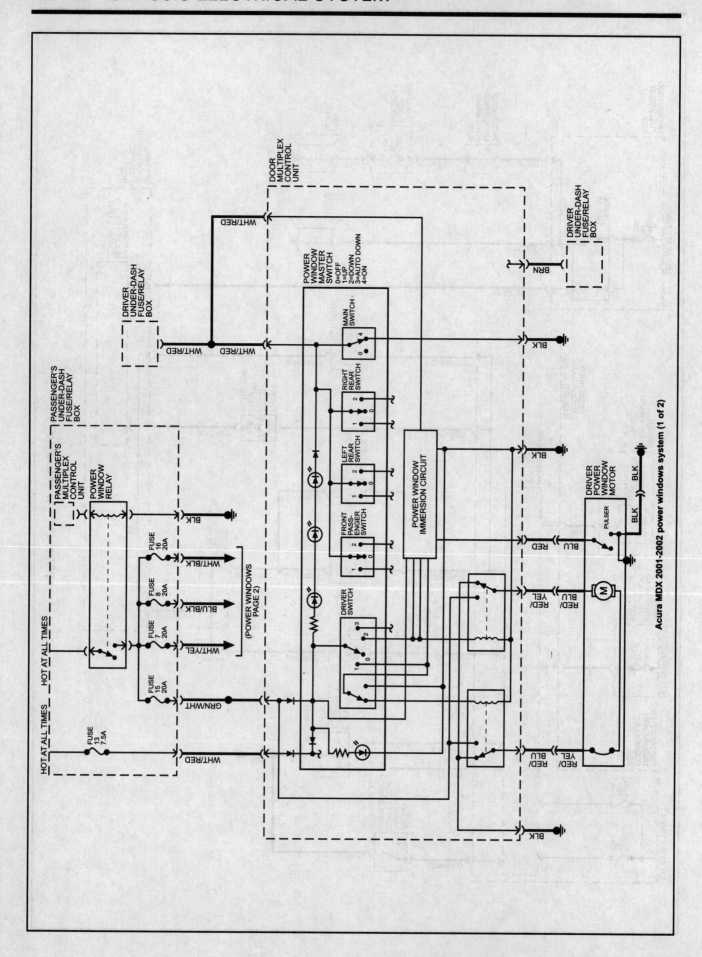

Acura MDX 2001-2002 power windows system (1 of 2)

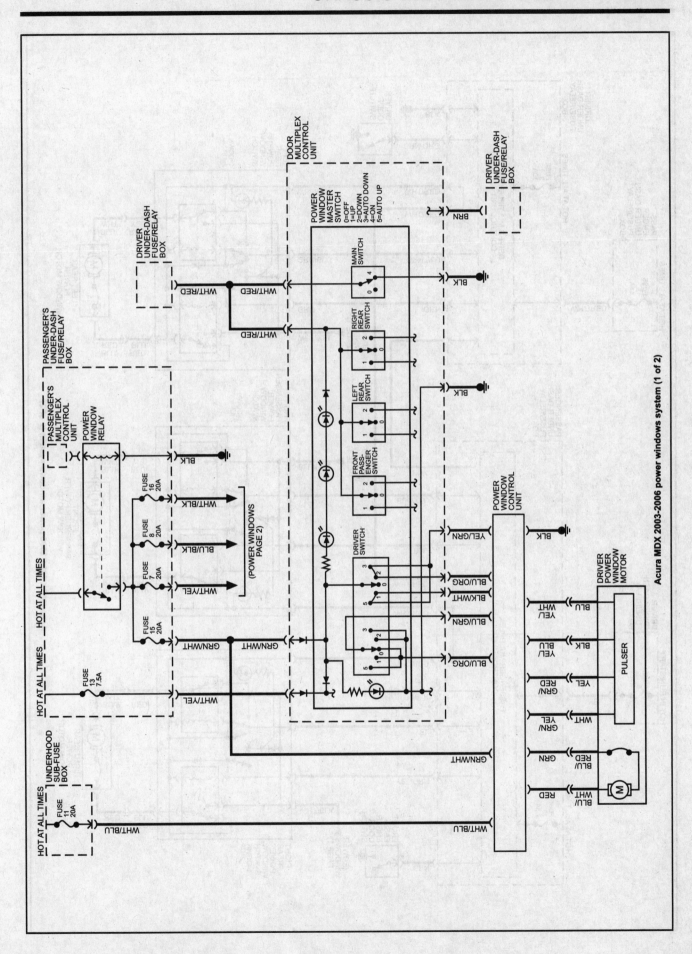

Acura MDX 2003-2006 power windows system (1 of 2)

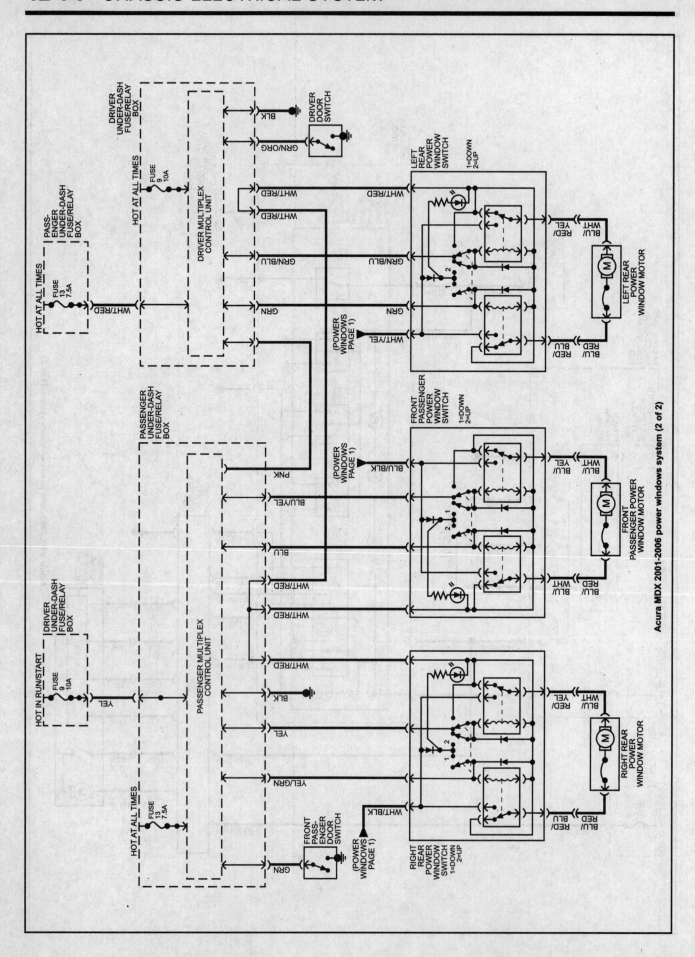

Acura MDX 2001-2006 power windows system (2 of 2)

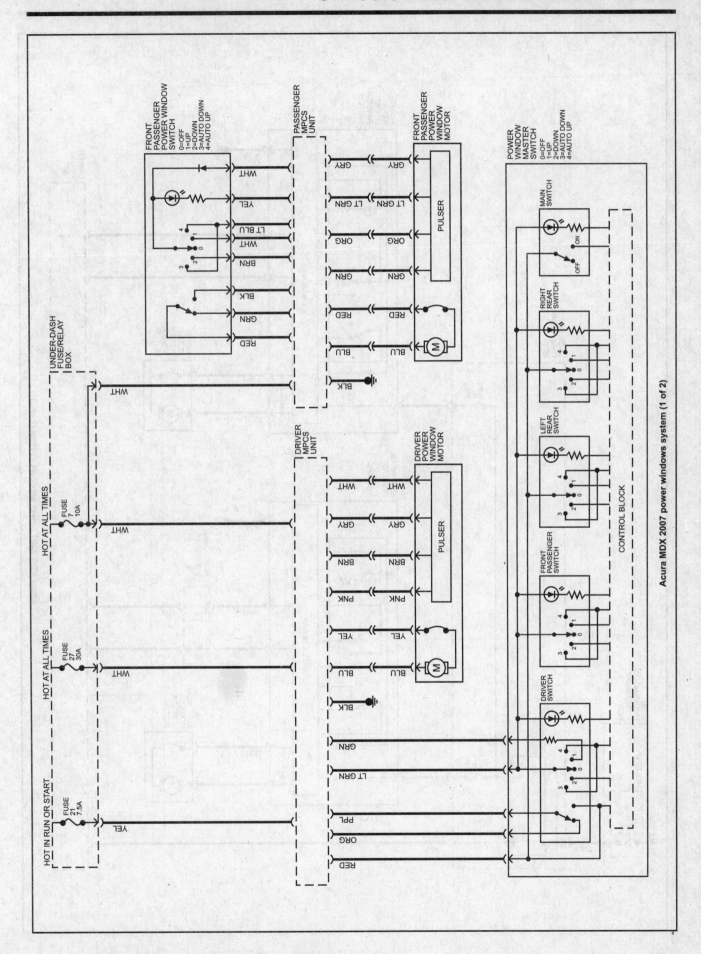

Acura MDX 2007 power windows system (1 of 2)

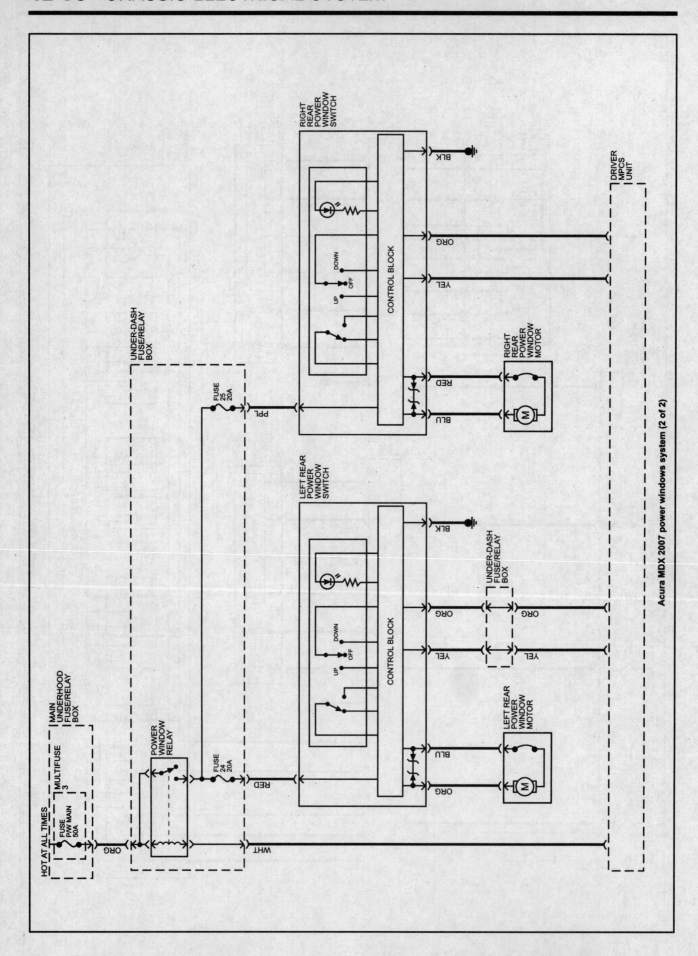

Acura MDX 2007 power windows system (2 of 2)

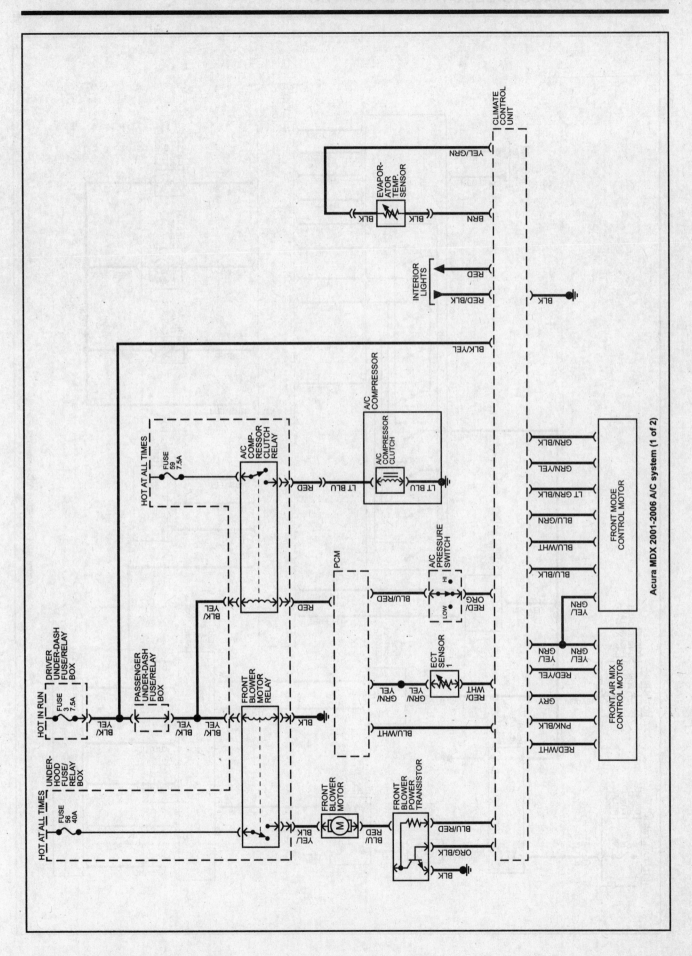

Acura MDX 2001-2006 A/C system (1 of 2)

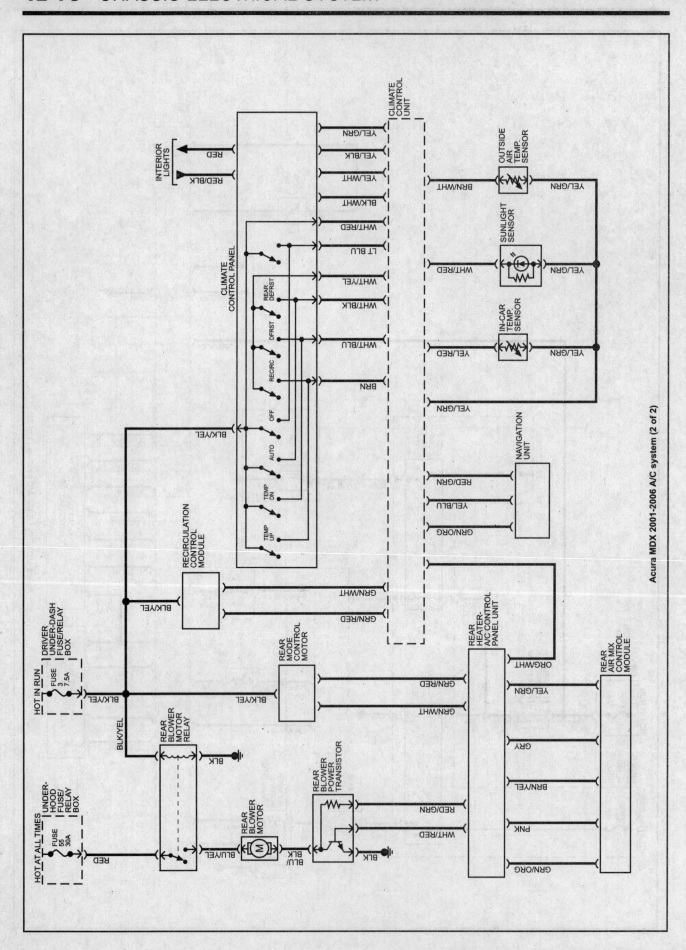

Acura MDX 2001-2006 A/C system (2 of 2)

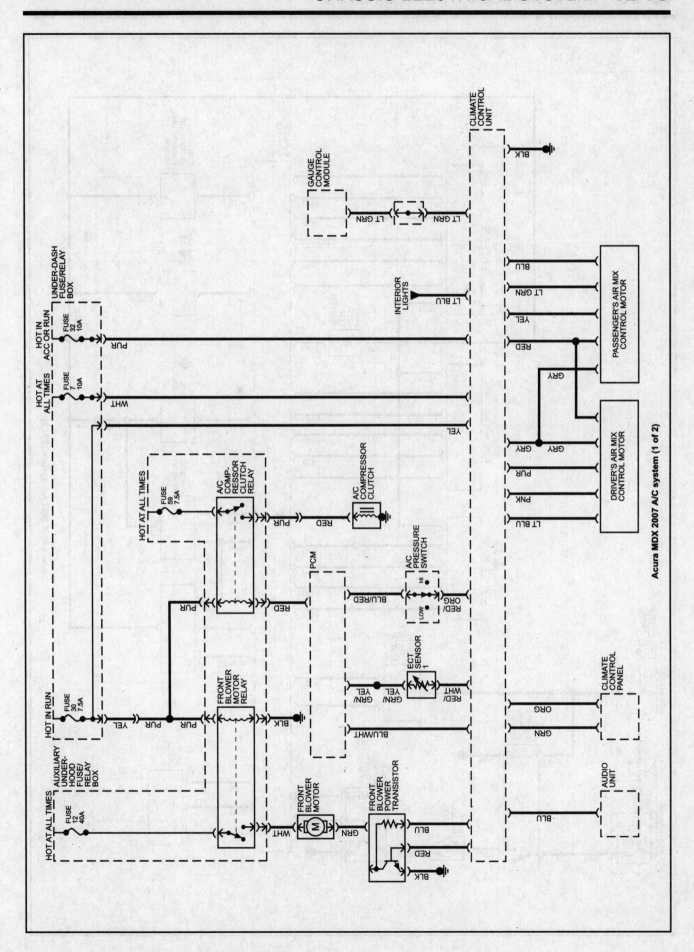

Acura MDX 2007 A/C system (1 of 2)

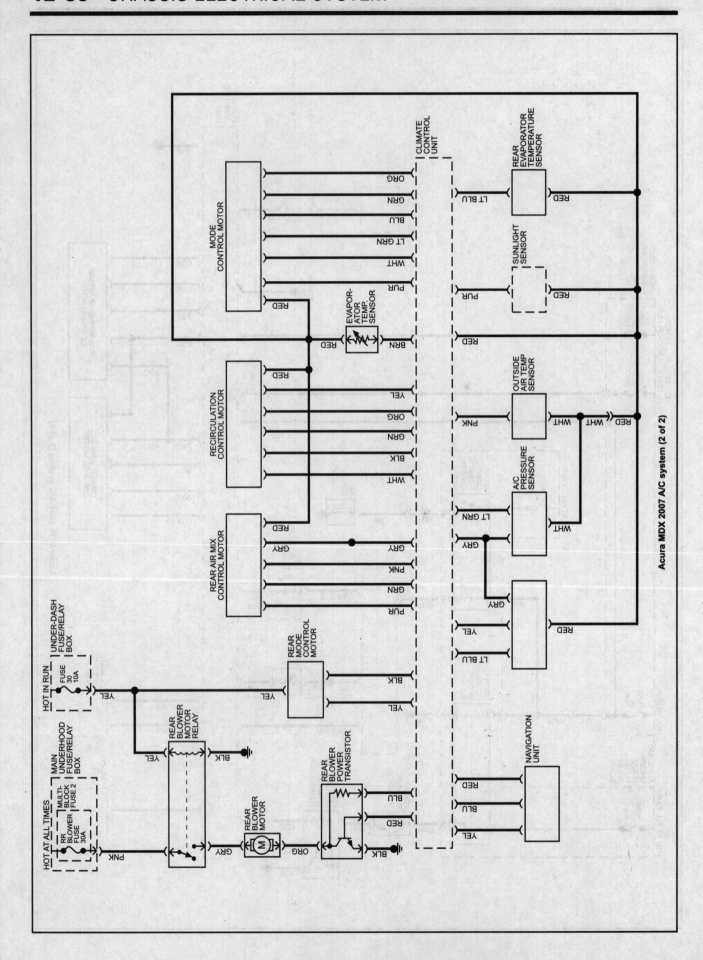

Acura MDX 2007 A/C system (2 of 2)

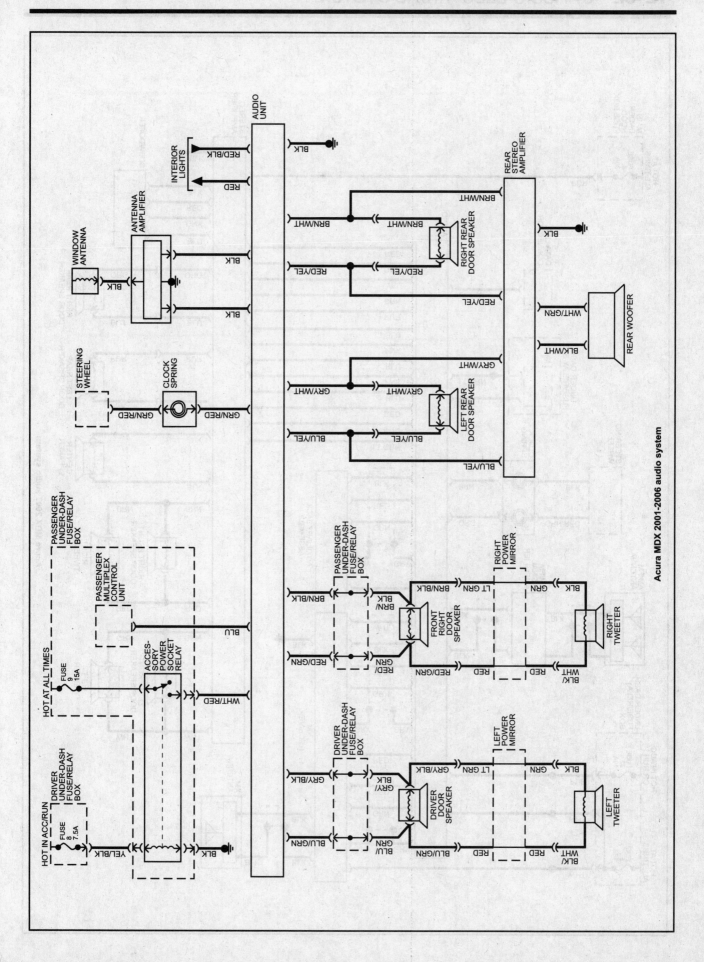

Acura MDX 2001-2006 audio system

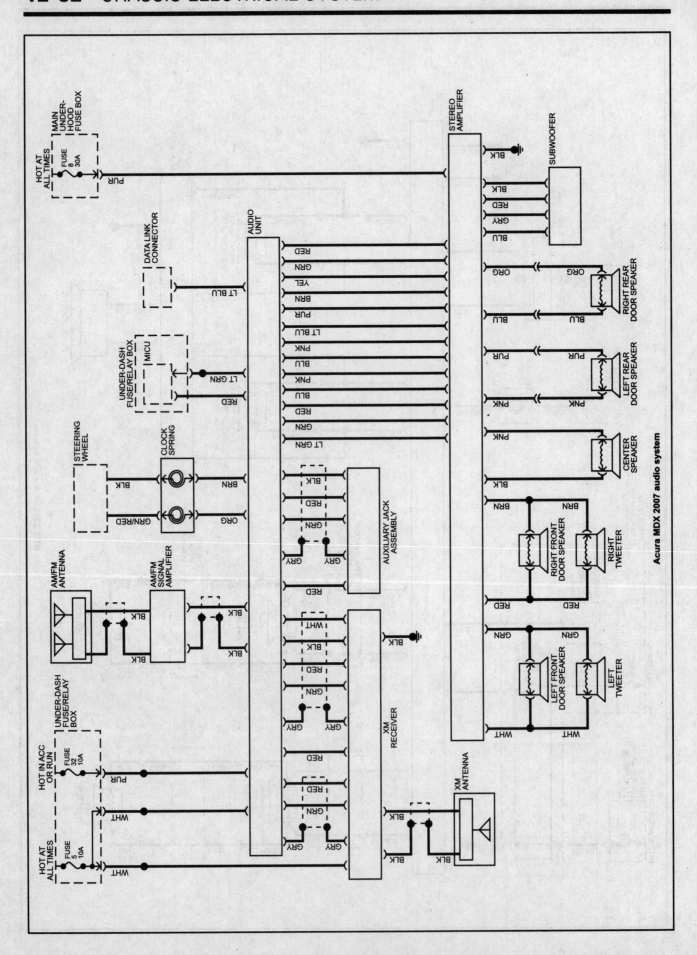

Acura MDX 2007 audio system

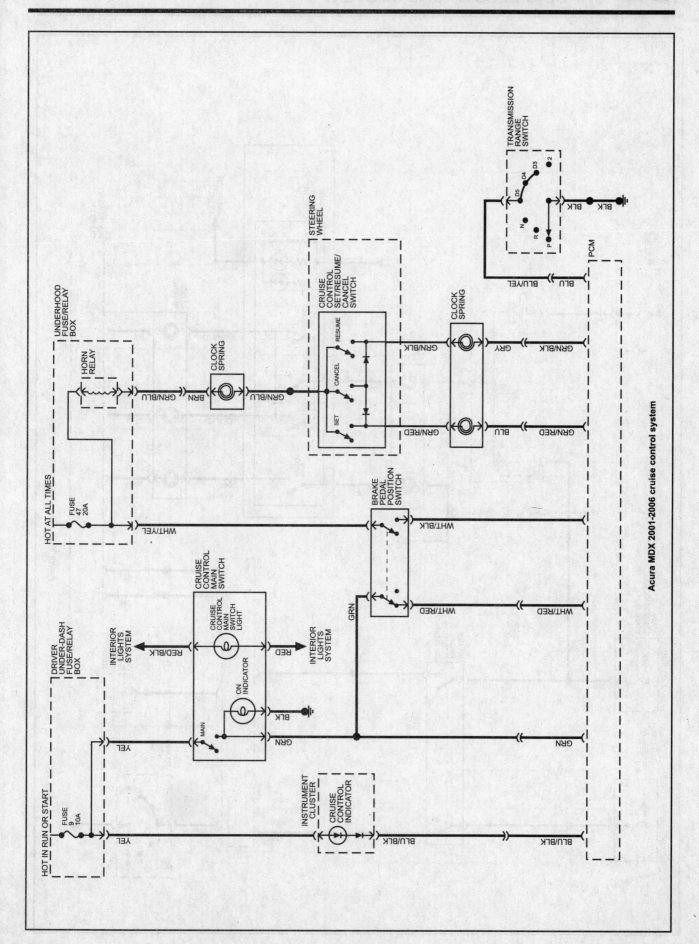

Acura MDX 2001-2006 cruise control system

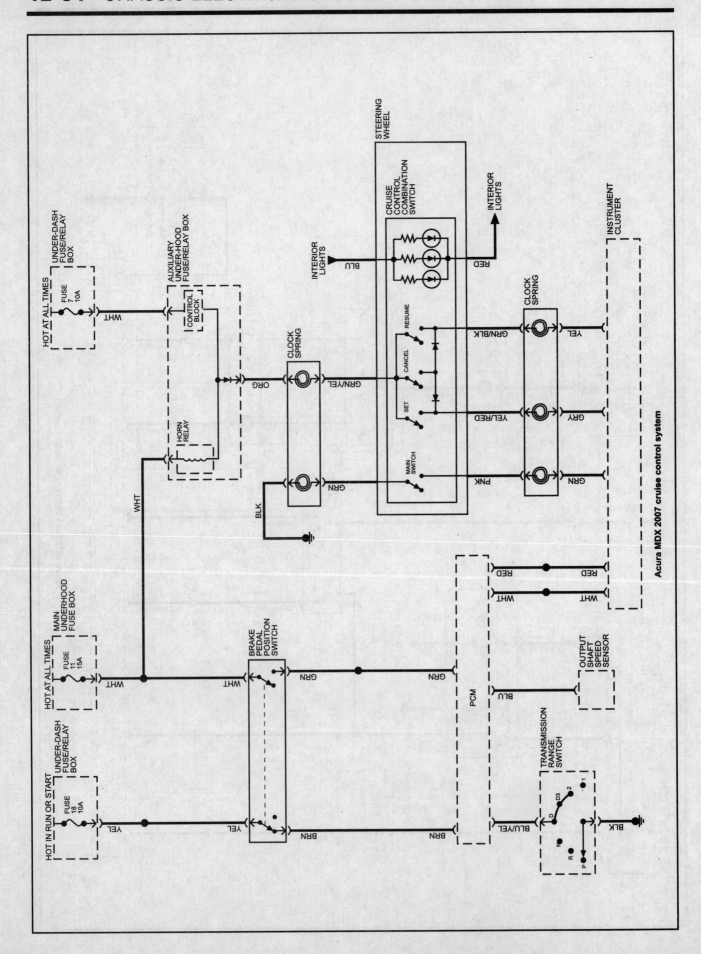

Acura MDX 2007 cruise control system

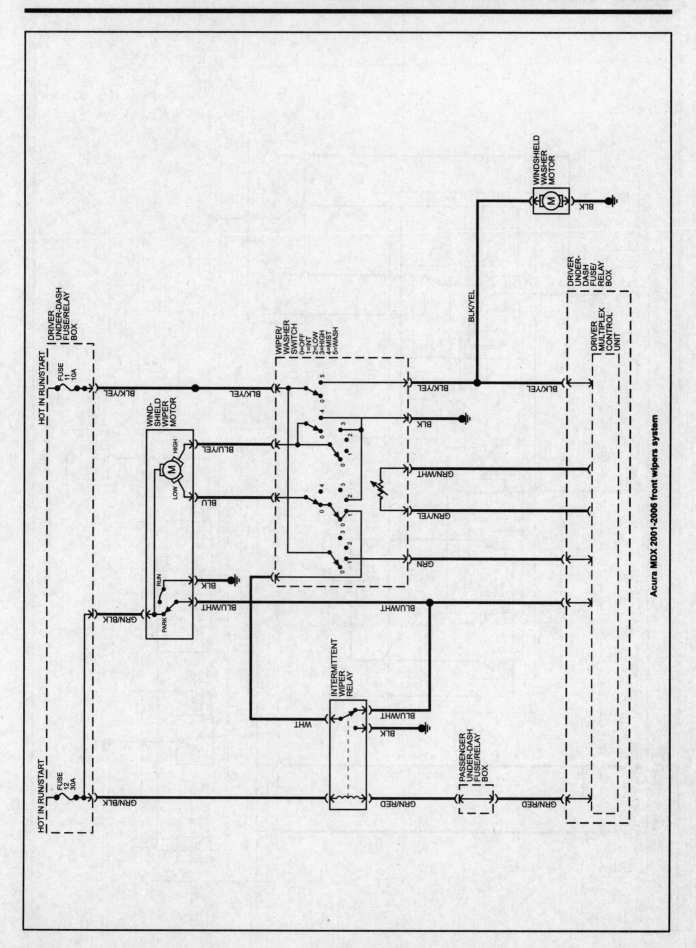

Acura MDX 2001-2006 front wipers system

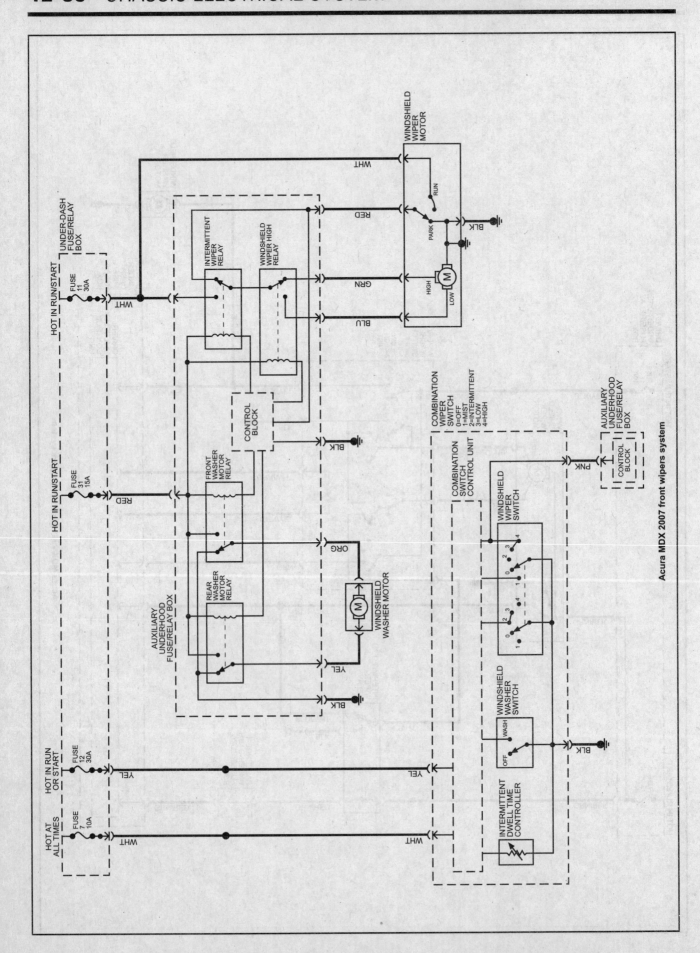

Acura MDX 2007 front wipers system

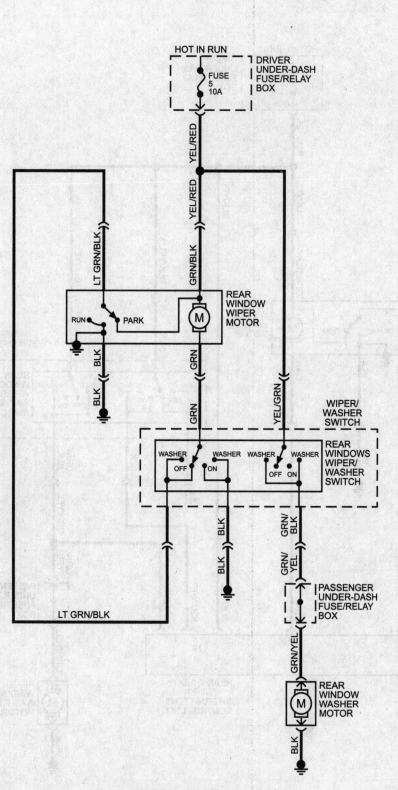

**Acura MDX 2001-2002 rear wipers system**

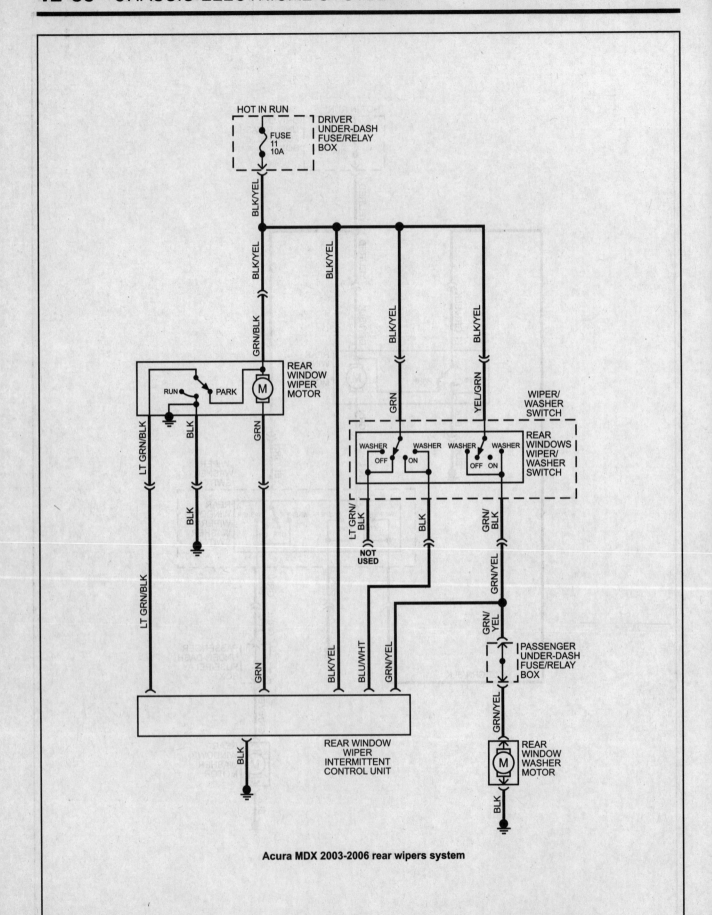

**Acura MDX 2003-2006 rear wipers system**

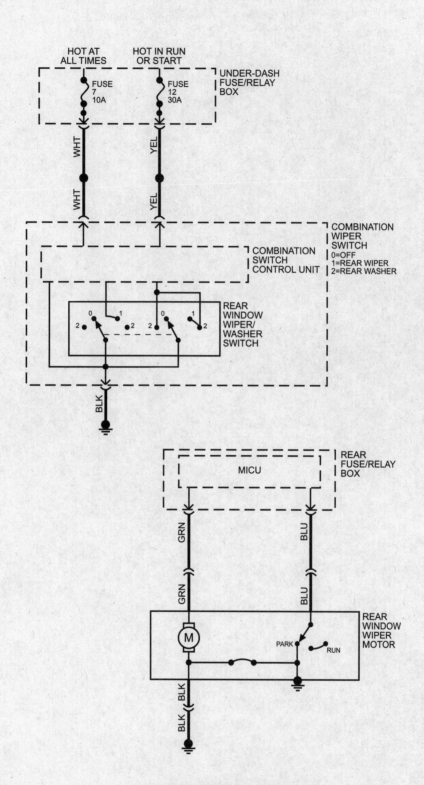

**Acura MDX 2007 rear wipers system**

**Notes**

## GLOSSARY

**AIR/FUEL RATIO:** The ratio of air-to-gasoline by weight in the fuel mixture drawn into the engine.

**AIR INJECTION:** One method of reducing harmful exhaust emissions by injecting air into each of the exhaust ports of an engine. The fresh air entering the hot exhaust manifold causes any remaining fuel to be burned before it can exit the tailpipe.

**ALTERNATOR:** A device used for converting mechanical energy into electrical energy.

**AMMETER:** An instrument, calibrated in amperes, used to measure the flow of an electrical current in a circuit. Ammeters are always connected in series with the circuit being tested.

**AMPERE:** The rate of flow of electrical current present when one volt of electrical pressure is applied against one ohm of electrical resistance.

**ANALOG COMPUTER:** Any microprocessor that uses similar (analogous) electrical signals to make its calculations.

**ARMATURE:** A laminated, soft iron core wrapped by a wire that converts electrical energy to mechanical energy as in a motor or relay. When rotated in a magnetic field, it changes mechanical energy into electrical energy as in a generator.

**ATMOSPHERIC PRESSURE:** The pressure on the Earth's surface caused by the weight of the air in the atmosphere. At sea level, this pressure is 14.7 psi at 32°F (101 kPa at 0°C).

**ATOMIZATION:** The breaking down of a liquid into a fine mist that can be suspended in air.

**AXIAL PLAY:** Movement parallel to a shaft or bearing bore.

**BACKFIRE:** The sudden combustion of gases in the intake or exhaust system that results in a loud explosion.

**BACKLASH:** The clearance or play between two parts, such as meshed gears.

**BACKPRESSURE:** Restrictions in the exhaust system that slow the exit of exhaust gases from the combustion chamber.

**BAKELITE:** A heat resistant, plastic insulator material commonly used in printed circuit boards and transistorized components.

**BALL BEARING:** A bearing made up of hardened inner and outer races between which hardened steel balls roll.

**BALLAST RESISTOR:** A resistor in the primary ignition circuit that lowers voltage after the engine is started to reduce wear on ignition components.

**BEARING:** A friction reducing, supportive device usually located between a stationary part and a moving part.

**BIMETAL TEMPERATURE SENSOR:** Any sensor or switch made of two dissimilar types of metal that bend when heated or cooled due to the different expansion rates of the alloys. These types of sensors usually function as an on/off switch.

**BLOWBY:** Combustion gases, composed of water vapor and unburned fuel, that leak past the piston rings into the crankcase during normal engine operation. These gases are removed by the PCV system to prevent the buildup of harmful acids in the crankcase.

**BRAKE PAD:** A brake shoe and lining assembly used with disc brakes.

**BRAKE SHOE:** The backing for the brake lining. The term is, however, usually applied to the assembly of the brake backing and lining.

**BUSHING:** A liner, usually removable, for a bearing; an anti-friction liner used in place of a bearing.

**CALIPER:** A hydraulically activated device in a disc brake system, which is mounted straddling the brake rotor (disc). The caliper contains at least one piston and two brake pads. Hydraulic pressure on the piston(s) forces the pads against the rotor.

**CAMSHAFT:** A shaft in the engine on which are the lobes (cams) which operate the valves. The camshaft is driven by the crankshaft, via a belt, chain or gears, at one half the crankshaft speed.

**CAPACITOR:** A device which stores an electrical charge.

**CARBON MONOXIDE (CO):** A colorless, odorless gas given off as a normal byproduct of combustion. It is poisonous and extremely dangerous in confined areas, building up slowly to toxic levels without warning if adequate ventilation is not available.

**CARBURETOR:** A device, usually mounted on the intake manifold of an engine, which mixes the air and fuel in the proper proportion to allow even combustion.

**CATALYTIC CONVERTER:** A device installed in the exhaust system, like a muffler, that converts harmful byproducts of combustion into carbon dioxide and water vapor by means of a heat-producing chemical reaction.

**CENTRIFUGAL ADVANCE:** A mechanical method of advancing the spark timing by using flyweights in the distributor that react to centrifugal force generated by the distributor shaft rotation.

**CHECK VALVE:** Any one-way valve installed to permit the flow of air, fuel or vacuum in one direction only.

**CHOKE:** A device, usually a moveable valve, placed in the intake path of a carburetor to restrict the flow of air.

**CIRCUIT:** Any unbroken path through which an electrical current can flow. Also used to describe fuel flow in some instances.

**CIRCUIT BREAKER:** A switch which protects an electrical circuit from overload by opening the circuit when the current flow exceeds a predetermined level. Some circuit breakers must be reset manually, while most reset automatically.

**COIL (IGNITION):** A transformer in the ignition circuit which steps up the voltage provided to the spark plugs.

**COMBINATION MANIFOLD:** An assembly which includes both the intake and exhaust manifolds in one casting.

**COMBINATION VALVE:** A device used in some fuel systems that routes fuel vapors to a charcoal storage canister instead of venting them into the atmosphere. The valve relieves fuel tank pressure and allows fresh air into the tank as the fuel level drops to prevent a vapor lock situation.

**COMPRESSION RATIO:** The comparison of the total volume of the cylinder and combustion chamber with the piston at BDC and the piston at TDC.

**CONDENSER:** 1. An electrical device which acts to store an electrical charge, preventing voltage surges. 2. A radiator-like device in the air conditioning system in which refrigerant gas condenses into a liquid, giving off heat.

**CONDUCTOR:** Any material through which an electrical current can be transmitted easily.

**CONTINUITY:** Continuous or complete circuit. Can be checked with an ohmmeter.

**COUNTERSHAFT:** An intermediate shaft which is rotated by a mainshaft and transmits, in turn, that rotation to a working part.

**CRANKCASE:** The lower part of an engine in which the crankshaft and related parts operate.

**CRANKSHAFT:** The main driving shaft of an engine which receives reciprocating motion from the pistons and converts it to rotary motion.

**CYLINDER:** In an engine, the round hole in the engine block in which the piston(s) ride.

**CYLINDER BLOCK:** The main structural member of an engine in which is found the cylinders, crankshaft and other principal parts.

**CYLINDER HEAD:** The detachable portion of the engine, usually fastened to the top of the cylinder block and containing all or most of the combustion chambers. On overhead valve engines, it contains the valves and their operating parts. On overhead cam engines, it contains the camshaft as well.

**DEAD CENTER:** The extreme top or bottom of the piston stroke.

**DETONATION:** An unwanted explosion of the air/fuel mixture in the combustion chamber caused by excess heat and compression, advanced timing, or an overly lean mixture. Also referred to as "ping".

**DIAPHRAGM:** A thin, flexible wall separating two cavities, such as in a vacuum advance unit.

**DIESELING:** A condition in which hot spots in the combustion chamber cause the engine to run on after the key is turned off.

**DIFFERENTIAL:** A geared assembly which allows the transmission of motion between drive axles, giving one axle the ability to turn faster than the other.

**DIODE:** An electrical device that will allow current to flow in one direction only.

**DISC BRAKE:** A hydraulic braking assembly consisting of a brake disc, or rotor, mounted on an axle, and a caliper assembly containing, usually two brake pads which are activated by hydraulic pressure. The pads are forced against the sides of the disc, creating friction which slows the vehicle.

**DISTRIBUTOR:** A mechanically driven device on an engine which is responsible for electrically firing the spark plug at a predetermined point of the piston stroke.

**DOWEL PIN:** A pin, inserted in mating holes in two different parts allowing those parts to maintain a fixed relationship.

**DRUM BRAKE:** A braking system which consists of two brake shoes and one or two wheel cylinders, mounted on a fixed backing plate, and a brake drum, mounted on an axle, which revolves around the assembly.

**DWELL:** The rate, measured in degrees of shaft rotation, at which an electrical circuit cycles on and off.

**ELECTRONIC CONTROL UNIT (ECU):** Ignition module, module, amplifier or igniter. See Module for definition.

**ELECTRONIC IGNITION:** A system in which the timing and firing of the spark plugs is controlled by an electronic control unit, usually called a module. These systems have no points or condenser.

**END-PLAY:** The measured amount of axial movement in a shaft.

**ENGINE:** A device that converts heat into mechanical energy.

**EXHAUST MANIFOLD:** A set of cast passages or pipes which conduct exhaust gases from the engine.

**FEELER GAUGE:** A blade, usually metal, or precisely predetermined thickness, used to measure the clearance between two parts.

**FIRING ORDER:** The order in which combustion occurs in the cylinders of an engine. Also the order in which spark is distributed to the plugs by the distributor.

**FLOODING:** The presence of too much fuel in the intake manifold and combustion chamber which prevents the air/fuel mixture from firing, thereby causing a no-start situation.

**FLYWHEEL:** A disc shaped part bolted to the rear end of the crankshaft. Around the outer perimeter is affixed the ring gear. The starter drive engages the ring gear, turning the flywheel, which rotates the crankshaft, imparting the initial starting motion to the engine.

**FOOT POUND (ft. lbs. or sometimes, ft.lb.):** The amount of energy or work needed to raise an item weighing one pound, a distance of one foot.

**FUSE:** A protective device in a circuit which prevents circuit overload by breaking the circuit when a specific amperage is present. The device is constructed around a strip or wire of a lower amperage rating than the circuit it is designed to protect. When an amperage higher than that stamped on the fuse is present in the circuit, the strip or wire melts, opening the circuit.

**GEAR RATIO:** The ratio between the number of teeth on meshing gears.

**GENERATOR:** A device which converts mechanical energy into electrical energy.

**HEAT RANGE:** The measure of a spark plug's ability to dissipate heat from its firing end. The higher the heat range, the hotter the plug fires.

**HUB:** The center part of a wheel or gear.

**HYDROCARBON (HC):** Any chemical compound made up of hydrogen and carbon. A major pollutant formed by the engine as a byproduct of combustion.

**HYDROMETER:** An instrument used to measure the specific gravity of a solution.

**INCH POUND (inch lbs.; sometimes in.lb. or in. lbs.):** One twelfth of a foot pound.

**INDUCTION:** A means of transferring electrical energy in the form of a magnetic field. Principle used in the ignition coil to increase voltage.

**INJECTOR:** A device which receives metered fuel under relatively low pressure and is activated to inject the fuel into the engine under relatively high pressure at a predetermined time.

**INPUT SHAFT:** The shaft to which torque is applied, usually carrying the driving gear or gears.

**INTAKE MANIFOLD:** A casting of passages or pipes used to conduct air or a fuel/air mixture to the cylinders.

**JOURNAL:** The bearing surface within which a shaft operates.

**KEY:** A small block usually fitted in a notch between a shaft and a hub to prevent slippage of the two parts.

**MANIFOLD:** A casting of passages or set of pipes which connect the cylinders to an inlet or outlet source.

**MANIFOLD VACUUM:** Low pressure in an engine intake manifold formed just below the throttle plates. Manifold vacuum is highest at idle and drops under acceleration.

**MASTER CYLINDER:** The primary fluid pressurizing device in a hydraulic system. In automotive use, it is found in brake and hydraulic clutch systems and is pedal activated, either directly or, in a power brake system, through the power booster.

**MODULE:** Electronic control unit, amplifier or igniter of solid state or integrated design which controls the current flow in the ignition primary circuit based on input from the pick-up coil. When the module opens the primary circuit, high secondary voltage is induced in the coil.

**NEEDLE BEARING:** A bearing which consists of a number (usually a large number) of long, thin rollers.

**OHM:** ($\Omega$) The unit used to measure the resistance of conductor-to-electrical flow. One ohm is the amount of resistance that limits current flow to one ampere in a circuit with one volt of pressure.

**OHMMETER:** An instrument used for measuring the resistance, in ohms, in an electrical circuit.

**OUTPUT SHAFT:** The shaft which transmits torque from a device, such as a transmission.

**OVERDRIVE:** A gear assembly which produces more shaft revolutions than that transmitted to it.

**OVERHEAD CAMSHAFT (OHC):** An engine configuration in which the camshaft is mounted on top of the cylinder head and operates the valve either directly or by means of rocker arms.

**OVERHEAD VALVE (OHV):** An engine configuration in which all of the valves are located in the cylinder head and the camshaft is located in the cylinder block. The camshaft operates the valves via lifters and pushrods.

**OXIDES OF NITROGEN (NOx):** Chemical compounds of nitrogen produced as a byproduct of combustion. They combine with hydrocarbons to produce smog.

**OXYGEN SENSOR:** Use with the feedback system to sense the presence of oxygen in the exhaust gas and signal the computer which can reference the voltage signal to an air/fuel ratio.

**PINION:** The smaller of two meshing gears.

**PISTON RING:** An open-ended ring with fits into a groove on the outer diameter of the piston. Its chief function is to form a seal between the piston and cylinder wall. Most automotive pistons have three rings: two for compression sealing; one for oil sealing.

**PRELOAD:** A predetermined load placed on a bearing during assembly or by adjustment.

**PRIMARY CIRCUIT:** the low voltage side of the ignition system which consists of the ignition switch, ballast resistor or resistance wire, bypass, coil, electronic control unit and pick-up coil as well as the connecting wires and harnesses.

**PRESS FIT:** The mating of two parts under pressure, due to the inner diameter of one being smaller than the outer diameter of the other, or vice versa; an interference fit.

**RACE:** The surface on the inner or outer ring of a bearing on which the balls, needles or rollers move.

**REGULATOR:** A device which maintains the amperage and/or voltage levels of a circuit at predetermined values.

**RELAY:** A switch which automatically opens and/or closes a circuit.

**RESISTANCE:** The opposition to the flow of current through a circuit or electrical device, and is measured in ohms. Resistance is equal to the voltage divided by the amperage.

**RESISTOR:** A device, usually made of wire, which offers a preset amount of resistance in an electrical circuit.

**RING GEAR:** The name given to a ring-shaped gear attached to a differential case, or affixed to a flywheel or as part of a planetary gear set.

**ROLLER BEARING:** A bearing made up of hardened inner and outer races between which hardened steel rollers move.

**ROTOR:** 1. The disc-shaped part of a disc brake assembly, upon which the brake pads bear; also called, brake disc. 2. The device

mounted atop the distributor shaft, which passes current to the distributor cap tower contacts.

**SECONDARY CIRCUIT:** The high voltage side of the ignition system, usually above 20,000 volts. The secondary includes the ignition coil, coil wire, distributor cap and rotor, spark plug wires and spark plugs.

**SENDING UNIT:** A mechanical, electrical, hydraulic or electro-magnetic device which transmits information to a gauge.

**SENSOR:** Any device designed to measure engine operating conditions or ambient pressures and temperatures. Usually electronic in nature and designed to send a voltage signal to an on-board computer, some sensors may operate as a simple on/off switch or they may provide a variable voltage signal (like a potentiometer) as conditions or measured parameters change.

**SHIM:** Spacers of precise, predetermined thickness used between parts to establish a proper working relationship.

**SLAVE CYLINDER:** In automotive use, a device in the hydraulic clutch system which is activated by hydraulic force, disengaging the clutch.

**SOLENOID:** A coil used to produce a magnetic field, the effect of which is to produce work.

**SPARK PLUG:** A device screwed into the combustion chamber of a spark ignition engine. The basic construction is a conductive core inside of a ceramic insulator, mounted in an outer conductive base. An electrical charge from the spark plug wire travels along the conductive core and jumps a preset air gap to a grounding point or points at the end of the conductive base. The resultant spark ignites the fuel/air mixture in the combustion chamber.

**SPLINES:** Ridges machined or cast onto the outer diameter of a shaft or inner diameter of a bore to enable parts to mate without rotation.

**TACHOMETER:** A device used to measure the rotary speed of an engine, shaft, gear, etc., usually in rotations per minute.

**THERMOSTAT:** A valve, located in the cooling system of an engine, which is closed when cold and opens gradually in response to engine heating, controlling the temperature of the coolant and rate of coolant flow.

**TOP DEAD CENTER (TDC):** The point at which the piston reaches the top of its travel on the compression stroke.

**TORQUE:** The twisting force applied to an object.

**TORQUE CONVERTER:** A turbine used to transmit power from a driving member to a driven member via hydraulic action, providing changes in drive ratio and torque. In automotive use, it links the driveplate at the rear of the engine to the automatic transmission.

**TRANSDUCER:** A device used to change a force into an electrical signal.

**TRANSISTOR:** A semi-conductor component which can be actuated by a small voltage to perform an electrical switching function.

**TUNE-UP:** A regular maintenance function, usually associated with the replacement and adjustment of parts and components in the electrical and fuel systems of a vehicle for the purpose of attaining optimum performance.

**TURBOCHARGER:** An exhaust driven pump which compresses intake air and forces it into the combustion chambers at higher than atmospheric pressures. The increased air pressure allows more fuel to be burned and results in increased horsepower being produced.

**VACUUM ADVANCE:** A device which advances the ignition timing in response to increased engine vacuum.

**VACUUM GAUGE:** An instrument used to measure the presence of vacuum in a chamber.

**VALVE:** A device which control the pressure, direction of flow or rate of flow of a liquid or gas.

**VALVE CLEARANCE:** The measured gap between the end of the valve stem and the rocker arm, cam lobe or follower that activates the valve.

**VISCOSITY:** The rating of a liquid's internal resistance to flow.

**VOLTMETER:** An instrument used for measuring electrical force in units called volts. Voltmeters are always connected parallel with the circuit being tested.

**WHEEL CYLINDER:** Found in the automotive drum brake assembly, it is a device, actuated by hydraulic pressure, which, through internal pistons, pushes the brake shoes outward against the drums.

## Notes

# A

# B

## U

UNDERHOOD HOSE CHECK AND REPLACEMENT, 1-20
UPHOLSTERY AND CARPETS, MAINTENANCE, 11-2

## V

V6 ENGINES, 2B-1 THROUGH 2B-28
camshafts, removal, inspection and installation, 2A-14
crankshaft front oil seal, removal and installation, 2A-12
cylinder heads, removal and installation, 2A-16
driveplate, removal and installation, 2A-20
Engine Mount Control System, description and check, 2A-23
exhaust manifolds, removal and installation, 2A-7
intake manifold, removal and installation, 2A-5
oil pan, removal and installation, 2A-18
oil pump, removal, inspection and installation, 2A-19
powertrain mounts, check and replacement, 2A-21
rear main oil seal, replacement, 2A-21
repair operations possible with the engine in the vehicle, 2A-2
rocker arm assembly, removal, inspection and installation, 2A-12
timing belt and sprockets, removal and installation, 2A-8
Top Dead Center (TDC) for number 1 piston, locating, 2A-2
valve clearance, check and adjustment, 2A-4
valve covers, removal and installation, 2A-3
VACUUM GAUGE DIAGNOSTIC CHECKS, 2B-5
VALVE CLEARANCE, CHECK AND ADJUSTMENT, 2A-4
VALVE COVERS, REMOVAL AND INSTALLATION, 2A-3
VARIABLE CYLINDER MANAGEMENT (VCM) SYSTEM, DESCRIPTION AND COMPONENT REPLACEMENT, 6-42

VARIABLE VALVE TIMING AND LIFT ELECTRONIC CONTROL (VTEC) SYSTEM, DESCRIPTION AND COMPONENT REPLACEMENT, 6-39
VEHICLE IDENTIFICATION NUMBERS, 0-6
VINYL TRIM, MAINTENANCE, 11-2

## W

WATER PUMP
check, 3-9
replacement, 3-10
WHEEL ALIGNMENT, GENERAL INFORMATION, 10-24
WHEEL BEARING ASSEMBLY, REPLACEMENT
front, 10-9
rear, 10-14
WHEEL SPEED SENSOR, ANTI-LOCK BRAKE SYSTEM, REMOVAL AND INSTALLATION, 9-3
WHEELS AND TIRES, GENERAL INFORMATION, 10-23
WINDOW GLASS
door, removal and installation, 11-14
regulator, removal and installation, 11-15
WINDSHIELD
and fixed glass, replacement, 11-6
washer fluid, level check, 1-8
wiper blade inspection and replacement, 1-14
WIPER MOTORS, CHECK AND REPLACEMENT, 12-13
WIRING DIAGRAMS, GENERAL INFORMATION, 12-31
WORKING FACILITIES, 0-8